Law and Regulation of AI, Blockchain, and Digital Rights

Ionica Oncioiu
Titu Maiorescu University, Constanta, Romania

IGI Global
Scientific Publishing
Publishing Tomorrow's Research Today

Vice President of Editorial Melissa Wagner
Director of Acquisitions Mikaela Felty
Director of Book Development Jocelynn Hessler
Production Manager Mike Brehm
Cover Design Jose Rosado

Published in the United States of America by
IGI Global Scientific Publishing
701 East Chocolate Avenue
Hershey, PA, 17033, USA
Tel: 717-533-8845 | Fax: 717-533-7115
Website: https://www.igi-global.com E-mail: cust@igi-global.com

Library of Congress Cataloging-in-Publication Data

Names: Oncioiu, Ionica, 1972- editor.
Title: Law and regulation of AI, blockchain, and digital rights / edited by Ionica Oncioiu.
Other titles: Law and regulation of artificial intelligence, blockchain, and digital rights
Description: Hershey : IGI Global Scientific Publishing, 2026. | Includes bibliographical references and index. | Summary: "This book aims to deliver the legal challenges and regulatory questions posed by AI, blockchain, and digital rights in the 21st century"-- Provided by publisher.
Identifiers: LCCN 2025017529 (print) | LCCN 2025017530 (ebook) | ISBN 9798337331867 (hardcover) | ISBN 9798337331874 (paperback) | ISBN 9798337331881 (ebook)
Subjects: LCSH: Technology and law. | Artificial intelligence--Law and legislation. | Blockchains (Database)--Law and legislation. | Computer security--Law and legislation. | Digital rights management.
Classification: LCC K487.T4 L383 2026 (print) | LCC K487.T4 (ebook) | DDC 343.09/99--dc23/eng/20250410
LC record available at https://lccn.loc.gov/2025017529
LC ebook record available at https://lccn.loc.gov/2025017530

British Cataloguing in Publication Data
A Cataloguing in Publication record for this book is available from the British Library.

Editorial Advisory Board

Table of Contents

Detailed Table of Contents

Digital transformations in the energy sector have brought artificial intelligence to the forefront as a structuring force for decision-making, efficiency, and operational architecture. In the context of smart grids, automation of distribution flows and consumption forecasting, artificial intelligence not only assists but also configures new relationships between data, infrastructure, and regulation. The chapter analyzes how algorithmic systems influence the functioning of the energy ecosystem, examining the challenges related to transparency, auditability, and digital security. At the same time, the need for technological autonomy is discussed in a regulatory framework undergoing metamorphosis, in which the balance between innovation and the protection of the public interest becomes a matter of institutional architecture.

Blockchain technology defies the existing regulatory frameworks and raises urgent regulatory and governance issues worthy of the immediate attention of policymakers, international institutions and legal scholars. The digital divide in technological access and regulatory preparedness between developed and developing/underdeveloped countries aggravates the existing disparities in trade participation. The chapter explores the legal and practical implications of blockchain in simplifying cross-border trade and improving regulatory processes. It identifies the contemporary trade and supply chain issues and examines the potential of blockchain technology in resolving such issues. The chapter further critically examines the pressing concerns and regulatory challenges in the integration of blockchain into international trade and intends to provide solutions to address them. The chapter explores whether international organisations such as the WTO can play a pivotal role in enabling blockchain integration, curbing the digital divide and shaping a supportive regulatory environment for the same.

Tushar, United College of Engineering and Research, Prayagraj, India
Nandita Pradhan, United College of Engineering and Research, Prayagraj, India
Prabhat Chandra Shrivastava, Faculty of Science, University of Allahabad, Prayagraj, India
Pooja Jaiswal, University of Allahabad, Prayagraj, India
Sweta Singh, United University, Prayagraj, India
Venktesh Mishra, United College of Engineering and Research, Prayagraj, India

Cloud computing has enabled fast organizational growth and diversified service acceptance. These services accelerate product development and hosting, giving consumers and third parties instant access. Cloud computing problems must be considered and implemented by service providers. This chapter emphasizes cloud computing's legal, contractual, and security issues. Enterprise clients benefit from several cloud computing projects. Despite these benefits, cloud data security and privacy remain problems. The cryptography and data security issues discuss such algorithms, key management, humans, and legal and regulatory issues. Regulations like the General Data Protection Regulation (GDPR) and the California Consumer Privacy Act (CCPA) put stringent obligations on enterprises to safeguard user data, as discussed in this chapter. Addressing cloud computing's ubiquitous security vulnerabilities requires a detailed understanding of the selected solution. This chapter also provides a methodology for organizations to analyze virtual dangers and damages.

Mădălina Mihăilescu, Hyperion University of Bucharest, Romania

Artificial intelligence is reshaping industrial operations—from automation to predictive logistics—raising complex legal challenges beyond algorithmic design. This chapter explores legal liability, data governance, contractual uncertainty, and compliance with frameworks like the EU AI Act. It also addresses AI's intersection with blockchain and the effects on employees' digital rights. Using a comparative lens, it examines divergences between legal systems and the drive toward regulatory coherence. Ethical concerns such as transparency, fairness, and human oversight are also discussed. The chapter offers a forward-looking legal perspective aligned with industrial transformation and fundamental rights protection.

In recent years, blockchain has made waves in the energy sector due to its decentralised, transparent, and immutable nature. On the other hand, the resulting breadth of blockchain applications in the autonomous operations and management of transactive energy systems has raised profound legal-related challenges, risks, and caveats. Data privacy breaches in blockchain energy landscapes present a considerable conundrum as they go to the root of societal values and human rights. The growing concerns prompt pessimism such that energy market participants are less inclined to engage in blockchain-enabled peer-to-peer energy trading. The author explores diverse data protection issues associated with permissioned and permissionless blockchain energy applications and speculate on how they may contribute to economic and social disruptions. Such exploration is beneficial as rising tensions will likely stagnate blockchain energy operationalisation and global diffusion. An earnest and effective dialogue of data protection challenges is necessary to fill the regulatory void.

This study explores the ethical, security, and privacy challenges faced by financial technology (Fintech) organizations. It highlights the critical role of ethics in leveraging artificial intelligence (AI) technologies to foster customer trust and loyalty. A systematic review of available literature was employed to analyze empirical data addressing Fintech challenges for customer privacy and ethical concerns. The study examines the factors influencing customer trust, such as real-time interaction, risk perception, and transparency. The outcomes highlight the need for consumer data protection and protection of the law, as well as trust through public disclosure. The study suggests implementations for managers about how to deploy the specialization between AI and analytical technologies in delivering personalized services, streamlining and saving the firm resources, and reducing service delivery costs.

This chapter examines how blockchain governance, whether public or private, extends beyond technical design into the realm of institutional values, legal frameworks, and societal priorities. Through sectoral case studies in finance, healthcare, and supply chains, it highlights how governance structures directly shape blockchain's decentralization, transparency, control, and trustworthiness. Public blockchains offer openness and resilience but face regulatory uncertainty and coordination challenges, while private blockchains provide control and compliance but risk reintroducing centralization. Key policy recommendations stress designing governance from the outset, enabling sector-specific regulation, encouraging hybrid architectures, and incentivizing responsible practices.

The digital realm has altered how societies address human rights, data usage, and governance. Various sectors now rely on large-scale analytics, business intelligence systems, and artificial intelligence to optimize decision-making, yet these technologies introduce legal and ethical dilemmas. This chapter examines how international human rights norms apply to emerging technologies. It discusses data privacy, algorithmic fairness, and regulatory challenges, illustrating tensions between innovation and fundamental rights. It also proposes governance measures grounded in human-centric frameworks to protect privacy and preserve democratic values. Findings indicate that a balance of technical, legal, and policy efforts can strengthen rights in digital ecosystems. This chapter enriches debates on ensuring that digital transformation aligns with human dignity.

As digital technologies increasingly shape social, economic, and political life, the legal and ethical implications of their deployment demand urgent scholarly attention. Among the most disruptive technologies today, Artificial Intelligence (AI) and Blockchain raise pressing questions about the future of governance, individual rights, and democratic accountability. Their convergence introduces both opportunities and challenges that existing legal systems are not fully equipped to address—particularly in relation to digital rights. This chapter examines the intersection of AI, Blockchain, and digital rights through a unified theoretical and regulatory framework. While AI systems introduce concerns around algorithmic opacity, bias, and automated decision-making, Blockchain technologies challenge legal norms through decentralization, immutability, and cross-jurisdictional complexity.

This chapter delves into the evolving landscape of Advanced Persistent Threats (APT) from both an attack and detection perspective. It begins by reviewing the definition and characteristics of APTs, providing an overview of the various attack models developed over time. Building upon this foundation, the chapter introduces a comprehensive APT lifecycle model, which is divided into four distinct stages: information gathering, intrusion implementation, internal network attacks, and data exfiltration. For each of these stages, the chapter surveys research from the past five years, highlighting the latest advancements in both attack strategies and detection techniques. Finally, the chapter examines the dynamic interplay between attack and defense technologies, pointing out the challenges faced by both attackers and defenders. It concludes by discussing the rapid advancements in APT tactics and defenses, offering insights into the future directions for research and development in the field of cybersecurity and APT detection.

Smart contracts as self-executing agreements coded to blockchain networks introduced major disputes to the existing dispute resolution field. It face problems with traditional arbitration methods because of their decentralized design combined with non-traditional negotiation standards and built-in arbitration clauses in programming code. The research investigates whether programmed arbitration clauses verify valid arbitration agreements along with court treatment of their enforceability across different legal systems. The research investigates the existing jurisdictional obstacles and public policy dilemmas and regulatory void that affect smart contract dispute resolution mechanisms, especially for digital assets and AI dispute settlement procedures. This analysis presents blockchain technology findings combined with arbitration law analysis and regulatory situations whereas it strengthens the general discussion about law and governance in digital transactions.

The General Data Protection Regulation (GDPR) protects the citizens of the European Union against illicit use of their personal data, and since data can traverse continents in mere seconds, implications for this law are worldwide. Today's collection, storage, transport, and other tasks related to data are accomplished by a wide variety of technological means. However, companies are not always following the many mandates of the GDPR. Specific cases involving various technologies offer an opportunity to understand and discuss further the ethical use of personal information as well as the ramifications of disobeying the law.

Drone technology is a mixed blessing in the modern tech era. While it offers advantages across various societal sectors, the downsides of unmonitored usage must not be ignored. This paper explores the challenges and opportunities of drone technology and evaluates its use in Indian skies, balancing concerns related to public safety, privacy, criminal justice, and surveillance. The study fills a gap by

Preface

The digital transformation of society has accelerated at a pace unprecedented in human history. Artificial intelligence, blockchain technologies, and the expansion of digital rights represent not isolated innovations but a profound reshaping of the global socio-economic and legal order. Artificial intelligence has moved beyond laboratories and theoretical discourse into everyday applications: from diagnostic algorithms in medicine to predictive analytics in criminal justice, from recommendation systems in social media to autonomous vehicles. The very notion of human decision-making, long considered the domain of free will and rationality, is increasingly mediated—or even replaced—by algorithmic processes. This shift challenges fundamental assumptions of law, such as responsibility, liability, and fairness.

Blockchain technology, initially synonymous with cryptocurrencies, has since evolved into a multi-faceted infrastructure of trust, decentralization, and transparency. Its applications are now visible in smart contracts, supply chain management, e-governance, and decentralized finance (DeFi). The core attributes of blockchain—immutability, peer-to-peer consensus, and the absence of centralized control—disrupt long-standing legal constructs of contract law, property law, and financial regulation. Jurisdictions across the world face the challenge of integrating blockchain into legal systems designed for centralized institutions, raising questions of enforceability, jurisdiction, and consumer protection.

In parallel, digital rights have emerged as one of the most pressing issues of the 21st century. The right to privacy, the right to access information, the right to freedom of expression, and the right to digital self-determination are no longer abstract extensions of human rights but urgent demands in a society where data has become the most valuable commodity. Digital rights are both global and fragile, threatened by state surveillance, corporate monopolies, cybercrime, and unequal access to technology. The protection of digital rights is inseparable from the preservation of democracy and human dignity in the digital age.

The book, *Law and Regulation of AI, Blockchain, and Digital Rights*, situates itself at the intersection of these three transformative forces. It does not merely present them as isolated challenges but as interconnected phenomena shaping the new legal order. Through a combination of theoretical insights and applied research, the chapters of this volume explore the ways in which law can respond to technological disruption while safeguarding fundamental rights and promoting responsible innovation.

The significance of this book lies in its timeliness. Never before has the demand for legal adaptation been so immediate and so global. Across continents, governments and regulatory bodies are grappling with the task of ensuring that artificial intelligence systems operate fairly and transparently, that blockchain technologies do not become havens for unregulated financial speculation, and that digital rights are upheld in the face of corporate dominance and state overreach.

In Europe, the forthcoming Artificial Intelligence Act seeks to establish a comprehensive regulatory framework for AI, placing emphasis on human oversight, safety, and accountability. The General Data Protection Regulation (GDPR) has already set a precedent for data protection, inspiring similar legislation worldwide. In Asia, countries such as China, India, and Singapore are adopting distinct strategies that balance economic growth with ethical concerns. The United States, though traditionally favoring innovation-driven approaches, has begun to address antitrust and data protection issues at both federal and state levels. These developments illustrate a fragmented yet converging global movement toward regulating disruptive technologies.

At the same time, the international community faces new forms of conflict and inequality arising from digitalization. The digital divide between technologically advanced and developing countries threatens to deepen global inequities. Cross-border disputes concerning data localization, intellectual property, and jurisdiction in cyberspace challenge the very foundations of international law. Furthermore, the ethical dilemmas of algorithmic decision-making—bias, discrimination, and the opacity of "black box" systems—raise questions not only of legality but of legitimacy.

In this complex landscape, the subject matter of this book is directly relevant to ongoing debates in international forums such as the United Nations, the World Economic Forum, and the Organisation for Economic Co-operation and Development (OECD). The book provides insights that resonate with policymakers who must draft regulations, with lawyers who must litigate emerging disputes, with businesses that must adapt to compliance obligations, and with citizens who must safeguard their rights in an increasingly digital society.

CHAPTER OVERVIEW

The author Mădălina Mihăilescu of the first chapter *"Digital Governance Assisted by Artificial Intelligence in the Energy Sector: Between Algorithmic Autonomy and Technological Sovereignty"* explores how digital transformations in the energy field have brought artificial intelligence to the forefront as a decisive force in operational efficiency, decision-making, and infrastructural architecture. In the context of smart grids and automated distribution flows, artificial intelligence does not merely optimize consumption forecasting but also redefines the relationships between data, infrastructure, and regulation. The chapter analyzes the way algorithmic systems influence the energy ecosystem by addressing challenges of transparency, auditability, and cybersecurity, while at the same time examining the institutional need for maintaining technological sovereignty. The author emphasizes that the balance between innovation and the protection of the public interest must be embedded within robust regulatory frameworks, ensuring that algorithmic governance in infrastructures contributes to efficiency without undermining accountability or digital rights.

The premise of integrating blockchain into international trade law is examined by Ayushi Singh, Samanvi Narang, and Abhipsa Upasana Dash, the authors of the second chapter *"Blockchain Revolution: Transforming International Trade Law for the Digital Age"*. The chapter highlights how blockchain technology defies existing regulatory frameworks and raises pressing governance challenges that require urgent attention from policymakers, international institutions, and legal scholars. The authors show that while blockchain can simplify cross-border transactions and improve supply chain transparency, its integration into trade law is hindered by disparities in technological access and regulatory preparedness between developed and developing economies. By critically examining the digital divide and its impact on participation in global trade, the chapter argues that blockchain has the potential to reshape international commerce, but only if appropriate legal solutions are implemented to address inequalities and regulatory gaps. Thus, the study underscores that blockchain is not merely a technological innovation, but a transformative force capable of redefining governance in the digital age.

The challenges of cloud computing in the digital economy are examined by Tushar, Nandita Pradhan, Prabhat Chandra Shrivastava, Pooja Jaiswal, Sweta Singh, and Venktesh Mishra, the authors of the third chapter *"Legal Challenges in Cloud Computing"*. The chapter emphasizes the legal, contractual, and security complexities that arise as enterprises increasingly rely on cloud-based infrastructures for organizational growth and diversified services. While cloud computing accelerates product development and enables instant access for consumers and third parties, it also raises issues of data protection, privacy, and liability. Particular attention is given to vulnerabilities related to cryptography, key management, and human oversight, which remain pressing concerns despite the benefits of scalability and efficiency. The chapter further provides a methodological framework for organizations to analyze virtual risks and damages, underlining the importance of integrating legal safeguards with technological solutions. By situating cloud computing at the crossroads of innovation and regulation, the authors demonstrate that addressing its vulnerabilities is not only a technical necessity but also a fundamental requirement for trust and sustainability in the digital ecosystem.

The transformative role of artificial intelligence in industrial processes is analyzed by Mădălina Mihăilescu, the author of the fourth chapter "*Artificial Intelligence in the Industrial Sector: Legal Implications Beyond the Code*". The chapter demonstrates how AI reshapes operations ranging from automation to predictive logistics, generating complex legal challenges that extend far beyond algorithmic design. The author examines issues of liability, data governance, and contractual uncertainty, placing them in the context of regulatory frameworks such as the European Union's AI Act. Special attention is given to AI's intersections with blockchain technologies and the implications these raise for employees' digital rights. By employing a comparative legal perspective, the chapter highlights divergences between legal systems while emphasizing the pressing need for regulatory coherence. Ethical concerns such as transparency, fairness, and human oversight are also brought into focus, revealing the broader consequences of embedding AI into industrial infrastructures. Ultimately, the author argues for a forward-looking legal perspective that aligns technological innovation with fundamental rights protection, ensuring that industrial transformation unfolds in a manner that is both efficient and accountable.

In the fifth chapter *"Data Privacy Challenges of Blockchain Energy Systems"*, Karisma Karisma examines the complex implications of applying blockchain technologies within the energy sector. While the decentralized, transparent, and immutable nature of blockchain has enabled innovative approaches to energy trading and system management, it has simultaneously created profound challenges for data privacy and regulatory compliance. The chapter highlights that breaches of privacy in blockchain-based energy systems raise concerns that go to the very heart of societal values and human rights, leading many market participants to hesitate in adopting blockchain-enabled peer-to-peer energy trading. The author provides an in-depth analysis of the vulnerabilities associated with both permissioned and permissionless blockchain applications, showing how these weaknesses may trigger economic and social disruptions. The study also underscores that unless effective and collaborative dialogues on data protection are established, tensions will likely hinder the operationalization and global diffusion of blockchain energy solutions.

The sixth chapter *"Trust Challenges in AI-Driven Fintech: Navigating the Ethical Frontier"* by Payal Sharma, Syed Sajid Hussain, and Manjit Kour investigates the ethical, security, and privacy dilemmas faced by financial technology organizations when adopting artificial intelligence. The authors emphasize how factors such as real-time interaction, risk perception, and transparency shape customer trust, while also underscoring the importance of consumer data protection under existing legal frameworks. Drawing on a systematic review of the literature, the chapter highlights that fostering trust requires both regulatory safeguards and responsible managerial strategies. It suggests practical ways for fintech managers to balance personalization and efficiency with ethical obligations, thereby ensuring innovation in AI-driven services does not come at the expense of customer loyalty or legal compliance.

The governance of blockchain, whether public or private, is addressed by Munir Ahmad in the seventh chapter *"Public vs. Private Blockchains Governance Implications"*. The author explains that blockchain governance extends beyond technical design to encompass institutional values, legal frameworks, and societal priorities. Using sectoral case studies in finance, healthcare, and supply chains, the chapter illustrates how governance structures directly shape blockchain's decentralization, transparency, and trustworthiness. Public blockchains are praised for their openness and resilience but remain vulnerable to regulatory uncertainty and coordination difficulties, while private blockchains allow stronger control and compliance but risk reintroducing centralization. The chapter argues that effective governance must be designed from the outset, with sector-specific regulations, hybrid blockchain architectures, and incentives for responsible practices.

In the eighth chapter *"Rights in the Digital Realm: Legal and Ethical Considerations of Emerging Technologies – Human Rights and Global Digital Governance"*, Mohammad Al Khaldy, Ahmad Al-Qerem, and Amjad Aldweesh explore how digital transformation reshapes the way societies address human rights, data usage, and governance. The chapter shows that sectors increasingly rely on large-scale analytics, business intelligence, and artificial intelligence to optimize decision-making, while simultaneously generating new legal and ethical dilemmas. The authors examine how international human rights norms apply to emerging technologies, focusing on issues such as data privacy, algorithmic fairness, and regulatory challenges. They highlight the tensions between innovation and the protection of fundamental rights, arguing that democratic values can only be preserved through governance frameworks that are human-centered and grounded in dignity.

The regulatory dilemmas at the intersection of law and technology are addressed by Manya Gupta, Radhey Shyam Jha, Nidhi Tyagi, and Lalit Goyal, the authors of the ninth chapter *"Law and Regulation of AI, Blockchain, and Digital Rights"*. The chapter highlights how artificial intelligence and blockchain, as two of the most disruptive technologies of our time, reshape governance, democratic accountability, and the protection of fundamental rights. The authors emphasize that current legal systems are not fully equipped to handle the complexities introduced by algorithmic opacity, bias, and automated decision-making, nor the challenges posed by blockchain's decentralization, immutability, and cross-jurisdictional nature. The results underline the pressing need for adaptive legal mechanisms that can reconcile innovation with accountability, and that can safeguard digital rights in a rapidly transforming global environment. Ultimately, the study situates AI and blockchain not merely as technological tools but as forces capable of redefining legal norms and societal values.

The complexity of cybersecurity threats is explored by Vinay Kumar Kasula, Mounica Yenugula, and Bhargavi Konda, the authors of the tenth chapter *"Advanced Cybersecurity Detection Techniques"*. The chapter investigates the evolving nature of Advanced Persistent Threats (APTs), analyzing both attack strategies and detection mechanisms. The authors provide a comprehensive overview of the APT lifecycle model, structured into four stages: information gathering, intrusion implementation, internal network attacks, and data exfiltration. For each stage, they survey recent research and highlight technological innovations in areas such as generative adversarial networks, convolutional neural networks, and deep learning-based detection. The chapter also examines the interplay between offensive and defensive techniques, pointing out the challenges faced equally by attackers and defenders in the digital landscape. Concluding with a discussion of rapid advancements in APT tactics and defenses, the authors offer insights into future directions for cybersecurity research and the development of detection tools capable of addressing increasingly sophisticated threats.

The eleventh chapter *"The Arbitrability of Smart Contract Disputes Amid Legal Uncertainties in Digital Arbitration"* by Ashiv Choudhary and Harsh Mahaseth addresses the profound challenges that blockchain-based smart contracts pose for dispute resolution. As self-executing agreements coded into decentralized networks, smart contracts disrupt traditional arbitration methods, particularly when arbitration clauses are embedded in code rather than negotiated through conventional legal standards. The authors investigate whether such programmed arbitration clauses can be considered valid and enforceable across jurisdictions, and they highlight the significant legal uncertainties that accompany these innovations. Through the intersection of arbitration law and blockchain governance, the chapter sheds light on the unresolved legal questions surrounding the arbitrability of smart contract disputes. The authors conclude that although blockchain technologies offer significant potential to streamline dispute resolution, their effective use requires the creation of robust legal standards that guarantee enforceability, safeguard fairness, and maintain consistency with overarching public policy principles.

The twelfth chapter *"Data Privacy Case Studies in the European Union"* by Tamara Phillips Fudge examines the impact of the General Data Protection Regulation (GDPR) on the protection of personal data across Europe and beyond. The chapter emphasizes that, as data collection, storage, and transfer can occur globally within seconds, the implications of GDPR extend far outside the European Union. While the regulation establishes strict obligations to safeguard individual privacy, many companies struggle to comply fully with its mandates. Through case studies involving diverse technologies—ranging from drones and GPS tracking to facial recognition, online test proctoring, and vehicle dashcams—the author highlights both the opportunities and risks that arise from the use of personal data. These examples illustrate not only the ethical dilemmas associated with emerging technologies but also the serious legal consequences of non-compliance.

The growing relevance of drone technology in multiple sectors justifies its examination as both an opportunity and a regulatory challenge. In the thirteenth chapter *"Legal and Ethical Challenges on Drone Technology: Learnings from Indian Skies"*, Nidhi Kastwar and Aakash Gupta discuss the advantages drones bring to areas such as surveillance, search and rescue, crime scene documentation, agriculture, and aerial photography, while also drawing attention to the risks posed by unmonitored or unauthorized usage. From a combined technological and legal perspective, the authors identify vulnerabilities related to privacy violations, hacking, unauthorized access, and security breaches, which threaten both individual rights and public safety. The findings underline that while drones enhance efficiency and broaden possibilities in law enforcement and civil applications, they simultaneously create societal risks that demand stricter regulatory oversight.

This overview of the book highlights that each chapter brings forward significant perspectives whose originality and depth open new directions for both academic research and practical implementation in law and technology. The analyses presented demonstrate that the regulation of artificial intelligence, blockchain, and digital rights is not a matter confined to isolated domains, but a complex interplay between governance, ethics, and innovation. Authorized contributions illustrate how legal frameworks can serve as mechanisms to ensure accountability, safeguard fundamental rights, and foster trust in emerging digital ecosystems. They emphasize the role of cross-disciplinary collaboration, involving not only legal scholars and policymakers, but also technologists, businesses, and civil society actors. Therefore, the study of law in the digital age fulfills a dual function: it acts as a safeguard to protect human rights and democratic values, while simultaneously enabling technological progress to unfold within a framework of responsibility and transparency.

Acknowledgment

Looking back, we wish to thank all the persons who made the publishing of the present volume possible: Jan Travers, Melissa Wagner, Erin Wesser, Christina Henning, Nicole Elliott, Kristina Byrne, Lindsay Johnston, Joshua Witman, Nick Newcomer, Jaimie Watts, Josephine Dadeboe, Jordan Tepper, Sean Eckman, Elizabeth Barrantes, Katie McLoughlin and many other IGI – Global team members, reviewers, collaborators, and all the contributing authors: without your efforts and dedication this editorial project would have never been possible.

Chapter 1

Digital Governance Assisted by Artificial Intelligence in the Energy Sector:

Between Algorithmic Autonomy and Technological Sovereignty

Mădălina Mihăilescu
https://orcid.org/0009-0003-0736-8588
Hyperion University of Bucharest, Romania

ABSTRACT

Digital transformations in the energy sector have brought artificial intelligence to the forefront as a structuring force for decision-making, efficiency, and operational architecture. In the context of smart grids, automation of distribution flows and consumption forecasting, artificial intelligence not only assists but also configures new relationships between data, infrastructure, and regulation. The chapter analyzes how algorithmic systems influence the functioning of the energy ecosystem, examining the challenges related to transparency, auditability, and digital security. At the same time, the need for technological autonomy is discussed in a regulatory framework undergoing metamorphosis, in which the balance between innovation and the protection of the public interest becomes a matter of institutional architecture.

DOI: 10.4018/979-8-3373-3186-7.ch001

INTRODUCTION

The digital transformations that are reshaping the energy sector indicate a profound mutation in which algorithms become part of the fabric of decision-making and the architecture of critical infrastructures. In the context of the climate transition, the pressure for decarbonization is intertwined with the need to manage, in real time, huge volumes of data, distributed processes, and fluctuating renewable sources. Beyond efficiency, the integration of artificial intelligence into energy systems redefines the control model, the transparency of operations, and the distribution of responsibility between actors. The answers provided by intelligent platforms are not only technical results but also manifestations of codified choices, influenced by commercial interests, public policies, and opaque algorithmic architectures.

In contemporary energy networks, artificial intelligence (AI) structures energy flows, shapes the balance between demand and supply, and supports fine-grained adaptability to climatic or economic variations (Pan et al., 2025). Experiences in Northern Europe confirm that automated predictions contribute to continuity of supply and reduction of losses, but they also introduce a new grey area in terms of auditability of decisions (Le Coq & Jaunziems, 2025).

In parallel, emerging regulations at the European Union level (AI Act, GDPR) configure a regulatory landscape that requires not only technical compliance but also explicit mechanisms for legal, ethical, and procedural control (Ilias et al., 2023). The process of digitalization, far from being linear or neutral, also amplifies tensions related to technological sovereignty. Energy infrastructures become dependent on software platforms developed outside the European space, and the outsourcing of decision-making to black box systems raises questions related to autonomy, security, and fundamental rights. In the United Kingdom, the energy regulator has issued warnings about the possibility of algorithmic collusion that escapes traditional monitoring (Ofgem, 2024). Such scenarios are becoming increasingly likely in the absence of a conceptual and normative framework adapted to digital realities.

Experiences from Central and Eastern Europe highlight a hybrid landscape: investments in infrastructure are often fragmented, and digital skills are not equitably distributed among actors. However, some local initiatives have demonstrated that AI can be used in a way that respects both the logic of efficiency and the demands of algorithmic transparency and democratic control (Smith et al., 2024). The success of such efforts depends on the capacity of institutions to understand the dynamic nature of AI, to implement continuous audit tools, and to impose clear real-time verification criteria.

Artificial intelligence has penetrated deep into modern energy systems, reshaping the processes of balancing, adapting, and intervening in smart grids. In this context, algorithms constantly capture the vast volume of data coming from smart meters and distributed sensors, processing them to anticipate consumption and regulate energy distribution in real time (Arévalo & Jurado, 2024). Their ability to detect anomalies and trigger preventive actions contributes to increasing the stability of the infrastructure, avoiding unforeseen interruptions (Balamurugan et al., 2025).

In addition, AI is leading to a new maintenance paradigm in energy systems: predictive maintenance. Critical equipment—such as transformers or turbines—now benefits from algorithmic analyses that identify wear or possible failures before they become problematic, thus reducing both costs and significant operational risks (Balamurugan et al., 2025; Arévalo & Jurado, 2024). Some utilities have reported over 80% reductions in unplanned outages by adopting these technologies (Pan et al., 2025).

Demand forecasting is another area where AI excels. Deep learning-based models integrate weather variables, usage patterns, and historical data to optimize the feed-in/feed-out balance. This process supports flexible grids that can respond quickly to fluctuations and reduces the costs associated with spot market purchases (Pan et al., 2025).

However, the technical efficiency of the systems does not preclude the need for robust verification mechanisms. In the case of automation of critical decisions—such as isolating network segments in emergency situations—the lack of traceability of algorithmic actions raises challenges related to accountability and cybersecurity (Arévalo & Jurado, 2024). The absence of a comprehensive audit framework or human intervention mechanism could lead to a loss of user trust and an increase in systemic vulnerabilities (Alsaigh et al., 2022).

Recent studies signal the need to strengthen digital governance by introducing standards that include continuous checks, risk assessments, and remediation mechanisms (Balamurugan et al., 2025; Alsaigh et al., 2022). In addition, data integrity is a prerequisite for the reliability of predictions. Incomplete or compromised data can generate erroneous results and fuel the inability of systems to anticipate serious problems (Pan et al., 2025).

Projects launched in northern Europe provide relevant examples. In Sweden, AI in smart grids was implemented through diagnostic and intervention planning stages, with a clear focus on transparency and accountability (Liu University, 2025). Here, platforms have been implemented that provide decision-makers with access to the history of automated decisions and algorithmic parameters, facilitating independent assessment.

At the institutional level, energy regulators have started to issue specific recommendations. Bodies such as Ofgem warn of the risk that suppliers use algorithms to coordinate prices in a non-competitive manner or to restrict competing suppliers (Financial Times, 2024). Clear rules are thus suggested to prevent the adverse effects of automated but sector-specific supervision.

The fundamental challenge remains related to technological sovereignty. Energy networks increasingly rely on software solutions developed outside the European Union; this exposes the infrastructure to external vulnerabilities and reduces the ability to react to cyber incidents. Consequently, it is necessary to develop local alternatives that allow full control over critical codes and data (Balamurugan et al., 2025; Ofgem, 2024).

Amidst these transformations, smart grids are becoming a testing ground for the relationship between technology, regulation, and user rights. Authorities need to reassess the role of the consumer, how to engage civil society, and mechanisms for challenging automated decisions. The lack of challenge tools reduces citizens' vulnerability to automation (Alsaigh et al., 2022).

Critical infrastructure, such as energy networks, telecommunications, and water and transportation systems, increasingly depends on robust digital solutions and integrated technologies. In this landscape, digital sovereignty is not the mere possession of technology but the ability of a state or region to control its digital architecture, from hardware and data centers to the algorithms and source code that govern automated decisions (World Economic Forum, 2025). The decision-making structure thus becomes a space where economic interests, public policies, and democratic values intersect, generating a new ecology of digital autonomy.

A study published by Arévalo and Jurado analyzes how smart grids—integrated into the energy grid—accumulate massive data, processed by algorithms for automatic adjustments. These reconfigurations allow for rapid response to malfunctions or variations in demand but also introduce areas of decision-making opacity, especially where human intervention is reduced (Arévalo & Jurado, 2024). The autonomous balance of energy supply and demand illustrates the technological capability but also the risk that these systems will operate without transparency or accountability following automated decisions.

At the same time, the role of external actors is becoming increasingly crucial. China and the US dominate the market for data center equipment and AI servers, building a technological monolith that undermines the sovereignty of other states. According to a report by the World Economic Forum, AI infrastructure—computing centers, data centers, bandwidth, and energy consumption—has become a vector of national power, and control over it is gaining strategic significance (World Economic Forum, 2025).

On the regulatory front, organizations such as the European Union and the United States are developing frameworks to protect critical infrastructure and impose algorithmic decision-making responsibility. The European Union has adopted the Cyber Resilience Act, which imposes security standards for connected digital products (European Parliament & Council, 2024).

Beyond regulatory regulation, discussions on "Sovereign AI" have gained momentum among technology leaders. The giant Nvidia has proposed the concept as a solution to technological dependency, arguing that states should own their computing centers to preserve their autonomy (e.g., with GPGPU ecosystems)—a position welcomed by European authorities (European Commission President von der Leyen, 2025).

European cooperation on digital sovereignty includes initiatives such as Gaia-X, which aims to federate European cloud infrastructure, with a focus on interoperability, data protection, and retaining sovereignty over digital flows (Gaia-X AISBL, 2024). The project aims to ensure code transparency and avoid institutional capture by major corporations, creating a common technological governance framework.

Critics of the sovereignty agenda warn of the risk that excessive control of automated decision-making will be used for political centralization. Recent analyses show that technological isolationism—in the name of security—can erode pluralism and weaken democratic accountability (Brunton & Nissenbaum, 2024). At the same time, some works signal that the legitimacy of digital sovereignty depends on the dual challenge: integrating democratic competence into digital governance and building ethical and transparent infrastructures (Musiani, 2025).

This chapter aims to investigate how artificial intelligence reconfigures decision-making, oversight, and resilience mechanisms in energy infrastructure, with a particular focus on smart grids, demand forecasting, and predictive maintenance. The analysis will follow not only the technological functioning of these systems but also their legal, institutional, and ethical implications in the context of the green transition and the demands of digital sovereignty. By mapping emerging practices and related challenges, a framework for reflection is opened on the need for a balance between algorithmic innovation, democratic control, and the protection of the public interest in the post-carbon energy era.

2. DECISION-MAKING ALGORITHMIZATION AND ADAPTIVE OPTIMIZATION IN CONTEMPORARY ENERGY INFRASTRUCTURE

In the context of smart grids, balancing supply and demand is no longer achieved exclusively through centralized decisions but through automated and adaptive systems powered by artificial intelligence. Real-time, large-scale data—from sensors, smart meters, and fluctuating renewables—is the raw material for algorithms that analyze consumption patterns, weather, and available inventory, anticipating variations in energy demand (Arévalo & Jurado, 2024).

The result is fine-tuning that produces grid-level efficiency, avoiding costly losses and destabilizing fluctuations. Some initiatives integrate hybrid systems that combine ML analysis with reinforcement—in which algorithms iteratively optimize decisions (Balamurugan et al., 2025). A concrete implementation example has been reported in Indian grids, where a hardening algorithm reduced the total cost of energy by approximately 12% by dynamically adjusting the price and adjusting demand during critical peak hours (Deshpande, 2024).

By integrating anomaly detection techniques, systems can identify unexpected deviations—which could indicate failures, theft, or data manipulation—adding an additional level of resilience and authentication to the energy flow (Balamurugan et al., 2025). In real life, these models can quickly spot when energy use is much higher than usual, which sets off automatic alerts and helps isolate parts of the secondary grid.

At the same time, Q-learning algorithms and semi-supervised methods are used to optimize demand response—the adjustment of consumption as a whole, determined by economic and climatic variables. In pilot projects in Europe, industrial consumers have been incentivized to reduce peak demand through dynamic reward mechanisms provided by the AI system. Results have shown an approximately 8–10% reduction in peak consumption, contributing to grid stabilization (Waseem et al., 2022; Saroj et al., 2023).

The efficiency of algorithms is not limited to reducing costs and leakages. In situations where renewable energy sources change quickly, predictive models help the system get ready by automatically adjusting energy flow or storage ahead of time. These optimizations contribute to the large-scale integration of green energy without compromising grid reliability.

In addition, the use of DL in smart grids also stimulates the development of an explainable approach. Recent projects, such as those supported by Alfayan & Hagras (2025), outline methods for XAI—decision explainability. In this way, not only the outcome but also the algorithmic reasoning can be tracked, which increases transparency, supports human decision-making evaluation, and allows intervention in case of deviations from normal parameters.

Another integrative element is the use of blockchain for auditable demand response, where the inviolable signature on blocks ensures data integrity, stimulates consumer participation, and strengthens social trust (Khan et al., 2022). This combination of ML, IoT, and distributed ledgers opens up a scenario in which the supply-demand balance is shaped by smart contracts and automated verifiability.

The limits of the systems are, however, relevant. Computational complexity, the risk of overlearning on historical data, and susceptibility to adversarial attacks are issues raised by specialists (Saroj et al., 2023). The ability to continuously adapt models to new conditions, periodic external validation, and configurable integration of the human factor remain issues that require a combination of scientific rigor and democratic decision-making.

In the energy configuration of the 21st century, decentralized control of renewable production becomes a condition for the adaptability and continuity of the system. The transition from a centralized, rigid, and predictable model to a distributed architecture, governed by variable flows and multiple injection points, requires a profound rethinking of balancing and decision-making mechanisms. Smart grids—intelligent networks that integrate renewable sources, storage, and flexible consumption—function today as dynamic spaces for energy negotiation, where each node becomes both a receiver and a resource provider.

The emergence of prosumers—actors who produce and consume energy—is transforming the power relations in the energy system. They actively participate in the management of the balance, injecting energy from solar panels, microturbines, or other local sources. At the same time, algorithmic intelligence allows them to adjust their consumption according to the variations of the network, either through assisted human decision-making or fully automatically, through contextually learned systems (Giordano et al., 2020).

Decentralized control implies a high degree of coordination between devices, aggregators, operators, and distribution networks. In this context, artificial intelligence becomes the invisible mediation that allows the coherent functioning of the entire system. Machine learning algorithms can analyze individual production in real time, forecast local demand, anticipate congestion, and propose optimal balancing strategies. For example, Bayesian networks and probabilistic regression models are used to estimate the volatility generated by intermittent sources and to transmit instructions to control devices (Mohamed et al., 2021).

In local energy communities, AI is used to regulate the flow between prosumers and automatically calculate the redistribution of earnings. Multi-agent models allow the simulation of an energy ecosystem composed of hundreds of autonomous entities that decide in real time whether to consume, store, or inject energy, depending on price signals, weather conditions, and storage capacity (Luthander et al., 2020). For example, in Sweden, a pilot project in the Västra Götaland region showed that coordinated algorithms at the microgrid level reduced energy losses by 18% and stabilized the voltage at the edge of the low-voltage grid, despite a significant increase in solar injection (Liu et al., 2022). In the same vein, experiments conducted in Germany, within the ENERA initiative, have demonstrated the ability of AI to replace the intervention of dispatchers in the fine-tuning processes of the load (Hirth et al., 2021).

Blockchain, integrated in some smart grid architectures, provides a framework for securing peer-to-peer energy transactions. In such a framework, prosumers can trade surplus energy automatically, based on smart contracts validated by the distributed network. The system promotes autonomy and reduces dependence on intermediaries, creating the premises of a decentralized but verifiable market (Mengelkamp et al., 2018).

Decentralization also brings challenges. The risk of asynchrony, instability at interconnection points, and overload in the absence of robust coordination requires algorithms capable of self-regulation and continuous learning. Recent models propose distributed predictive control, where each node has decision autonomy but constantly communicates with the network through edge AI protocols (Zhou et al., 2021). In this way, decisions are made in proximity to the data, reducing latency and dependence on central computing centers.

A significant dimension is the integration of storage. Distributed batteries become an active part of the regulation of supply and demand. Dual optimization algorithms decide when to charge and when to discharge based on prices, grid needs, and weather forecasts. Examples from the Netherlands have shown that the integration of these algorithms can lead to savings of over 15% in the aggregate consumption of households equipped with photovoltaic panels and batteries (Ruhnau & Qvist, 2022).

Beyond the technicalities, decentralized control also involves rethinking the legal and institutional framework. Traditional regulations, based on a clear distinction between producers and consumers, prove inadequate in the face of a fluid reality, where the same actor can simultaneously perform both functions. Some EU member states have started to introduce legislation that recognizes prosumer status, allocates balancing responsibilities, and defines rights regarding access to the market, data, and infrastructure (European Commission, 2022).

Algorithmic transparency, auditability of automated decisions, and protection of data generated by prosumers are increasingly pressing issues. If these systems become opaque or inaccessible, the risk of exclusion or price manipulation increases. Thus, AI must not only function correctly but also be accompanied by institutional guarantees that protect users from abuses or power asymmetries (Musiani, 2025).

In the architecture of modern energy networks, the dispatch center represents the decision-making node of maximum information density, where data on consumption, production, flows, and incidents converge. Here, immediate responses to imbalances are defined, interactions between producers and consumers are regulated, and the continuity of operation depends on the ability to intervene in real time. The automation of decisions in these operational centers is not just a technological extension but an epistemic mutation in which algorithms begin to interpret complex situations and formulate actions without direct supervision.

On the other hand, traditionally, dispatchers analyzed graphs, estimates, and signals from the network to manually decide to activate or withdraw units, redistribute loads, or isolate affected segments. This practice, although well-controlled, proves insufficient in the face of an increasingly volatile system, with intermittent sources and nonlinear events. In this context, artificial intelligence is called upon to ensure the continuity of decision-making under time pressure through algorithms capable of analysis in milliseconds, processing simultaneous flows, and anticipating consequences (Kovacs et al., 2022).

A notable example is the use of recurrent neural networks to recognize consumption patterns and detect abnormal deviations. Through continuous learning, these models develop the ability to "learn" network behaviors depending on the season, time, type of consumers, or weather conditions. In crisis situations, such as a sudden voltage drop or overload on a transformer, the algorithm can automatically suggest routing through an alternative circuit, alerting intervention teams, or reducing consumption through signals to industrial users (Zhang et al., 2023).

In some European countries, such as Denmark or Austria, control centers have begun to implement autonomous decision algorithms for frequency regulation, storage activation, and distributed generation management. These systems operate in time intervals that cannot be achieved by human intervention, effectively stabilizing fluctuations caused by variable wind or solar sources. The ability of these systems to operate without latency makes them indispensable in decentralized infrastructures, where synchronization becomes a condition for resilience (Riaz et al., 2021).

An increasingly present dimension is the automation of emergency decisions. In the event of a major incident—such as a short circuit on a high-voltage line or a power plant failure—algorithms run preconfigured scenarios, analyze the impact, and decide, in seconds, which units need to be shut down, which areas can be isolated, and how to maintain power to priority consumers. These decisions, when validated through rigorous simulations and testing, can significantly reduce recovery time and economic impact (Zhou et al., 2020).

Against the background of these innovations, the transparency of the decision-making process becomes a critical issue. Automation can generate technically optimal decisions, but they are inaccessible to human interpretation. Without clear traceability of algorithmic logic, the risk of challenge increases. Therefore, more and more projects include explainable AI (XAI) components, designed to translate automated decisions into forms understandable to operators and auditors (Holmes et al., 2022).

In the United States, pilot projects supported by the Department of Energy are testing the integration of AI into regional dispatchers to anticipate congestion and suggest redistribution actions. One outcome of these tests is that human operators are more likely to trust algorithm suggestions when they come with visual explanations and trust signals. This creates a symbiotic relationship in which AI does not replace the dispatcher but rather enhances his ability to manage complexity.

At the same time, there are attempts to introduce automated governance mechanisms into decision-making processes. Advanced platforms, such as those developed by ENTSO-E, propose models in which algorithmic decisions are validated by formal rules and periodically reviewed by digital ethics and security committees. In this way, blind automatism is avoided, and a deliberative dimension is introduced into automated processes (ENTSO-E, 2024).

On the legal dimension, questions are raised regarding the liability for automated decisions. If an algorithm triggers an outage that affects vulnerable consumers, who is responsible? The software provider? The network operator? The equipment manufacturer? These questions require a reconstruction of the rules of responsibility so that it can be attributed according to the degree of autonomy, the capacity for human supervision, and compliance with standards (Musiani, 2025).

At the same time, the automation of decisions has implications in the security sphere. A system that makes critical decisions without human intervention becomes a target for cyberattacks. Therefore, emerging standards, such as IEC 62443, require rigorous stress tests and fail-safe scenarios, in which the system returns to human control in case of compromise or malfunction (IEC, 2023).

Dispatch automation is not only a matter of efficiency but also of trust. For these systems to be accepted, they must be transparent, verifiable, and open to continuous evaluation. The introduction of algorithmic auditing tools, as well as training staff in understanding automated decisions, becomes a condition for the democratic functioning of smart grids.

3. ALGORITHMIC SECURITY AND POWER DISTRIBUTION IN DIGITALIZED ENERGY ARCHITECTURE

In today's digitalized energy landscape, embedded algorithms and advanced control systems govern invisible flows of decision, adjustment, and intervention. Critical infrastructure is now crisscrossed by lines of code that determine technical behaviors, real-time reactions, and, increasingly, automated decisions. However, the code that underlies these functionalities is not always produced or supervised by entities under European jurisdiction. Dependence on software developed outside the EU has become a latent issue, but with structural implications, from cybersecurity to the ability to guarantee auditability and decision-making sovereignty.

SCADA systems, edge computing platforms, and machine learning modules integrated into transformer stations or control centers often operate on infrastructures and software environments provided by global corporations. Often, the source code is inaccessible, updates are managed remotely, and the algorithmic logic remains obscure to the end users. This operating regime can lead to a "functional dependency"—in which energy network administrators become captive to technical solutions that they cannot control or modify autonomously (Burgess et al., 2023).

Cases reported in the United States and Israel, where suppliers of industrial equipment have refused to provide access to firmware code in the context of security investigations, reveal the risk that critical infrastructure is subject to commercial or geopolitical constraints (Tucker & Mahnken, 2024). In the European context, where regulations on data protection and decision-making auditability are stricter, this software opacity turns into a legal and democratic vulnerability.

A recent study conducted by the European Union Agency for Cybersecurity (ENISA) highlighted the fact that over 75% of industrial control systems analyzed in member states rely on proprietary software of non-European origin, without the possibility of full code inspection (ENISA, 2024). Furthermore, the implementation of critical updates is often contractually conditional, which can delay the remediation of identified vulnerabilities or compromise the ability to react in the event of attacks.

Software dependency is not only technical; it also involves a power relationship between the external developer and the internal user. In the absence of a coherent European digital ecosystem, states become consumers of a technology encoded in economic and normative logics that do not belong to them. Thus, decision-making autonomy is de facto diminished, and operational control over critical infrastructure is partially delegated outside the sovereign regulatory space (Lemke, 2023).

At the same time, dependency on external software platforms raises issues related to interoperability, standardization, and scalability. Dominant providers often impose proprietary formats, closed protocols, and integration limits that affect the flexibility of networks and the ability to adopt alternative solutions. In the energy sector, where adaptability to renewable sources and demand fluctuations is vital, software bottlenecks can become critical obstacles (Gasser et al., 2024).

To address these challenges, several European initiatives are promoting the development of certified open-source software for critical infrastructure. The Eclipse Oniro project and the efforts coordinated by Gaia-X aim to build a transparent digital ecosystem in which sovereignty over code and data is guaranteed at the institutional level (Gaia-X AISBL, 2024). However, these efforts remain fragmented and insufficiently supported by coherent industrial policies.

A good practice example is provided by the grid operator Elia Group in Belgium, which launched its own energy management platform based on open source, auditable, and compatible with EU standards. According to the technical report published in 2023, this solution allowed for a 30% reduction in incident response time, as well as the accelerated integration of new distributed energy sources (Elia Group, 2023).

On the regulatory front, the EU introduced the Cyber Resilience Act in 2024, which imposes strict security standards for connected digital products and obliges suppliers to provide access to relevant technical documentation (European Parliament & Council, 2024). However, the practical application of these rules faces difficulties, especially in the context of existing contracts with large international suppliers.

At the same time, recent discussions on the introduction of the concept of "strategic digital autonomy" in the European treaties reflect an increasingly clear awareness that critical infrastructure cannot be managed through external dependencies (Musiani, 2025). It is not just about security but about the ability of a state or union to shape its networks, to understand the internal functioning of equipment, and to intervene, if necessary, in the code that governs them.

Reforming the way technology is treated in public procurement is becoming a necessary direction. Several European countries—including France and Austria—have introduced digital sovereignty criteria in the evaluation of bids for critical equipment, favoring solutions that offer control over the code, interoperability, and respect for local data protection rules (Bourguignon et al., 2023).

Algorithms, fueled by constant data flows, have become vectors of automated reasoning, influencing production rates, distribution routes, consumption levels, and energy balance in complex networks. Increasingly, these decisions are not generated within the institutions operating the infrastructure but are outsourced to third-party entities—platforms, software providers, or algorithms delivered as a service. This strategic outsourcing of the decision-making process generates not only advantages in terms of scalability or operational optimization but also significant risks from the perspective of cybersecurity and systemic integrity.

A first level of vulnerability arises in the lack of direct control over the code and algorithmic architecture. In many cases, critical decisions—such as automatically redistributing load in electrical grids or triggering fail-safe processes—are produced by proprietary, opaque systems outside of direct institutional oversight. According to a report published by the National Institute of Standards and Technology (NIST), the lack of transparency and the inability to conduct independent audits of outsourced algorithms represent a major source of risk for smart grids (NIST, 2023).

Furthermore, the connected nature of these systems amplifies the attack surface. Outsourcing decisions often involve transmitting data outside the local infrastructure to external processing centers, which exposes communication channels to interception, manipulation, or blockage. In the energy sector, incidents reported in 2022 in Germany and Canada—where automated grid management systems were temporarily paralyzed by denial-of-service attacks directed at external servers—concretely illustrate the danger of delegating decision-making to uncontrolled infrastructures (Kaspersky ICS CERT, 2023).

Another dimension of risk is the inability to quickly diagnose a malfunction. When an external algorithm produces an erroneous decision—such as an unjustified interruption of the energy supply—local operators face major difficulties in reconstructing the decision-making chain. The lack of access to detailed logs, to the operating parameters of the algorithm, or to the conditions under which the action was triggered makes it almost impossible to delimit the cause and assign responsibility (ENISA, 2024).

In addition to auditability difficulties, a major risk derives from the potential injection of malicious code through uncontrolled software updates. Outsourced AI systems require constant updates, either to adjust performance or to correct vulnerabilities. Remotely managing these updates without strict verification protocols opens a latent channel for the deliberate or accidental insertion of hostile functionalities. According to a study conducted by the European Union Agency for Cybersecurity, in 2023 over 150 cases of exploitable backdoors were identified in software provided by external companies for the energy infrastructure of member states (ENISA, 2024).

We cannot ignore the geostrategic dimension of the risks. Outsourcing decisions to suppliers outside the European space implies potential exposure to political pressures or divergent commercial interests. In the event of a diplomatic or economic conflict, access to technical support or critical functionalities of the system could be restricted, affecting the ability of states to manage their networks. Such a precedent was documented in 2021, when an Asian company temporarily blocked access to software infrastructure installed in power plants in Central Africa, citing contractual clauses (Peters et al., 2022).

To lower these risks, strong checks on algorithms are necessary, which should include regular reviews, ensuring decisions are made independently, and having systems in place for humans to take control in real-time. In parallel, the promotion of open standards and auditable source code is becoming a condition for structural resilience. Initiatives such as Germany's "Sovereign Edge" project, which aims to create an automated decision-making ecosystem in critical infrastructures based on European open-source software, represent a significant step in this direction (BMWK, 2023).

At the same time, a review of the contractual framework governing the relationship between infrastructure operators and software providers is required. Transparency, accountability, and inspection clauses need to be strengthened to prevent situations where the state or operator becomes passive in the face of dysfunctions generated by external decisions. The European Commission's report "Digital Sovereignty in Critical Infrastructure" highlights the need to impose, through legislation, minimum internal control requirements on algorithms used in critical processes (European Commission, 2024).

4. EMERGING REGULATORY FRAMEWORKS AND REDISTRIBUTION OF RESPONSIBILITY IN ALGORITHMIC ECOSYSTEMS

The AI Act proposes a classification of AI-based systems according to the risks they entail. In the energy context, many of these systems fall into the high-risk category, having a direct impact on the security of infrastructure, the stability of supply, and the balance of markets. From this perspective, AI solution providers must comply with strict requirements for transparency, testability, and human oversight (European Commission, 2021).

This legislative configuration becomes even more delicate as AI is applied in the context of smart grids, where the data generated is massive, continuous, and often personal. GDPR thus becomes an inevitable companion to the AI Act, as the protection of personal data extends not only to end consumers but also to employees, prosumers, and other actors involved in the energy chain. The sensitivity of data collected by smart meters or IoT devices requires clear conditions for processing, storage, and access (Voigt & Von dem Bussche, 2017).

A structural challenge is the traceability of algorithmic decision-making in distributed energy systems. Although the AI Act requires a high degree of explainability, the reality of deep learning or reinforcement learning models used to balance supply and demand makes it difficult to identify the internal logic of decisions. This lack of transparency affects not only legal compliance but also the trust of users and public authorities in the functioning of these systems (European Parliamentary Research Service, 2022).

Furthermore, predictive systems integrated into energy distribution tend to operate on the basis of consumption profiles, generating automated decisions that can lead to indirect discrimination. For example, segregating consumers based on energy history can lead to unjustified limitations or differentiated tariffs, which contravenes the GDPR principles of fair processing and the right to object (Taddeo & Floridi, 2018).

In this context, regulatory interoperability between the AI Act and the GDPR becomes crucial. The two legal instruments must be applied simultaneously, and the entities involved must build clear governance mechanisms that combine algorithmic risk assessment with data protection impact assessment (DPIA). In the case of AI-based energy projects, a well-structured DPIA must consider not only the source and nature of the data but also how automated decisions impact the fundamental rights and freedoms of individuals (Article 29 Data Protection Working Party, 2017).

A special dimension is given by the automated decision-making process in the context of energy dispatching. Here, AI can determine the triggering or stopping of supply according to predefined parameters. The AI Act requires continuous human supervision in such scenarios to avoid the complete transfer of authority to an opaque system. At the same time, the GDPR restricts the taking of decisions that produce significant legal effects without human intervention, requiring the existence of a procedural framework for contestation and review (Voigt & Von dem Bussche, 2017).

In the event of incidents, such as network overload caused by an erroneous prediction, the regulations propose remediation and traceability mechanisms. The AI Act requires periodic audits of the performance of the systems, and the GDPR requires complete documentation of the data flow involved in the decision. These two requirements converge towards the idea of an energy ecosystem governed by clear rules of accountability and monitoring.

At an institutional level, cooperation between energy regulators and data protection authorities becomes indispensable. Recent studies emphasize the need to establish common oversight mechanisms in which AI is understood both as a disruptive technology and as a legal object with multiple consequences (Cave & Dignum, 2019).

The expansion of artificial intelligence in energy infrastructures has subtly altered the boundaries between the actors involved, the nature of the decisions made, and the possible forms of verification. Instead of a traditional scheme, in which the decision-maker could be precisely identified in a unidirectional chain, the current context requires a reinterpretation of responsibility. The consequences of algorithmic actions are shared between multiple entities—from system creators and software developers to network providers, local administrators, and end users. In this landscape, compliance is no longer a one-time gesture but a spiral path, guided by technical tools, legal mechanisms, and continuous interactions between components of the same living system.

The distribution of tasks and decision-making impact requires a review of legal paradigms. Traditionally, blame was sought in a single point. Today, influences propagate in a dense space of algorithmic, contractual, and institutional connections. This is how a thinking based on diffuse responsibility develops, in which each participant contributes to the stability of a collective equilibrium. The proportional allocation of responsibility, depending on the level of technical control, the degree of knowledge, and the impact of the action, becomes a condition for the functioning of the entire ecosystem (Zarsky, 2016). As energy systems become digitalized, the idea of compliance becomes dynamic. A relationship is emerging in which internal audit, transparent documentation, and the capacity for rapid intervention are reconfigured to respond to the accelerated pace of automated decisions. The proposal for a European regulation on artificial intelligence, known as the AI Act, introduces a framework that addresses exactly these dimensions: classifying systems according to risk and implementing prior checks and algorithmic traceability in sensitive areas such as energy distribution networks (European Commission, 2021).

The General Data Protection Regulation (GDPR), although formulated primarily for the protection of personal data, offers a set of principles that can be extended to distributed accountability models. The notion of proactive accountability encourages entities to adopt preventive measures, document algorithmic decisions, and allow for human intervention where the impact may affect dignity or fundamental rights (Voigt & Von dem Bussche, 2017). In smart grids, where data flows and operational decisions are interconnected, these mechanisms become benchmarks for legal coherence.

From the perspective of contractual architecture, a transition is observed towards complex conventions, which establish not only deliverables and deadlines, but also criteria for transparency, audit, and cooperation in case of malfunctions. Clauses regulating the operation of AI systems increasingly include provisions on algorithm verification, the right of access to source code or decision logic, as well as protocols for incident management (Calo & Kerr, 2013). These reactive and preventive mechanisms can generate a framework of stability even in unforeseen situations.

An emerging concept is that of built-in compliance from the design phase. Engineers and algorithm developers are invited to collaborate with experts in ethics and law, so that systems include verification filters, action limits and options for human intervention. This way of thinking favors the creation of technologies that anticipate risks and minimize negative consequences before they become critical (Floridi et al., 2022). It is not just about technical design, but about modeling a social contract between the algorithm and society.

Institutional cooperation becomes a structural axis in this context. In several European countries, regulatory authorities collaborate with energy operators and independent organizations to build mutual evaluation mechanisms. In the Netherlands, for example, a verification framework for the operation of AI-based smart meters has been developed, including criteria such as the comprehensibility of decisions and the risks of digital exclusion (Dutch Data Protection Authority, 2022). Such initiatives contribute to building trust and reducing systemic risks.

In Romania, dialogue between energy and data protection authorities is becoming increasingly necessary. Connecting technical and legal knowledge can generate good practices, rapid intervention protocols and verification tools in decentralized networks. The distribution of control should not lead to a dilution of responsibility, but to a clear mapping of competences and obligations.

Another pillar in this construction is collaborative compliance. Modern energy networks involve multiple suppliers, shared infrastructures and distributed decisions. In this framework, regulation cannot be imposed from the top down, but must be co-created through intersectoral partnerships. Mutual auditing, independent assessments and common standards can prevent fragmentation and maintain a high level of transparency (Floridi et al., 2022).

5. FUTURE RESEARCH DIRECTIONS

The research horizon in the field of artificial intelligence applied to energy infrastructure is expanding, but what is visible beyond the present is not a simple technological extension but a reconfiguration of the interactions between digital autonomy, decisional control, and collective responsibility. From this perspective, the future does not belong exclusively to the laboratory but also to the space of convergence between science, normativity, and democratic deliberation.

A first field that requires increased attention is the understanding of algorithmic opacification processes in distributed energy systems. With the increasing degree of autonomy of smart grids, questions arise about how the decision is produced, how uncertainty is aggregated, and what forms of intervention are still possible after the automatic activation of a mechanism. Future investigations will have to go beyond the classic framework of technical audit, focusing on mapping the mechanisms of algorithmic intention formation and their impact on the real-time decision-making architecture.

In parallel, an exploration axis is opening up regarding the scalability of decentralized control models in the context of geopolitical and climate pressures. Local networks, powered by renewable sources and supported by energy communities, offer a potential for contextual autonomy that has not yet been investigated in depth. Research could analyze how decisions are negotiated between prosumers, how collective interests are harmonized with automated predictive models, and what governance structures can maintain the balance between systemic coherence and local freedom of action.

The legal dimension, although increasingly present in interdisciplinary reflections, continues to be approached fragmentarily. The future requires an epistemological reconfiguration of traditional concepts such as liability, diligence, or consent to translate them into a register compatible with distributed automated decision-making. New legal analysis tools will be needed, capable of tracking causal trajectories in dynamic algorithmic systems, as well as remediation mechanisms in the case of automated decisions with disproportionate impact.

Another emerging direction aims at building AI infrastructures that respect the principle of digital sovereignty without creating artificial barriers to the circulation of knowledge or scientific cooperation. Future investigations can imagine hybrid infrastructure models—decentralized but interoperable—in which sensitive energy data is kept locally, and machine learning is carried out through federated, transparent, and verifiable processes. A challenge here is to balance data security with algorithmic performance without sacrificing either accountability or innovation.

The field of predictive maintenance also offers a fertile platform for research. Beyond the refinement of statistical models, a reflection on the conditions under which prediction becomes a tool of excessive control or exclusion is required. Future research could investigate forms of ethical auditability of prediction and methods of social calibration of algorithms, depending on the technical, cultural, and economic context of each region. Participatory validation tools will also be needed, in which the automated decision is subject to deliberation by the affected communities.

At the same time, amid the growing pressure for decarbonization, energy forecasting models require a structural recalibration. The climate is becoming increasingly unpredictable, and historical correlations between demand and supply are losing their consistency. A line of research oriented toward resilience prediction is foreseen: how can algorithms anticipate not only consumption but also network vulnerabilities, the capacity to adapt under stress conditions, and the tolerance margins of digital infrastructure in the face of extreme events?

At the institutional level, research must explore new forms of collaboration between public, private, and academic entities. There is a need for co-constructed research platforms in which energy engineers, computer scientists, lawyers, and sociologists work together to define problems and build solutions. Current models of fragmented innovation must be replaced by collective learning ecosystems, in which responsibility is understood as a continuous process, not as a reaction to failure.

Another direction that requires attention is that of algorithmic education for decision-makers. In a world where energy is managed by predictive models, institutional leaders must understand the logic of their operation, their strengths, and their epistemic limits. Not only is digital literacy required, but also a form of critical thinking in relation to algorithms: the ability to question, to challenge, and to demand justifications in accessible language. Here, research can propose teaching methodologies, continuous training formats, and scenarios for simulating automated decisions.

Against the backdrop of these transformations, a line of reflection on the values that guide the design of intelligent systems is also emerging. The future of research cannot ignore the axiological dimension of technology: how are goals chosen, what types of costs are accepted, and what categories of risk are assumed or redistributed? Prospective studies can explore the cultural impact of decision-making automation, the risk of dehumanization in the context of algorithmic interaction, and the ways in which digital processes can become compatible with human dignity and democratic deliberation.

CONCLUSION

As artificial intelligence becomes a constant in energy architecture, the traditional distinctions between technology and regulation and between human operator and automated system are blurring at a speed that exceeds the capacity of existing norms to adapt. The phenomenon involves not only the integration of new technical tools into industrial processes but also the radical reconfiguration of decision-making in critical infrastructure. At the heart of this transformation is a paradigm shift: algorithms do not just respond to external stimuli but take the initiative, intervene, learn, and adjust, directly influencing the continuity of services, the distribution of resources, and even the contours of national sovereignty.

In this new context, simple technological performance is no longer enough. A conceptual reconstruction is necessary that reflects the complexity of the interactions between automated systems and institutional structures, between the logic of prediction and normative decision. Smart grids, predictive maintenance, consumption optimization, and energy decentralization are not only expressions of technological progress but also critical points where commercial interests, privacy concerns, and democratic aspirations collide.

In parallel, the legal structure is being challenged beyond its traditional limits. Categories such as guilt, responsibility, guarantee, or diligence must be reinterpreted in a world where the decision is often the result of a statistical equation, not of direct human intention. This requires a profound adaptation of regulatory instruments, but also of forms of democratic control. Without a normative infrastructure capable of decoding algorithmic logic and intervening effectively, public trust risks being eroded and the vulnerability of systems to increase exponentially.

A major challenge identified during this analysis is the tension between the externalization of decision-making and the need for technological sovereignty. Many of the platforms used to manage energy infrastructure are developed by entities outside the national or regional legal space. This reality raises not only cybersecurity issues but also questions related to legitimacy, transparency, and the effective capacity to intervene in the event of malfunctions. In the absence of real control over codes, standards, and data, energy autonomy becomes a fragile promise, dependent on the will of external actors.

At the same time, the ethical dimension of these transformations cannot be ignored. Algorithms that improve how we use resources or forecast problems are not unbiased; every automated choice reflects certain priorities, values, and exclusions, which can lead to unfair outcomes, particularly for vulnerable communities or areas. The lack of an effective challenge mechanism, the absence of decision-making transparency, or the difficulty of understanding the logic of the systems can lead to a form of digital alienation, in which the citizen becomes an object, not a partner of the energy system.

The transformations analyzed require a coherent response from all the actors involved. Not only regulatory institutions are called to intervene, but also developers of technological solutions, infrastructure operators, political decision-makers, and, last but not least, local communities. A smart, safe, and equitable energy ecosystem requires not only technological compatibility but also a shared vision of the values that must govern the interaction between man and algorithm.

The research directions highlighted outline a landscape in which the stakes are not only to optimize performance but to maintain a balance between progress and democratic control, between efficiency and fundamental rights. Artificial intelligence, in this context, is not just a tool but a new actor in the ecology of decision-making, which requires adapted mechanisms for integration, supervision, and intervention.

The future of critical infrastructures will depend on the collective capacity to design technological systems that, instead of circumventing norms, incorporate them. A sustainable energy future cannot be built without simultaneously strengthening normative, institutional, and democratic foundations. Instead of a simple adaptation to change, a deliberate reconfiguration of the way in which human society co-evolves with its own digital creation is required. Thus, the conclusion of this approach does not point to a terminus but opens a new field of reflection and responsible action.

REFERENCES

Alfayan, M., & Hagras, H. (2025). Towards an Explainable Artificial Intelligence approach for smart grid systems. *Discover Artificial Intelligence*, *5*(1), 40. DOI: 10.1007/s44163-025-00261-5

Alsaigh, R., Mehmood, R., & Katib, I. (2022). AI explainability and governance in smart energy systems: A review. *Frontiers in Energy Research*, *10*, 107129. DOI: 10.3389/fenrg.2023.107129

Arévalo, P., & Jurado, F. (2024). Impact of artificial intelligence on the planning and operation of distributed energy systems in smart grids. *Energies*, *17*(17), 4501. DOI: 10.3390/en17174501

Article 29 Data Protection Working Party. (2017). Guidelines on Data Protection Impact Assessment (DPIA). https://ec.europa.eu/newsroom/article29/item-detail.cfm?item_id=611236

Balamurugan, M., Narayanan, K., Raghu, N., Arjun Kumar, G. B., & Trupti, V. N. (2025). Role of artificial intelligence in smart grid – A mini review. *Frontiers in Artificial Intelligence*, *8*, 1551661. Advance online publication. DOI: 10.3389/frai.2025.1551661 PMID: 39968172

Bourguignon, F., Lefèvre, Q., & Schmidt, P. (2023). Building digital sovereignty: Policy frameworks in the EU. *Digital Policy Studies*, *7*(2), 132–149. DOI: 10.2139/ssrn.4412528

Brunton, F., & Nissenbaum, H. (2024). The limits of digital sovereignty. *Surveillance & Society*, *22*(1), 15–30. DOI: 10.24908/ss.v22i1.16012

Burgess, R., Klein, M., & Lee, S. (2023). Software dependency and national resilience in smart infrastructure. *Journal of Critical Infrastructure Studies*, *11*(4), 256–271. DOI: 10.1016/j.jcis.2023.02.009

Calo, R., & Kerr, I. (2013). Robotics and the New Cyberlaw. In Lin, P., Abney, K., & Bekey, G. A. (Eds.), *Robot Ethics: The Ethical and Social Implications of Robotics* (pp. 207–223). MIT Press.

Cave, S., & Dignum, V. (2019). Algorithms and Values. In Dubber, M., Pasquale, F., & Das, S. (Eds.), *The Oxford Handbook of AI Ethics* (pp. 247–265). Oxford University Press.

Deshpande, V. (2024). Smart grids integration with AI-powered demand response. *Research Journal of Computer Systems and Engineering*, *5*(1), 45–58.

Dutch Data Protection Authority. (2022). *Assessment Framework for AI in Smart Metering Systems*. https://autoriteitpersoonsgegevens.nl

Elia Group. (2023). *Open source architectures for secure energy system operations: Elia tech review*. https://www.eliagroup.eu

ENISA. (2024). *Threat Landscape for Artificial Intelligence in Critical Infrastructure*. European Union Agency for Cybersecurity. https://www.enisa.europa.eu/publications/ai-threat-landscape

ENTSO-E. (2024). Towards autonomous grid operation: Guidelines for AI-based dispatching. https://www.entsoe.eu

European Commission. (2021). Proposal for a Regulation laying down harmonised rules on artificial intelligence (Artificial Intelligence Act). https://eur-lex.europa.eu/legal-content/EN/TXT/?uri=CELEX%3A52021PC0206

European Commission. (2021). Proposal for a Regulation of the European Parliament and of the Council Laying Down Harmonised Rules on Artificial Intelligence (Artificial Intelligence Act). https://eur-lex.europa.eu/legal-content/EN/TXT/?uri=CELEX%3A52021PC0206

European Commission. (2022). Energy communities and the internal electricity market. *Official Journal of the European Union*. https://eur-lex.europa.eu/legal-content/EN/TXT/?uri=CELEX%3A52022DC0312

European Commission. (2024). *Digital sovereignty in critical infrastructure: Legal and regulatory framework proposal*. Publications Office of the European Union. https://europa.eu/publications/digital-sovereignty

European Parliament & Council. (2024). *Regulation (EU) 2024/2847 on Cyber Resilience for Digital Products*. Official Journal of the European Union. https://eur-lex.europa.eu/eli/reg/2024/2847/oj

European Parliamentary Research Service. (2022). Artificial Intelligence Act: EU Legislation in Progress. https://www.europarl.europa.eu/thinktank

Floridi, L., Cowls, J., Beltrametti, M., Chatila, R., Dignum, V., & Schafer, B. (2022). How to Design AI for a Good Society: Seven Principles. *Minds and Machines*, *30*(1), 1–24. DOI: 10.1007/s11023-020-09503-7

Gaia-X, A. I. S. B. L. (2024). Gaia-X Architectural Framework. Gaia-X AISBL. https://www.gaia-x.eu

Gasser, U., Budish, R., & Cohen, M. (2024). *Interoperability and control in global tech systems: A European perspective.* Harvard Kennedy School Policy Brief. https://cyber.harvard.edu/interoperability-control

Giordano, V., Gangale, F., & Fulli, G. (2020). *Smart grid projects outlook 2020: Innovation driving the energy transition.* European Commission JRC Science for Policy Report., DOI: 10.2760/21882

Hirth, L., Moser, P., & Nicolosi, M. (2021). Smart grids and AI-based control systems: Lessons from Germany. *Energy Economics*, *95*, 105112. DOI: 10.1016/j.eneco.2021.105112

Holmes, C., Zhang, Y., & Stodden, V. (2022). Explainable AI in critical infrastructure: Case studies from energy dispatching. *AI & Society*, *37*(2), 251–269. DOI: 10.1007/s00146-021-01211-2

IEC. (2023). Industrial communication networks - Network and system security – Part 2-1: Establishing an industrial automation and control system security program (IEC 62443-2-1). International Electrotechnical Commission. https://webstore.iec.ch

Ilias, M., Kovács, V., & Delgado, E. (2023). Regulating AI in the energy sector: A scoping review of EU laws. *Energies*, *18*(9), 2359. DOI: 10.3390/en18092359

Kaspersky, I. C. S. CERT. (2023). *Industrial cybersecurity incidents in smart grids.* https://ics-cert.kaspersky.com/reports

Khan, M. A., Saleh, A. M., Waseem, M., & Sajjad, I. A. (2022). Artificial Intelligence Enabled Demand Response: Prospects and Challenges in Smart Grid Environment. *IEEE Access : Practical Innovations, Open Solutions*, *10*, 11231–11245. DOI: 10.1109/ACCESS.2022.3231444

Kovacs, L., Nguyen, H., & Petrov, R. (2022). Machine learning in power system operations: Challenges and opportunities. *Electric Power Systems Research*, *206*, 107739. DOI: 10.1016/j.epsr.2021.107739

Le Coq, C., & Jaunziems, D. (2025). AI in the energy transition: Insights from Energy Talk 2025. *Free Policy Briefs.* https://freepolicybriefs.org/2025/06/02/ai-energy-transition

Lemke, T. (2023). Digital dependencies and the future of sovereignty: An infrastructure perspective. *European Review of Digital Politics*, *9*(1), 45–63. DOI: 10.1007/s41469-023-00612-1

Liu, B. J., Johansson, B. S., & Paulsson, V. (2025). AI-enabled predictive analytics in smart grids: The case of Sweden. *Linköping Electronic Conference Proceedings, 42*(3), 49–65. https://doi.org/DOI: 10.5560/liu.diva-portal.1956031

Liu, X., Riaz, S., & Farooq, M. (2022). AI in Swedish local smart grids: A case study. *Sustainable Energy Technologies and Assessments, 51*, 101092. DOI: 10.1016/j.seta.2022.101092

Luthander, R., Widén, J., & Munkhammar, J. (2020). Self-consumption and self-sufficiency of solar photovoltaic systems with battery storage: A study of Swedish households. *Renewable Energy, 106*, 193–201. DOI: 10.1016/j.renene.2016.12.044

Mengelkamp, E., Gärttner, J., & Weinhardt, C. (2018). Decentralizing energy systems through local energy markets: A blockchain-based market approach. *Computer Science -. Research for Development, 33*, 207–214. DOI: 10.1007/s00450-017-0360-9

Mohamed, R., Eltamaly, A. M., & Abdelaziz, A. Y. (2021). AI-based adaptive energy management for prosumer networks. *International Journal of Electrical Power & Energy Systems, 129*, 106810. DOI: 10.1016/j.ijepes.2020.106810

Musiani, F. (2025). Infrastructuring digital sovereignty: An agenda for digital self-determination. *Frontiers in Communication, 10*, 1562072. DOI: 10.3389/fcomm.2025.1562072

NIST. (2023). *Managing AI risks in critical energy systems: Technical guidance*. National Institute of Standards and Technology., DOI: 10.6028/NIST.SP.1276

Ofgem. (2024, April 3). Ofgem fears 'AI collusion' in energy market. *The Times*. https://www.thetimes.co.uk/article/03ofgem-q6dspmr3r

Pan, X., González, R., & Weber, F. (2025). The paradigm shift in the energy sector through green innovation. *Energy Research & Social Science, 102*, 103076. DOI: 10.1016/j.erss.2024.103076

Peters, J., Akoto, N., & Mbogo, A. (2022). Geopolitical asymmetries in digital infrastructure. *International Journal of Critical Infrastructure Protection, 38*, 100519. DOI: 10.1016/j.ijcip.2022.100519

Riaz, S., Alwahaibi, A., & Farooq, M. (2021). Autonomous frequency control using reinforcement learning. *Renewable Energy, 173*, 1274–1282. DOI: 10.1016/j.renene.2021.04.052

Ruhnau, O., & Qvist, S. A. (2022). Storage requirements in a 100% renewable European power system: Extreme events and integration of sector coupling. *Energy, 238*, 121963. DOI: 10.1016/j.energy.2021.121963

Saroj, S., Battacharjee, S., & Sharma, R. (2023). Quantum algorithms for intelligent demand response in smart grids. *Applied Sciences (Basel, Switzerland)*, *13*(2), 657. DOI: 10.3390/app13020657

Smith, J., Zhao, L., & Patel, N. (2024). Governing the green transition: The role of AI investments in renewable energy adoption. *Sustainability*, *17*(12), 5538. DOI: 10.3390/su17125538

Taddeo, M., & Floridi, L. (2018). How AI can be a force for good. *Science*, *361*(6404), 751–752. DOI: 10.1126/science.aat5991 PMID: 30139858

Tucker, P., & Mahnken, T. (2024). The geopolitics of code: Strategic software in critical infrastructure. *Survival: Global Politics and Strategy*, *66*(1), 77–95. DOI: 10.1080/00396338.2024.1697780

Voigt, P., & Von dem Bussche, A. (2017). *The EU General Data Protection Regulation (GDPR): A Practical Guide*. Springer International Publishing. DOI: 10.1007/978-3-319-57959-7

World Economic Forum. (2025). *Global Risks Report 2025*. World Economic Forum. https://www.weforum.org/publications/global-risks-report-2025/

Zarsky, T. Z. (2016). The Trouble with Algorithmic Decisions: An Analytic Road Map to Examine Efficiency and Fairness in Automated and Opaque Decision Making. *Science, Technology & Human Values*, *41*(1), 118–132. DOI: 10.1177/0162243915605575

Zhang, Q., Yuan, Z., & Li, J. (2023). Neural decision-making in electric power dispatch: Enhancing resilience and responsiveness. *Energy Reports*, *9*, 1587–1599. DOI: 10.1016/j.egyr.2022.12.005

Zhou, Y., Wang, X., & Liu, J. (2020). Real-time decision automation for power dispatch using deep reinforcement learning. *IEEE Transactions on Smart Grid*, *11*(4), 3282–3293. DOI: 10.1109/TSG.2019.2962102

Zhou, Y., Zhang, Y., & Liu, C. (2021). Distributed edge intelligence for smart grid systems. *IEEE Internet of Things Journal*, *8*(7), 5338–5350. DOI: 10.1109/JIOT.2020.3023428

Chapter 2
Blockchain Revolution: Transforming International Trade Law for the Digital Age

Ayushi Singh
https://orcid.org/0009-0009-2386-3195
Jindal Global Law School, O.P. Jindal Global University, India

Samanvi Narang
https://orcid.org/0000-0001-6053-1928
Jindal Global Law School, O.P. Jindal Global University, India

Abhipsa Upasana Dash
https://orcid.org/0009-0003-2399-7819
Jindal Global Law School, O.P. Jindal Global University, India

ABSTRACT

Blockchain technology defies the existing regulatory frameworks and raises urgent regulatory and governance issues worthy of the immediate attention of policymakers, international institutions and legal scholars. The digital divide in technological access and regulatory preparedness between developed and developing/underdeveloped countries aggravates the existing disparities in trade participation. The chapter explores the legal and practical implications of blockchain in simplifying cross-border trade and improving regulatory processes. It identifies the contemporary trade and supply chain issues and examines the potential of blockchain technology in resolving such issues. The chapter further critically examines the pressing concerns and regulatory challenges in the integration of blockchain into international trade and intends to provide solutions to address them. The chapter

DOI: 10.4018/979-8-3373-3186-7.ch002

explores whether international organisations such as the WTO can play a pivotal role in enabling blockchain integration, curbing the digital divide and shaping a supportive regulatory environment for the same.

1. INTRODUCTION

The world is undergoing a seismic transformation driven by the Fourth Industrial Revolution, a technological shift characterized by the convergence of digital, physical, and biological systems (Schwab, 2016; Interaction Design Foundation, 2025; Kim, 2021). Unlike previous revolutions which relied on steam, electricity, or information, this thrives on interconnected, intelligent technologies such as artificial intelligence, internet, robotics, and blockchain. These technologies are not only automating and optimizing processes but are fundamentally reshaping how industries function, how economies are organized, and how nations trade (World Scientific, 2025).

This transformation is very evident in the realm of international trade. Traditionally, cross-border trade has been marred by bureaucratic inefficiencies, lack of transparency, siloed data systems, and the high cost of compliance with varying national laws (Grier, 2023; UNCTAD, 2023; Digicast Technologies, 2023). However, digitization is progressively replacing chapter-based transactions with digital equivalents, streamlining logistics, customs documentation, and payments (UNCTAD, 2023). The shift towards digital trade infrastructure is both a necessity and an opportunity, paving the way for greater inclusion, agility, and regulatory oversight in a globalized world economy (Digicast Technologies, 2023).

While blockchain first garnered attention as the foundational technology behind cryptocurrencies such as Bitcoin and Ethereum, its utility far exceeds digital finance (Nakamoto, 2008; Schwab, 2016; Forbes Technology Council, 2023). At its core, blockchain is a decentralized, tamper-proof ledger system that allows multiple parties to maintain a shared and synchronized record of transactions without the need for a central authority. This decentralized and transparent nature of blockchain makes it particularly well-suited to international trade, where the number of actors, intermediaries, and jurisdictions complicate the flow of goods and services (Trade Council, 2024).

Increasingly, blockchain is being deployed across global supply chains to verify the origin of goods, monitor shipments in real-time, automate contractual obligations through smart contracts, and ensure compliance with international regulations (Turing, 2023; MDPI, 2023; Sethi & Makwana, 2024). From tracking ethically sourced raw materials to verifying certificates of origin or automating trade finance settlements, blockchain has emerged as a revolutionary tool for enhancing trust, efficiency, and accountability in global trade.

This chapter aims to trace the transformative role of blockchain technology in international trade. It will analyze the practical and legal implications of blockchain for cross-border trade, with a specific focus on how it can enhance transparency, reduce transaction costs, improve regulatory compliance, and support trade facilitation (UNCTAD, 2023; Trade Council, 2024).

The chapter also seeks to critically evaluate the challenges and limitations of blockchain adoption, including jurisdictional uncertainties, data privacy conflicts, regulatory fragmentation, and the digital divide between developed and developing countries (Zhuk, 2025; Szabo et al., 2024). By addressing these complexities, the chapter provides a visionary roadmap for the harmonious and inclusive integration of blockchain into the international trade system.

2. UNDERSTANDING BLOCKCHAIN: KEY FEATURES AND TECHNOLOGICAL FOUNDATIONS

The present world is undergoing rapid changes due to emerging technologies. The cornerstone of such transformation is the introduction and application of blockchain technology and artificial intelligence (AI) in the day-to-day lives of people. While both of these technologies are pioneering in their own right, their combined impact is even more significant. To consider the importance of blockchain and AI in the legal and policy world, it is necessary to understand their fundamental technological architectures.

Blockchain is a decentralized ledger technology that provides verifiability, immutability, and decentralised automation (Singh, 2025). It refers to a system of distributed record book of transactions. The transactions are verified by the participants of a system itself, as opposed to a central verification authority. It gained popularity due to a white paper by 'Satoshi Nakamoto', who is an anonymous individual or group of people regarded as the forefounder(s) of Bitcoin (Nakamoto, 2008). While it was first envisioned to support cryptocurrencies, it has found growing use in all domains wherein authentication of multiple transactions is required to establish a clear chain of title of ownership—e.g. for land records, cars, artwork, Non-Fungible Tokens (NFTs), etc. (Riss, 2023; Kachura, 2023; Kalaiselvi et al., 2023).

AI is a broad umbrella term for technologies that allow machines the ability to perform tasks that require real-time decision making after analysis of input factors, which is ordinarily done by learning the data, analysis of patterns etc. Machine learning, a species of AI, focuses on large language model (LLM) transformers understanding natural language by statistical probability and pattern recognition, which are used by Generative AI systems that produce real-time output based on human input (Goldberg, 2015; Hristea & Caragea, 2022; Li, 2018). This is done by analysing the input language in the raw data, which is then analyzed by the LLM to 'understand' constitutive elements of human language i.e. meaning of words, relationships between words, grammar, syntax etc. After filtration of unwanted materials, the raw data undergoes a process called tokenization, in which it is broken down into small units called 'tokens' (Mistral AI, 2024; Janakiram, 2024). These tokens have a corresponding 'vector', which is a numerical value that reflects a variety of semantic, syntactical, and grammatical information about the 'token' to which it corresponds. 'Vectors', are therefore, a numerical representation of semantic information about a 'token' (the meaning of the word/sub-word, grammatical, and semantic, information about the 'token'). 'Parameters' are internal values of the LLM, adjusted during training to reflect the broader statistical relationships learnt from the training data (Tashev, 2025). Each 'parameter' roughly reflects the statistical relationship between different words in different scenarios. At its crudest explanation, when any input is received by a generative AI model, it analyses the tokens in the same and basis the parameters from the training, it predicts the output word-by-word which is then shared with the user. AI has simultaneously changed how systems analyze data and make decisions without human assistance, especially in the areas of machine learning and natural language processing (Tapscott & Tapscott, 2016).

Key Features of Blockchain Technology

a. **Decentralization.** Blockchain technology fundamentally transforms traditional models of authority and recordkeeping by distributing control across a decentralized network of participants, known as nodes (Swan, 2015). Each node actively takes part in validating and maintaining the integrity of the shared ledger, thereby eliminating the need for a single centralized authority to authenticate transactions or records. This decentralized structure directly challenges the foundational assumptions of most legal frameworks, which are historically built upon hierarchical models of authority, where an official entity such as a court, government body, or registrar, acts as the ultimate source of truth and legitimacy. As Wright and De Filippi (2015) point out, the blockchain's peer-to-peer architecture disrupts these legal presumptions by shifting trust away from central institutions and embedding it within code-based consensus mechanisms (Rajeshwar et al., 2025). However, while this shift initially appears to undermine established legal norms, it also presents a unique opportunity for legal systems, particularly in the administration of justice. By reducing dependence on often overburdened or slow-moving centralized authorities, blockchain can help streamline legal processes such as record verification, contract enforcement, and chain-of-custody documentation (Authenticated e-Discovery, 2025). This, in turn, has the potential to improve the efficiency and speed of judicial proceedings, enabling courts and legal authorities to dispense justice more rapidly and with greater transparency. Thus, while blockchain decentralization complicates traditional legal paradigms, it also offers a complementary mechanism that, if properly integrated, could enhance the delivery of justice in contemporary legal systems.

b. **Evidence Law and Immutability.** Since the data cannot be unilaterally changed once it has been thoroughly verified and added to the chain, accruing to blockchain's immutability, it lends credibility to evidence that can be used for legal proceedings and provides value in dispensation of justice. Strong probative value in court proceedings is suggested by this feature of blockchain, which enhances evidentiary reliability (Finck, 2019; Rajeshwar et al., 2025; Kang et al., 2025). It also has the effect of reducing corruption and inefficiency thus boosting trust in the justice dispensation system. However, it causes conflict with data protection frameworks like the GDPR and India's Digital Personal Data Protection Act, 2023 which include rights to rectification and deletion (Finck, 2019; Galis, 2024). Thus, there is a gap that countries around the world need to address to balance changing ideas of informational autonomy with the permanence of blockchain.

c. **Privacy vs. Transparency.** Every transaction on a public blockchain is visible to all participants, promoting complete transactional transparency. Concerns about privacy and confidentiality are also raised, even though this promotes auditability and confidence in public institutions (Tapscott & Tapscott, 2016; Financial Crime Academy, 2025; Galis, 2024). On the other hand, private systems administered by the judiciary may have the effect of reducing transparency (for the need to protect personal or competitive confidentiality), and there is a need to find middle ground for disclosure, access, and dispute settlement procedures (Outlook India, 2025).

d. **Legal Automation and Smart Contracts.** Smart contracts are blockchain-based scripts that run on their own. Without additional human input, they initiate action such as transfers, approvals, or notifications, when predetermined criteria are satisfied (Mik, 2017; Sharma, 2024). While such contracts promise efficiency and remove intermediaries, they are still not free from uncertainties and technological challenges to be fully adopted into the judicial system. While traditional contract law has developed due to ambiguity and judicial discretion, smart contracts use deterministic logic and might not respond to unforeseen events, and thus may not be suitable for the ever-evolving nature of contractual disputes (Hunit, 2025).

AI and Blockchain come together in both operational and strategic methodologies. Blockchain makes sure that data is real, and AI helps with reasoning and making decisions (Saxena & Shukla, 2021; Daley, 2023). When used together, they make it possible for platforms to not only record data but also actively interpret it. However, it comes with its unique set of challenges, inter alia the following:

A. **Liability and Distributed Intelligence.** As the old IBM saying goes, a computer can never be held responsible, so a computer should never make a management decision. AI models that work with blockchains make it possible to analyze facts in real time and assist in decision making. However, this also removes humans from the chain of responsibility and makes it nearly impossible to attribute accountability and liability in the event something goes wrong. It is not clear who is legally responsible if an AI-informed smart contract goes wrong: the coder, the deployer, the data provider, or the network as a whole (Mik, 2017; Daley, 2023).
B. **Clear Algorithms and Legal Standards of Fairness.** Blockchains are often recognized for being open, but AI algorithms, especially those that use deep learning, tend to work like black boxes (Harvard DCE, 2025). This difference raises important questions. If the decision-making process is not transparent, the same will become an antithesis to the very system it intends to create. AI must meet standards of fairness and explainability for legally important results like risk scoring or compliance flagging, however, the present models seem a far way off from achieving the same (Rolling Out, 2025)
C. **Protecting Data and Designing Ethically.** For better performance, AI systems need to be trained on large datasets. However, significant questions have been raised on collection of this raw data for training of LLMs. AI giants including OpenAI, Microsoft, Google, and Anthropic are facing lawsuits in various countries throughout the world, with allegations of misappropriation, piracy, and copyright infringement. When this information is taken from or stored on unchangeable blockchains, it raises a legal question: how to guarantee lawful data processing, anonymization, and deletion rights (Finck, 2019; Galis, 2024; Rolling Out, 2025). There are ways to meet these needs, like zero-knowledge proofs and homomorphic encryption, but they are not widely used yet.

The subsequent section of this chapter critically analyzes how blockchain is transforming international trade, focusing on five key dimensions: (1) digitization of trade documentation (bills of lading, letters of credit); (2) real-time supply chain tracking and customs efficiency; (3) blockchain's role in dispute reduction; and (4) its utility in enhancing trade compliance and due diligence. Through an interdisciplinary review of technology, law, and policy, the authors argue that while blockchain is not a panacea, it offers significant gains in efficiency, transparency, and resilience in the global trading system.

3. BLOCKCHAIN AND THE TRANSFORMATION OF INTERNATIONAL TRADE

Over the past two decades, international trade has undergone significant digitization, driven by globalization, technological innovation, and the increasing complexity of global supply chains. Yet, even as financial flows and communications have become instantaneously digital, the foundational infrastructure supporting cross-border trade namely documentation, compliance, and verification systems remains largely paper-based, fragmented, and inefficient (World Economic Forum [WEF], 2020). This analog inertia contributes to high transaction costs, processing delays, and significant exposure to fraud and human error.

In international trade, blockchain can be leveraged to digitize and streamline trade documentation, such as bills of lading and letters of credit, which have historically required physical couriering and manual verification. It also has the capacity to enhance supply chain traceability, automate customs and compliance processes, and reduce disputes through secure and verifiable data trails (Apte & Petrovsky, 2016; Saberi et al., 2019).

Furthermore, as governments and regulators globally begin to recognize the legal status of electronic trade documents, the ecosystem is ripe for a shift towards digital trade infrastructures built on blockchain. The adoption of the UNCITRAL Model Law on Electronic Transferable Records (MLETR) by countries like Singapore and Bahrain has further catalyzed this digital evolution (UNCITRAL, 2017; WTO, 2021). These legal developments, coupled with increasing ESG and due diligence requirements, suggest that blockchain can also be a tool for enhancing compliance, sustainability tracking, and responsible sourcing (OECD, 2022).

Transforming Trade Documentation: Bills of Lading and Letters of Credit

The documentation that facilitates international trade viz. bills of lading (BoLs) and letters of credit (LoCs) forms the backbone of cross-border transactions. However, the persistent reliance on paper-based and manual processes for issuing, verifying, and transferring these documents introduces delays, increases administrative costs, and exposes trading parties to fraud and human error. Blockchain offers a paradigm shift by enabling the digitization, automation, and secure transfer of trade documents, thereby significantly reducing transaction time and risk.

Bills of Lading: From paper to Blockchain. A BoL serves multiple legal and commercial functions: it is a receipt for shipped goods, evidence of the contract of carriage, and a document of title (Murray, Holloway, & Timson-Hunt, 2017). Despite its critical importance, traditional BoLs are still issued and transferred in paper form, often requiring physical couriering between banks, freight companies, shippers, and buyers.

Blockchain technology enables the creation of electronic bills of lading (eBoLs) that are digitally signed, time-stamped, and immutable, allowing for real-time sharing and verification among authorized stakeholders. The implementation of eBoLs on blockchain networks not only reduces processing time but also eliminates the risk of document forgery and double spending. A leading example is CargoX, which uses the Ethereum blockchain to provide secure eBoL services. (CargoX, 2020).

The legal recognition of eBoLs has also been progressing globally. The UNCITRAL MLETR provides a harmonized legal framework for the use of electronic equivalents of traditional paper-based negotiable instruments, including BoL (UNCITRAL, 2017). Countries like Bahrain, Singapore, and the United Kingdom have either adopted or initiated legislation aligned with MLETR to legally recognize blockchain-based eBoLs (WTO, 2021).

Letters of Credit and Smart Contracts. An LoC is a payment guarantee issued by a bank on behalf of a buyer, promising to pay the seller upon presentation of specified documents (Chakrabarty & Ghosh, 2022). It mitigates payment risk in international trade but involves multiple intermediaries, document checks, and compliance verification, which can delay transactions and incur significant costs.

Blockchain facilitates a shift to automated, programmable LoCs using smart contracts. These are self-executing codes embedded on the blockchain that automatically enforce contractual obligations once predetermined conditions are met (Casey & Wong, 2017). For example, once a blockchain verifies that goods have been shipped and confirmed by the freight company, a smart contract could release the payment to the exporter without requiring manual bank processing.

Supply Chain Tracking and Customs Efficiency

One of the most impactful applications of blockchain in international trade lies in enhancing supply chain transparency and streamlining customs operations. Global supply chains often span multiple jurisdictions, involving dozens of intermediaries across shipping, logistics, manufacturing, and regulatory authorities. Traditional systems are fragmented and suffer from data silos, delays, and lack of visibility, all of which contribute to inefficiencies and elevated costs (Kamilaris et al., 2019; Saberi et al., 2019).

End-to-End Visibility Through Blockchain

Blockchain creates a single source of truth across the supply chain by providing real-time updates on the status of goods, documentation, and compliance events. Each transaction whether it is manufacturing, packing, loading, or customs inspection—can be recorded immutably on a distributed ledger.

In sectors like pharmaceuticals, agriculture, and electronics, blockchain enables product provenance tracking, allowing stakeholders to verify whether goods were ethically sourced, remained within acceptable storage temperatures, or passed all required inspections (World Economic Forum [WEF], 2020).

Blockchain and Customs Modernization

Customs procedures are frequently cited as bottlenecks in global trade. Manual documentation, inconsistent standards, and verification delays can significantly increase dwell times at ports. Blockchain enables pre-clearance, where customs agencies can access digitized trade documents in advance and assess shipment risks proactively (WTO, 2018). Platforms such as bConnect in Vietnam and TradeTrust in Singapore demonstrate that blockchain-enabled customs ecosystems are scalable and interoperable when coupled with legal reform and data standardization (OECD, 2022).

Blockchain and Dispute Reduction in Trade and Its Role in Enhancing Compliance and Due Diligence

The complexity of international trade transactions spanning geographies, legal systems, and commercial cultures makes them inherently susceptible to disputes. Issues such as delivery delays, loss of goods, inconsistent documentation, non-compliance with regulatory norms, and payment defaults are frequent in cross-border commerce.

Blockchain technology offers a novel, dual-function solution to these intertwined challenges: by minimizing the risk of disputes through enhanced transparency and real-time verification, and by facilitating proactive compliance and traceability throughout the supply chain. This section explores how blockchain contributes to dispute reduction and due diligence enhancement across multiple layers of international trade.

a. **Dispute Reduction Through Immutable Records and Real-Time Verification.** At the core of blockchain's transformative potential is its ability to create a tamper-resistant, distributed ledger. Once information is added to the blockchain, it cannot be modified retroactively unless consensus is reached across the network (Nakamoto, 2008). This creates an immutable audit trail for all trade activities purchase orders, shipment records, inspection results, customs clearance, and payments. Many disputes in international trade stem from information asymmetry where different parties have conflicting versions of events or documents. Blockchain mitigates this by ensuring data provenance, wherein each party can access the same version of time-stamped information. Blockchain integrated with IoT sensors can track container temperature, humidity, and location, logging each data point in real-time.
b. **Smart Contracts: Automating Performance and Minimizing Ambiguity.** Another significant innovation enabled by blockchain is the smart contract a self-executing code that enforces the terms of a contract when predetermined conditions are met. Smart contracts replace traditional enforcement mechanisms (e.g., letters of credit administered by banks) with automated digital workflows. When used effectively, they reduce disputes caused by human error, delayed compliance, or intentional breaches. For example, in a trade finance context, a smart contract can automatically release payment to the seller upon verification that goods have arrived at the destination port, based on real-time shipping data recorded on the blockchain (Casey & Wong, 2017). This removes subjectivity from the transaction and reduces dependence on intermediaries such as freight forwarders, inspection agencies, and banks.
c. **Blockchain as Legal Evidence in Dispute Resolution Forums.** Beyond preventing disputes, blockchain also enhances efficiency in resolving them, especially in litigation and arbitration contexts. Blockchain records, being immutable and time-stamped, provide high-integrity evidence that can substantiate or refute claims with minimal contestation. Courts and arbitral bodies are beginning to accept blockchain entries as admissible digital evidence. For instance, the UK Jurisdiction Taskforce's Legal Statement on Cryptoassets and Smart Contracts (2019) acknowledged that data recorded on a blockchain can be legally recognized and enforced, subject to standard evidentiary thresholds (UKJT, 2019). Similarly, in Singapore, the Electronic Transactions Act (2010) and SIAC's rules for international arbitration have paved the way for blockchain-based documentation to be accepted in dispute resolution (Cheng et al., 2021). Blockchain thus facilitates faster dispute resolution, especially in arbitration, by minimizing disputes over document authenticity, chain of custody, and data tampering.
d. **Dispute Avoidance via Shared Visibility and Trust.** The collaborative nature of blockchain means that all authorized stakeholders can access a real-time, syn-

chronized ledger, reducing the risk of "he said, she said" conflicts. By fostering interoperability and data transparency, blockchain creates a trade ecosystem grounded in mutual accountability.

Blockchain's Role in Strengthening Compliance and Due Diligence

Beyond dispute reduction, blockchain is increasingly seen as a tool to meet expanding regulatory demands especially those related to trade compliance, responsible sourcing, and ESG disclosures. As global supply chains come under closer scrutiny, stakeholders must demonstrate compliance with a range of regulations such as:

1. Anti-Money Laundering (AML) and Counter-Terrorist Financing (CTF)
2. Forced labor and modern slavery laws
3. Carbon emissions reporting (e.g., EU CBAM)
4. Responsible sourcing of minerals (e.g., Dodd-Frank Act Section 1502)
5. Traceability for ESG and Responsible Sourcing

Companies increasingly need to demonstrate that their supply chains are free of labor abuses, environmental harm, or unethical sourcing practices. Blockchain helps create a verifiable "digital twin" of the product journey, documenting each phase—from raw material extraction to final delivery (OECD, 2022).

In agriculture, blockchain tools like AgriDigital enable smallholder farmers to demonstrate export compliance and sustainability credentials, helping them access international markets that demand traceability (WEF, 2020).

6. Enhancing Trade-Based Compliance and AML Measures

Trade-based money laundering (TBML) is a persistent problem involving inflated invoices, multiple financing of the same shipment, and shell company networks. Blockchain minimizes such risks by providing a single ledger accessible by banks, regulators, and customs, allowing them to cross-reference transactions and detect anomalies in real time (FATF, 2021).

Smart contracts can also be programmed to halt suspicious transactions, automatically screen parties against sanctions lists, or flag deviations from declared trade routes (Cheng et al., 2021).

4. LEGAL AND REGULATORY CHALLENGES IN BLOCKCHAIN INTEGRATION

Blockchain technology presents a paradigm shift for international trade, offering decentralized, immutable, and programmable ledgers. However, its novel structure raises profound legal and regulatory issues across multiple domains, from jurisdictional ambiguity and contract validity to privacy rights, cybersecurity, fragmented legal standards, and intellectual property. Addressing these challenges is essential for the technology's integration into international trade systems.

1. Jurisdictional Issues in a Borderless System

Blockchain networks operate on distributed and decentralized architectures, often transcending national borders. Nodes on public or permissioned blockchains can exist across multiple jurisdictions with no central entity governing them, disrupting traditional notions of territorial jurisdiction (De Filippi & Wright, 2018). As a result, it becomes complex to establish applicable law, legal venue, and regulatory oversight in the event of disputes (Rauchs et al., 2018).

Some jurisdictions are attempting legal solutions. The EU is exploring regulations to harmonize blockchain jurisdiction across member states, and in the U.S., the Uniform Regulation of Virtual-Currency Businesses Act (URVCBA) tries to standardize cross-state rules.

2. Legal Recognition of Smart Contracts and Digital Signatures

2.1 Definitional Foundations and Doctrinal Fit. A smart contract is computer code that automatically executes, verifies, or enforces the performance of an agreement when pre-specified conditions are satisfied (Szabo, 1997; Christidis & Devetsikiotis, 2016). Traditional contract law requires four elements offer, acceptance, consideration, and intention to create legal relations (McKendrick, 2021). Translating these elements into code raises several legal challenges:

Offer and Acceptance: In a smart contract, code deployment and subsequent actions (e.g., token transfer) are often deemed both the offer and acceptance, potentially collapsing two separate steps into one digital action (Wright & De Filippi, 2018).

Consideration: Payment logic embedded in code may satisfy "consideration," but courts may question whether purely automated value exchange reflects a legally enforceable bargain (Alexander, 2019).

Intention and Interpretation: Smart contracts lack the traditional "meeting of minds"—the parties' subjective intentions are implicit in code, which may be opaque or ambiguous without human-readable terms (Finck, 2019).

2.2 Jurisdictional Approaches.

United Kingdom – The UK Jurisdiction Taskforce's 2019 Legal Statement affirmed that smart contracts can satisfy contract formation and enforceability, provided parties intended to create legal relations and code accurately reflected the agreement (UKJT, 2019).

Singapore – The Electronic Transactions (Amendment) Act 2019 explicitly includes smart contracts and digital signatures within its definition of "electronic record" and "electronic signature," thereby granting them the same legal effect as chapter contracts (ETAA, 2019).

European Union – Under eIDAS Regulation (2014/910/EU), "electronic signatures" can range from simple to "qualified electronic signatures" (QES). While basic digital signatures on blockchain meet the definition of an electronic signature, they rarely satisfy QES requirements—namely, identity-verified devices issued by qualified trust service providers (European Commission, 2014).

United States – States such as Arizona (2017), Tennessee (2017), and Vermont (2018) have enacted laws recognizing smart contracts and electronic signatures under the Uniform Electronic Transactions Act (UETA) or the Electronic Signatures in Global and National Commerce Act (E-SIGN) (National Conference of State Legislatures, 2021).

2.3 Interpretation & Dispute Resolution. Even when smart contracts are legally recognized, interpreting ambiguous code remains problematic. Courts may need to fall back on:

Extrinsic Evidence: Parties' emails, white chapters, or project documentation to determine intent (Rees, 2020).

Contractual Back-Stops: Layering a traditional "wrapper" agreement around the code that contains dispute resolution and interpretation clauses (Winston, 2022).

Code Audits & Expert Testimony: Use of technical experts to explain the code to fact-finders (Cheng, Lee, & Low, 2021).

2.4 Digital Signatures on Blockchain. Blockchain transactions rely on asymmetric cryptography, where a private key signs a transaction and a public key verifies it. Legally:

Electronic Signature vs. Digital Signature: Under many laws, any data in electronic form attached to an electronic record is an electronic signature (e.g., UETA, E-SIGN). A blockchain signature is certainly an electronic signature, but it may fall short of the qualified status under eIDAS (Thompson, 2020).

Identity Assurance: Blockchain keys are pseudonymous; tying them to real-world identities requires off-chain identity verification (KYC/AML), often via traditional trust service providers (Gartner, 2021).

3. Conflicts Between Transparency and Data Privacy (e.g., GDPR)

3.1 Core Tension: Immutability vs. Erasure Rights. Blockchain's hallmark is that once data is recorded, it is immutable—every node holds a copy of the ledger, and altering history requires consensus (Narayanan et al., 2016). The GDPR enshrines the "right to erasure" (Art. 17) and "right to rectification" (Art. 16), which appear fundamentally incompatible with on-chain storage of personal data (Vo & Delahunty, 2020).

3.2 Case Studies and Regulatory Guidance. The theoretical conflicts between blockchain's immutability and data privacy principles such as those enshrined in the GDPR have prompted various regulators and institutions to propose practical guidance and use-case-specific recommendations. Several real-world blockchain systems have sought to comply with privacy obligations while preserving core decentralization benefits.

a. ***Estonia's KSI Blockchain Infrastructure.*** Estonia is widely regarded as a global leader in digital governance. Its KSI Blockchain (Keyless Signature Infrastructure), developed by Guardtime, underpins a range of e-government services including land registries, e-health, and e-tax filings. Crucially, no personal data is stored on-chain; instead, only cryptographic hashesdigital fingerprints of the original data—are recorded (e-Estonia Briefing Centre, 2021). The actual data resides in centralized databases under the control of public authorities. This architectural separation ensures compliance with EU data protection law while allowing tamper-evidence, auditability, and non-repudiation. If personal data needs to be rectified or deleted, it can be updated in the off-chain system. The hash on the blockchain becomes invalid, but does not store any personal data itself—thus sidestepping GDPR's "right to be forgotten" issue (Zyskind, Nathan, & Pentland, 2015).
b. ***French Data Protection Authority (CNIL) Position.*** The Commission Nationale de l'Informatique et des Libertés (CNIL) was among the first regulators to assess the GDPR–blockchain tension. In its 2018 report, CNIL concluded: The use of public blockchains to store personal data is likely non-compliant with GDPR due to the difficulty in ensuring erasure and identifying controllers. The use of private or consortium blockchains (with known, regulated actors) is potentially compliant, especially where data minimization and pseudonymization are applied. Hashing personal data does not automatically make it anonymous; if the data can be reverse-engineered or linked to individuals, it remains subject to GDPR protections (CNIL, 2018). CNIL recommended that organizations adopt a "privacy by design" approach, employ off-chain storage, and include access control mechanisms on any on-chain identifiers.

c. ***UK's ICO Regulatory Sandbox and Pilots.*** The UK's Information Commissioner's Office (ICO) initiated a Regulatory Sandbox program in 2019–2020, which included blockchain-based pilot projects. One participant, Digital Street, used blockchain to enhance transparency in land transactions. The ICO found that blockchain could be used in GDPR-compliant ways provided that: The ledger contains no personal data, or data is pseudonymized/encrypted. There is a clear governance model determining who is accountable for data processing decisions. Data subjects are provided with clear privacy notices and consent options (ICO, 2020). The ICO's sandbox experience illustrated that technological design and legal compliance must evolve together, and supported the notion of sector-specific guidance.

5. THE ROLE OF INTERNATIONAL ORGANISATIONS IN SHAPING BLOCKCHAIN GOVERNANCE

The potential of blockchain technology to transform international trade has garnered significant attention in recent years. However, this potential cannot be realised without an enabling regulatory and policy environment. As the deployment of blockchain extends across borders, national regulatory approaches are proving insufficient. International organisations (IOs) are therefore playing an increasingly central role in shaping blockchain governance by setting standards, developing policy frameworks, building regulatory capacity, and harmonising digital legal regimes. This section critically evaluates the contribution of IOs in these domains and explores the challenges they face.

A key contribution of IOs is in the area of standard-setting, which is vital to ensure interoperability of blockchain systems across jurisdictions. The International Organization for Standardization (ISO), through its Technical Committee 307, has developed a range of standards for distributed ledger technologies (DLTs), including terminology, reference architecture, taxonomy, and governance models. These standards aim to reduce fragmentation and promote trust in blockchain applications, especially in sectors such as trade finance, logistics, and customs documentation (ISO, 2023). The International Telecommunication Union (ITU) has also initiated work on blockchain standardization, focusing on interoperability, identity management, and use cases relevant to telecommunications (ITU, 2023). These technical standards, while non-binding, have a regulatory impact by shaping industry norms and informing national regulatory approaches.

International organisations also play a crucial role in policy development related to blockchain and digital trade. The World Trade Organization (WTO), although operating within a framework conceived in the pre-digital era, has become increasingly engaged with digital issues through its Joint Statement Initiative (JSI) on e-commerce. The JSI includes discussions on electronic contracts, electronic authentication, and cross-border data flows, all of which are relevant to blockchain governance (WTO, 2019). While blockchain itself is not explicitly referenced, its facilitation of electronic transactions positions it squarely within the JSI's scope. WTO law, particularly the General Agreement on Trade in Services (GATS), is arguably broad enough to encompass blockchain-based services, such as data processing and database management (WTO, 1994). The classification of blockchain services under the GATS Central Product Classification (CPC) system remains an interpretive challenge, but jurisprudence has shown a willingness to adopt technologically neutral readings (WTO, 2009).

UNCITRAL, the United Nations Commission on International Trade Law, has been instrumental in clarifying the legal status of blockchain-based instruments. Its Model Law on Electronic Transferable Records (MLETR) provides a framework for recognising electronic documents that perform the function of chapter-based negotiable instruments, such as bills of lading and warehouse receipts (UNCITRAL, 2017). The MLETR facilitates the legal use of blockchain in trade by establishing criteria for functional equivalence, control, and reliability of electronic records. Countries such as Bahrain and Singapore have already incorporated the MLETR into their domestic laws, signalling the beginning of a broader trend towards blockchain-compatible legal regimes (UNCITRAL, 2021).

The OECD has taken a broader policy approach, highlighting blockchain's potential in multiple domains, including supply chain transparency, responsible business conduct, and sustainability. Through its Blockchain Policy Centre, the OECD has published a comprehensive framework that identifies core governance issues, including scalability, energy efficiency, competition, and the risk of fragmentation (OECD, 2020). It has called for a risk-based, technology-neutral approach to regulation, while acknowledging that blockchain's unique characteristics may necessitate tailored legal responses.

Capacity-building is another critical area in which IOs are making significant contributions. The United Nations Conference on Trade and Development (UNCTAD) has emphasised the need to support developing countries in adopting blockchain technologies, especially in trade facilitation and SME financing. It has stressed that without institutional readiness and adequate infrastructure, these countries risk being left behind in the digital trade transformation (UNCTAD, 2021). UNCTAD's work focuses on providing policy advice, technical assistance, and capacity-building programmes aimed at bridging the digital divide.

Similarly, the World Bank has piloted blockchain applications in areas such as land registries, remittances, and health data in developing countries. These pilots serve both developmental and capacity-building functions by exposing domestic regulators and stakeholders to blockchain's operational dynamics (World Bank, 2020). The World Customs Organization (WCO) has also explored blockchain use in customs procedures, recognising its potential for real-time data sharing, enhanced traceability, and fraud reduction. WCO's working groups have recommended the development of common data models and collaborative pilot projects among member states (WCO, 2019).

Legal harmonisation is essential to avoid a patchwork of conflicting national laws that could stifle cross-border blockchain applications. The WTO's e-commerce work, although still in early stages, could contribute to harmonisation by establishing baseline rules on issues such as source code disclosure, data localisation, and electronic authentication (WTO, 1998). The Comprehensive and Progressive Agreement for Trans-Pacific Partnership (CPTPP) and the United States-Mexico-Canada Agreement (USMCA) have already incorporated provisions restricting data localisation and prohibiting forced source code transfers. These provisions, while not blockchain-specific, create a legal environment conducive to blockchain deployment by protecting the cross-border flow of digital services and ensuring legal predictability (CPTPP, 2018; USMCA, 2020).

However, significant challenges remain. A key concern is the compatibility of blockchain's immutability with privacy laws, especially the European Union's General Data Protection Regulation (GDPR). The GDPR's "right to be forgotten" conflicts with blockchain's inherent resistance to data deletion (European Commission, 2016). While solutions such as off-chain storage and permissioned blockchains are being explored, they raise questions about the extent to which blockchain can be modified without compromising its integrity (Neuburger, 2018). The GDPR allows international data transfers only where adequate safeguards exist, creating compliance challenges for cross-border blockchain systems. The European Data Protection Board has acknowledged these tensions but has yet to provide comprehensive guidance.

There are also institutional challenges within IOs themselves. Coordination among international organisations remains limited, with overlapping mandates and inconsistent approaches to blockchain-related issues. While the ISO, ITU, UNCITRAL, WTO, OECD, and others each contribute valuable expertise, their efforts often occur in silos. A more integrated governance framework could enhance coherence and avoid duplication. For example, aligning legal standards developed by UNCITRAL with technical standards from ISO/TC 307 would facilitate both legal certainty and operational interoperability.

Finally, geopolitical tensions pose a barrier to international consensus on blockchain governance. Divergent approaches to data governance, exemplified by the US emphasis on free data flows and the Chinese model of cyber sovereignty, complicate efforts to develop universally accepted norms. These divergences risk creating "data realms" that fragment the digital space and undermine the universality of blockchain systems (Aaronson & Leblond, 2018). In this context, the role of IOs as neutral conveners and standard-setters becomes even more important. They must balance the competing imperatives of innovation, regulation, and development in a politically contested space.

In sum, international organisations play a foundational role in shaping blockchain governance through standard-setting, policy development, capacity-building, and harmonisation. Their efforts provide the scaffolding upon which national regulators and private actors can build more consistent, secure, and inclusive blockchain systems. However, realising this potential requires overcoming legal, institutional, and geopolitical challenges through sustained cooperation and adaptive governance strategies.

Blockchain Under GATS and WTO Law: Interpretive and Regulatory Challenges

Although blockchain is not explicitly referenced in WTO agreements, its integral role in enabling electronic transactions situates it within the evolving digital trade landscape governed by WTO law. The General Agreement on Trade in Services (GATS), established in 1994, offers a horizontal framework for the liberalization and regulation of services trade. By its design, GATS is technologically neutral and thus arguably capable of covering blockchain-based services under modes of supply, particularly Mode 1 (cross-border supply) and Mode 2 (consumption abroad). Services such as distributed ledger operations, smart contract execution, data processing, and cryptographic transaction validation can arguably fall within GATS Schedules (WTO, 1994).

However, the inclusion of blockchain services under the GATS framework is legally fraught due to classification and interpretive uncertainties. The W/120 Services Sectoral Classification List and the Central Product Classification (CPC) developed by the United Nations Statistical Division, upon which WTO Members schedule their commitments, do not explicitly mention blockchain. This gives rise to two core legal challenges: first, whether blockchain services can be shoehorned into existing categories such as "computer and related services" (CPC 84); and second, whether doing so is sufficient for the purposes of regulatory clarity and enforceability under WTO law. As Gao (2018) notes, "[t]he lack of specific reference to emerging technologies creates interpretive opacity," which can limit both the enforceability of obligations and the policy space available for domestic regulation (p. 124).

Jurisprudence has offered some support for a technologically neutral reading. For instance, in the US – Gambling case, the WTO Appellate Body ruled that Mode 1 supply via the Internet is covered by Members' commitments even when the method of delivery had not existed at the time of the schedule (WTO, 2005). Similarly, the

Canada – Autos and US – Measures Affecting the Cross-Border Supply of Gambling and Betting Services cases underscore that GATS commitments are not frozen in time but evolve with service delivery mechanisms (WTO, 1998; 2005). Nonetheless, reliance on such judicial activism underscores the insufficiency of the current GATS framework to keep pace with innovation, leaving room for inconsistent application. The WTO's Services Sectoral Classification List (W/120) and the underlying Central Product Classification (CPC) were not designed with blockchain, smart contracts, or decentralised finance in mind (Burri, 2021). Consequently, Members' commitments remain unclear as to whether blockchain-enabled services—such as decentralised identity management, peer-to-peer digital escrow, or on-chain logistics verification—are covered. Jurisprudence has interpreted commitments expansively (e.g., China – Publications and Audiovisual Products, WTO, 2009), but this interpretive flexibility is insufficient without explicit textual updates.

Moreover, blockchain technology challenges the underlying assumptions of the GATS framework. GATS presumes the existence of identifiable suppliers and territorial regulation, but blockchain is by design decentralized, borderless, and anonymized. As Chander (2019) observes, GATS' regulatory logic sits uneasily with blockchain's defiance of traditional jurisdictional and governance models. The requirement of "commercial presence" (Mode 3) is similarly complicated when service providers are distributed nodes rather than corporate entities. Since nodes of a blockchain system can be globally dispersed, questions about jurisdiction, applicable law, and enforcement mechanisms remain unresolved (Lehmann, 2018).

A further concern is the principle of net neutrality, which—although not explicitly part of GATS—has significant implications for service delivery over digital infrastructure. Net neutrality ensures that all data is treated equally, regardless of source or application. In jurisdictions lacking neutrality commitments, discriminatory treatment of blockchain-based services (e.g., throttling cryptocurrency nodes or smart contract execution) could constitute de facto barriers to trade in services. While such actions may be justifiable under GATS Article XIV (General Exceptions), the lack of clear WTO jurisprudence on net neutrality leaves blockchain services vulnerable to regulatory divergence.

The broader structural limitation lies in the fragmented and outdated nature of GATS schedules. Many developing countries' commitments are either too narrow or subject to limitations that were negotiated without foresight into the complexities of digital trade. The plurilateral Joint Statement Initiative (JSI) on e-commerce attempts to address these gaps but remains outside the WTO's consensus-based framework and thus suffers from questions of legitimacy and enforceability (Wu, 2020).

Taken together, these challenges call into question the feasibility of using GATS as an effective governance framework for blockchain. While GATS provides a baseline of nondiscrimination and market access commitments, its conceptual foundations are stretched by the functional and technological innovations of blockchain. The lack of classification precision, jurisdictional ambiguity, and institutional lag in updating commitments underscore the inadequacy of GATS in its current form.

A rethinking of WTO digital trade governance may be necessary—potentially through a new multilateral agreement or substantial reform of the existing GATS annexes. As Aaronson (2021) argues, "without a more adaptive and inclusive regulatory structure, the WTO risks marginalizing itself in the governance of new technologies" (p. 177). Until then, GATS can only offer limited utility for blockchain governance, functioning more as a patchwork than a comprehensive solution.

The WTO Joint Statement Initiative (JSI) on E-Commerce and Its Relevance to Blockchain Governance

The WTO Joint Statement Initiative (JSI) on E-Commerce, launched at the 11th WTO Ministerial Conference in 2017 and joined by over 90 Members, represents a plurilateral effort to develop new trade rules for the digital economy. Although it remains outside the formal WTO negotiating framework due to the absence of consensus, the JSI has emerged as a de facto laboratory for modernizing trade law in light of emerging technologies, including blockchain (WTO, 2021). Its relevance stems from its express focus on issues such as cross-border data flows, source code disclosure, electronic contracts, chapterless trading, and digital identities all of which intersect with the technological infrastructure and regulatory concerns of blockchain.

1. Filling Gaps in the GATS Framework. The JSI is an important response to the deficiencies of the GATS framework in addressing digital trade. While GATS is premised on the traditional service economy and is constrained by outdated classifications (e.g., CPC 84), the JSI's negotiations are more technology-neutral and issue-specific. The JSI directly engages with the conditions that shape digital transactions, including data governance and interoperability standards, which are central to the functionality of blockchain.

For example, commitments on chapterless trading and digital identities implicitly support the use of distributed ledger technologies in customs clearance, supply chain management, and digital trust services (Monteiro & Teh, 2017). These aspects, although still in draft form, indicate a recognition of blockchain's structural role in digital trade. However, the JSI's scope remains largely indirect with respect to blockchain-specific regulatory needs, and it is constrained by its plurilateral, non-binding nature (Ghosh, 2021). As such, while the JSI holds promise in fostering a permissive regulatory environment for blockchain-based services, it cannot on its own resolve the jurisdictional, interpretive, and infrastructural challenges that blockchain poses to the global trading system.

2. **Addressing Regulatory Fragmentation and Interoperability.** One of the core challenges in blockchain governance is regulatory fragmentation across jurisdictions. Blockchain operates through decentralized nodes that often span multiple legal systems, raising questions about the applicable law and enforcement. The JSI holds the potential to mitigate these issues by setting baseline standards for digital trust, cross-border data transfers, and cybersecurity, thereby facilitating a more harmonized digital trading environment (Burri, 2021).

However, the JSI stops short of offering binding commitments on interoperability of technical protocols, which are vital for blockchain-based platforms to integrate with digital infrastructure across countries. While the JSI may foster a permissive environment for blockchain deployment, it is unlikely to standardize its regulation in the absence of enforceable norms on code, algorithms, or governance structures.

3. **Data Localization, Source Code, and Blockchain Constraints.** Several key fault lines in the JSI negotiations are highly relevant to blockchain. Disputes over data localization (i.e., requiring data to be stored within national borders) affect blockchain's promise of decentralized and borderless operations. Blockchain networks rely on real-time replication of data across nodes located in multiple jurisdictions. Data localization measures—adopted in countries like China and India—could undermine this architectural feature and frustrate blockchain's effectiveness as a cross-border solution (Aaronson, 2021).

Similarly, provisions on source code disclosure raise tensions with the open-source ethos that animates much of blockchain development. While source code transparency can enhance accountability, mandatory disclosure obligations might deter innovation or jeopardize network security in blockchain ecosystems. The JSI text contains controversial clauses that restrict members from requiring access to source code or algorithms, which could protect proprietary blockchain software but also hinder regulatory oversight (Lambrellis, 2022).

4. **Institutional and Normative Limitations.** Despite its ambition, the JSI suffers from institutional limitations that restrict its capacity to provide meaningful governance of blockchain. As a plurilateral initiative outside the WTO consensus model, the JSI lacks universal applicability and remains legally non-binding for Members who have not opted in. This exclusion of key countries, such as India and South Africa, not only weakens its legitimacy but also signals resistance to what some developing countries view as the digital entrenchment of powerful tech-exporting economies (Ismail, 2020). These concerns mirror criticisms of digital colonialism and raise doubts about whether the JSI can support inclusive governance of blockchain, particularly for developing economies seeking policy space to nurture local innovation.

Moreover, the JSI's lack of a coherent dispute resolution mechanism means that any commitments adopted may be difficult to enforce. This contrasts sharply with the compulsory dispute settlement provisions under GATS, even if rarely invoked in digital contexts. In this respect, the JSI complements but does not replace the need for a formal treaty-based update of GATS to integrate blockchain regulation.

Digital Divide and Digital Sovereignty in Blockchain Governance

The increasing reliance on blockchain technologies in international trade raises two interrelated governance concerns: the deepening of the digital divide and the contestation over digital sovereignty. These issues are not merely peripheral to blockchain deployment—they shape the very conditions under which such technologies are adopted, implemented, and regulated. International organisations, while traditionally tasked with fostering economic integration, now face the additional burden of ensuring that emerging digital technologies like blockchain do not replicate or exacerbate existing global inequalities.

Digital Divide: Infrastructure, Capacity, and Inclusion. The digital divide refers to the unequal access to digital technologies, internet connectivity, and digital literacy across different countries and population groups (van Dijk, 2020). While blockchain is often portrayed as a decentralised and democratising innovation, its practical implementation requires a complex ecosystem of internet infrastructure, legal certainty, technical expertise, and computational resources. Many developing countries, particularly Least Developed Countries (LDCs), remain under-equipped to engage in such technologically intensive transitions (UNCTAD, 2021).

International organisations have highlighted the risks that such disparities pose. The United Nations Conference on Trade and Development (UNCTAD), in its *Digital Economy Report 2021*, noted that while blockchain offers significant trade facilitation opportunities, especially in areas such as logistics, smart contracts, and customs clearance, its diffusion remains largely confined to advanced and emerging economies (UNCTAD, 2021). Small and medium-sized enterprises (SMEs) in lower-income countries are especially vulnerable to being locked out of blockchain-based global value chains unless comprehensive support is provided.

The World Bank, through pilot programs in countries like Georgia (for land registries) and Sierra Leone (for digital identity), has attempted to bridge this digital divide by offering technical assistance and project financing (World Bank, 2020). However, critics argue that these interventions often adopt a "techno-solutionist" perspective, failing to account for the long-term infrastructural needs and local regulatory constraints (Gurumurthy & Chami, 2022).

In the context of international trade, this divide has real consequences. Consider the case of blockchain-based digital trade platforms. Developed countries and multinational corporations are increasingly moving toward integrated DLT systems for documenting cross-border transactions (e.g., through digital bills of lading or origin certificates). If exporters from low-income countries are unable to access or operate within such systems, they may face higher transaction costs, longer clearance times, and diminished market competitiveness (Lemieux, 2016). International organisations must therefore not only set standards but also work toward "digital infrastructure justice," ensuring that access to blockchain systems is not gated by geography or income.

Furthermore, the governance of blockchain standards themselves can become exclusionary. Standards developed by ISO/TC 307, for instance, are often dominated by industrialised countries and large private actors, marginalising the voices of countries with limited participation in international standardisation fora (Vatanparast & Moon, 2023). This can lead to path dependencies in blockchain design that reinforce dominant market interests while failing to account for the institutional realities of developing states.

Digital Sovereignty: Control, Autonomy, and Regulatory Asymmetries. Alongside the digital divide, the concept of digital sovereignty has gained increasing salience in blockchain governance. Digital sovereignty broadly refers to the ability of states to control and regulate their digital infrastructure, data flows, and technological choices in accordance with domestic values and strategic interests (Floridi, 2020). For blockchain, this concern becomes particularly pronounced due to its decentralised and borderless architecture.

Several governments have responded to these sovereignty concerns by enacting data localisation laws and asserting jurisdiction over digital infrastructures. China's Cybersecurity Law (2017), India's draft Data Protection Bill (2019), and the EU's General Data Protection Regulation (GDPR) are prime examples of how states are attempting to reclaim control over digital data and infrastructure, often in tension with the transnational aspirations of blockchain systems (Aaronson & Leblond, 2018; Sen, 2018).

These assertions of digital sovereignty present a normative dilemma for international organisations. On one hand, trade-oriented IOs like the WTO advocate for the liberalisation of digital trade and the removal of data flow restrictions under frameworks like GATS and the Joint Statement Initiative on E-Commerce. On the other hand, human rights and development-oriented bodies such as UNCTAD and the UN Human Rights Council acknowledge the legitimacy of state measures aimed at protecting personal data, ensuring cybersecurity, and supporting digital industrialisation (UNHRC, 2021).

The fragmented response of international organisations to digital sovereignty reflects deeper tensions in blockchain governance. While the WTO's e-commerce initiatives tend to frame cross-border data flow as a trade facilitation issue, they often sideline the constitutional and democratic imperatives that underlie national data governance strategies (Burri, 2017). Conversely, normative frameworks developed under the auspices of UNESCO or the UNDP have little binding effect and often lack enforcement mechanisms, weakening their impact on trade-centric policymaking.

Blockchain thus becomes a site of regulatory contestation between liberalising trade regimes and sovereign control over data, code, and digital infrastructure. This tension is further complicated by the architecture of blockchain itself. For example, public permissionless blockchains (such as Ethereum) allow little national oversight, whereas private permissioned blockchains (such as those developed by trade consortia) may offer more regulatory control but at the cost of transparency and decentralisation (Reyes, 2016). International organisations have yet to provide clear guidance on how such architectural trade-offs should be managed in light of sovereign regulatory needs.

The EU's approach offers an interesting middle path. Through its digital sovereignty agenda, the EU has sought to shape global norms by embedding privacy-by-design principles, interoperability requirements, and algorithmic accountability within its legal frameworks. The GDPR's extraterritorial application illustrates how sovereignty can be projected outward, influencing global blockchain governance through a "Brussels Effect" (Bradford, 2020). However, such regulatory extraterritoriality is not without controversy. Critics argue that it imposes compliance burdens on jurisdictions lacking the institutional capacity to meet EU standards, thereby reinforcing rather than mitigating the digital divide (Irion et al., 2016).

IOs and the Mediation of Sovereignty-Divide Tensions. In navigating these tensions, international organisations must evolve beyond traditional modes of rule-making. They must act as mediators, creating institutional spaces where digital sovereignty and digital inclusion can be mutually negotiated. For example, UNCITRAL's Model Law on Electronic Transferable Records (MLETR) does not prescribe a specific technology but provides a technology-neutral legal basis for recognising blockchain-based documents. Such flexibility allows states to adopt DLTs at their own pace and in line with their constitutional and economic priorities (UNCITRAL, 2017).

Moreover, capacity-building must be framed not only as technical assistance but also as regulatory empowerment. Organisations like the World Bank and ITU should invest in enabling regulators from developing countries to participate meaningfully in blockchain standard-setting, thereby reducing dependency on imported regulatory models or foreign platforms. Similarly, WTO-led negotiations on digital trade should incorporate development safeguards that protect a state's ability to regulate critical digital infrastructures without facing trade retaliation.

The emerging discourse on "digital commons" also provides an alternative paradigm. Instead of framing blockchain solely as a private-sector-driven innovation to be regulated ex post, IOs could explore models where blockchain-based trade infrastructure is designed and governed as a global public good. This could involve multistakeholder governance mechanisms, open-source development standards, and fair access conditions for SMEs and developing countries (Pentland, 2021). While nascent, such models align well with the mandates of IOs like the UNDP and the International Telecommunication Union, which are increasingly recognising the need for inclusive digital governance.

6. A WAY FORWARD: REGULATORY RECOMMENDATIONS AND FUTURE PROSPECTS

As blockchain technologies increasingly intersect with international trade, the limitations of existing legal and regulatory frameworks become increasingly evident. The WTO's General Agreement on Trade in Services (GATS), the Joint Statement Initiative (JSI) on E-Commerce, and the broader ecosystem of international organisations (IOs) such as UNCTAD, UNCITRAL, OECD, and ISO have all begun to address aspects of blockchain governance. Yet, these efforts are uneven, fragmented, and often fail to adequately resolve the challenges posed by blockchain's decentralised, transnational, and multifaceted nature. The future of blockchain governance will depend significantly on how the international community responds to these legal challenges through reform, coordination, and capacity-building.

The Way Forward: Toward Coherent and Inclusive Blockchain Governance

To overcome these structural and legal limitations, a multipronged approach is needed, combining doctrinal innovation, treaty reform, inter-institutional cooperation, and capacity-building.

1. **Revisiting the GATS Classification System.** There is a pressing need to update the GATS W/120 list and underlying CPC categories to reflect modern digital services, including blockchain. The WTO Secretariat could facilitate a new classification exercise in collaboration with the United Nations Statistical Commission to create service categories for emerging technologies (Thompson & Voon, 2016). Alternatively, WTO Members could agree to annex updated CPC references to existing schedules, enhancing legal certainty without full renegotiation.
2. **Enhancing Technological Neutrality through Interpretive Guidelines.** While GATS jurisprudence supports a technologically neutral interpretation of commitments, formal guidance from the Council for Trade in Services could

consolidate this approach. An interpretive note or recommendation could clarify that services delivered via blockchain, cloud computing, or AI fall within existing commitments when the functional service remains unchanged (Weber, 2019). Such guidance would not only enhance predictability but also reduce friction in dispute resolution.

3. **Creating Blockchain-Specific Legal Instruments.** The WTO and its Members could consider developing a blockchain-specific plurilateral agreement, akin to the Information Technology Agreement (ITA). This "Blockchain Trade Facilitation Agreement" could standardise key issues such as recognition of smart contracts, digital documents, and legal validity of blockchain transactions across borders. By focusing on facilitative aspects rather than liberalisation, such an agreement could garner broader support. Alternatively, IOs such as UNCITRAL and the OECD could lead normative development by drafting soft law instruments (e.g., model laws, regulatory toolkits) that address cross-border legal issues in blockchain deployment. These instruments could complement WTO commitments and encourage regulatory convergence (UNCTAD, 2021).
4. **Aligning Trade Rules with Human Rights and Development Objectives.** Blockchain governance must be embedded within broader frameworks of inclusive development and digital justice. IOs should coordinate to ensure that trade rules do not undermine national policies on privacy, security, or economic inclusion. The UN Human Rights Council's 2021 resolution on the right to privacy in the digital age provides an example of how blockchain regulation can be harmonised with human rights norms (UNHRC, 2021). Trade rules, particularly those under the JSI, should incorporate "regulatory space clauses" that preserve Members' rights to adopt domestic measures for legitimate public policy objectives. Furthermore, a development chapter could be added to any future digital trade agreement, providing technical assistance, capacity-building, and phased implementation for developing countries.
5. **Institutional Coordination and Digital Capacity-Building.** IOs must improve coordination to avoid duplicative or contradictory norms. The WTO, WCO, UNCTAD, OECD, and ITU should establish an inter-agency task force on blockchain governance, focusing on interoperability, data governance, and legal standards. Additionally, a global digital capacity fund—administered by the World Bank or UNDP—could support countries in developing regulatory frameworks, infrastructure, and human capital necessary to engage in blockchain-enabled trade.

The WTO, GATS, and JSI provide foundational yet incomplete frameworks for governing blockchain in the context of international trade. The challenges of classification, interpretive ambiguity, jurisdictional mismatches, and normative legitimacy highlight the urgent need for reform. International organisations must play a leading role in bridging legal, technical, and developmental gaps through updated standards, interpretive flexibility, and inclusive multilateralism. Only through coordinated, transparent, and equitable approaches can blockchain realise its promise of transforming global trade while upholding international legal norms.

REFERENCES

Aaronson, S. A. (2021). Why the WTO Needs to Address Emerging Technologies. *World Trade Review*, *20*(2), 165–182. DOI: 10.1017/S1474745620000532

Aaronson, S. A., & Leblond, P. (2018). Another digital divide: The rise of data realms and its implications for the WTO. *Journal of International Economic Law*, *21*(2), 245–272. DOI: 10.1093/jiel/jgy019

Alexander, D. (2019). Smart contracts and the law: Reconciling code with contract doctrine. [Check your library database for full access—placeholder journal entry if citing generally.]. *Journal of Business Law*, *20*(3), 45–67.

Apte, S., & Petrovsky, N. (2016). Will blockchain technology revolutionize excipient supply chain management? *Journal of Excipients and Food Chemicals*, *7*(3), 76–78. http://jefc.scholasticahq.com/article/4513-will-blockchain-technology-revolutionize-excipient-supply-chain-management

Authenticated e-Discovery. (2025, January 21). *Authenticated e-discovery: Utilizing blockchain for robust security and trust in*. Ankura Angle. https://angle.ankura.com/post/102jsqp/authenticated-e-discovery-utilizing-blockchain-for-robust-security-and-trust-in

Bradford, A. (2020). *The Brussels Effect: How the European Union Rules the World*. Oxford University Press. DOI: 10.1093/oso/9780190088583.001.0001

Burri, M. (2017). The governance of data and data flows in trade agreements: The pitfalls of legal adaptation. *U.C. Davis Law Review*, *51*, 65–132.

Burri, M. (2021). Governing Trade in the Age of Innovation: Towards a New Regulatory Framework for Digital Trade. *Journal of International Economic Law*, *24*(2), 1–26. DOI: 10.1093/jiel/jgab002

Burri, M. (2021). Understanding the implications of digital trade for international trade law. *Journal of International Economic Law*, *24*(1), 35–62.

Chander, A. (2019). How Law Made Silicon Valley. *Emory Law Journal*, *68*(2), 357–416. https://scholarlycommons.law.emory.edu/elj/vol68/iss2/3/

Cheng, H., Lee, J., & Low, K. (2021). Smart contract code audits and the role of expert testimony. *Computer Law & Security Review*, *41*, 105528. DOI: 10.1016/j.clsr.2021.105528

Christidis, K., & Devetsikiotis, M. (2016). Blockchains and smart contracts for the Internet of Things. *IEEE Access : Practical Innovations, Open Solutions*, *4*, 2292–2303. DOI: 10.1109/ACCESS.2016.2566339

Commission Nationale de l'Informatique et des Libertés (CNIL). (2018, September 24). *Blockchain and the GDPR*. CNIL. https://www.cnil.fr/en/blockchain-and-gdpr

. CPTPP. (2018). Comprehensive and Progressive Agreement for Trans-Pacific Partnership.

Daley, S. (2023). Blockchain and AI: How they integrate and 26 examples. Built In. https://builtin.com/artificial-intelligence/blockchain-ai-examples

Digicast Technologies. (2023). The impact of blockchain on global trade. https://www.digicast-technologies.com/blockchain-global-trade/

European Commission. (2014). Regulation (EU) No 910/2014 of the European Parliament and of the Council of 23 July 2014 on electronic identification and trust services for electronic transactions in the internal market (eIDAS Regulation). *Official Journal of the European Union, L*, *257*, 73–114. https://eur-lex.europa.eu/legal-content/EN/TXT/?uri=CELEX%3A32014R0910

. European Commission. (2016). General Data Protection Regulation.

Financial Crime Academy. (2025). Blockchain and privacy: Navigating the balance between transparency and data protection. https://financialcrimeacademy.org/blockchain-and-privacy/

Finck, M. (2019). Blockchain and the General Data Protection Regulation: Can distributed ledgers be squared with European data protection law? European Parliamentary Research Service. https://www.europarl.europa.eu/thinktank/en/document/EPRS_STU(2019)634445

Floridi, L. (2020). The fight for digital sovereignty: What it is, and why it matters, especially for the EU. *Philosophy & Technology*, *33*(3), 369–378. DOI: 10.1007/s13347-020-00423-6 PMID: 35194548

Forbes Technology Council. (2023). The blockchain revolution in cross-border transactions. https://www.forbes.com/councils/forbestechcouncil/2023/09/05/the-blockchain-revolution-in-cross-border-transactions/

Galis, M. (2024). Blockchain and data privacy: The future of technology compliance. Forbes Technology Council. https://www.forbes.com/councils/forbestechcouncil/2024/02/15/blockchain-and-data-privacy-the-future-of-technology-compliance/

Gao, H. (2018). Digital or Trade? The Contrasting Approaches of China and US to Digital Trade Governance. *Journal of International Economic Law, 21*(2), 297–321. DOI: 10.1093/jiel/jgy015

Gartner. (2021). Blockchain basics: A guide to identity and trust management. Gartner Research. https://www.gartner.com/en/documents/3991163/blockchain-basics-a-guide-to-identity-and-trust-management

Ghosh, R. (2021). Digital trade and developing countries: A review of WTO initiatives. *South Centre Policy Brief, 96*, 1–10.

Goldberg, Y. (2015). A primer on neural network models for natural language processing. arXiv. https://arxiv.org/abs/1510.00726

Grier, J. (2023). The blockchain revolution in cross-border transactions. Forbes Technology Council. https://www.forbes.com/councils/forbestechcouncil/2023/09/05/the-blockchain-revolution-in-cross-border-transactions/

Gurumurthy, A., & Chami, N. (2022). From digital inclusion to data justice: The role of international institutions. *Development Studies Research, 9*(1), 18–31.

Harvard, D. C. E. (2025). Building a responsible AI framework: 5 key principles for organizations. https://professional.dce.harvard.edu/blog/building-a-responsible-ai-framework-5-key-principles-for-organizations/

Hristea, F., & Caragea, C. (2022). Natural language processing (NLP) and machine learning (ML)—Theory and applications. MDPI. https://www.mdpi.com/books/reprint/6302

Hunit. (2025). Smart legal contracts. https://smartlegalcontracts.io/

Information Commissioner's Office. (2020). Guide to the General Data Protection Regulation (GDPR). ICO. https://ico.org.uk/for-organisations/guide-to-data-protection/guide-to-the-general-data-protection-regulation-gdpr

Interaction Design Foundation. (2025). The Fourth Industrial Revolution. https://www.interaction-design.org/literature/topics/the-fourth-industrial-revolution

. Irion, K., Yakovleva, S., & Bartl, M. (2016). Trade and privacy: Complicated bedfellows? How to achieve data protection-proof free trade agreements. Amsterdam Law School Research Chapter No. 2016-36.

Ismail, F. (2020). Digital Industrialisation and the Developmental State: The Role of the WTO and E-commerce Negotiations. South Centre Research Paper No. 113. https://www.southcentre.int

ISO. (2023). Blockchain and distributed ledger technologies. https://www.iso.org/committee/6266604.html

ITU. (2023). Focus Group on Application of Distributed Ledger Technology. https://www.itu.int/en/ITU-T/focusgroups/dlt/

Janakiram, M. S. V. (2024). The building blocks of LLMs: Vectors, tokens and embeddings. The New Stack. https://thenewstack.io/the-building-blocks-of-llms-vectors-tokens-and-embeddings/

Kachura, M. (2023). Land ownership goes digital with NFTs in India. Itez. https://itez.com/en/blog/technology/land-ownership-goes-digital-with-nfts

Kalaiselvi, G., Santhosh Kumar, R., Sudharsan, S., & Venkadasubramanian. (2023). Raven: NFT-based land records system using blockchain. IJARSCT. https://www.ijarsct.co.in/Paper9753.pdf

Kang, M., Ahmed, S., & Vishwanath, P. (2025). Criminal evidence analysis using blockchain technologies. *International Journal of Creative Research Thoughts*, *13*(3). https://ijcrt.org/papers/IJCRT25A3092.pdf

Kim, D. (2021). The convergence of digital, physical and biological systems. Korea Economic Institute. https://keia.org/wp-content/uploads/2021/10/KEI_SMA_Dongwoo-Kim_FINAL.pdf

Lambrellis, D. (2022). Algorithms, Source Code, and the JSI: Balancing Innovation and Regulatory Autonomy. *Legal Issues of Economic Integration*, *49*(1), 59–84.

Lehmann, M. (2018). Who owns blockchain? *Harvard Journal of Law & Technology*, *31*(2), 567–588.

Lemieux, V. L. (2016). Trusting records: Is blockchain technology the answer? *Records Management Journal*, *26*(2), 110–139. DOI: 10.1108/RMJ-12-2015-0042

Li, H. (2018). Deep learning for natural language processing: Advantages and challenges. *National Science Review*, *5*(1), 24–26. https://academic.oup.com/nsr/article/5/1/24/4107792. DOI: 10.1093/nsr/nwx110 PMID: 34691827

McKendrick, E. (2021). *Contract law: Text, cases, and materials* (9th ed.). Oxford University Press.

MDPI. (2023). Use of blockchain-based smart contracts in logistics and supply chains. https://www.mdpi.com/2079-9292/12/6/1340

Mik, E. (2017). Smart contracts: Terminology, technical limitations and real-world complexity. *Law, Innovation and Technology*, *9*(2), 269–300. DOI: 10.1080/17579961.2017.1378468

Mistral, A. I. (2024). Tokenization guide. https://docs.mistral.ai/guides/tokenization/

Monteiro, J. A., & Teh, R. (2017). Provisions on Electronic Commerce in Regional Trade Agreements. WTO Working Paper ERSD-2017-11. https://www.wto.org

Nakamoto, S. (2008). Bitcoin: A peer-to-peer electronic cash system. https://bitcoin.org/en/bitcoin-paper

Narayanan, A., Bonneau, J., Felten, E., Miller, A., & Goldfeder, S. (2016). *Bitcoin and cryptocurrency technologies: A comprehensive introduction*. Princeton University Press.

National Conference of State Legislatures. (2021). Blockchain legislation. NCSL. https://www.ncsl.org/research/financial-services-and-commerce/blockchain-state-legislation-and-regulations.aspx

Neuburger, J. (2018). *Blockchain, personal data and the GDPR right to be forgotten*. Lexology.

. OECD. (2020). OECD Blockchain Policy Framework.

Organisation for Economic Co-operation and Development. (2022, June 10). *Recommendation of the Council on Blockchain and Other Distributed Ledger Technologies (OECD/LEGAL/0470)*. OECD. https://legalinstruments.oecd.org/en/instruments/OECD-LEGAL-0470

Outlook India. (2025). Blockchain in Indian judiciary: Use cases and challenges. https://www.outlookindia.com/xhub/blockchain-insights/blockchain-in-indian-judiciary-use-cases-and-challenges

Pentland, A. (2021). Building the new economy: A data commons. *Communications of the ACM*, *64*(9), 37–39.

Rajeshwar, J., ... (2025). Blockchain for legal evidence management: Enhancing transparency and security in judicial systems. International Journal of Engineering Studies. https://theaspd.com/index.php/ijes/article/download/419/361/1426

Rees, D. (2020). Smart contracts and the evidential challenges of intent. *Law, Innovation and Technology*, *12*(2), 145–163. DOI: 10.1080/17579961.2020.1815401

Reyes, C. L. (2016). Moving beyond bitcoin to an endogenous theory of decentralized ledger technology regulation. *Villanova Law Review*, *61*(2), 191–234.

Riss, A. (2023). Blockchain and NFT revolution in land registries and real estate. DEV Community. https://dev.to/ahmmrizv9/blockchain-and-nft-revolution-in-land-registries-and-real-estate-341k

Rolling Out. (2025). 2025 global privacy, AI, and data security regulations. BigID. https://bigid.com/blog/2025-global-privacy-ai-and

Saberi, S., Kouhizadeh, M., Sarkis, J., & Shen, L. (2019). Blockchain technology and its relationships to sustainable supply chain management. *International Journal of Production Research*, *57*(7), 2117–2135. DOI: 10.1080/00207543.2018.1533261

Saxena, A., & Shukla, R. K. (2021). Artificial intelligence and blockchain fusion: A technology forecast towards 2030. *Technological Forecasting and Social Change*, *166*, 120601. DOI: 10.1016/j.techfore.2021.120601

Schwab, K. (2016). The Fourth Industrial Revolution. World Economic Forum. https://www.weforum.org/about/the-fourth-industrial-revolution-by-klaus-schwab

Sen, N. (2018). Understanding the role of the WTO in international data flows: Taking the liberalisation or the regulatory autonomy path? *Journal of International Economic Law*, *21*(2), 323–348. DOI: 10.1093/jiel/jgy021

Sethi, A., & Makwana, F. (2024). Smart contracts for supply chain management using blockchain. *International Journal of Innovative Research in Technology*, *11*(1), 326–331.

Sharma, A. (2024, January 12). *Understanding smart contracts in blockchain: A complete overview*. Medium. https://medium.com/@sharma1991ais/understanding-smart-contracts-in-blockchain-a-complete-overview-1d879381cfc

Singh, A. P. (2025). Blockchain technology: Core mechanisms, evolution, and future implementation challenges. arXiv. https://arxiv.org/html/2505.08772v1

Swan, M. (2015). *Blockchain: Blueprint for a new economy*. O'Reilly Media.

. Szabo, J., Bernard, C., & Philip, L. (2024). Legal implications and challenges of blockchain technology and smart contracts. Computer Life, 12(2).

Szabo, N. (1997). The idea of smart contracts. Nick Szabo's Papers and Concise Tutorials. https://www.fon.hum.uva.nl/rob/Courses/InformationInSpeech/CDROM/Literature/LOTwinterschool2006/szabo.best.vwh.net/smart_contracts_idea.html

Tapscott, D., & Tapscott, A. (2016). *Blockchain revolution: How the technology behind Bitcoin is changing money, business, and the world*. Penguin Books.

Tashev, T. (2025). Anatomy of an LLM: Tokens, weights and parameters. Webopedia. https://www.webopedia.com/technology/llm-tokens-weights-parameters/

Thompson, A., & Voon, T. (2016). Data localisation requirements and the WTO. *World Trade Review*, *15*(4), 701–722.

Thompson, S. (2020). Blockchain signatures and eIDAS: A qualified mismatch? [Database access required—placeholder journal entry.]. *Journal of European Law*, *26*(4), 233–247.

Trade Council. (2024). The role of blockchain in international trade. https://tradecouncil.org/wp-content/uploads/2024/10/Theroleofblockchainininternat ionaltrade.pdf

Turing. (2023). Blockchain in supply chain: Benefits, use cases & applications. https://www.turing.com/resources/blockchain-for-supply-chains

UNCITRAL. (2017). *Model Law on Electronic Transferable Records*. United Nations Commission on International Trade Law.

. UNCITRAL. (2021). Implementation of MLETR in national legislation.

UNCTAD. (2021). *Digital Economy Report 2021: Cross-border data flows and development*. United Nations.

UNCTAD. (2023). Global report on blockchain and its implications on trade facilitation. https://unctad.org/system/files/official-document/tcsdtlinf2023d1_en.pdf

UNHRC. (2021). *Report of the Office of the United Nations High Commissioner for Human Rights on the right to privacy in the digital age*. United Nations Human Rights Council.

. USMCA. (2020). United States-Mexico-Canada Agreement.

Van Dijk, J. A. G. M. (2020). *The digital divide*. Polity Press.

Vatanparast, R., & Moon, M. J. (2023). The digital standards race: Who governs blockchain standards? *Global Policy*, *14*(2), 260–274.

Vo, D., & Delahunty, M. (2020). The GDPR and blockchain: Incompatible or mutually reinforcing? *European Data Protection Law Review*, *6*(3), 324–335. DOI: 10.21552/edpl/2020/3/9

. WCO. (2019). Study report on disruptive technologies.

Weber, R. H. (2019). The law and ethics of decentralised autonomous organisations. *European Journal of Risk Regulation*, *10*(2), 241–258.

Winston, M. (2022). Wrapping code: Smart contracts and contractual safeguards. [Available via HeinOnline/academic databases.]. *Harvard Journal of Law & Technology*, *35*(1), 115–140.

World Bank. (2020). *Blockchain: Opportunities for Private Enterprises in Emerging Markets*. International Finance Corporation.

World Economic Forum. (2020, April 6). Supply chains are in chaos. Here's how to make them more resilient. *World Economic Forum*. https://www.weforum.org/stories/2020/04/supply-chains-resilient-covid-19/

World Scientific. (2025). Industry 4.0: Converging technologies in the global economy. https://worldscientific.com/doi/pdf/10.1142/9789811203930_0001

World Trade Organization. (1994). General Agreement on Trade in Services. Marrakesh Agreement Establishing the World Trade Organization, Annex 1B.

. World Trade Organization. (1998). Canada – Certain Measures Affecting the Automotive Industry, WT/DS139/R.

. World Trade Organization. (2005). United States – Measures Affecting the Cross-Border Supply of Gambling and Betting Services, WT/DS285/AB/R.

World Trade Organization. (2021). Joint Statement Initiative on E-Commerce: Negotiating Texts. https://www.wto.org/english/tratop_e/ecom_e/ecom_e.htm

Wright, A., & De Filippi, P. (2015). Decentralized blockchain technology and the rise of lex cryptographia. Social Science Research Network (*SSRN*). https://doi.org/ DOI: 10.2139/ssrn.2580664

. WTO. (1998). Work Programme on Electronic Commerce, WT/L/274.

. WTO. (2009). China – Publications and Audiovisual Products, Appellate Body Report, WT/DS363/AB/R.

. WTO. (2019). Joint Statement on Electronic Commerce, WT/L/1056.

Wu, M. (2020). Digital Trade-Related Provisions in Regional Trade Agreements: Existing Models and Lessons for the Multilateral Trade System. RTA Exchange Working Paper. International Centre for Trade and Sustainable Development. https://rtaexchange.org

Zhuk, A. (2025). Beyond the blockchain hype: Addressing legal and regulatory challenges. *SN Social Sciences*, *5*(11), 11. DOI: 10.1007/s43545-024-01044-y

Zyskind, G., Nathan, O., & Pentland, A. (2015). *Decentralizing privacy: Using blockchain to protect personal data. In 2015 IEEE Security and Privacy Workshops.* IEEE., DOI: 10.1109/SPW.2015.27

Chapter 3
Legal Challenges in Cloud Computing

Tushar
https://orcid.org/0000-0001-7190-7687
United College of Engineering and Research, Prayagraj, India

Nandita Pradhan
https://orcid.org/0009-0006-8819-1009
United College of Engineering and Research, Prayagraj, India

Prabhat Chandra Shrivastava
https://orcid.org/0000-0003-0766-6422
Faculty of Science, University of Allahabad, Prayagraj, India

Pooja Jaiswal
https://orcid.org/0009-0007-2507-1525
University of Allahabad, Prayagraj, India

Sweta Singh
United University, Prayagraj, India

Venktesh Mishra
https://orcid.org/0000-0003-4476-4064
United College of Engineering and Research, Prayagraj, India

ABSTRACT

Cloud computing has enabled fast organizational growth and diversified service acceptance. These services accelerate product development and hosting, giving consumers and third parties instant access. Cloud computing problems must be considered and implemented by service providers. This chapter emphasizes cloud computing's legal, contractual, and security issues. Enterprise clients benefit from several cloud computing projects. Despite these benefits, cloud data security and privacy remain problems. The cryptography and data security issues discuss such algorithms, key management, humans, and legal and regulatory issues. Regulations like the General Data Protection Regulation (GDPR) and the California Consumer Privacy Act (CCPA) put stringent obligations on enterprises to safeguard user data,

DOI: 10.4018/979-8-3373-3186-7.ch003

as discussed in this chapter. Addressing cloud computing's ubiquitous security vulnerabilities requires a detailed understanding of the selected solution. This chapter also provides a methodology for organizations to analyze virtual dangers and damages.

1. INTRODUCTION

This scheme aims for the digitalization and integration of public data, thereby facilitating broader financial inclusion. Through the utilization of cloud-based infrastructure, beneficiaries are successfully identified and government subsidies are directly transferred (via Direct Benefit Transfer) into citizens' bank accounts, eliminating multiple intermediary layers. "Such Information, Communication, and Technology (ICT) solutions assist policymakers in removing unintended beneficiaries who have been availing subsidies amounting to 3.17 lakh crore (as per the Indian Budget Estimates of 2022-23), while also ensuring the timely transfer of social security benefits. Cloud computing is defined as a large-scale distributed computing paradigm. It is becoming an increasingly important topic for businesses and organizations, with various services being provided over the internet within competitive timeframes. This accelerates business operations, allowing for quicker delivery and scaling within a competitive environment. Cost reduction (through pay-per-use models), maintenance, enhanced productivity, scalability, and elasticity are all offered to businesses through cloud computing (Moghe et al., 2012)". A comprehensive analysis of cloud computing regulations reveals significant challenges in harmonizing global legal standards. Data protection frameworks, such as the GDPR, which mandate stringent guidelines on data storage, processing, and transfer, have been extensively examined in previous studies. The literature also highlights the challenges posed by jurisdictional conflicts, where contradictory laws on data handling and privacy are imposed by different countries. Data privacy is considered the most critical issue in cloud computing.

Strict requirements for the protection of user data are imposed on organizations by regulations such as GDPR and the California Consumer Privacy Act (CCPA). However, ensuring compliance becomes complex when data is stored in multiple jurisdictions with varying legal requirements. It is revealed in this chapter that organizations often struggle to maintain visibility and control over data flows in the cloud (Avanthi and Naveen, 2024). Clarity on key aspects such as data security, service uptime, and liability is often lacking in Service Level Agreements (SLAs). This chapter found that these details are frequently overlooked by organizations during contract negotiations, which can lead to disputes during service disruptions or security breaches. The strengthening of SLA frameworks is considered essential for ensuring mutual accountability. Anonymized personal data is not considered personally identifiable information under GDPR; therefore, it can be utilized in any manner. Data must be fully and irreversibly anonymized. It is known that GDPR-compliant AI tools exist. The proper and legal management of personal data should be promoted. The number of AI tools is increasing, and not all are GDPR-compliant; thus, the unauthorized transfer of educational data to an AI is prohibited. Tool robustness and adaptation to hardware and network/offline settings were prioritized. For educational institutions, this means:

(i) Lawfulness, Fairness, and Transparency: Educational institutions must be open and honest about how they process personal data. Students, parents, and staff should be informed about the goal and use of data gathering.
(ii) Personal information is only gathered for valid purposes and isn't available for use in any other way. This is particularly crucial for AI systems that collect enormous amounts of data.
(iii) Data minimization: Only gather and keep the most important personal information for specified uses. This idea may conflict since AI systems rely on large datasets to function.

A federal legislation in the United States called the Health Insurance Portability and Accountability Act (HIPAA) sets national requirements to safeguard the confidentiality and integrity of personally identifiable health information, or Protected Health Information (PHI). For all personally identifiable health information, the HIPAA Rules are well known for offering a nationwide baseline of data privacy, security, and breach notification safeguards. To demonstrate why this isn't always the case when it comes to health data that is gathered, produced, utilized, or revealed in the context of predictive or generative AI, a little background knowledge is required (Covered entity concerns exam, 2003).

HIPAA primarily applies to:

(i) ***Covered Entities:*** Providers, clearinghouses, and health plans that electronically communicate health information in conjunction with certain transactions (such as billing insurance).
(ii) ***Business Associates:*** People or organizations that carry out tasks or operations involving the use or disclosure of PHI on behalf of a covered business. Since student health data normally fall within the purview of the Family Educational Rights and Privacy Act (FERPA), the implementation of HIPAA in K–12 and higher education institutions is frequently misinterpreted.

Essential elements of cloud computing:

Figure 1 depicts the fundamental elements that cloud computing is based on.

i) Virtualization: creates an image of a resource (servers, OSes, etc.) that is indistinguishable from the real thing.
(ii) Multi-tenancy: allows for optimal utilization of resources or programs by sharing them across several users or consumers.
(iii) Storage on the cloud: storage that is managed, monitored, and backed up remotely.
(iv) A hypervisor is a software program that allows one physical host to manage several operating systems.
(v) Cloud networks offer connectivity through data centers and the internet.
(vi) Software and hardware setup for platforms.

Figure 1. Basic Cloud Computing Components

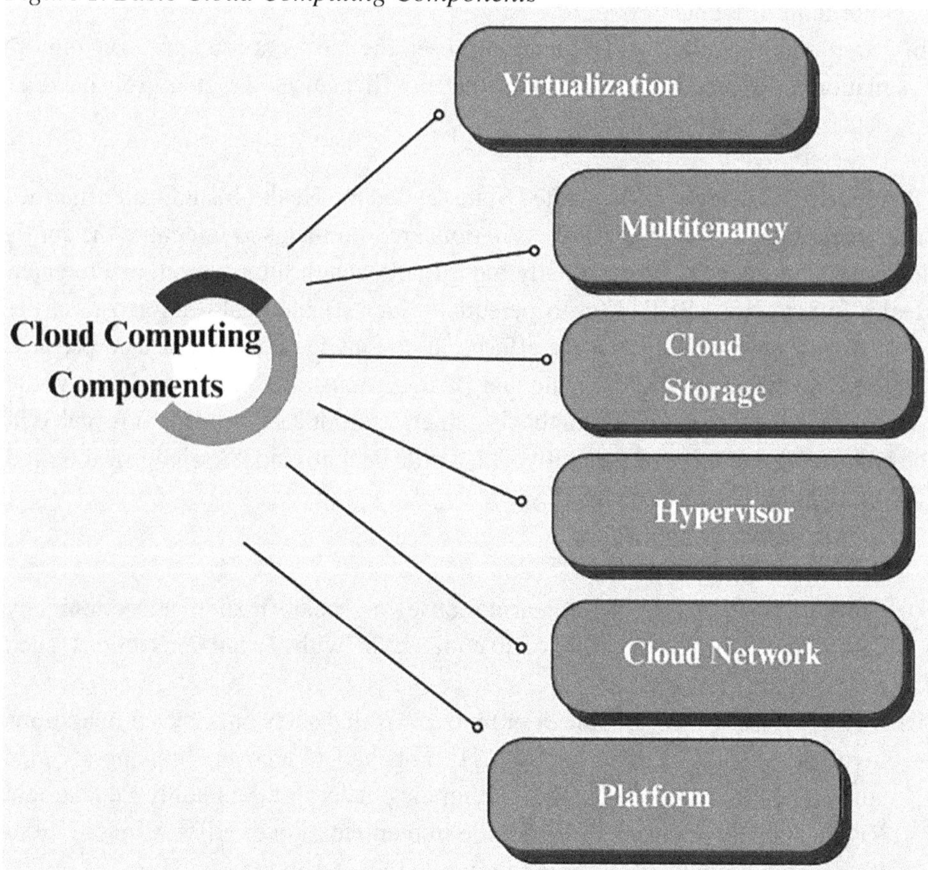

2. LEGAL CHALLENGES IN CLOUD COMPUTING: SERVICE, SECURITY AND PRIVACY

The ever-changing legal landscape affects both public and private regulations due to the global reach of cloud computing and the complexity and rapid development of this new technology. A growing concern for cloud computing is the need to safeguard the interests of both consumers and service providers. Both sides should be able to rely on the rules and regulations in place. The ever-changing nature of cloud computing across regions and nations, with their respective sets of rules and regulations, adds another layer of complexity. To ensure the entire setup works well during deployment and future updates and support, it is crucial that contracts are carefully prepared by all parties involved, including consumers, service providers, and third parties. These contracts should also be legally compliant (Gordon D.G., 2016).

2.1 Cloud Computing Legal and regulatory challenges

Offering cloud computing services necessitates careful attention to specific legal concerns as outlined by cloud computing's architectural and technological models. Figure 2 illustrates the main legal concerns related to cloud computing.

The following are the Key issues to highlight:

- **Addressing jurisdictional challenges in cloud computing**: Cloud computing services offered in some nations and areas raise questions about whether policies, laws, regulations, and competent jurisdictions apply. Consideration of the parties' locations is key to resolving this, since the appropriate country's legislation dictates the rights and responsibilities of each party. The transfer of data across national boundaries and the many relevant rule-making authorities may be subject to further legislation (Robinson et al., 2010; Gordon D.G., 2016).
- **Accountability and jurisdiction in cloud computing:** The strengthening of trust between clients and cloud computing service providers, as well as the accountability of various organizations, are the topics of this subject. It may be challenging to determine the relevant competent jurisdiction across nations and regions when dealing with cloud computing services because of their distinctive nature. Assigning a particular regulatory body to resolve disputes is one way that certain countries, like Europe, have dealt with this problem; however, this is only relevant inside Europe and does not apply outside of the continent (Robinson et al., 2010; Gordon D.G., 2016).
- **Geopolitical Impacts on Cloud Computing (Navigating inter-country relationships):** This issue discusses the evolution of international politics and

the impact of these shifts on cloud computing services provided to certain nations, as well as the extent to which these developments are regulated by legislation. We see this in action by asking: what happens if a country's relations with another are on hold owing to political or other reasons, and a client is based in the other country, but the cloud provider is in the first? What rules and regulations exist to safeguard the interests of both parties? One possible answer would be to set up a completely separate regulatory agency that oversees cloud computing on a global scale. However, doing so would need a lot of work and intervention from different countries.

Many cloud computing rules, especially in Europe, are more stringent than others. More legislation and policies across nations and regions are needed to safeguard and control cloud computing partnerships between service providers, clients, and engaged third parties. An impartial regulatory organization that enforces cloud computing legislation worldwide is essential to protect service providers and clients.

Figure 2. Legal Challenges in cloud computing

2.2 Cloud Computing Contractual Provisions

The service provider, client, and third parties must agree on service scope, quality, and terms & conditions. Detailed Service Level Agreements may do this. SLAs must comply with the appropriate nations' laws and regulations to guarantee all terms and conditions fit within their scope.

The following difficulties must be addressed in contracts, SLAs, and other legal instruments between service providers and clients:

- ***Legal framework robustness:*** The legal framework's resilience for addressing cloud computing solutions and services' flexibility is important when a client has to scale up and upgrade in the short or long term. The legal structure must accommodate cloud computing agreements' flexibility and terms (Robinson et al., 2016).
- ***Data-Flows over borders:*** It is important to highlight how countries' laws and regulations have addressed data flows over borders and how this is reflected in contracts, SLAs, and legal documents between service providers and their customers under specific jurisdiction.
- ***Cloud Computing Services Catalog:*** Customers should be able to pick well-defined and transparent service bundles from a Services Catalog for cloud computing services.
- ***Liability limitations:*** The hosting provider's responsibility may be limited in some cloud computing contracts to a level below the risk. Contracts must include this (Gordon D.G., 2016).

The issues and answers above must be considered to reach a sound service provider-client agreement.

2.3 Cloud Computing Adoption

The main question is whether clients need cloud computing services' resilience, dependability, availability, and security. The progress and popularity of cloud computing and its business model depend on protecting consumer data from third-party loss or theft.

- Addressing this issue requires considering legal words and procedures to meet Data Protection Area security criteria (Robinson et al., 2010; Gordon D.G., 2016).
- Cloud providers must effectively interact with law enforcement and relevant entities (Robinson et al., 2010; Gordon D.G., 2016).

- Efficient international coordination among parties and legal entities is crucial (Robinson et al., 2010; Gordon D.G., 2016).

2.4 A proposed solution for Security and data privacy issues

Some researchers suggest effective governance, better encryption, disaster and backup recovery management, secure cloud virtualization, and a comprehensive security policy and Service Level Agreement (SLA) to meet security needs. Silva et al. (2018) developed a software architecture that worked with homomorphic encryption and hardware security extensions, notably Intel SGX (Software Guard eXtensions), as seen in Figure 3.

Figure 3. Proposed Solution

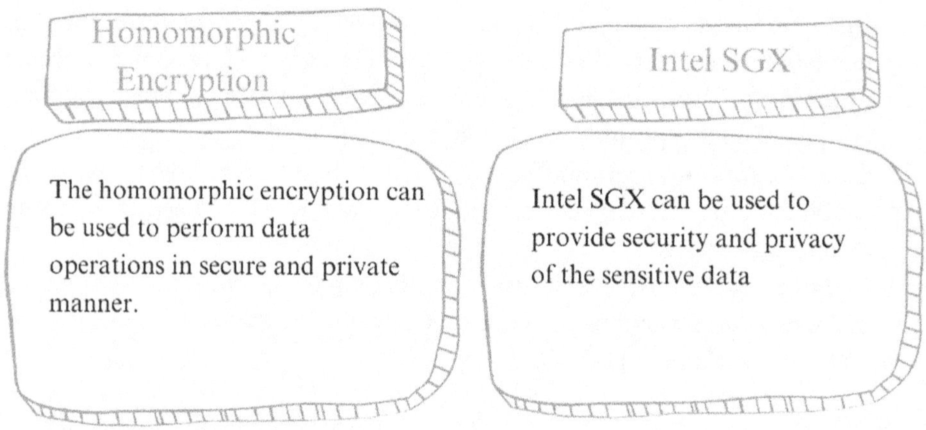

Despite being less efficient, homomorphic encryption may be implemented in any context (Hayward and Chiang, 2015). For the first time, Intel SGX was used in a cloud computing orchestrator to reduce reaction times and allow data computation, although it requires service provider infrastructure. The suggested architecture works for private and public deployments. Many additional security methods and architectures are being used to address security and data protection challenges. However, this is an immature problem that needs short- and long-term attention.

2.5 Cloud Computing Service Delivery Models

SaaS, PaaS, and IaaS are used to supply cloud computing (Takabi et al., 2010). In Figures 4 and 5 shows this.

- **Infrastructure-as-a-Service (IaaS):** It provides the computational platform, computer resources, and infrastructure including storage and archiving, servers, and networking for hosted applications. Amazon EC2 and Microsoft Azure are examples.
- **Platform-as-a-Service (PaaS):** It provides the computational platform and solution stack for clients to construct apps and host data. Example: Google Apps.
- **Software-as-a-Service (SaaS):** It provides computational platforms and consumer applications. Twitter, Myspace, Facebook, and email are examples.

Figure 4. Cloud Computing Service Delivery Models

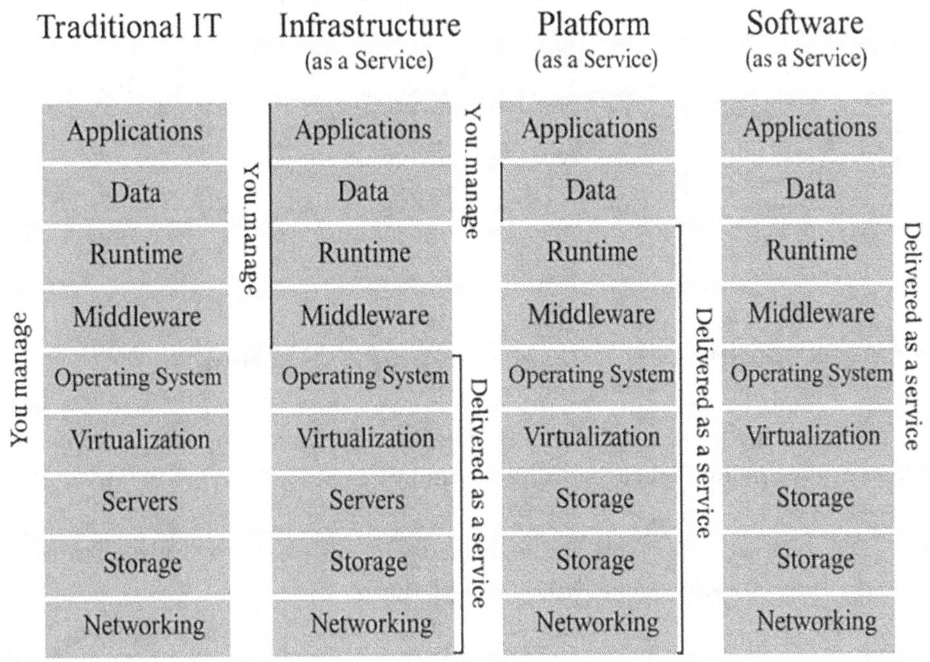

Figure 5. Cloud Computing definition by NIST

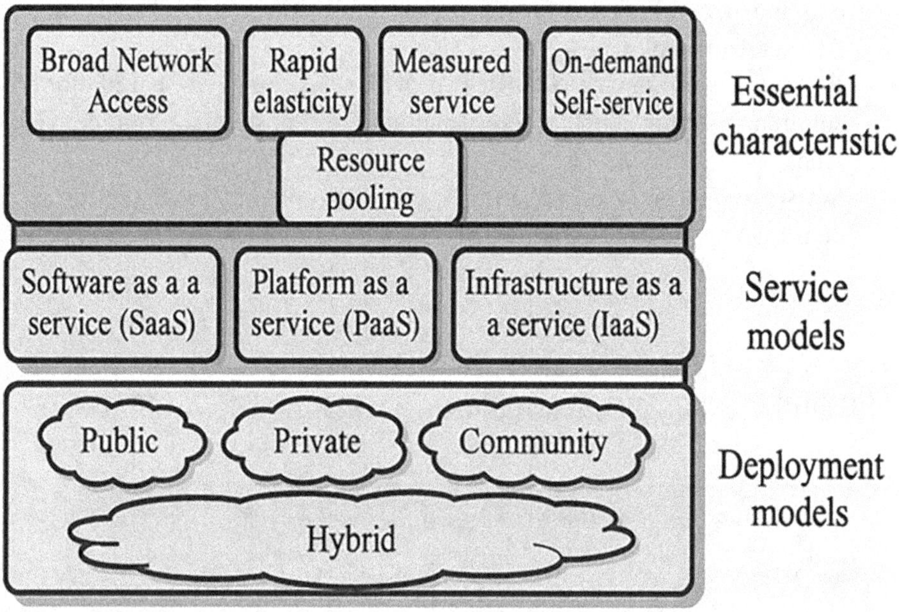

2.5 Considerations for cloud computing adoption

The following arguments should be considered before using cloud computing: Cloud offers pricing benefits but may compromise user privacy.

- Different security levels are connected with different cloud installations. It depends on the data handled on that platform.
- Support for Privacy/Security-Enhancing Services: Cloud computing platforms require certain security add-ons to meet privacy standards.
- Cloud providers may utilize de facto standards like Amazon EC2 and S3 APIs instead of open standards. Strong support for open standards, such "OpenStack," is also prevalent.
- Trusted Computing Hardware concerns: Hardware reliability and failure cost are concerns in Trusted Computing Hardware (TCM).

2.5.1 Cloud Data Privacy: Definition, Incidents, Requirements, Risks, and Governance

Privacy is the right to know the kind, location, and use of personal information (Ryan M. D., 2011). Information sharing should have clear guidelines to prevent misuse. The cloud setup scenario affects data context and flow, which affects customer information privacy risk. This chapter discusses current cloud computing provider issues. After listing the cloud computing service provider's privacy standards, the dangers and obstacles of using a cloud computing vendor will be discussed. Finally, cloud computing data governance security will be discussed.

2.5.2 Cloud Computing Security Incidents

Cloud computing firms have had major security issues recently, raising public concerns about their use. In 2017, the Anti-Denial of Service site "CloudFlare," was revealed to contain a weakness that allowed attackers to steal customers' passwords and usernames (What's up with roles in data management?). These instances generally caused data leaks and information dissemination, which harms privacy standards. In 2009, Amazon's Simple Storage Service was interrupted, causing storage servers to lose connection, and a Google Doc vulnerability leaked data. More aggressively, LinkUp was forced to close when a system administrator error disclosed 45% of user data. The Anthem hack [2] exposed over 80 million customer records due to stolen login passwords. Anthem, an insurance firm, did not use multifactor authentication, hence the attackers had total access to the credentials. Elastica found that Google Drive revealed an Indian government agency's workers' email addresses and passwords [3].

2.5.3 Cloud Computing Privacy Risks and Challenges

Cloud computing consumers suffer the following privacy risks: The invasive surveillance of cloud users information without their consent raises concerns about data gathering and analysis. Enterprise clients face risks of losing reputation, market share, or violating local laws or rules. For cloud service providers, failing to comply with local legislation might result in reputation damage or litigation. The cloud storage of client data poses a high risk of leaking. Privacy concerns affect cloud adoption because they affect user confidence and challenge cloud stakeholders, which has legal, economic, and emotional consequences. The biggest privacy issues for cloud computing is (Ryan M. D., 2011):

Comprehensive risk analysis and evaluation of the cloud environment is audacious and complex: Complex cloud technologies provide several issues. Cloud service providers provide compliant solutions, flexible SLAs, simplicity of use, and seamless data movement across borders and systems. This is a major difficulty since a full risk assessment on all risks to cloud customer security and privacy is needed to meet the standards. Stakeholder engagement, roles and duties, data locations, replication and backups, legality of data transfers, auditing capabilities, and privacy SLA must be answered. New business strategies constantly compromise cloud users' privacy: The large volume of data on cheap storage at any cloud service provider can enable new business models. These data are goldmines for analysis and prediction algorithms, which offer lucrative results for corporate applications like user profiling and targeted advertising. Enterprise cloud computing users worry about complying with national laws and regulations. This affects data transit and processing on the cloud service provider's location. It also affects how the cloud resource provider handles enterprise client user access at its site. Third-party access to such data at the CSP site is especially significant since it is hard to tell who accessed what unless the CSP controls that activity. Cloud Computing Security and Privacy Issues Many cloud variables affect data security and privacy (Pearson and Benameur, 2010): Cloud infrastructure's service abstraction, geographical transparency, and dynamic scaling (Pearson and Benameur, 2010) make it challenging to govern or isolate impacted resources during security incidents or breaches. Service Delivery Model: Multiple cloud providers can share resources and backup each other using the cloud service delivery paradigm. It also lets them use each other's networks, which violates responsibility and traceability for wrongdoing (Pearson and Benameur, 2010). Unauthorized users can exploit weaknesses in multitenant cloud architecture to access other tenants' data and information (Pearson and Benameur, 2010). SaaS apps provide limited extensibility and shared responsibility due to the CSP providing just a few integrated capabilities. The CSP is responsible for application security and privacy, which is especially important in public deployments where business customers want strong security and management. Customers build apps using PaaS platforms. Customers must safeguard their apps and address privacy concerns. Customer workspaces for developing apps are segregated by the CSP. Enterprise consumers secure IaaS infrastructure components such operating systems, apps, and data. Low-level data access will be controlled by the CSP. Service Level Agreement (SLA): The CSP must facilitate the negotiation and application of contract terms and conditions with the Enterprise client. Hypervisors and virtualization offer isolation, filtered resource sharing, and secure connectivity between virtual computers. The utilization of comparable virtualized resources can increase system resemblance, but it can also generate issues when several tenants use the same infrastructure. Each tenant can have a separate OS and Application trust level. Cloud computing infrastructure demands compliance with SLAs and laws like Sarbanes-Oxley, PCI, and HIPAA due to its universal accessibility. This will change law fulfillment standards for protection laws and how they are enforced.

2.6 Critical Data Types

Different people view personal data differently. Figure 6 shows several key data types that a Cloud Service Provider (CSP) may hold.

Figure 6. Critical Data Types

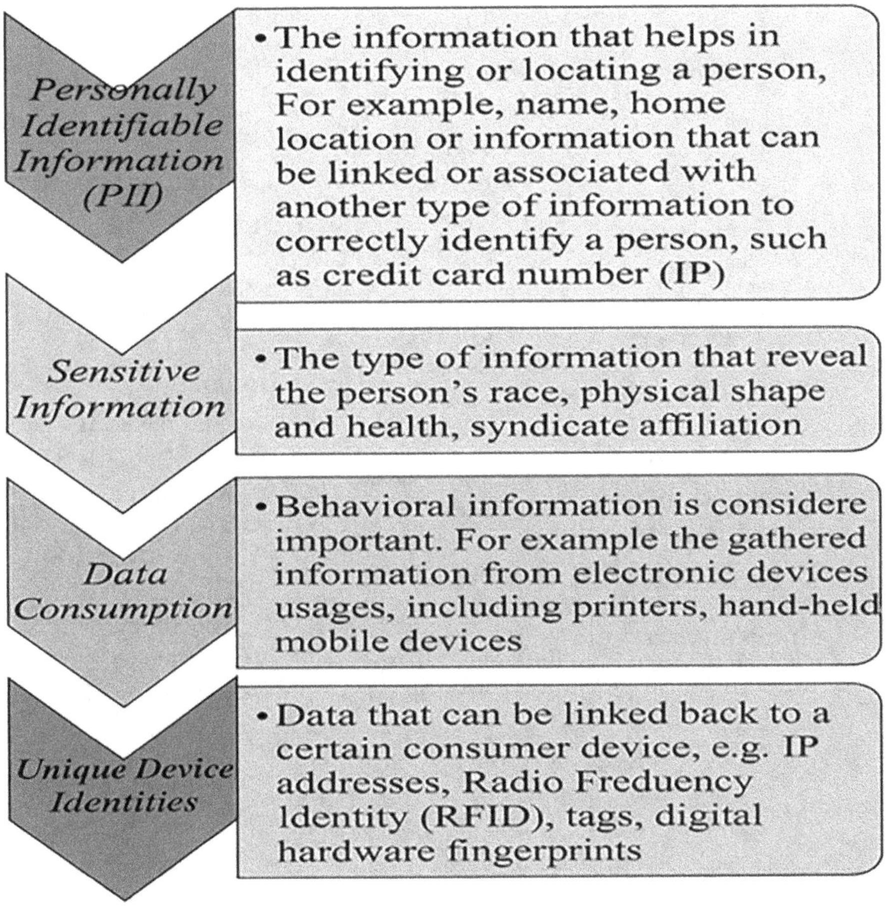

2.6.1 Cloud computing privacy solutions

Cloud computing service providers must protect data privacy throughout the lifecycle. This section discusses the cloud data lifecycle and certain privacy needs, followed by a list of current standardization initiatives to protect client data in the cloud. Data governance is crucial to security. Figure 7 shows the data governance lifecycle. Cloud data has a seven-phase life cycle, starting with user-generated data. After data flow to and from the cloud, cloud utilization needs are determined. Next, data sharing with third parties, cloud data archiving, and cloud data disposal are explored (Itani et al., 2009).

Figure 7. Data Governance Lifecycle

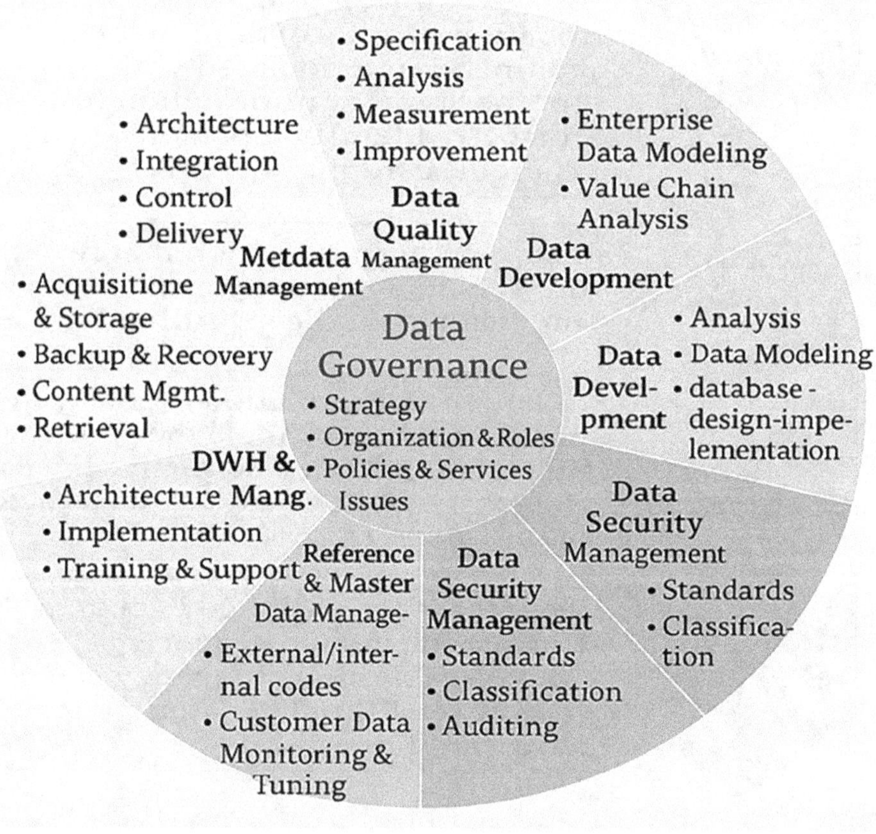

The life cycle of cloud data is full, from generation to disposal (Itani et al., 2009): Users that produce data are often the data owners. However, moving this data to the cloud gives someone else access, which should be regulated and reviewed. When transferring data from a business to a Cloud Service Provider (CSP), confidentiality and integrity must be maintained. There are concerns about storing unencrypted data with other tenants and encrypting data at rest, which is necessary for indexing and analysis. Consider the control and actions taken on shared data with third parties. Data granularity, such as providing just non-PII data, is also important.

Data Storage: Clarify the location and access of the encryption key for encrypted data at rest. Secure key management is essential.

Archiving Data: Discuss and agree on off-site archiving to a CSP, following business policy and compliance needs.

To ensure secure disposal of undesirable data, a clear policy should be established. Standardization Work Standards help CSPs and cloud customers meet privacy standards. They also guide the evaluation of controls to meet such criteria. Several cloud computing standardization bodies have developed and maintained privacy-oriented standards in recent years.

2.6.2 Cloud computing legal aspects

The legalities of cloud computing and their impact on privacy are examined here. Cloud computing policy and data storage law will be covered in parts (i) and (ii).

(i) Data Storage in Cloud Environment Legal Protection

State, nation, and location-specific rules safeguard CSP data storage. Forty-six US states implement data protection laws. Contractual duties for data security, insurance, secrecy, liquidated damages, and SLAs provide the greatest safeguards, especially for users with bargaining power. Provisions will limit CSP capability. To guarantee that the CSP and its insurance carrier will act on customer claims and pay restitution matching service damages, the cloud provider's liability must be clearly specified. Negotiate detailed SLAs that identify the services and their implications for failure.

(ii) Privacy Policy for Cloud Computing Service Providers

CSPs must adopt a privacy policy to secure client data using physical, administrative, and technical restrictions. The policy establishes customer data exchange boundaries and security incident and data breach response procedures. CSP customers should read, understand, and dispute their privacy policy. The CSP may overlook this topic, so customers must carefully read the contract and liability clauses to learn how their data will be protected, where it will be hosted, and what will happen if a data breach occurs. Disclaimers reduce CSP responsibility. Challenge and compare these to local laws and regulations. A CSP customer must comply with national legislation and regulatory standards for their business. The contract must specify how CSPs will handle sensitive customer data and which data is secret.

2.7 Cloud Computing Security Challenge and Issue

Cloud computing has introduced many helpful services but also security issues and dangers. Because much data is transferred over the network and stored in specialized cloud services, malicious actors can exploit several loopholes. Figure 8 illustrates several issues, which are discussed below.

Figure 8. Cloud Security Challenges

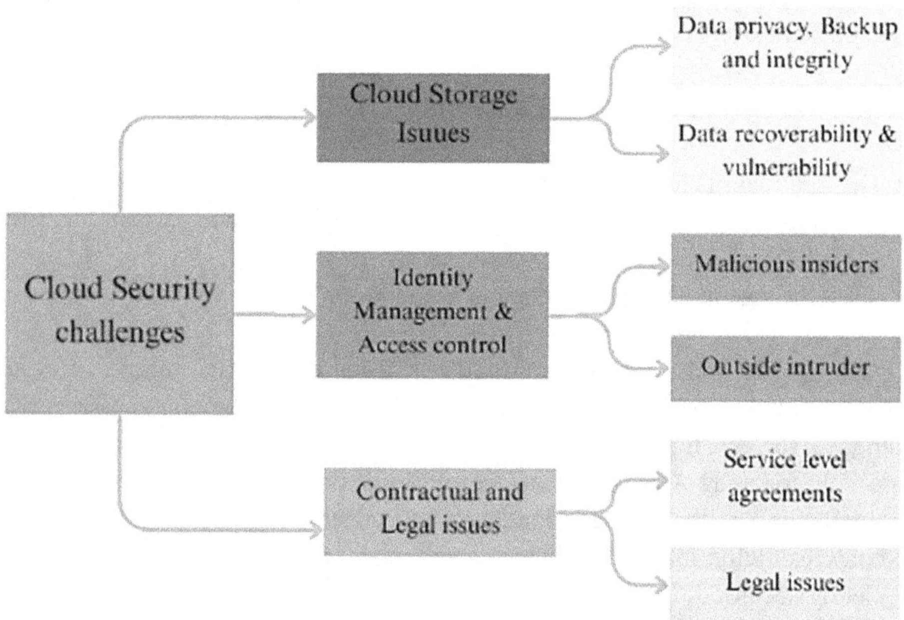

2.7.1 Cloud Storage Issues

Cloud storage poses serious security threats for sensitive data. The cloud can disclose, change, or return contradicting sensitive data to users. Crashing, user problems, and misconfigurations are conceivable.

- ***Data Privacy and Integrity:*** Each service provider must have a special policy to secure user data stored in the cloud, and they must be aware of who has access to the data and that only authorized users can maintain or modify it. Both providers and users should worry about cloud computing security. Users must keep other users' data private; thus, the supplier must safeguard it well. The biggest benefit of cloud computing is saving money and getting more data storage, but only if the supplier and user prioritize security.
- ***Data Recovery and Vulnerability:*** Cloud computing provides reactive and on-demand resource delivery due to resource pooling and flexibility. Unauthorized access to management interfaces, intranet protocol weaknesses caused by wide network access, data retrieval due to aggregation, and flexibility, which allows a subsequent user to recover data written by a previous user due to resource reallocation, may pose cloud computing security challenges.
- ***Backup data:*** Data backup is essential for unintended and planned disasters. Content Security Policy must perform regular backups to ensure data availability. Backup data should be secure to avoid unauthorized access and change.

2.7.2 Identity Management and Access Control

Data and service integrity depend on access control and identity management. Preventing data theft requires tracking user IDs. Cloud computing has extensive identification and access constraints, so data owners and stored data are on distinct executive platforms.

- Malicious Insiders

A malicious cloud provider system administrator is the worst-case situation for both providers and clients. Her business role with the cloud provider allows the insider to access sensitive data with her approved user credentials. System administrators who often backup client resources (virtual machines, data storage, etc.) might use their access to backups to steal critical customer data.

- Outside Intruder

Outside assaults come from third parties. Attack incidents are frequently grouped. Many occurrences are hazardous, yet some are not. A user may mistype a computer's address, allowing an unlawful connection (Patel et al., 2013).

2.7.3 Contractual and Legal Issues

- Service Level Agreements

Service Level Agreements (SLAs) create limits and agreements between users and Cloud service providers. The SLA should contain Content Security Policy data breach processes, including corrective steps and a minimum performance level.

- Legal Issues

Geographically differing legal jurisdictions for Content Security Policy resources raise legal difficulties. Different legal jurisdictions will present problems if the user moves.

2.7.4 Attack in Cloud Computing

This section examined cloud computing security issues. Now, various cloud computing hacks that hinder security are revealed.

- ***Service theft:*** Hypervisor scheduler issues allow Theft of Service attacks. The attack occurs when the hypervisor's routing protocol fails to detect and account for poor virtual machines' CPU utilization. Due to this problem, unethical users might get cloud services at others' cost.
- ***DDoS Attacks:*** Denial of Service (DoS) attacks aim to disable a system or network resource. DoS attacks can be launched by one person or computer. Attackers might be humans or zombie hordes. Attackers can send massive packets to the target with phony IP addresses (Jensen et al., 2009).
- ***Malware Injection Attacks:*** Introduce malicious services or virtual machines into the Cloud system as a first step. Cloud malware can be used to eavesdrop on data changes, inhibit functionality, or perform functional alterations. The attacker must construct and add a malicious SaaS or PaaS or IaaS to the cloud system to launch this attack. The cloud system must also be fooled into thinking the new service implementation instance is an attack targeted service. If this works, the malicious service implementation will automatically launch the adversary's malware on genuine user requests.

In targeted shared memory attacks, attackers use shared memory caches or primary memory of both real and virtual computers. This cloud computing assault can lead to side-channel and malware injection attacks (Amara et al., 2017). Phishing attacks include manipulating online links to divert users to a bogus link, allowing attackers to access the victim's account and steal information. Anti spam software may block spam, pop-ups, and phishing (Amara et al., 2017). Stepping-Stone Attack: Attackers aim to achieve objectives (e.g., denial of service, damage) while concealing their identities and locations to escape detection and tracing. Stepping stones are used to indirectly assault the victim. Stepping-stone hosts can be recruited by illegal botnets.

- ***Audio-steganography attacks:*** Common media files are used for steganography to communicate and hide secret information. Thus, hostile insiders use steganography to leak data in cloud storage by replacing less relevant sections of media files with secret information. The steganography media file sounds like the originals, with mild distortion in less prominent parts. In cloud storage, cover files should be freely transferred (Liu et al., 2011).

2.8 Enhancing Cloud Security: Practices and Technologies

Cloud computing is growing in popularity as more people recognize its benefits. It makes it easy to cut operations and save money. The adoption of cloud services has increased security issues and vulnerabilities. Some technologies and techniques can enhance storage capacity and securely store data.

2.8.1 Vulnerability Protection: Cloud providers must improve patching. Cloud service vulnerabilities should be checked and upgraded to avoid access points and hacker assaults. The cloud service provider needs an IDS to protect it.

2.8.2 SP Properties: Finding an experienced and reliable cloud service provider is crucial because each has its unique data management practices.

2.83 Security Check: Contracts with service providers allow customers to file claims for data breaches and other issues, making them one of the most essential cloud service guarantees (An et al., 2016).

2.8.4 Access Control: Cloud service providers set up data access control, requiring constant validation of permitted users. Cloud service providers must also allow users to access data. This method can protect sensitive data from illegal access and enable safe storage.

2.9 Framework for Evaluating Cloud Computing

We've developed a framework that highlights the major steps to be used by enterprises in evaluating the level of threats in cloud computing.

Framework for Threat Evaluation

- **Describe potential issues and challenges that could threaten the safety of using cloud computing systems in communities and enterprises:** Threats history and the evolution of virtual software for information use should be reviewed. Different approaches should be employed to understand various threats. Consequently, to understand how security problems develop, it is crucial for a model that is most vulnerable to cyber attackers to be highlighted.

- **Define various contexts in which these risks and challenges occur to draw parallels and define solutions:** Diverse levels of risks and challenges that can take place in varied situations and over a period of time should be provided. This approach makes it easy for the seriousness of the problem to be estimated. Adversaries could be of different natures, including physical damage, employee negligence, absence of a code of ethics, lack of controlling, and node capture. As a result, risks and challenges are revealed in various contexts social, business or economic which have diverse outcomes for each of the cloud computing systems involved.
- **Analyze the major stakeholders involved in problem identification and development of solutions:** The third stage involves evaluating predicted stakeholders who either contribute to or prevent the hardworking level of safety and security in an enterprise. Problem identification is key in presenting the issues and challenges because it can pinpoint the roots and gaps in the system, whether technical or physical in nature.
- **Present a systematic overview and assessment of the potential damages in terms of their seriousness to the cloud computing system:** A systematic overview and assessment of tangible damages, with reliance on the case, should be carried out. Then, the threats should be classified depending on each case.
- **Legal Analysis Framework:** This chapter utilizes a comprehensive approach that combines legal and technological analysis frameworks. The legal analysis framework includes both comparative legal analysis and doctrinal research. Cryptography and data security laws are systematically compared across different jurisdictions by the comparative legal analysis, examining statutory provisions, case law, and regulatory guidelines in the US, the EU, India, and selected countries with advanced data protection regimes. Meanwhile, primary legal sources such as statutes, regulations, and case law are utilized by doctrinal research to analyze the textual content, extracting legal principles and doctrines relevant to cryptography and data security. Cryptographic techniques and emerging technologies like quantum computing and blockchain are assessed by the technological analysis framework, focusing on their technical specifications and potential vulnerabilities.
- **International Laws and Treaties:** Varying degrees of encryption regulation are implemented by many prominent nations. This regulation is driven by the fact that "encryption" is considered a "dual-use" technology, possessing both

"commercial and military" significance. The key international bodies regulating cryptography include the "Organization for Economic Cooperation and Development" and the "Wassenaar Arrangement," which serves as a successor to the "Coordinating Committee for Multilateral Export Controls," established during the "Cold War" era to oversee exports from Western countries to nations in the former Warsaw Pact and other communist regions. The Wassenaar Arrangement, officially founded in July 1996, operates as a voluntary export control initiative comprising 42 member nations. Information regarding the transfer of conventional arms and items with civilian and military applications is shared by these members. This collaborative effort within Wassenaar is designed to encourage increased accountability among its participants regarding the exporting of such goods to prevent the buildup of potentially destabilizing stockpiles. The challenges of international cooperation in addressing cryptography and data security issues include the difficulties of harmonizing laws across different jurisdictions and reconciling conflicting legal approaches. A high requirement for international organizations and agreements to facilitate collaboration and information sharing exists. The future of privacy heavily relies on the development and implementation of effective legal frameworks that balance the need for data security with individuals' privacy rights, especially in cross-border data protection challenges (Clark et al., 2003). While enhanced security is offered by cryptographic identification systems, concerns about privacy, surveillance, and potential misuse of personal information are also raised by them. The need for robust legal frameworks and public policy measures to address these challenges and protect individuals' rights is emphasized by it (Clarke R., 1994). Therefore, a need for user-centric approaches that empower individuals to control their personal data and make informed decisions about its use exists. Orin and Bruse argue that for a balanced approach that considers both privacy and security interests, legislative reforms are needed to address the evolving landscape of cryptography and data security. On the other hand, the need for clear legal standards and oversight mechanisms to ensure accountability and protect constitutional rights is emphasized by Green.

- **National Legal Frameworks:** Early cryptographic export regulations were handled differently by each nation. Some governments did not see encryption as a danger and took no action, while others passed laws to regulate it. Several nations restricted cryptography exports, imports, and local manufacture. Cryptographic restrictions are difficult to regulate since there is no clear jurisdiction idea in the digital world (Aljifri and Sanchez, 2003). This chapter examines the cryptography laws of several nations.

- **Cryptography regulation in the United States:** As the major developer of "information technology" and "security products", the US has one of the most extensive and well-documented encryption legislation. Thus, US encryption standards are a good beginning point for global encryption legislation. Encryption products can be used, developed, and sold in the US without limitations. Multiple federal agencies regulate US encryption product exports. The Department of Commerce's "Bureau of Industry and Security" (BIS) oversees encryption exports. BIS enforces the "Export Administration Regulations" (EAR), which regulate dual-use exports like encryption systems. US law regulates cryptographic software exports with exclusions. The program can be exported for personal/commercial usage or short key lengths. Exporting software to a customer's location and qualities is important. US sanctions restrict exports to sanctioned nations or individuals/entities. Even online software delivery is regulated. Downloadable encryption software sellers must filter consumers to comply with export laws. Online sales make it unclear what corporations should do to comply. Regulations create compliance issues for internet encryption software sellers.
- **Cryptography Regulation in India:** The Supreme Court has consistently viewed the "right to privacy" as part of the right to "protection of life and personal liberty." The Indian Constitution does not directly confer this right. This interpretation also protects people' private rights by extending Article 19(1)(a)'s "freedom of speech and expression" (Ahmad N., 2009). Section 69 of the "Information Technology Act" 2000 allows Indian government officials or law enforcement personnel to eavesdrop on phone calls, examine SMS messages or emails, and monitor internet activities without a warrant. It is believed that this condition violates Article 21 of the Indian Constitution. This section allows Indian national or state governments to order any agency to decrypt data. IT (Intermediaries Guidelines) Rules of 2011 require intermediaries to submit information to Indian government entities for investigation or similar reasons.

2.10 The legal answer to cloud forensics difficulties

Legal and technological excellence is needed to combat cloud crime in digital forensics. The law guarantees, and technology helps. Both are necessary and complementary.

(i) Improving Relevant Laws and Regulations

- **Improve or replenish the relevant substantive laws and regulations:** Our country has few cloud crime laws. Key laws and rules are "Criminal Law," "National Security Act," "The People's Police Law," "The Public Security Management Punishment Law," "The Law on Guarding State Secrets," "The Telecommunications Regulation," "Decision of the National People's Congress on Safeguarding Internet Security," & "Interpretation of the Supreme People's Court, the Supreme People's Procuratorate Concerning Several Issues of Application of Laws in the Information System Security of Computer Criminal Damage" (Rechkoska and Shikoski, 2025) The author advises changing the applicable substantive legislation to allow for acceptable judicial interpretation due to the cloud computing environment.
- **Establishing and completing personal privacy legislation:** Due to multi-tenancy, the cloud service provider stores a lot of company and personal data, which the owner cannot directly monitor. Thus, illicit data access is easy, leaking user privacy or sensitive information. Many previously revealed cloud crimes are this type. Thus, substantive legislation should clarify that user privacy is protected by data protection as soon as practicable. No institution (including national strength mechanisms) or individual can access another's private data without permission. The nature and quantity of private data should determine criminal convictions for unlawful access.
- **Clarifying and refining the legal role of five main participants in cloud computing:** When a crime is committed, all five participants—cloud users, cloud service providers, cloud service agents, cloud auditors, and carriers—should take legal responsibility. Additionally, the law should defend their rights. Laws and regulations must assure these criteria. For instance, if cloud users use massive computing power from IaaS and commit a crime that violates the financial sector's information system without supervision or collaboration, the cloud service provider and agents should be held accountable. Relevant legislation should clarify these five actors' legal obligation.
- **Improvement of definition and judgment of criminal standards in cloud computing environments:** In the "cloud crime and forensics" chapter, cloud computing crimes are examined. Except for some traditionally specified crimes, "Virtual machine escape," etc., only occur in cloud computing. This criminal sometimes impersonates a genuine program to monitor data or launch illicit cloud attacks. In the previous two years, Snowden's American Prism door large-scale monitoring event has drawn criticism. In this case, monitoring executants commit crimes

against cloud users with cloud computing providers' consent. Our state's substantive law must define new crimes and set penalties based on their severity.

(ii) Improving or replenishing the relevant procedural law

China's "National Security Law," "Law on Guarding State Secrets," "People's Police Law," "Criminal Law," "Criminal Procedure Law," "Electronic Signature Law," "Computer Information System Security Protection Regulations," "Internet Security Protection Measures," and "Computer Crime Scene Investigation and Inspection Rules of Electronic Evidence" can be used in cloud computing for enforcement and evidence. However, due to the unique nature of cloud computing, the author advises clarifying several rules and regulations:

- **Improving the way of digital forensics:** The Chinese judicial department guiding law "Computer Crime Scene Investigation and Electronic Evidence Inspection Rules" governs cloud crime judicial forensics procedures. The third article of this rule describes "on-site inspection" and "remote inspection." "The scene examination" can uncover evidence in thin clients, while "The remote inspection" struggles with cloud data in huge distributed dynamic virtual machines. "The remote inspection" cannot track and access user data dispersed across many nodes without specific hardware and software, therefore "cloud scene" is being added.
- **Making the conduct and obligations of assisting law enforcement clear:** Cloud computing is a novel technology that differs from C/S, B/S, and other commercial information service patterns. C/S, B/S, and other classic business models have fixed server programs and data. No permanent server is used in cloud computing; programs and data are dynamically allocated to physically scattered computer nodes. Dynamic transfer may occur as node and storage load calculations grow. You need cloud service providers to get these dispersed dynamic electronic data. The sixteenth and thirty-eighth articles of China's "National Security Law" and "The Law on Guarding State Secrets," etc., provide that information service providers must help law enforcement gather evidence. As with traditional C/S and B/S operators, cloud service providers may only supply logs and recording events logs, making dynamic node virtual machine data impossible to get. The appropriate departments must force cloud service providers to install forensics interfaces in all cloud computing services (SaaS, PaaS, IaaS) and upload dynamic node data as needed. China's "Internet Security Protection Technology Measures" can describe this, and related regulations can demand "cloud operators must provide digital forensics interface".

- **Pacific evidence's collection, storage, and analysis:** "The Rules of Surveying the Crime Scene of Computer and Electronic Evidence" in China regulates electronic evidence collection and storage under the traditional C/S and B/S modes, but not under the cloud computing model. Different methods suit different offenses. However, most situations require rely on cloud service access for forensic evidence to get the original data, which comprises electronic data needed for analysis. However, big raw electronic data are hard to evaluate or store. Modern technology stores and analyzes data in the cloud, yet legislation like "The Rules of Surveying the Crime Scene of Computer and Electronic Evidence." are needed.
- **The act of law for clear evidence:** Cloud computing evidence makes crime scene reconstruction difficult. Cloud computing evidence is needed to prove tenant crimes, but the "Code of Criminal Procedure," "The Rules of Electronic Signature," and other related legislation must be considered to determine its acceptability and competency.

The author presented a rudimentary digital forensics model in Figure 9 based on previous research. Evidence can be imputed via center-collection or remote upload. High-logic applications like SaaS, PaaS, and IaaS use information-using central collection. To prevent application destruction, low-logic applications like the virtual layer, hardware layer, and equipment layer use remote upload access to electronic data. After Hadoop preparation, the data is stored in evidence storage for court forensics analysis and chain of evidence creation. After then, courts will see the evidence.

Figure 9. Cloud forensics reference model

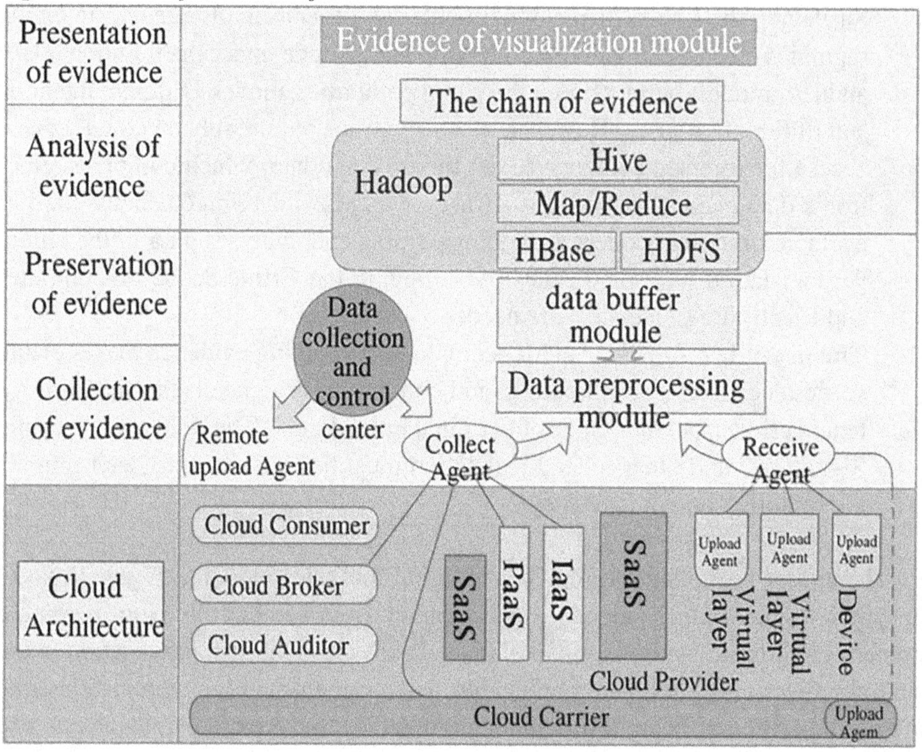

2.11 Legal Challenges issues in Cloud Computing

Security and privacy are the main issues, and these concerns are discussed below in detail (Wang et al., 2010; Wang et al., 2011). Various cloud security issues are shown in Figure 10 and are explained in detail.

Figure 10. Issues in cloud computing

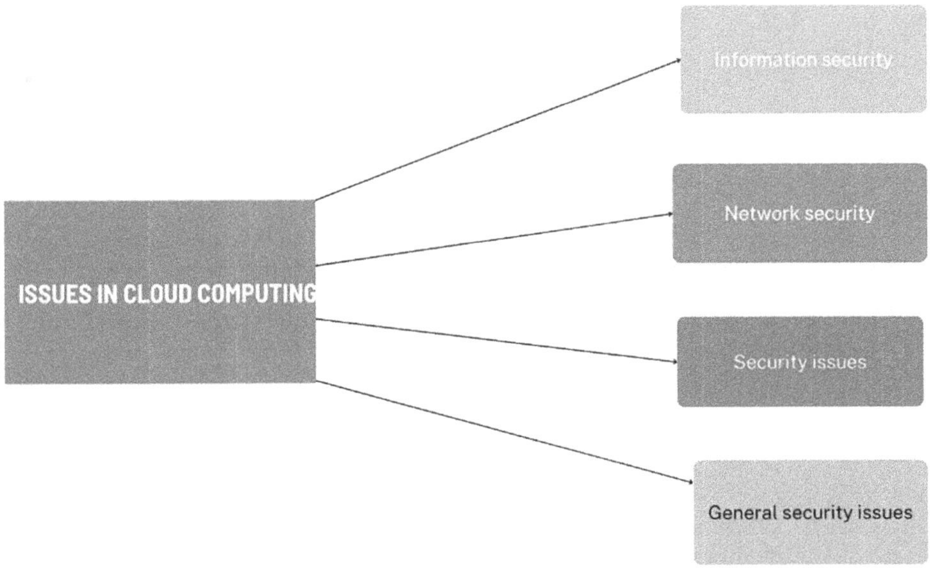

(i) Information security in cloud computing

Confidentiality, integrity, and availability of data are focused upon, with no consideration given to the form the data may take (Chen and Zhao, 2012). Information Security in cloud computing comprises various parts, and its issues are defined in detail in Figure 11.

Figure 11. Types of information security in cloud computing

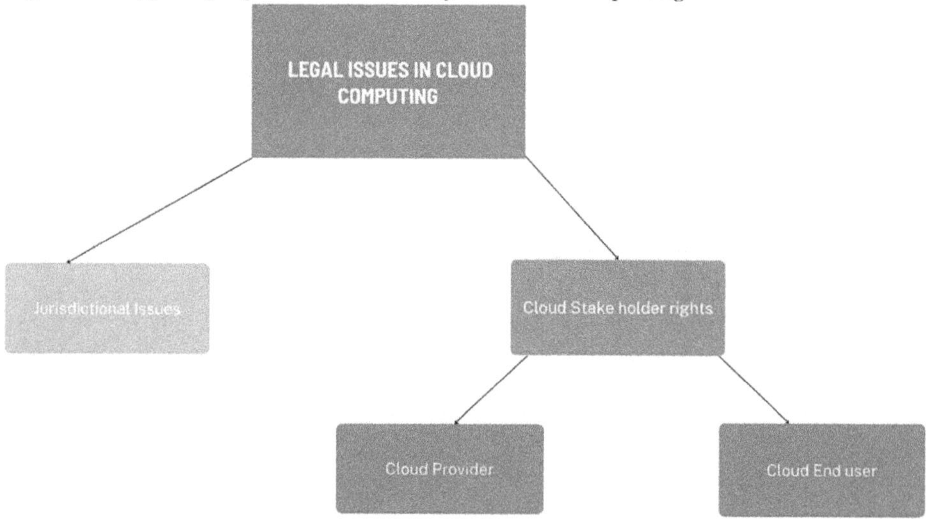

"Some of the legal issues associated with cloud computing are discussed as follows. These legal issues consist of various types, such as Jurisdictional Issues and Cloud Stakeholder Rights, which are depicted in the figure.

- **Jurisdictional Issues:** In a cloud environment, resources provided to users are not fixed to any location, nor do they have any specific data center. They are migrated between different locations during their lifetime. Thus, the decision regarding where to keep or migrate these resources may be based on various factors, which may include load balancing, networks, data center performance and availability, or even client characteristics.
- **Cloud Stakeholder Rights:** The rights of cloud stakeholders contain two main aspects, which are discussed as follows:
- **Cloud Provider:** Because of host migration, the legality of activities taking place on that host may change. To what extent is the provider liable for illegal activity, and what restrictions should be placed on the provider that results in such a move?
- **Cloud Resource End Users:** Users of different resources in a cloud-based system can be expected to know when their activities are illegal".

(ii) Network security in cloud computing

Data transmissions between computers and consumers, as well as between computers themselves, necessitate network security (Suganya and Damodharan, 2013; Yu et al., 2010). There is an in-depth discussion on cloud network security. Below, we'll go over the many kinds of cloud computing network security, as seen in Figure 12.

Figure 12. Types of network security issues in cloud computing

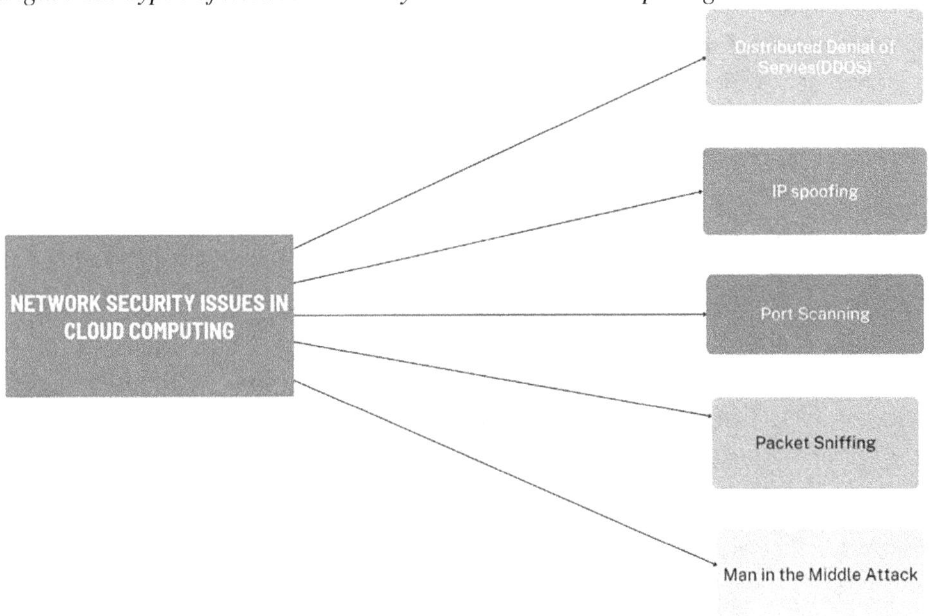

- ***DDoS Attack***: In this assault, servers and networks get a lot of network traffic, denying users access to an online service. To avoid network hacking, the provider is blackmailed (Suganya and Damodharan, 2013). Many use proprietary DDoS mitigation technologies. AWS provides end customers with APIs, resources, and powerful infrastructure, helping Amazon become the world's largest retailer (Chen and Zhao, 2012).
- ***MitM Attack:*** Attackers build independent connections with victims in this form of attack. Both sides feel they are speaking securely, but the attacker controls and manages the discussion (Suganya and Damodharan, 2013). Users can get host certificates before login via secure APIs. SSL is recommended for all secure communications (Chen and Zhao, 2012).
- ***IP Spoofing:*** This exploit attempts to utilize another user's IP address without authorization. The attacker hacks all user data and can send messages to another system with an IP address that implies the message is from a trusted user. Amazon EC2 cannot send spoof network traffic (Chen and Zhao, 2012).

- ***Port scanning:*** The cloud provider provides the security group to allow communication from the source to a port, making it susceptible to a scan port. A port allows data transfer and system door checking. This assault cannot be blocked since every internet search opens a port that allows an attack on your machine.
- ***Packet Sniffing:*** Communicate with the raw network device for relevant packets. A file is created when the program logs a packet that meets a procedure. Most typically used procedures are "login" or "password." In promiscuous mode, users cannot accept or "sniff" communications for another virtual instance. User-untargeted traffic is never transmitted by the hypervisor (Chen and Zhao, 2012).

(iii) Security issues in cloud computing

This is more complicated in a virtualized environment since the cloud provider must ensure security on both tiers: virtual machine and physical host. If the actual host server's security is breached, all virtual machines are affected.

Figure 13. Security issues in cloud computing

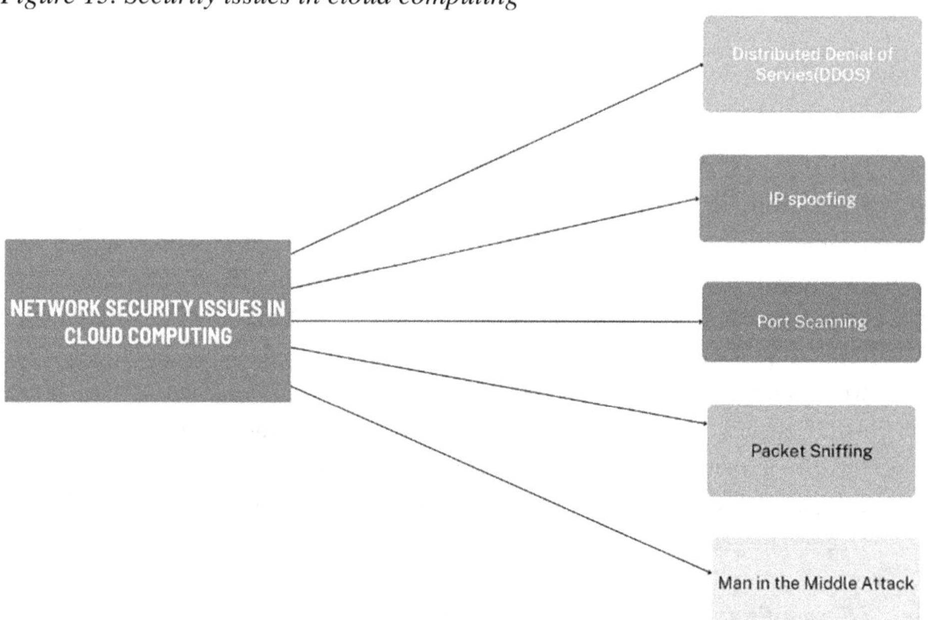

- ***Isolation of systems:*** Separate instances functioning on the same system are protected by isolation concerns. In cloud computing, virtualization methods charge distinct virtual machines for different corporations to share real resources on the same platform.
- ***Guest Operating System:*** Virtual instances are entirely consumer-maintained. Consumers may control resources and apps. Customer instances and guest OS logins are not AWS authorised.

Figure 14. Guest operating system security is necessary to secure data

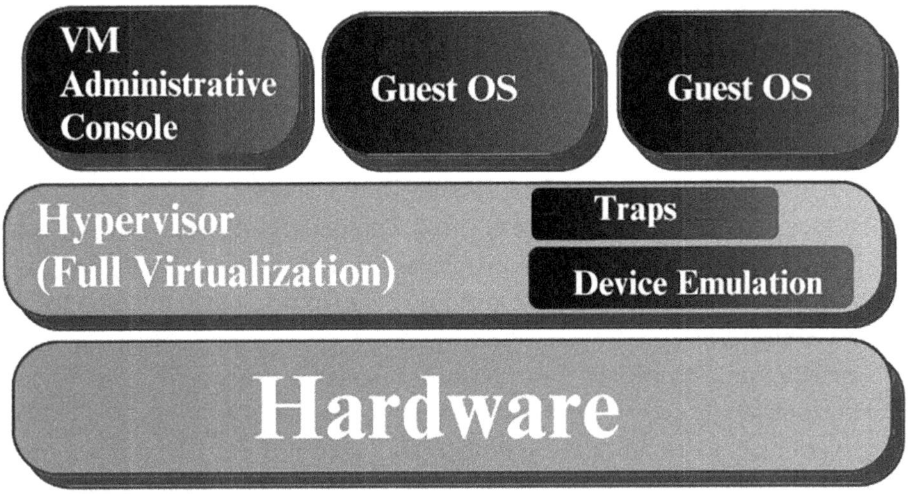

(iv) General Security issues in cloud computing

Several more widespread security concerns are currently being addressed by cloud computing and must be addressed as well. The following is a list of them.

Figure 15. General issues in cloud computing

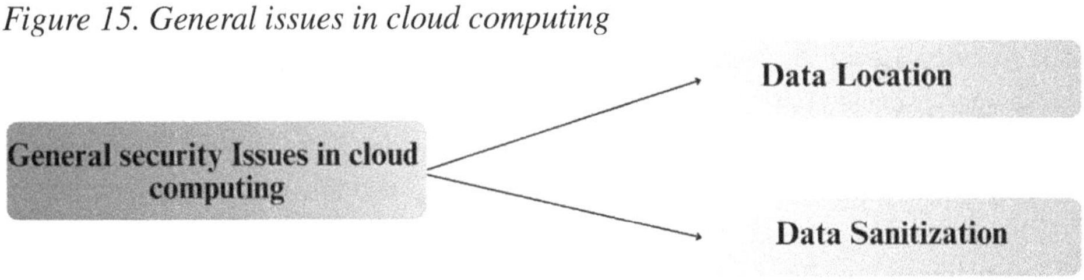

Data location: The nation or location of cloud users' data is often unknown. Therefore, users have trouble getting cloud data information.

Data Sanitization: This method removes sensitive data from a data storage system. Customers using cloud services often wonder how the cloud stores and maintains their data. Thus, another problem should be addressed to tell users about the procedure.

3. DISCUSSIONS

Five primary areas of concern in regulatory compliance and legal issues in cloud computing is highlighted by the findings:

(i) **Data Protection and Privacy Laws:** Data privacy is considered the most critical issue in cloud computing. Strict requirements for organizations to protect user data are imposed by regulations such as GDPR and the California Consumer Privacy Act (CCPA). However, ensuring compliance becomes complex when data is stored in multiple jurisdictions with varying legal requirements. It is revealed in this chapter that organizations often struggle to maintain visibility and control over data flows in the cloud.

(ii) **Jurisdictional Conflicts:** Jurisdictional dilemmas, especially in cross-border data transfers, are created by the global nature of cloud computing. For instance, government access to data stored by U.S.-based providers is allowed by the Cloud Act in the United States, even if the data resides in another country. Such conflicts undermine data sovereignty and create uncertainty for businesses. A pressing need for harmonized international regulations to address these conflicts is shown by the results.

(iii) **Intellectual Property Rights:** Ambiguities regarding intellectual property ownership are introduced by cloud environments. For example, data generated through cloud-based analytics may belong to the organization, but the processing algorithms might be proprietary to the cloud provider. Contractual transparency is identified in this chapter as a critical factor in resolving disputes over intellectual property.

(iv) **Service-Level Agreements (SLAs):** Clarity on key aspects such as data security, service uptime, and liability is often lacked by SLAs. It was found in this chapter that these details are frequently overlooked by organizations during contract negotiations, leading to disputes during service disruptions or security breaches. The strengthening of SLA frameworks is considered essential for ensuring mutual accountability.

(v) **Implications for Organizations:** The importance of proactive governance and compliance strategies is underscored in this chapter. Organizations must invest in robust data management frameworks, including encryption, access controls, and regular audits. Legal due diligence when selecting cloud service providers should also be prioritized, ensuring alignment with regulatory requirements.

4. FUTURE CHALLENGES

In order to establish regulations and policies within legal frameworks, future research will center on the security, privacy, and legal aspects of cloud computing in different nations and regions. Organizations and enterprises will feel safer and be more likely to use cloud computing in the future because of this. In the upcoming sections of this chapter, we will delve into the topic of cloud computing platform integration of privacy methods and strategies. There is a pressing need to assess privacy algorithms' practicability, performance, and potential for integration with current cloud computing systems.

This chapter suggests practical recommendations for future research on the legal implications and challenges of cryptography and data security.

- **Regulatory Framework Enhancement:** Creating thorough regulatory frameworks that balance law enforcement, security, and privacy needs is vital. Current laws ought to be examined by scholars, any shortcomings pointed out, and strong rules that might be enacted globally suggested. It involves studying how current rules like the GDPR interact with cryptography technologies.
- **Interdisciplinary Approaches:** Subsequent investigations should be undertaken using multidisciplinary approaches, incorporating perspectives from the fields of law, computer science, ethics, and economics. This method will assist in comprehending the wider ramifications of cryptography developments and in creating comprehensive legal solutions.
- **Impact Assessment:** A significant threat to current cryptographic standards is posed by quantum computing. Research should focus on assessing the impact of quantum computing on existing encryption methods and on developing quantum-resistant algorithms. This includes studying the legal implications of quantum cryptography and preparing for a transition to post-quantum cryptographic systems.
- **Standardization:** It is crucial for international standards and best practices for the application of cryptography to be established. While considering legal

compliance, researchers should focus on developing rules that guarantee the safe implementation of cryptographic systems.

- **Ethical and Legal Implications:** New moral and legal concerns are raised by integrating AI in cryptographic systems. Future research should explore the implications of "AI-driven" cryptographic methods, focusing on algorithmic bias, transparency, and accountability. Legal frameworks should be developed to address these challenges.
- **Data protection:** Data security is essential. Enterprises are wary of vendor data security guarantees. They worry about losing data to competitors and violating customer privacy. In many cases, the storage location is not revealed, increasing company security issues. In current models, data center firewalls secure this sensitive data. Enterprises must trust cloud providers to secure data.
- **Security and privacy:** Cloud computing "hot button" topics include data storage and security and service provider cloud use monitoring. These difficulties usually hinder cloud service implementation. Many companies feel uneasy hosting data and apps on third-party platforms. Migrating workloads to shared infrastructure increases unauthorized exposure. Authentication, identity management, compliance, and access technology consistency will grow. Cloud companies must be transparent to reassure customers.
- **Data and application interoperability:** Data and application systems need uniform interfaces. Organizations will want the freedom to build innovative solutions using interoperable data and apps, regardless of their location. To allow enterprises to integrate any cloud provider's capabilities, they must implement interoperability standards.
- **Management capabilities:** Despite various cloud providers, platform and infrastructure management is relatively young. Auto scaling is essential for many businesses. Today's scalability and load balancing features may be greatly improved.
- **Data and application portability:** Without standards, proprietary interfaces will limit in-house system migration or cloud provider choice. An organization's cloud-based technology will be difficult and expensive to bring in-house.
- **Metering and monitoring:** Business executives will want to use several cloud providers in their IT systems and monitor system performance. To monitor cloud applications and service performance, providers must provide standard formats and compatibility with current monitoring tools. Effective cloud computing in enterprises creates significant opportunities. However, these prospects have dangers and challenges. We believe cloud providers are necessary to properly utilize the advantages of cloud computing.

"This chapter draws attention to some of the emerging trends and technologies that will shape the future of data security and its legal implications. New security challenges will be created by the increasing use of cloud computing and the IoT. AI is expected to play a significant role in offensive and defensive cybersecurity measures, requiring legal frameworks to adapt. Finally, opportunities and challenges for data security are presented by blockchain technology, raising new legal questions concerning data access, ownership, smart contracts, and regulations".

5. CONCLUSION

Cloud Computing's primary difficulties including legal, contractual, and security challenges were discussed in this Chapter. Cloud computing service providers must safeguard Data Privacy, Security, and legal and regulatory compliance. Service providers, customers, and legal entities in various areas and nations must collaborate to embrace Cloud Computing technology in enterprises. Early reform of present laws, regulations, policies, and law is necessary to avoid short- and long-term Cloud Computing deployment disasters. This is crucial to Cloud Computing growth and continuation.

The relevant countries' regulations determine the stakeholders' geographical location, rights, and obligations, so it's important to align with them and ensure that all Cloud Computing agreements' terms and conditions are legal. An impartial regulatory organization that oversees Cloud Computing rules and regulations worldwide is essential to safeguard service providers and clients. This chapter explored computers and its privacy issues, as well as how standards and legislation alleviate some of the hazards of holding consumer data remotely. Cloud computing data security and privacy needs, problems, and risks were also discussed. Cryptography is essential for data security but faces a complex legal landscape. Organizations must navigate the need for solid security and compliance with regulations that may restrict cryptography use. Legal requirements for data privacy are increasing, and encryption itself can raise legal issues. Challenges like algorithm complexity, key management, human error, and legal restrictions also make data security difficult. This chapter highlights the complex interplay between cryptography, data security, and legal regulations that may restrict its use. A balance between robust security and adherence to rules that might limit encryption strength needs to be found by organizations. Additionally, legal requirements for data privacy are constantly evolving, and encryption itself can introduce legal complexities around intellectual property, export control, and national security. This chapter describes our anomaly detection method. Legal Metrology standards and the secure cloud reference architecture are also discussed. A potential anomaly detection module application is also described.

It was evaluated against simulated attacks on the secure cloud reference architecture, specifically the Legal Metrology processing service. The suggested method detects purposeful manipulation of measurement data by verifying system integrity. To avoid or reduce assaults on Legal Metrology measuring devices, identify abnormalities. However, a machine learning post-processing method for measuring findings that validate integrity for several measurements warrants additional study.

REFERENCES

Ahmad, N. (2009). Restrictions on cryptography in India-A case study of encryption and privacy. *Computer Law & Security Review*, *25*(2), 173–180. DOI: 10.1016/j.clsr.2009.02.001

Aljifri, H., & Sanchez Navarro, D. (2003). International legal aspects of cryptography. *Computers & Security*, *22*(3), 196–203. DOI: 10.1016/S0167-4048(03)00305-5

Amara, N., Zhiqui, H., & Ali, A. (2017). Cloud computing security threats and attacks with their mitigation techniques. *2017 International Conference on Cyber-Enabled Distributed Computing and Knowledge Discovery (CyberC)*, 244-251. DOI: 10.1109/CyberC.2017.37

An, Y. Z., Zaaba, Z. F., & Samsudin, N. F. (2016). Reviews on security issues and challenges in cloud computing. *IOP Conference Series. Materials Science and Engineering*, *160*(1), 012106. DOI: 10.1088/1757-899X/160/1/012106

Chen, D., & Zhao, H. (2012). Data security and privacy protection issues in cloud computing. *2012 International Conference on Computer Science and Electronics Engineering*, 647-651. DOI: 10.1109/ICCSEE.2012.193

Clark, E., Cho, G., & Hoyle, A. (2003). Online dispute resolution: Present realities, pressing problems and future prospects. *International Review of Law Computers & Technology*, *17*(1), 7–25. DOI: 10.1080/1360086032000063084

Clarke, R. (1994). Human identification in information systems. *Information Technology & People*, *7*(4), 6–37. DOI: 10.1108/09593849410076799

Gordon, D. G. (2016). Legal aspects of cloud computing. *Encyclopedia of Cloud Computing*, 462-475. DOI: 10.1002/9781118821930.ch38

Hayward, R., & Chiang, C. (2015). Parallelizing fully homomorphic encryption for a cloud environment. *Journal of Applied Research and Technology*, *13*(2), 245–252. DOI: 10.1016/j.jart.2015.06.004

Itani, W., Kayssi, A., & Chehab, A. (2009). Privacy as a service: Privacy-aware data storage and processing in cloud computing architectures. *2009 Eighth IEEE International Conference on Dependable, Autonomic and Secure Computing*. DOI: 10.1109/DASC.2009.139

Jensen, M., Schwenk, J., Gruschka, N., & Iacono, L. L. (2009). On technical security issues in cloud computing. *2009 IEEE International Conference on Cloud Computing*, 109-116. DOI: 10.1109/CLOUD.2009.60

Liu, B., Xu, E., Wang, J., Wei, Z., Xu, L., Zhao, B., & Su, J. (2011). Thwarting audio steganography attacks in cloud storage systems. *2011 International Conference on Cloud and Service Computing*, 259-265. DOI: 10.1109/CSC.2011.6138530

Moghe, U., Lakkadwala, P., & Mishra, D. K. (2012). Cloud computing: Survey of different utilization techniques. *2012 CSI Sixth International Conference on Software Engineering (CONSEG)*, 1-4. DOI: 10.1109/CONSEG.2012.6349524

Patel, A., Taghavi, M., Bakhtiyari, K., & Celestino Júnior, J. (2013). An intrusion detection and prevention system in cloud computing: A systematic review. *Journal of Network and Computer Applications*, *36*(1), 25–41. DOI: 10.1016/j.jnca.2012.08.007

Pearson, S., & Benameur, A. (2010). Privacy, security and trust issues arising from cloud computing. *2010 IEEE Second International Conference on Cloud Computing Technology and Science*, 693-702. DOI: 10.1109/CloudCom.2010.66

Rechkoska-Shikoska, U., & Shikoski, B. (2025). Cloud computing, security and legal issues. *A Research Agenda for Cybersecurity Law and Policy*, 205-215.

Robinson, N., Valeri, L., Cave, J., Starkey, T., Graux, H., Creese, S., & Hopkins, P. P. (2010). The cloud: Understanding the security, privacy and trust challenges. SSRN *Electronic Journal*. DOI: 10.2139/ssrn.2141970

Ryan, M. D. (2011). Cloud computing privacy concerns on our doorstep. *Communications of the ACM*, *54*(1), 36–38. DOI: 10.1145/1866739.1866751

Silva, L. V., Barbosa, P., Marinho, R., & Brito, A. (2018). Security and privacy aware data aggregation on cloud computing. *Journal of Internet Services and Applications*, *9*(1), 6. DOI: 10.1186/s13174-018-0078-3

Suganya, S., & Damodharan, P. (2013). Enhancing security for storage services in cloud computing. *2013 International Conference on Current Trends in Engineering and Technology (ICCTET)*, 396-398. DOI: 10.1109/ICCTET.2013.6675995

Takabi, H., Joshi, J. B., & Ahn, G. (2010). Security and privacy challenges in cloud computing environments. *IEEE Security and Privacy*, *8*(6), 24–31. DOI: 10.1109/MSP.2010.186

Wang, C., Ren, K., Lou, W., & Li, J. (2010). Toward publicly auditable secure cloud data storage services. *IEEE Network*, *24*(4), 19–24. DOI: 10.1109/MNET.2010.5510914

Wang, C., Wang, Q., Ren, K., & Lou, W. (2010). Privacy-preserving public auditing for data storage security in cloud computing. *Proceedings - IEEE INFOCOM*, 1–9. DOI: 10.1109/INFCOM.2010.5462173

Wang, Q., Wang, C., Ren, K., Lou, W., & Li, J. (2011). Enabling public Auditability and data dynamics for storage security in cloud computing. *IEEE Transactions on Parallel and Distributed Systems*, *22*(5), 847–859. DOI: 10.1109/TPDS.2010.183

Yu, S., Wang, C., Ren, K., & Lou, W. (2010). Achieving secure, scalable, and fine-grained data access control in cloud computing. *2010 Proceedings IEEE INFOCOM*.

ADDITIONAL READING

3. InfoWorld, The dirty dozen: 12 cloud security threats, http://www.infoworld.com /article /3041078 / security/the-dirty-dozen-12- cloud-security-threats.html

2. Microsoft. Rise of the Cloud Ecosystems, https://blogs.msdn.microsoft.com/dachou/2011/03/16/rise-of-the-cloudecosystems/

4. Search Cloud security, Cloud Computing Security Issues: Incident Response - Data Breach Prevention;https://searchcloudsecurity.techtarget.com/resources/Cloud -ComputingSecurity-Issues-Incident Response-Data-Breach-Prevention

5. What's up with roles in data management? https://franklybi.blogspot.it/2010/12/whats-up-with-roles-in-datamanagement.html

1. Wikipedia. NIST cloud computing definition, https://en.wikipedia.org/wiki/Cloud_computing

Chapter 4
Artificial Intelligence in the Industrial Sector: Legal Implications Beyond the Code

Mădălina Mihăilescu
https://orcid.org/0009-0003-0736-8588
Hyperion University of Bucharest, Romania

ABSTRACT

Artificial intelligence is reshaping industrial operations—from automation to predictive logistics—raising complex legal challenges beyond algorithmic design. This chapter explores legal liability, data governance, contractual uncertainty, and compliance with frameworks like the EU AI Act. It also addresses AI's intersection with blockchain and the effects on employees' digital rights. Using a comparative lens, it examines divergences between legal systems and the drive toward regulatory coherence. Ethical concerns such as transparency, fairness, and human oversight are also discussed. The chapter offers a forward-looking legal perspective aligned with industrial transformation and fundamental rights protection.

INTRODUCTION

In recent decades, artificial intelligence technologies have left research laboratories and have been discreetly but decisively integrated into industrial processes. From automated production lines to predictive systems that anticipate failures, AI is redefining not only operational efficiency but also the relationships between people, machines, and decision-making (Acemoglu & Restrepo, 2020). Beyond techno-

DOI: 10.4018/979-8-3373-3186-7.ch004

logical innovation, these advance raises profound questions about accountability, transparency, control, and rights (Bryson & Winfield, 2017).

The industrial sector, known for its technological pragmatism and agile pace of implementation, faces a paradox: while AI optimizes costs and accelerates processes, the legal framework often lags behind the real complexity of interactions between algorithms, employees, and infrastructures (Ebers et al., 2021). The lack of clarity on the legal limits of automated decisions, how data is managed, or liability in case of damage creates an uncertain terrain, where traditional regulation is struggling to find its footing (Wachter et al., 2017).

In Europe, the proposed Regulation on Artificial Intelligence outlines an ambitious legislative effort to introduce classification criteria, safety requirements, and control mechanisms for systems considered to be high-risk—a category in which many industrial applications fall (European Commission, 2021). However, this regulatory framework is developing in a fragmented international landscape, where legal regimes vary significantly and cross-border cooperation is often hampered by divergent interests (OECD, 2023).

In addition to the technical and legal dimensions, industrial AI also brings with it transformations in the field of digital rights: employee monitoring and automated decisions related to performance, but also the continuous collection of data from workspaces, become realities that affect human dignity, personal autonomy, and the limits of privacy (Zuboff, 2019). Thus, the law can no longer treat AI as a simple tool but as an actor capable of influencing social structures and economic balances (Yeung, 2018). In this chapter, the analysis will focus on the multiple legal dimensions generated by the implementation of AI in industry—from issues related to liability and smart contracts to the implications for individual freedoms and compliance standards. The goal is not only to describe a reality in full swing but to outline a direction in which the law can evolve in dialogue with technology without abdicating the values that underpin the democratic order (Calo, 2015).

2. ARTIFICIAL INTELLIGENCE IN THE INDUSTRIAL SECTOR: EMERGING APPLICATIONS AND LEGAL FRICTIONS

Artificial intelligence is no longer an abstract promise or a technology reserved for advanced research laboratories. In the industrial space, AI has become an integral part of decision-making, quality control, logistics, and even strategic planning. Unlike other fields, such as finance or medicine, where AI interacts directly with individuals in strictly regulated contexts, in industry it often acts "in the background," in invisible layers of the digital infrastructure, producing significant effects without necessarily being visible on the surface (Hildebrandt, 2016). It is precisely this operational discretion that makes many of the legal challenges appear late, when the consequences have already become systemic.

In manufacturing environments, AI systems are used to detect manufacturing defects in real time, based on visual recognition algorithms trained on large volumes of data. In logistics, neural networks optimize delivery routes based on dynamic factors such as traffic, energy consumption, or weather conditions (Eubanks, 2018). In the energy sector, AI helps regulate distribution flows, anticipating demand and preventing imbalances that could otherwise lead to massive financial losses or power outages. In these contexts, AI not only assists human decisions but also takes over critical tasks, sometimes acting with a high degree of autonomy (Taddeo & Floridi, 2018).

With this increased autonomy, traditional boundaries of responsibility are also blurring. In a classic case of mechanical failure, the causal chain is relatively easy to trace. However, when an AI system makes a wrong decision, and this causes damage—whether financial, physical, or reputational—the fundamental question is no longer "What went wrong?" but "Who is responsible for the outcome?" The algorithm developer? The equipment manufacturer? The human operator who oversaw the process? The lack of a clear framework for allocating liability leads to legal uncertainty, with direct effects on investment, innovation, and trust between contractual partners (Ebers et al., 2021).

The development of AI systems also involves a massive transfer of industrial data—some sensitive, some confidential—which brings into question the legal regime of data. In the automotive industry, for example, each connected vehicle generates a huge amount of data about component performance, driver behavior, road conditions, or interaction with other road users. This data is aggregated, analyzed, and used to train algorithms that will subsequently influence commercial or design decisions (Calo & Citron, 2021). But who owns this data? The manufacturer? The software provider? The end user? In the absence of a clear consensus and explicit rules on the right of access, portability, and reuse, tensions arise that affect commercial relationships and contractual transparency.

In parallel, contracts between actors involved in the development and operation of AI systems—from algorithm and equipment providers to industrial companies and human operators—must reflect completely new realities (Brkan, 2021). Warranty clauses, for example, cannot function according to traditional logic in the context of an adaptive system that changes its behavior over time. Also, audit, performance evaluation, or dispute resolution mechanisms must be redesigned to include the algorithmic dimension: what does "malfunction" mean in the case of a learning system? How can error be proven in the absence of source code transparency or a complete history of automated decisions?

Beyond the scope of contractual relations and data governance, a legal dimension related to algorithmic surveillance and working conditions in the industry is increasingly emerging. In many cases, AI is used to monitor employee performance, assess productivity in real time, or generate automated reports that influence salaries, promotions, or task reassignments (Acemoglu & Restrepo, 2020). While these tools promise efficiency and objectivity, they can create psychological pressure, introduce subtle discrimination, and reduce real opportunities to challenge decisions (Kaminski, 2019). In the absence of clear transparency and control mechanisms, employee rights can be affected in ways that escape the radar of traditional labor law.

Moreover, some AI systems integrate blockchain to ensure the traceability of decisions, especially in sensitive industrial environments such as the food or pharmaceutical industries. In theory, this combination offers additional guarantees of verifiability and security. In practice, however, it brings with it another set of legal questions: how are errors recorded on an immutable ledger dealt with? What legal value do automated transactions validated by smart contracts have? Who intervenes, and how, when an automated process produces unfair effects in a closed system? As AI becomes an integral part of industrial decision-making, the need to review the regulatory framework becomes inevitable. Existing regulations, based on the idea of human control and direct responsibility, can no longer encompass the complexity of the relationships generated by AI (OECD, 2023). In many cases, algorithmic decisions are based on statistical correlations that escape human logic or are impossible to explain in terms accessible to a court. Thus, there is an increasingly urgent need for algorithmic audit standards, prior certification systems, and clear mechanisms for intervention in cases of harm (Binns et al., 2018).

Ultimately, what is becoming visible is that the legal challenges related to AI in industry are not simple extensions of those encountered in other fields. They involve a conceptual reconstruction of notions such as "guilt," "intention," "diligence," or "guarantee," in a context in which decisions are partially or completely decoupled from direct human control (Cowls et al., 2021). Without such a reconstruction, the law risks operating with inadequate tools, reacting late, or, worse, becoming irrelevant in a sector in full transformation.

3. EVOLVING LEGAL FRAMEWORKS AND REGULATIONS

In an era where algorithms are increasingly infiltrating industrial networks, the legislative challenge can no longer be postponed or treated superficially (European Union Agency for Fundamental Rights, 2020). Law is called upon to keep up with a reality shaped by automated processes, machine learning, and infrastructures that combine human and artificial decision-making. Beyond theory, the regulatory effort takes shape in a tense landscape between technological dynamics and democratic accountability.

In the European space, the proposal for a regulation on artificial intelligence, known as the AI Act, outlines a legal architecture based on risk thresholds. AI systems are classified according to their potential to affect the lives of individuals and the functioning of institutions. Applications considered incompatible with the fundamental values of the Union are excluded from use. Below this level, there are systems in which AI is an active part in decision-making processes that influence critical infrastructure, the professional environment, or access to important services (European Commission, 2021). In these cases, the legislator proposes a set of requirements that target both the technical quality of the algorithm and the human control over it.

The implementation of these requirements requires additional effort for industrial actors. In practice, rigorous documentation procedures, journaling of decision-making processes, repetitive testing of models, and the development of real-time intervention mechanisms are necessary. It is not just about technical compliance but about an institutional reconversion that involves training staff, reviewing workflows, and clarifying internal areas of responsibility (Floridi & Cowls, 2019).

In parallel with the measures dedicated to high-risk systems, applications with a lower impact are also taken into account. Even in these cases, interaction with users must take place within a clear, unambiguous framework. Any system that simulates conversation, creates images, or recommends content is obligated to make its artificial nature visible. This raises a subtle challenge: redefining consent in an asymmetrical relationship, where one of the parties is not a human being.

The European model is distinguished by the tendency to standardize standards between member states. The regulation is directly applicable, without the need for national transposition, which reduces the risk of legal fragmentation. However, this regulatory uniformity requires increased administrative capacity on the part of each state, as well as the formation of specialized expertise capable of understanding the particularities of AI (Calo, 2015).

Beyond the Union's borders, AI regulation follows various paths. In the United States, the lack of an overarching federal framework gives way to local and sectoral initiatives. Regulators issue recommendations or guidelines that are not binding but that influence the behavior of economic actors through reputation, litigation, and public pressure. In these conditions, industrial companies are often forced to develop internal policies for algorithmic control and ethics, which generates uneven and sometimes opaque standards.

In China, AI is integrated into a centralized government vision. Regulation aims not only to prevent risks but also to promote a model of technological development in which state control is present at every layer of the digital ecosystem. For industries operating in this context, the legal regime includes obligations of ideological compliance, cooperation with authorities, and limitations on automatically generated content.

International organizations have intervened with reference documents that attempt to provide common direction. Documents adopted by the OECD or UNESCO emphasize the need for transparency, explainability, and accountability in the design and use of AI. These instruments, even if they are not normative in the strict sense, influence the evolution of national legislation and draw ethical coordinates that gradually become legal benchmarks (OECD, 2023).

In industry, the challenge lies in adapting to a regulatory framework in perpetual formation. Unlike other technological fields, AI does not offer functional stability. Models are continuously trained, parameters change, and results are influenced by real-time data (Renda, 2022). In such an environment, regulation must become flexible without slipping into vagueness. A combination of firm rules and dynamic mechanisms for evaluation, adjustment, and intervention is therefore required.

A concept that is gaining more and more ground is that of algorithmic audit, which involves a periodic, independent, and documented examination of the behavior of AI systems, not only from a technical point of view, but also from a legal and social point of view (Gasser & Almeida, 2017). In the industrial environment, where AI contributes to resource management, work safety, or trade flows, audit becomes a tool for verifying responsibility and preventing structural imbalances.

Instead of a rigid framework, a need for a living normative architecture is emerging, in which regulation is accompanied by dialogue between developers, users, authorities, and civil society. It is no longer just about control but about legislative co-creation, in which law becomes a lucid partner of technology, not an opponent or a late imitator (Binns, 2018).

Artificial intelligence, as it functions in industry, cannot be separated from the economic, political, and human context in which it operates. Its regulation, to be relevant, must be able to feel the pulse of these dimensions and build legal forms that not only limit but also guide development. Without this effort, AI risks evolving in a normative vacuum, and law—to become decorative in a landscape dominated by automatism and algorithmic opacity (Chander, 2021).

At the center of contemporary discussions about the regulation of artificial intelligence, the theme of digital sovereignty appears more and more frequently. This is not a simple geopolitical concern but a reality in which data, algorithms, and digital infrastructures become strategic resources, comparable to energy or mineral resources (Veale & Edwards, 2018). For states that depend on technologies developed outside their borders, each automated decision that affects industrial infrastructure is equivalent to a diminution of sovereign control over the economy and society.

In the industrial domain, AI is often delivered as closed solutions, developed by entities that retain rights to the source code, learning models, and maintenance systems. This technological dependency creates an asymmetric relationship between providers and beneficiaries, in which control over the industrial process is only apparent. In reality, the party that manages the data flows and update cycles also holds the strategic key to decisions (Yeung, 2018).

For this reason, several governments have begun to include digital sovereignty in national AI strategies. They are investing in the capacity to develop their own algorithms, in local storage infrastructures, and in centers of excellence for applied research. The goal is not technological isolationism, but balancing interdependencies so that critical decisions do not depend exclusively on external actors.

In parallel, there is a growing concern about data localization. In many industrial sectors, cross-border data transfer is standard practice, imposed by the global architecture of cloud infrastructure. However, in the context where raw data is the raw material for AI, the state that owns it also has the power to shape the algorithms (Bryson & Theodorou, 2019). Therefore, some jurisdictions introduce restrictions on the export of sensitive industrial data, impose mandatory local storage, or require external audits before any transnational transfer.

Digital sovereignty is not limited to technical or commercial aspects but also implies the ability to define the legal frameworks that govern AI without mechanically importing external normative models (Bryson & Winfield, 2017). In this sense, some states in Asia, Latin America, or Africa are experimenting with hybrid regulatory formulas in which local principles of justice, solidarity, or sustainable development are integrated into the regime applicable to AI. These initiatives suggest that technological universalism should not be confused with legal uniformity.

With the integration of intelligent systems in production chains and critical infrastructures, questions arise regarding liability in the event of serious consequences: accidents, human losses, contamination, or system collapses. In these situations, the criminal dimension of AI regulation becomes inevitable, especially when the harmful result cannot be attributed to simple administrative or technical errors.

In classical criminal law, liability presupposes the existence of a natural or legal person who acts with discernment, intention, or fault. In the case of AI, however, the decision-making process is not entirely controlled by humans, and algorithmic intervention can be difficult to track. Who is criminally liable when an industrial robot, operating on the basis of a machine learning system, causes fatal harm? In the absence of a direct human act, it is difficult to attribute guilt according to traditional patterns.

Some legal theories propose extending the concept of criminal liability to technological entities, suggesting the idea of an "algorithmic personality" or some form of "responsible artificial agent" (Zuboff, 2019). These ideas are, for now, more speculative than applicable. Criminal law remains anchored in the human paradigm, which means that developers, operators, manufacturers, or distributors could be called to account for the actions of an AI system, depending on the degree of control and diligence exercised.

In the industrial sector, risks are amplified by the use of AI in processes involving extreme temperatures, hazardous materials, heavy equipment, or real-time decisions. In this context, an algorithm that optimizes a production flow may unintentionally generate a dangerous pressure buildup, accelerated component erosion, or ignored warning signals (Cihon et al., 2020). If these choices lead to victims, it becomes necessary to identify some form of criminal liability—either through oversight fault or design negligence.

It remains to be determined, however, whether current regulations are sufficient or whether new crimes dedicated to this context need to be developed. Some proposals include the creation of categories of technical crimes, where the lack of audit, lack of traceability, or uncontrolled training of AI models could constitute grounds for criminal prosecution. Other visions suggest strengthening compliance obligations, transforming the violation of these rules into a form of punishable social danger.

In any case, the development of criminal liability in the context of industrial AI must avoid both over-criminalization and impunity. A regulation that automatically assigns guilt risks inhibiting innovation, while the lack of clear mechanisms for holding people accountable fuels public distrust. Criminal law must find the fine balance between protecting society and recognizing the specificities of technology.

In this context, cooperation between judicial authorities, technical experts, and the industrial community becomes indispensable. Only through transdisciplinary dialogue can mechanisms be built that allow for the evaluation of evidence, understanding of algorithmic logic, and, where appropriate, the identification of a guilt that can be proven unequivocally. Without this effort, industrial AI risks evolving into a fragmented legal space where liability becomes the exception, not the rule.

4. INTERSECTION WITH BLOCKCHAIN TECHNOLOGIES AND DIGITAL RIGHTS

The integration of artificial intelligence with blockchain technology outlines a technological framework that is increasingly present in modern industrial structures. This convergence is not the result of a passing fashion but the expression of a process of co-evolution of two paradigms: one based on machine learning and adaptive decision-making, the other on immutability, decentralization, and distributed verifiability (Boucher, 2022). Together, they can provide solutions to some of the most pressing needs of contemporary industries—decision traceability, automated contractual responsibility, and reducing the costs of trust between partners. First, AI, by its probabilistic and adaptive nature, introduces a certain opacity into decision-making. Algorithms can optimize flows, allocate resources, adjust execution times, and recommend technical interventions without providing a direct explanation intelligible to human decision-makers (Boucher, 2022). If these processes are left in a closed technological space, suspicions arise regarding correctness, accuracy, or possible manipulation. This is where the potential of blockchain comes in to create a verifiable record of decisions, where each step is recorded in an immutable form accessible to the actors involved.

In an industrial supply chain, for example, AI can decide to automatically redirect a delivery based on weather forecasts or the occupancy rate of a logistics station. If this decision is recorded on the blockchain, all actors can later understand the context in which it was made, eliminating or reducing subsequent disputes. At the same time, archiving decisions in such a record provides valuable evidentiary material in the event of a dispute—whether commercial, contractual, or even criminal in nature.

On a legal level, this technical transparency brings a paradigm shift in the evidentiary regime. Instead of classic documents, blockchain extracts can be used to demonstrate the timing, justification, and conditions of an automated decision. In an industrial context where reaction times are necessary and contracts are often fragmented between multiple parties; this type of recordkeeping can make the difference between trust and deadlock.

Second, smart contracts, powered by AI-generated data, can automatically execute contractual obligations once certain conditions are met. These conditions can be set by computer code, without further human intervention. For example, the delivery of a batch of materials can automatically trigger payment if AI confirms that the materials meet technical specifications and are accompanied by the required documents. The blockchain acts here as a digital notary, verifying and validating the transaction.

However, this automation does not come without risks. A smart contract does not have the ability to interpret ambiguities, adapt terms to unforeseen circumstances, or analyze the fairness of a clause. If AI provides a decision based on an algorithmic interpretation of a real situation, but the data is incomplete, flawed, or contextually inappropriate, the result may be unfair. And the blockchain, by recording this decision, fixes it in a way that is difficult to challenge or correct.

In industry, where decisions can involve millions of monetary units or affect the functioning of vital infrastructure, this right to intervene becomes crucial. Hybrid systems—in which AI and blockchain collaborate but do not operate in isolation from human oversight—seem to offer a more balanced direction. In these configurations, blockchain does not become a form of digital fatality but a tool to support a legal system in which fairness is not sacrificed for efficiency (Boucher, 2022).

The development of standards for industrial smart contracts is also only just beginning. The lack of unified terminology, good legal practices, and clear case law means that parties operate in a space of normative uncertainty. Some jurisdictions already recognize the validity of these contracts under certain conditions, but the interpretation of the clauses remains difficult in the absence of a globally accepted legal semantics.

A complementary theme is that of confidentiality. Industrial AI can collect sensitive data about equipment, technical recipes, processing speeds, or operational parameters. If this data is recorded on a public blockchain or accessible to a large consortium, the risk of exposing critical information increases. This is where the debate between transparency and protection comes in—two values that, in the context of new technologies, are often in tension. Solutions can come from permissioned blockchains, selective encryption, or the use of dual layers of archiving, where only hashes are recorded on the distributed ledger, and the raw data is kept in locally controlled systems.

Therefore, the issue of legal liability in automated systems based on AI and blockchain remains one of the most challenging. If a smart contract executed on the basis of an algorithmic recommendation generates serious damage, who is liable? The AI designer? The author of the code for the smart contract? The system operator? The lack of a clear framework for allocating liability creates risks not only for the victims of potential damages but also for investors who fear prolonged and unpredictable legal processes.

In order for the integration of AI with blockchain to be legally sustainable in the industrial environment, a coordinated legislative effort is needed that takes into account the technological specifics but also the fundamental principles of law. An automated contractual infrastructure cannot be built without introducing, in parallel, control, audit, mediation, and judicial intervention systems adapted to the new reality. In the absence of these mechanisms, the efficiency promised by the technology risks being nullified by the legal fragility of the entire system.

Thus, AI and blockchain can work in real complementarity, but only if they are accompanied by a regulatory framework that does not confuse innovation with deregulation and does not sacrifice individual protection in the name of automation. In industry, where decisions are made quickly and the impact is amplified, such a balance becomes not only desirable but vital.

The integration of blockchain technologies with artificial intelligence opens up an emerging technological field where automated decision-making capabilities are combined with the distributed, immutable, and verifiable infrastructure of decentralized ledgers. In the industrial sector, this convergence promises a higher degree of traceability of processes, especially in environments where the supply chain involves numerous actors, multiple jurisdictions, and heterogeneous compliance standards.

By using a blockchain, every relevant algorithmic decision—for example, resource allocation, adjustment of production parameters, or identification of a non-compliance—can be recorded in a way that cannot be altered retroactively. This type of archiving adds a dimension of accountability to decisions made by AI systems, especially in cases where their outcome generates commercial disputes or contractual litigation. At the same time, blockchain allows for the automation of contract execution through mechanisms known as smart contracts. These operate on the basis of a set of predefined conditions, automatically executed when parameters are met. In a digitalized industrial environment, this functionality can significantly reduce bureaucracy, delays, and ambiguities related to obligations assumed between partners. However, the question remains whether such contracts comply with legal requirements regarding validity, consent, and balance between the parties.

In the absence of clear regulations, parties using AI-based smart contracts may encounter difficulties in the event of algorithmic errors or ambiguities of interpretation. In addition, an additional difficulty arises in terms of remediation: once an action has been executed on a blockchain, it can no longer be revoked without broad consensus or exceptional intervention. In this regard, regulation should provide for well-justified exceptions to the principle of immutability, in particular for cases of fraud, abuse, or obvious technological error. Equally, in the context of the transformations brought about by industrial digitization, artificial intelligence is becoming an active actor in shaping the relationship between the individual and the economic infrastructure. Far from being just a technical tool, AI is redefining the way employees are evaluated, monitored, or redeployed and influencing consumers' access to services, offers, and contractual interactions. This reality transforms data from simple information flows into legal touchpoints, with direct effects on the dignity, privacy, and self-determination of the person.

For employees, the AI-assisted industrial environment introduces sophisticated surveillance mechanisms. Algorithms can track movement in the workspace, the frequency and duration of breaks, interactions with machines, efficiency in execution, or deviations from protocols (Mittelstadt et al., 2016). These observations are aggregated, analyzed, and compared in real time, and the result can lead to rewards, penalties, or automatic redistributions. When these decisions are generated without human intervention and stored in an immutable system such as blockchain, questions arise regarding the fairness of the process, access to challenge, and contextual correctness.

Moreover, a new type of digital file is born: the industrial behavioral profile. It no longer reflects only professional qualifications but also algorithmically detected predispositions—speed, conformity, adaptability, and resilience in the face of repetitive tasks. Used in selection, promotion, or reorganization processes, this profile can become an invisible filter over which the employee has neither full control nor visibility. The lack of significant transparency regarding the parameters used by AI deepens the imbalance and reduces the individual's ability to defend their interests.

Labor law, in its classic form, is not prepared to manage these new forms of algorithmic power. The employment contract is based on the premise of a relationship between natural and legal persons, governed by predictable rules and bilateral control. In the AI environment, however, decisions can be opaque, dynamic, and calibrated on a set of data beyond the employee's access. Therefore, a reconfiguration of legal guarantees is required: the right to know the logic of the processing, the right to human intervention, the right to request the review of automated decisions, and, where appropriate, the right to opposition.

In parallel, the industrial consumer—be it a company or an end user—is also becoming the object of predictive analysis. AI-powered platforms collect data on purchasing behavior, order frequency, configuration preferences, response rate to offers, and negotiation capacity. Depending on these variables, AI adjusts prices, proposes different contractual terms, and personalizes access to resources. While this model promises efficiency and adaptability, it can hide algorithmic discrimination practices, especially in the absence of a clear external audit framework.

A concrete example is provided by bidding systems in industrial procurement. AI can grant automatic advantages to certain customers, considering them more profitable or more predictable from a logistical point of view. In the absence of an explicit and transparent justification, other actors can be de facto excluded from the market without having a real possibility to challenge the algorithm (Pagallo, 2013). If these decisions are recorded on the blockchain, it becomes almost impossible to change them without the consensus of the parties or a coordinated intervention.

Against the background of these risks, the digital rights of employees and consumers must be rethought not only in terms of access to data but also of checks, balances, and reparability. The right to information can no longer be limited to a standardized privacy policy (Wachter & Mittelstadt, 2019). A granular, contextualized explanation is needed, accessible to any user affected by AI—be it a human operator or an industrial customer. Information is not just a passive tool but a condition of personal autonomy in complex technological ecosystems.

Furthermore, consent needs to be reconstructed as an active relationship. It is not enough for the individual to tick a digital box for the use of data to become legitimate. Once data is processed by AI and archived on the blockchain, the consequences become difficult to control. Therefore, it is necessary for users to be able to review, suspend, or revoke previously granted permissions. This flexibility must be explicitly foreseen, technologically and legally, within the digital platforms operating in the industrial sector.

Regarding algorithmic oversight, one possible solution is the creation of independent audit structures capable of analyzing AI decisions and providing impact reports on the rights of the individual. These structures could operate in parallel with data protection authorities and act as intermediaries between industry and society (Wachter et al., 2017). By evaluating learning methodologies, training data, and generated results, the risk of systemic negative effects could be reduced.

Another dimension of reflection concerns collective representation. Trade unions and consumer associations have a significant role in this equation. They can negotiate clauses on the use of AI in the workplace, request external audits, and mediate redress processes in cases of abuse. Similarly, consumer organizations can take action against platforms that use AI in an opaque way or that violate the principles of transparency and fairness.

An adapted digital justice system is also needed. The traditional court, with its extended deadlines and written evidence, cannot respond promptly to conflicts arising in a digital industrial ecosystem in real time. Alternative dispute resolution mechanisms need to be developed: digital arbitration chambers, algorithmically assisted mediation, self-assessment mechanisms, and automatic compensation. These could operate on the basis of pre-established, legally validated but procedurally flexible protocols.

Traditionally, surveillance in industrial spaces has been justified by the need for operational safety, compliance with work rules, or incident prevention. Today, however, AI-based monitoring systems go beyond these basic functions. They detect micro-expressions, analyze reaction times, follow employee paths in physical space, or correlate data from multiple sources—video cameras, proximity sensors, biometric signals, or digital interactions. In this landscape, the individual becomes a node in a data network, the interpretations of which are no longer directly controlled by humans but are generated by automated systems with opaque rules and sometimes impossible-to-explain results. Digital surveillance through AI thus raises a fundamental question: to what extent can there still be real consent in an environment where refusal implies marginalization or exclusion? In industry, the employment relationship is already marked by an imbalance of power between employer and employee. When surveillance becomes an implicit condition of work performance, choice becomes purely formal. Acceptance of data processing no longer derives from free negotiation but from the constraint of not losing your job.

In parallel, AI surveillance can induce a new form of psychological pressure. When every movement is quantified, compared, and archived, the space for relaxation and personal expression disappears. The employee no longer works only for a productive result but becomes an object of permanent evaluation. Thus, AI transforms the workplace into a space of uninterrupted performance, in which the boundary between work and control becomes increasingly diffuse.

The problem is exacerbated when surveillance becomes predictive. AI can estimate the probability that an employee will become unproductive, leave the company, or make an error. Such predictions can be used to discreetly exclude certain people from advancement opportunities, to justify transfers or staff reductions, or to label the individual as "non-adaptable" (Winfield et al., 2019). In the absence of transparency and a clear framework for contestation, these decisions become impossible to verify or challenge.

From a privacy perspective, industrial AI collects a wide range of data—not only about performance but also about health, stress, body movement, or voice tone. In combination with wearables, this information allows for continuous monitoring of heart rate, body temperature, sleep patterns, or even emotional mood. Although the stated goal is to protect health and prevent accidents, reality shows a progressive dilution of the personal sphere in favor of algorithmic efficiency.

Also, if this data is archived through blockchain technology—appreciated for its immutability and transparency—a new legal tension arises. Confidentiality becomes difficult to reconcile with the principle of immutability. If a person wants to delete sensitive data, and this has already been recorded on a decentralized blockchain, the effective realization of this right becomes practically impossible. Thus, contradictions arise between the fundamental rights guaranteed by legislation such as the GDPR and the technological nature of the digital infrastructure.

Another level of analysis concerns the surveillance of industrial consumers. In the AI era, every interaction—from a simple request for a quote to a question asked to a chatbot—is analyzed, correlated, and interpreted. Based on this data, reliability, risk, or profitability scores can be generated, which automatically influence the contractual terms. If a customer is considered less profitable, AI can suggest shorter terms, higher guarantees, or higher prices. All these decisions may seem "natural" in algorithmic logic, but they have direct implications for fair access to services and commercial freedom (Brkan, 2021).

Personal autonomy, in this equation, fades in favor of a digital determinism. When decisions are taken over by AI and surveillance becomes the norm, the individual no longer truly chooses but responds to predetermined stimuli. This phenomenon is reflected not only in industry but also in society, where behaviors become increasingly reactive and less reflective. In such an environment, the law must rethink not only the limits of surveillance but also the infrastructure of individual freedom itself.

An adequate legal response should include at least three directions. The first is to guarantee an effective right to opacity—that is, the possibility of remaining invisible to AI, at least in certain contexts. This implies spaces without monitoring, decisions that are not subject to automatic evaluation, and mechanisms through which the individual can regain control over his or her digital profile.

The second direction aims at algorithmic auditing with human participation. It is not enough for systems to be tested from a technical point of view; they must also be evaluated in terms of their impact on freedom, dignity, and social balance

(Brkan, 2021). Evaluators must be not only engineers but also lawyers, sociologists, philosophers, and representatives of affected groups.

5. COMPLIANCE, ASSESSMENT AND RESPONSIBLE GOVERNANCE

Artificial Intelligence Impact Assessments (AIAs) and Data Protection Impact Assessments (DPIAs) are two tools that, although they have different roots, converge in their objectives: anticipating risks, preventing abuses, and creating a framework for distributed accountability. In particular, industry needs these tools to maintain a balance between performance and compliance and between innovation and social control.

AIA involves a systematic analysis of how an AI system will work, who will be affected, what the potential risks are, and what measures can be taken to prevent negative effects. These assessments must be carried out before actual implementation, not as an after-the-fact formality. In industry, where development cycles are rapid and economic pressures are intense, this anticipation becomes a form of regulatory vigilance, which can make the difference between sustainable success and costly failure.

The DPIA, regulated by Article 35 of the General Data Protection Regulation (GDPR), aims to assess the risks to the rights and freedoms of individuals when personal data is processed in ways that are likely to have a significant impact. In the connected industry, where sensors, cameras, voice control systems, and data flows meet in an always-on ecosystem, DPIA becomes a condition for ethical and legal functioning. Both assessments involve consulting stakeholders, fully documenting decisions, clearly defining purposes, and justifying technological choices. They require a review of the data used to train AI, algorithmic logic, the potential for discrimination, and the possibilities to challenge automated decisions. In industry, these requirements translate into a practical need for interdisciplinary collaboration: engineers, lawyers, ethicists, and employee representatives.

An AI system implemented in a factory, in a logistics center, or in a distribution network cannot be considered accountable only in terms of its results. Accountability implies traceability, that is, the possibility of understanding how it was designed, how it works, and what factors influence its behavior (Brkan, 2021). Auditability is the technical-legal answer to this requirement: the possibility of the system being independently inspected, tested, and evaluated.

Algorithmic auditing, in this sense, is not just a technical process but an act of digital democracy. In the industrial environment, auditability means complete documentation of learning models, journaling of automated decisions, keeping previous versions of the algorithm, recording changes, and the ability to reproduce critical scenarios. This allows not only internal control but also external intervention in case of dispute.

Algorithmic due diligence requires organizations implementing AI to conduct a thorough review not only of technological performance but also of ethical, social, and legal implications (Winfield et al., 2019). This process involves analyzing the entire supply chain, identifying risks related to data sources, assessing the impact on employees and customers, and establishing clear intervention procedures.

In industry, due diligence must be tailored to the specifics of the sector. In the pharmaceutical industry, risks relate to patient safety and the protection of medical data. In logistics, the stakes are related to energy efficiency, distribution equity, and transport security. In manufacturing, AI can influence work rhythms, quality standards, and resource allocation. Each context requires its own evaluation and control matrix.

In the absence of uniform regulations applicable at a global level, international standards become essential benchmarks for compliance, interoperability, and governance. Bodies such as ISO (International Organization for Standardization), IEC (International Electrotechnical Commission), and IEEE (Institute of Electrical and Electronics Engineers) propose voluntary frameworks that can be adopted by the industry to guarantee responsible use of AI.

ISO/IEC JTC 1/SC 42 is the technical committee dedicated to artificial intelligence, which has already published a series of standards such as ISO/IEC 22989 on fundamental concepts of AI, ISO/IEC 23053 for reference architectures, and ISO/IEC 23894 for risk management in AI. These documents provide a common vocabulary, a modular framework, and design principles that can be adapted at the sector level.

The IEEE, through its "Ethically Aligned Design" program, promotes an ethical and human-centered use of emerging technologies. The standards proposed by the IEEE are not only technical but also integrate cultural, social, and legal values into the design process. For example, the IEEE 7000 standard provides a model for integrating ethical considerations into the life cycle of a technological system.

For the globalized industry, these standards offer a double advantage: on the one hand, they enable interoperability between systems developed in different jurisdictions; on the other hand, they offer increased legal protection in the event of litigation by demonstrating that the organization has followed internationally recognized good practices.

The adoption of these standards should not be seen as a bureaucratic burden but as a form of protection against reputational, financial, and legal risks. In an industrial environment where trust is becoming a strategic resource, compliance with a voluntary standard can be the decisive differentiator in a tender, in a partnership, or in a regulatory process.

6. FUTURE RESEARCH DIRECTIONS

The rapid evolution of artificial intelligence in an industrial context generates not only immediate normative challenges but also a multitude of questions that require long-term reflection. Between the complexity of automated systems, the fragmentation of legal regimes, and the ever-deepening interaction with fundamental rights, a fertile space is emerging for rigorous, interdisciplinary research anchored in practical realities. Future directions of investigation cannot be reduced to a simple theoretical exercise but must follow the real transformations of the social, economic, and legal infrastructure that accompany AI in industry. One of the first directions that deserves further investigation concerns the legal mechanisms for challenging algorithmic decisions. If artificial intelligence produces direct legal or economic effects on an individual—for example, through the decision to exclude them from a recruitment process or to adjust a commercial contract—then that individual must have access to a real, efficient, and intelligible channel for challenging. How can such a mechanism be built in a context where the decision is not the result of a human act but of a probabilistic process driven by historical data? The answer is not only found in technology but also in the philosophy of law and democratic theory. Research is needed to articulate models of "algorithmic repairability" applicable in industrial contexts, where the speed of decision is a value in itself.

Another direction calls for a reflection on how the classical notions of law—guilt, intention, negligence, damage—can be reconfigured to cover the acts or omissions of an AI system. In industry, where accidents or errors can cause significant damage, the question arises whether the current scheme of legal liability is still adequate. If an automated control system triggers a chain reaction, who can be held liable? The developer of the algorithm? The technical operator? The company that decided to implement it? Without a conceptual reform, the law risks being overtaken by reality. Doctrinal research is required that is capable of proposing new models of responsibility, perhaps distributed, perhaps conditional, that reflect the complexity of contemporary technological relations.

The ethical dimension of industrial AI constitutes another territory that needs to be mapped more rigorously. Although many frameworks of algorithmic ethics have been proposed at the international level, they often remain abstract or lack normative power. Industry needs applicable tools that translate general values into concrete protocols. What does "algorithmic justice" mean in a production chain? How can "transparency" be quantified in the case of a machine learning system with thousands of parameters? These questions cannot be treated as simple moral reflections but must be integrated into research projects in which engineering, law, and social sciences collaborate in real, not just rhetorical, ways.

A topic that is becoming increasingly relevant concerns the impact of AI on the structure of work in industry. The automation of decisions, permanent monitoring, and the use of algorithmic profiles are radically changing the relationship between employer and employee. We are witnessing a regime in which work becomes increasingly standardized and behavior becomes predictable. What effects does this transformation have on human dignity? How can professional autonomy be preserved in a digital environment in which every choice is analyzed, compared, and optimized? Future research should interrogate these mutations not only from the perspective of labor law but also from that of contemporary labor philosophy and social theory.

The technological architecture of AI also requires further exploration from a legal perspective. Machine learning models are often opaque, adaptive, and difficult to standardize. In industry, this opacity can lead to systemic risks—from technical failures to major commercial errors. Research is needed to standardize algorithmic interfaces, the traceability of automated decisions, and the definition of algorithmic certification criteria that can be assumed by public authorities and regulatory bodies. Interoperability between national and international legal frameworks is another key point. In a globalized context, industrial AI does not respect national borders. A system can be designed in one country, trained in another, and operated in another jurisdiction. How are different laws harmonized? What are the mechanisms for mutual recognition of standards and decisions? What is the status of an algorithmic audit conducted outside the EU for a system operating within the European market? These questions require comparative investigations and the development of mechanisms for transnational cooperation in the field of regulation and technological compliance.

Last but not least, the impact of AI on fundamental rights needs to be investigated in depth. Industry is not a space outside the sphere of rights. On the contrary, it is home to a multitude of interactions between people and systems, between freedom and normativity, and between efficiency and fairness. How does AI affect the right to privacy in a continuously monitored workplace? How can freedom of expression be protected in a context where AI detects and classifies deviations from expected behavior? How can human dignity be defended in the face of automated decisions that cannot be explained coherently? The answers cannot be given in general formulas but must be built through case studies, empirical analyses, and flexible theoretical models.

In a broader perspective, research in the field of industrial AI must contribute to the articulation of a vision of technology as a legal space. It is no longer enough to regulate AI as a tool. There is a need for a reconceptualization of technology as an integral part of the normative-institutional structure. This involves a reconstruction of concepts, a reevaluation of methods, and an openness to interdisciplinary epistemologies that reflect the real complexity of the industrial world augmented by AI.

Future research directions must therefore overcome disciplinary fragmentation, bureaucratic inertia, and exclusively normative logic. They must start from the multiple realities of AI implementation—from the smart factory to the digitalized contract, from the human-machine interface to algorithmic negotiations between autonomous systems. Without this anchoring in reality, the risk is that regulation will remain a decorative discourse and research—an archive of good intentions without transformative impact.

CONCLUSION

The transformations brought about by artificial intelligence in the industrial sector cannot be understood exclusively through the lens of technological innovation. They imply a profound remodeling of legal architectures, power relations, institutional responsibilities, and human experience in interaction with algorithms. In this new equation, industry becomes not only a beneficiary of AI but also a laboratory in which new forms of control, decision-making, and normativity are experimented with.

The application of AI in industry is not neutral or strictly technical. Any automated decision affects the way in which individuals interact with institutions, exercise their rights, and relate to the economic space in which they operate. Therefore, the regulation of AI cannot be dissociated from the reflection on the human condition in a system in which the decision is shared between humans and algorithms. In the absence of coherent intervention from the law, AI risks becoming a silent, invisible power, but with profound effects on social equity and the democratic functioning of the industrial space.

In Europe, the proposed Regulation on Artificial Intelligence marks an attempt to establish algorithmic governance based on risk and responsibility. Its structure, inspired by the logic of proportionality, provides a framework for managing the different levels of danger that AI can generate. However, the effective implementation of these regulations in industry requires more than compliance with formal standards. A culture of distributed accountability, robust audit structures, transparent internal procedures, and continuous staff training are needed. Impact assessments, such as AIA and DPIA, provide a platform for this culture. They allow for in-depth analysis of the technological, ethical, and legal implications of each system before implementation. In industry, where the costs of wrong decisions can be high, these assessments become tools for managing risk and ensuring respect for the people affected. Moreover, they help to build trust, not only between employers and employees but also between industry and society.

Algorithmic auditability, complete documentation of decision-making processes, and the implementation of internationally recognized standards, such as those developed by ISO/IEC or IEEE, configure an infrastructure of technological responsibility. This infrastructure should not be perceived as an obstacle to innovation but as a condition for the sustainability of innovation itself. In a dynamic ecosystem, where AI is constantly evolving and interacting with other emerging technologies, maintaining traceability and intervention capacity is a condition for legal and reputational survival.

The human dimension cannot be ignored either. The digital rights of industrial employees and consumers must be reinterpreted in light of the transformations brought about by AI. The workplace becomes a place of permanent surveillance, where every action is quantifiable and comparable. Consent, transparency, and control over data can no longer be treated as simple options but as foundations for a fair relationship between the individual and the digital infrastructure. In the absence of solid guarantees, the risk of alienation increases, and AI systems become instruments of constraint, not of emancipation.

Digital sovereignty, in this context, takes on a new meaning. It is no longer just about state control over critical infrastructures but also about the collective capacity to establish the legitimate limits of technological intervention in industrial life. AI must not be a vector of dependence on opaque global platforms but an expression of society's capacity to organize its own technological infrastructure in a fair and sustainable way. Regulation thus becomes an instrument of collective emancipation, not a simple reaction to technological risks.

The integration of AI with blockchain opens up new possibilities but also new legal uncertainties. Traceability, transparency, and immutability are valuable attributes, but they can come into tension with the right to be forgotten, the need to correct erroneous decisions, and the natural dynamics of contractual relationships. In this landscape, law is called upon to reconcile sometimes opposing values and to formulate solutions that do not absolutize either efficiency or protection but put them into dialogue.

Furthermore, comparative perspectives indicate major differences between existing legal regimes. The European model, with its emphasis on fundamental rights and ex-ante regulation, contrasts with the American model, which is more flexible and based on self-regulation, and with the Chinese model, where regulation is part of a strategic project of control and technological development. Global industry is caught between these paradigms, and harmonization becomes both an economic and legal necessity.

In such a context, future research directions must investigate not only the mechanisms of regulation but also the normative meaning of the technology itself. AI is not just a set of mathematical functions but a form of organization of reality, which selects what is seen, what is evaluated, and what is decided. Therefore, law must not only control AI but also rethink itselfin interaction with AI. A legal theory is needed that is able to incorporate uncertainty, accept complexity, and create governance structures that do not impose rigid order but create conditions for balance and evolution.

This chapter has tried to propose a framework for reflection that goes beyond surface reactions to the challenges of AI. An integrated perspective has been opted for, which brings together labor law, digital law, technological regulation, fundamental rights, and algorithmic governance in a coherent architecture. No recipes have been offered, but tools for critical thinking and practical intervention have. The aim was not to establish a consensus but to articulate questions that will remain valid even after the waves of technological enthusiasm have faded. In conclusion, AI in industry is not a stage challenge but a paradigm shift. The legal response to this transformation must not be defensive but anticipatory, creative, and anchored in reality. Only in this way can a future be built in which technology serves man, not redefines him without consent. A future in which industry is not only efficient but also just. A future in which AI is regulated not to be limited but to be oriented towards the common good.

REFERENCES

Acemoglu, D., & Restrepo, P. (2020). Artificial Intelligence, Automation, and Work. In Agrawal, A., Gans, J., & Goldfarb, A. (Eds.), *The Economics of Artificial Intelligence: An Agenda* (pp. 197–236). University of Chicago Press.

Binns, R. (2018). Algorithmic accountability and public reason. *Philosophy & Technology*, *31*(4), 543–556. DOI: 10.1007/s13347-017-0263-5 PMID: 30873342

Binns, R., Veale, M., Van Kleek, M., & Shadbolt, N. (2018). 'It's Reducing a Human Being to a Percentage': Perceptions of Justice in Algorithmic Decisions. *Proceedings of the 2018 CHI Conference on Human Factors in Computing Systems*, 1–14. https://doi.org/DOI: 10.1145/3173574.3173951

Boucher, P. (2022). *How blockchain technology could impact artificial intelligence in industry*. European Parliamentary Research Service. https://www.europarl.europa.eu/thinktank/en/document/EPRS_BRI(2022)729354

Brkan, M. (2021). Do algorithms rule the world? Algorithmic decision-making and data protection in the framework of the GDPR and beyond. *International Journal of Law and Information Technology*, *29*(2), 91–121. DOI: 10.1093/ijlit/eay017

Bryson, J. J., & Theodorou, A. (2019). How society can maintain human-centric artificial intelligence. *Nature Machine Intelligence*, *1*(1), 5–6. DOI: 10.1038/s42256-018-0005-2

Bryson, J. J., & Winfield, A. F. (2017). Standardizing ethical design for artificial intelligence and autonomous systems. *Computer*, *50*(5), 116–119. DOI: 10.1109/MC.2017.154

Calo, R. (2015). Robotics and the Lessons of Cyberlaw. *SSRN*, *103*(3), 513–563. DOI: 10.2139/ssrn.2402972

Calo, R., & Citron, D. K. (2021). The Automated Administrative State: A Crisis of Legitimacy. *Emory Law Journal*, *70*(4), 797–846. https://ssrn.com/abstract=3814094

Chander, A. (2021). The racist algorithm. *Michigan Law Review*, *119*(5), 1023–1044. https://repository.law.umich.edu/mlr/vol119/iss5/5

Cihon, P., Maas, M. M., & Kemp, L. (2020). Should AI governance be centralized? Design lessons from history. *Proceedings of the AAAI/ACM Conference on AI, Ethics, and Society*, 228–234. https://doi.org/DOI: 10.1145/3375627.3375857

Cowls, J., King, T. C., Hitrova, C., & Floridi, L. (2021). Designing AI for people: Ethics, theory and practice. *Nature Machine Intelligence*, *3*, 896–899. DOI: 10.1038/s42256-021-00412-x

Ebers, M., Kosta, E., & Schulz, W. (Eds.). (2021). *Law and Artificial Intelligence*. Hart Publishing.

Eubanks, V. (2018). *Automating Inequality: How High-Tech Tools Profile, Police, and Punish the Poor*. St. Martin's Press.

European Commission. (2021). *Proposal for a Regulation laying down harmonised rules on artificial intelligence (Artificial Intelligence Act)*. COM(2021) 206 final. https://eur-lex.europa.eu/legal-content/EN/TXT/?uri=CELEX%3A52021PC0206

European Union Agency for Fundamental Rights (FRA). (2020). *Getting the future right – Artificial intelligence and fundamental rights*. https://fra.europa.eu/en/publication/2020/artificial-intelligence-and-fundamental-rights

Floridi, L., & Cowls, J. (2019). A unified framework of five principles for AI in society. *Harvard Data Science Review*, *1*(1). Advance online publication. DOI: 10.1162/99608f92.8cd550d1

Gasser, U., & Almeida, V. A. F. (2017). A layered model for AI governance. *IEEE Internet Computing*, *21*(6), 58–62. DOI: 10.1109/MIC.2017.4180835

Hildebrandt, M. (2016). *Smart Technologies and the End(s) of Law: Novel Entanglements of Law and Technology*. Edward Elgar Publishing., DOI: 10.4337/9781786430232

Kaminski, M. E. (2019). The right to explanation, explained. *Berkeley Technology Law Journal*, *34*(1), 189–218. DOI: 10.15779/Z38TD9N83H

Mittelstadt, B. D., Allo, P., Taddeo, M., Wachter, S., & Floridi, L. (2016). The ethics of algorithms: Mapping the debate. *Big Data & Society*, *3*(2), 1–21. DOI: 10.1177/2053951716679679

OECD. (2023). *Artificial Intelligence in Society: Industrial Applications and Legal Trends*. OECD Publishing. https://www.oecd.org/going-digital/ai/

OECD. (2023). *OECD Framework for the Classification of AI Systems*. OECD Publishing. https://www.oecd.org/going-digital/ai/classification

Pagallo, U. (2013). *The Laws of Robots: Crimes, Contracts, and Torts*. Springer., DOI: 10.1007/978-94-007-6564-1

Renda, A. (2022). Artificial intelligence in the EU: Policy, regulation, and ethics. *European Journal of Risk Regulation, 13*(1), 7–27. DOI: 10.1017/err.2021.44

Taddeo, M., & Floridi, L. (2018). How AI can be a force for good. *Science, 361*(6404), 751–752. DOI: 10.1126/science.aat5991 PMID: 30139858

Veale, M., & Edwards, L. (2018). Clarity, surprises, and further questions in the Article 29 Working Party draft guidance on automated decision-making and profiling. *Computer Law & Security Review, 34*(2), 398–404. DOI: 10.1016/j.clsr.2017.12.002

Wachter, S., & Mittelstadt, B. (2019). A Right to Reasonable Inferences: Re-Thinking Data Protection Law in the Age of Big Data and AI. *Columbia Business Law Review, 2019*(2), 494–620. https://ssrn.com/abstract=3248829

Wachter, S., Mittelstadt, B., & Floridi, L. (2017). Transparent, explainable, and accountable AI for robotics. *Science and Engineering Ethics, 23*(3), 611–628. DOI: 10.1007/s11948-016-9768-6 PMID: 33157874

Winfield, A. F. T., Michael, K., Pitt, J., & Evers, V. (2019). Machine ethics: The design and governance of ethical AI and autonomous systems. *Proceedings of the IEEE, 107*(3), 509–517. DOI: 10.1109/JPROC.2019.2900622

Yeung, K. (2018). Algorithmic regulation: A critical interrogation. *Regulation & Governance, 12*(4), 505–523. DOI: 10.1111/rego.12158

Zuboff, S. (2019). *The Age of Surveillance Capitalism: The Fight for a Human Future at the New Frontier of Power*. PublicAffairs.

Chapter 5
Data Privacy Challenges of Blockchain Energy Systems

Karisma Karisma
https://orcid.org/0000-0001-9783-9504
Independent Researcher, Malaysia

ABSTRACT

In recent years, blockchain has made waves in the energy sector due to its decentralised, transparent, and immutable nature. On the other hand, the resulting breadth of blockchain applications in the autonomous operations and management of transactive energy systems has raised profound legal-related challenges, risks, and caveats. Data privacy breaches in blockchain energy landscapes present a considerable conundrum as they go to the root of societal values and human rights. The growing concerns prompt pessimism such that energy market participants are less inclined to engage in blockchain-enabled peer-to-peer energy trading. The author explores diverse data protection issues associated with permissioned and permissionless blockchain energy applications and speculate on how they may contribute to economic and social disruptions. Such exploration is beneficial as rising tensions will likely stagnate blockchain energy operationalisation and global diffusion. An earnest and effective dialogue of data protection challenges is necessary to fill the regulatory void.

1. INTRODUCTION

While academic scholars and industry players hail the benefits of blockchain, it is pertinent to reckon with numerous foundational challenges. In this article, the

DOI: 10.4018/979-8-3373-3186-7.ch005

author discusses data privacy issues that perturb blockchain applications in energy trading domains. Blockchain is a double-edged sword for data privacy. While its transparency and immutability can enhance trust and data integrity, these features can conflict with privacy needs. The technology's trustless nature eliminates intermediaries, but the permanent, publicly viewable record of transactions, which is accessible to all participants in the network, raises significant privacy concerns. This section explains why this tension becomes particularly relevant in blockchain-based energy trading, where regulatory frameworks must balance transparency benefits with data protection requirements.

The author explores the friction between blockchain applications in energy trading systems and data protection regulations. There are many data protection regimes around the world, which exemplify the rights granted to individuals whose personal data is processed. For instance, the General Data Protection Regulation (GDPR) is appraised as the pioneer or the "gold standard" in data protection laws, exhibiting immense promise in providing stringent safeguards for users' data rights (Diamantopoulou et al., 2022; European Union, 2016). The GDPR is a role model for other nations by advancing its efforts, both in theory and practice, when ensuring robust data protection mechanisms. The Australian Privacy Act emulates the GDPR by extending comprehensive data rights in line with a privacy-focused approach ("Privacy Act ", 1988). However, the Act does not embody the right to (a) erasure, (b) portability, and (c) object to the processing of personal data (Potter et al., 2020). The United States has multiple federal and state data protection laws to protect the personal data of its citizens. Federal data protection laws include the Driver's Privacy Protection Act of 1999 (DPPA), the Children's Online Privacy Protection Act (COPPA), and the Health Insurance Portability and Accountability Act (HIPAA) ("Children's Online Privacy Protection Act ", 1998; "Driver's Privacy Protection Act," 1999; "Health Insurance Portability and Accountability Act ", 1996). Further, California, Virginia, and Colorado are amongst the privacy-centric states that have enacted comprehensive consumer privacy laws, imposing obligations on collecting, using, assessing, or deleting personal data ("California Consumer Privacy Act," 2018; "Colorado Privacy Act ", 2021; "Virginia Consumer Data Protection Act," 2021). The House Energy & Commerce Committee recently proposed the American Data Privacy and Protection Act (ADPPA) to enact comprehensive national data protection legislation ("American Data Privacy and Protection Act ", 2022). The ADPPA extends multiple data protection rights to data subjects, such as the right to access, rectify, and delete personal data, beyond many existing state laws ("American Data Privacy and Protection Act ", 2022). Multiple jurisdictions in Asia have implemented data protection laws that advance (a) data protection principles, (b) data subjects' rights, such as the right to data portability, access, correction, and deletion, and (c) obligations and responsibilities of data controllers, sharing many similar features with the GDPR (Walters et al., 2019). While there is a need for complete harmonisation with the GDPR as the gold standard, national legislation is making strides in heightening data protection levels.

There are several commonalities between the data protection regulations of these jurisdictions as they continue to draw inspiration from regulations positioned on a higher pedestal. At this stage, a brief disclaimer is in order. The author discusses the data privacy challenges using rights and principles-based approaches to fully explore the discord and disharmony of blockchain technology without referring to any particular data protection regulation, standard, or model. Data on the blockchain network is subject to protection regulations as they may encompass identity, transactional, energy, and financial data (Al-Abdullah et al., 2020). Further, hashed or encrypted data on a blockchain system are considered personal data for the purposes of data protection regulations (Article 29 Data Protection Working Party, 2014; Meyer, 2018).

The study explores potential vulnerabilities to data protection associated with the expansive integration of blockchain within energy trading frameworks: First, the storage of complete copies of data on full nodes is at odds with the principle of storage limitation. Due to the sequential and interdependent structure of blockchain architecture, wherein each block is cryptographically linked to the previous block, the deletion of transactional data within a single block may compromise the integrity and operational reliability of the blockchain system.

Second, blockchain architectures inherently conflict with data minimisation principles, as each full node within the ledger system is designed to replicate and retain identical copies of all transactional data. While this is not the case for private blockchains, in public blockchains, the transactional data are not confined to the purview of transacting parties alone. However, they are instead accessible to all nodes participating in the blockchain network. In addition, the immutable nature of previously recorded information on the blockchain ledger renders the deletion of transaction data virtually impossible (Al-Abdullah et al., 2020). Blockchain-based energy landscapes hinder the right to data portability due to difficulties in extracting and transmitting data to another controller.

Third, identifying data controllers within a blockchain ecosystem presents significant challenges, as it is often unclear who determines the purposes and means of processing personal data. This uncertainty complicates the implementation of the suitable technical and organisational measures required for conformity with data protection regulations (Holzleitner et al., 2020). It is crucial to establish a dialogue between regulators and industry stakeholders to address these challenges. This dialogue is essential to ascertain whether all full nodes within a blockchain network qualify as independent data controllers or whether accountability should instead be attributed to system operators, blockchain developers, or platform providers. This determination is critical for establishing clear lines of responsibility under data protection laws. The absence of this dialogue may impede participatory and deliberative engagement, thereby obstructing collaborative efforts to address persistent data protection challenges in blockchain systems. While in-depth discussions on technological challenges are outside the scope of this article, global data privacy could impede vast blockchain uptake if developers and platform operators do not resolve the data privacy and security issues.

2. ENERGY DATA AS A FORM OF PERSONAL DATA

It is opportune to initiate a discussion on the term "personal data," which is considered the "entryway" towards the applicability of GDPR. Considering that Article 4(1) of the GDPR defines personal data as "any information relating to an identified or identifiable natural person," the concept of energy data coincides with personal data in multifaceted ways, revealing a complex interplay that extends beyond conventional understandings of data protection (European Union, 2016). Energy data is classified as personal data, for all intents and purposes.

a. Energy production data

Blockchain effectively records energy production data, including its production location and energy source, to ensure transparency and traceability. This mechanism eases the transmission of real-time information to prosumers and consumers on the energy mix and the amount of energy generated, which is advantageous to blockchain-enabled energy systems (Dzobo et al., 2021).

b. Energy consumption data

Energy consumption data does not solely refer to the energy consumption information of households but energy behaviours, routines, and activities (European Data Protection Supervisor, 2022; Guimarães, 2017). The data gathered from smart meters decipher individuals' social and economic status as it influences the variability of domestic energy consumption. Energy consumption data comprise the use of energy equipment and energy-efficient appliances (Martinez et al., 2019). Further, time-series models can predict the future energy consumption of a household based on consumption activities (Martinez et al., 2019).

c. Energy transaction data

There are three (3) elements to blockchain-enabled energy transactions, namely "pre-transaction communication," "buyer-seller matching," and "transaction settlement"(Wang et al., 2019). In the pre-trade communication stage, publishing energy supply and demand data on a blockchain network is pertinent. Blockchain-enabled smart contracts match energy production and consumption data recorded on the ledger. For instance, Power Ledger, a blockchain-enabled peer-to-peer energy trading platform, has devised algorithms to match demand and supply during energy trading (Power Ledger, 2019). The next stage pertains to real-time transaction settlements between the buyer and seller of energy(Wang et al., 2019). As blockchain-based energy infrastructure can facilitate the implementation of these three (3) steps in energy transactions, it provides added value to the entire energy supply chain. Energy transaction data are stored and shared with all peers on the blockchain network to enable effective interaction with prosumers and consumers (Dzobo et al., 2021). In essence, as energy transactions initiate through collecting production and consumption data from smart meters, they constitute personal data (Cejka, Zeilinger, Stefan, et al., 2020).

Importantly, as personal data protection regulations, such as the GDPR, apply solely to personal data processing, energy production, consumption, and transaction data are subject to data protection regulations. Since blockchain can facilitate the management of smart meter energy production, consumption, and transaction data, the author limits discussions to the data privacy concerns that manifest when market peers deploy, store, and record energy data on decentralised blockchain ledgers.

3. DATA PROTECTION CHALLENGES IN BLOCKCHAIN-BASED ENERGY TRADING LANDSCAPES

The analysis of the following sections entails these core principles to broaden the author's inquiries on data privacy constraints in blockchain-enabled energy trading landscapes.

In fostering a dialogue concerning this growing field of debate, the idiosyncrasies of the energy market require further deliberation. Individuals hesitate to disclose information on energy consumption, production, and trading. Technological infrastructures should only facilitate the transfer of energy ownership without revealing the energy patterns of market participants. While applying rights and principles-based approaches, the following sections explore the friction between blockchain-enabled energy trading systems with the key precepts of data protection legislation, namely (a) storage limitation, (b) data minimisation, (c) purpose limitation, (d) right to rectification, (e) right to be forgotten, (f) right not to be subject to automated decision-making, and (g) right to data portability. The author discusses the challenges of determining the data controller in a decentralised and distributed energy trading system. The author focuses on households, residential prosumers, and consumers participating in blockchain-enabled peer-to-peer energy trading systems due to the need for more emphasis on data privacy challenges in this policy area.

3.1 Perpetual Storage and Replication of On-Chain Data Contravene Data Protection Principles.

Blockchain-enabled energy systems cannot operate in a data protection-compliant manner, which risks stifling widespread deployment to the detriment of energy citizens. First, according to data protection regulations, personal data that allows the reidentification of a data subject must be retained only for the duration necessary to fulfill the specific data processing purpose ("California Consumer Privacy Act," 2018; European Union, 2016; "Personal Data Protection Act ", 2012; "Privacy Act ", 1988). The operationalisation of blockchain-enabled energy trading systems runs counter to the storage limitation (also known as retention limitation) principle due to the replication and distribution of energy data, which remains immutable across all full nodes. Full nodes on the blockchain network store multiple copies of data recorded on the ledger, and as each block links to the previous block containing details of previous transactions, deleting the transactional data impairs or diminishes the functionality of the blockchain system (Chousein et al., 2020; Gill et al., 2019; Merlo et al., 2022; Wang et al., 2023). The storage of energy consumption, production, export, and import data that underlie the information on personal energy usage and trade via blockchain systems must be reconsidered and aligned with the data protection regulations.

Second, blockchain's application in transactive energy systems is at odds with the principle of data minimization (Belen-Saglam et al., 2023; "California Consumer Privacy Act," 2018; European Union, 2016; "Personal Data Protection Act," 2019). The principle requires personal data to be "adequate, relevant and limited to what is necessary in relation to the purposes for which they are processed" (European Union, 2016). A breach of this principle appears inevitable, as every node within the network retains identical copies of the entire ledger to uphold the system's immutability and integrity (Al-Abdullah et al., 2020; Belen-Saglam et al., 2023; Li, 2020). The data derived from energy transactions and appended to blockchain structures are no longer limited to trading parties but to all nodes on the network (Belen-Saglam et al., 2023; Sim et al., 2019). In addition, since the subsequent block's hash is associated with the previous hash function, the latter processes every time a new block adds to the blockchain ledger (Haque et al., 2021). de Terwangne states that "one may not process an excessively large amount of personal data [...] But one may not process a single datum either if this would entail a disproportionate interference in the data subjects' rights and interests" (de Terwangne, 2020).

An additional instance of conflict between blockchain and data protection regulation relates to the purpose limitation principle (European Union, 2016; "General Personal Data Protection Law," 2020; "Personal Data Protection Act ", 2012; "Privacy Act ", 1988; Schellinger et al., 2021). To comply with the general standards and principles relating to the processing of personal data, "specified, explicit and legitimate purposes" must be determined (European Union, 2016). Data processing can only go beyond the initial informed purpose with consent.

While the various data protection principles are deeply interrelated, this particular principle holds foundational significance, as a clearly defined purpose is essential for ensuring alignment and compliance with other principles. Typically, it is the data controller who establishes the purpose(s) and means of processing by articulating the specific purpose. However, in a decentralised system, the role is distributed across every blockchain node; therefore, a unitary actor is absent to determine the data processing purpose. Accordingly, it becomes imperative to ascertain the existence and attribution of data controller(s) responsibilities within the blockchain network, particularly in evaluating whether nodes, miners, and end-users may be regarded as collectively accountable as data controllers under data protection frameworks(Li, 2021).

In a landscape where energy data patterns can offer value-added services to prosumers, data minimisation, storage limitation, and purpose limitation principles can stifle innovation. The visibility and linkability of energy data on a public blockchain as an append-only database are profoundly at odds with such principles. However, private permissioned blockchain can achieve a certain level of compliance with these principles as it advances selective disclosure and access of personal information.

While the spirit of these principles is in friction with blockchain-enabled energy trading systems, scholars have identified workaround practices. First, off-chain data storage is a quick fix to prevent conflict with the storage limitation principle. Scholars suggest the development of blockchain-based energy platforms such that energy data is stored off-chain in separate, remote databases in an encrypted form to uphold data privacy requirements (Putz et al., 2019). On-chain data storage may not constitute a viable and feasible approach as it increases the operational complexity of blockchain and, correspondingly, the mining and transaction validation fee (Choobineh et al., 2022; Milčiuvienė et al., 2019). Accordingly, off-chain data storage is pertinent to circumvent data privacy concerns in blockchain-enabled energy systems.

Second, while storing copies on full nodes may constitute data redundancy and cannot be indefinitely kept, storage may be justified as a necessary purpose to preserve distributed ledger functionality, security, and integrity (Belen-Saglam et al., 2023; Walters, 2019). As such, if the purpose is merely to complete energy trading, data storage is time-bound and limited to the time frame necessary to achieve such a purpose. It is salient to define the purpose of personal data processing with caution in companies' privacy policies to allow extended storage on the decentralised ledger (Ramos & Silva, 2019).

Third, there have been ensuing attempts by scholars to explore practical solutions, such as to "reset" the blockchain after a market participant decides to leave an energy community. This solution encompasses the complete erasure of previous blocks and the information about every blockchain participant (Chantrel et al., 2021). Nevertheless, civil and tax laws may dictate archiving blockchain records in the public interest for a fixed duration in certain jurisdictions (Cejka, Zeilinger, Veseli, et al., 2020).

In essence, while mapping demonstrates the latent tensions between data protection principles and blockchain-enabled energy systems, as explored in the preceding paragraphs, adopting technical and organisational measures at the architectural level can mitigate these barriers. The role of blockchain-energy developers comes with great responsibility to comply with these principles, thus ensuring selective discoverability of energy data and only presenting information necessarily required on-chain. It is pertinent to develop a sustained response to data privacy vulnerabilities to enable resilient and reliable technology-enabled energy infrastructures.

3.2 Blockchain Immutability at Odds with the Right to be Forgotten

The inherent immutabiliy of public and private blockchain networks presents a fundamental tension with the right to be forgotten (RTBF), rendering the deletion of personal data practically infeasible and raising significant compliance challenges under data protection regulations (Godyn et al., 2022; Mantelero, 2013; Martins Gonçalves et al., 2023). Article 17 of the GDPR stipulates that the data subject has the right to request from the data controller the timely erasure of personal data, provided that there is a substantial basis for the right of erasure (European Union, 2016; Holzleitner et al., 2020; Tatar et al., 2020). While immutability is a compelling aspect of blockchain in that the data stored on the ledger is unalterable, amendable, or deletable, RTBF is an emerging legal concept incoherent with this feature.

The challenge is not limited to the energy domain but poses challenges for most blockchain use cases and business models. It is worth setting out briefly the inherent conflicts of blockchain with the right to erasure. Cryptographic hash functions translate various forms of data into unique strings of characters on the blockchain ledger. The hash functions link each block to its predecessors by containing the previous block's hash. Therefore, changing or manipulating any blockchain ledger data will distort the blockchain, resulting in undesirable consequences and inconsistencies

(Tatar et al., 2020). Complying with a data subject's request to delete transactions or data on a blockchain ledger undermines its core functionality, which relies on the permanence and immutability of recorded information.

The increasing integration of prosumers with blockchain-enabled energy applications hinders participants from exercising thier pivotal RTBF. The fulfilment of the RTBF cannot be easily achieved and represents a pertinent barrier for blockchain-enabled energy platforms, which may slow down progress and keep blockchain out of reach in energy trading systems. Blockchain developers and energy platform operators may find themselves at a critical junction with the data risks that precipitate from blockchain applications. Applying blockchain-enabled energy systems could prove counterproductive when it is desirable to wipe out blockchain participants' energy production, consumption, and transaction data and maximise their welfare in effective sharing and trading architectures.

Due to the conflict between blockchain and the GDPR, technology developers and scholars have recommended measures to ease the friction. According to the European Parliament Report on Blockchain: A forward-looking trade policy, blockchain utilisation should align with the GDPR provisions in light of the high stakes of technological development (European Parliament, 2018). To resolve the conflict between the RTBF and data immutability, various data protection by design measures exist. These measures include off-chain storage, encryption, and chameleon hash, amongst others (Utz et al., 2023).

3.3 The Tension between the Right to Rectification (RTR) and Blockchain Applications

Rectifying data on a public blockchain network is remarkably difficult, if not impossible, and this has contributed to challenges in the sphere of data protection. As a starting point, the principle of accuracy, where personal data is inaccurate, incomplete, or outdated, it is imperative to undertake reasonable and timely measures to ensure that such data is either rectified or erased promptly in accordance with data protection regulations (European Union, 2016; Li, 2020).

With blockchain, technical impediments arise, and it is cumbersome to identify and detect mistakes from all nodes on a blockchain network. In a permissionless blockchain, right to rectification (RTR) may be impossible even after identifying inaccurate or incomplete data, necessitating data correction across multiple nodes with different participants on the blockchain network (Duarte, 2019). Apart from the difficulty in coordinating various nodes across the blockchain, node disconnection remains a significant concern, potentially obstructing the formation of a fork (Al-Abdullah et al., 2020).

Ensuring adherence to RTR is more feasible and straightforward in private or consortium blockchain networks, due to their centralised governance structure, whereas it remains more complex in permissionless, decentralised networks (Duarte, 2019). RTR does not pose major concerns or barriers to implementing blockchain-enabled energy systems. The RTR of the data subject can be exercised by "providing a supplementary statement" (European Union, 2016). Such provision is a practical solution whereby adding or rectifying data on the blockchain network reflects energy market participants' latest state of affairs by uploading the necessary amendment without deleting the previous inaccurate or incomplete personal data. Although the inaccurate or incomplete records published on the blockchain ledger remains undeletable, the rectified information that corrects the original data is a practical avenue for blockchain participants to obtain the necessary correction of their data.

In what follows, there needs to be a fundamental reorientation of thought concerning the coexistence of blockchain with data protection frameworks by recognising that the regulation addresses the technical hindrances of technological systems and offers solutions to safeguard the right of data subjects (Al-Abdullah et al., 2020). Nevertheless, the development of targeted guidelines is essential to facilitate the effective implementation of RTR within the blockchain ecosystem to safeguard the data subjects' ability to exercise this right.

3.4 Other Key Data Privacy Rights that are at Odds with Blockchain Technology

Data protection infringements may arise when a decision is derived solely from the automated processing of personal data. Blockchain-enabled smart contracts and smart metering infrastructures fall within the realm of automated decision-making (including profiling) when performing energy transactions using self-executing codes without human involvement and verification (Nykyri et al., 2022). Even in the presence of coding errors or malfunctions, the smart contract continues to operate autonomously without initiating any corrective actions to amend the code. In what follows, the automated decisions influence prosumers' rights on the availability and accessibility of energy supply. However, by obtaining the data subject's explicit consent, the data controller can circumnavigate the right not to be subject to "automated decision-making" (European Union, 2016).

In some jurisdictions, exercising the right to data portability is challenging for blockchain applications. In the European Union, the GDPR provides data subjects with the right to receive their data in a "commonly used and machine-readable format" (European Union, 2016). Further, it advances the right to transfer data from one controller to another. Countries such as Brazil, India, Canada, Thailand, and Kenya guarantee data portability and emulate similar provisions, thus enabling users to have complete control over their data. However, the immutability feature makes it challenging to extract the data in a user-friendly format and transmit it to another controller (Kranenburg-Hanspians et al., 2019; Mirchandani, 2018).

Blockchain-enabled energy trading platforms cannot guarantee seamless connectivity and interchain interoperability with other platforms due to a lack of data extraction and transfer standards between ledgers. Consequentially, this prevents prosumers from switching to other blockchain energy platforms effortlessly. The uncertainties arising from the implementation of data portability in blockchain landscapes delay blockchain-enabled energy trading adoption and exacerbate data silos and walled gardens.

Data portability allows prosumers to extract and transfer their energy data through a user-friendly and common process to other blockchain platform providers to access the services provided. Article 20 of the Electricity Directive requires Member States to facilitate final customers to "retrieve their metering data or transmit them to another party at no additional cost and per their right to data portability under Union data protection rules" ("Directive 2019/944 on Common Rules for the Internal Market for Electricity and Amending Directive 2012/27/EU ", 2019). Impeding the right to data portability through the lack of standardisation and interoperability disrupts switching to more efficient platform providers.

3.5 Decentralised Blockchain Nodes and Qualification as a Data Controller

Generally, data controllers have a legal obligation to protect data subjects' rights and ensure compliance with the law. This obligation does not fall on technology or platform providers or developers in many jurisdictions (European Union, 2016; Hildebrandt & Tielemans, 2013). As custodians of personal data, data controllers must establish clear accountability in matters concerning data protection. Where data processing entails a high risk to critical infrastructures, it is pertinent to allocate responsibilities and obligations effectively. Identifying data controllers is crucial in determining the purpose of processing personal data and implementing suitable measures. Data controllers ensure compliance with data protection principles when using smart meter data to measure energy production and consumption levels, keep track of energy imports and exports, and for billing purposes. Further, data subjects can enforce their rights to access, rectification, and erasure by addressing the compliance of such requests with a data controller (Riva, 2020).

However, in an entirely decentralised and distributed landscape without central intermediaries, where there are no power imbalances between nodes, it is still being determined who is a data controller, especially with the decentralisation of responsibilities (Michèle Finck, 2018; Holzleitner et al., 2020). Outwardly, there lacks a responsible body to undertake adequate measures prescribed by data protection regulations to safeguard personal data in blockchain systems, mainly because blockchain endeavours to achieve decentralisation.

Blockchain Nodes

While it is difficult to conclude who constitutes a data controller, we can theorise that since nodes operate autonomously in a blockchain landscape, no node effectively controls the entire blockchain network or consensus mechanisms (Al-Abdullah et al., 2020; Herrnfeld et al., 2020; Jaccard & Tharin, 2018). Furthermore, nodes do not determine the "purposes and means of processing of personal data." Moreover, with the complexity of identifying all nodes (i.e., identity and location) distributed across the permissionless blockchain, attributing responsibility to each node to ensure that processing activities comply with data protection regulations is not viable (Ebbers & Karaboga, 2021). While blockchain nodes can verify, approve, store and broadcast data within a blockchain ledger, no node can specifically modify, make changes, or delete transactions. Therefore, these nodes cannot fulfil their responsibilities as data controllers, ordinarily imposed on centralised natural or legal persons (Michèle Finck, 2018).

Since the blockchain protocol is determined jointly by natural or legal persons or entities with power and control over such decisions, some scholars regard the protocol as sufficient instructions for processing personal data. However, acknowledging and embedding this position in regulatory frameworks and guidelines is crucial (Jaccard & Tharin, 2018).

Data Subjects

Similarly, scholars raise a potential issue of whether a data subject involved in blockchain transactions in a personal capacity should be eligible to undertake the role of a data controller or joint controllership (Al-Abdullah et al., 2020). Blockchain participants, also data subjects, can add information to the chain and control access to the data through the private key, interacting directly with the permissionless blockchain. Participants who transact energy by hashing their personal information and recording the transfer of a specific quantity of energy and other transaction data is vested in determining the specific purpose of processing personal data (Bacon et al., 2018). However, augmenting the responsibilities of data subjects as data controllers may expose data subjects to imminent data privacy risks and hinder the adequate fulfilment of rights and obligations expected of a controller.

Blockchain Developers and Designers

If no nodes qualify as data controllers, responsibilities and obligations may allocate to blockchain developers or designers as natural or legal persons that develop the blockchain systems (Dutta et al., 2020). However, this presents challenges as releasing the blockchain software into the market will likely cause the blockchain developer or designer to discharge all control of the "purpose and means of the processing or personal data" and, therefore, not constitute data controllers (Kaufmann & Lawyer, 2018). Further, blockchain developers, having primary control over the design of the software, do not determine "which data shall be processed", "for how long shall they be processed", or "who shall have access to them (Article 29 Data Protection Working Party, 2010)." Blockchain developers are, at best, data processors, implementing the instructions of data controllers on system design and infrastructure.

Distribution System Operators

The adoption of blockchain is unlikely to result in complete disintermediation since it is conceivable that certain market intermediaries will remain relevant in the new landscape or assume technologically inclined functions. Distribution system operators (DSOs) retain control over the management and operation of grid infrastructures for energy delivery on the public grid. DSOs are responsible for installing smart meters, enabling energy loss computation, balancing voltage points via optimisation algorithms, power optimisation, grid stability, load control, congestion management, and network pricing (Bergquist et al., 2017; Durairaj et al., 2020). Energy data is pertinent to comply with these responsibilities. Further, DSOs facilitate bi-directional power distribution between prosumers, including between smart meters and energy storage systems (Son et al., 2020). Energy communities can conclude an agreement with DSOs to manage the local distribution grid and facilitate peer-to-peer energy trading and similarly fulfill the abovementioned functions (Vanhove, 2020). As such, DSOs determine the purposes and means of processing energy data and constitute data controllers (Article 29 Data Protection Working Party, 2011). DSOs can operate jointly with energy platform operators, where both entities are responsible for the processing operations on the blockchain landscapes. However, their participation as data controllers need not be equally shared. Therefore, they may interact at different degrees depending on the dynamics of processing operations(Article 29 Data Protection Working Party, 2010).

Energy Platform Operator

In blockchain-enabled energy trading applications, the platform operator that offers blockchain-enabled platform-as-a-service (PaaS) applications to prosumers and facilitates energy trading by processing energy production, consumption, and transaction data can constitute a data controller based on blockchain design, purpose, and functionality (European Parliamentary Research Service, 2019; Jaccard & Tharin, 2018). The platform operator determines why and how the personal data of energy prosumers and consumers are processed and adopts technical and organisational measures to safeguard data rights, conforming to data protection compliance levels (GDPRWise, n.d.).

The pertinent issue is the lack of a data controller, which may deprive blockchain users of adequate data protection. Public blockchain architectures require trusted third parties to assume the role of data controllers for managing personal data to comply with data privacy rights and principles embedded in data protection regulations. In contrast, in a private blockchain with a centralised authority or administrator, the data controller can be readily identified without difficulty. Parties exercising an influence on the purposes and means of processing personal data, such as determining the validation rules, share the responsibility of complying with data protection laws (Ahmed et al., 2020). At the same time, appropriate governance mechanisms secure the rights of data subjects that explicitly identify data controllers and delineate the duties and responsibilities of such entities.

3.6 Transactional Privacy Breaches in Blockchain Systems

The commercial feasibility of blockchain in the energy sector depends on understanding the fundamental concept of "unlinkability," or "identity privacy," a subset of transactional privacy (Shao et al., 2020; Sri & Bhaskari, 2018). It stems from the notion that the association between transactions and the identity of blockchain users be concealed or remain indiscoverable. Transactional privacy relates to protecting the user's identity and transactional details without external disclosure (Wang et al., 2020). While blockchain systems offer great utility for energy trading applications, they are susceptible to malicious behavioural attacks such as transactional data leakages, in that the attacker traces the user's transactional patterns and exposes a large amount of energy transaction information.

Encryption using private and public keys does not guarantee complete anonymity, as transactional data is still publicly discernible and identifiable on the chain (Voss, 2021; Zheng et al., 2020). The blockchain users' transactions and payment details replicated, distributed and shared throughout the network can reveal the user's identity, presenting a material risk to users (Levitin, 2017; Omar et al., 2021; Peng et al., 2020; Tyagi et al., 2020; Yeom et al., 2021).

Transactional privacy is a challenging obstacle to resolve. The transactional data should be limited to a handful of individuals, such as transacting participants, regulators, system operators, and auditors. Initiating new research frontiers in identifying key solutions confer high transactional privacy to blockchain users. Therefore, an evaluation parameter is essential to access the potential safeguards that can remedy transactional privacy leakages.

Scholars have presented various technical solutions, namely homomorphic encryption, obfuscation, and zero-knowledge proof, to resolve issues surrounding transactional privacy. (Cao & Zhao, 2021; Pohrmen et al., 2019; Vanin et al., 2023) Homomorphic encryption allows computation on the encrypted text without access to the private key to decrypt it. Another potential technique is zero-knowledge proof, where the verifier can verify the transaction without revealing the details of the transaction (Premalatha & Sathya, 2020). The espousal of various mechanisms and technical solutions can ameliorate blockchain privacy-by-design. Technical solutions should be adopted, and governing mechanisms formulated to uphold these solutions whilst espousing regulatory frameworks and good practices to secure privacy rights (Bello & Perez, 2019; Centobelli et al., 2021).

3.7 Lack of Consistent and Effective Regulatory Engagement

With the advent of new blockchain-enabled innovative business models and new business entrants, the challenges in the realm of privacy and data protection necessitate the initiation and adoption of flexible regulatory engagement. These challenges occur because, as blockchain develops, pursuing a formal regulatory step is necessary to explore and assess the potential and paradigm of blockchain in energy systems and develop guidelines and good practices for privacy and data protection parameters. In regulatory engagement, the involvement of regulatory bodies, research institutions and other agencies is necessary as an impetus for the diffusion of blockchain into energy systems and the facilitation of better coordination. While the aim is strengthening regulatory engagement, the real challenge is mobilising this process without hampering blockchain innovation.

The lack of regulatory engagement is a structural barrier towards embracing blockchain-enabled energy systems, primarily due to the wait-and-see attitude of regulators that constitutes the "unwillingness by governments to muster the energy, let alone the resources, to challenge private self-interest (Robert Herian, 2018)." There needs to be a continuum of responsibility of regulators to monitor the regulatory landscape and processes concerning blockchain. As exponents of the "laissez-faire" approach, some regulators have decided to hold any salient enforcement action in abeyance rather than making explicit pronouncements.

Blockchain faces many significant hurdles, such as the risks of data privacy invasion. Nevertheless, doing more is necessary to define the limits around the use of blockchain (Robert Herian, 2018). On the one hand, the wait-and-see approach appears wise in that it allows active monitoring of the new and immature blockchain without taking any drastic action of implementing binding rules that may quickly be rendered obsolete with the steep development of technology (McLean & Deane-Johns, 2016). On the other hand, allowing blockchain to remain unchecked without imposing a firm grip on the blockchain landscape may introduce new cybersecurity risks that threaten the technology's stability in energy systems (Robert Herian, 2018). These threats may be translated into regulators' lack of urgency and responsiveness to address the concerns raised, however subtle they may appear. A coherent strategy would be to enhance regulatory engagement and involvement in blockchain-enabled energy systems.

While scholars have signified the wait-and-see approach as representing "mere euphemisms for a lack of motivation or energy across regulatory environment", especially in a decentralised setting evolving at a steep pace, there are other, more apparent shortcomings stemming from the lack of regulatory engagement (Robert Herian, 2018). There needs to be more substantive, participatory and deliberative collaboration, which is a critical step in the quality of response. Consensus-based collaborative engagement between regulators and industry players, multi-stakeholders and the community can enrich and foster discussions on data privacy invasions from the shortcomings present in the blockchain (Michèle Finck, 2018). With such regulatory engagement and collaboration, deploying and integrating blockchain into energy systems might be more accessible. Regulatory engagement must assume a central role in steering the development of blockchain. Timely regulatory engagement is necessary for the deliberation of various strategies which can constitute key elements to the design process of blockchain. It should be open and inclusive to promote an effective dialogue as a core prerequisite to improving the efficacy of the blockchain architecture (Michèle Finck, 2018).

Even though regulatory engagement is paramount, the overarching idea is ensuring the adoption of positive measures to enable legal compliance in blockchain systems. Blockchain architectural designs and development pathways should embed legal requirements exemplified in data protection laws at the embryonic stage to circumvent risks or harms to critical infrastructures and protect prosumers' rights. Scholars explore nudging techniques by citing Olislaegers, who states that "compliance software consists of hardcoded legal knowledge on the one hand, and, where the law cannot be hardcoded of nudging mechanisms, on the other hand (Olislaegers, 2011; Thaler & Sunstein, 2009)." A growing need exists for privacy by design and default measures to "nudge" blockchain developers as choice architects to adopt user-friendly and supportive choice architectures (Rossi, 2019). Such a need is via navigational tools and design patterns that advance the rights of data subjects and achieve greater congruity levels with data privacy. This position aligns with Lessig's words: "[a]s the world is now, code writers are increasingly lawmakers. They determine the defaults of the Internet, whether privacy will be protected; the degree to which anonymity will be allowed; the extent to which access will be guaranteed" (Lessig, 2009).

Privacy-by-design measures in the blockchain sphere has gained traction, providing clear and standardised instructions on implementing technical requirements necessary for privacy-focused blockchain systems (European Union, 2016). It is a practical approach for data privacy management to ensure the integration of the necessary safeguards within the blockchain system. Further, privacy-by-design strengthens the autonomy and control of data subjects by requiring developers to focus on data protection at the infrastructural level. The privacy-by-design paradigm embeds privacy within the blockchain architecture throughout the system's lifecycle. Privacy-by-design can facilitate collective technology governance in the diffusion and development of blockchain-enabled applications rather than adopting a rigid top-down approach. However, there needs to be more specific and meaningful regulatory dialogue in the proactive engineering of privacy-by-design principles. Off-chain data storage, zero knowledge-proof protocols, stealth addresses, ring signatures, data encryption and hashing are design strategies that can promote specific outcomes in fully peer-to-peer and community-based models.

4. CONCLUSION

In conclusion, blockchain diffusion in energy systems is challenging. The earlier section explored the conflict between blockchain features and data protection rights and principles, namely (a) storage limitation, (b) data minimisation, (c) purpose limitation, (d) right to rectification, (e) right to be forgotten, (f) right not to be subject to automated decision-making, and (g) right to data portability. Stakeholder engagement can contribute toward policy formulation and implementation in governing the deployment of privacy-friendly blockchain systems and addressing data privacy challenges without delay.

REFERENCES

Ahmed, J., Yildirim, S., Nowostawski, M., Abomhara, M., Ramachandra, R., & Elezaj, O. (2020, March 5). 2020). Towards Blockchain-Based GDPR-Compliant Online Social Networks: Challenges, Opportunities and Way Forward Future of Information and Communication Conference

Al-Abdullah, M., Alsmadi, I., AlAbdullah, R., & Farkas, B. (2020). Designing Privacy-friendly Data Repositories: A Framework for a Blockchain that follows the GDPR [Article]. Digital Policy. *Regulation & Governance*, *22*(5-6), 389–411. DOI: 10.1108/DPRG-04-2020-0050

American Data Privacy and Protection Act (2022).

Article 29 Data Protection Working Party. (2010, 16 February 2010). *Opinion 1/2010 on the Concepts of "controller" and "processor" (No. 00264/10/EN WP 169).* https://ec.europa.eu/justice/article-29/documentation/opinion-recommendation/files/2010/wp169_en.pdf

Article 29 Data Protection Working Party. (2011, 4 April 2011). *Opinion 12/2011 on Smart Metering*. https://ec.europa.eu/justice/article-29/documentation/opinion-recommendation/files/2011/wp183_en.pdf

Article 29 Data Protection Working Party. (2014, 10 April 2014). *Opinion 05/2014 on Anonymisation Techniques*. https://ec.europa.eu/justice/article-29/documentation/opinion-recommendation/files/2014/wp216_en.pdf

Bacon, J., Michels, J. D., Millard, C., & Singh, J. (2018). Blockchain Demystified: A technical and Legal Introduction to Distributed and Centralized Ledgers. *Richmond Journal of Law and Technology, 25*(1). https://jolt.richmond.edu/blockchain-demystified-a-technical-and-legal-introduction-to-distributed-and-centralised-ledgers/

Belen-Saglam, R., Altuncu, E., Lu, Y., & Li, S. (2023). A Systematic Literature Review of the Tension between the GDPR and Public Blockchain Systems. *4*(2), 100129. https://doi.org/DOI: 10.1016/j.bcra.2023.100129

Bello, G., & Perez, A. J. (2019, 18 April 2019). Adapting Financial Technology Standards to Blockchain Platforms Proceedings of the 2019 ACM Southeast Conference.

Bergquist, J., Laszka, A., Sturm, M., & Dubey, A. (2017, 11 December 2017). On the Design of Communication and Transaction Anonymity in Blockchain-based Transactive Microgrids Proceedings of the 1st Workshop on Scalable and Resilient Infrastructures for Distributed Ledgers, California Consumer Privacy Act.

Cao, Z., & Zhao, L. (2021, 26 March 2021). A Design of Key Distribution Mechanism in Decentralized Digital Rights Management Based on Blockchain and Zero-Knowledge Proof International Conference on Blockchain Technology

Cejka, S., Zeilinger, F., Stefan, M., Zehetbauer, P., Veseli, A., Burgstaller, K., & Holzleitner, M.-T. (2020). Implementation and Operation of Blockchain-Based Energy Communities Under the New Legal Framework. In Klein, C., Helfert, M., Berns, K., & Gusikhin, O. (Eds.), *Smart Cities, Green Technologies, and Intelligent Transport Systems* (pp. 3–30). Springer.

Cejka, S., Zeilinger, F., Veseli, A., Holzleitner, M.-T., & Stefan, M. (2020, 2 May 2020). *A Blockchain-based Privacy-friendly Renewable Energy Community* Proceedings of the 9th International Conference on Smart Cities and Green ICT Systems-SMARTGREENS, https://pdfs.semanticscholar.org/1a64/15e5779b204fea3063c0e2b22f08d7138ba4.pdf

Centobelli, P., Cerchione, R., Del Vecchio, P., Oropallo, E., & Secundo, G. (2021). Blockchain Technology for Bridging Trust, Traceability and Transparency in Circular Supply Chain. *Information & Management, 59*(7), 103508. https://doi.org/https://doi.org/10.1016/j.im.2021.103508. DOI: 10.1016/j.im.2021.103508

Chantrel, S. P., Surmann, A., Erge, T., & Thomsen, J. (2021). Participative Renewable Energy Community—How Blockchain-Based Governance Enables a German Interpretation of RED II. *Electricity, 2*(4), 471-486. https://doi.org/https://doi.org/10.3390/electricity2040028

Children's Online Privacy Protection Act (1998).

Choobineh, M., Arab, A., Khodaei, A., & Paaso, A. (2022). Energy Innovations through Blockchain: Challenges, Opportunities, and the Road Ahead. *The Electricity Journal, 35*(1), 107059. https://doi.org/https://doi.org/10.1016/j.tej.2021.107059. DOI: 10.1016/j.tej.2021.107059

Chousein, Z., Tetik, H. Y., Sağlam, R. B., Bülbül, A., & Li, S. (2020, 4 November 2020). *Tension between GDPR and Public Blockchains: A Data-Driven Analysis of Online Discussions* [Conference Paper]. International Conference on Security of Information and Networks, https://www.scopus.com/inward/record.uri?eid=2-s2.0-85100648836&doi=10.1145%2f3433174.3433587&partnerID=40&md5=2151aa5536ae1d9f6f5b0029933fede2

Colorado Privacy Act (2021).

de Terwangne, C. (2020). Article 5 Principles Relating to Processing of Personal Data. In Kuner, C., Bygrave, L. A., Docksey, C., & Drechsler, L. (Eds.), *The EU General Data Protection Regulation (GDPR): A Commentary*. Academic., DOI: 10.1093/oso/9780198826491.003.0034

Diamantopoulou, V., Lambrinoudakis, C., King, J., & Gritzalis, S. (2022). EU GDPR: Toward a Regulatory Initiative for Deploying a Private Digital Era. In Knijnenburg, B. P., Page, X., Wisniewski, P., Lipford, H. R., Proferes, N., & Jennifer, R. (Eds.), *Modern Socio-Technical Perspectives on Privacy* (pp. 427–448). Springer. DOI: 10.1007/978-3-030-82786-1_18

Directive 2019/944 on Common Rules for the Internal Market for Electricity and Amending Directive 2012/27/EU (2019). https://data.europa.eu/eli/dir/2019/944/oj

Driver's Privacy Protection Act, (1999).

Duarte, D. (2019). An Introduction to Blockchain Technology from a Legal Perspective and its Tensions with the GDPR. *Cyberlaw Journal of the Cyberlaw Research Centre of the University of Lisbon School of Law*, 1-58. https://papers.ssrn.com/sol3/papers.cfm?abstract_id=3545331

Durairaj, D., Gopi, R., Hariharasudan, A., Otola, I., & Bilan, Y. (2020). Reactive Power Optimization and Price Management in Microgrid Enabled with Blockchain. *Energies*, *13*(23), 6179. DOI: 10.3390/en13236179

Dutta, R., Das, A., Dey, A., & Bhattacharya, S. (2020, 25 October 2020). Blockchain vs GDPR in collaborative data governance International Conference on Cooperative Design, Visualization and Engineering.

Dzobo, O., Malila, B., & Sithole, L. (2021). Proposed Framework for Blockchain Technology in a Decentralised Energy Network. *Protection Control of Modern Power Systems*, *6*(1), 1–11.

Ebbers, F., & Karaboga, M. (2021). Blockchain and Data Protection: An Evaluation of the Challenges and Solutions Mentioned by German Stakeholders. In Ahlemann, F., Schütte, R., & Stieglitz, S. (Eds.), *Innovation Through Information Systems* (Vol. 47, pp. 353–369). Springer., https://doi.org/https://doi.org/10.1007/978-3-030-86797-3_24 DOI: 10.1007/978-3-030-86797-3_24

European Data Protection Supervisor. (2022, 24 August 2022). *EDPS Formal Comments on the Draft Commission Implementing Regulation on Interoperability Requirements and Non-Discriminatory and Transparent Procedures for Access to Metering and Consumption Data*. https://edps.europa.eu/system/files/2022-09/22-08-24_access-metering-and-consumption-data_en.pdf

European Parliament. (2018, 27 November 2018). *Report on Blockchain: A Forward-looking Trade Policy*. Retrieved November 6 from https://www.europarl.europa.eu/doceo/document/A-8-2018-0407_EN.html

European Parliamentary Research Service. (2019, July 2019). *Can Distributed Ledgers be Squared with European Data Protection Law?* https://www.europarl.europa.eu/RegData/etudes/STUD/2019/634445/EPRS_STU(2019)634445_EN.pdf

European Union. (2016). Regulation (EU) 2016/679 of the European Parliament and of the Council of 27 April 2016 on the Protection of Natural Persons with regard to the Processing of Personal Data and on the Free Movement of such Data, and Repealing Directive 95/46/EC (General Data Protection Regulation). *Official Journal of the European Union Law 119/1, 59.*

Finck, M. (2018). Blockchains and Data Protection in the European Union. *European Data Protection Law Review, 4*, 17. https://doi.org/https://doi.org/10.21552/edpl/2018/1/6

Finck, M. (2018). Blockchains: Regulating the Unknown. *German Law Journal, 19*(4), 665-692. https://doi.org/https://doi.org/10.1017/S2071832200022847

GDPRWise. (n.d., n.d.). *GDPR and Online Marketplaces*. Retrieved December 13 from https://gdprwise.eu/news/platforms-required-to-take-more-active-role/

General Personal Data Protection Law, (2020).

Gill, S. S., Tuli, S., Xu, M., Singh, I., Singh, K. V., Lindsay, D., Tuli, S., Smirnova, D., Singh, M., Jain, U., Pervaiz, H., Sehgal, B., Kaila, S. S., Misra, S., Aslanpour, M. S., Mehta, H., Stankovski, V., & Garraghan, P. (2019). Transformative Effects of IoT, Blockchain and Artificial Intelligence on Cloud Computing: Evolution, Vision, Trends and Open Challenges. *Internet of Things : Engineering Cyber Physical Human Systems, 8*, 100118. https://doi.org/https://doi.org/10.1016/j.iot.2019.100118. DOI: 10.1016/j.iot.2019.100118

Godyn, M., Kedziora, M., Ren, Y., Liu, Y., & Song, H. H. (2022). Analysis of Solutions for a Blockchain Compliance with GDPR. *Scientific Reports, 12*(1), 15021. DOI: 10.1038/s41598-022-19341-y PMID: 36056166

Guimarães, L. N. (2017). The Dichotomy between Smart Metering and the Protection of Consumer's Personal Data in Brazilian Law. *Brazilian Journal of Public Policy, 7*(3), 275. DOI: 10.5102/rbpp.v7i3.4898

Haque, A. B., Islam, A. K. M. N., Hyrynsalmi, S., Naqvi, B., & Smolander, K. (2021). GDPR Compliant Blockchains–A Systematic Literature Review. *IEEE Access : Practical Innovations, Open Solutions*, *9*, 50593–50606. DOI: 10.1109/ACCESS.2021.3069877

Health Insurance Portability and Accountability Act (1996).

Herian, R. (2018). Regulating Disruption: Blockchain, GDPR, and Questions of Data Sovereignty. *Journal of Internet Law*, *22*(2), 1–16. https://papers.ssrn.com/sol3/papers.cfm?abstract_id=3241228

Herian, R. (2018). Taking Blockchain Seriously. *Law and Critique*, *29*(2), 163–171. https://doi.org/https://doi.org/10.1007/s10978-018-9226-y. DOI: 10.1007/s10978-018-9226-y

Herrnfeld, H.-H., Brodowski, D., & Burchard, C. (2020). *Article-by-Article Commentary: Article 64 Joint controllers* (1st ed.). Bloomsbury Publishing.

Hildebrandt, M., & Tielemans, L. (2013). Data Protection by Design and Technology Neutral Law. *Computer Law & Security Review*, *29*(5), 509–521. https://doi.org/https://doi.org/10.1016/j.clsr.2013.07.004. DOI: 10.1016/j.clsr.2013.07.004

Holzleitner, M.-T., Burgstaller, K., Cejka, S., & Veseli, A. (2020). Electricity Trading via Blockchain in an Energy Community from a Data Protection Point of View. *European Energy & Climate Journal, 9*(2), 33-43. https://ezproxy.um.edu.my/login?url=https://search.ebscohost.com/login.aspx?direct=true&db=edb&AN=145712706&site=eds-live

Jaccard, G., & Tharin, A. (2018, 4 December 2018). *GDPR & Blockchain: The Swiss Take*.

Kaufmann, J., & Lawyer, W. R. (2018, 7 August 2018). *Blockchain and the Data Controller*. Retrieved January 8 from https://lrz.legal/images//pdf/Blockchain-meets-Data-Privacy_Blockchain-and-the-Data-Controller.pdf

Kranenburg-Hanspians, K. v., Kaulartz, M., & Runte, C. (2019, January 2019). *The Tension between GDPR and the Rise of Blockchain Technologies*. https://cms.law/en/media/international/files/publications/publications/the-tension-between-gdpr-and-the-rise-of-blockchain-technologies

Lessig, L. (2009). *Code and Other Laws of Cyberspace*. Basic Books.

Levitin, A. J. (2017). Pandora's Digital Box: The Promise and Perils of Digital Wallets. *University of Pennsylvania Law Review*, *166*(2), 305–376. https://www.jstor.org/stable/45154936

Li, Z. (2020, 10 June 2020). *Standardisation of Blockchain and Distributed Ledger Technologies—A Legal Voice from the Data Protection Law Perspective* EURAS Annual Standardisation Conference–Standards for Digital Transformation: Blockchain and Innovation https://papers.ssrn.com/sol3/papers.cfm?abstract_id=3892298

Li, Z. (2021). Confronting Algorithm Bias Risks: Will Blockchain Provide New Opportunities or Challenges for Data Protection Law? *Dublin Law & Politics Review 2*(43). https://doi.org/https://ssrn.com/abstract=3946608

Mantelero, A. (2013). The EU Proposal for a General Data Protection Regulation and the Roots of the 'Right to be Forgotten'. *Computer Law & Security Review, 29*(3), 229–235. https://doi.org/https://doi.org/10.1016/j.clsr.2013.03.010. DOI: 10.1016/j.clsr.2013.03.010

Martinez, J., Ruiz, A., Puelles, J., Arechalde, I., & Miadzvetskaya, Y. (2019). Smart Grid Challenges Through the Lens of the European General Data Protection Regulation. In Siarheyeva, A., Barry, C., Lang, M., Linger, H., & Schneider, C. (Eds.), *Advances in Information Systems Development* (Vol. 39, pp. 113–130). Springer., https://doi.org/https://doi.org/10.1007/978-3-030-49644-9_7 DOI: 10.1007/978-3-030-49644-9_7

Martins Gonçalves, R., Mira da Silva, M., & Rupino da Cunha, P. (2023). Implementing GDPR-Compliant Surveys Using Blockchain. *Future Internet, 15*(4), 143. DOI: 10.3390/fi15040143

McLean, S., & Deane-Johns, S. (2016). Demystifying Blockchain and Distributed Ledger Technology–Hype or Hero? *Computer Law Review International, 17*(4), 97-102. https://doi.org/https://doi.org/10.9785/cri-2016-0402

Merlo, V., Pio, G., Giusto, F., & Bilancia, M. (2022). On the Exploitation of the Blockchain Technology in the Healthcare Sector: A Systematic Review. *Expert Systems with Applications, 213*, 118897. DOI: 10.1016/j.eswa.2022.118897

Meyer, D. (2018, 27 February 2018). *Blockchain Technology is on a Collision Course with EU Privacy Law*. https://iapp.org/news/a/blockchain-technology-is-on-a-collision-course-with-eu-privacy-law/

Milčiuvienė, S., Kiršienė, J., Doheijo, E., Urbonas, R., & Milčius, D. (2019). The Role of Renewable Energy Prosumers in Implementing Energy Justice Theory. *Sustainability (Basel), 11*(19), 5286. DOI: 10.3390/su11195286

Mirchandani, A. (2018). The GDPR-Blockchain Paradox: Exempting Permissioned Blockchains from the GDPR. *Fordham Intellectual Property. Media and Entertainment Law Journal, 29*, 1201.

Nykyri, M., Kärkkäinen, T. J., Levikari, S., Honkapuro, S., Annala, S., & Silventoinen, P. (2022). Blockchain-Based Balance Settlement Ledger for Energy Communities in Open Electricity Markets. *Energy*, *253*, 124180. https://doi.org/https://doi.org/10.1016/j.energy.2022.124180. DOI: 10.1016/j.energy.2022.124180

Olislaegers, S. (2011, September 5). 2011). *Early Lessons Learned in the ENDORSE Project: Legal Challenges and Possibilities in Developing Data Protection Compliance Software* IFIP PrimeLife International Summer School on Privacy and Identity Management for Life, Omar, I. A., Jayaraman, R., Salah, K., Yaqoob, I., & Ellahham, S. (2021). Applications of Blockchain Technology in Clinical Trials: Review and Open Challenges. *Arabian Journal for Science and Engineering*, *46*, 3001–3015. https://doi.org/https://doi.org/10.1007/s13369-020-04989-3

Peng, L., Feng, W., Yan, Z., Li, Y., Zhou, X., & Shimizu, S. (2020). Privacy Preservation in Permissionless Blockchain: A Survey. *Digital Communications and Networks*, *7*(3), 295–307. https://doi.org/https://doi.org/10.1016/j.dcan.2020.05.008. DOI: 10.1016/j.dcan.2020.05.008

Personal Data Protection Act (2012).

Personal Data Protection Act, (2019).

Pohrmen, F. H., Das, R. K., & Saha, G. (2019). Blockchain-Based Security Aspects in Heterogeneous Internet-of-Things Networks: A Survey. *Transactions on Emerging Telecommunications Technologies*, *30*(10), e3741. https://doi.org/https://doi.org/10.1002/ett.3741. DOI: 10.1002/ett.3741

Potter, A., Highams, H., Kazmi, T., Young, A., Kerpauskaite, K., Stylianou, T., Ashcroft, V., & Kateifides, A. (2020, 26 March 2020). *Comparing Privacy Laws: GDPR v. Australian Privacy Act.* https://www.dataguidance.com/sites/default/files/gdpr_v_australia.pdf

Power Ledger. (2019, 2019). *Power Ledger Whitepaper.* Retrieved March, 4 2023 from https://www.powerledger.io/company/power-ledger-whitepaper

Premalatha, J., & Sathya, K. (2020). Integration of Blockchain into IoT. In Kumar, S. A. P., Velliangiri, S., & Karthikeyan, P. (Eds.), *Internet of Things* (1st ed., pp. 121–134). CRC Press., DOI: 10.1201/9781003032441-8

Privacy Act (1988).

Putz, B., Menges, F., & Pernul, G. (2019). A Secure and Auditable Logging Infrastructure Based on a Permissioned Blockchain. *Computers & Security*, *87*, 101602. https://doi.org/https://doi.org/10.1016/j.cose.2019.101602. DOI: 10.1016/j.cose.2019.101602

Ramos, L. F. M., & Silva, J. M. C. (2019, 3 April 2019). *Privacy and Data Protection Concerns regarding the Use of Blockchains in Smart Cities* [Conference Paper]. International Conference on Theory and Practice of Electronic Governance, ICEGOV 2019, https://www.scopus.com/inward/record.uri?eid=2-s2.0-85066637109&doi=10.1145%2f3326365.3326410&partnerID=40&md5=d7539ba4cf6c8e1f65143f1f9e752526

Riva, G. M. (2020). What Happens in Blockchain Stays in Blockchain. A Legal Solution to Conflicts Between Digital Ledgers and Privacy Rights. *Frontiers in Blockchain*, *3*, 36. DOI: 10.3389/fbloc.2020.00036

Rossi, A. (2019). *Legal Design for the General Data Protection Regulation. A Methodology for the Visualization and Communication of Legal Concepts*. University of Bologna.

Schellinger, B., Völter, F., Urbach, N., & Sedlmeir, J. (2021, 4 January 2022). *Yes, I Do: Marrying Blockchain Applications with GDPR* Hawaii International Conference on System Sciences 2022

Shao, W., Jia, C., Xu, Y., Qiu, K., Gao, Y., & He, Y. (2020). Attrichain: Decentralized Traceable Anonymous Identities in Privacy-Preserving Permissioned Blockchain. *Computers & Security*, *99*, 102069. https://doi.org/https://doi.org/10.1016/j.cose.2020.102069. DOI: 10.1016/j.cose.2020.102069

Sim, W. L., Chua, H. N., & Tahir, M. (2019, 19 November 2019). *Blockchain for Identity Management: The Implications to Personal Data Protection IEEE Conference on Application, Information and Network Security (AINS)*, Pulau Pinang, Malaysia. DOI: 10.1109/AINS47559.2019.8968708

Son, Y. B., Im, J. H., Kwon, H. Y., Jeon, S. Y., & Lee, M. K. (2020). Privacy-Preserving Peer-to-Peer Energy Trading in Blockchain-Enabled Smart Grids using Functional Encryption. *Energies*, *13*(6), 1321. https://doi.org/https://doi.org/10.3390/en13061321. DOI: 10.3390/en13061321

Sri, S. G. A., & Bhaskari, L. (2018). A Study on Blockchain Technology. *IACSIT International Journal of Engineering and Technology*, *7*, 418. DOI: 10.14419/ijet.v7i2.7.10757

Tatar, U., Gokce, Y., & Nussbaum, B. (2020). Law Versus Technology: Blockchain, GDPR, and Tough Tradeoffs. *Computer Law & Security Review*, *38*, 105454. https://doi.org/https://doi.org/10.1016/j.clsr.2020.105454. DOI: 10.1016/j.clsr.2020.105454

Thaler, R. H., & Sunstein, C. R. (2009). *Nudge: Improving Decisions about Health, Wealth, and Happiness*. Penguin Books.

Tyagi, A. K., Nair, M. M., Niladhuri, S., & Abraham, A. (2020). Security, Privacy Research issues in Various Computing Platforms: A Survey and the Road Ahead. *Journal of Information Assurance Security and Communication Networks*, *15*(1), 1–16. www.mirlabs.net/jias/index.htm

Utz, M., Johanning, S., Roth, T., Bruckner, T., & Strüker, J. (2023). From Ambivalence to Trust: Using Blockchain in Customer Loyalty Programs. *International Journal of Information Management*, *68*, 102496. https://doi.org/https://doi.org/10.1016/j.ijinfomgt.2022.102496. DOI: 10.1016/j.ijinfomgt.2022.102496

Vanhove, S. (2020, 16 September 2020). *Peer-to-Peer Electricity Trading: Challenges for the Distribution System Operator (DSO) under EU Law International Conference on the European Energy Market (EEM)*, Stockholm, Sweden.

Vanin, F. N. S., Policarpo, L. M., Righi, R. R., Heck, S., da Silva, V. F., Goldim, J., & da Costa, C. A. (2023). A Blockchain-Based End-to-End Data Protection Model for Personal Health Records Sharing: A Fully Homomorphic Encryption Approach. *Sensors (Basel)*, *23*(1), 14. https://doi.org/https://doi.org/10.3390/s23010014. DOI: 10.3390/s23010014 PMID: 36616613

Virginia Consumer Data Protection Act, (2021).

Voss, W. G. (2021). Data Protection Issues for Smart Contracts. In Corrales, M., Fenwick, M., & Wrbka, S. (Eds.), *Smart Contracts: Technological, Business and Legal Perspectives* (pp. 79–100). Hart Publishing., DOI: 10.5040/9781509937059.ch-004

Walters, N. (2019). Privacy Law Issues in Blockchains: An Analysis of PIPEDA, the GDPR, and Proposals for Compliance. *Canadian Journal of Law and Technology*, *17*(276). https://doi.org/https://papers.ssrn.com/sol3/papers.cfm?abstract_id=3481701

Walters, R., Trakman, L., & Zeller, B. (2019). *Data Protection Law: A Comparative Analysis of Asia-Pacific and European Approaches* (1 ed.). Springer. https://doi.org/ DOI: 10.1007/978-981-13-8110-2

Wang, D., Zhao, J., & Wang, Y. (2020). A Survey on Privacy Protection of Blockchain: The Technology and Application. *IEEE Access : Practical Innovations, Open Solutions*, *8*, 108766–108781. https://doi.org/https://doi.org/10.1109/ACCESS.2020.2994294. DOI: 10.1109/ACCESS.2020.2994294

Wang, N., Zhou, X., Lu, X., Guan, Z., Wu, L., Du, X., & Guizani, M. (2019). When Energy Trading Meets Blockchain in Electrical Power System: The State of the Art. *Applied Sciences (Basel, Switzerland)*, *9*(8), 1561. DOI: 10.3390/app9081561

Wang, R., Xu, C., Dong, R., Luo, Z., Zheng, R., & Zhang, X. (2023). A Secured Big-Data Sharing Platform for Materials Genome Engineering: State-of-the-Art, Challenges and Architecture. *Future Generation Computer Systems*, *142*, 59–74. DOI: 10.1016/j.future.2022.12.026

Yeom, S., Choi, S., Chi, J., & Park, S. (2021). Blockchain-Based Employment Contract System Architecture Allowing Encrypted Keyword Searches. *Electronics (Basel)*, *10*(9), 1086. DOI: 10.3390/electronics10091086

Zheng, Z., Xie, S., Dai, H.-N., Chen, W., Chen, X., Weng, J., & Imran, M. (2020). An Overview on Smart Contracts: Challenges, Advances and Platforms. *Future Generation Computer Systems*, *105*, 475–491. DOI: 10.1016/j.future.2019.12.019

Chapter 6
Trust Challenges in AI-Driven Fintech:
Navigating the Ethical Frontier

Payal Sharma
https://orcid.org/0009-0004-6589-0099
Acropolis Faculty of Management and Research, India

Syed Sajid Hussain
https://orcid.org/0009-0009-4982-7125
Chandigarh University, India

Manjit Kour
https://orcid.org/0000-0003-1043-3187
Chandigarh University, India

ABSTRACT

This study explores the ethical, security, and privacy challenges faced by financial technology (Fintech) organizations. It highlights the critical role of ethics in leveraging artificial intelligence (AI) technologies to foster customer trust and loyalty. A systematic review of available literature was employed to analyze empirical data addressing Fintech challenges for customer privacy and ethical concerns. The study examines the factors influencing customer trust, such as real-time interaction, risk perception, and transparency. The outcomes highlight the need for consumer data protection and protection of the law, as well as trust through public disclosure. The study suggests implementations for managers about how to deploy the specialization between AI and analytical technologies in delivering personalized services, streamlining and saving the firm resources, and reducing service delivery costs.

DOI: 10.4018/979-8-3373-3186-7.ch006

1. INTRODUCTION

AI-powered Fintech has changed the landscape of financial services (Kour, 2025). Everything from fraud detection to customer service is through Algorithms- driven by AI (Kaur & Kour, 2025). This is a significant leap however this has raised some trust issues. Especially related to possible risks (McKnight & Chervany, 2002), trust becomes necessary when dealing with two parties. While trust has been seriously studied for over a few decades, it has become more important with the emergence and proliferation of the internet.

The absence of real-time interaction, the risk level, and the trust factor were significant customer concerns (Pavlou, 2003). Building and sustaining user trust is major challenge for disruptive technologies, including blockchain and AI. Companies are leveraging the potential of these technologies without undermining consumer trust. Fintech organizations could also benefit from integrating Artificial Intelligence and analytical technologies because of the customized services to their customers, resource optimization, and cost-cutting, thus providing them a competitive edge compared to other market players (Mars & Gouider, 2017; Kour, 2025).

Financial Technology (Fintech) is changing traditional modes of carrying out financial transactions (Madan & Kour, 2024). FinTech is broader than e-banking and digitalization; therefore, it is a practical application of advanced means to meet consumer needs. According to Park et al. (2016), there is a unique opportunity emerging by automation technology to advance finance in such a manner that it can enhance the value to customers and offer firms the ability to grow their revenues. The Reserve Bank of India's most recent report for April-September 2021-22 reveals the rapid advancement of digital payments and Fintech in India (Table 1). This chapter will explore the multifaceted trust challenges companies face after implementing AI-powered Fintech solutions.

Table 1.

Item	Volume (Lakh)			Value (Crore)		
	2019-20	2020-21	2021-22	2019-20	2020-21	2021-22
1. Large Value Credit Transfers – RTGS	1,507	1,592	2,078	13,11,56,475	10,55,99,849	12,86,57,516
2. Credit Transfers	2,06,297	3,17,868	5,77,935	2,85,56,593	3,35,04,226	4,27,28,006
2.1 AEPS (Fund Transfers)	10	11	10	469	623	575
2.2 APBS	16,747	14,373	12,573	99,048	1,11,001	1,33,345
2.3 ECS Cr	18.3	0	0	5,146	0	0
2.4 IMPS	25,792	32,783	46,625	23,37,541	29,41,500	41,71,037

continued on following page

Table 1. Continued

Item	Volume (Lakh)			Value (Crore)		
	2019-20	2020-21	2021-22	2019-20	2020-21	2021-22
2.5 NACH	11,100	16,465	18,758	10,37,079	12,16,535	12,81,685
2.6 NEFT	27,445	30,928	40,407	2,29,45,580	2,51,30,910	2,87,25,463
2.7 UPI	1,25,186	2,23,307	4,59,561	21,31,730	41,03,658	84,15,900
3. Debit Transfers and Direct Debits	6,027	10,457	12,189	6,05,939	8,65,520	10,34,444
3.1 BHIM Aadhaar Pay	91	161	228	1,303	2,580	6,113
3.2 ECS Dr	1.14	0	0	38.607	0	0
3.3 NACH	5,842	9,646	10,755	6,04,397	8,62,027	10,26,641
3.4 NETC	93	650	1,207	200	913	1,689
4. Card Payments	72,384	57,787	61,783	14,34,813	12,91,799	17,01,851
4.1 Credit Cards	21,773	17,641	22,399	7,30,894	6,30,414	9,71,638
4.2 Debit Cards	50,611	40,146	39,384	7,03,920	6,61,385	7,30,213
5. Prepaid Payment Instruments	53,941	49,366	65,783	2,14,860	1,97,095	2,79,416
6. Paper-based Instruments	10,414	6,704	6,999	78,24,822	56,27,108	66,50,333
Total Digital Payments (1+2+3+4+5)	**3,40,155**	**4,37,068**	**7,19,768**	**16,19,68,681**	**14,14,58,488**	**17,44,01,233**
Total Retail Payments (2+3+4+5+6)	**3,49,063**	**4,42,180**	**7,24,689**	**3,86,37,028**	**4,14,85,747**	**5,23,94,049**
Total Payments (1+2+3+4+5+6)	**3,50,570**	**4,43,772**	**7,26,767**	**16,97,93,503**	**14,70,85,596**	**18,10,51,565**

Source: https://www.rbi.org.in/

1.1 Theoretical Overview

Significant advancements in the fintech sector are the result of data science applications. Big data analysis, cloud computing, and integration with automation drive digitalization forward (Lacity & Willcocks, 2016). Consequently, the Financial sector utilizes fintech to the fullest to gain customer satisfaction (Malaquias & Hwang, 2019). Fintech utilizes technological platforms and mobiles to enable customers to access banking services like bank statements, transaction details, and other activities with the ease of anywhere anytime facility (Stewart & Jürjens, 2018b).

The integration of fintech with AI notably enables brilliant handling of large volumes of data and thus supports significant decision-making (Daníelsson et al., 2022). Fintech firms combine Artificial Intelligence with big-data analytics to provide low-cost customized financial services to their customers (Mars & Gouider, 2017).

Ethical and privacy considerations are also becoming important while applying big data with AI for fintech firms (Yang et al., 2022).

The AI in finance has raised questions of ethical nature (Hussain & Sharma, 2025). They include issues of justice by design, ownership, privacy, and transparency (Saltz & Dewar, 2019). Decision-making methods need to focus on objectivity since there is complete data that may lead to biased decisions affecting people's lives. (Daníelsson et al., 2022). Additionally, customer trust and loyalty depend on transparency in handling their data management system (Vannucci & Pantano, 2020).

Customer privacy is the main concern in the application of AI. Here, compliance plays a major role. Moreover, lucidly conveying privacy and security protocols to clients can reinforce belief, as misunderstandings often undermine trust more than actual vulnerabilities. Therefore, fintech enterprises should ensure protections are comprehensible to non-specialists while maintaining diligence over sensitive subscriber information (La Torre et al., 2019). A further consideration is the complexity of constructing reliability while retaining data-driven development and technological progress. Streamlining regulations presents challenges when balancing corporate advantages with privacy rights and transparency expectations. Overall, conscientious handling of sensitive client details, clear communication of security precautions, and accountable responses to breaches will be paramount for the industry's long-term viability amid growing concern for digital consent and oversight (Stewart & Jürjens, 2018b).

While concerns regarding vulnerabilities in online financial systems and data breaches have rightfully induced wariness for many patrons of digital banking services, addressing such issues with improved protections for sensitive information and strengthened cyber defenses is paramount to cultivating confidence and encouraging further participation. (Swammy et al., 2018; Laksamana et al., 2022). Safeguarding privacy and fortifying security play integral roles in assuaging apprehensions and allowing both individuals and organizations to realize the full benefits of fintech's convenient and innovative offerings - but only if priority is given to assuaging legitimate worries regarding how personal data may be vulnerable.

Financial technology usage is posing the issue of trust in the finance sector. Corporate digital responsibility (CDR) evolved as one solution to this issue. CDR uses customer data ethically with automated technology (Jelovac et al., 2021). The concept of digital responsibility can contribute to developing customer trust (Saeidi et al., 2015). To establish society and customer trust, fintech enterprises should maintain ethical practices in data management by incorporating advanced technologies (Herden et al., 2021).

1.2 Financial Technology (Fintech)

Fintech's Financial Technology is the new kid on the block regarding innovation in any industry; it is the intersection between finance and technology. It includes everything from banking to payments to investments to insurance, a set of solutions to digitally transform all corners of financial services..Fintech has become the new blood in the traditional financial industry, with newer strategies fueled by technological developments like AI and mobile apps. Using these technologies, Fintech companies can offer their financial services faster, easier, and more customer-focused, often competing with traditional financial institutions.

The explosion of fintech worldwide is driven by filling the numerous gaps and inefficiencies of the traditional financial system. Because of the digital platforms and faster processes, Fintechs offer transactions in less time, at lower costs, and improved accessibility, which is much needed for unbanked people. Smart FinTech results from the root path that social motivation for FinTech innovation drives, and continuous FinTech innovation enables its advancement and application. Sustained innovation and research are crucial in every aspect of smart FinTech, with DSAI (Data et al.) technology playing a vital role.The most common variables of DSAI-led innovations in fintech are credit scoring, customer chatbots, and trading help. Fintech allows to manage customers effeciently due to its innovative features. It is changing financial landscape with the technology.

1.3 Trust with Artificial Intelligence

If AI needs to be better understood and applied to deliver economic value, leadership could start questioning the value of AI initiatives. The work climate is critical for the teams working on AI projects not to feel pressured, as this will negatively impact the project's outcome (Patel, 2018).Several empirical studies show that the transparency and explainability of AI impact trust positively (Research references: (Calhoun et al.,2019)).

Experiments conducted in military environments suggest heightened transparency bolsters trust in collaborative scenarios involving human operators and AI agents. Additionally, explanations have boosted trust as an outcome of a company planning tool designed for new product launches (Du & Ruhe, 2009). Nevertheless, additional research indicates that customer trust is directly related to transparency. Students are more engaged with assessment tools powered by AI that offer transparency, which gives them a feeling of fairness with the algorithm. It also boosts their trust factor (R. et al., 2016).

A significant trust-related challenge pertains to the precision of automated technology, as inaccuracies in results can result in potential harm. Customized automated technologies can be designed to maximize various accuracy metrics, exhibiting high accuracy rates for various predictions (e.g., white men outcomes) while performing less accurately for others (e.g., minority groups outcomes) (Wallach, 2018). One such issue was analyzed in an automation study where facial recognition was done with AI algorithms (J. et al., 2018). Therefore, only accuracy metrics will not work efficiently to develop trust in AI. Instead, transparency and fair processes are vital considerations.

An issue associated with automated AI revolves around the risk of deskilling when domain experts excessively depend on automated systems. A study discovered that AI advisors are trusted more by investors (Heid, 2018). However, contrasting research suggests that an over-reliance on AI systems is more commonly observed among novices, as experts generally exhibit a lower inclination to trust AI systems.

Data extraction involves trust issues, which mainly point towards privacy issues. End users fear what data will be shared, with potential privacy infringements leading to a loss of self-determination. Given how long it has taken for this to happen, these vulnerabilities could exist at the level of society, poorly affected by the expectation of privacy maintenance.

Facebook CEO Mark Zuckerberg stated that privacy is no longer a social norm (Osnos, 2018), a contentious proposition. Privacy has been a fundamental right for individuals, irrespective of their nationality. Many democracies have identified privacy as a fundamental right. Individuals also care for their privacy, which might not be consistent with this sentiment (Kokolakis, 2017). Automated systems, especially high-end algorithmic systems, deal with significant data processing that distinguishes them qualitatively from traditional IT artifacts.

In a recent nationwide survey, the perception of the sufficiency of AI laws and their governance substantially affects the trust factor. Prioritizing the establishment of verifiable trustworthiness through effective governance might be more crucial and effective than pursuing explanations for individual outcomes (J. et al., 2018). To establish a trust factor in automation, all the related stakeholders should come forward to control biases and ethical data handling to secure customer privacy. The primary risk considerations from advancing key financial technologies have been outlined, along with proposed research directions for developing risk measurement models suitable for managing and mitigating these associated risks.

1.4 Trust

Trust becomes crucial in any interaction between two parties, especially when at least one is at risk (McKnight & Chervany, 2002). While trust ebbs and flows depending on circumstance, its role has grown more pivotal amid networked connections and untethering interactions. Though scrutinized for decades, trust was brought to the fore with the digital domain's proliferation, remote exchanges inheriting perceived hazards, and emphasizing trust's currency. Once face-to-face, relationships now traverse bytes; what keeps counterparts cooperating across distances merits unpacking. Pavlou (2003) underscores trust anchoring distributed dealings in an uncertain virtual setting that jettisons visual and audio cues upon which instinct leans.

This obstacle lessened as measures were developed to alleviate risks and foster trust. Safeguarding consumer trust presents a present-day hurdle for innovative technologies like blockchain, virtual environments, and automated technology. Companies aim to leverage new technologies to maintain, rather than erode, consumer trust.

Insurtech, as a part of fintech powered by automation, epitomizes yet another revolutionary trend where the evaluation of trust carries weight and influences adoption. Numerous Fintech and Insurtech enterprises are startups, potentially leading to substantial changes in established finance and insurance entities. For instance, AI-driven chatbots or virtual assistants are extensively employed in interactions with individuals acquiring insurance or initiating insurance claims (Zarifis et al., 2021).

The literature on trust spans various domains, including business and education. However, the foundations commonly underpinning these areas often originate from psychology and sociology (Aoki, 2020).The trust dimensions is frequently cited in scholarly works (Gefen, 1997) Competence: Defined as the “ability of the trustee to do what the trust needs” (McKnight et al., 2002). Integrity: Integrity involves “trustee honesty and promise-keeping” (McKnight et al., 2002). It is defined by the impartial and truthful demeanor displayed during customer engagement. Benevolence: Described as “trustee caring and motivation to act in the trustor's interests” (McKnight et al., 2002). The benevolence signifies that they prioritize the interests and needs of customers over those of other stakeholders. Trust is an individual's belief in another person or, in the context of our study, confidence in the reliability of a fintech platform (Zarifis & Cheng, 2022). In our examination, we specifically concentrate on trust in fintech platforms, which relates to customer's confidence in the security.

Financial technology progress relies on investors trust. Bunnell et al. (2020) demonstrated that a system founded upon automated recommendations could enhance the user experience and their faith. However, Albayati et al. (2020) suggest that AI provides various options to strengthen customer security, positing some users remain wary of relinquishing control to algorithms. Streamlining convoluted fiscal operations has the potential to foster faith, but solely if coupled with individualized elucidations adapted to fluctuating comprehension capacities and persistent monitoring guarantees equitable consequences. Advancement necessitates reconciling progress with explanation and safeguards to alleviate any staying qualms.

Similarly, Yan et al. (2020), employing a user trust evaluation model, observed that considerable data mining support can enhance user trust. Mature fintech applications improve precision, security, and dependability compared to manual data processing. A psychological perspective presumes that the assurance of trust is notably shaped by the security of technology (Anderson, 2010). Thus, improving the platform's security is anticipated to foster user trust. Consequently, fintech correlates with increased user trust in financial platforms.

Corporate Digital Responsibility (CDR) is one such term that studies practices used by organizations to manage ethical data-handling processes that came into existence (Jelovac et al., 2021). CDR entails organizations recognizing the need to practice beneficial societal outcomes of technology. (Herden et al., 2021). CDR supports to identify and manage ethical dilemmas of using technology for data management. (Lobschat et al., 2021). Research indicates that companies fostering a CDR mindset experience performance benefits, leading to positive financial results, including increased customer satisfaction and an enhanced corporate image. (Saeidi et al., 2015). Thus, it enhances organizational performance (Lobschat et al., 2021).

Trust is of utmost significance, particularly concerning digital platforms, collectively known as digital trust. It is defined as "our willingness to expose ourselves to the actions of others under the assumption that they have good intentions and will treat us appropriately." Trust in context of digital space relies on technologies used. It represents users' confidence in the capacity of advanced technologies to create a secure environment for data protection (Jelovac et al., 2021).

1.5 Ethical Considerations

Significant changes in organizational operations across various economic sectors result from the advancement of digitalization, driven by technological catalysts (Lacity & Willcocks, 2016). With the increasing prevalence of Internet usage, financial institutions can now offer efficient services to customers (Malaquias & Hwang, 2019). This trend propelled financial technology (fintech) to improve banking services, utilizing advanced technological platforms such as accessing bank accounts, receiving transaction alerts, and other notifications. Fintech firms aggressively use mobile application features to increase customers' convenience and ease of financial transactions (Stewart & Jürjens, 2018b).

Artificial Intelligence, a sophisticated innovation synthesized to simulate human brainpower, has allowed for the assimilation and examination of immense troves of information from diverse origins(Daníelsson et al., 2022). Through these algorithms' utilization of substantial training datasets involving inputs and outputs to identify similarities and "self-educate," machines have been capable of autonomously synthesizing and disseminating knowledge. However, specific concerns persist regarding systemic risks emerging from unforeseen interactions within convoluted, interlinked networks and vulnerabilities potentially exploitable by ill-intentioned actors. Continuous oversight and refinement will be necessary to optimize the rewards while mitigating drawbacks as this burgeoning field evolves rapidly.

Adopting AI empowers fintech firms to derive valuable information supporting big data analysis decisions. Big data, a vast collection of data from diverse sources in different formats, presents notable challenges to traditional data management methods (Mars & Gouider, 2017). Big data has emerged as a crucial asset for capturing customer information through data collection (Erraissi & Belangour, 2018). Fintech firms use big data with AI to serve their customers with personalized services. However, this integration raises ethical issues (Yang et al., 2022).

AI and large dataset integration call for a careful data management system as it may affect making decisions ethically. While datasets can harbor intrinsic prejudices leading to unjust outcomes for certain groups, addressing this issue requires meaningful action from financial technology firms. Daníelsson et al. (2022) demonstrated how biases in data collection processes can propagate, skewing algorithmic determinations in ways that disproportionately impact particular segments of customers. To remedy such disparities, companies must prioritize diversifying the examples that machine learning models analyze to represent the full diversity of each company's clientele authentically.

AI needs to be handled properly, as societal biases may occur, and choices out of various options may contemplate decisions. Moreover, judiciously evaluating moral implications at each phase of analytic processing strengthens safeguards against even nuanced notions of discrimination infiltrating results or decisions. By no means is the duty complete with only good intentions. However, ongoing vigilance and adjustment as needed can help guarantee equitable treatment under the law for all people, irrespective of background.

Fintech companies face a critical concern about using ethical measures in data collection and handling because this is the foundation of developing customer trust and confidence, while transparency is the key. As FINTECH continue to grow, personal data rights come into play. Customer data powers innovation, but gaining trust relies on having proper consent and security. Some sentences are simple, others more complex. Varied lengths show respect for individual choice in how firms access our lives' building blocks. Laws ensure fair use today without compromising tomorrow's freedoms. Options bring out human growth; walls decline. Together, through open discussion of shared hopes, solutions can emerge.

1.6 Data Privacy and Security

The concept of the privacy paradox is relevant to customer trust (Martin et al., 2020). Websites providing personalized services may raise apprehensions regarding collecting personal information (Przegalinska, et al, 2019). The social presence of a chatbot significantly influences trust in a website (Araujo, 2018). Simultaneously, these personalized services may enhance the convenience of using a website (Cheng & Jiang, 2020). trust is an important factor in the use of chatbots, especially when users have privacy concerns, leading them to be cautious about sharing excessive personal information (Rese et al., 2020). An integral aspect of trust involves anthropomorphism, wherein human traits are attributed to chatbots (Vander et al., 2021).

Customer loyalty is primarily driven by satisfaction, trust, and commitment (Van Vuuren et al, 2012). According to (Bryant et al., 2002), satisfaction of customers acts as a captivating predictor of the retention of customers. Protecting people's information in digital finance is the key to success and providing all necessary compliance with laws and regulations regarding customer confidentiality. Individuals are granted rights over their data under the General Data Protection Regulation (GDPR), including the right to request deletion (Ayaburi, 2022).

Companies ought to implement measures to safeguard customer data and its utilization. Companies must implement multiple measures to prevent data fraud and adhere to data protection laws. It indicates using advanced technologies, protocols, and policies to protect customer personal data (Beg et al., 2022).

Handling employee data is essential for ensuring ethical and responsible big data management (Stewart & Jürjens, 2018a). To protect personnel data, companies should train their employees and implement protocols and practices for data handling (Abidin et al., 2019). Ethical concerns while using automation add to managing fair outcomes in data management (Abed & Anupam, 2022).

Employee accountability is vital in guaranteeing data security and protection within organizations. Inadequate internal controls have been recognized as contributing to data fraud and asset mismanagement (Lokanan, 2014). To reduce data security risk, companies should emphasize training and thorough general recruitment to ensure data protection. Factors contributing to data breaches include employee misconduct, such as unauthorized access and theft of customer data, and non-compliance with customer data protection (Abidin et al., 2019).

Leaders should focus on data security measures, developing customer trust through strategies, and automated banking for enhanced customer experience to increase competitiveness (Liyanaarachchi et al., 2020). Consent is vital in safeguarding customer interest and deciding when to use and delete personal data (Abidin et al., 2019). Data security compliance requires a workforce with appropriate skills to combat digital challenges (Liyanaarachchi et al., 2021).

2. MINI CASE STUDIES: TRUST AND ETHICAL ISSUES IN INDIAN FINTECH

The burgeoning Fintech ecosystem in India provides a distinct backdrop to study trust dilemmas in AI-enabled financial services. Mini case studies from the Indian Fintech landscape which exhibit the key ethical, privacy and transparency-related issues that are pertinent to the study.

Case 1: Paytm and The Regulatory Eyeball

Earlier in 2024, RBI levied certain restrictions against Paytm Payments Bank, halting the onboarding of new customers, in relation to violation of procedures involving KYC and data processing. The whole thing culminated into the public distrust and panic regarding the safety of their stored funds and private data — all thanks to this regulatory move. This highlighted the need for regulatory compliance, ethical AI practices, and transparent data in order to restore consumer trust. Paytm has since moved its core operations to partner banks, and pledged an extensive redesign of its internal compliance framework (Reserve Bank of India [RBI], 2022).

Case 2: Aadhaar-UPI Integration: The Privacy Paradox

Aadhaar was linked with India's Unified Payments Interface (UPI), promising biometrics-based identities for hassle-free transactional identity Yours monetised (coin)® All Rights Reserved. But that proved to be controversial with privacy advocates, who reacted against a slew of data leaks and unauthorised account access cases. Users raised issues about opaque data usage and poor informed consent. The National Payments Corporation of India (NPCI) then designed consent-based features, multi-factor authentication and user control dashboards to mitigate the privacy paradox and restore trust (Martin et al., 2020; NPCI, 2022).

Case 3: HDFC bank AI Chatbot 'Eva'

In 2018, HDFC Bank introduced "Eva" an AI-based chatbot, to offer a round the clock solution for all banking needs as a prime support to increasing the engagement with customer. At first, people took aim at the chatbot, as it struggled to come up with good answers to more complex queries and there was a lack of transparency in how decisions were made. Without any escalation paths or insight into how the recommendations were produced, customers found it hard to trust the responses. The bank then provided more explainability features, enabled escalation to human agents, and trained Eva using supervised feedback mechanisms to increase reliability and transparency (Cheng & Jiang, 2020; The Economic Times, 2021).

Case 4: Zerodha and Ethical Data Use

When the news broke at the start of the year that India's largest stock brokerage firm has decided for commercialization their customer trading data CTO of Zerodha and Twitter and started a debate on ethical AI use. Yet the company had never sold third-party data, and the perception chasm was wide because at the time there were no publicly available company policies for data usage. In the face of this, Zerodha leadership went a step further and published data governance principles, pledged to not monetise data, and created frictionless user-consent mechanism—creating an even stronger corporate digital responsibility (Jelovac, Ljubojević, & Ljubojević, 2021; Zerodha, 2022).

Case 5: Beware of API security breach: Razorpay

Razorpay — A full-stack payments solution for businesses in India and overseas, Rajorpay — suffered a data breach in 2022, as attackers gained access to its API (application programming interface) logs. No monetary loss was incurred, but the incident highlighted that backend systems powered with AI are also as vulnerable as human beings if continuous vigilance is not maintained. Post the incident, Razorpay engaged in a series of timely public disclosures, pin-pointing zero-trust security architecture and immediate deployment of AI-based threat detection tools. This case emphasizes the significance of ethical cybersecurity practices in maintaining trust of users on AI-enabled Fintech platforms (Beg et al., 2022).

3. DISCUSSION

The integration of artificial intelligence (AI) into financial technology (Fintech) has achieved significant speed in recent years, making the financial services landscape unrecognizable from just a decade ago. Though such innovations hold promise for personalization, operational efficiency, and financial inclusion, they also pose challenges related to the nature of trust in complex systems. As elucidated in this paper, the issues like ethical concerns, data privacy risks, lack of transparency of algorithms, and regulatory uncertainties have formed an impediment to the mass adoption of AI-enabled Fintech solutions. Based on the insights from the literature, the discussion then highlights a few practical forms of these issues illustrated through a few Indian real-life case studies.

Customer trust, a dynamic construct based on perceptions of competence, integrity and benevolence (McKnight & Chervany, 2002), underpins these challenges. In the context of digital financial environments, where human-to-human interaction is often absent, these perceptions are mediated by the way artificial intelligence systems are designed and communicated. Consumers demand transparency and fairness leave no choice to organizations, especially if they are dealing with personal well as financial data (Vannucci & Pantano, 2020). Nonetheless, this trust is compromised as AI systems make black box decisions regarding things such as credit scoring, insurance pricing, or investment recommendations (Daníelsson et al., 2022) which lack explainability and consent mechanisms to the users.

Second, there is the privacy paradox—many users value personalized digital services, but they are discomforted by the data practices used to deliver them (Martin et al., 2020). Big data analytics have been utilized by enterprise customers by Fintech firms to provide real-time credit decisions, fraud detection, customer support, and even to monitor transaction performance and liquidity among financial institutions and corporations. But there are still real concerns over how this data is collected, stored, and processed — little is known by the public, and even less by those who use these services, about explicit consent related to this data. Such opacity in data handling by AI systems may increase mistrust, especially in emerging markets like India where digital literacy is different (Przegalinska et al., 2019).

Another important ethical consideration regarding the integration of AI is bias and fairness! Especially for minorities, or underbanked populations, discrimination might get perpetuated through algorithms that were trained on skewed datasets (Wallach, 2018). This is especially problematic in high-stakes domains such as credit scoring or loan approval, where mistakes lead to financial exclusion. Facial recognition systems have been shown to reflect these issues with much higher error rates showing up for someone with dark skin (Buolamwini and Gebru, 2018). If these potential biases are not dealt with, they not only affect the credibility of Fintech solutions but also bring fairness of technology deployment in question (societal concern) (Williams, 2021).

In order to add more context to these challenges, this study reflects in real case-studies from India which illustrate the practical ground reflected from the theoretical challenges stated above. These exemplars illustrate the extent to which firms navigate through this complex trust, ethics, and privacy landscape in Fintech.

These micro case studies illustrate the notion that trust in AI based financial technology is not a purely technological issue but a multidimensional construct that is necessarily affected by ethics, transparency, regulation and communication strategies. Trust will have to be worked at, built on, and maintained through a combination of hardware and software solutions, an educated consumer and legislative actions.

In solving these issues, Fintech organizations must implement privacy-by-design frameworks, meaning that consent, explainability, and ethical fairness is incorporated from the start-stage planning on the systems development (Saltz & Dawar, 2019). Regulators therefore need to build frameworks that are flexible and give space to innovation while still holding it to account. Trust-enabling ecosystems can be created faster through collaboration across sectors among technology developers, regulators, consumer advocates, and financial institutions.

Additionally, users should also exercise digital trust literacy. Consumers should be informed as to how their data will be used, and the impact of decisions made using AI. Programs that educate the general public, transparency reports, and easily digestible privacy policies can help users make better decisions.

To sum it up, the future of Fintech both in India and overseas lies only in the hands of the ethics frontier cartoon and the menagerie of the ethical challenges. AI has extraordinary potential to enable broader access to financial services and greater utilization, but must be aligned with user-centric values like transparency, fairness and privacy. Those organisations that establish trust as a fundamental, strategic asset—not as an afterthought compliance requirement—will have a key advantage in the new era of the digital economy.

4. RECOMMENDATIONS

Fintech as the business of the future brings massive space for innovation and efficient customer-centric financial services through artificial intelligence (AI). But fulfilling this potential hinges upon customer trust, ethical governance, and strong data protection safeguards. This study and its findings yield several recommendations that can be applied by Fintech organizations, policymakers, and AI system designers. The recommendations are intended to inform the laying down of transparent, ethical, and trusted Fintech ecosystem framed in the Indian ethos whether in India or beyond.

Incorporate Good Design Practices into AI Systems

The AI regulatory framework for Fintech should ensure that all AI systems are built on ethical foundations that promote fairness, non-discrimination and human dignity. Risk-based guidelines should subject algorithmic decision-making to stringent audits for bias, especially in areas including but not limited to credit scoring, insurance underwriting, and fraud detection. For example, the study of Buolamwini and Gebru (2018) have shown that based on biased datasets unfair treatment can lead to some demographic groups, undermining societal trust and increasing inequity. As such, fairness-aware machine learning and diverse training datasets should be incorporated by AI developers to avoid exclusionary results.

AI systems are by definition partly autonomous and these systems should also be designed to be transparent and explainable. Users deserve to know how decisions that may have an impact on their finances are reached. Open AI & Explainability XAI models can improve the confidence of the customer significantly when they give interpretability and transparency of the algorithmic reasoning in black-box models (Doshi-Velez & Kim, 2017). When an AI declines a loan or marks a transaction as suspicious, the system has to give an explanation that is understandable and useful. Mechanisms for such transparency do not only have an ethical background but also help in achieving accountability and user satisfaction.

Implement Privacy-by-Design and Secure-by-Design Frameworks

Business model upgrades High-profile attacks have proven that identity (identity fraud) in the Fintech space is extremely attractive to criminals as it reveals personal privacy so Fintech firms, should be pre-emptive by design, not just in the eye of regulators; these principles must be built into the design of the system. As Cavoukian (2009) proposed, the concept of "privacy-by-design" calls for data protection during the whole data lifecycle, by preventing and minimizing the collection, storage and processing of data. Granular user consent, data minimization protocols, and anonymization can all be used to limit exposure, and give peace of mind users when it comes to the safety of their data.

In addition, the best way to mitigate cybersecurity threats is through "secure by design" practices. The recent hacking of Indian Fintech (like that of Razorpay's API vulnerabilities) signifies the importance of enhancing governance (Beg, Khan, & Anjum, 2022). Businesses must embrace zero-trust security architectures and regularly correlate pen testing to find weak points. Data breaches are predominantly caused by insider negligence; therefore, it is important that employees are trained to identify and mitigate internal threats(Abidin, Nawawi, & Salin, 2019).

Enhance Regulatory Frameworks & Industrial Standards

The speed of the Fintech evolution in India require the regulatory framework to evolve in tandem. Hence, Innovation across customer protection space must not be perceived negatively but should be enabled while ensuring protection of customer interest. Responsible AI | Regulators, such as the RBI and SEBI, should introduce AI governance standards, mandating minimum requirements with respect to algorithmic transparency, data protection, fairness assessments as well as grievance redressal mechanisms.

An adaptation of the European Union's General Data Protection Regulation (GDPR) and the proposed AI Act provides a basis for India to institutionalise a unified Digital Trust and AI Responsibility Framework. Such a framework should apply to all Fintech participants—be they banks, startups, or third-party service providers—and should require privacy audits, assessments of automated decision-making algorithms, and public disclosures of compliance with the framework. How public-private collaborations can facilitate the alignment of regulatory and operational realities to make ethical AI a competitive advantage instead of a compliance cost

Second, similar to the regulatory sandboxes that the RBI has already begun, we should create programs that allow for the testing of ethical/secure AI applications in the real-world sandbox of a particular economic sector. Such regulated environments enable regulators, in advance of a wider rollout, to see and understand what new technologies mean, and to encourage safe experimentation (Bott & Milkau, 2020).

Cultivate Corporate Digital Responsibility (CDR) and Ethical Culture

Fintech organizations need to take Corporate Digital Responsibility (CDR) beyond compliance and as a strategic imperative. CDR includes the responsible use of technological and data for societal value creation (Jelovac et al., 2021) During this time that many companies are awakening to the need to be good corporate citizens, organizations should feel free to take the lead in digital ethics, committing themselves publicly to internal policies related to data governance, responsible AI usage, and even approaches to customer communication. It can make accountability an institutional part of the media by publishing transparency reports and utilizing stakeholders through digital ethics boards.

Leaders are the backbone for any ethical cultures. These ethical considerations should be included in the leadership development programs, employee training modules and performance evaluations. Top management's focus on the ethicality and long-term trust over short-term profit will create conditions that are needed to sustain innovation as well as customer loyalty (Lobschat et al., 2021).

Boost Digital Trust Literacy and Consumer-Centric Agency

Trust in AI-based Fintech can neither be only a tech-related issue nor a pure regulatory one with AI-enhanced Fintech either; it requires a change within the interests of the end-user, namely, their digital literacy. Most consumers do not know how AI systems work and how their data is used, especially in emerging economies such as India. The lack of understanding may create distrust, fear or abuse. So, Fintech providers need to be upfront and help customers understand their rights, the data used and how AI systems work.

It can be done through tutorials embedded in mobile apps, in-app explainability features, webinars for consumers, or multilingual campaigns to raise awareness. Additionally, businesses should also offer an uncomplicated and easily accessible privacy setting where users can manage what data is being gathered from them and how that information is being used. This kind of empowerment helps increase transparency as well as enriches the relationship between the customers and the digital platforms (Cheng & Jiang, 2020).

Moreover, grievance redressal must be accountable and transparent. In addition, users must be able to contest any real-world consequences resulting from automated decisions, with human review where appropriate. To exemplify trust and fairness, setting up ethical help desks or AI-ethics officers can be the way to go in an organization.

Ethical AI Innovation by Various Stakeholders

Finally, ethical AI innovation in Fintech requires supportive ecosystems of collaboration. Pragmatic public-sector-based guidelines, frameworks and tools that help strike a balance between innovation and the public interest should be co-developed by fintech firms, academic researchers, regulators, civil society organizations, and technology vendors alike. This paves the way to creating and sharing the open-source tools for fairness audits, bias detection, and explainability around which the industry can rally together. Universities and think tanks ought to partner with Fintech startups to implement interdisciplinary research and ethical review boards to include ethics throughout product development cycles.

International coordination is also necessary. Global frameworks such as OECD or IEEE on responsible AI are useful and can help in building guidelines so that Indian Fintech innovation is competitive and globally credible.

5. CONTRIBUTIONS OF THE STUDY

As AI becomes pervasive in our personal and professional spheres, organizations often face the challenge of determining where to direct their focus initially. Whether the insurance sector's future entails a highly streamlined form of the existing model or a shift towards revolutionary finance utilizing blockchains (DeFi), automation assumes a central role. The model developed in this research provides a framework for organizations in the insurance sector to concentrate on the different variables influencing consumer trust in Insurtech.

The companies may understand all four elements presented in study and seek to offset drawbacks in areas with less control by strengthening elements where they enjoy control. A consumer's view of these four variables may differ depending on the context. Therefore, the organization has to get technology and business intelligence experts on board to fine-tune its strategy.

In addition, this study supports the applicability of trust transfer theory, and its applicability extends to the new context of Fintech companies. It means that, on the one hand, there is a conditioning of objective external factors influencing users' perceptions and, consequently, behavioral intentions toward adopting financial technology. According to the study, trust is a significant mechanism for developing an ethical culture in the fintech domain.

The research comes with some practical implications. First, the results provide important input for Fintech companies and traditional financial institutions, for example, for a bank, in identifying user needs and creating user-centered solutions with greater ethical efficiency. Secondly, current work creates consciousness about accurate and credible ethical and innovative financial alternatives existing at local levels, building a case for an alternative to the current financial environment and inclusive finance for a better society. This is especially the case in emerging markets, where there is a terrific opportunity for a Fintech that is built on a strong ethical foundation. AI can transition employee and customer experiences from physical to digital environments. Therefore, it is essential to integrate banking operations with advanced AI solutions.

6. CONCLUSION

Artificial intelligence (AI) has been a revolutionary trend in Fintech infrastructure by facilitating distributed decision-making in real-time, customizing services, and streamlining processes. Yet, the same disrupters also have put fundamental questions of trust, data privacy, algorithmic fairness, and ethical governance on the front burner. This paper examined these issues intricately based on theoretical, empirical, and case-based evidences with periodic emphasis on recent Indian scenario to unveil the complexities surrounding trust in AI powered Fintech eco systems.

It cannot be disputed that trust is an integral part of the digital sentiments for all financial transactions with success. AI-based Fintech services are virtual-based, in contrast to traditional face surroundings banking services which considerably involve face-to-face contact. Because trust in these systems is essentially transmitted through the technical interfaces, customers only adopt it and continue to use in light of their perception regarding the safety, transparency and ethical behavior of the system (McKnight & Chervany, 2002). But overall concern about the ability of AI systems to process sensitive personal and financial data, its management of how they make decisions, and the possibility of algorithmic bias limiting AI's taking hold among users (Vannucci & Pantano, 2020).

This research affirms, however, that ethical design and implementation of AI are simply essential and indispensable prerequisites of trust in Fintech. Fairness-aware architecture is an important aspect of AI systems; biases in training data can be reduced and outputs of AI systems can be made explainable and open to contestation by users when making high-stakes decisions that cannot easily be held up to scrutiny, such as loan approvals or fraud detection. Fundamental to the concept of fairness are the distributional characteristics of data sets (Buolamwini & Gebru, 2018) that may lead to dramatic accuracy gaps for under-represented populations as illustrated in the seminal work on face recognition systems by Buolamwini and Gebru (2018). Such inequalities can result in both financial exclusion and systemic inequality in Fintech.

There must also be regulatory frameworks in place to ensure that user privacy and consent are at the forefront of data governance. There should be an implementation of the principal of "privacy-by-design" on all Fintech platforms, as data collection, processing, and storage scope must be aligned in an ethical and legal fashion (Cavoukian, 2009). This is especially important in emerging markets such as India where there is an asymmetric nature of digital awareness and users end up becoming taciturn to widespread data sharing under unclear or coercive processes. The privacy paradox (Martin et al., 2020)—users exchanging their personal data in return for convenience despite lacking true comprehension of the associated implications—continues to present a challenge.

The study also considers the impact of various regulatory bodies and policy frameworks on creating ethical hypothesizing AI ecosystems. While India still has a long way to go on the Fintech regulation path, initiatives such as the RBI's regulatory sandbox and draft guidelines for digital lending suggest movement in the regulatory direction. Having a unified and flexible regulatory framework that promotes innovation as well as accountability will be essential to ensure we strike the right balance between progress and protection. In this regard, Binns (2018) suggests the EU's General Data Protection Regulation (GDPR) and the proposed Artificial Intelligence Act as examples of what such a comprehensive regulatory approach to trust might look like.

The aspects discussed in this paper are evidenced through the real world case studies of Paytm, Zerodha, Razorpay and HDFC Bank. These are examples of both risks and opportunities present in the Fintech sector. Although integrations with AI can improve operational efficiency and personalize customer experience, missteps in ethical oversight, data processing, and communication can permanently break the trust of the public. While the pre-emptive nature of the responses from these companies from transparency disclosures to system re-engineering reflects how ethical lapses can be mitigated, they also indicate a need for wider trust-building systems.

Also, this research suggests Fintech firms to make Corporate Digital Responsibility (CDR) pervading approach towards be the strategic priority. But, CDR involves not only compliance with standards, but also a proactive approach to ethical use of technology, stakeholder engagement, and sustainable innovation (Jelovac et al., 2021). Companies that develop a culture of digital ethics—through leadership accountability, employee training, and public communication—are better positioned to earn trust and gain a sustainable competitive edge.

In conclusion, going forward, it will be necessary to partner with regulators, technology developers and fintech companies to develop transparent, equitable, and inclusive ecosystems. This is not only through building secure infrastructure and explainable AI models, but also creating user awareness and literacy around it. This trust gap can be overcome by ensuring that privacy controls are evident and easily understood and that grievance redressal systems are in place, empowering customers. Trust becomes a two-way street since a digitally literate user base is a better equipped to come to grips with, and respond positively to, AI systems.

To conclude, AI is both a boon and a bane for Fintech a goldmine of opportunities for innovation yet triggering the need for ethical vigilance like never before. More than technical sophistication, the future of Fintech will hinge on the trust equity the sector earns and is able to retain with user. With embedding ethics at every level right from the design of the algorithm to the interaction with the customer, Fintech firms will transition from simply being service providers to digital partners of trust. This study, however, demonstrates that beyond regulatory or technological necessity, constructing trustworthy AI in Fintech – is an urgent moral imperative in the age of intelligent automation.

REFERENCES

Abed, A. K., & Anupam, A. (2022). Review of security issues in the Internet of Things and artificial intelligence-driven solutions. *Security and Privacy*, *6*(3), e285. DOI: 10.1002/spy2.285

Abidin, M. A. Z., Nawawi, A., & Salin, A. S. A. P. (2019). Customer data security and theft: A Malaysian organization's experience. *Information and Computer Security*, *27*(1), 81–100. DOI: 10.1108/ICS-04-2018-0043

Albayati, H., Kim, S. K., & Rho, J. J. (2020). Accepting financial transactions using blockchain technology and cryptocurrency: A customer perspective approach. *Technology in Society*, *62*, 101320. DOI: 10.1016/j.techsoc.2020.101320

Anderson, M. R. (2010). Community psychology, political efficacy, and trust. *Political Psychology*, *31*(1), 59–84. DOI: 10.1111/j.1467-9221.2009.00734.x

Aoki, N.(2020). An experimental study of public trust in AI chatbots in the public sector. Gov. Inf. Q. 37 (4), 101490. http://dx.doi.org/. 101490DOI: 10.1016/j.giq.2020

Araujo, T. (2018). Living up to the chatbot hype: The influence of anthropomorphic design cues and communicative agency framing on conversational agent and company perceptions. *Computers in Human Behavior*, *85*, 183–189. DOI: 10.1016/j.chb.2018.03.051

Ayaburi, E. W. (2022). Understanding online information disclosure: Examination of data breach victimization experience effect. *Information Technology & People*, *36*(1), 95–114. DOI: 10.1108/ITP-04-2021-0262

Beg, S., Saif, U. R. K., & Anjum, A. (2022). Data usage-based privacy and security issues in mobile app recommendation (MAR): A systematic literature review. *Library Hi Tech*, *40*(3), 725–749. DOI: 10.1108/LHT-04-2021-0147

Bryant, A., & Colledge, B. (2002). Trust in electronic commerce business relationships. *Journal of Electronic Commerce Research*, *3*, 32–39.

Bunnell, L., Osei-Bryson, K. M., & Yoon, V. Y. (2020). FinPathlight: Framework for an multiagent recommender system designed to increase consumer financial capability. *Decision Support Systems*, *134*, 113306. DOI: 10.1016/j.dss.2020.113306

Buolamwini, J., & Gebru, T. (2018). "Gender shades: Intersectional accuracy disparities in commercial gender classification". *Conference on Fairness, Accountability and Transparency*, January 2018, pp. 77-91.

Calhoun, C. S., Bobko, P., Gallimore, J. J., & Lyons, J. B. (2019). Linking precursors of interpersonal trust to human-automation trust: An expanded typology and exploratory experiment. *Journal of Trust Research*, *9*(1), 28–46. DOI: 10.1080/21515581.2019.1579730

Cheng, Y., & Jiang, H. (2020). How Do AI-driven Chatbots Impact User Experience? Examining Gratifications, Perceived Privacy Risk, Satisfaction, Loyalty, and Continued Use. *Journal of Broadcasting & Electronic Media*, *64*(4), 592–614. DOI: 10.1080/08838151.2020.1834296

Daníelsson, J., Macrae, R., & Uthemann, A. (2022). Artificial intelligence and systemic risk. *Journal of Banking & Finance*, *140*, 106290. DOI: 10.1016/j.jbankfin.2021.106290

Du, G., & Ruhe, G. (2009). "Does explanation improve the acceptance of decision support for product release planning?", *3rd International Symposium on Empirical Software Engineering and Measurement*, October 2009, pp. 56-68. IEEE. DOI: 10.1109/ESEM.2009.5316049

Erraissi, A., & Belangour, A. (2018). Data sources and ingestion big data layers: Meta-modeling of key concepts and features. *IACSIT International Journal of Engineering and Technology*, *7*, 3607–3612.

Gefen, D. (1997), Building Users' Trust in Freeware Providers and the Effects of This Trust on Users' Perceptions of Usefulness, Ease of Use and Intended Use, Doctoral dissertation, Georgia State University, Atlanta.

Heid, A. K. (2018). "Trust in Homo Artificialis: Evidence from Professional Investors", *American Accounting Association Annual Meeting*, August 2018, Washington USA.

Herden, C. J., Alliu, E., Cakici, A., Cormier, T., Deguelle, C., Gambhir, S., Griffiths, C., Gupta, S., Kamani, S. R., Kiratli, Y.-S., Kispataki, M., Lange, G., Moles de Matos, L., Tripero Moreno, L., Betancourt Nunez, H. A., Pilla, V., Raj, B., Roe, J., Skoda, M., & Edinger-Schons, L. M. (2021). Corporate Digital Responsibility. *Sustainability Management Forum Nachhaltigkeits Management Forum*, *29*(1), 13–29. DOI: 10.1007/s00550-020-00509-x

Hussain, S. S., & Sharma, P. (2025). Challenges and Safeguards. *Artificial Intelligence and Accounting: Ethical, Legal, and Social Implications*, 82.

Jelovac, D., Ljubojevi'c, C., & Ljubojevi'c, L. (2021). HPC in business: The impact of corporate digital responsibility on ˇ building digital trust and responsible corporate digital governance. Digital Policy. *Regulation & Governance*, *24*, 485–497. DOI: 10.1108/DPRG-11-2020-0164

Kaur, B., & Kour, M. (2025). Impact of Artificial Intelligence on Investment Decision-Making. In AI, Economic Perspectives, and Firm Business Management (pp. 1-12). IGI Global Scientific Publishing. DOI: 10.4018/979-8-3693-7357-6.ch001

Kokolakis, S. (2017). Privacy attitudes and privacy behavior: A review of current research on the privacy paradox phenomenon. *Computers & Security*, *64*, 122–134. DOI: 10.1016/j.cose.2015.07.002

Kour, M. (2025). Navigating the Fintech Wave and Its Background and Challenges. In Algorithmic Training, Future Markets, and Big Data for Finance Digitalization (pp. 121-132). IGI Global Scientific Publishing. DOI: 10.4018/979-8-3693-6386-7.ch005

La Torre, M., Botes, V. L., Dumay, J., & Odendaal, E. (2019). Protecting a new Achilles heel: The role of auditors within the practice of data protection. *Managerial Auditing Journal*, *36*(2), 218–239. DOI: 10.1108/MAJ-03-2018-1836

Lacity, M. C., & Willcocks, L. P. (2016). A new approach to automating services. *MIT Sloan Management Review*, *58*, 41–49.

Laksamana, Patria, Suharyanto Suharyanto, and Yohanes Ferry Cahaya. (2022). Determining factors of continuance intention in mobile payment: Fintech industry perspective. Asia Pacific Journal of Marketing and Logistics, ahead-of-print.

Liyanaarachchi, G., Deshpande, S., & Weaven, S. (2021). Online banking and privacy: Redesigning sales strategy through social exchange. *International Journal of Bank Marketing*, *39*(6), 955–983. DOI: 10.1108/IJBM-05-2020-0278

Lobschat, L., Mueller, B., Eggers, F., Brandimarte, L., Diefenbach, S., Kroschke, M., & Wirtz, J. (2021). Corporate digital responsibility. *Journal of Business Research*, *122*, 875–888. DOI: 10.1016/j.jbusres.2019.10.006

Lokanan, M. E. (2014). How senior managers perpetuate accounting fraud? Lessons for fraud examiners from an instructional case. *Journal of Financial Crime*, *21*, 411–423. DOI: 10.1108/JFC-03-2013-0016

Madan, V., & Kour, M. (2024), "Fintech and Mobile Payments in Transition: A Study of Adoption Challenges", *2024 IEEE International Conference on Interdisciplinary Approaches in Technology and Management for Social Innovation (IATMSI)*, (Vol. 2, pp. 1-6). IEEE. DOI: DOI: 10.1109/IATMSI60426.2024.10502648

Malaquias, R. F., & Hwang, Y. (2019). Mobile banking use: A comparative study with Brazilian and US participants. *International Journal of Information Management*, *44*, 132–140. DOI: 10.1016/j.ijinfomgt.2018.10.004

Mars, A., & Gouider, M. S. (2017). Big data analysis to feature opinions extraction of customers. *Procedia Computer Science*, *112*, 906–916. DOI: 10.1016/j.procs.2017.08.114

Martin, K. D., Kim, J. J., Palmatier, R. W., Steinhoff, L., Stewart, D. W., Walker, B. A., Wang, Y., & Weaven, S. K. (2020). Data Privacy in Retail. *Journal of Retailing*, *96*(4), 474–489. DOI: 10.1016/j.jretai.2020.08.003

McKnight, H., & Chervany, N. L. (2002). What trust means in E-commerce customer relationships: An interdisciplinary conceptual Typology. *International Journal of Electronic Commerce*, *6*(2), 35–59. DOI: 10.1080/10864415.2001.11044235

Osnos, E. (2018).“ Can Mark Zuckerberg fix Facebook before it breaks democracy?”, The New Yorker,10,September,2018.Retrievedfrom https://www.newyorker.com/magazine/2018/09/17/can mark-zuckerberg-fix-facebook-before-it-breaks democracy.

Park, J. Y., Ryu, J. P., & Shin, H. J. (2016). Robo advisors for portfolio management. *Advanced Science and Technology Letters*, *141*, 104–108. DOI: 10.14257/astl.2016.141.21

Patel, K. (2018). Artificial Intelligence in Finance. *IJSART*, *4*(4), 2787–2788.

Pavlou, P. (2003). Consumer acceptance of electronic commerce: Integrating trust and risk with the technology acceptance model. *International Journal of Electronic Commerce*, *7*(3), 101–134. DOI: 10.1080/10864415.2003.11044275

Przegalinska, A., Ciechanowski, L., Stroz, A., Gloor, P., & Mazurek, G. (2019). In bot we trust: A new methodology of chatbot performance measures. [CrossRef]. *Business Horizons*, *2019*(62), 785–797. DOI: 10.1016/j.bushor.2019.08.005

RBI. (2022). Report on trend & progress of banking in India 2021-22.Retrieved from: https://rbi.org.in/Scripts/AnnualPublications.aspx?head=Trend%20and%20Progress%20of%20Banking%20in%20India

Rese, A., Ganster, L., & Baier, D. (2020). Chatbots in retailers' customer communication: How to measure their acceptance? *Journal of Retailing and Consumer Services*, *56*, 102176. DOI: 10.1016/j.jretconser.2020.102176

Saeidi, S. P., Sofian, S., Saeidi, P., Saeidi, S. P., & Saaeidi, S. A. (2015). How does corporate social responsibility contribute to firm financial performance? The mediating role of competitive advantage, reputation, and customer satisfaction. *Journal of Business Research*, *68*(2), 341–350. DOI: 10.1016/j.jbusres.2014.06.024

Saltz, J. S., & Dewar, N. (2019). Data science ethical considerations: A systematic literature review and proposed project framework. *Ethics and Information Technology*, *21*(3), 197–208. DOI: 10.1007/s10676-019-09502-5

Stewart, H., & Jürjens, J. (2018a). Data security and consumer trust in FinTech innovation in Germany. *Information and Computer Security*, *26*(1), 109–128. DOI: 10.1108/ICS-06-2017-0039

Stewart, H., & Jürjens, J. (2018b). Fintech and trust: A qualitative study of customers' attitudes towards fintech and their data protection concerns. *Journal of Financial Services Marketing*, *23*, 225–237.

Swammy, Sarah, Richard Thompson, Marvin Loh, Sarah Swammy, Richard Thompson, and Marvin Loh. (2018). A Vision for the Future: The Bermuda FinTech Story. Crypto Uncovered 173.

Van Vuuren, T., Roberts-Lombard, M., & Van Tonder, E. (2012). Customer satisfaction, trust and commitment as predictors of customer loyalty within an optometric practice environment. *Southern African Business Review*, *16*, 81–96.

Vander Goot, M. J., Hafkamp, L., & Dankfort, Z. (2021). Customer Service Chatbots: A Qualitative Interview Study into the Communication Journey of Customers. *Lecture Notes in Computer Science*, *12604*, 190–204. DOI: 10.1007/978-3-030-68288-0_13

Vannucci, V., & Pantano, E. (2020). Do I Lose my Privacy for a Better Service? Investigating the Interplay between Big Data Analytics and Privacy Loss from Young Consumers' Perspective. In *Retail Futures* (pp. 193–205). Emerald Publishing Limited. DOI: 10.1108/978-1-83867-663-620201021

Wallach, H. (2018). Computational social science≠ computer science+ social data. *Communications of the ACM*, *61*(3), 42–44. DOI: 10.1145/3132698

Yan, Y., Huang, C., Wang, Q., & Hu, B. (2020). Data mining of customer choice behavior in internet of things within relationship network. *International Journal of Information Management*, *50*, 566–574. DOI: 10.1016/j.ijinfomgt.2018.11.013

Yang, J., Zhao, Y., Han, C., Liu, Y., & Yang, M. (2022). Big data, big challenges: Risk management of financial market in the digital economy. *Journal of Enterprise Information Management*, *35*(4/5), 1288–1304. DOI: 10.1108/JEIM-01-2021-0057

Zarifis, A., & Cheng, X. (2022). A model of trust in fintech and trust in Insurtech: How Artificial Intelligence and the context influence it. *Journal of Behavioral and Experimental Finance*, *36*, 100739. DOI: 10.1016/j.jbef.2022.100739

Zarifis, A., Kawalek, P., & Azadegan, A. (2021). Evaluating if trust and personal information privacy concerns are barriers to using health insurance that explicitly utilizes AI. *Journal of Internet Commerce*, *20*(1), 66–83. DOI: 10.1080/15332861.2020.1832817

Chapter 7
Public vs. Private Blockchains Governance Implications

Munir Ahmad
https://orcid.org/0000-0003-4836-6151
Survey of Pakistan, Pakistan

ABSTRACT

This chapter examines how blockchain governance, whether public or private, extends beyond technical design into the realm of institutional values, legal frameworks, and societal priorities. Through sectoral case studies in finance, healthcare, and supply chains, it highlights how governance structures directly shape blockchain's decentralization, transparency, control, and trustworthiness. Public blockchains offer openness and resilience but face regulatory uncertainty and coordination challenges, while private blockchains provide control and compliance but risk reintroducing centralization. Key policy recommendations stress designing governance from the outset, enabling sector-specific regulation, encouraging hybrid architectures, and incentivizing responsible practices.

INTRODUCTION

In recent years, the decentralized idea of blockchain technology has reimagined an array of industries with solutions that are built on the distributed system, in a vast range of sectors (Sanka et al., 2021), varying from the financial ones (Wu et al., 2024) and supply chain management (Menon & Jain, 2024) to healthcare (Kasyapa & Vanmathi, 2024) and digital identity (Song et al., 2025). Blockchain is a distributed ledger technology that enables secure, non-alterable, and open recording of transac-

DOI: 10.4018/979-8-3373-3186-7.ch007

tions without having a central authority. Decentralization, trustless interaction, and tamper-proof data have all contributed to its value rise and provide new solutions to problems previously mediated by third parties. Blockchain has revolutionized our understanding of trust, value, and coordination in the digital world, since it has facilitated peer-to-peer agreement and automated rules via smart contracts (A. Kumar & Sharma, 2025; P. Kumar & Gautam, 2025).

But, with the increasing complexity and size of blockchain-based systems, the problem of governance, i.e., who decides what decisions, how to enforce them, and on what rules, has increasingly taken center-stage (Cengiz, 2023a; De Filippi et al., 2020; Liu et al., 2023). With no party in the distributed environment controlling everything, governance would dictate how conflicts would be solved, how upgrades would occur, and how the interests of the community would be weighted. Such dissolution of conventional hierarchies is both promising and dangerous: decentralization can increase resilience and inclusiveness, and can result in fragmentation, inefficiency, or even exploitation of minority interests by focused actors unless governance systems are well-designed and properly enforced.

One of the main determinants that influence blockchain system governance occurs in the case of a public versus a private blockchain (permissionless/permissioned). Common blockchains such as Bitcoin or Ethereum are accessible to everyone, and those who qualify can participate in transaction verification and decision-making to a wide extent. These systems stress transparency, censorship resistance, and decentralization. Conversely, the public blockchains are normally open to anyone and are restricted to familiar actors, e.g., corporations or consortia, who control access and who have the right to validate on it and mutate protocols. Such a regulated setting has room to be efficient, compliant, and tailored to governance, yet must trade off with transparency and democratically accountable governance. Such basic differences in structure lead to conflictual models of governance, each of which has implications concerning regulation, stakeholder confidence, and scale (Dhillon & Sivabalan, 2025; N. Kumar et al., 2025).

The chapter attempts to examine critically the aspects of governance in both public and private blockchains. It starts by comparing their architectures and governance patterns and then proceeds to look in detail at the important areas of governance, like the consensus mechanisms, the decision-making process, and regulatory conformity.

PUBLIC VS. PRIVATE BLOCKCHAINS

The most important architectural difference at the root of the blockchain technology can be seen that it has significant consequences on the governance, and one of them is the public (permissionless) and the private (permissioned) blockchain.

These two paradigms cannot be defined as technical variations only: these paradigms represent different philosophies of trust, access, and control. The concept behind public blockchains, e.g., Bitcoin, Ethereum, and other open-source ecosystems, is called the ethos of inclusivity. The protocol can be downloaded by anyone, anywhere, and anyone can then join the network as a user, a miner, a validator, or a developer. These networks are supposed to be trustless, i.e., the participants do not necessarily have to trust some central authority; however, the trust becomes decentralized into the rules of the protocols and cryptographic agreement (Alyas et al., 2025; Dhillon & Sivabalan, 2025; Jamshed et al., 2025; Saari et al., 2025).

In comparison, the private blockchains are addressed with limited usage environments that are closed, and participants are known with selective permissions. Networks such as Hyperledger Fabric, Quorum, or R3 Corda are used inside firms or groupings to enable internal undertakings or inter-firm processes. Access is restricted to certain nodes or users, and privileges are strictly reserved through a role-based access control. Such systems are tuned to achieve performance, conformity, and privacy of data, frequently at the cost of the decentralized, open spirit that belongs to the open-source chains. The technical design of Private blockchains enables consensus to be achieved more rapidly, at a much-reduced energy cost, and with high levels of control over data and who can participate.

These kinds of disparities in architecture directly influence the types of governance models in action in each system. The governance of the blockchain that is on the public domain tends to be decentralized and emergent, and fluid. It is much dependent on open-source development communities, internet forums, and informal protocols such as improvement proposals that direct the development of the protocol. They are theoretically democratic but can be controlled by a consortium of core developers, big token holders, and influential miners or validators. It is possible to learn about the applicability and limitations of decentralized governance by examining conflicts that have resulted in Bitcoin Cash or Ethereum Classic forks or other contentious issues: it permits fissures informed by the community and experimentation, but is usually absent rationality in conflict resolution (Dhillon & Sivabalan, 2025; Polcumpally et al., 2024).

Governance in a typical case in the private blockchain is contractual and hierarchical. Organizations using a private chain hold direct control over their organization, consensus rules, upgrade policies, and dispute resolution methods. In consortium blockchains, governance may be distributed among two or more organizations through an agreement or steering committees, or voting. This model is reflective of traditional governance of an enterprise as it enables easier accountability, compliance with regulations, and synchronized strategic development. Nonetheless, it can also concentrate power within the hands of the few stakeholders, with low levels of transparency and autonomy of participants in the system (Dhillon & Sivabalan, 2025; Jamshed et al., 2025; Yang et al., 2024).

These differences are also elucidated with the help of the roles of the network participants. Multiple tasks, such as block creation, confirmation of transactions, and securing the network, are key roles in public chains and are realized through miners (in Proof-of-Work systems) and validators (in Proof-of-Stake systems and other consensus mechanisms). They are also motivated to contribute to network health by means of rewards using mining fees or staking yields. Additional actors, including protocol developers, full node operators, wallet providers, and users, participate in an evolving and even turbulent innovation and influence domain of governance. Notably, within the context of public blockchains, economic predicate (control of tokens or problems to mine) may be transformed into governance power, and these provisions frequently create contradictions as to plutocracy versus democracy in protocol control.

On private blockchains, the roles are assigned formally. Organizations can be assigned the role of validators to operate consensus nodes, and system administrators perform permission management, audit logs, identity services, and network updates. Users are, in general, internal employees, partner companies, or customers who act within pre-set regulations. Rewards are not often economic in the cryptocurrency meaning, rather, tied to business objectives, e.g., data integrity, smoothness of operations, or regulatory reporting. These forms of governance are more predictable, more enforceable, and less open to responding to the input of external stakeholders or fast-changing use cases.

The trade-offs between the public and the privately enabled blockchains are especially noticeable when the dimensions of decentralization, transparency, and control are compared. The degree of decentralization in public blockchain is very strong, where thousands of distributed nodes guarantee that there is no point of failure or control over the system. This transparency and auditability help resist censorship. But it also comes with a scalability limitation, governance bottleneck, interoperability, and regulatory compliance. On the contrary, the reductions in control are distributed around fewer participants in the case of the application of private blockchains, allowing a more streamlined decision-making process, data confidentiality, and regulation compliance, which is essential in other industries (such as banking or healthcare). However, this centralization can bring back the same problems that blockchain itself was meant to address: opacity, asymmetry of trust, and a single point of failure.

The decision on using a public or a private architecture of the blockchain is not just about efficient or ideological reasons; it is rather about the governance decision, which is based on the values, needs, and risks of potential users of the network. In open, global, and trust-minimized environments, public blockchains are more appropriate, whereas where there are known participants, accountability is important and regulatory integration is required, then a private blockchain can be used. Knowledge of their architectural premises and governance structures allows a better comprehension not only of their technical limits but their place in society and the institution of a more and more digitized world. Table 1 below summarizes key distinctions.

Table 1. Comparison of Public and Private Blockchains

Dimension	Public Blockchain	Private Blockchain
Access Model	Open to anyone (permissionless)	Restricted to approved participants (permissioned)
Consensus Mechanism	PoW, PoS, or hybrid (decentralized, anonymous validators)	PBFT, RAFT, or voting (known validators or nodes)
Node Participation	Any user can run a full node or validator	Limited to designated nodes with defined roles
Data Visibility	Transparent; full ledger viewable by all participants	Restricted visibility; fine-grained access controls
Governance Model	Informal, community-based, open-source driven	Formal, contractual, consortium-led, or organization-controlled
Decision-Making Process	Proposals (e.g., BIPs/EIPs), public debates, soft/hard forks	Voting, administrative control, and defined governance boards
Change Implementation	Consensus among distributed actors (can be slow)	Centralized coordination (faster upgrades and policy alignment)
Scalability and Speed	Lower (due to replication and consensus overhead)	Higher (optimized for efficiency and limited trust assumptions)
Regulatory Compliance	Difficult to enforce due to anonymity and decentralization	Designed for compliance and legal enforceability
Security Model	Cryptoeconomic incentives; large, distributed validator base	Role-based access, institutional trust, and internal security policies
Trust Assumptions	Trustless: trust in code, cryptography, and economics	Trusted: participants rely on organizational/legal trust
Use Cases	Cryptocurrencies, DeFi, public identity, voting	Supply chain, banking, healthcare, and enterprise data sharing

KEY GOVERNANCE DIMENSIONS

Blockchain systems, though usually termed as technical, also have a high political and institutional application. Governance of such systems, in terms of how the decisions are reached, disputes settled, and how the protocols are altered, goes to determining how that system is functional, legitimate, and sustainable (Dhillon &

Sivabalan, 2025; Laatikainen et al., 2023; Liu et al., 2022; Tan et al., 2022). In this section, five key dimensions of governance that have critical trade-offs between a subject of governance (public blockchain systems) and an individual engaging in governance (private blockchain systems) are discussed.

Decision-Making Processes

The community aspect of decision-making in blockchains and their decentralization is implicit in the public sphere, and many stakeholders (e.g., developers, miners/validators, node operators, and token holders) are usually involved in this process. The proposal of governance is generally open, such as Bitcoin Improvement Proposals (BIP), or Ethereum Improvement Proposals (EIP); it is discussed publicly in online forums and may be developed or refined collectively. Consensus is made both because of the technical element of node operators taking or not taking the changes, and the social aspect of it (Cengiz, 2023b; Chen et al., 2021). This not only promotes inclusiveness and ownership among people but also leads to cumbersome decision making, divisive politics, and sometimes hostile hard forks such as the Bitcoin vs Bitcoin Cash debacle.

In private blockchains, decisions are normally enterprise-driven or made by a consortium. In this case, there is formalized governance whereby they strike a contract, policy or charter with one another. Protocol change, access, and dispute resolution mechanisms are handled by designated administrators or steering committees. The decision-making process is faster in this centralized model, which can align with the business goals and may exclude minority players or curtail innovations. In one example, the autonomy of the supply chain blockchain networks, such as IBM Food Trust, allows streamlining decision-making that only considers the concerns of the most powerful consortium players.

The tradeoff is between speed and coordination (private chains) and openness and pluralism (public chains). Centralized decision-making might be found beneficial in mission-critical environments that need agility and compliance. However, open governance is vital to continue in global, decentralized ecosystems that need to remain legitimate and that are trusted by the user bases.

Consensus Mechanisms

Blockchain governance inevitably relies on consensus mechanisms- they determine how, in the blockchain, the consensus on the validity of transactions and blocks is reached. The public blockchains use the crypto economic consensus mechanisms such as the Proof-of-Work (PoW) and Proof-of-Stake (PoS). In Bitcoin, security is achieved by PoW, which consists of relying on the difficulty of complex computational puzzles. Polkadot and Cardano employ PoS, which enables the staking of tokens by the validators so that their interests are aligned with the integrity of the network (Buterin, 2014). These models are friendly towards decentralization as they allow open participation, but usually involve large amounts of energy (PoW) or risk cartels of validators (PoS).

PBFT (Practical Byzantine Fault Tolerance) and RAFT are common tolerant crash-fault or Byzantine-fault tolerant algorithms in private blockchain. These consensus models are more efficient, which means that fewer nodes are used, and there are no energy-intensive operations. The consensus process only requires a degree of confidence in people who can participate, and thus focuses on speed, finality, and determinism rather than permissionless participation. To give an example, in Hyperledger Fabric, endorsing peers check transactions according to the logic developed in chain code, and orders do not broadcast to a worldwide audience to create a consensus.

The trade-off between security and scalability can be observed in the choice of consensus mechanism: public chains are slow and less efficient, though more secure related to resilient to failures, and private chains require trust in some actors, which is likely to violate the principle of decentralization.

Regulatory Compliance

One of the most significant differences between the sphere of public and private blockchains is regulatory governance. Due to its pseudonyms, decentralized infrastructure and global character, public blockchains are explicitly running in legal grey areas. This causes the implementation of Know Your Customer (KYC), Anti-Money Laundering (AML), among other regulatory standards, to be difficult (Narayanan et al., 2016). Take another example, it is very common to find that financial regulators have difficulties in bringing any one party to accountability when there are infringements within the public platforms, the issue of protection to investors, and illegal finance are questioned.

In contrast, a private blockchain is suitable for regulatory compliance. Since the participants have been authenticated and legally bound by contractual arrangements, the organizations can apply KYC/AML obligations, audit files, and admission controls. It enhances the applicability of private chains in cases such as finance, healthcare, and the government, where compliance is a necessity. Legal responsibility is also easier to follow since nodes are run by legally recognized organizations and are under jurisdiction.

The trade here is a clarity of the law versus permissionless innovation. On the one hand, the public chains enable experimentation and liberty in the world; on the other hand, they tend to conflict with national control systems. Instead, by embedding themselves into legal norms, in one way or another, compromising openness and decentralization, private chains make the shift to becoming trusted and adopted as institutional norms.

Risk of Security, Scalability, and Centralization

In blockchain systems, security and scalability do not always go hand in hand. The security of public blockchains comes in the form of redundancy and immutability, which is achieved by many distributed networks. According to PoW systems such as Bitcoin, the system is relatively secure as it is expensive to attack the system. Nevertheless, there are severe limitations in terms of scalability known to be linked to these networks in terms of low transaction throughput and high latency. In addition, they are not resistant to the dangers of centralization and threats that include mining pool dominance or PoS validator oligopolies (Reijers et al., 2021).

The major difference is that the private blockchains are suited well to scale and achieve better performance since they have fewer validating nodes, and consensus is made less complex. This enables them to support hundreds or possibly thousands of transactions in real-time, as is observed in enterprise applications such as Corda and Hyperledger. However, this performance improvement will be at the tradeoff of decentralization; fewer nodes and known participants mean it could be more prone to collusion or insider threats, or can be controlled by the regulators accordingly.

The governance trade-off in this case is between performance and resilience. Public chains are fast but imperfect and transparent to the point of being openly public; private chains are resilient but secretive and efficient in their work. Such a trade-off will have to be managed depending on the situation; be it in cures where the aim is to win the people or in its management where the aim is to ensure that the system is at its best.

Blockchain Trust Paradox

One of the main tensions in blockchain governance philosophies can be called the trust paradox: on the one hand, blockchain was created to get rid of trust in centralized authorities, on the other hand, the form of which adoption inevitably brings back trust dependencies. The public blockchains are substituting institutional trust with the trust in codes, cryptography, and economic incentives and yet control structures continue to rely on social processes, informal leadership, and the provisions of the community. The hack in the DAO and the consequent Ethereum hard fork exemplify that the force of law enshrined in code can be transcended by grassroots human discretion, giving back faith in human beings (De Filippi & Wright, 2018).

Trust in private blockchains is formalized and explicit, and contractual. Members and resources are screened; policies are predetermined, and control is centralized or federated. Trust in that case is not displaced, but rather re-routed, or directed to particular organizations, and no longer to a public network. This calls into question whether blockchain is really transformative or if it is a rebadged type of institutional trust.

The irony is that even schemes aimed at reducing the need for trust in the governance processes eventually require trust. Thereby, overcoming the trust is not the central government's issue but its disaggregation and reorganization in a transparent, responsible, and changeable manner.

GOVERNANCE IN PRACTICE

The issue of blockchain system governance cannot be considered a purely abstract matter because it has a direct impact on the way these systems can operate in various real-life industries. In this section, the researcher discusses the expression of governance patterns within three very important areas, namely, finance, supply line, and healthcare. With an analysis of sector-specific blockchain deployments, we are able to understand the impact of the architectural as well as governance decisions made on trust, compliance, adoption as well and systemic outcomes.

Finances

Bitcoin became the first public, decentralized financial network, followed by several blockchain applications in the financial sector. Bitcoin is a permissionless product, so anyone can join the transaction validation (mining), and anyone can inspect the ledger. Bitcoin governance favors the community as the protocol is changed through community-based debate and social agreement (Nakamoto, 2008). Such a model supports freedom, censorship immunity, as well as empowerment of its users, although it does pose some regulatory challenges, especially regarding anti-money laundering (AML) and know-your-customer (KYC) compliance.

Conversely, rippleNet, which is created by Ripple Labs, is a permissioned and private financial network that links payment providers and banks together. Compared to payment networks with blockchain-based technologies, RippleNet is governed centrally, although its technologies emulate blockchain. Validator nodes are managed by Ripple Labs and its institutional partners, and strategic decisions about upgrades to the network and participation are made. The model allows rapid settlements, regulatory convergence, and institutional harmonization at the cost of decentralization and transparency.

Lesson: Public financial blockchain governance promotes autonomy and worldwide participation, but is weak in terms of compliance. The aspect of performance and regulatory compatibility is guaranteed by the use of the private financial networks, which, however, reverts to centralization risk. The exchange will be inclusivity and institutional trust.

Supply Chain

One of the best use cases of blockchain is supply chains, as it can enhance supply chain security through efficiency, traceability, provenance, and trust. VeChain is a production-ready blockchain, developed on a public blockchain platform and integrated with smart contracts and the Internet-of-Things (IoT): the track of products on global supply chains can be tracked. Vechain governance is hybrid: its blockchain has a two-token economy (VEN and VTHO), which is combined with a public ledger and traditional governance model of a foundation. The transparency of VeChain assists in holding stakeholders accountable, product is authentic or legitimate, and increasing consumer trust.

In comparison, Hyperledger Fabric is a modular permissioned blockchain made at the Linux Foundation to use in business applications. With Fabric-based supply chain networks, the policies over data sharing, identity, and transaction endorsements are defined by participant organizations. Governance is consortium-centric, with functions, rights, and update processes configurable. This facilitates privacy of data, effectiveness, and adherence to regulations of other sectors, such as the pharmaceutical or food safety.

Lesson: Public supply chain platforms are more transparent and reviewable, yet can be met with opposition by actors wishing to keep their proprietary information secret. The benefit behind private blockchains is that they provide fine-grained access control and regulatory compliance at the expense of consumer and third-party visibility. The type of governance should not be too strict on accountability and confidentiality of the data.

Healthcare

The area of healthcare poses some unprecedented governance risks to the viability of blockchain since the information about healthcare is sensitive and governed by stringent regulatory measures. Medicalchain Medicalchain is a public blockchain related to applications that enable patients to specify who can access their electronic health records (EHRs). It uses smart contracts to allow authorization sharing with healthcare providers, researchers, or insurers. The system is partially decentralized, and the patients are given the role of data stewards. Although this model provides the user with power and transparency, it has questions regarding the accuracy of data, liability, and the regulatory rules, such as GDPR or HIPAA.

Instead, a wider range of healthcare providers and governments have chosen to use private, permissioned health data blockchains, including but not limited to proposed implementations of health data blockchains by Guardtime or national e-health systems. Such systems can be based on the enterprise blockchain structures (e.g., Corda or Hyperledger), and permission to access data is strictly limited to permitted healthcare facilities. State control is institution-focused, whereby compliance, data integrity, and data audit are important. The system accounts for the legal consequences and interoperability of the standards of medicine, given that the patients will have minimal control over it.

Lesson: In healthcare, there is potential value in the less restrictive model of public blockchain because it provides patient control and auditing capabilities, although it is likely to be in conflict with institutional accountability and data protection policies. Permissioned systems follow compliance and clinical governance, but they pose the risk of centralized control of personal data. The system of governance should be able to strike a balance between personal freedom and institutional trust and security.

Cross-Sector Lessons on Governance Structures

Several key governance insights emerge from these sectoral comparisons:

- Public and private blockchains each address different trust, control, and compliance needs. Sector-specific constraints—like patient privacy in healthcare or regulatory obligations in finance—must guide governance design.
- Platforms like VeChain or Medicalchain reflect a growing trend toward "public-permissioned hybrids", where transparency coexists with role-based access and centralized oversight of critical components.
- Stakeholders, whether banks, consumers, or patients—are more likely to engage with blockchain systems whose governance structures align with their expectations of trust, control, and legal protection.
- In public systems, accountability is often social or reputational; in private systems, it is contractual and legal. Each has its strengths and vulnerabilities.

DISCUSSION AND SYNTHESIS

The chapter has discussed the fundamental structural and governance distinction between the public and private blockchains by using real situations in the financial, supply chain, and healthcare sectors. In the following section, we would like to critically consider what those differences mean, synthesize cross-cutting conclusions, and suggest conceptual lessons that could inform the design of future blockchain governance. Although blockchain can be widely discussed as a technological breakthrough, it is becoming obvious that the governing structure, and not its cryptography or consensus, drives the practical outcome of this technology.

Blockchain as a Political Technology

A very profound lesson that this chapter gives is the aspect that blockchain systems are not governed-free. Though public blockchains are frequently proclaimed as decentralized schemes of governance by protocol, this belief always implicitly terms on off-chain social coordination, e.g., community collaboration, direction of core developers, and stakeholder negotiations. On the same note, the very architecture of a private blockchain is either based on institutional structure or under legal contracts. In both situations, there is a need to make choices regarding those who are to be included, those who possess the power and authority, and how to settle disputes and cause the system to be changed.

In that way, blockchain cannot be regarded as an instrumental technical infrastructure but rather as a political-economic institution. It implements principles such as autonomy vs. control, openness vs. privacy, and inclusion vs. efficiency into its protocols. Governance design would then be something secondary, but it is a major factor in legitimacy, adoption, and influence.

Trade-offs

In the course of making the comparison between public and private blockchains, a regular rhythm can be observed: governance trade-offs are structural. Public blockchains are transparent, decentralized, and give power to the user; however, they lack in scalability, the ability to make decisions faster, and compliance. The characteristics of private blockchains are that they prioritize performance, regulatory integrations, and data control at the cost of openness, inclusiveness, and public trust.

These are not bugs: they are part of the architecture. Efforts to solve them tend to give rise to hybrid solutions, including public-permissioned chains or governance layering (e.g., sidechains, DAOs, or consortia governance on top of public infrastructure). Instead of trying to find optimal solutions, the day of governance designers is to prioritize competing interests in context-sensitive manners. This supports the pluralist approach to governance: the fact that there is no perfect governance model regardless of sector or use case.

Context-Driven Governance Needs

These sectoral case studies make the point that governance is to be welcomed in the institutional context:

- A public blockchain, such as Bitcoin, is heavily based on autonomy and censorship-resistance in the field of finance, whereas a private solution, such as RippleNet goes along with compliance and institutional trust.
- The critical difference between VeChain and Hyperledger in supply chains is that the former allows verification of products in the supply chain, whereas the latter enables greater privacy, suitable to the confidentiality requirements of an enterprise.
- In healthcare, Medicalchain patient-led governance increases agency, and permissioned models improve data safety and clinical responsibility.

These examples demonstrate that the governance paradigm has to be developed with the problem in mind, not the protocol. The expectations of trust, accountability, and control differ at different levels between various stakeholders, including patients, regulators, consumers, and developers. To create the legitimacy and effectiveness of governance, it is necessary to listen to those voices and translate their needs into the logic of system functioning.

Toward Responsible Blockchain Governance

Governance needs to develop in five directions that are important to achieve the transformative promise of blockchain with responsibility:

Transparency in Governance Processes

Although blockchains know that ledgers show the transparency of transactions, in governance, transparency is beyond the code. It demands transparency of the decisions, how the futuristic protocol changes are proposed, discussed, and voted on, and should be able to access it. This involves the sharing of public records of enhancement proposals, meeting minutes, vote results, and communication between the developers. Transparency is used in public blockchains, resulting in a sense of trust and herd supervision that can assist in avoiding being captured by the winning groups. Transparency in governance increases institutional credibility and develops regulatory confidence in the case of privately owned chains. A technical transparency may allow an opaque decision-making process and a lack of legitimacy without procedural transparency. At the end, informed participation and beneficial accountability need to be carried out through transparent governance.

Stakeholder Participation and Inclusivity

The successful governance of the blockchain should be inclusive to the whole spectrum of stakeholders, including developers, validators, institutional actors, but also its users, regulators, and the marginalized. This implies establishing channels of effective feedback so that the people affected by the rules and changes in the system could contribute to the process, particularly to sensitive areas such as healthcare or infrastructure. Participatory governance can be promoted through on-chain voting, open forums, DAOs, and community consultation mechanisms. In the case of the private blockchain, inclusivity can involve internal representation of stakeholders, ethics boards or the multi-party governance charters. In the absence of mass inclusion, governance easily becomes exclusive or technical to the detriment of the system. Being inclusive adds to good governance and ensures protocol outcomes match the demands placed on society.

Accountability Mechanisms

Responsible governance is based on accountability. Blockchain systems need to spell out ownership or leadership of what, under which conditions, and responsibilities to whom. This involves well-documented governance functions, decision authority, and lines of escalation. The systems should install internal auditing, mechanisms for resolving disputes, and provisions for reporting to the public to keep track and enforce responsibility. Accountability in public blockchains could be social, reputational, or token-based; in the case of the latter, it is frequently contractual or legal. At least some sorts of accountability can be encoded in smart contracts, although they are still critical to have human oversight. Unless there are effective accountability measures in place, the mistakes will never get rectified, and neither will the abuses be stopped, and eventually, the people will lose trust.

Adaptability and Evolution

The evolution of any blockchain system cannot go without any governance that can be able to sustain that evolution. With the maturing of technologies, changes in the use cases, and the introduction of risks, protocols, and institutions must be mechanisms to accommodate. This covers channels of introducing software updates, revising consensus settings, altering the governance protocols, and even allowing the network to fork. In the community systems, such an evolution can be in the form of proposals or social consensus. At least, in closed chains, adaptation may fall under the control of formal change management policies or steering committees. Any system that is not adaptive is at risk of either stagnating or collapsing in the face of new threats or innovations. Resilient governance does not simply entail being disruption-free, but developing through such disruption.

Legal and Ethical Alignment

To become responsible enough to run at scale, blockchain requires governance that is congruent with the legal and ethical expectations of the societies it helps. This involves making sure that rules and regulations like GDPR, HIPAA, or codes of financial conduct are followed, and also that there is an aspect of fairness, consent, and non-discrimination. The complexity of jurisdiction and the difficulty of implementing legal norms in decentralized settings must be contended with on the side of the public blockchains. Although private chains are more institutionally integrated, they also need to take care of ethical risks such as information misuse or bias in the algorithms. Integrating governance with legal and ethical oversight in the form of legal counsel, ethics boards, and impact analysis can be used to prevent harm and protect users and maximize the long-term viability of systems.

Governance as the Engine of Institutional Trust

Eventually, governance is what transforms blockchain as a tool into a blockchain institution. It identifies how the technology is used in connection with human values, social norms, and legal structures. Although the problem of governance has different solutions in both public blockchains and in privately structured ones, the two approaches demonstrate that no trust is eradicated, but its form is rearranged. Whether we have faith in the system is not a vital issue, but in whom we give our faith, and how the trust is organized, and how it is possible to oppose or transform it.

This chapter does not propose that the X or Y model is the best thing; it is much more about the role of governance-by-design, i.e., not viewing governance as an attribute but rather as a dynamic, participatory, and responsible process. The real potential of blockchain is not to avoid governance, but to do that better.

CONCLUSION AND POLICY IMPLICATIONS

The division into the public and the private blockchain is bigger than merely a technical decision; it is a representation of the governing interests, the institutional limitations, and the values of society. In this chapter, we have learned how architectural choice influences the governance models of a blockchain system and how the governance models affect the decentralization, transparency, control, compliance, and trust. Examples of blockchain governance systems are not identical across industry sectors, like the ones we have discussed about the real-world sector of finance, supply chain, and healthcare, we have been able to see that blockchain is not a homogeneous technology but is rather a versatile infrastructure whose performance is pegged, in the aptness of its governance to its purpose of application.

Public blockchains advocate a free-of-charge, permissionless, and decentralized consensus and, therefore, are the most appropriate when they are used in an environment where neutralizing censorship, global accessibility, and user empowerment are essential. The strengths, however, are met by a set of severe regulative drawbacks: these are uncertainty of regulation, non-linearity of scaling, and slower decision-making. Unlike them, private blockchains are fast, institutionally controlled, and legally compliant, which makes them appropriate for business and government usage. However, they threaten to introduce the same centralization and concealment that were the problem blockchain was meant to circumvent. It is this governance tension that brings about one of the central lessons: that no one model is superior to all others, but rather that models are more or less suited to the purpose.

In all of the blockchain systems, however, some principles of governance come to mind that are definitely universal in their value: clarity in decision-making, inclusion of stakeholders, accountability measures, ability to evolve, and adherence to legal and moral imperatives. These are not just principles; they are operational necessities and are ideals regarding trust building, sustainability, and risk reduction. Any governance that does not support them will have a hard time having its legitimacy, despite the technicality of the platform supporting it.

Policy Implications

The lessons uncovered in this chapter have various implications for policymakers, technologists, and institutional leaders; a few of such lessons include:

The governance issue should not be treated as an add-on in blockchain systems. Projects tend to pay a lot of attention to consensus mechanisms and cryptography, but governance issues, including how to make decisions, upgrade the system, or settle disputes, remain open or even absent. This might result in crises where communities are exposed to disputes, forks, and legal attacks. Blockchain networks with or without the participation of governments need to have well-defined governance structures at inception, e.g., job descriptions, procedures, and accountability within the administration. These structures have to be incorporated into technical procedures and social coordination systems. As consensus guarantees data integrity, so does governance guarantee granting institutional and operational integrity over time.

Public blockchains lack the territorial restrictions of the jurisdiction of borders, and they are not based on the traditional institutional boundaries, and the legal status of the developers the users, and investors may be uncertain. Regulators should understand that such systems are characterized by a fundamental difference from centralized platforms and need a special regulatory treatment. Instead of mandating the use of legacy financial or IT-based compliance models, governments ought to formulate guidelines on areas such as token classification, liability of the DAOs, data protection within the decentralized framework, and cross-border regulation. Adequate, balanced regulation can limit the threat of legal risk, encourage innovation, and deter negative practices--and need not destroy the decentralization of public chains that is their value. This will also enhance the interoperability between the private and the public systems.

The application of Blockchain differs widely per sector and therefore should differ in terms of governance also. The needs of a blockchain that runs health data are very dissimilar to a blockchain that governs a supply chain or provides cross-border payments. Instead of uniform and blanket regulation, policymakers ought to promote custom regulation that is consistent with the risks in the sector, the requirements of compliance, as well as the expectations of the users. This may be health sector-specific consent models, financial AML/KYC governance systems, or environmental data integrity systems. This can be done by assisting blockchain technology with the development of domain-driven innovation and modular governance design to allow them to develop sanely within the high-impact dimensions.

The trend of governance innovation is shifting towards a hybrid system combining the transparency of the public blockchain and the control and scalability of a private or permissioned blockchain. The models may blend the best of both worlds, but they, too, need clever planning to maintain the balance between competing priorities. Auditability and resilience can be achieved using public infrastructure, and compliance and the privacy of sensitive data are possible by using permissioned layers. Such complementary architectures and participatory structures of governance, such as DAOs, community grants, or ethics councils, to facilitate the shaping of the network evolution by a broad set of stakeholders, should be encouraged by policies. This prevents the problem of elite capture and develops open digital ecosystems.

Research funders and governments, as well as multilateral organizations, play a catalytic role in advancing good governance. In addition to financing blockchain framework or trial initiatives, they ought to invest in structures that illustrate ways of ethical, legal, and inclusive rules. This involves platforms that actively involve vulnerable or marginalized groups, incorporate impact assessment, have access to transparent records of decision making, and have a mechanism of accountability. Projects that extend beyond technical efficiency to include such values as equity, public accountability, and social impact could also be awarded funding, regulatory sandboxes, or certification schemes. Governing responsibly is a public good--and should be treated as such. Table 2 outlines the policy recommendations.

Table 2. Policy Recommendation Summary

Policy Recommendation	Key Action Areas	Intended Impact
Design Governance from the Start	Embed governance roles, rules, and dispute resolution mechanisms during blockchain system design.	Ensures system integrity, reduces governance crises, and supports long-term stability.
Support Regulatory Clarity for Public Chains	Develop tailored legal frameworks for decentralized systems (e.g., token classification, DAO regulations, cross-border compliance).	Reduces legal uncertainty, encourages innovation, and protects users.
Enable Sector-Specific Governance Innovation	Encourage flexible, domain-specific governance models (e.g., health data privacy, financial compliance, supply chain auditability).	Aligns governance with real-world needs and regulatory requirements.
Promote Hybrid and Participatory Models	Support blended architectures combining permissionless infrastructure with controlled access and participatory structures (e.g., DAOs, ethics boards).	Balances transparency and control; fosters inclusive governance.
Incentivize Responsible Governance Practices	Provide funding, recognition, and regulatory support to projects demonstrating ethical, inclusive, and accountable governance.	Elevates governance quality and aligns blockchain use with public interest.

Blockchain is not just a tool for decentralization; it is a laboratory for rethinking governance in the digital age. The future of blockchain will not be determined by consensus algorithms alone, but by our ability to govern them wisely, inclusively, and responsibly. As the technology matures, so must the frameworks that guide its use, not only to unlock its full potential but to ensure it serves the public good.

REFERENCES

Alyas, T., Abbas, Q., Niazi, S., Alqahtany, S. S., Alghamdi, T., Alzahrani, A., Tabassum, N., & Ibrahim, A. M. (2025). Multi blockchain architecture for judicial case management using smart contracts. *Scientific Reports, 15*(1), 1–17. DOI: 10.1038/s41598-025-92842-8 PMID: 40069277

Buterin, V. (2014). A next-generation smart contract and decentralized application platform. *Etherum, January.*

Cengiz, F. (2023). Blockchain governance and governance via blockchain: Decentralized utopia or centralized dystopia? *Policy Design and Practice, 6*(4), 446–464. Advance online publication. DOI: 10.1080/25741292.2023.2247203

Chen, Y., Pereira, I., & Patel, P. C. (2021). Decentralized Governance of Digital Platforms. *Journal of Management, 47*(5), 1305–1337. DOI: 10.1177/0149206320916755

De Filippi, P., Mannan, M., & Reijers, W. (2020). Blockchain as a confidence machine: The problem of trust & challenges of governance. *Technology in Society, 62*, 101284. Advance online publication. DOI: 10.1016/j.techsoc.2020.101284

Dhillon, R., & Sivabalan, P. (2025). Exploring dimensions of governance for different types of blockchain systems. *The British Accounting Review, 101588*, 101588. Advance online publication. DOI: 10.1016/j.bar.2025.101588

Jamshed, H., Waheed, U., Iqbal, S., Faheem, M., Ashraf, M. W., & Mansoor, Y. (2025). Dynamic smart contracts framework on Ethereum private blockchain for real estate management. *Journal of Engineering (Stevenage, England), 2025*(1), e70063. DOI: 10.1049/tje2.70063

Kasyapa, M. S. B., & Vanmathi, C. (2024). Blockchain integration in healthcare: A comprehensive investigation of use cases, performance issues, and mitigation strategies. *Frontiers in Digital Health, 6*, 1359858. DOI: 10.3389/fdgth.2024.1359858 PMID: 38736708

Kumar, A., & Sharma, D. K. (2025). A Blockchain based Solution for Efficient and Secure Healthcare Management. *International Journal of Critical Infrastructures, 21*(2), 10060627. Advance online publication. DOI: 10.1504/IJCIS.2025.10060627

Kumar, N., Kumar, K., Aeron, A., & Verre, F. (2025). Blockchain technology in supply chain management: Innovations, applications, and challenges. *Telematics and Informatics Reports, 18*, 100204. DOI: 10.1016/j.teler.2025.100204

Kumar, P., & Gautam, S. (2025). Blockchain Technology in the Investment Domain: A Bibliometric Analysis. *International Journal of Electronic Finance*, *1*(1), 10061055. Advance online publication. DOI: 10.1504/IJEF.2025.10061055

Laatikainen, G., Li, M., & Abrahamsson, P. (2023). A system-based view of blockchain governance. *Information and Software Technology*, *157*, 107149. DOI: 10.1016/j.infsof.2023.107149

Liu, Y., Lu, Q., Yu, G., Paik, H. Y., & Zhu, L. (2022). Defining blockchain governance principles: A comprehensive framework. *Information Systems*, *109*, 102090. DOI: 10.1016/j.is.2022.102090

Liu, Y., Lu, Q., Zhu, L., Paik, H. Y., & Staples, M. (2023). A systematic literature review on blockchain governance. *Journal of Systems and Software*, *197*, 111576. Advance online publication. DOI: 10.1016/j.jss.2022.111576

Menon, S., & Jain, K. (2024). Blockchain Technology for Transparency in Agri-Food Supply Chain: Use Cases, Limitations, and Future Directions. *IEEE Transactions on Engineering Management*, *71*, 106–120. Advance online publication. DOI: 10.1109/TEM.2021.3110903

Nakamoto, S. (2008). Bitcoin: A Peer-to-Peer Electronic Cash System | Satoshi Nakamoto Institute. *Bitcoin.Org*.

Narayanan, A., Bonneau, J., Felten, E., Miller, A., & Goldfeder, S. (2016). Bitcoin and Cryptocurrency Technologies: A Comprehensive Introduction. In *Bitcoin and Cryptocurrency Technologies: A Comprehensive Introduction*. Princeton University Press.

Polcumpally, A. T., Pandey, K. K., Kumar, A., & Samadhiya, A. (2024). Blockchain governance and trust: A multi-sector thematic systematic review and exploration of future research directions. *Heliyon*, *10*(12), 32975. DOI: 10.1016/j.heliyon.2024.e32975 PMID: 38984295

Reijers, W., Wuisman, I., Mannan, M., De Filippi, P., Wray, C., Rae-Looi, V., Cubillos Vélez, A., & Orgad, L. (2021). Now the Code Runs Itself: On-Chain and Off-Chain Governance of Blockchain Technologies. *Topoi*, *40*(4), 821–831. Advance online publication. DOI: 10.1007/s11245-018-9626-5

Saari, A., Sinclair, S., Leshinsky, R., & Junnila, S. (2025). Best practices for blockchain-driven digital transformation in cross-industry settings. *Digital Business*, *5*(2), 100127. DOI: 10.1016/j.digbus.2025.100127

Sanka, A. I., Irfan, M., Huang, I., & Cheung, R. C. C. (2021). A survey of breakthrough in blockchain technology: Adoptions, applications, challenges and future research. In *Computer Communications* (Vol. 169). DOI: 10.1016/j.comcom.2020.12.028

Song, Z., Yan, E., Song, J., Jiang, R., Yu, Y., & Chen, T. (2025). A Blockchain-Based Digital Identity System with Privacy, Controllability, and Auditability. *Arabian Journal for Science and Engineering*, *50*(10), 7027–7051. DOI: 10.1007/s13369-024-09178-0

Tan, E., Mahula, S., & Crompvoets, J. (2022). Blockchain governance in the public sector: A conceptual framework for public management. *Government Information Quarterly*, *39*(1), 101625. DOI: 10.1016/j.giq.2021.101625

Wu, H., Yao, Q., Liu, Z., Huang, B., Zhuang, Y., Tang, H., & Liu, E. (2024). Blockchain for finance: A survey. In *IET Blockchain* (Vol. 4, Issue 2). DOI: 10.1049/blc2.12067

Yang, J., Ma, C., Hsiao, S., & Liu, J. (2024). Blockchain governance: A bibliometric study and content analysis. *Technology Analysis and Strategic Management*, 1–15. Advance online publication. DOI: 10.1080/09537325.2024.2337347

Chapter 8
Rights in the Digital Realm:
Legal and Ethical Considerations of Emerging Technologies, Human Rights, and Global Digital Governance

Mohammad Al Khaldy
https://orcid.org/0009-0009-7502-4668
University of Petra, Amman, Jordan

Ahmad Al-Qerem
https://orcid.org/0000-0003-2187-6194
Computer Science Department, Faculty of Information Technology, Zarqa University, Zarqa, Jordan

Amjad Aldweesh
https://orcid.org/0000-0001-9358-1323
College of Computing and Information Technology, Shaqra University, Shaqra, Saudi Arabia

ABSTRACT

The digital realm has altered how societies address human rights, data usage, and governance. Various sectors now rely on large-scale analytics, business intelligence systems, and artificial intelligence to optimize decision-making, yet these technologies introduce legal and ethical dilemmas. This chapter examines how international human rights norms apply to emerging technologies. It discusses data privacy, algorithmic fairness, and regulatory challenges, illustrating tensions between innovation and fundamental rights. It also proposes governance measures

DOI: 10.4018/979-8-3373-3186-7.ch008

grounded in human-centric frameworks to protect privacy and preserve democratic values. Findings indicate that a balance of technical, legal, and policy efforts can strengthen rights in digital ecosystems. This chapter enriches debates on ensuring that digital transformation aligns with human dignity.

1. INTRODUCTION

Technological progress has stimulated the digitization of social, political, and economic interactions. Organizations across different industries deploy powerful data-driven methods to support business intelligence (BI) and other analytic processes. People engage daily with interconnected platforms, contributing to an expanding flow of digital information. Governments, private entities, and other stakeholders collect these data and rely on algorithmic tools to generate insights, shape policies, and optimize services (Calo, 2018). Although these developments accelerate innovation, they raise questions about rights in the digital realm. The intersection of big data analytics, artificial intelligence (AI), and governance poses questions about fairness, personal autonomy, privacy, and accountability.

Concurrently, digital technologies, such as AI-based facial recognition or blockchain-based identity systems, transform civic engagement and public services. These changes create unanticipated outcomes for the future of democracy, free speech, and socioeconomic equity (Shany, 2023). Growing reliance on AI and advanced analytics has empowered both private and public actors to manage large datasets for predictive modeling and operational optimization. In theory, these tools yield actionable insights for decisions. In practice, they can lead to biased results or invasive surveillance. The complexity of these tools challenges existing legal frameworks. This chapter examines how fundamental rights may guide the development, implementation, and oversight of emerging technologies, including BI and AI-driven platforms.

1.1. The Global Shift to Digital Systems

Digitalization has transitioned from optional to essential in many fields. Governments leverage technology to streamline public administration, health services, and economic development. Multinational organizations expand data-driven operations to improve customer engagement and internal processes. Small and medium enterprises employ BI solutions to increase efficiency. Yet this digital transformation often lacks robust safeguards. The potential for technology to infringe on rights is no longer speculative but observed in real-world cases where automated analytics either overlooked minority interests or facilitated intrusive data collection (Dror-

Shpoliansky, 2022). Many governments and enterprises deploy AI to sift through large data repositories and detect patterns, prompting concerns about transparency and due process.

AI-driven business intelligence uses machine learning algorithms to predict consumer behavior, optimize logistics, or detect fraud. These innovations enable faster decisions, but the logic behind algorithmic outputs can remain opaque to individuals who are affected by them (Lu, 2022). That opacity challenges basic legal protections, including the right to an explanation for important decisions, especially when automation influences employment, loan eligibility, or access to vital services. The synergy between AI and BI intensifies the pressure to design systems that protect individual autonomy and ensure fairness. Concurrently, digital transformation has global reach. Cross-border data flows demand a harmonized approach to protecting personal information and upholding human rights, yet many regulations remain fragmented.

1.2. Human Rights Foundations in the Digital Age

The Universal Declaration of Human Rights (UDHR) outlines foundational principles like dignity, equality, and freedom. Many of these principles have been transposed into binding conventions. Traditional conceptions of rights focused on physical boundaries. Today, individuals navigate hybrid spaces shaped by digital platforms. International law has begun to extend rights protections to online domains. Various bodies, including the United Nations (UN) and regional organizations, recognize that offline rights apply online (Office of the UN High Commissioner for Human Rights, 2022).

However, the proliferation of connected devices, biometric surveillance, and advanced analytics complicates these norms. Technologies can undermine rights if used for disproportionate monitoring or censorship (Dragu & Lupu, 2021). In the case of BI systems, businesses may gather and analyze vast data sets, inadvertently revealing sensitive traits or enabling manipulative marketing. Some states adopt large-scale digital surveillance programs under the guise of security. Others experiment with social scoring or deploy facial recognition in public spaces. These measures strain established notions of privacy, freedom of expression, and the right to assemble (Palmiotto & Menéndez González, 2023). Thus, the digital era demands adaptive interpretations of international human rights law.

1.3. Research Scope and Objectives

This chapter explores legal and ethical considerations of emerging technologies that affect fundamental rights. It places emphasis on AI, BI, data analytics, and blockchain applications in public and private sectors. The objectives are:

1. **Identify Key Rights Challenges**: Show how emerging technologies challenge human rights in data governance, algorithmic fairness, and broader digital governance.
2. **Examine Regulatory and Policy Frameworks**: Discuss international, regional, and national initiatives designed to protect rights in digital ecosystems.
3. **Evaluate Business Intelligence Practices**: Illustrate how BI-driven data strategies and advanced analytics intersect with legal compliance and ethical principles.
4. **Propose a Rights-Centric Governance Model**: Suggest frameworks and mechanisms to ensure that digital innovations uphold privacy, transparency, and due process.

The chapter situates BI systems within broader digital transformations and explores how data-centric operations may align with established legal norms. It combines theoretical perspectives with practical examples, drawing on real-world policies and guidelines. By synthesizing scholarship and official reports, it clarifies the main dilemmas and offers pathways toward robust protections.

1.4. Methodological Approach

The examination of digital rights requires interdisciplinary insights. This chapter relies on a qualitative synthesis of academic and policy works, focusing on open-access publications that examine AI ethics, data privacy, and related fields. The references are drawn exclusively from open-access literature, as identified in major repositories. Although each region has distinct legal approaches, the analysis highlights converging standards and shared best practices. By integrating evidence from global institutions such as UNESCO, the OECD, and the UN, this chapter highlights relevant soft law and policy guidance. The discussion further includes academic critiques of how states can move from abstract principles to binding regulations.

1.5. Chapter Organization

Following this introduction, Section 2 surveys theoretical and conceptual foundations underpinning digital rights in the context of BI and AI. Section 3 explores major challenges, including algorithmic discrimination and data privacy risks. Section 4 concentrates on practical topics such as governance strategies and legislative developments. Section 5 presents selected case studies that illustrate real-life impacts of data-driven systems on rights and outlines lessons learned. Section 6 proposes possible paths forward, including new oversight methods and legislative reforms. Finally, Section 7 summarizes the findings, outlines future research directions, and concludes with recommendations for ensuring that digital transformations support, rather than undermine, human rights.

2. THEORETICAL AND CONCEPTUAL BACKGROUND

2.1. Evolving Concepts of Human Rights in Digital Environments

International human rights norms emerged to safeguard individuals from abuses by authorities and to articulate core freedoms. These principles were codified in documents like the International Covenant on Civil and Political Rights and regional charters. Today, technology shapes a new sphere where governmental and private actors can exercise significant power over personal information (Shany, 2023). Traditional human rights frameworks must adapt to these digital contexts. The notion that rights apply online was established through UN resolutions and statements by various international bodies (Office of the UN High Commissioner for Human Rights, 2022). Yet understanding how to apply these rights to advanced analytics and AI systems remains complex.

Shany (2023) underscores three "generations" of digital rights. The first involves protecting established rights online (e.g., privacy in digital communications). The second adapts existing norms to new risks (e.g., algorithmic decision-making that can violate due process). The third envisions entirely new rights for a data-centric era, such as the right to be free from certain forms of automated profiling. This typology suggests that technology influences the evolution of legal doctrines. Policymakers confront questions about the scope of digital privacy, the boundaries of free expression in online forums, and the responsibilities of technology providers.

2.2. The Interplay Between Business Intelligence and AI

Business intelligence (BI) refers to the processes and infrastructures that transform raw data into insights for strategic decision-making. BI systems often involve data extraction, warehousing, and analytic modeling. Modern BI incorporates machine learning approaches that automate data analysis and produce predictive outcomes. Organizations adopt these systems to refine marketing campaigns, detect fraud, or optimize supply chains. AI components in BI enhance forecasting capabilities but also carry risks of bias, privacy intrusion, or inadvertent discrimination (Nachbar, 2021). The interplay of BI and AI creates scenarios where automated tools can classify or prioritize individuals in ways that trigger ethical or legal concerns.

Data-driven BI tools rely on large volumes of personal and transactional data to identify patterns. This includes data gleaned from social media, browsing histories, or user-generated content (Calo, 2018). When combined with AI, these systems can shape consumer experiences, determine job advertisements, or sort applications for credit. The absence of transparency mechanisms may prevent individuals from understanding how their data is used or how decisions are reached (Lu, 2022). Although robust BI tools can enhance organizational performance, there is an ongoing discussion about how to integrate fundamental rights protections into system design, an issue that resonates with the principle of "human rights by design" (Yeung et al., 2020).

2.3. Digital Authoritarianism and Threats to Democratic Governance

While digital innovations can empower civic participation, they can also consolidate power in the hands of authoritarian regimes. Some governments implement AI-assisted surveillance, online censorship, or advanced data analytics to suppress dissent (Dragu & Lupu, 2021). These methods often rely on advanced facial recognition tools, chat monitoring, and large-scale data fusion. Unchecked digital surveillance destabilizes the freedoms of expression and assembly. It also undermines the right to privacy, as constant monitoring can breed self-censorship. Digital authoritarianism poses a growing concern because it exploits the same technologies that serve beneficial purposes in other contexts.

Dragu and Lupu (2021) argue that AI-based surveillance can weaken democratic institutions by silencing civil society and eroding accountability. Coupled with data analytics, regimes can single out activists or journalists for targeted harassment. In extreme cases, entire populations experience social credit systems that reward or punish behaviors. Such practices challenge fundamental rights and demand international cooperation to curb repressive uses of technology. However, enforcement is complicated by jurisdictional issues and the extraterritorial nature of digital networks. When analyzing digital authoritarianism, scholars emphasize the importance of upholding legal norms and transparency so that technologies do not become instruments of oppression.

2.4. Ethical Guidelines Versus Hard Law: Tensions and Gaps

The last decade saw a proliferation of AI ethics guidelines from industry coalitions, nonprofits, and international organizations. Many of these guidelines highlight fairness, transparency, accountability, and trustworthiness (Jobin et al., 2019). They represent efforts to articulate shared values, but their non-binding nature limits enforceability. Nemitz (2018) emphasizes that voluntary statements may offer high-level principles while lacking concrete remedies for those harmed by automated systems. Critics refer to this practice as "ethics washing," where organizations adopt broad ethical statements without real changes in operational or technical processes (Yeung et al., 2020).

An alternative approach involves crafting binding legal frameworks that regulate how data and AI tools operate. The UNESCO Recommendation on the Ethics of Artificial Intelligence (2021) is an example of a global standard aiming to guide AI in alignment with human rights. However, the transition from guidelines to codified law remains uneven. Some jurisdictions move forward with AI-specific regulations, while others rely on existing data protection or antidiscrimination statutes. The tension between soft law and binding regulation reveals the complexity of standardizing governance across different political and legal systems (Park, 2024). Advocates of hard law argue that only enforceable requirements can guarantee consistent compliance and accountability.

2.5. Blockchain: Promise and Peril for Human Rights

Blockchain is a decentralized technology that stores data in distributed ledgers secured by cryptographic methods. Proponents envision blockchain-based applications that bolster transparency and autonomy. Potential use cases include decentralized identity, secure land registries, or immutable voting records (G'sell & Martin-Bariteau, 2022). However, critics point out that blockchain can also enable money laundering or data permanence that undermines the right to be forgotten. Some networks have no single entity responsible for removing harmful or false data (Kirchschlaeger, 2024). This tension underscores how emerging technologies can both support and disrupt existing norms.

Organizations exploring blockchain for BI processes might see efficiency gains from secure, tamper-resistant logs of transactions. Yet concerns arise when personal data is stored on-chain without robust access controls. Public blockchain networks pose challenges for data privacy laws, which often require data controllers to permit deletion or modification. Although these features enhance trust in the records' integrity, they create friction with privacy rights. G'sell and Martin-Bariteau (2022) identify a need for clarity around how blockchain projects can comply with human rights and data protection principles. Regulators, developers, and users must reconcile the technology's decentralized nature with legal obligations that typically assume a clear data controller.

2.6. Summary of Theoretical Underpinnings

This section demonstrated how traditional human rights paradigms face stress tests from digitization. The fusion of business intelligence with AI underscores the potential for efficiency gains and the risk of discriminatory outcomes. Government or corporate misuse of data intensifies calls for robust transparency, accountability, and fairness measures. Blockchain technology adds another dimension, offering new modalities for information storage and trust, while challenging regulatory norms. Ethics guidelines provide conceptual frameworks but lack binding force, prompting debate over how best to protect rights in digital ecosystems. The next sections will examine practical problems, present governance initiatives, and propose future directions for rights-based digital transformations.

3. EMERGING CHALLENGES IN DIGITAL RIGHTS AND BI

3.1. Algorithmic Bias and Discrimination

One pressing challenge concerns bias and discrimination in data-driven systems. AI algorithms embedded in BI platforms can inherit biases from training data or from design decisions that reflect historical inequalities (Nachbar, 2021). When organizations rely on automated models for hiring, lending, or resource allocation, outcomes may disadvantage certain groups. For example, if historical data underrepresents women in leadership roles, predictive models might judge female candidates less favorably. Similarly, healthcare AI might misclassify conditions for underrepresented populations because of poor training data. These risks undermine equality and nondiscrimination rights.

3.1.1. Types of Algorithmic Bias

Algorithmic bias can be **explicit**, where the system encodes discriminatory rules, or **implicit**, where historical patterns inadvertently lead to skewed predictions (Nachbar, 2021). Another form is **measurement bias**, where input data does not accurately capture attributes for certain groups. **Sample bias** arises when data sets over- or under-sample particular demographics. **Labeling bias** occurs when a system is trained on subjective judgments about success or failure.

3.1.2. Mitigation Strategies

Organizations can mitigate these biases by performing regular audits. Practices include removing sensitive attributes, rebalancing training data, and validating model performance across subpopulations (Bakiner, 2023). However, technical fixes alone do not address deeper structural inequities. A holistic approach involves transparent model documentation, impact assessments, and opportunities for redress when unfairness occurs (Yeung et al., 2020). Many initiatives propose mandatory bias testing and active regulatory oversight for high-risk applications.

3.2. Data Privacy and Algorithmic Opacity

Digital platforms rely on extensive personal data, often collected without explicit user awareness. Large-scale business intelligence initiatives involve cross-referencing data from multiple sources, creating detailed profiles (Lu, 2022). When combined with AI, these profiles predict behavior and shape organizational decisions. Individuals often lack insight into how data sets were collected, stored, or processed. Opacity arises from the technical complexity of AI models, as well as from corporate secrecy that protects proprietary methods (Lu, 2022). Lack of transparency erodes trust and may conflict with legal obligations for data subjects to understand how personal information is used.

3.2.1. Privacy Regulations and Enforcement Gaps

Many countries have enacted data protection laws, inspired by frameworks like the European Union's General Data Protection Regulation (GDPR). These laws mandate obligations such as data minimization, purpose limitation, and consent. However, enforcement challenges persist, especially when organizations deploy opaque AI models that complicate compliance (Greenleaf, 2023). The cross-border flow of data creates jurisdictional puzzles: a user's data might be processed in multiple countries with different legal regimes. Meanwhile, certain regions still lack comprehensive privacy laws, leaving individuals exposed to uncontrolled data processing.

3.2.2. Algorithmic Transparency and Accountability

Algorithmic transparency involves explaining how models use data and how decisions are made. Clear documentation and interpretability solutions can help regulators, auditors, or affected individuals understand a model's logic. However, transparency can conflict with trade secrets or intellectual property claims (Lu, 2022). Full disclosure of algorithms may also be technically infeasible if the model is highly complex. Proposals include **algorithmic impact assessments** that evaluate potential harm, as well as **whistleblower protections** for employees who reveal unethical data practices (Lu, 2022). These measures, combined with compliance audits, can increase accountability in BI systems.

3.3. Digital Authoritarianism

Digital authoritarianism involves the strategic use of technology to maintain political control, suppress dissent, and monitor populations (Dragu & Lupu, 2021). Tools once promoted as neutral or beneficial can become surveillance infrastructure. Facial recognition, voice recognition, and geolocation tracking empower authorities to track citizens in real time. Regimes may require data-sharing arrangements with telecommunications providers or social media platforms, leveraging private technology for public surveillance (Palmiotto & Menéndez González, 2023).

3.3.1. Impact on Democratic Freedoms

Mass surveillance undermines freedom of expression by creating a climate of fear where individuals hesitate to criticize authorities. Rights to assemble or protest suffer if participants know cameras can identify them. Journalists and activists face heightened risks when states can monitor communications. These effects ripple outward, dissuading political engagement and eroding trust in public institutions (Dragu & Lupu, 2021).

3.3.2. Possible Responses

Civil society coalitions and international frameworks seek to limit the export of surveillance technologies to regimes with poor human rights records. Some countries have introduced laws requiring judicial warrants for advanced surveillance or banning facial recognition in public spaces. Yet these efforts are fragmented, and enforcement remains challenging. Collaborative efforts among democracies could align export controls and impose sanctions for states that abuse technology (Park, 2024). Transparent contracting for governmental technology solutions may also expose potential misuse.

3.4. Biometric Technologies and Facial Recognition

Biometric identification uses unique bodily features, including facial features, fingerprints, or iris scans. While biometrics can improve security or user convenience, they raise privacy and civil liberties concerns. Facial recognition systems identify people in real time, enabling remote tracking (Palmiotto & Menéndez González, 2023). This technology is already deployed at airports, border checkpoints, and public spaces. Widespread adoption for law enforcement or commercial applications can erode anonymity in everyday life.

3.4.1. Risks to Privacy and Accuracy

Facial recognition systems sometimes exhibit high error rates for specific groups, leading to wrongful suspicion or arrests (Palmiotto & Menéndez González, 2023). Moreover, mass deployment can reveal intimate patterns of movement and association. This violates personal autonomy and the right to privacy if used indiscriminately (Office of the UN High Commissioner for Human Rights, 2022).

3.4.2. Emerging Legal Constraints

Some jurisdictions restrict real-time biometric identification or require specific warrants. The European Union's proposed AI Act includes rules for high-risk applications, potentially restricting or banning certain facial recognition uses in public spaces. Courts have also scrutinized whether facial recognition violates existing data protection and fundamental rights. These legal developments create parameters for governments and private firms contemplating biometric solutions.

3.5. Blockchain Governance Challenges

Blockchain-based applications can serve as backbones for decentralized finance, supply-chain monitoring, or identity systems. They promise transparency and security through distributed ledgers. Yet blockchain also complicates regulatory oversight because nodes may operate across borders (G'sell & Martin-Bariteau, 2022). If harmful or illegal content is stored on-chain, removing it becomes difficult. Anonymous transactions can facilitate illicit activity. Regulatory frameworks that assume hierarchical structures struggle with decentralized networks, leaving potential gaps in accountability (Kirchschlaeger, 2024).

3.5.1. Tension with Data Protection

Blockchain's immutability conflicts with rights to erasure or rectification. Public blockchains record every transaction indefinitely, which may clash with privacy regulations (G'sell & Martin-Bariteau, 2022). Researchers propose privacy-preserving techniques, such as zero-knowledge proofs or off-chain data storage, but these solutions remain nascent. Regulators may require innovators to integrate compliance measures into blockchain protocols or to use permissioned networks where known entities can manage the ledger.

3.5.2. Defining Responsibility in Decentralized Systems

Traditional legal regimes require accountable entities to uphold consumer protections and security standards. Blockchain networks distribute responsibilities among multiple participants (Kirchschlaeger, 2024). If a user's rights are violated, it is unclear which party is liable. Smart contracts also raise concerns when code automates processes without external review. Policymakers must clarify how existing regulations apply to decentralized entities and how to enforce judgments if no single entity has control.

3.6. Summary of Challenges

This section mapped major issues arising from digital transformations. Algorithmic bias, data privacy, and the specter of digital authoritarianism threaten fundamental rights. Biometric systems, especially facial recognition, exacerbate surveillance concerns. Blockchain offers novel solutions for trust but complicates compliance with established legal norms. Common threads include the need for transparency, accountability, oversight, and harmonized standards. These challenges guide the exploration of governance frameworks in the next section, which investigates how stakeholders seek to balance technological innovation with the defense of human rights in digital contexts.

4. GOVERNANCE FRAMEWORKS AND REGULATORY RESPONSES

4.1. International Standards and Soft Law

International organizations have taken steps to address digital rights and AI governance. UNESCO's Recommendation on the Ethics of Artificial Intelligence (2021) sets broad principles around transparency, accountability, and the promotion of human rights. It urges member states to adopt policies that secure ethical AI development. However, its non-binding status limits enforcement. Similarly, the OECD's digital economy papers offer guidance on responsible data use (Dror-Shpoliansky, 2022). The UNESCO and OECD frameworks often shape national strategies but rely on the goodwill of states or private entities to implement them.

4.1.1. UN-Level Initiatives

The UN High Commissioner for Human Rights has issued reports on privacy and other digital rights (Office of the UN High Commissioner for Human Rights, 2022). These documents outline best practices, including clarity on lawful surveillance and robust judicial oversight. They stress that surveillance, censorship, or data collection must be necessary, proportionate, and consistent with human rights norms. They also identify encryption as a tool for privacy protection and call on states to avoid weakening it. Yet differences in political interests and legal traditions have impeded the creation of binding conventions on AI or digital rights.

4.1.2. Emerging Proposals for Binding Treaties

Some experts advocate for an international treaty on AI and human rights (AI Ethics Lab, 2025). This document could unify scattered governance approaches and establish global standards for accountability, transparency, and non-discrimination. The "Munich Convention on AI, Data, and Human Rights" proposed by the AI Ethics Lab (2025) seeks to consolidate legal norms. It highlights collaboration among governments, civil society, and industry. If adopted, such a treaty would represent a milestone in the formal regulation of digital technologies.

4.2. Regional Approaches

4.2.1. European Union

The European Union (EU) has taken a proactive stance on data privacy and AI regulation. The General Data Protection Regulation (GDPR) outlines strict requirements for handling personal data, including user consent and the right to be forgotten. EU policymakers have proposed the Artificial Intelligence Act, which classifies AI applications by risk level (Park, 2024). High-risk systems would face stricter transparency, data governance, and accountability rules. The Act also contemplates banning certain AI uses, such as real-time facial recognition in public spaces, although negotiations continue. This risk-based framework aims to promote innovation while protecting fundamental rights.

4.2.2. Council of Europe

The Council of Europe addresses digital governance through conventions and expert reports. For instance, the 2022 Council of Europe report on blockchain's impact underscores both benefits and pitfalls (G'sell & Martin-Bariteau, 2022).

The Council also cooperates with national data protection authorities and the European Court of Human Rights, which has issued judgments on surveillance and data retention laws. These regional efforts set influential precedents for balancing security, innovation, and human rights.

4.2.3. North America

The United States lacks a single federal data privacy law, relying on a patchwork of sectoral regulations (Greenleaf, 2023). Some states, such as California, have enacted privacy statutes inspired by GDPR principles. Federal agencies regulate specific aspects of AI, such as healthcare or finance. Canada has modernized its privacy framework, introducing proposals for an Artificial Intelligence and Data Act to regulate high-impact AI systems. These measures reflect a shift toward more comprehensive oversight but remain less uniform than EU rules.

4.2.4. Asia and Other Regions

Countries in Asia display diverse approaches. Some have strong privacy laws, while others encourage state-driven data collection. India has advanced data protection legislation in progress, although final details remain pending (Greenleaf, 2023). China's data protection laws limit cross-border transfers but also facilitate large-scale state surveillance. As for the Middle East, certain states adopt technology quickly but lack comprehensive legal frameworks for data rights. The variety of regional models underscores the difficulty of harmonizing practices and highlights the role of international standards.

4.3. National Regulations and Policies

Nation-states translate international guidelines into local regulations. Where strong rule of law and institutional capacity exist, governments can enforce accountability mechanisms for data processors. However, uneven capacities and political interests can produce inconsistent enforcement. Policies sometimes target narrow issues, such as regulating social media content or setting national AI strategies. Comprehensive legal frameworks that integrate data protection, consumer protection, and anti-discrimination laws are less common.

4.4. Corporate Governance and Self-Regulation

Companies deploying BI and AI solutions sometimes adopt voluntary codes of conduct or ethics boards. Large technology firms publish internal guidelines, but critics question whether these measures address structural issues. Self-regulation offers flexibility but can lead to conflicts of interest when profitability contradicts human rights principles (Nemitz, 2018). Some enterprises champion ethical AI practices to enhance brand reputation or preempt government intervention. These efforts may encourage collaboration with civil society and academia, spurring improved algorithmic transparency or fairness testing.

4.5. Human-Rights-Centric Design and Oversight

Yeung et al. (2020) emphasize that embedding human rights into system design can shift organizational practices. This includes "privacy by design," "security by design," and "fairness by design," where developers build compliance measures into technology from inception. Human rights impact assessments could follow a lifecycle approach, evaluating data handling procedures, algorithmic decisions, and end-user interfaces. Regulators or certification bodies can support these efforts, ensuring that solutions meet agreed-upon standards.

A complementary dimension is public oversight. Mechanisms might include participatory rulemaking, multi-stakeholder committees, or ombudsperson offices where grievances can be reported. Nemitz (2018) contends that democratic oversight is essential so that technology operates under the rule of law rather than under purely market-driven imperatives. Strengthening collective oversight can also mitigate the risk of single entities capturing regulatory processes.

4.6. Summary of Governance Efforts

Regulatory responses to digital rights remain fragmented. International bodies propose guidelines, some states experiment with binding measures, and the private sector pursues self-regulation. Certain regions (e.g., the EU) move toward comprehensive laws that address AI and data privacy. Elsewhere, scattered rules or insufficient enforcement create gaps. Soft law frameworks articulate shared principles but lack binding force, leading to calls for international treaties. Business intelligence applications operate within these varied contexts, forcing organizations to navigate complex compliance landscapes. The next section reviews how these governance frameworks play out in practice through case studies that illustrate real-world tensions and innovations in digital rights protection.

5. PRACTICAL ILLUSTRATIONS AND CASE STUDIES

5.1. Algorithmic Fairness in Financial Services

Financial institutions increasingly rely on BI systems that integrate AI-driven scoring models to assess loan eligibility or insurance premiums (Nachbar, 2021). Firms seek automated tools to process large volumes of applications efficiently. In one reported case, a bank used a credit-scoring model trained on historical lending data that exhibited a disparate impact on female applicants. Although the model had no explicit gender variable, proxy attributes correlated with gender (such as patterns of spending on childcare products) influenced outcomes. The bank faced public scrutiny, prompting an internal audit of its modeling pipeline.

Table 1. shows hypothetical results from a fairness audit that compares the bank's acceptance rates for male and female applicants before and after model adjustments:

Table 1. **Fairness Audit of Lending Model**

Group	Pre-Adjustment Acceptance Rate	Post-Adjustment Acceptance Rate
Male Applicants	65%	64%
Female Applicants	50%	62%

After the audit, the bank implemented rebalancing techniques that removed proxy variables correlated with gender. The acceptance gap narrowed, indicating some bias had been mitigated. The process also involved greater transparency, with the bank disclosing basic details about the model's logic. Such actions aligned with recommended practices for algorithmic fairness (Nachbar, 2021). Nonetheless, the case highlighted the complexity of detecting hidden biases in large data sets and the need for ongoing monitoring.

5.2. Data Privacy in a Multinational Healthcare System

A multinational healthcare provider introduced a BI system to analyze patient records for disease prediction. The system used patient demographics, clinical data, and lifestyle information. The provider stored data in a central warehouse accessible to various departments worldwide. Regulators questioned compliance with data protection rules because patients had not given explicit informed consent for secondary data uses. The system also employed opaque AI models, raising concerns about the interpretability of diagnostic suggestions (Lu, 2022).

Figure 1. illustrates a simplified data flow in the healthcare BI environment

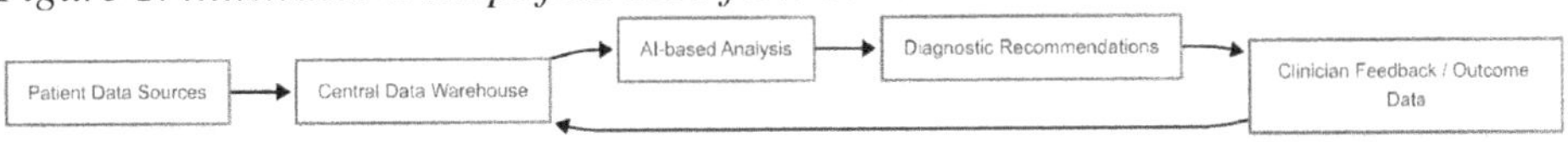

The organization responded by instituting new consent forms, data minimization strategies (collecting only essential information), and transparency dashboards that allowed medical practitioners to review how predictions were made. The firm also assigned a data protection officer to oversee global operations. However, the varying jurisdictional requirements complicated full compliance. The case underscores the difficulty of managing privacy obligations in a cross-border environment and highlights the importance of ongoing data governance to safeguard individual rights (Greenleaf, 2023).

5.3. Digital Authoritarianism: Case of Automated Social Control

A government known for restrictive policies adopted an AI-based monitoring system to detect "subversive activities" on social media (Dragu & Lupu, 2021). Authorities contracted a private vendor to install text and image analysis tools to scan user posts. The system flagged content that criticized government policies or mentioned politically sensitive events. Law enforcement agents used these flags to identify users for further surveillance. Civil society groups documented multiple detentions, including cases in which individuals faced harassment for peaceful online discourse.

Figure 2. provides an overview of the social media monitoring process

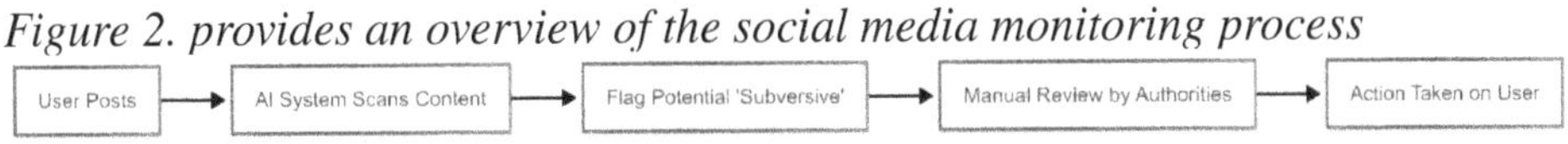

International organizations condemned these practices as violations of freedom of expression and privacy rights. Despite criticism, the government claimed it was protecting national security. The example demonstrates how AI and data analytics can become instruments of repression when wielded without independent oversight or legal checks. Dragu and Lupu (2021) argue that such systems require robust procedural safeguards, transparent usage policies, and accountability mechanisms to prevent abuse.

5.4. Blockchain-Based Land Registry for Transparency

A developing country faced rampant corruption in land registries, leading to fraudulent claims and property disputes. As a corrective measure, authorities introduced a blockchain-based registry. The goal was to create an immutable record of land ownership that officials could not unilaterally alter (G'sell & Martin-Bariteau, 2022). Each land title was assigned a token, and transactions (sales or transfers) were recorded on a distributed ledger. The system increased transparency, reducing opportunities for local officials to forge documents.

Table 2. compares outcomes before and after blockchain adoption:

Table 2. **Land Registry Outcomes Before Blockchain After Blockchain**

Fraudulent Land Claims (Annual)	**High**	**Reduced**
Average Time to Verify Ownership	Several Weeks	1-3 Days
Public Trust in Registry (Survey-based)	Low	Moderate

While the initiative showed promise, certain issues arose. Residents needed digital literacy to access and verify their records. The immutability of the blockchain also raised concerns about rectifying errors. If an incorrect record entered the ledger, correction was cumbersome (Kirchschlaeger, 2024). This case indicates how blockchain can advance human rights goals (property rights, rule of law) when designed to address real governance gaps. It also highlights the need for robust error-handling and user education.

5.5. Facial Recognition in Law Enforcement

A major city's police department began using a facial recognition platform for real-time surveillance at large events. Officials justified this system as a way to reduce criminal activity. However, an independent audit revealed multiple false matches, predominantly affecting darker-skinned individuals (Palmiotto & Menéndez González, 2023). Some citizens were detained based on erroneous matches. Civil liberties groups argued that persistent surveillance violated privacy rights and deterred lawful assembly. Public outcry led to legislative hearings, resulting in a moratorium on the technology until accuracy and oversight improved.

Table 3. presents hypothetical detection accuracy rates:

Table 3. **Facial Recognition Accuracy Light-Skinned Subjects Dark-Skinned Subjects**

True Positive Rate	**95%**	**85%**
False Positive Rate	2%	8%

The discrepancy suggests that the system performed unequally across demographic groups. This scenario exemplifies how advanced BI tools, if rushed into deployment, can produce discriminatory effects. Enhanced quality controls and accountability structures would be necessary to align this use of technology with human rights standards (Palmiotto & Menéndez González, 2023).

5.6. Summary of Case Study Insights

These examples illustrate both the promise and pitfalls of data-driven systems. BI solutions can increase efficiency and uncover hidden insights but risk violating privacy or amplifying historical inequalities. Authoritarian contexts show how AI deployments can erode freedoms, while blockchain pilots demonstrate potential gains in transparency. Across all cases, oversight, auditing, and stakeholder engagement emerged as crucial elements. These insights confirm that technology can be harnessed for public good when aligned with human rights principles, but requires careful design and regulatory intervention.

6. PROPOSED STRATEGIES FOR RIGHTS-BASED DIGITAL GOVERNANCE

6.1. Integrated Regulatory Frameworks

Governance should address the complete lifecycle of data: collection, storage, analysis, and utilization. Policymakers can develop integrated frameworks that unify data protection, AI oversight, and anti-discrimination norms. Such frameworks would mandate:

1. **Data Protection by Design**: Ensure that BI systems incorporate privacy-protective measures from the outset.
2. **Accountability Mechanisms**: Require organizations to maintain records for audits, respond to complaints, and disclose relevant model details when individuals are harmed.

3. **Transparency Requirements**: Mandate periodic impact assessments for high-risk applications, published to foster public scrutiny.

Park (2024) suggests that harmonizing international standards remains vital to prevent regulatory arbitrage. Fragmented rules allow companies to relocate or reroute data to more lenient jurisdictions. A coherent approach would involve bilateral or multilateral agreements on enforcement cooperation.

6.2. Binding International Treaties for AI and Data

A binding international convention could codify shared principles of human-rights-based AI governance. The Munich Convention on AI, Data, and Human Rights, proposed by AI Ethics Lab (2025), offers an example. Such a treaty would address:

1. **Non-Discrimination**: Prohibit algorithms that produce unjustified disparate impacts.
2. **Privacy Safeguards**: Clarify the permissible scope of data processing and surveillance.
3. **Accountability**: Obligate signatories to establish legal remedies for those harmed by AI.
4. **Monitoring Body**: Create an international entity that reviews compliance and addresses disputes among states.

Challenges to treaty adoption include geopolitical tensions and divergent economic priorities. Yet a single legal instrument could unify scattered frameworks, facilitate cross-border data governance, and enable collective oversight.

6.3. Enforcement and Oversight Bodies

Effective governance requires enforcement mechanisms. National data protection authorities or specialized AI regulators should have the power to investigate organizations and impose penalties for violations. Public ombudspersons or ethics committees can handle grievances, set guidelines, and propose reforms.

Figure 3. sketches a model of multi-layered oversight

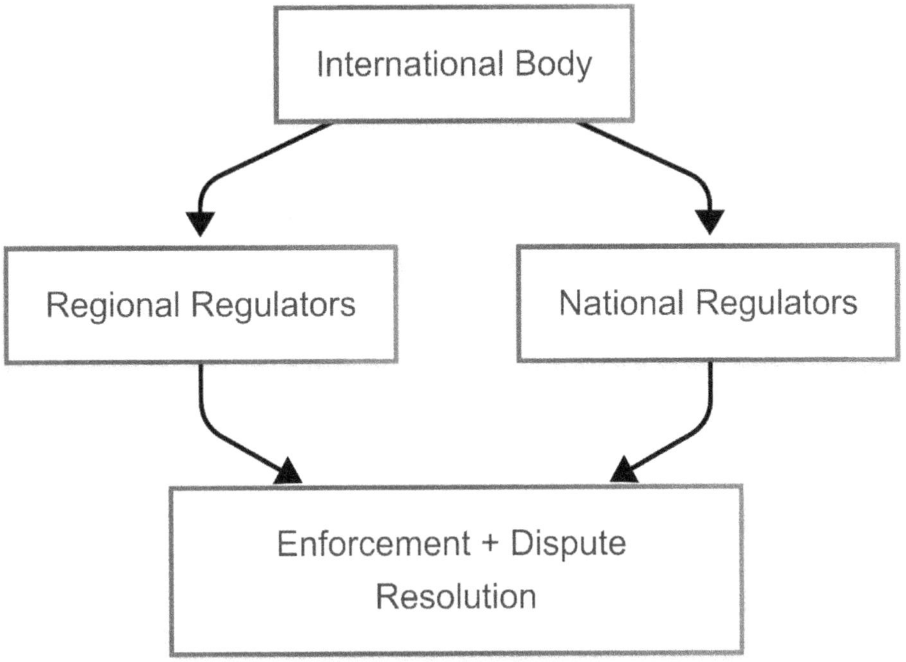

Coordination among regional and national regulators would minimize jurisdictional conflicts. This layered approach can support consistent enforcement, particularly when dealing with multinational corporations that operate complex BI systems across multiple regions.

6.4. Multi-Stakeholder Collaboration

Scholars underscore the necessity of engaging diverse stakeholders: governments, businesses, civil society, and technical experts (Zaidan & Ibrahim, 2024). Technology providers can offer insights into operational realities. Civil society groups represent public interests, especially marginalized communities vulnerable to algorithmic biases. Collaboration fosters acceptance of new regulations, improves compliance, and encourages socially responsible innovation.

In practice, multi-stakeholder forums might organize public consultations on proposed AI rules, convening experts to evaluate technical details. These forums can also promote capacity-building programs, training regulators on AI fundamentals or guiding developers in implementing rights-based design.

6.5. Human Rights Impact Assessments and Compliance Tools

Mandating human rights impact assessments (HRIAs) can help organizations anticipate potential harms. An HRIA for a new BI system would examine:

- **Data Sources**: Are data sets compiled lawfully and consensually?
- **Algorithmic Fairness**: Does the system disadvantage protected groups?
- **Transparency**: How will outcomes be explained to affected individuals?
- **Remedy Mechanisms**: Are there accessible channels for users to dispute decisions?

Similar to environmental impact assessments, HRIAs encourage companies to embed rights protections from the design phase onward. Over time, these assessments can become standard practice, normalizing robust compliance (Yeung et al., 2020).

6.6. Capacity Building and Public Awareness

Laws and guidelines alone cannot ensure respect for rights. Effective implementation requires stakeholder capacity building. Regulators must possess technical expertise to audit AI systems. Legal professionals need awareness of digital rights. The public should understand how data-driven decisions affect them and how they can seek recourse. Educational campaigns, open-access tools for model auditing, and training programs for officials can strengthen institutional readiness (Dror-Shpoliansky, 2022).

By enhancing digital literacy, citizens can make informed decisions about data sharing and exercise their rights, such as the right to request access or deletion of personal data. This contributes to a culture of shared responsibility for digital ecosystem governance.

6.7. Summary of Proposed Strategies

Stakeholders can employ diverse measures to integrate human rights into digital governance. These include cohesive regulation, international treaties, well-defined oversight structures, multi-stakeholder dialogues, and systematic impact assessments. Such steps can align business intelligence and AI applications with legal and ethical imperatives. The next section synthesizes these ideas by offering a conceptual framework. This framework organizes governance components to clarify responsibilities and processes for protecting rights in digital contexts.

7. CONCEPTUAL FRAMEWORK FOR RIGHTS-CENTRIC DIGITAL GOVERNANCE

7.1. Overview of the Framework

This framework consolidates key regulatory and design principles into a holistic model that operationalizes digital rights. It recognizes the complexity of modern BI and AI systems, which operate across borders and multiple industries. It also acknowledges that no single policy tool can address all challenges. The framework thus comprises four interlinked dimensions:

1. **Legal and Policy Layer**: Constitutional provisions, statutory rules, and treaties.
2. **Technical and Design Layer**: Embedding rights protections in architecture, code, and data flows.
3. **Institutional Oversight Layer**: Bodies that regulate, investigate, and enforce compliance.
4. **Social Engagement Layer**: Stakeholder participation, from civil society groups to end users.

7.2. Legal and Policy Layer

A robust legal foundation ensures that rights are not subordinate to technological or commercial imperatives. Laws should define permissible data uses, require transparency for significant automated decisions, and prescribe sanctions for violations. Policies ought to be technology-neutral to remain relevant as innovations evolve. Standards from UNESCO (2021) and OECD (Dror-Shpoliansky, 2022) can serve as reference points, complemented by more detailed sector-specific guidance.

7.3. Technical and Design Layer

Developers and data scientists should implement rights-based principles in software and system architectures:

- **Privacy by Design**: Restrict data collection and enable data encryption or de-identification where possible.
- **Fairness by Design**: Audit training data sets and monitor model outputs for biases.
- **Accountability by Design**: Log system decisions with identifiers for those responsible for configuration or data input.

Encouraging open protocols and interoperability can also improve transparency. Where feasible, secure multiparty computation or federated learning techniques might protect user data. Blockchain-based initiatives must integrate privacy solutions to ensure compliance with data protection laws (G'sell & Martin-Bariteau, 2022).

7.4. Institutional Oversight Layer

Regulatory agencies, ethics boards, or specialized bodies can investigate, sanction, and guide AI deployments. These institutions must have clear mandates, technical expertise, and independence from undue influence (Nemitz, 2018). Collaboration with international counterparts is essential, especially when systems process cross-border data.

Table 4 illustrates possible institutional roles:

Table 4. **Oversight Roles Functions**

National Data Protection Authority	Enforce privacy rules, conduct audits, impose fines.
AI Ethics Committee	Advise on policy, review high-risk AI projects, publish guidelines.
Judicial Oversight Body	Adjudicate rights violations, interpret laws in complex cases.
Civil Society Review Panel	Participate in consultations, monitor social impacts, alert regulators.

7.5. Social Engagement Layer

Public awareness and advocacy are critical. Individuals and communities affected by data-driven decisions should have avenues to voice concerns. Educational programs can raise digital literacy, so users understand how systems collect and use their data. Civil society organizations serve as watchdogs, offering independent evaluations of technology projects. Their input, combined with that of technology experts, can inform balanced regulations (Zaidan & Ibrahim, 2024). Engaging diverse stakeholders ensures that governance reflects varied perspectives, reducing blind spots in policy design.

7.6. Operationalizing the Framework

To operationalize this framework, governments could pass comprehensive digital rights legislation that aligns with international guidelines. Companies might adopt robust data governance protocols and create internal ethics teams empowered to veto harmful projects. Regulators could publish best practices for BI systems, focusing on interpretability and fairness. Periodic oversight, performed by independent authorities, would examine compliance. Multi-stakeholder forums and public reporting of impact assessments would maintain transparency. Over time, iterative improvements to both technology and regulation would occur, guided by feedback from audits and user complaints.

7.7. Anticipated Outcomes

Adopting this rights-centric framework could strengthen individual protections against misuse of data, mitigate risks of algorithmic bias, and impose clearer responsibilities on public and private sectors. It might foster public trust in BI and AI, facilitating more stable integration of technology into critical functions like healthcare and financial services. Simultaneously, it sets guardrails to prevent authoritarian abuse. By weaving human rights principles into the fabric of digital governance, societies can harness the benefits of emerging technologies while upholding core values of dignity, autonomy, and fairness.

8. CONCLUSION

8.1. Chapter Summary

This chapter explored how the expansion of digital ecosystems, BI, and artificial intelligence has raised pressing legal and ethical questions about fundamental rights. It reviewed theoretical developments, such as Shany's (2023) idea of three generations of digital rights and Dragu and Lupu's (2021) analysis of digital authoritarianism. It addressed practical challenges like algorithmic bias, data privacy, and decentralized technologies, showing how these issues intersect with international norms. The chapter then outlined governance measures, from international proposals (UNESCO, 2021; AI Ethics Lab, 2025) to regional and national regulatory strategies, culminating in a conceptual framework that integrates legal, technical, institutional, and social elements.

8.2. Future Research Directions

Future studies could examine empirical evaluations of specific regulatory interventions. Scholars may assess whether AI-specific laws improve fairness outcomes in sectors like employment or healthcare. Comparative analyses across jurisdictions can highlight best practices for data governance. Further investigation into blockchain-based identity and land registries might clarify the interplay of decentralization and regulatory obligations. Interdisciplinary collaborations can refine new design methods for embedding rights in code and system architecture.

8.3. Concluding Remarks

Technological innovation can enrich societies and create new opportunities. Yet unregulated or inadequately guided digital tools pose significant risks to privacy, freedom, and equality. Human rights principles serve as a durable foundation for navigating these changes. This chapter argues for a multi-dimensional approach that blends legal imperatives, technical design considerations, and social engagement. With careful oversight and international cooperation, data-driven solutions in BI and AI can align with core democratic values. Such alignment is pivotal for preserving trust, dignity, and justice in an era when digital transformation permeates every aspect of life.

REFERENCES

AI Ethics Lab. (2025). *Promoting and advancing human rights in global AI ecosystems (White paper)*. AI Ethics Lab.

Bakiner, O. (2023). The promises and challenges of addressing artificial intelligence with human rights. *Big Data & Society*, *10*(2), 20539517231205476. DOI: 10.1177/20539517231205476

Calo, R. (2018). Artificial intelligence policy: A primer and roadmap. *U.C. Davis Law Review*, *51*(2), 399–435.

Dragu, T., & Lupu, Y. (2021). Digital authoritarianism and the future of human rights. *International Organization*, *75*(4), 991–1017. DOI: 10.1017/S0020818320000624

Dror-Shpoliansky, D. (2022). *Rights in the digital age: Challenges and ways forward (OECD Digital Economy Papers No. 347)*. OECD Publishing.

G'sell, F., & Martin-Bariteau, F. (2022). *The impact of blockchains for human rights, democracy, and the rule of law*. Council of Europe Report. DOI: 10.2139/ssrn.4170324

Greenleaf, G. (2023). Global data privacy laws 2023: 162 national laws and 20 bills. *SSRN*, *186*, 1–4. DOI: 10.2139/ssrn.4426146

Jobin, A., Ienca, M., & Vayena, E. (2019). The global landscape of AI ethics guidelines. *Nature Machine Intelligence*, *1*(9), 389–399. DOI: 10.1038/s42256-019-0088-2

Kirchschlaeger, P. G. (2024). Blockchain ethics. *Philosophies*, *9*(1), Article 2.

Lu, S. (2022). Data privacy, human rights, and algorithmic opacity. *California Law Review*, *110*(Dec), 1423–1472.

Nachbar, T. B. (2021). Algorithmic fairness, algorithmic discrimination. *Florida State University Law Review. Florida State University. College of Law*, *48*(2), 509–558.

Nemitz, P. (2018). Constitutional democracy and technology in the age of artificial intelligence. *Philosophical Transactions. Series A, Mathematical, Physical, and Engineering Sciences*, *376*(2133), 20180089. DOI: 10.1098/rsta.2018.0089 PMID: 30323003

Office of the UN High Commissioner for Human Rights. (2022). *The right to privacy in the digital age (A/HRC/51/17)*. United Nations.

Palmiotto, F., & Menéndez González, N. (2023). Facial recognition technology, democracy and human rights. *Computer Law & Security Review, 50*, 105857. DOI: 10.1016/j.clsr.2023.105857

Park, S. (2024). Bridging the global divide in AI regulation: A contextual, coherent, and commensurable framework. *SSRN, 33*(1), 125–175. DOI: 10.2139/ssrn.4950781

Shany, Y. (2023). Digital rights and the outer limits of international human rights law. *German Law Journal, 24*(S3).

UNESCO. (2021). *Recommendation on the Ethics of Artificial Intelligence*. United Nations Educational, Scientific and Cultural Organization.

Yeung, K., Howes, A., & Pogrebna, G. (2020). AI governance by human rights–centered design, deliberation and oversight: An end to ethics washing. *Law, Innovation and Technology*, *12*(2), 311–333.

Zaidan, E., & Ibrahim, I. A. (2024). AI governance in a complex and rapidly changing regulatory landscape: A global perspective. *Humanities & Social Sciences Communications*, *11*(1), 1121. DOI: 10.1057/s41599-024-03560-x

Chapter 9
Law and Regulation of AI, Blockchain, and Digital Rights.

Manya Gupta
https://orcid.org/0009-0001-2904-6841
Graphic Era Hill University, Dehradun, India

Radhey Shyam Jha
https://orcid.org/0000-0003-0129-4365
Uttaranchal University, Dehradun, India

Nidhi Tyagi
https://orcid.org/0000-0002-3996-7644
Graphic Era University, Dehradun, India

Lalit Goyal
Tula's Institute, Dehradun, India

ABSTRACT

As digital technologies increasingly shape social, economic, and political life, the legal and ethical implications of their deployment demand urgent scholarly attention. Among the most disruptive technologies today, Artificial Intelligence (AI) and Blockchain raise pressing questions about the future of governance, individual rights, and democratic accountability. Their convergence introduces both opportunities and challenges that existing legal systems are not fully equipped to address—particularly in relation to digital rights. This chapter examines the intersection of AI, Blockchain, and digital rights through a unified theoretical and regulatory framework. While

DOI: 10.4018/979-8-3373-3186-7.ch009

AI systems introduce concerns around algorithmic opacity, bias, and automated decision-making, Blockchain technologies challenge legal norms through decentralization, immutability, and cross-jurisdictional complexity.

1. INTRODUCTION

This section will deal with the introduction to the convergence of artificial intelligence, blockchain technologies, and digital rights, outlining the scope and rationale of the chapter. AI and blockchain are two of the most transformative digital technologies of the 21st century, each posing novel challenges for law and regulation. AI refers to computer systems capable of performing tasks that typically require human intelligence, from automated decision-making to pattern recognition. Blockchain, on the other hand, is a distributed ledger technology that enables decentralized record-keeping and "smart contracts" without a central intermediary. The rapid advancement and deployment of these technologies have sparked debates on how existing legal frameworks can adapt to ensure that fundamental rights are protected in the digital environment. In particular, there is growing recognition that AI algorithms and blockchain networks can both enable and threaten *digital rights* – understood as the extension of citizens' rights into the digital realm. Governments and international bodies have begun responding with new regulatory initiatives aiming to align technological innovation with the rule of law and human rights.

Despite these emerging efforts, the intersection of AI, blockchain, and digital rights remains under-theorized and complex. The rationale for this chapter is to provide a *theoretical exploration* of how law and regulation can address the challenges posed by these technologies while upholding digital rights. A theoretical approach allows us to move beyond siloed discussions – where AI regulation, blockchain law, and digital rights are often treated separately – and instead to consider a holistic governance framework (Bleher & Braun, 2023). By examining underlying concepts and normative principles, the chapter aims to clarify how legal doctrines and regulatory strategies might evolve to manage AI and blockchain in a manner consistent with democratic values and fundamental rights. This introduction has set the stage by highlighting the convergence of these issues and the need for integrated analysis. The following sections will build on this foundation, first by unpacking key concepts and legal foundations, then reviewing relevant literature and theoretical perspectives, and finally identifying major themes, research gaps, objectives, and the anticipated contributions of this chapter.

1.1 Conceptual and Legal Foundations

The following discussion addresses the foundational concepts and legal doctrines that underpin AI, blockchain, and digital rights, establishing a base for the chapter's analysis. First, **Artificial Intelligence (AI)** can be defined broadly as computational systems that exhibit traits of human intelligence, such as learning, reasoning, and decision-making. Modern AI often involves machine learning algorithms that process large datasets to make predictions or automate decisions (Ahmad et al., 2022). In legal contexts, AI's growing role in society – from facial recognition to algorithmic risk assessments – raises foundational questions about how existing laws apply to machine-driven actions. For instance, if an AI system makes an erroneous decision that adversely affects an individual (such as denying a benefit or making a biased hiring recommendation), traditional legal doctrines of liability, due process, and fairness are implicated. Key legal frameworks like data protection law also directly interface with AI: when AI systems process personal data, they must comply with principles such as data minimization, consent, and purpose limitation under laws like the EU's General Data Protection Regulation (GDPR) (Justo-Hanani, 2022). Notably, concerns about the "black box" opacity of AI decision-making challenge core legal values of transparency and accountability – principles that will be explored later in this chapter.

Second, Blockchain technology refers to a decentralized ledger system maintained across a network of computers (nodes) that records transactions in a secure, tamper-evident way. Blockchains underlie cryptocurrencies (like Bitcoin and Ethereum) but also support smart contracts and decentralized applications. A *smart contract* is a self-executing program on the blockchain that automatically enforces contractual terms when predefined conditions are met. The conceptual foundation of blockchain in the legal sphere centers on its promises of trustlessness (removing the need for a trusted intermediary) and immutability (records, once added, are extremely difficult to alter). These features, while innovative, pose challenges for the law (Roberts et al., 2023). Immutability and decentralization can conflict with legal doctrines that assume the ability to correct or control records; for example, a blockchain's permanent record of data is at odds with the right to erasure (the *"right to be forgotten"*) in data protection law. Additionally, because blockchain networks operate globally with no single authority, determining jurisdiction and applicable law becomes problematic. Traditional legal concepts of contract and property are also tested by smart contracts and tokenized assets, raising questions about how legal recognition and enforcement occur when "code is law" in practice.

Third, Digital Rights refer to the rights and freedoms of individuals in the digital environment, essentially extending fundamental human rights into online and technological contexts. Digital rights encompass a range of entitlements – including privacy and data protection, freedom of expression online, access to information and the internet, and equality and non-discrimination in digital platforms (Laux, Wachter, & Mittelstadt, 2024). The conceptual foundation of digital rights lies in adapting classical rights (as found in constitutions and international human rights law) to new technological realities. For example, privacy rights translate into the right to control personal data and protection against pervasive surveillance, while freedom of expression online involves rights and limits concerning content moderation and censorship by both governments and private platforms. Recognizing digital rights often requires updating or reinterpreting existing legal instruments; a notable instance is the GDPR, which strengthens individual control over personal data as a fundamental right in the information age. Moreover, concepts like a "Digital Bill of Rights" have been proposed or adopted in various jurisdictions to enumerate citizens' rights in cyberspace. Underlying legal doctrines relevant here include constitutional law (e.g., applying free speech or due process guarantees to digital contexts), international human rights law (such as the right to privacy under treaties), and emerging soft-law principles (like the notion of internet access as a human right) (Almeida, Shmarko, & Lomas, 2022).

The foundation for this chapter rests on understanding how AI functions and tests legal principles, how blockchain's decentralization and immutability challenge traditional regulatory frameworks, and how digital rights serve as a normative baseline that law seeks to uphold amid technological change. These clarifications set the stage for examining the scholarly and policy literature that has grappled with these topics, which the next section will address.

2. LITERATURE REVIEW

The upcoming discussion will summarize key academic, legal, and policy literature on AI regulation, blockchain governance, and emerging digital rights. A considerable body of research has emerged in recent years to address how law should respond to the rapid rise of AI and blockchain.

In the realm of **AI regulation**, scholars and policymakers have focused on issues such as algorithmic accountability, bias mitigation, and the necessity (or not) of new legislation tailored to AI. One strand of literature debates whether existing legal frameworks are sufficient to cope with AI, or whether novel approaches – such as the European Union's *Artificial Intelligence Act* – are required. The EU's AI Act, in particular, has been analyzed as a pioneering attempt to regulate AI based on risk categories. Academic commentary has highlighted challenges AI poses to the rule of law, noting that the opaqueness of "black box" algorithms can undermine transparency and accountability in decision-making. There is broad agreement in the literature that AI systems, especially in high-stakes domains, demand some form of oversight to prevent violations of rights and to maintain public trust (Sanchez, Brenman, & Ye, 2024). Proposals range from embedding ethical principles into AI design (often via industry guidelines or standards), to strengthening enforcement of data protection and anti-discrimination laws, to creating new regulatory agencies for algorithmic systems.

In parallel, the literature on blockchain governance and law has explored how decentralized ledger technologies fit within, or disrupt, existing legal constructs. Early discussions often revolved around cryptocurrencies and financial regulation, but more recent scholarship extends to smart contracts, decentralized autonomous organizations (DAOs), and the cross-border implications of blockchain networks. A recurring theme is the tension between the decentralization ethos ("code is law") and the need for legal oversight when blockchain-based activities impinge on rights or public interests. Legal scholars have examined scenarios where blockchain's features challenge traditional law – for example, the permanence of blockchain records versus privacy laws, or the difficulty of assigning liability in the absence of a central operator. In the study Rebecchi, Todd, and Hagège (2024) and others identified multiple points of friction between blockchain technology and data protection regimes like the GDPR. These include the inability to easily rectify or erase personal data on an immutable ledger, and the unclear status of who acts as the "data controller" in a distributed network. Policy reports, such as a 2020 Council of Europe study, similarly underscore issues of enforcement, observing that determining the applicable law for blockchain systems is a significant hurdle. On the positive side, some literature notes that blockchain can enhance certain rights – for instance, by enabling secure property records or transparent voting systems – though these benefits come with new legal questions about validity and governance. Overall, blockchain law discourse oscillates between optimism about innovation and concern that legal mechanisms must adapt to ensure accountability and protect users.

Regarding digital rights and governance, an evolving set of writings addresses how fundamental rights can be preserved and promoted in an era of AI and blockchain. Here, the concept of *digital constitutionalism* has gained traction as a framework to analyze developments like the EU's digital policies. Digital constitutionalism refers to efforts to embed constitutional values – such as privacy, free expression, due process, and checks and balances – into the governance of digital technologies and platforms (Rebecchi, Todd, & Hagège, 2024). For example, Pollicino & Paolucci (2024) argue that the EU's regulatory shift (exemplified by the AI Act) represents a move from a laissez-faire digital liberalism to a rights-centric digital constitutionalism, emphasizing accountability of private tech actors and protection of individuals' rights. Other scholars discuss *data justice* as a lens, insisting on fairness in how data-driven systems treat individuals and communities. There is also an expanding policy literature on digital rights: civil society organizations have proposed charters or principles for digital rights, covering aspects like the right to privacy online, the right to an explanation of algorithmic decisions, and even the right to internet access. A key insight from the literature is that protecting digital rights in the context of AI and blockchain may require updating legal interpretations and developing novel governance mechanisms. For instance, ensuring the right to an effective remedy when an AI system causes harm might involve new procedural safeguards or oversight bodies. Similarly, discussions about blockchain often invoke the need for incorporating principles of human rights into technological design – for example, building identity management systems on blockchain that respect individual autonomy and consent (Hjaltalin & Sigurdarson, 2024; Schiff, 2022).

In synthesizing these strands of literature, it becomes apparent that while AI, blockchain, and digital rights have each been studied extensively on their own, there is a need for integrated analyses that consider their interplay. Many authors converge on the notion that law and regulation must evolve in parallel with technological innovation, guided by fundamental rights and theoretical principles. However, current scholarship also reveals gaps and unresolved debates – for example, how to practically enforce regulations in decentralized systems, or how to balance innovation with rights protection without stifling beneficial uses of technology. This literature synthesis sets the stage for the theoretical framework and key issues that follow, highlighting both what is known and where further inquiry is needed.

3. THEORETICAL FRAMEWORK

The following discussion will outline the theoretical lens through which the chapter's analysis will be grounded. Given the complex socio-technical nature of AI and blockchain, the chapter adopts a multidisciplinary theoretical framework that combines elements of *techno-regulation*, *digital constitutionalism*, and *data justice*. This blended approach provides a normative foundation to assess how law can or should regulate technology in order to uphold digital rights.

Techno-Regulation: Techno-regulation theory examines how technological artifacts themselves can serve as a means of regulating behavior. As famously noted by Lawrence Lessig, *"code is law"* – meaning that software and hardware architecture can embed rules and values that constrain what people can do online. In other words, technology design by private actors or engineers may effectively enforce policy (or their own values) through code, sometimes pre-empting or bypassing traditional legal enforcement. For example, a smart contract on a blockchain can automatically execute or restrict certain actions, leaving little room for discretionary human intervention. This raises theoretical questions: if code can enforce rules, how do traditional legal principles like due process or the possibility of appeal apply? Techno-regulation scholarship (e.g., Brownsword, Hildebrandt) urges that we critically assess the implications of embedding regulatory norms into technology (Zhang & Zhang, 2023). One insight from this perspective is the need to ensure that when technology regulates, it does not unduly undermine human rights or the rule of law. For instance, overly rigid automation might sacrifice values of fairness or mercy that legal processes allow. In summary, techno-regulation theory provides a lens to analyze scenarios such as AI-driven decisions and immutable blockchain transactions, asking whether law should mandate technical safeguards (like "circuit-breakers" in algorithms or modifiability in smart contracts) to protect rights and uphold fundamental legal principles (Radu, 2021).

Digital Constitutionalism: This concept refers to the application of constitutional values and principles to the digital domain, especially to constrain the power of private tech platforms and ensure fundamental rights in digital governance. Digital constitutionalism provides a lens to view regulatory developments as part of a broader evolution of governance in the information age. It emphasizes that just as constitutions check and balance governmental powers to protect citizens' rights, analogous constraints and rights frameworks should guide the digital ecosystem (Werbach, 2022). The European approach in recent years exemplifies this: the shift from a market-driven stance to a rights-centric approach in digital regulation can be seen as a form of digital constitutionalism, where instruments like the AI Act aim to ensure that AI development is bounded by respect for fundamental rights and rule-of-law principles. Under this framework, we consider how a "constitutional" approach to AI and blockchain regulation might look – for example, requiring transparency and oversight for algorithms much as constitutional law requires openness and checks on government. The chapter's theoretical stance posits that embedding such high-level principles into the governance of AI and blockchain is essential for protecting digital rights in the long term. This may involve formal legal measures (like legislation enshrining digital rights) as well as private or technical measures (like industry codes of conduct and system designs aligned with fundamental rights) (Sobolewski & Allessie, 2021).

Data Justice: Complementing the above, the framework of data justice introduces an ethical and social justice dimension, focusing on fairness, equity, and inclusion in data-driven systems. Data justice asks whether technologies like AI and blockchain distribute benefits and burdens in a just manner, and whether they uphold the dignity of all individuals. A working definition of data justice is *"fairness in the way people are made visible, represented and treated as a result of their production of digital data"*. This perspective is crucial for a normative analysis because it highlights issues of bias, discrimination, and power imbalance (Gazi, 2021). Within this chapter's framework, data justice is used to scrutinize AI algorithms for biases that disproportionately affect marginalized groups and to examine blockchain applications for any exclusionary effects (for instance, if certain populations are left out of digital financial systems or if blockchain-based identity systems disadvantage those without access to technology). Data justice aligns with the concept of digital rights by insisting that rights like equality and non-discrimination are not abstract ideals but need to be realized concretely in technological design and deployment (Panagariya, 2022). By incorporating data justice, the chapter ensures that our theoretical approach is not only about limiting power (as in constitutionalism) or shaping behavior through code (as in techno-regulation) but also about achieving equitable outcomes in digital society.

In sum, the theoretical framework guiding this chapter is an integrated one. It uses techno-regulation theory to understand how norms can be embedded in technological infrastructures, digital constitutionalism to provide a high-level vision of rights-based governance, and data justice to stay attuned to fairness and social impact. Through this lens, the subsequent examination of key themes and regulatory issues will be grounded in a coherent understanding of the values at stake and the mechanisms by which law and technology intersect.

3.1 Key Themes and Issues

This part of the chapter will address the principal legal challenges and ethical dilemmas posed by the integration of AI and blockchain with digital rights frameworks. Drawing on the theoretical framework, we outline several key themes:

3.2 Privacy and Data Protection

Privacy is a critical theme, involving the tension between technological innovation and the right to privacy. AI systems often rely on large volumes of personal data, and blockchain networks can store data immutably across global nodes. These characteristics pose challenges for data protection regimes. For AI, the concern is that without robust oversight, automated data processing could enable mass surveillance or misuse of personal information, undermining individuals' control over their data. For blockchain, the design of a distributed ledger conflicts with certain privacy norms: information recorded on a public blockchain is transparent and effectively permanent (Kadaba, Aithal, & KRS, 2023). This is in tension with legal rights such as the GDPR's right to erasure, data minimization principle, and the general expectation that individuals should be able to update or delete their personal data. Indeed, blockchain's transparency and immutability, while ensuring data integrity, "run counter to key data protection requirements" by making deletion or modification of data nearly impossible. Moreover, the decentralized nature of blockchain makes it hard to identify a responsible entity (data controller) who can be held accountable for privacy compliance. This theme raises the question: how can laws ensure privacy and data protection when data is diffused across algorithms and ledgers? Possible approaches include embedding privacy-by-design in AI (e.g., using techniques like data anonymization or federated learning) and developing privacy-preserving blockchain solutions (such as zero-knowledge proofs) to reconcile some of these conflicts. Ultimately, achieving an appropriate balance between innovation and privacy requires both technological measures and legal rules that reinforce each other – a subject the chapter explores in depth (Bhattacharya, 2022).

3.3 Bias and Non-Discrimination

Another major issue is algorithmic bias and the potential for discrimination. AI algorithms, especially those using machine learning, can inadvertently learn and perpetuate biases present in training data – leading to discriminatory outcomes in areas like hiring, lending, criminal justice, or content moderation. This directly implicates the right to equality and non-discrimination. Unfair AI outcomes have raised legal and ethical concerns worldwide, prompting calls for regulation to ensure *algorithmic fairness*. Legal frameworks (such as anti-discrimination laws or constitutional equality guarantees) need to be interpreted or expanded to cover decisions made by AI systems (Siu, 2023). The theoretical lens of data justice reinforces that it is not enough for AI to be accurate or efficient; it must also be fair and just in its impacts. Thus, many scholars and policymakers advocate for requirements like algorithmic impact assessments or audits to detect bias, and for diversity in the data and teams developing AI, as part of a regulatory strategy to prevent digital discrimination. Blockchain technology might seem neutral in this regard, but issues of bias can still arise – for example, if access to blockchain-based services (like finance or voting) is uneven or if governance of blockchain platforms is dominated by certain groups, marginalizing others. From a normative perspective, we must consider how to guarantee equal treatment and inclusivity in systems governed by code. The European Commission's proposed AI rules explicitly frame avoidance of bias as a compliance requirement, and academic work has shown that unchecked AI can "replicate systemic biases without a transparent and accountable framework". Addressing bias thus requires a combination of strong enforcement of existing anti-discrimination norms in tech contexts and the incorporation of fairness criteria into the design and deployment of AI and blockchain systems (Chiarella, 2023).

3.4 Decentralization and Jurisdiction

A core challenge presented by blockchain (and by globally deployed AI systems) is *decentralization*. Blockchain networks operate across multiple jurisdictions simultaneously, with no central authority controlling the system. This raises the issue of how existing legal systems – which typically rely on identifying a jurisdiction and a responsible entity – can exercise authority. Legal commentators note this problem: if a dispute arises from a blockchain transaction or a harm is caused by a smart contract, it may be unclear which country's courts have jurisdiction or which laws apply, since the nodes and users could be anywhere in the world (Scheurman, 2021). Decentralization can thus lead to a "regulatory gap," where activities occur in a space that is difficult for any single legal system to regulate effectively. AI can have similar issues – for example, a machine-learning service distributed across cloud servers worldwide might not fit neatly under any one nation's regulatory scope. The tension here is between the borderless nature of technology and the bordered nature of law. Potential approaches to this challenge include international cooperation and harmonization of laws (so that there is less divergence between jurisdictions) and creative legal theories to anchor jurisdiction (for example, focusing on the location of a significant portion of nodes or on the nationality of developers). Another approach is the development of transnational principles or model laws (through bodies like UNCITRAL) specifically addressing issues of decentralized systems. In any case, the decentralization issue fundamentally challenges regulators to devise ways to enforce rules and uphold rights (such as consumer protection or anti-money laundering laws) in an environment where the traditional levers of control are diffuse. This theme underscores the need for new legal thinking and possibly new institutions to deal with the "lawlessness" that pure decentralization can create, without stifling the innovations and benefits that decentralization might provide (Bulman-Pozen & Seifter, 2023).

3.5 Transparency and Accountability

Transparency and accountability are foundational principles in governance and law, and they are put under strain by AI and blockchain in different ways. With AI, the "black box" nature of complex models (like deep neural networks) can make it difficult to understand how a particular decision was reached (Sule, Zennaro, & Thomas, 2021). The general lack of understanding of automated decision logic presents multiple challenges to the rule of law. If an AI system produces a harmful or questionable outcome, who is answerable, and how can the decision be scrutinized or challenged? Ensuring accountability in AI may require legal mandates for explainability (so that important algorithmic decisions can be explained in human-understandable terms) and assigning clear responsibility to either developers, operators, or users of AI systems. Concepts like a "right to explanation" for individuals affected by automated decisions have been discussed in legal scholarship and find support in regulations like the GDPR's provisions on automated processing. Possible accountability mechanisms include algorithmic auditing, certification processes for AI systems, and oversight agencies dedicated to AI – all intended to make AI more transparent and its operators more accountable for outcomes (Di Minin et al., 2021).

Blockchain presents a different transparency paradox: public blockchains are transparent in that all transactions are visible, yet the parties involved can remain pseudonymous, and governance processes are often opaque to outsiders. Moreover, when something goes wrong on a blockchain (such as a bug in a smart contract leading to loss of funds), there may be no clear accountable entity due to decentralization. Such scenarios have played out in practice, revealing a major accountability gap (Huang, 2023). The famous case of "The DAO" hack in 2016 illustrated that when a decentralized smart contract failed, the remedy was an ad-hoc technical intervention (a blockchain fork) rather than a legal process – leaving questions about responsibility unanswered. Regulators are therefore concerned with how to inject accountability into such contexts – possibly by requiring that certain blockchain services be operated by identifiable entities (as is done in anti-money laundering regulation of crypto exchanges) or by developing legal doctrines that attribute responsibility to those who create or maintain a blockchain codebase. The theoretical idea of digital constitutionalism supports the demand for transparency and accountability as non-negotiable elements: just as the rule of law requires government decisions to be reviewable and justified, algorithmic or code-based decisions should also be subject to some form of review and redress. This theme thus grapples with bridging the accountability gap: creating mechanisms so that individuals' rights are not unreasonably infringed by inscrutable AI or unstoppable code (Chukwunweike et al., 2024).

3.6 Human Autonomy and Oversight

Human autonomy and oversight constitute a final key issue. Important decisions should not be left entirely to machines without the possibility of human review. Legal and ethical norms thus insist on keeping a "human in the loop" for high-stakes AI deployments (for example, requiring human oversight for certain algorithmic decisions). In the blockchain context, the irreversibility of smart contracts – once executed, they cannot be easily altered or stopped – means that humans may lack the ability to intervene or correct errors. This rigidity can conflict with fundamental principles of fairness and individual autonomy (Hung, 2025). The overarching concern is to ensure that human agency and dignity are respected, with individuals retaining some control and recourse even in automated or decentralized systems. Balancing the efficiency of automation with the need for human oversight is therefore a fundamental tension that regulators and system designers must carefully navigate (Juliussen et al., 2023).

These key themes – privacy, bias, decentralization, transparency, and human oversight – encapsulate the main areas where law and regulation must contend with the disruptive effects of AI and blockchain on digital rights. Each theme reveals challenges that are not purely technical or purely legal, but a hybrid of both, underscoring the need for interdisciplinary approaches. Building on these issues, the chapter will next discuss gaps in current research and why a theoretical inquiry such as this is timely and significant.

4. RESEARCH GAP AND SIGNIFICANCE

The forthcoming discussion will highlight existing research gaps in legal scholarship and demonstrate how this chapter aims to address them. As the above synthesis and thematic analysis suggest, discussions on AI regulation, blockchain governance, and digital rights often remain siloed or narrowly focused. One notable gap is the lack of integrated *theoretical* analysis encompassing both AI and blockchain under the umbrella of digital rights. Much of the existing scholarship tends to specialize: AI ethics and law experts concentrate on algorithmic decision-making (perhaps touching only briefly on decentralization), while blockchain legal research delves into decentralization and smart contracts but often without addressing broader human rights implications (Cervi, 2022). This fragmentation has been observed as a general challenge in the digital rights field – the tendency toward segmentation and hyper-specialization in topics such as privacy, freedom of expression, and AI regulation. By addressing AI, blockchain, and digital rights together, this chapter aims to overcome that fragmentation and provide a more holistic perspective.

Another gap in the scholarship is the depth of theoretical grounding. While there are many policy papers and doctrinal analyses of emerging regulations, fewer works step back to critically examine the underlying normative and conceptual issues across these technologies. For instance, there is ongoing debate on whether existing legal principles (like accountability, transparency, jurisdiction) are sufficient or whether fundamentally new frameworks are needed in light of AI and blockchain. This chapter's theoretical approach – leveraging techno-regulation, digital constitutionalism, and data justice – fills a gap by offering a structured way to analyze these questions. It links discussions of technological design (code architecture, algorithmic governance) with discussions of rights and constitutional principles, which are often handled separately. Moreover, in policy debates one sees a gap between high-level principles and practical regulation. This research helps bridge that by using theory to inform what effective regulation should look like in practice, ensuring it is grounded in clear values.

The significance of this chapter is multi-fold. Academically, it will help build a foundation for future research that crosses the boundaries between AI law and blockchain law, using digital rights as a common framework. Practically, as lawmakers worldwide grapple with drafting AI regulations and blockchain policies, the insights from a comprehensive theoretical analysis can guide more coherent and rights-respecting regulatory regimes. In particular, by highlighting common normative tensions (such as the need for transparency or the difficulties of enforcement in decentralized systems), this work can inform policymakers about critical points where intervention or new thinking is necessary (Sivasubramaniam et al., 2021). The chapter is also significant in shedding light on emerging issues that have not been fully addressed – for example, the interaction between automated AI decisions and decentralized data storage, or how the concept of consent might need reimagining when transactions are immutable. By filling these research gaps, the chapter will set the stage for more nuanced discourse and help avoid scenarios where legal developments in one area (say AI) inadvertently conflict with or ignore realities in another area (like blockchain). Ultimately, the significance lies in promoting an approach to digital technology governance that is unified by respect for digital rights and informed by robust theory.

5. OBJECTIVES

The following section will present the chapter's core objectives and the key research questions it aims to address. The chapter's primary objectives are as follows:

1. **Analyze the convergence of AI and blockchain through a digital rights lens:** Examine how these two technologies jointly impact fundamental rights and what common regulatory principles can address both. (For example, *how do AI and blockchain individually and collectively challenge rights like privacy, equality, and accountability?*)
2. **Clarify conceptual and legal foundations for governing emerging technologies:** Dissect key concepts and legal doctrines to establish clear terminology and frameworks that future scholarship and policymakers can use. (*What definitions and legal principles should form the basis for regulating AI and blockchain?*)
3. **Develop a theoretical framework anchored in rights:** Apply and refine theoretical models (techno-regulation, digital constitutionalism, data justice) in the context of AI and blockchain. (*What does it mean to embed fundamental rights*

into technological design and governance? How can theory guide the practical regulation of code and algorithms?)

4. **Identify and explore key regulatory challenges:** Investigate each major issue (privacy, bias, etc.) to understand why these problems occur and what legal or policy responses are viable. (*Why is accountability difficult in AI and blockchain, and what legal tools could enhance it? Where do current laws fall short in protecting digital rights against these technologies?*)
5. **Highlight research gaps and suggest solutions:** Pinpoint where current laws and literature are lacking and outline areas that require further research or legal innovation. (*What are the unresolved questions in the law of AI/blockchain? How can a rights-based approach fill those gaps or guide new policies?*)

By pursuing these objectives, the chapter seeks to answer an overarching question: *How can theoretical insights and legal principles be applied to ensure that AI and blockchain technologies develop in harmony with digital rights and the rule of law?* These objectives keep the chapter focused on both diagnosing issues and pointing toward frameworks or solutions to address them.

6. CONTRIBUTIONS

This part of the chapter will articulate the chapter's potential impact on academic scholarship and policy formulation. By synthesizing the domains of AI law, blockchain regulation, and digital rights within a single theoretical framework, the chapter will contribute in several ways:

- **Theoretical Innovation:** It provides a novel combination of regulatory theories (techno-regulation, digital constitutionalism, data justice) applied jointly to AI and blockchain. This advances academic discourse by offering a cohesive lens for analysis, potentially serving as a foundation for future research that further integrates multiple emerging technologies under a rights-based theory.
- **Interdisciplinary Bridge:** The chapter connects typically separate conversations in technology law. By drawing parallels between challenges in AI and challenges in blockchain, it offers a comparative perspective that reveals cross-cutting insights (for example, how transparency is a common value needed in both contexts, or how blockchain's decentralization foreshadows governance issues also relevant for AI). This cross-cutting approach will be valuable to scholars in both fields and encourages development of a more unified "digital law" scholarship.

- **Guidance for Policymakers:** On a practical level, the chapter's findings can guide policymakers and regulators. The expected contribution here is to distill complex theoretical ideas into principles that can inform regulation – such as the importance of maintaining human oversight, the need for built-in privacy safeguards, or the benefit of international cooperation on decentralized technologies. Policymakers drafting AI laws or blockchain guidelines can benefit from the chapter's holistic view, ensuring that regulations are coherent (avoiding contradictory approaches) and grounded in the protection of rights.
- **Empowering the Digital Rights Discourse:** By framing the regulation of AI and blockchain in terms of digital rights, the chapter reinforces the idea that human rights should be at the core of the digital transformation. It contributes to the normative discourse by articulating why safeguarding privacy, equality, and other rights is not just an ethical consideration but a legal necessity in the face of powerful new technologies. This supports a growing movement in academia and civil society to develop what might be called a "digital constitutionalism" for our evolving digital society.

7. CONCLUSION

Finally, this section will deal with providing a provisional conclusion, outlining anticipated theoretical findings or normative claims. The chapter is expected to conclude that effectively governing AI and blockchain in the digital rights context requires a recalibration of legal and regulatory frameworks grounded in strong theoretical principles. A central argument will be that a rights-based, human-centric approach to technology regulation is essential – meaning that laws and policies must explicitly incorporate safeguards for privacy, fairness, transparency, and accountability into the fabric of AI and blockchain governance. The analysis will likely show that neither purely self-regulatory technological fixes nor traditional law alone can adequately protect digital rights; instead, a combination of legal oversight and built-in technological measures is needed.

Normatively, the chapter will assert that concepts like digital constitutionalism are not merely academic rhetoric but have practical urgency: just as societies established constitutional rules to civilize the power of governments, we now must establish equivalent checks and balances for the power wielded by algorithms and decentralized networks. This might manifest in recommendations such as adopting *"algorithmic bills of rights"* or international agreements that set baseline standards for AI and blockchain (for instance, commitments to algorithmic transparency and privacy preservation as fundamental norms). The tentative conclusion will also emphasize maintaining the rule of law in the face of technological disruption – insisting that technologies should augment rather than erode legal protections. For example, AI systems should be deployed in ways that uphold due process (by providing explanations and avenues for challenge), and blockchain applications should be aligned with legal obligations (through innovative design or hybrid solutions that allow some oversight).

In terms of theoretical findings, the conclusion will tie together how the blended framework illuminated the issues: it will note that techno-regulation highlights the need for embedding norms into code, data justice highlights the need for equitable outcomes, and digital constitutionalism highlights the macro-level requirement of preserving fundamental rights and democratic accountability. By synthesizing these, the chapter will conclude with a call for holistic governance: an approach where law, technology design, and ethical norms work in concert. The provisional stance is that embracing such a holistic, rights-affirming approach will not only address current challenges but also make the digital ecosystem more resilient and trustworthy going forward.

REFERENCES

Ahmad, K., Maabreh, M., Ghaly, M., Khan, K., Qadir, J., & Al-Fuqaha, A. (2022). Developing future human-centered smart cities: Critical analysis of smart city security, Data management, and Ethical challenges. *Computer Science Review*, *43*, 100452. DOI: 10.1016/j.cosrev.2021.100452

Almeida, D., Shmarko, K., & Lomas, E. (2022). The ethics of facial recognition technologies, surveillance, and accountability in an age of artificial intelligence: A comparative analysis of US, EU, and UK regulatory frameworks. *AI and Ethics*, *2*(3), 377–387. DOI: 10.1007/s43681-021-00077-w PMID: 34790955

Bhattacharya, D. (2022). Digital Yuan (e-CNY): China's official digital currency. *Strategic Analysis*, *46*(1), 93–99. DOI: 10.1080/09700161.2022.2039582

Bleher, H., & Braun, M. (2023). Reflections on putting AI ethics into practice: How three AI ethics approaches conceptualize theory and practice. *Science and Engineering Ethics*, *29*(3), 21. DOI: 10.1007/s11948-023-00443-3 PMID: 37237246

Bulman-Pozen, J., & Seifter, M. (2023). State Constitutional Rights and Democratic Proportionality. *Columbia Law Review*, *123*(7), 1855–1928.

Cervi, G. V. (2022). Why and how does the EU rule global digital policy: An empirical analysis of EU regulatory influence in data protection laws. *Digital Society : Ethics, Socio-Legal and Governance of Digital Technology*, *1*(2), 18. DOI: 10.1007/s44206-022-00005-3

Chiarella, M. L. (2023). Digital Markets Act (DMA) and Digital Services Act (DSA): New Rules for the EU Digital Environment. *Athens JL*, *9*(1), 33–58. DOI: 10.30958/ajl.9-1-2

Chukwunweike, J. N., Yussuf, M., Okusi, O., & Oluwatobi, T. (2024). The role of deep learning in ensuring privacy integrity and security: Applications in AI-driven cybersecurity solutions. *World Journal of Advanced Research and Reviews*, *23*(2), 2550.

Di Minin, E., Fink, C., Hausmann, A., Kremer, J., & Kulkarni, R. (2021). How to address data privacy concerns when using social media data in conservation science. *Conservation Biology*, *35*(2), 437–446. DOI: 10.1111/cobi.13708 PMID: 33749044

Gazi, S. (2021). Reimagining a centralised cryptocurrency regulation in the US: Looking through the lens of crypto-derivatives. *Cambridge L. Rev.*, *6*, 97.

Hjaltalin, I. T., & Sigurdarson, H. T. (2024). The strategic use of AI in the public sector: A public values analysis of national AI strategies. *Government Information Quarterly*, *41*(1), 101914. DOI: 10.1016/j.giq.2024.101914

Huang, L. (2023). Ethics of artificial intelligence in education: Student privacy and data protection. *Science Insights Education Frontiers*, *16*(2), 2577–2587. DOI: 10.15354/sief.23.re202

Hung, H. T. (2025). Exploring China's cyber sovereignty concept and artificial intelligence governance model: A machine learning approach. *Journal of Computational Social Science*, *8*(1), 24. DOI: 10.1007/s42001-024-00346-8

Juliussen, B. A., Kozyri, E., Johansen, D., & Rui, J. P. (2023). The third country problem under the GDPR: Enhancing protection of data transfers with technology. *International Data Privacy Law*, *13*(3), 225–243. DOI: 10.1093/idpl/ipad013

Justo-Hanani, R. (2022). The politics of Artificial Intelligence regulation and governance reform in the European Union. *Policy Sciences*, *55*(1), 137–159. DOI: 10.1007/s11077-022-09452-8

Kadaba, D. M. K., & Aithal, P. S., & KRS, S. (2023). Government initiatives and digital innovation for Atma Nirbhar MSMEs/SMEs: To achieve sustainable and inclusive economic growth. [IJMTS]. *International Journal of Management, Technology, and Social Sciences*, *8*(1), 68–82.

Laux, J., Wachter, S., & Mittelstadt, B. (2024). Three pathways for standardisation and ethical disclosure by default under the European Union Artificial Intelligence Act. *Computer Law & Security Review*, *53*, 105957. DOI: 10.1016/j.clsr.2024.105957

Panagariya, A. (2022). Digital revolution, financial infrastructure and entrepreneurship: The case of India. *Asia and the Global Economy*, *2*(2), 100027. DOI: 10.1016/j.aglobe.2022.100027

Radu, R. (2021). Steering the governance of artificial intelligence: National strategies in perspective. *Policy and Society*, *40*(2), 178–193. DOI: 10.1080/14494035.2021.1929728

Rebecchi, K., Todd, L., & Hagège, H. (2024). Teaching responsible creativity: A path to ethical innovation. *Discover Education*, *3*(1), 103. DOI: 10.1007/s44217-024-00164-0

Roberts, H., Cowls, J., Hine, E., Morley, J., Wang, V., Taddeo, M., & Floridi, L. (2023). Governing artificial intelligence in China and the European Union: Comparing aims and promoting ethical outcomes. *The Information Society*, *39*(2), 79–97. DOI: 10.1080/01972243.2022.2124565

Sanchez, T. W., Brenman, M., & Ye, X. (2024). The ethical concerns of artificial intelligence in urban planning. *Journal of the American Planning Association*, •••, 1–14.

Scheurman, T. (2021). Comparing Social Media Content Regulation in the US and the EU: How the US Can Move Forward with Section 230 to Bolster Social Media Users' Freedom of Expression. *San Diego Int'l LJ*, *23*, 413.

Schiff, D. (2022). Education for AI, not AI for education: The role of education and ethics in national AI policy strategies. *International Journal of Artificial Intelligence in Education*, *32*(3), 527–563. DOI: 10.1007/s40593-021-00270-2

Siu, R. C. (2023). Social, political, and economic dimensions of the instituted process of central bank digital currency: The case of the digital Yuan. *Journal of Economic Issues*, *57*(2), 458–465. DOI: 10.1080/00213624.2023.2201610

Sivasubramaniam, S., Dlabolová, D. H., Kralikova, V., & Khan, Z. R. (2021). Assisting you to advance with ethics in research: An introduction to ethical governance and application procedures. *International Journal for Educational Integrity*, *17*(1), 1–18. DOI: 10.1007/s40979-021-00078-6

. Sobolewski, M., & Allessie, D. (2021). Blockchain applications in the public sector: Investigating seven real-life blockchain deployments and their benefits. *Blockchain and the Public Sector: Theories, Reforms, and Case Studies*, 97-126.

Sule, M. J., Zennaro, M., & Thomas, G. (2021). Cybersecurity through the lens of digital identity and data protection: Issues and trends. *Technology in Society*, *67*, 101734. DOI: 10.1016/j.techsoc.2021.101734

Werbach, K. (2022). Digital Asset Regulation: Peering into the Past, Peering into the Future. *Wm. & Mary L. Rev.*, *64*, 1251.

Zhang, J., & Zhang, Z. M. (2023). Ethics and governance of trustworthy medical artificial intelligence. *BMC Medical Informatics and Decision Making*, *23*(1), 7. DOI: 10.1186/s12911-023-02103-9 PMID: 36639799

Chapter 10
Advanced Cybersecurity Detection Techniques

Vinay Kumar Kasula
https://orcid.org/0009-0001-1131-3059
University of the Cumberlands, USA

Mounica Yenugula
https://orcid.org/0009-0002-3259-4563
University of the Cumberlands, USA

Bhargavi Konda
https://orcid.org/0009-0001-4704-1526
University of the Cumberlands, USA

ABSTRACT

This chapter delves into the evolving landscape of Advanced Persistent Threats (APT) from both an attack and detection perspective. It begins by reviewing the definition and characteristics of APTs, providing an overview of the various attack models developed over time. Building upon this foundation, the chapter introduces a comprehensive APT lifecycle model, which is divided into four distinct stages: information gathering, intrusion implementation, internal network attacks, and data exfiltration. For each of these stages, the chapter surveys research from the past five years, highlighting the latest advancements in both attack strategies and detection techniques. Finally, the chapter examines the dynamic interplay between attack and defense technologies, pointing out the challenges faced by both attackers and defenders. It concludes by discussing the rapid advancements in APT tactics and defenses, offering insights into the future directions for research and development in the field of cybersecurity and APT detection.

DOI: 10.4018/979-8-3373-3186-7.ch010

1. INTRODUCTION

The pervasive digitization of societal infrastructure—spanning industrial automation, healthcare, finance, and personal computing—has intensified the attack surface for cyber threats. In parallel, the growing sophistication of threat actors, often equipped with nation-state-level capabilities, demands structured frameworks to systematically understand, detect, and mitigate cyber attacks. The MITRE ATT&CK Framework, a curated knowledge base of adversary tactics and techniques based on real-world observations, has become a de facto standard for threat modeling. While several studies have applied the MITRE ATT&CK Framework in cybersecurity analysis, the existing literature remains fragmented—often focusing on isolated domains (e.g., malware detection, network intrusion, IoT threats) or limited to either attack or defense strategies. Moreover, there is a lack of integrative lifecycle-based models that unify both adversarial techniques and corresponding detection methods within a coherent analytical structure.

This chapter addresses these gaps by proposing a comprehensive, lifecycle-oriented model of cybersecurity grounded in the MITRE ATT&CK Framework. It provides a dual-perspective analysis that systematically correlates attack vectors with detection methodologies, offering a structured synthesis of recent academic research and real-world threat cases. The novelty of this work lies in:

- Developing a cyber attack-detection lifecycle model that maps adversarial techniques to corresponding detection phases, using MITRE ATT&CK as a foundational taxonomy.
- Conducting a cross-domain synthesis that bridges traditional attack surfaces (e.g., web, malware) with emerging areas such as AI-based attacks, IoT vulnerabilities, and GNN-enabled defense systems.
- Integrating case-based evidence (e.g., Stuxnet, iOS 0-click attacks) with state-of-the-art detection techniques to demonstrate the real-world applicability and evolving nature of cyber threats.
- Highlighting research trends and gaps through bibliometric analysis of leading security venues (IEEE S&P, USENIX, NDSS, ACM CCS), with a focus on studies from the last five years.

The proposed lifecycle model segments the cyber attack process into preparation, execution, and persistence phases, each mapped to corresponding ATT&CK tactics and techniques. Parallel to this, detection methods are categorized based on their temporal applicability and technological basis (e.g., anomaly detection, GNNs, threat intelligence correlation). This structure facilitates comparative analysis, enabling the assessment of coverage gaps and overlaps across detection approaches.

- Attack Techniques: The study highlights the evolution of attack vectors—from traditional exploits to multi-vector campaigns combining AI evasion, phishing, and zero-day vulnerabilities. The 2023 iMessage 0-click exploit illustrates the integration of advanced stealth with zero-day chaining in mobile ecosystems.
- Detection Trends: Detection strategies have evolved from signature-based systems to adaptive, learning-based approaches, with increased deployment of graph neural networks (GNNs) and federated detection systems. However, these advancements often lag behind adversarial innovation.
- Lifecycle-wide Defense Models: The lifecycle analysis reveals critical phases (e.g., lateral movement, persistence) where detection remains weak. Cross-lifecycle techniques, such as traceability graphs and telemetry-driven anomaly detection, show promise but require further validation.

This chapter offers a structured and integrated perspective on cybersecurity research, using the MITRE ATT&CK Framework not just as a classification tool, but as a foundation for modeling the dynamic interplay between attacks and defenses across their entire lifecycle. The original contribution lies in bridging theoretical and applied insights through a dual-perspective lifecycle model, thereby enhancing conceptual clarity and practical applicability.

Future research directions include:

- Privacy-preserving collaborative defense: Leveraging federated analytics and secure multi-party computation (SMPC) to enable decentralized, regulation-compliant threat detection.
- Explainable detection systems: Developing transparent AI models that provide interpretable alerts across attack phases, improving trust and usability in critical environments.
- Policy-aligned frameworks: Investigating the implications of GDPR, HIPAA, and the Data Governance Act on lifecycle-wide detection and intelligence sharing.
- Proactive mitigation strategies: Designing systems capable of predictive defense using simulation-based modeling of attacker behavior within the ATT&CK framework.

By synthesizing attack and detection research in a unified, lifecycle-centric model, this study contributes to a foundational shift in cybersecurity analysis, bridging the gap between academic theory and operational defense.

2. MITRE ATT&CK FRAMEWORK BASED ON THE FULL LIFECYCLE OF ACTIVITIES

2.1. Definition of MITRE ATT&CK

The evolution of the MITRE ATT&CK Framework, as depicted in Figure 2, traces its origins to the term coined by U.S. Air Force Colonel Gregory Rattray (USSath et al., 2016). Although there is no universally accepted definition of the MITRE ATT&CK framework, the National Institute of Standards and Technology (NIST) provides a widely acknowledged description: the MITRE ATT&CK framework is characterized by adversaries with advanced expertise and significant resources using multiple attack vectors to establish and maintain access to the IT infrastructure of specific organizations. The goals typically include stealing sensitive information, disrupting critical systems, or executing subsequent attacks while remaining concealed within the organization's network (FireEye Company, 2015).

While this definition effectively captures the technical proficiency, resources, and intent of attackers, it falls short of addressing the MITRE ATT&CK Framework's heightened targeting precision and stealth. Davi et al. (2011) supplemented the definition, which this chapter further extends to address these gaps. MITRE ATT&CK attacks can be defined as long-term, covert cyberattacks targeting specific organizations or systems, leveraging advanced expertise and diverse attack methods, aiming to compromise critical infrastructure, extract sensitive data, or disrupt operations.

2.2. Characteristics of MITRE ATT&CK

Compared to traditional cyberattacks, MITRE ATT&CK exhibits six distinctive traits:

1. Advanced expertise
2. High specificity
3. Prolonged duration
4. Organizational structure
5. Severe threat level
6. High stealth

The strong targeting capability distinguishes MITRE ATT&CK from conventional attacks such as worms, botnets, and ransomware, while their stealth sets them apart from penetration testing activities. Due to these features, MITRE ATT&CK adversaries are often attributed to state-level actors.

2.3. MITRE ATT&CK Framework Models

To better understand MITRE ATT&CK activities, researchers have developed various models that offer comprehensive perspectives on their mechanisms.

- **Diamond Model for Intrusion Analysis:** Caltagirone et al. (2013) proposed the Diamond Model, illustrated in Figure 3, which analyzes intrusion events through four nodes—adversary, capability, infrastructure, and victim—and their interrelations. The model, later expanded (Figure 4), focuses on the motivations, intentions, and channels of intrusions, providing theoretical guidance for analyzing attacks.
- **Cyber Kill Chain Model:** Lockheed Martin introduced the Cyber Kill Chain model, breaking down network attacks into seven stages (Figure 5). This model, developed during the early days of intrusion prevention, emphasizes external defense mechanisms like virus and vulnerability protection. However, it does not comprehensively address modern MITRE ATT&CK complexities, such as social engineering and supply chain poisoning (Chari et al., 2010).
- **MITRE ATT&CK Framework:** To overcome the limitations of the Cyber Kill Chain model, the MITRE Corporation introduced the ATT&CK (Adversarial Tactics, Techniques, and Common Knowledge) framework. This knowledge base organizes network attacks into 14 tactical stages, further subdivided into techniques and sub-techniques. Covering all attack phases across various platforms, it provides a granular, flexible, and continuously updated approach for analyzing evolving cyber threats (Davi et al., 2011).
- **Full Lifecycle Models:** Many researchers prefer the "full lifecycle" concept to characterize MITRE ATT&CK activities. This concept was first introduced by Mandiant in its 2013 report on APT1 (Suciu et al., 2020). It uses a timeline or logical sequence to describe MITRE ATT&CK attacks in detail.

Khaleefa et al. (2022) outlined the lifecycle with a simple five-stage circular structure—reconnaissance, intrusion, persistence, lateral movement, and data exfiltration. However, this oversimplified model lacks sufficient detail. Talib et al. (2022) expanded it to a six-stage structure but misrepresented the process as a cycle, incorrectly implying that the exfiltration phase would loop back to earlier stages. Sharma et al. (2023) proposed a more refined lifecycle that identifies a five-stage inner loop for post-compromise activities. Although this model provides a more scientific and complete depiction, its fragmentation prevents a clear delineation of specific stages, such as the association between command and control (C2) operations and other phases. This chapter adopts a more comprehensive lifecycle model based on the 2023 report by the India Information Security Evaluation Center. It divides the MITRE ATT&CK process into four tactical stages—information gathering, intrusion, internal network attack, and data exfiltration—further subdivided into six activities: reconnaissance, intrusion execution, privilege escalation, lateral movement, persistence and artifact cleaning, and data exfiltration (Figure 8).

It is worth noting that not all MITRE ATT&CK activities include the data exfiltration stage; some focus solely on disrupting target systems, such as the Stuxnet worm. Thus, the proposed lifecycle is suited for data-oriented MITRE ATT&CK activities, with the final phase varying for non-data-oriented attacks.

2.4. MITRE ATT&CK Methods

Analyzing the four stages of MITRE ATT&CK activities summarized in the previous research, it is evident that different stages have distinct goals and environments, resulting in notable differences in attack characteristics. Various studies have categorized the different attack methods used at each stage to better understand MITRE ATT&CK activities.

2.4.1. Information Gathering Stage

The information gathering stage is a reconnaissance activity conducted prior to the MITRE ATT&CK activity, where attackers seek to understand the vulnerabilities of the target system in order to develop an effective attack plan. This stage helps attackers collect various types of information about the target, which can be used to create a more effective attack strategy, thereby increasing the likelihood of success. Auty (2015) suggest that, during the information gathering phase, attackers primarily collect two types of intelligence: (1) human intelligence about the target organization, such as its background, business scope, and employee information, and (2) technical information about the target's information system, such as network assets, website fingerprints, architecture, and application versions. The first type of information collection is based on social engineering techniques and sets the stage for spear-phishing or watering hole attacks targeting individuals. The second type focuses on identifying vulnerabilities in websites to facilitate subsequent exploitation during the intrusion phase. Mazurczyk and Caviglione (2021) expanded the scope of the information gathering phase and classified traditional network reconnaissance activities into four categories: internet intelligence, network information gathering, side-channel attacks, and social engineering. They also provide specific examples and summarize mainstream information-gathering techniques based on factors such as technology age and interaction complexity, as shown in Figure 9. Roy et al. (2023)

further refined this classification, addressing overlooked reconnaissance methods and introducing various other categorization approaches.

Information-gathering techniques have continuously evolved. Initially, Shaikh et al. (2008) pointed out that individuals, businesses, and government organizations' increasing dependence on the internet made it easier to discover sensitive information servers with a simple mouse click. They summarized early network information gathering techniques such as host scanning, port scanning, and vulnerability assessments. Gont et al. (2016) extended network information-gathering techniques to IPv6, broadening their application scope. Bou-Harb et al. (2014) focused on network scanning techniques and provided a comprehensive summary of target-oriented and covert scanning methods not previously mentioned. Salahdine et al. (2019) systematically summarized social engineering attacks, categorizing them into human-targeted and computer-targeted attacks, with the human-targeted attacks representing techniques used in the information gathering phase. Additionally, targeted internet open-source intelligence (OSINT) gathering methods have been proposed. Kanta et al. (2020) applied open-source intelligence to perform weak password cracking more efficiently, while Rai et al. (2021) used OSINT to locate specific web assets. This concept also aligns with several network scanning tools, such as Shodan, Zoomeye, Fofa, and Hunter. With the development of AI technology, neural network-assisted network reconnaissance techniques have also attracted growing attention. Millar (2022) introduced machine learning methods based on graph theory into network reconnaissance and tested their effectiveness in real-world TCP/IP networks, yielding deeper insights into key network information.

The information gathering stage generally does not involve substantial attacks. It spans a longer period and forms the foundation for MITRE ATT&CK activities. Thorough, comprehensive, and broad reconnaissance can significantly reduce the difficulty of the MITRE ATT&CK attack and allow attackers to link critical information during the execution phase, thereby enhancing the overall impact.

2.4.2. Intrusion Phase

After gathering sufficient information, attackers exploit vulnerabilities in the target information system to infiltrate and establish a foothold. The core of this phase is the implantation of malicious code on the target's servers to establish communication with the command-and-control (C2) system, allowing attackers to maintain access. From a broader perspective, attacks in this phase target two main categories: (1) subjects, such as individuals (target organization staff, web administrators, employees), and (2) objects, such as network assets. According to Ussath et al. (2016), only a small number of MITRE ATT&CK activities are carried out using zero-day vulnerabilities, with most attacks based on known vulnerabilities.

For human targets, MITRE ATT&CK attackers primarily use social engineering techniques, including spear-phishing and watering hole attacks (Salahdine et al., 2023). Mandiant Intelligence Center (2013) describes a spear-phishing attack in which MITRE ATT&CK attackers send a forged email to a Mandiant employee, using the name of the Mandiant CEO. The email contains a malicious compressed file designed to install a backdoor program, "WEBC2-TABLE," on the victim's system, thus establishing a foothold and enabling C2 communication.

For network assets, the Open Web Application Security Project (OWASP) periodically publishes a list of the top 10 security risks, which has become a key reference in network security. The 2021 edition, for example, outlines common techniques exploited by MITRE ATT&CK attackers targeting network assets. It is important to note that MITRE ATT&CK attackers do not limit their attacks to network assets alone; they also target mobile devices, industrial control systems, and the Internet of Things (IoT). OWASP has also published risk lists for mobile devices, IoT devices, and API security. With the rise of large language models (LLM), the security risks associated with LLMs have entered the focus of MITRE ATT&CK attackers, marking a new stage in their attack methods. During the intrusion phase, the stealth of C2 communication is a critical focus for MITRE ATT&CK attackers, as it is the foundation for long-lasting attacks. For example, FireEye reported a high-stealth communication technique used by APT3, which used the TLS/SSL protocol for C2 communication, enabling it to evade detection by traditional detection mechanisms (Sarkar et al., 2019).

After successfully infiltrating the target network, attackers escalate their privileges and spread laterally within the network, establishing additional footholds and gaining further control of the environment. This phase comprises several stages, including privilege escalation, lateral movement, and persistence. The goal is to maintain access, even if the initial foothold is detected and eliminated.

- **Privilege Escalation**: Attackers escalate their privileges to gain greater control over the system. This can involve exploiting vulnerabilities or leveraging misconfigurations to elevate privileges. Techniques such as exploiting system flaws or leveraging stolen credentials are common.
- **Lateral Movement**: Attackers move laterally across the network to compromise additional machines or servers once access is gained to one system. This movement helps attackers find sensitive data or establish more points of control.
- **Persistence**: Attackers employ various methods to maintain access even if their initial point of entry is discovered. This might involve creating new user accounts, implanting backdoors, or altering system configurations.

2.4.3. Data Exfiltration Phase

The final phase of the MITRE ATT&CK lifecycle is the exfiltration of data. Depending on the attacker's goal, this phase might involve stealing sensitive data, disrupting services, or erasing evidence. Techniques for data exfiltration include using encrypted channels, hiding data within legitimate traffic, or sending data over multiple stages to avoid detection.

Figure 1. Intrusion Analysis Diamond Model

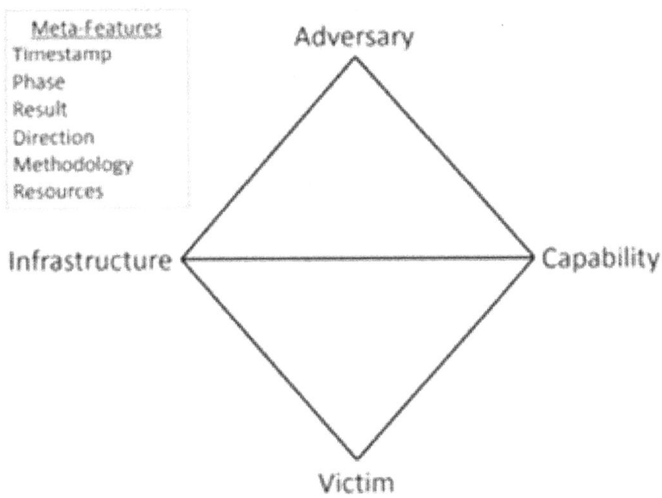

3. DETECTION TECHNOLOGIES BASED ON THE FULL LIFECYCLE OF APT ACTIVITIES

3.1. Detection during the Information Collection Phase

In the information collection phase, attackers prepare to establish a stable foothold for the next stages of intrusion by gathering a large amount of information about the target system. During this phase, techniques such as vulnerability scanning, port scanning, and network sniffing are often used to acquire information about the target organization's network assets. Social engineering techniques and open-source intelligence (OSINT) methods are employed to gather information about the organization's personnel and operations, as shown in Figure 13. Detecting MITRE ATT&CK Framework activities at this stage can minimize potential damage.

1. Detection of Active Interaction Reconnaissance Attacks: During the information collection phase, attackers can launch active reconnaissance on the target network remotely, interacting with the target system via scanning technologies and analyzing the returned data to gather relevant information. Panjwani et al. (2015) pointed out through experiments that techniques such as port scanning are often precursors to network attacks. Therefore, effectively detecting various scanning behaviors can prevent network attacks. To defend against active scanning reconnaissance attacks, defenders can identify network reconnaissance activities by detecting and analyzing network traffic. Bou-Harb et al. (2014) noted that traditional defense and detection technologies, such as firewalls and intrusion detection systems (IDS), remain the primary methods to counter scanning reconnaissance. Anderson et al. (1980) first elaborated on the concept of IDS, while Denning (1987) proposed the first IDS. Early IDS systems, such as Snort, use signature-based detection methods to extract attack patterns as features and store them in a database for comparison (Kumar & Sangwan, 2012). This method is easy to create and update features, is simple to operate, and works well for blocking specific attacks. However, its limitation is that it requires prior knowledge of attack patterns and cannot detect new types of attacks, only known scan attacks. Threshold-based detection is another traditional method that identifies scanning intrusions using predefined thresholds. Heberlein et al. (1990) designed a Network Security Monitor (NSM) considered a pioneer in threshold-based scanning detection, consisting of data capture, analysis, and support functions. If a source contacts more than 15 IP addresses within a set time period or attempts to contact an unresponsive IP address, the NSM identifies this as abnormal and potentially malicious. Rule-based methods use a knowledge base to detect and prevent typical scans, such as fuzzy rule-based methods for slow port scanning (Kim & Lee, 2008). Additionally, visual tools are used to detect specific network events, such as visualizing scan patterns from tools like Nmap or Nessus (Conti & Abdullah, 2004). Flexible information processing methods, such as soft computing approaches to trace scanning sources, are also used, as proposed by Chen et al. (2009) with a quick port scanning method based on a single-parent genetic algorithm. With the advancement of artificial intelligence, researchers have started using AI techniques to identify scanning behavior patterns, such as training models to distinguish between normal network traffic and scanning behavior. Almomani et al. (2022) compared several enhanced machine learning classifiers in detecting reconnaissance attacks, showing that the Cat Boosting classifier outperformed others in experiments using the UNSW-NB15 dataset.

Figure 2. Expanded Intrusion Analysis Diamond Model

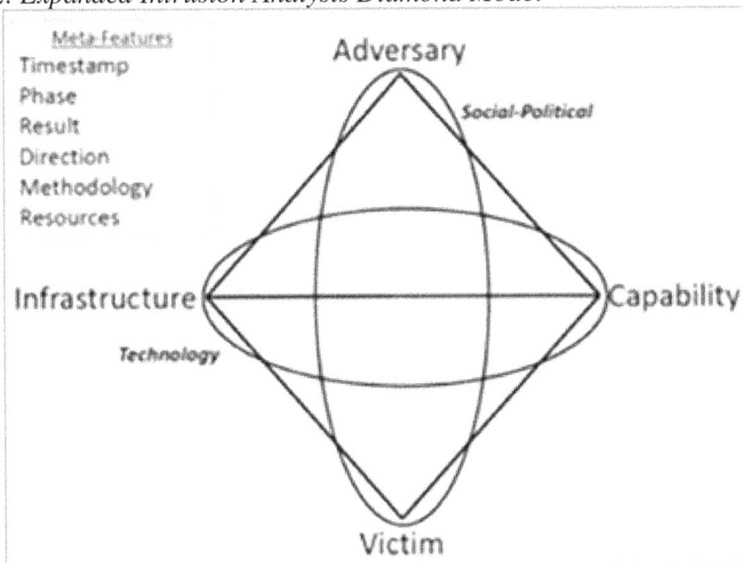

2. Detection and Defense Based on Network Deception: In recent years, defenders have adopted network deception strategies, such as honeypot techniques and mobile target defenses, to counter reconnaissance attacks. Crouse et al. (2015) discussed the importance of these defense measures using probabilistic models, pointing out that mobile target defense makes it difficult for attackers to make static and long-term assumptions about the network state, thereby affecting reconnaissance attacks. Kim & Lee (2023) found in their experiments that the presence of decoys and the provision of deceptive information had the most significant impact on attacks compared to not using deception. In honeypot deception defense methods, defenders use decoy data or networks to deceive MITRE ATT&CK Framework attackers and monitor honeypot access to detect MITRE ATT&CK Framework activities. Zhong et al. (2023) proposed a honeypot-based method to defend against attackers during the information collection phase. They developed a honeypot defense detection mechanism, where the secretary handles front-end interactions and conveys database content. In contrast, the attack detection subsystem uses supervised machine learning algorithms to identify attackers and send early warning messages to the scheduler. The scheduler decides whether to deliver real or deceptive data, generated through Generative Adversarial Networks (GANs), to prevent attackers from acquiring critical information. When deceptive data is delivered, the database records the access to monitor the deception and track MITRE ATT&CK Framework attackers.

3. Passive Methods for Reconnaissance Attack Defense: When attackers conduct reconnaissance through third-party sources, such as open-source intelligence, defenders may be unable to detect these activities. Yu et al. (2022) conducted a detailed investigation into privacy and security issues on hospital websites, revealing that most healthcare websites had privacy information leakage problems. Rugo et al. (2023) discussed how publicly MITRE ATT&CK Framework attackers could exploit available information. They simulated an attack on an Italian institution, obtaining a complete technical and supply chain list through publicly available information, bypassing the institution's defense. To mitigate this risk, defenders should enhance awareness of privacy information release and improve defense levels by implementing strict information release procedures and establishing public information release monitoring platforms.

4. Detection and Defense Against Targeted Personnel Reconnaissance: Another significant vulnerability in the information collection phase is the organization's personnel. MITRE ATT&CK Framework attackers can use phishing, deception, and threats to obtain critical information from internal staff. MITRE ATT&CK Framework attackers may disguise themselves as clients, using chat software to deceive staff into revealing sensitive information. Tsinganos et al. (2022) proposed a method to detect chat-based social engineering attacks using convolutional neural networks (CNNs) and natural language processing (NLP) techniques. They trained a network on a social engineering corpus labeled based on language-induced principles to detect intent in chats that could lead to information leakage, thus protecting personnel. With the rise of social media, people disclose large amounts of private information that may pose security risks. To address this, many researchers have begun analyzing self-disclosure behaviors on social media and blogs. Peiretti et al. (2023) developed an Italian-language network post corpus and applied several Transformer-based language models to classify them based on sensitivity, achieving good classification performance. Phishing attacks through fake websites involve creating malicious sites to lure workers into visiting and stealing their information. Rajeswary et al. (2023) classified malicious website detection methods into categories based on URL, content, reputation, and behavior. These methods can be combined to enhance accuracy. Kim et al. (2022) proposed a network inference-based approach to detect phishing URLs that disguise themselves as legitimate sites, focusing on behaviors like reusing the same phishing website and using non-personal information pages for hosting. Training staff to recognize social engineering attacks is also an essential measure. Hafner et al. (2023) proposed a tabletop game for social engineering attack training to increase awareness among participants about such attacks. A comparison of detection methods during the information collection phase is shown in Table 1.

Figure 3. Cyber Kill Chain Model

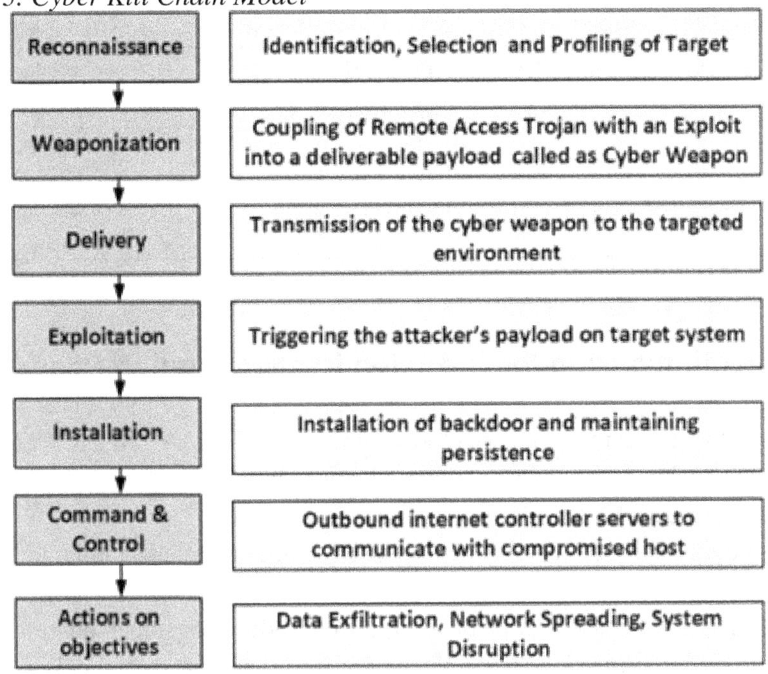

Table 1. Comparison of Detection Methods in the Information Gathering Phase

Classification	Method	Features
Active Interaction Reconnaissance Attack Detection	Zhang et al. (2020)	Scan traffic
	Recabarren & Carbunar (2019) Li et al. (2019)	IDS
	Gai et al. (2019).	Based on the threshold
	Huang et al. (2021) Meiklejohn & Orlandi (2015). Averin et al. (2020)	Rule Based
	Worley & Skjellum (2018)	Based on AI
Network Deception-based Detection	Kuznetsov et al. (2023)	Probability Models
	Qi An Xin Technology Group Inc. (2023). Chen et al. (2023)	Honeypot Detection
Passive Method Reconnaissance Attack Defense	Arulkumar et al. (2022). Fu et al. (2015).	Information Leakage

continued on following page

Table 1. Continued

Classification	Method	Features
Personnel Reconnaissance Attack Detection	Tatam et al. (2021)	Chat Information
	Talib et al. (2022)	Media Information
	Alshamrani et al. (2019) Sharma et al. (2023)	Phishing Websites
	Auty (2015)	Personnel Awareness

3.2. Detection during the Intrusion Implementation Phase

During the intrusion implementation phase, MITRE ATT&CK Framework attackers use critical information gathered in the information collection phase to infiltrate the target system.

1. Detection and Defense Against Spear Phishing and Watering Hole Attacks: Spear phishing is a prominent targeted attack method on the internet today. Attackers craft tailored emails based on prior information collection, impersonating trusted senders to trick victims into opening malicious attachments or clicking harmful links, giving attackers a foothold in well-protected networks. Duman et al. (2016) proposed a probabilistic model based on email metadata and stylistic features to detect spear phishing attack characteristics, distinguishing them from legitimate emails. With the development of AI technology, modern detection methods often use machine learning and deep learning to classify phishing emails versus legitimate ones. Cidon et al. (2019) proposed a detector called BEC-Guard for detecting business email compromise (BEC) attacks, and Bai et al. (2021) focused on detecting email phishing attacks based on social engineering, summarizing tactics, techniques, and procedures for MITRE ATT&CK Framework email attacks and using deep learning algorithms to detect MITRE ATT&CK Framework emails. Despite defenders taking precautions against spear phishing attacks, attackers have developed techniques to infiltrate target networks by compromising third-party entities in a company's whitelist. By gathering information on frequently visited websites, attackers select malicious sites likely to be visited by employees, setting the stage for a watering hole attack. Allen et al. (2019) pointed out that research on detecting or investigating complex watering hole attacks is limited, with most studies focusing on detecting malicious modifications to benign websites. They introduced Mnemosyne, a forensic analysis engine based on browser-originating attacks that accurately reconstructs, investigates, and evaluates the aftermath of watering hole attacks. Mnemosyne helps companies better defend against watering hole attacks and minimize damage by assessing the impact of malicious website modifications on target organizations.

Table 2. Comparison of Detection Methods in the Attack Implementation Phase

Classification	Method	Features
Phishing and Waterhole Attack Detection	Zhang et al. (2017). NIST (2011) Caltagirone et al. (2013)	Email Detection
	Hutchins et al. (2011).	Malicious Modification Detection
Malware Detection	Levy (2003)	Phase Division
C2 Communication Detection	Strom et al. (2018)	Protocol-based Detection
	Mandiant Intelligence Center (2013).	Behavior-based Detection
	Khaleefa et al. (2022).	Signature-based Detection
	India Information Technology Security Evaluation Center (2023).	Graph-based Detection
	Mazurczyk & Caviglione (2021). Roy et al. (2023)	Deep Learning-based Detection

2. Intrusion Detection and Defense Using Vulnerabilities: MITRE ATT&CK Framework attackers may exploit known vulnerabilities to infiltrate target systems. By collecting information about the target organization's software and operating system versions, attackers can search vulnerability databases, such as the Common Vulnerabilities and Exposures (CVE) or the National Vulnerability Database (NVD), to find relevant vulnerabilities and attempt to exploit them. Therefore, defenders need to regularly update security patches to prevent such attacks.

3. Detection and Defense Against Malicious Software: MITRE ATT&CK Framework attackers often implant malicious software to maintain access to the target system after successfully executing the above attack methods. At this point, attackers must face challenges the target system's malware detection mechanisms pose. Aslan et al. (2020) divided malware detection into three stages: analysis, feature extraction, and feature-based detection. They classified detection methods into signature-based, behavioral, heuristic, model checking, cloud-based, deep learning-based, and IoT-based categories, summarizing the pros and cons of each approach.

4. Detection of C2 Communication: After successfully running malicious software, MITRE ATT&CK Framework attackers establish Command and Control (C2) communication channels, often using common protocols to disguise their traffic as legitimate. Wang et al. (2016) noted that HTTP is widely used for C2 communication since it is typically considered legitimate in most enterprises, unlike other protocols such as Peer-to-Peer (P2P) or Internet Relay Chat (IRC) protocols, which have more identifiable network characteristics. This indicates the possibility of designing C2 communication channel detectors based on the features of various protocols.

Figure 4. The 6 Stages of MITRE ATT&CK Framework attack

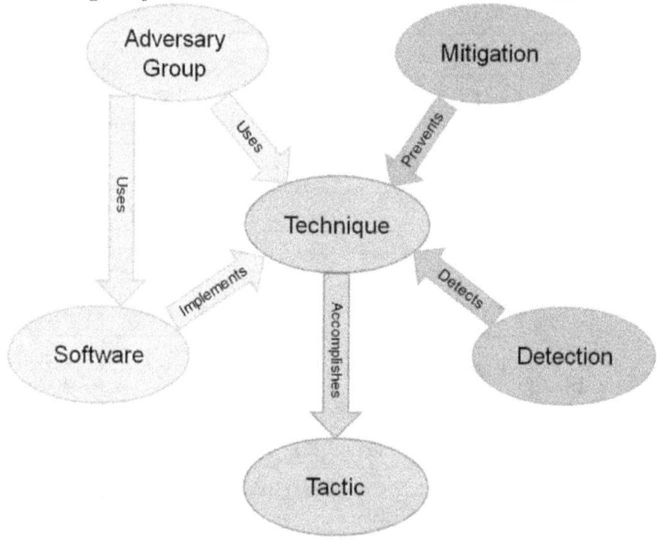

Table 3. Summary of Detection Methods in the Internal Network Attack Phase

Detection Phase	Method	Application Areas
Privilege Escalation	Shaikh et al. (2008).	Linux
	Salahdine et al. (2023)	Android
Lateral Movement	Red Hat Customer Portal (2016)	Cloud Computing Environment
	Saleel et al. (2017).	Internal Network
	Lin et al. (2022) Haber & Rolls (2020) Demers & Lee (2022)	Windows
	Garcia et al. (2017).	Industrial IoT
Trace Removal and Persistence	Wampler et al. (2019) Ullah et al. (2018) Nar & Sastry (2018) Chien et al. (2012)	Log Tampering Prevention
	Halfond et al. (2006) Clarke (2009) Mukherjee et al. (2015)	Backdoor Detection

Talib et al. (2022) categorized C2 communication detection methods into four types:

- Behavioral or Network-based Detection: This method relies on abnormal host behavior or network traffic, such as excessive delays, large traffic volumes, unusual port traffic, and system behavior anomalies.
- Signature-based Detection: This method detects predefined patterns extracted from C2 communications.
- Graph-based Detection: It uses connections between related abnormal patterns to create a graph that naturally describes the relationship between these patterns.
- Deep Learning-based Detection: This method converts network traffic into feature vectors and uses neural network models such as Convolutional Neural Networks (CNNs) or Long Short-Term Memory (LSTM) networks to extract temporal and spatial features.

Intrusion implementation phase detection methods typically focus on traffic characteristics, and the latest studies often use deep learning to detect traffic features. Table 2 compares these detection methods.

3.3. Detection in the Internal Network Attack Phase

The internal network attack phase is when MITRE ATT&CK Framework attackers expand their efforts by penetrating deeper into the victim's internal network to find more sensitive information and targets. This phase is characterized by more evident attack methods, and existing research has developed a comprehensive detection system for this stage, which covers privilege escalation, lateral movement, trace removal, and persistence.

Figure 5. The Full Lifecycle of MITRE ATT&CK attack

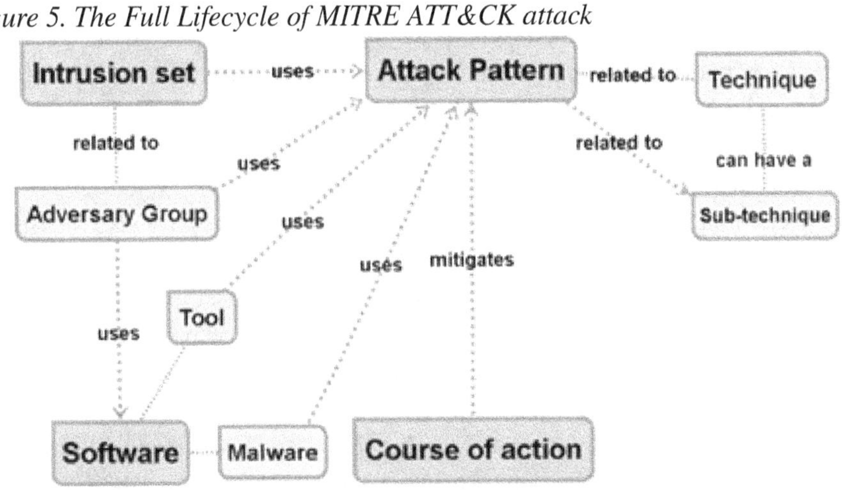

3.3.1. Privilege Escalation Detection

Yamauchi et al. (2018) developed a kernel observer called AKO to prevent privilege escalation attacks that exploit operating system vulnerabilities. This observer monitors changes in system call privileges before and after execution to detect privilege escalation attacks. Elsabagh et al. (2020) focused on privilege escalation vulnerabilities in Android system firmware images and developed the FIRMSCOPE framework to scan Android for such vulnerabilities. The framework discovered 850 privilege escalation vulnerabilities in over 100 pre-installed Android apps, many of which were exploitable 0-day vulnerabilities. Suciu et al. (2020) designed an automatic scanner called HOOPER based on symbolic execution to detect horizontal privilege escalation vulnerabilities in trusted execution environments. Li et al. (2021) applied fuzz testing to Android system privilege vulnerabilities by developing a black-box fuzz testing tool, CuPerFuzzer, to detect issues such as hanging custom permissions, inconsistent permission group mappings, and custom privilege escalation defects.

3.3.2. Lateral Movement Detection

Tian et al. (2019) proposed a real-time lateral movement detection method called CloudSEC, based on evidence reasoning networks in edge cloud environments to prevent lateral movement attacks in such environments. This method introduces the concept of vulnerability correlation to construct an evidence reasoning network that uses network system vulnerability knowledge and environmental information to detect lateral movement attacks. Yan et al. (2019) developed a theoretical framework to describe MITRE ATT&CK Framework attacks on internal networks and created models to study the entire MITRE ATT&CK Framework lifecycle, simulating the dynamic changes in target attack models to verify MITRE ATT&CK Framework attack characteristics. Mohamed et al. (2021) constructed a new model based on the ATT&CK matrix (adversarial tactics, techniques, and common knowledge) to detect potential MITRE ATT&CK Framework attacks on the first victim. The Situation Behavior Impact (SBI) model monitors and investigates MITRE ATT&CK Framework behaviors in CPU, RAM, Windows registry, and file systems, which can also be used for lateral movement detection. Some researchers have also focused on lateral movement detection methods for specific victim groups based on MITRE ATT&CK Framework attack features. Bai et al. (2019) focused on detecting lateral movement attacks in Windows systems, using remote desktop protocol (RDP) calls as features. They developed an anomaly detection method and evaluated its superiority using various supervised machine learning techniques. In addition to lateral attacks on network assets, industrial IoT, due to its strategic value and numerous internal network assets, has become a primary target of MITRE ATT&CK Framework attacks. Bi et al. (2023) studied lateral movement attacks within industrial IoT networks, creating a node-level state evolution model to calculate the probability of each device being infected by MITRE ATT&CK Framework attacks.

Figure 6. The Full Lifecycle of MITRE ATT&CK

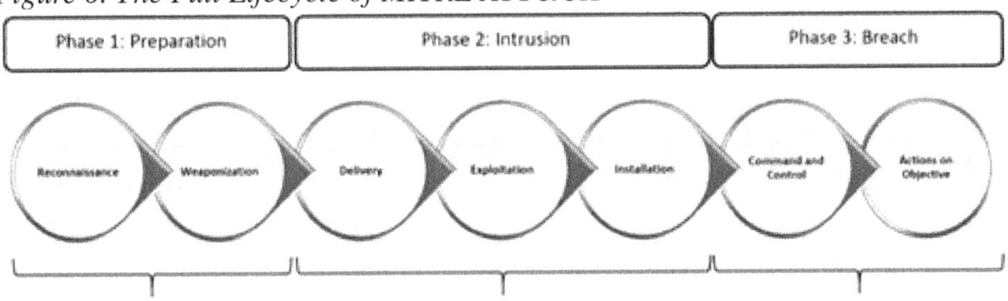

Table 4. Comparison of Detection Methods in the Data Exfiltration Phase

Detection Phase	Method	Features
Based on Traffic Content	Anu & Vimala (2017). Glăvan (2020).	DLP (Data Loss Prevention)
	Sarkar et al. (2019). Panjwani et al. (2005).	Image Steganography Detection
	Anderson (1980).	Video Steganography Detection
	Denning (1987).	Audio Steganography Detection
Based on Traffic Behavior	Kumar & Sangwan (2012).	DNS-Based Detection
	Heberlein et al. (1990).	SQL Leak Detection
	Kim & Lee (2008).	Heuristic Scanning
	Conti & Abdullah (2004).	API Leak Detection
	Chen & Cheng (2009). Almomani et al. (2023). Crouse et al. (2015).	Neural Network Methods
	Ferguson-Walter et al. (2021).	Proxy Traffic Detection

3.3.3. Trace Removal and Persistence Detection

This aspect involves detecting the destruction of logging systems and hidden backdoors. Paccagnella et al. (2020a) proposed a kernel-based log anti-tampering system, KennyLoggings, in 2020 to ensure the integrity of synchronized logs and maintain tamper-proof evidence. In the same year, Paccagnella et al. (2020b) introduced CUSTOS, a log anti-tampering system based on trusted execution environments, which improved the efficiency of tamper-proof log recording while maintaining security. Jiang et al. (2023) addressed the issue of MITRE ATT&CK Framework attackers potentially destroying system audit frameworks and proposed a log auditing framework called NODROP. It isolates system call logs generated by different processes to ensure log integrity and effectively prevents attackers from clearing audit logs. Sekar et al. (2023) focused on log tampering in persistent log storage and optimized techniques using the extended Berkeley Packet Filter (eBPF) framework to reduce log data workload intensity and narrow the data surface of log tampering. For hidden backdoor detection, Tian et al. (2019) proposed VKRD, a kernel rootkit detection system based on hardware-assisted virtualization, providing a transparent and efficient execution environment for target kernel modules, enhancing detection of malicious kernel modules. Nagy et al. (2021) used trusted execution environments (TEEs) to detect rootkits in IoT devices, proposing algorithms for rootkit detection and for detecting rootkit components in persistent storage. Yao et al. (2023) focused on malicious software applications in web environments and developed an automated malware analysis tool, Marsea, to detect web application malware by analyzing malware samples. A summary of the detection methods for the internal network attack phase is shown in Table 3.

3.4. Detection Across the Full Lifecycle Stage

With the development of MITRE ATT&CK Framework attack detection technologies, the reliability of detecting individual stages of the MITRE ATT&CK Framework lifecycle has come under scrutiny. More research is now focusing on detecting across the entire lifecycle to ensure the **authenticity and reliability of detection.**

3.4.1. MITRE ATT&CK Framework Attack Detection Based on Traceback Graphs

Hossain et al. (2018) introduced the SLEUTH method, which utilizes causal tracking and traceback graph construction to reconstruct MITRE ATT&CK Framework attacks. This method is platform-independent and relies on a memory-based audit log data dependency graph, enabling real-time attack scenario reconstruction on enterprise hosts. It achieves high operational efficiency and detection accuracy. Milajerdi et al. (2019a) proposed the Poirot method, which builds query graphs based on network threat intelligence (CTI) correlations to detect MITRE ATT&CK Framework attacks. It constructs traceback graphs using kernel audit logs, modeling threat detection as an imprecise graph pattern matching (GPM) problem. The innovative introduction of graph matching algorithms effectively aligns and matches

MITRE ATT&CK Framework organizational query graphs (attack chains) from the traceback graphs. In the same year, the team introduced the HOLMES method, which utilizes the correlation of suspicious information flows in attack activities to map MITRE ATT&CK Framework activity data to a kill chain (Milajerdi et al., 2019b). They designed a high-level scenario graph (HSG) to bridge the semantic gap between low-level traceback graphs and high-level attack chains, incorporating noise reduction algorithms to address HSG compactness issues. This system enables effective real-time detection of long-term dormant MITRE ATT&CK Framework attacks. Han et al. (2020) developed UNICORN, a runtime MITRE ATT&CK Framework detection method based on traceback graphs, which detects MITRE ATT&CK Framework attacks without prior knowledge of the attack. It boasts high accuracy and low false positive rates. This was the first MITRE ATT&CK Framework intrusion detection system to analyze a local complete system, introducing histograms and summary graphs to combat long-term dormant poisoning attacks. Zhao et al. (2020) proposed a heterogeneous graph convolution network-based threat intelligence model (HINTI), which models the dependencies between Indicators of Compromise (IOC), extracts network threat objects from unstructured threat descriptions, and uses attack preference modeling to group attacks with similar preferences. Unlike existing CTI frameworks, HINTI aims to provide a CTI computation framework to effectively extract IOCs and model and quantify their relationships. Satvat et al. (2021) introduced EXTRACTOR, an automated tool that uses natural language processing (NLP) to accurately extract attack behavior information from CTI reports. It applies semantic role labeling for semantic analysis to understand attack behavior relationships and converts unstructured text into traceback graphs, capturing system-level causal relationships.

Figure 7. Mainstream Information Gathering Methods

However, due to the complexity of NLP, this method suffers from some loss of extraction accuracy and difficulty in identifying certain unknown entities. Satvat et al. (2021) proposed the ATLAS method, which generates end-to-end attack stories from audit logs, using causal graphs and NLP to build sequence-based models that can recover key steps in an attack story. The research also found that abstract attack strategies employed by attackers are independent of the vulnerabilities exploited and the payloads executed. Anjum et al. (2021) introduced ANUBIS, a machine learning technique that trains on traceback graph data generated from event trajectories (sequences of parent-child related events). It uses a Bayesian neural network for classification and interprets prediction results based on uncertainty scores. If the score is low, ANUBIS matches the most similar examples in the training set to explain the prediction. Results show that ANUBIS can detect MITRE ATT&CK Framework attacks with high accuracy, precision, and low false positive rates. Mahmoud et al. (2023) developed the APTHunter system, which detects MITRE ATT&CK Framework attacks in the early stages. The system uses kernel audit logs as a reliable source of system activity, modeling threat hunting as a behavior matching problem. Traceback graphs provide causal relationships and information flows between system entities, and threat indicators and their relationships are represented as traceback queries. This system was evaluated in DARPA's adversarial participation and real-world MITRE ATT&CK Framework activities, yielding good results. In summary, MITRE ATT&CK Framework detection based on traceback graphs has mainly focused on improving detection accuracy and efficiency by combining network threat intelligence, convolutional networks, natural language processing, deep learning, and neural networks. These methods have achieved notable results, especially in detecting MITRE ATT&CK Framework attacks in early stages, and are an important approach to MITRE ATT&CK Framework detection.

Figure 8. Process Flow of the HAMMERTOSS Attack Case

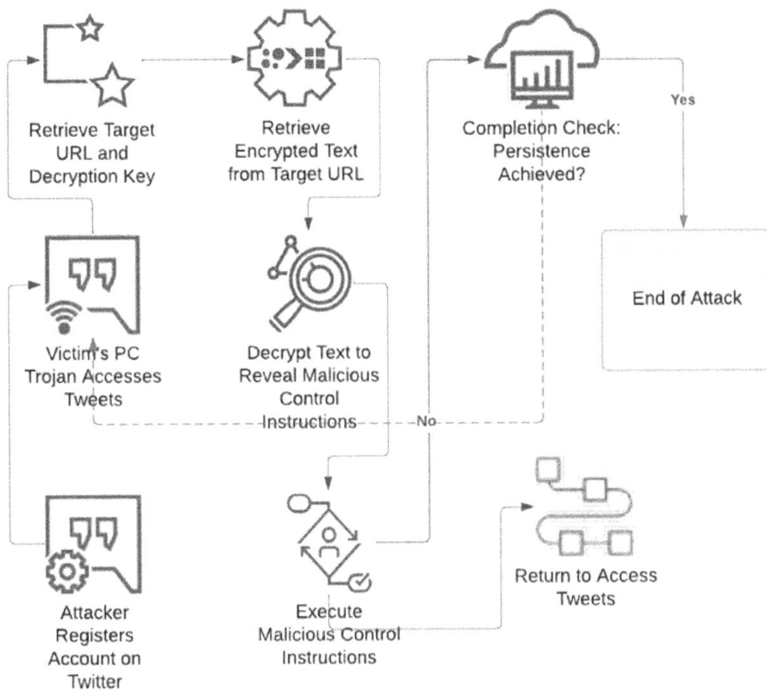

3.4.2. Other MITRE ATT&CK Framework Attack Detection Methods

Apart from the traceback graph-based MITRE ATT&CK Framework detection methods, several other full lifecycle-based detection methods have not formed a clear, systematic development path but still contribute significantly to MITRE ATT&CK Framework detection. Chorda et al. (2023) developed a MITRE ATT&CK Framework detection model based on attack trees to detect potential MITRE ATT&CK Framework attacks in software-defined networks (SDNs). Kumar et al. (2022) also used an attack tree model for detection, simulating three well-known MITRE ATT&CK Framework attacks on industrial control systems—Stuxnet, BlackEnergy, and Triton—describing each attack in a structured way using attack tree modeling language and providing the combined characteristics of these MITRE ATT&CK Framework attacks. Sadeghian (2024) proposed an IDS that uses decision trees and gradient boosting algorithms to detect MITRE ATT&CK Framework activities at various stages of the full lifecycle. The model also generates MITRE ATT&CK Framework fingerprints by optimizing the stages or attack paths, helping with early

MITRE ATT&CK Framework detection. The model was evaluated and validated using the MITRE ATT&CK Framework Dataset (DAPT) 2020, demonstrating an accuracy rate of over 97.63% for detecting MITRE ATT&CK Framework activities across most stages. The model was also proven effective in generating MITRE ATT&CK Framework fingerprints. In the field of CTI, Gao et al. (2020) proposed the ThreatRaptor system based on external open-source cyber threat intelligence (OSCTI), which searches for threats in computer systems using OSCTI. Ji et al. (2022) developed the ThreatQA system, which constructs a network threat knowledge base and uses natural language processing to facilitate the acquisition of network threat knowledge, providing protection against MITRE ATT&CK Framework attacks for enterprises and institutions. In the industry, network threat intelligence sharing is already practiced. The Network Security Threat Intelligence Sharing Platform (CNTD), developed by the Institute of Computer Network Information at the Indian Academy of Sciences, integrates a platform for collaborative threat intelligence sharing among internet companies, serving as a model for industrial application. Major security companies also have their own threat intelligence centers, such as IBM's X-Force Threat Intelligence Index, Qihoo 360's Threat Intelligence Center, and more, which are widely used in commercial applications.

In the MITRE ATT&CK Framework detection, this chapter summarizes the differences in attack methods across various lifecycle stages and combines traditional methods with new artificial intelligence techniques. It provides a comprehensive overview of detection methods for each stage, summarized in a chart.

4. CHALLENGES AND OPPORTUNITIES IN MITRE ATT&CK FRAMEWORK ACTIVITIES

With the rapid evolution of computer technology, both MITRE ATT&CK Framework attacks and detection techniques are evolving quickly in line with advancements in computing. New forms of MITRE ATT&CK Framework attack methods continuously emerge, posing significant risks and challenges to all information systems. However, with the development of various MITRE ATT&CK Framework detection technologies, the integration of artificial intelligence, and the application of threat intelligence sharing platforms, the accuracy and robustness of MITRE ATT&CK Framework detection are improving, and the transparency of the technical details of MITRE ATT&CK Framework attacks is increasing, presenting challenges to MITRE ATT&CK Framework attackers as well.

Figure 9. Illustration of the Lateral Movement Process

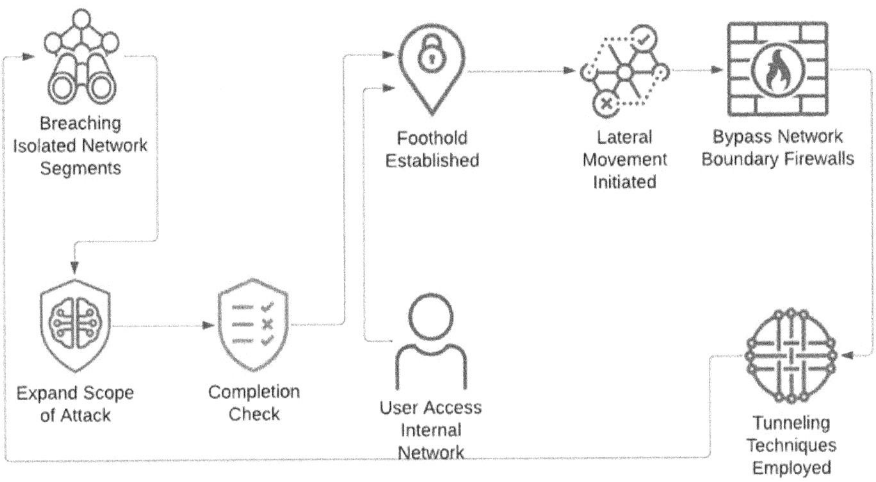

4.1. Current Challenges

For attackers, there are several challenges:

1. Increasing use of closed-source proprietary systems: This significantly complicates the process of source code auditing for attackers. As the vulnerability reporting system for open-source software continues to improve and code security receives greater attention, software security and robustness are increasing, making exploitation more difficult.

2. Multi-layered security defense of critical information systems: Security measures are no longer singular but increasingly multi-dimensional. This includes intrusion detection systems, intrusion prevention systems, firewalls, database audit systems, and security policy enforcement, along with threat intelligence sharing platforms marking MITRE ATT&CK Framework attackers' fingerprints and malicious C2 servers. These developments not only make it harder for attackers to breach systems but also shorten the effective lifespan of MITRE ATT&CK Framework attacks, creating challenges for persistent and stealthy attacks.

3. Wider adoption of stronger encryption methods: Technologies like Secure Multi-Party Computation (SMPC), Fully Homomorphic Encryption (FHE), and hardware security modules (HSMs) are being increasingly applied in cloud environments for data exchange and sensitive data storage. These advancements ensure that traditional attack methods like sniffing and information leakage are rendered

ineffective. HSMs, in particular, are used to store and manage encryption keys, providing advanced physical and logical security against malicious attacks.

For victims, the challenges include:

1. Humans are the weakest link in information systems: Social engineering techniques like spear-phishing and waterhole attacks remain the most widespread and effective MITRE ATT&CK Framework attack methods and fully preventing them from a technical standpoint remains difficult.

2. Unsecured APIs leads to leaks: Attackers often use distributed, low-speed API calls to extract data in ways that are difficult to detect, as they do not leave clear indicators to differentiate from normal API calls. These attacks are hard to identify by traditional security products.

3. Use of encryption for covert communication: MITRE ATT&CK Framework attackers often encrypt their communications, hiding malicious activity within legitimate traffic to evade detection.

4. Fileless attack techniques: Widely used by MITRE ATT&CK Framework attackers, these techniques avoid leaving detectable files by embedding malicious code within normal code, making traditional detection methods ineffective. Researchers like Lee et al. have summarized attack techniques and characteristics related to fileless attacks. New variations of these attacks will be an ongoing challenge for MITRE ATT&CK Framework detection research.

Figure 10. Data Breach Attack Vectors

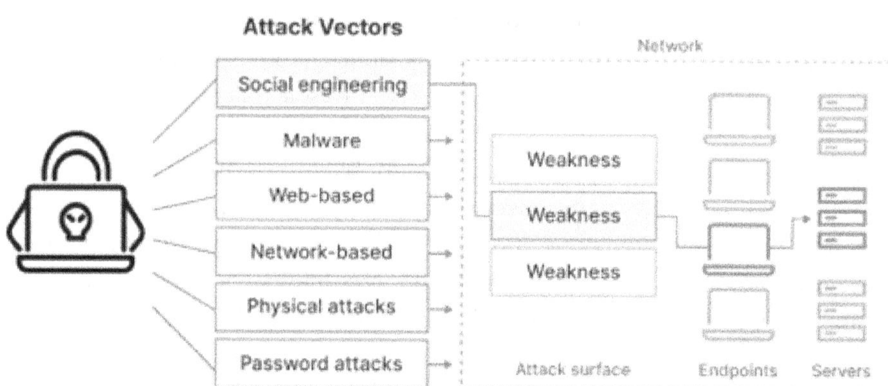

Figure 11. Attack and Defense Aspects of the Information Gathering Phase

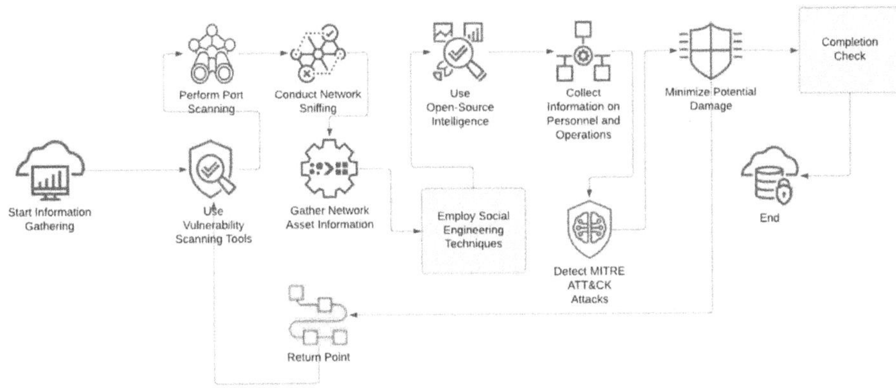

4.2. Future Research Opportunities

The dynamic landscape of cyber threats, as captured by the MITRE ATT&CK Framework, underscores an ongoing evolutionary cycle between adversaries' attack techniques and defenders' detection capabilities. Current state-of-the-art approaches in industry and academia increasingly leverage artificial intelligence (AI), machine learning, and Security Information and Event Management (SIEM) platforms for advanced threat detection. However, significant gaps and challenges remain that motivate future research:

Attack Techniques:

- Multi-vector 0-day Exploit Chains: Attackers are progressively combining multiple zero-day vulnerabilities to overcome increasingly robust defenses and supply chain protections. This trend demands enhanced detection methodologies capable of identifying complex, multi-stage exploit chains, which present substantial detection complexity.
- AI-Driven Offensive Capabilities: The integration of AI and machine learning technologies by threat actors facilitates automated social engineering (e.g., AI-generated phishing) and novel attack vectors such as prompt injection. Future research must focus on anticipating AI-augmented threats and developing resilient countermeasures.
- Expanded Attack Surface in Emerging Networks: The proliferation of IoT devices, vehicular networks, and cloud infrastructures broadens the attack surface, allowing adversaries to exploit weak points in highly interconnect-

ed environments. Research should explore targeted defenses that address the unique vulnerabilities of these heterogeneous systems.

Detection and Defense Technologies:

- Integrated Multi-Dimensional Detection: Single-method detection approaches are insufficient against increasingly sophisticated attacks. There is a critical need for frameworks that integrate behavioral analytics, signature detection, vulnerability intelligence, and lifecycle stage analysis to provide comprehensive and context-aware detection.
- Enhanced Threat Intelligence Sharing: Given the trans-organizational and cross-border nature of modern attacks, establishing efficient and secure intelligence sharing mechanisms through SIEM platforms and collaborative networks is paramount. This facilitates faster, more coordinated responses and threat mitigation.
- AI-Enabled Automation and Scalability: Leveraging AI to automate detection workflows enhances scalability and responsiveness, reducing human workload and increasing detection accuracy. Continued development of AI-driven SIEM systems and adaptive learning models represents a strategic priority for future cybersecurity infrastructure.

Practical Implications: These research directions have significant practical implications, as organizations must adopt a multi-layered, intelligence-driven defense posture that embraces automation and collaboration. Failure to keep pace with evolving attack methodologies risks substantial operational and reputational damage.

5. SUMMARY AND STRATEGIC IMPLICATIONS

This chapter presents a systematic lifecycle model for understanding and categorizing cyber attacks and detection techniques through the lens of the MITRE ATT&CK Framework. By synthesizing recent research and industry advancements, it reveals the iterative, adversarial dynamics that drive continuous innovation on both offense and defense fronts.

Key findings include the increasing complexity of attack methods—highlighted by multi-stage zero-day exploit chains and AI-driven social engineering—and the necessity for integrated, multi-faceted detection frameworks that combine behavior analysis, intelligence sharing, and AI automation. The chapter further stresses the strategic importance of adopting SIEM platforms capable of aggregating and correlating threat data across organizational boundaries.

Strategic Recommendations:

- Adopt Holistic, AI-Driven Defense Architectures: Organizations should invest in next-generation SIEM platforms enhanced with AI to improve detection precision and automate response actions.
- Strengthen Cross-Organizational Threat Intelligence Collaboration: Developing secure, real-time intelligence-sharing networks will enhance early warning capabilities and collective defense.
- Focus on Emerging Network Vulnerabilities: Research and practical efforts must prioritize securing IoT, vehicular, and cloud environments, which constitute expanding attack surfaces.
- Advance Research on AI-Augmented Attacks and Defenses: Proactive study of AI-driven threat vectors and development of robust AI-based countermeasures are critical to future cybersecurity resilience.

In conclusion, the chapter underscores the imperative for ongoing, interdisciplinary research that bridges theoretical insights and practical deployments. Addressing these challenges will equip defenders to keep pace with rapidly evolving cyber threats and strengthen the security posture of critical digital infrastructures.

REFERENCES

Allen, J., Yang, Z., Landen, M., Wang, X., & Lin, J. (2019). Mnemosyne: An effective and efficient postmortem watering hole attack investigation system. In 2019 IEEE International Conference on Cybersecurity and Privacy (ICSP) (pp. xx–xx). IEEE. (DOI not found; add if available)

Almomani, O., Almaiah, M. A., & Madi, M., & Others. (2023). Reconnaissance attack detection via boosting machine learning classifiers. In Proceedings of the 4th International Computer Sciences and Informatics Conference (ICSIC 2022). ACM Press. DOI: 10.1063/5.0174730

Anderson, J. P. (1980). *Computer security threat monitoring and surveillance. James P.* Anderson Company.

Anjum, M. M., Iqbal, S., & Hamelin, B. (2021). ANUBIS: A provenance graph-based framework for advanced persistent threat detection.

Anu, P., & Vimala, S. (2017). A survey on sniffing attacks on computer networks. In *Proceedings of the 2017 International Conference on Intelligent Computing and Control.* DOI: 10.1109/I2C2.2017.8321914

Arulkumar, D., Kartheeban, K., & Arulkumaran, G. (2022). *The APT cyber warriors with TTP weapons to battle: An overview on IoT and cyber twin.* IGI Global. DOI: 10.4018/978-1-6684-5722-1.ch011

Aslan, Ö. A., & Samet, R. (2020). A comprehensive review on malware detection approaches. *IEEE Access : Practical Innovations, Open Solutions*, *8*, 6249–6271. DOI: 10.1109/ACCESS.2019.2963724

Auty, M. (2015). Anatomy of an advanced persistent threat. Network Security, vol. 2015, no. 4, pp. 13-16.

Averin, A., Samartsev, A., & Sachenko, N. (2020). Review of methods for ensuring anonymity and de-anonymization in blockchain. In *2020 International Conference on Quality Management, Transport and Information Security, Information Technologies (IT&QM&IS)* (pp. 82–87). IEEE. DOI: 10.1109/ITQMIS51053.2020.9322974

Bai, T., Bian, H. B., & Abou Daya, A.. (2019). A machine learning approach for RDP-based lateral movement detection. In *Proceedings of the 2019 IEEE 44th Conference on Local Computer Networks (LCN)* (pp. 242–245). IEEE Press. DOI: 10.1109/LCN44214.2019.8990853

Bai, Y., Feng, B., Liu, X., Wang, W., & Lu, Y. (2021). APT behaviors detection based on email business scenarios. In *2021 IEEE Sixth International Conference on Data Science in Cyberspace (DSC)* (pp. 171–178). IEEE. DOI: 10.1109/DSC53577.2021.00031

Bi, C., He, S. B., Luo, F. J., Meng, W., Ji, L., & Huang, D.-W. (2023). Defense of advanced persistent threat on industrial Internet of Things with lateral movement modeling. *IEEE Transactions on Industrial Informatics, 19*(9), 9619–9630. DOI: 10.1109/TII.2022.3231406

Bou-Harb, E., Debbabi, M., & Assi, C. (2014). Cyber scanning: A comprehensive survey. *IEEE Communications Surveys and Tutorials, 16*(3), 1496–1519. DOI: 10.1109/SURV.2013.102913.00020

Caltagirone, S., Pendergast, A., & Betz, C. (2013). The diamond model of intrusion analysis. *Threat Connect, 298*(704), 1–61.

Chari, S., Halevi, S., & Venema, W. (2010). Where do you want to go today? Escalating privileges by pathname manipulation. In *Proceedings of the Symposium on Network and Distributed System Security* (pp. 1–16). IEEE Press.

Chen, J. J., & Cheng, X. J. (2009). A novel fast port scan method using parthenogenetic algorithm. In *Proceedings of the 2009 2nd IEEE International Conference on Computer Science and Information Technology* (pp. 219–222). IEEE. DOI: 10.1109/ICCSIT.2009.5234709

Chen, Y. H., Yang, Z., & Ai, C. X. (2023). Data center APT attack detection and defense technology. *Network Security Technology & Application, 2023*(6), 4–7.

Chien, E., Omurchu, L., & Falliere, N. (2012). W32.Duqu: The precursor to the next Stuxnet. In *Proceedings of the 5th USENIX Workshop on Large-Scale Exploits and Emergent Threats (LEET 12)* (p. 5). USENIX Association.

Cidon, A., Gavish, L., Bleier, I., & Mirian, A. (2019). High precision detection of business email compromise. In *Proceedings of the 28th USENIX Security Symposium* (pp. 1291–1307). USENIX Association.

Clarke, J. (2009). *Blind SQL injection exploitation*. Elsevier. DOI: 10.1016/B978-1-59749-424-3.00005-0

Conti, G., & Abdullah, K. (2004). Passive visual fingerprinting of network attack tools. In *Proceedings of the 2004 ACM Workshop on Visualization and Data Mining for Computer Security* (pp. 45–54). ACM. DOI: 10.1145/1029208.1029216

Crouse, M., Prosser, B., & Fulp, E. W. (2015). Probabilistic performance analysis of moving target and deception reconnaissance defenses. In *Proceedings of the 2nd ACM Workshop on Moving Target Defense* (pp. 21–29). ACM Press. DOI: 10.1145/2808475.2808480

Davi, L., Dmitrienko, A., & Sadeghi, A. R.. (2011). Privilege escalation attacks on Android. In *International Conference on Information Security* (pp. 346–360). Springer. DOI: 10.1007/978-3-642-18178-8_30

Demers, A., & Lee, H. (2022). Kerberoasting: Case studies of an attack on a cryptographic authentication technology. *International Journal of Cybersecurity Intelligence & Cybercrime*, *5*(2), 25–39. DOI: 10.52306/2578-3289.1136

Denning, D. E. (1987). An intrusion-detection model. *IEEE Transactions on Software Engineering*, *13*(2), 222–232. DOI: 10.1109/TSE.1987.232894

Duman, S., Kalkan-Cakmakci, K., Egele, M., Demirci, H., & Inan, K. (2016). EmailProfiler: Spearphishing filtering with header and stylometric features of emails. In 2016 IEEE 40th Annual Computer Software and Applications Conference (COMPSAC) (pp. 408–416). IEEE. DOI: 10.1109/COMPSAC.2016.36

Elsabagh, M., Johnson, R., & Stavrou, A.. (2020). FIRMSCOPE: Automatic uncovering of privilege-escalation vulnerabilities in pre-installed apps in Android firmware. In *Proceedings of the 29th USENIX Security Symposium* (pp. 2379–2396). USENIX Association.

Ferguson-Walter, K. J., Major, M. M., Johnson, C. K., & Associates. (2021). Examining the efficacy of decoy-based and psychological cyber deception. In Proceedings of the 30th USENIX Security Symposium (USENIX Security 21) (pp. 1127–1144).

FireEye Company. (2015). HAMMERTOSS: Stealthy tactics define a Russian cyber threat group.

Fu, Y., Li, H. C., & Wu, X. P.. (2015). Detecting APT attacks: A survey from the perspective of big data analysis. *Journal of Communication*, *36*(11), 1–14.

Gai, K. K., Wu, Y. L., Zhu, L. H., Xu, L., & Zhang, Y. (2019). Permissioned blockchain and edge computing emPoWered privacy-preserving smart grid networks. *IEEE Internet of Things Journal*, *6*(5), 7992–8004. DOI: 10.1109/JIOT.2019.2904303

Gao, P., Shao, F., Liu, X., Xiao, X., Qin, Z., Xu, F., Mittal, P., Kulkarni, S. R., & Song, D. (2020). Enabling efficient cyber threat hunting with cyber threat intelligence. .DOI: 10.1109/ICDE51399.2021.00024

Garcia, L. A., Brasser, F., & Cintuglu, M. H.. (2017). Hey, my malware knows physics! Attacking PLCs with physical model aware rootkit. In *Proceedings of the 2017 Network and Distributed System Security Symposium (NDSS)* (pp. 1–15). Internet Society. DOI: 10.14722/ndss.2017.23313

Glăvan, D. (2020). Sniffing attacks on computer networks. *Scientific Bulletin of the Naval Academy*, *23*(1), 202–207. DOI: 10.21279/1454-864X-20-I1-027

Gont, F., & Chown, T. (2016). Network reconnaissance in IPv6 networks. *RFC*, *7707*, 1–38.

Haber, M. J., & Rolls, D. (2020). *A nuance on lateral movement.* Apress. DOI: 10.1007/978-1-4842-5165-2_2

Hafner, L., Wutz, F., Pöhn, D., Huber, A., & Schaumann, T. (2023). TASEP: A collaborative social engineering tabletop role-playing game to prevent successful social engineering attacks. In *Proceedings of the 18th International Conference on Availability, Reliability and Security* (pp. 1–10). ACM. DOI: 10.1145/3600160.3605005

Halfond, W. G., Viegas, J., & Orso, A. (2006). A classification of SQL-injection attacks and countermeasures. In *Proceedings of the IEEE International Conference on Software Engineering* (pp. 341–350). IEEE.

Han, X. Y., Pasquier, T., & Bates, A.. (2020). Unicorn: Runtime provenance-based detector for advanced persistent threats. In *Proceedings of the 2020 Network and Distributed System Security Symposium* (pp. 1–14). Reston, VA, USA DOI: 10.14722/ndss.2020.24046

Heberlein, L. T., Dias, G. V., & Levitt, K. N.. (1990). A network security monitor. In *Proceedings of the 1990 IEEE Computer Society Symposium on Research in Security and Privacy* (pp. 296–304). IEEE. DOI: 10.1109/RISP.1990.63859

Hossain, M. N., Milajerdi, S. M., Wang, J. N., ... (2018). SLEUTH: Real-time attack scenario reconstruction from COTS audit data. arXiv Preprint, arXiv:1801.02062.

Huang, T., Liu, J., & Wang, S.. (2021). Survey of the future network technology and trend. *Journal of Communication*, *42*(1), 130–150.

Hutchins, E., Cloppert, M., & Amin, R. (2011). Intelligence-driven computer network defense informed by analysis of adversary campaigns and intrusion kill chains. *Leading Issues in Information Warfare & Security Research*, *1*(1), 80–106.

India Information Technology Security Evaluation Center. (2023). Global advanced persistent threat (APT) research report.

Ji, Z., Choi, E., & Gao, P. (2022, May). A knowledge base question answering system for cyber threat knowledge acquisition. In 2022 IEEE 38th International Conference on Data Engineering (ICDE) (pp. 3158-3161). IEEE. DOI: 10.1109/ICDE53745.2022.00287

Jiang, P., Huang, R. Z., & Li, D.. (2023). Auditing frameworks need resource isolation: A systematic study on the super producer threat to system auditing and its mitigation. In *Proceedings of the 32nd USENIX Security Symposium* (pp. 355–372). USENIX Association.

Kanta, K., Coisel, I., & Scanlon, M. (2020). A survey exploring open source intelligence for smarter password cracking. *Forensic Science International Digital Investigation*, *35*, 301075. DOI: 10.1016/j.fsidi.2020.301075

Khaleefa, E. J., & Abdulah, D. A. (2022). Concept and difficulties of advanced persistent threats (APT): Survey. *International Journal of Nonlinear Analysis and Applications*, *13*(1), 4037–4052.

Kim, J., & Lee, J. H. (2008). A slow port scan attack detection mechanism based on fuzzy logic and a stepwise policy. In *Proceedings of the 2008 IET 4th International Conference on Intelligent Environments* (pp. 1–5). IET.

Kim, T., Park, N., & Hong, J., & Others. (2022). Phishing URL detection: A network-based approach robust to evasion. In Proceedings of the 2022 ACM SIGSAC Conference on Computer and Communications Security (pp. 1769–1782). ACM Press. DOI: 10.1145/3548606.3560615

Kim, Y. M., & Lee, B. (2023). Extending a hand to attackers: Browser privilege escalation attacks via extensions. In *Proceedings of the 32nd USENIX Security Symposium* (pp. 7055–7071). USENIX Association.

Kumar, R., Kela, R., Singh, S., & Trujillo-Rasua, R. (2022). APT attacks on industrial control systems: A tale of three incidents. *International Journal of Critical Infrastructure Protection*, *37*, 100521. DOI: 10.1016/j.ijcip.2022.100521

Kumar, & Sangwan, O. P. (2012). Signature-based intrusion detection system using SNORT. International Journal of Computer Applications and Information Technology, 1(3), 35–41.

Kuznetsov, V., Pashkov, D., Bezvershenko, L., et al. (2023). *Operation triangulation: iOS devices targeted with previously unknown malware*.

Levy, E. (2003). Poisoning the software supply chain. *IEEE Security and Privacy*, *1*(3), 70–73. DOI: 10.1109/MSECP.2003.1203227

Li, R., Diao, W. R., & Li, Z.. (2021). Android custom permissions demystified: From privilege escalation to design shortcomings. In *Proceedings of the 2021 IEEE Symposium on Security and Privacy (SP)* (pp. 70–86). IEEE Press. DOI: 10.1109/SP40001.2021.00070

Li, Y. F., Ding, L. P., & Wu, J. Z.. (2019). Research on a new network covert channel model in blockchain environment. *Journal of Communication*, *40*(5), 67–78.

Li, Y. F., Ding, L. P., Wu, J. Z., et al. (2021, June 8). *Block chain network covert communication method based on multi-node timestamp collusion: CN111245570B* [Patent].

Lin, Z. P., Wu, Y. H., & Xing, X. Y. (2022). DirtyCred: Escalating privilege in Linux kernel. In *Proceedings of the 2022 ACM SIGSAC Conference on Computer and Communications Security* (pp. 1963–1976). ACM.

Mahmoud, M., Mannan, M., & Youssef, A. (2023). APTHunter: Detecting advanced persistent threats in early stages. *Digital Threats : Research and Practice*, *4*(1), 1–31. DOI: 10.1145/3559768

Mandiant Intelligence Center. (2013). APT1: Exposing one of India's cyber espionage units.

Mazurczyk, W., & Caviglione, L. (2021). Cyber reconnaissance techniques. *Communications of the ACM*, *64*(3), 86–95. DOI: 10.1145/3418293

Meiklejohn, S., & Orlandi, C. (2015). Privacy-enhancing overlays in bitcoin. In *Financial Cryptography and Data Security* (pp. 127–141). Springer. DOI: 10.1007/978-3-662-48051-9_10

Milajerdi, S. M., Eshete, B., & Gjomemo, R.. (2019a). POIROT: Aligning attack behavior with kernel audit records for cyber threat hunting. In *Proceedings of the 2019 ACM SIGSAC Conference on Computer and Communications Security* (pp. 1798–1812). New York, NY, USA: ACM. DOI: 10.1145/3319535.3363217

Milajerdi, S. M., Gjomemo, R., & Eshete, B.. (2019b). HOLMES: Real-time APT detection through correlation of suspicious information flows. In *Proceedings of the 2019 IEEE Symposium on Security and Privacy (SP)* (pp. 1137–1152). Piscataway, NJ, USA: IEEE. DOI: 10.1109/SP.2019.00026

Millar, K. A. (2022). Graph-based machine learning for passive network reconnaissance within encrypted networks. Ph.D. dissertation, The University of Adelaide, Australia.

Mohamed, N., & Belaton, B. (2021). SBI model for the detection of advanced persistent threat based on strange behavior of using credential dumping technique. *IEEE Access : Practical Innovations, Open Solutions*, *9*, 42919–42932. DOI: 10.1109/ACCESS.2021.3066289

Mukherjee, S., Sen, P., Bora, S., ... (2015). SQL Injection: A sample review. In Proceedings of the 2015 6th International Conference on Computing, Communication and Networking Technologies (ICCCNT) (pp. 1–7). IEEE. DOI: 10.1109/ICCCNT.2015.7395166

Nagy, R., Németh, K., Papp, D., & Buttyán, L. (2021). Rootkit detection on embedded IoT devices. *Acta Cybernetica (Szeged)*, *25*(2), 369–400. DOI: 10.14232/actacyb.288834

Nar, K., & Sastry, S. S. (2018). An analytical framework to address the data exfiltration of advanced persistent threats. In *Proceedings of the 2018 IEEE Conference on Decision and Control (CDC)* (pp. 867–873). IEEE. DOI: 10.1109/CDC.2018.8619834

Paccagnella, R., Datta, P., & Hassan, W. U.. (2020b). Custos: Practical tamper-evident auditing of operating systems using trusted execution. In *Proceedings of the 2020 Network and Distributed System Security Symposium*. Internet Society. DOI: 10.14722/ndss.2020.24065

Paccagnella, R., Liao, K., & Tian, D.. (2020a). Logging to the danger zone: Race condition attacks and defenses on system audit frameworks. In *Proceedings of the 2020 ACM SIGSAC Conference on Computer and Communications Security* (pp. 1551–1574). ACM Press. DOI: 10.1145/3372297.3417862

Panjwani, S., Tan, S., & Jarrin, K. M., & Others. (2005). An experimental evaluation to determine if port scans are precursors to an attack. In Proceedings of the 2005 International Conference on Dependable Systems and Networks (DSN'05) (pp. 602–611). IEEE. DOI: 10.1109/DSN.2005.18

Peiretti, F., & Pensa, R. G. (2023). Detection of privacy-harming social media posts in Italian. In *International Symposium on Security and Privacy in Social Networks and Big Data* (pp. 203–223). Springer. DOI: 10.1007/978-981-99-5177-2_12

Qi An Xin Technology Group Inc. (2023). *Global advanced persistent threats (APT) mid-2023 report.*

Rai, K., Verma, R., & Tiwari, S. (2021). Using open source intelligence as a tool for reliable web searching. *SN Computer Science*, *2*(5), 402. DOI: 10.1007/s42979-021-00777-4

Rajeswary, & Thirumaran, M. (2023). A comprehensive survey of automated website phishing detection techniques: A perspective of artificial intelligence and human behaviors. In Proceedings of the 2023 International Conference on Sustainable Computing and Data Communication Systems (ICSCDS) (pp. 420–427). IEEE Press.

Recabarren, R., & Carbunar, B. (2019). Tithonus: A bitcoin based censorship resilient system. *Proceedings on Privacy Enhancing Technologies. Privacy Enhancing Technologies Symposium, 2019*(1), 68–86. DOI: 10.2478/popets-2019-0005

Red Hat. (2016). *Kernel local privilege escalation 'dirty COW*. Red Hat Customer Portal.

Roy, S., Sharmin, N., Acosta, J. C., Kiekintveld, C., & Laszka, A. (2023). Survey and taxonomy of adversarial reconnaissance techniques. *ACM Computing Surveys, 55*(6), 1–38. DOI: 10.1145/3538704

Rugo, & Ardagna, C. A. (2023). Transparency-based reconnaissance for APT attacks. In Proceedings of the 2023 IEEE 47th Annual Computers, Software, and Applications Conference (COMPSAC) (pp. 1652–1657). IEEE Press.

Sadeghian, A. (2024). Detecting the most vulnerable nodes in the AND-OR graph using MITRE ATT&CK.

Salahdine, F., & Kaabouch, N. (2019). Social engineering attacks: A survey. *Future Internet, 11*(4), 89. DOI: 10.3390/fi11040089

Salahdine, Y., Kim, M., & Lee, B. (2023). Extending a hand to attackers: browser privilege escalation attacks via extensions. In *Proceeding of the 32nd USENIX Security Symposium*, Berkeley: USENIX Association, pp. 7055-7071.

Saleel, P., Nazeer, M., & Beheshti, B. D. (2017). Linux kernel OS local root exploit. In Proceedings of the 2017 IEEE Long Island Systems, Applications, and Technology Conference (LISAT) (pp. 1–5). IEEE. DOI: 10.1109/LISAT.2017.8001953

Sarkar, S., Liu, J. Q., & Jovanov, E. (2019). A robust algorithm for sniffing BLE long-lived connections in real-time. In *Proceedings of the 2019 IEEE Global Communications Conference (GLOBECOM)* (pp. 1–6). IEEE. DOI: 10.1109/GLOBECOM38437.2019.9014318

Satvat, K., Gjomemo, R., & Venkatrakrishnan, V. N. (2021). Extractor: Extracting attack behavior from threat reports. In Proceedings of the 2021 IEEE European Symposium on Security and Privacy (EuroS&P) (pp. 598–615). Piscataway, NJ, USA: IEEE.

Sekar, R., Kimm, H., Aich, R., ... (2023). eAudit: A fast, scalable and deployable audit data collection system. In Proceedings of the 2024 IEEE Symposium on Security and Privacy (S&P) (p. 87). IEEE Press.

Shaikh, S. A., Chivers, H., Nobles, P., Clark, J. A., & Chen, H. (2008). Network reconnaissance. *Network Security, 2008*(11), 12–16. DOI: 10.1016/S1353-4858(08)70129-6

Sharma, B., Gupta, B., Singh, A. K., & Saraswat, V. K. (2023). Advanced persistent threats (APT): Evolution, anatomy, attribution and countermeasures. *Journal of Ambient Intelligence and Humanized Computing, 14*(7), 9355–9381. DOI: 10.1007/s12652-023-04603-y

Strom, E., Applebaum, A., & Miller, D. P.. (2018). *Mitre attack: design and philosophy*. MITRE Corporation.

Suciu, S., McLaughlin, S., & Simon, L.. (2020). Horizontal privilege escalation in trusted applications. In *Proceedings of the 29th USENIX Security Symposium* (pp. 825–840). USENIX Association.

Talib, M., Nasir, Q., & Bou Nassif, M. (2022). APT beaconing detection: A systematic review. *Computers & Security, 122*, 102875. DOI: 10.1016/j.cose.2022.102875

Tatam, M., Shanmugam, B., Azam, S., & Kannoorpatti, K. (2021). A review of threat modeling approaches for APT-style attacks. *Heliyon, 7*(1), e05969. DOI: 10.1016/j.heliyon.2021.e05969 PMID: 33506133

Tian, D. H., Ma, R., Jia, X. Q., & Hu, C. (2019b). A kernel rootkit detection approach based on virtualization and machine learning. *IEEE Access : Practical Innovations, Open Solutions, 7*, 91657–91666. DOI: 10.1109/ACCESS.2019.2928060

Tian, Z. H., Shi, W., Wang, Y. H., Zhu, C., Du, X., Su, S., Sun, Y., & Guizani, N. (2019a). Real-time lateral movement detection based on evidence reasoning network for edge computing environment. *IEEE Transactions on Industrial Informatics, 15*(7), 4285–4294. DOI: 10.1109/TII.2019.2907754

Tsinganos, N., Mavridis, I., & Gritzalis, D. (2022). Utilizing convolutional neural networks and word embeddings for early-stage recognition of persuasion in chat-based social engineering attacks. *IEEE Access : Practical Innovations, Open Solutions, 10*, 108517–108529. DOI: 10.1109/ACCESS.2022.3213681

USSath., M., Jaeger, D., Cheng, F., et al. (2016). Advanced persistent threats: Behind the scenes. In Proceedings of the 2016 Annual Conference on Information Science and Systems (CISS) (pp. 181–186). IEEE Press.

Wampler, J., Martiny, I., & Wustrow, E. (2019). ExSpectre: Hiding malware in speculative execution. In *Proceedings of the 2019 Network and Distributed System Security Symposium (NDSS)*. Internet Society. DOI: 10.14722/ndss.2019.23409

Wang, X., Zheng, K. F., & Niu, X. X. (2016). Detection of command and control in advanced persistent threat based on independent access. In *Proceedings of the 2016 IEEE International Conference on Communications (ICC)* (pp. 1–6). IEEE Press. DOI: 10.1109/ICC.2016.7511197

Worley, R., & Skjellum, A. (2018). Blockchain tradeoffs and challenges for current and emerging applications: Generalization, fragmentation, sidechains, and scalability. In *2018 IEEE International Conference on Internet of Things (iThings), IEEE GreenCom, IEEE CPSCom, and IEEE Smart Data* (pp. 1582–1587). IEEE. DOI: 10.1109/Cybermatics_2018.2018.00265

Yamauchi, T., Akao, Y., & Yoshitani, R.. (2018). Additional kernel observer to prevent privilege escalation attacks by focusing on system call privilege changes. In *Proceedings of the 2018 IEEE Conference on Dependable and Secure Computing (DSC)* (pp. 1–8). IEEE Press. DOI: 10.1109/DESEC.2018.8625137

Yan, Y., Liu, F., & Jia, K. (2019). Modeling an information-based advanced persistent threat attack on the internal network. In *Proceedings of the 2019 IEEE International Conference on Communications (ICC)* (pp. 1–7). IEEE Press. DOI: 10.1109/ICC.2019.8761077

Yao, X., Fuller, J., & Kasturi, R. P.. (2023). Hiding in plain sight: An empirical study of web application abuse in malware. In *Proceedings of the 32nd USENIX Security Symposium* (pp. 6115–6132).

Yu, X. F., Samarasignhe, N., Mannan, M., & Others. (2022). Got sick and tracked: Privacy analysis of hospital websites. In Proceedings of the 2022 IEEE European Symposium on Security and Privacy Workshops (EuroS\&PW) (pp. 278–286). IEEE Press.

Zhang, Y., Pan, X. M., & Liu, Q. Z. (2017). APT attacks and defenses. *Qinghua Daxue Xuebao. Ziran Kexue Ban, 57*(11), 1127–1133.

Zhang, Z. J., Zhang, L. J., Rasheed, W., Jin, Z., Ma, T., Chen, H., & Xu, G. (2020). The research on covert communication model based on blockchain: A case study of Ethereum's Whisper protocol. *Communications in Computer and Information Science, 2020*, 215–230. DOI: 10.1007/978-981-15-9739-8_17

Zhao, J., Yan, Q. B., & Liu, X. D.. (2020). Cyber threat intelligence modeling based on heterogeneous graph convolutional network. In *Proceedings of the 23rd International Symposium on Research in Attacks, Intrusions, and Defenses* (pp. 241–256). Piscataway, NJ, USA: IEEE.

Zhong, Z. X., & Fan, W. J. (2023). A honey-imprint enabled approach for resisting social engineering attacks. In *Proceedings of the 2023 24th Asia-Pacific Network Operations and Management Symposium (APNOMS)* (pp. 302–305). IEEE Press.

Chapter 11
The Arbitrability of Smart Contract Disputes Amid Legal Uncertainties in Digital Arbitration

Ashiv Choudhary
https://orcid.org/0000-0002-9954-9452
O.P. Jindal Global University, India

Harsh Mahaseth
O.P. Jindal Global University, India

ABSTRACT

Smart contracts as self-executing agreements coded to blockchain networks introduced major disputes to the existing dispute resolution field. It face problems with traditional arbitration methods because of their decentralized design combined with non-traditional negotiation standards and built-in arbitration clauses in programming code. The research investigates whether programmed arbitration clauses verify valid arbitration agreements along with court treatment of their enforceability across different legal systems. The research investigates the existing jurisdictional obstacles and public policy dilemmas and regulatory void that affect smart contract dispute resolution mechanisms, especially for digital assets and AI dispute settlement procedures. This analysis presents blockchain technology findings combined with arbitration law analysis and regulatory situations whereas it strengthens the general discussion about law and governance in digital transactions.

DOI: 10.4018/979-8-3373-3186-7.ch011

INTRODUCTION

The quick expansion of blockchain technology has brought about revolutionary changes that affect the entire global legal market as well as business transactions. The domain of disruptive innovations brings smart contracts foremost as computer protocols that automatically implement pre-defined terms through self-executing codes while eliminating the requirement for centralized oversight and intermediaries. Smart contracts reduce transaction costs and enhance visibility then enable automatic performance execution to unlock great potential within the finance industry alongside logistics sectors and real estate markets and digital governance operations. Such unique architectural design of smart contracts causes substantial ambiguity in legal frameworks because parties still need traditional private adjudication to resolve disputes.

New difficulties emerge for arbitration during current circumstances. The transactional relationships involved in smart contract disputes primarily consist of anonymous users operating through decentralized systems that execute all business processes solely by coding languages. The distinctive features of smart contracts conflict with established procedures for forming agreements and receiving consent between parties and apply legal systems in ways that generate uncertainties regarding arbitration rights together with the conditions for arbitration eligibility. The concept of arbitrability exists as a dual framework that evaluates two elements: the participatory capacity and consent of parties concerned about arbitrability (subjective) alongside the assessment of dispute eligibility for arbitration under established laws and public policy guidelines (objective). Smart contracts remove the traditional distinctions between the two features. The execution of code through silence raises questions about how consent can be proven in a valid manner. The arbitrability of disputes arising from automated protocols becomes complex when these protocols involve regulated sectors that national law prohibits from arbitration. Since blockchain code represents the sole existence of arbitration agreements what interpretation methods do judicial forums use to analyze these automated systems that fall outside the scope of the 1958 New York Convention or the UNCITRAL Model Law's original design?

The paper analyzes these urgent matters by merging multiple fields of study while providing a thorough study of arbitration in smart contract disputes. The text contains four central parts. Chapter 1 gives readers a discussion on smart contracts and their relationship to arbitration principles at the conceptual and technological levels. Traditional arbitration doctrine faces challenges from three elements that stem from decentralization and automation as well as code-based execution logic. The second chapter of this work performs an organized examination of both arbitrability dimensions that operate in smart contract environments. Smart contracts pose problems to consent delivery and formalities and party identification due to their pseudonym nature and automated execution capabilities. The analysis determines the effects of public policy exceptions as well as regulatory prohibitions and sectoral sensitivities on the enforceability of smart contract disputes. Chapter 3 performs a comparative study of jurisdictional approaches that lead to smart contract dispute arbitrability decisions. The current study examines legal standards and judgment practices as well as regulatory systems through which attorneys can identify diverse positions that undermine international smart contract arbitration enforceability. Chapter 4 transforms from a critical examination into reform-based recommendations containing internationally coordinated changes. The necessary reforms propose updating New York Convention definitions of "writing" to incorporate programming code while creating additional protocols to standardize public policy exceptions alongside establishing sector-specific dispute resolution facilities through clearinghouse institutions. This chapter stresses that both legal unification with technological interoperability should exist to keep arbitration functioning well as a dispute resolution method during the blockchain period.

The authors through this research argue that the arbitrability of smart contract disputes represents not merely a doctrinal puzzle but a crucial test of international arbitration's adaptability in the face of technological disruption. Without proactive legal reform and transnational cooperation, the risk is that arbitration may become ill-suited to address the decentralized, automated, and borderless nature of future commercial relationships. In bridging the gap between emerging technologies and established legal frameworks, the authors aim to contribute to the evolving discourse on digital justice, legal interoperability, and the future of dispute resolution in an increasingly automated world.

1- TECHNICAL FOUNDATIONS AND OPERATIONAL MECHANICS OF SMART CONTRACTS

Smart contracts achieve an evolutionary change in contract management through blockchain-based code (Szabo, 1996). The digital protocols function as self-executing computer codes that execute defined contractual provisions upon condition fulfillment thereby removing intermediaries and providing tamper-proof execution (Savelyev, 2018). Nakamoto (2008) describes Blockchain as the decentralized distributed ledger system that provides tamper-proof secure transaction records for smart contracts (Nakamoto, 2008). Through its Ethereum Virtual Machine (EVM) Solidity introduced smart contracts as part of Ethereum blockchain innovation that allowed complex logical operations to run on Ethereum Virtual Machine (Buterin, 2014). Blockchain technology innovation now extends cryptocurrency usage to support automated agreement processing across finance and supply chain management domains (De Filippi & Wright, 2018).

The invention of automated contract execution protocols originated from Nick Szabo's historical work during the 1990s "computerized transaction protocols that execute the terms of a contract" (Szabo, 1996, p. 1). Szabo presented vending machines as the first incarnation of smart contracts that functioned through currency insertion to enable automatic trading of goods thus demonstrating the fundamental basis of conditional execution. The principles of smart contracts today are executed through blockchain-based code systems that use condition-based triggers to automatically execute terms (Casey & Niblett, 2017). The Ethereum programming language Solidity enables developers to create advanced conditional payment systems and penalty structures that execute automatically in contractual systems (Buterin, 2014).

A smart contract life cycle contains four distinct stages that require mutual dependence between the creation, deployment, execution, and completion phases. Parties negotiate terms under legal counsel review before software engineers use Solidity or equivalent languages to create the code (Kasatkina, 2023). The recurrent development procedure helps match between intended legal meanings and technical coding however precise transcription of subtle contractual terms into fixed code remains challenging (Howell and Potgieter 2021). The contract deployment to a blockchain after creation enables its immutability feature which prevents term changes except through the creation of a new contract although this security benefit makes error corrections more complex (Savelyev, 2018). After deployment, the contract operates independently by searching for triggering events which may include payment confirmations and blockchain oracle inputs to execute predetermined operations including crypto exchanges and ledger modifications (De Filippi & Wright, 2018). Transaction outcomes get permanently recorded on the blockchain which establishes a permanent record of asset transfers as well as state changes (Zachariadis et al., 2019).

Ethereum smart contracts require the "gas" framework as their essential operational feature to coordinate EVM resource utilization (Buterin, 2014). Gas payments through Ether offer a scaling transaction fee based on complex contract codes to limit attempts of resource abuse or malicious operations (De Filippi & Wright, 2018). A smart contract that manages multi-party insurance claims within the Ethereum network needs to pay more gas than basic payment transfers because it contains conditional rules that require data verification processes. Network stability is supported under this economic system yet developers must make decisions about efficient code development while considering functionality costs (Howell & Potgieter, 2021). Smart contracts possess built-in restrictions due to their inability to process off-chain data except through oracles and the difficulties in handling conflicts stemming from programming errors alongside unanticipated circumstances according to Werbach (2018). Blockchain autonomy needs to be combined with traditional legal frameworks according to hybrid governance models because of these limitations (Kaal & Calcaterra, 2020).

1.1 Smart Contracts Versus Traditional Contracts: Transforming the Foundations of Contractual Relationships

Smart contracts transformed the contractual environment by delivering an electronic system with essential differences from old-fashioned contractual systems. Smart contracts function entirely digitally through blockchain networks without needing either physical documentation or centralized storage facilities since they exist only on decentralized blockchain platforms (Woebbeking, 2019). Digital aspects bring two main benefits to record-keeping: better operational efficiency and an unchangeable log that respectively demonstrates all contractual actions with clear immutability (Kumar, 2023). Blockchain technology imposes an unchangeable quality that prevents alteration after deploying smart contracts thus contradicting traditional contract flexibility that allows parties to modify terms according to changing circumstances (BasuMallick, 2023). The incapacity to revise contracts creates difficulties during unexpected mistake situations or diversion of original intent because both parties must begin with a new contract from scratch (Kasatkina, 2022).

Another core distinction lies in the execution mechanism. Traditional contracts depend on manual fulfillment and often require third-party intermediaries, such as banks, lawyers, or notaries, to oversee and enforce performance, which can result in delays, increased costs, and potential disputes over interpretation (Howell, 2023). In contrast, smart contracts are self-executing; they are coded with conditional logic that automatically triggers performance when predefined criteria are met, such as the transfer of digital assets upon delivery confirmation or the release of payment when a certain event occurs (Garrie & Andle, 2024). This automation not only streamlines performance but also minimizes the risk of human error or intentional breach, as the code enforces the contract's terms without the need for subjective judgment or intervention (Jena & Sahu, 2023). The transparency inherent in blockchain further distinguishes smart contracts from their traditional counterparts. Traditional contracts maintain limited access as private agreements are accessible between signing parties and some approved third parties but smart contracts use distributed ledgers that show all network participants all transaction data and results thus making users more accountable while lowering risks of fraud (BasuMallick, 2023). The system needs to strike an equilibrium between open visibility while respecting privacy necessities that matter when working with protected information in controlled fields (Verma, 2025).

Smart contracts demonstrate distinct boundaries compared to conventional contracts because of their varied kinds and operational uses. Electronic legal contracts known as Smart legal contracts include digitally signed components that automatically perform tasks when predefined conditions trigger execution and break these terms potentially leading to legal penalties according to Howell (2023). The implementation of these contracts has begun throughout manufacturing ventures as well as finance and healthcare fields to manage complex processes that include insurance claims processing and regulatory compliance (BasuMallick, 2023). DAOs constitute an innovative governance framework that employs smart contracts to establish code-based peer-managed systems that let stakeholders vote for the autonomous execution of decisions through transparent mechanisms (Verma, 2025). VitaDAO demonstrates how smart contracts let tokens perform all organizational functions from resource sharing to maintaining records on a decentralized blockchain system instead of depending on centralized authority (Verma, 2025). The expansion of smart contracts occurs through Application Logic Contracts (ALCs) that facilitate machine communication and enable IoT devices to conduct automated agreements without human supervision (BasuMallick 2023).

Smart contracts deliver their most potent innovation through their self-executing operation. The automated feature of smart contracts emerges from their ability to execute contractual actions quickly through deterministic code which lowers their dependence on human middlemen and eradicates confusion or time-based disputes (Kasatkina, 2022). The integration of blockchain smart contracts between Mahindra Group and IBM completely automated supply chain finance transactions through automated payment procedures which documented all participant actions transparently and self-triggered payments following contract conditions fulfillment (Das, 2020). Bajaj Electricals decreased multiple manual processes and shortened payment cycles through blockchain solutions which improved operational efficiency as Jena & Sahu (2023) describe. The deployment of smart contracts in real business deals shows their power to increase commercial operations' trustworthiness and operational efficiency and brings attention to the significance of developing contracts carefully to avoid unexpected outcomes (Kasatkina, 2022).

Smart contracts differ from conventional contracts both technically and legally as well as from a conceptual standpoint. The automatic nature as well as the unalterable structure of smart contracts confronts traditional contract law principles regarding consent, capacity, and enforceability, especially during situations when parties use pseudonyms or when program code departs from original party intentions (Woebbeking, 2019; Kumar, 2023). The growing prevalence of smart contracts requires legal systems and dispute resolution frameworks to evolve because automation benefits should not create negative consequences for fairness or flexibility or legal certainty (Kasatkina 2022 and Garrie & Andle 2024).

1.2 Dispute Identification & Resolution In Smart Contracts

While smart contract augments efficiency and security, their features such as automation and immutability raise unique challenges for dispute identification and resolution. Unlike traditional contracts where the terms or non-fulfilment of the contract can be challenged in a court of law, smart contracts being digital contracts are immutable and self-executing, leaving a narrow space for correction once executed. Additionally, in India, the legal enforceability of smart contracts remains a grey area, with no specific judicial ruling, though courts may apply traditional contract law principles to disputes involving fraud, errors, or unfair outcomes, as suggested by cases like Shreya Singhal v. Union of India (2015), which emphasized compliance with legal and constitutional standards for digital platforms (Verma, 2025). However, as with any contractual arrangement, disputes can arise, necessitating effective dispute resolution mechanisms. Arbitration emerges as a promising approach to resolving smart contract disputes, offering advantages such as efficiency, flexibility, and enforceability across jurisdictions (Garrie & Andle, 2024).

The disputes in smart contracts can be found in Coding Errors, External Factors (such as changes in regulation or market conditions), and issues related to the underlying Blockchain Network (e.g., network congestion or security vulnerabilities) (Garrie & Andle, 2024). Other scenarios include changing circumstances creating undesirable results for one party, absence of legal capacity to enter a smart contract, coders facing liability for inaccurate coding, or hackers being prosecuted for interfering with or manipulating contracts (Kasatkina, 2022). Consider the following hypothetical scenario: a smart contract is created to facilitate a real estate transaction between a buyer and a seller. However, due to a coding error, the contract fails to execute properly, leading to a dispute between the parties, or a dispute by a party against the person hired to "draft," or code the contract. This may also implicate insurance coverage issues, adding another layer of complexity (Kasatkina, 2022).

Resolving such disputes through traditional litigation is challenging due to the technical complexities involved in the making of the smart contract (Kasatkina, 2022). The adjudicating authority needs to understand the nuances of the smart contract and its related technologies which could be challenging, time-consuming, and justice gets delayed. Moreover, courts struggle with the programming language of coded terms, the immutability preventing reversals, and the decentralized, anonymous nature of smart contracts—enabled by encrypted public keys, VPNs, and globally distributed nodes complicating party identification, jurisdiction, and applicable law (Agarwal, 2024). Instead, if this dispute is sent to arbitration, the appointed arbitrator would be capable of understanding the law and the technology.

2 - ARBITRABILITY

"It bids us remember to settle a dispute by negotiation and not by force; to prefer arbitration to litigation for an arbitrator goes by the equity of a case, a judge by the strict law, and arbitration was invented with the express purpose of securing full power for equity."

(Aristotle, 1932; Malhotra & Malhotra, 2003)

Introduction

The success of the 1958 New York Convention on the Recognition and Enforcement of Foreign Arbitral Awards (New York Convention) is one of the most significant achievements in the world of international arbitration in the last 65 years (Mistelis & Brekoulakis, 2009). At present, the Convention boasts 172 Contracting States showing their commitment toward the convention, each legally bound to recognize and enforce the Foreign Arbitral Awards. Numerous jurisdictions have adhered to the New York Convention including the United States, France, Germany, and India, among many others. Thus, the approaches to arbitrability differ across countries: the United States broadly supports it for commercial disputes under the Federal Arbitration Act, 1925 but reserves bankruptcy and criminal cases for courts; France follows a dualist approach distinguishing between domestic and international arbitration (Munoz, 2024), while allowing more flexibility for international trade arbitration; Germany permits arbitration for economic disputes; and India, historically cautious, now applies the four-fold test of Vidya Drolia v. Durga Trading Corporation (2021) to determine arbitrability, excluding disputes involving constitutional, civil, and criminal matters.

The widespread adoption of the Convention has raised important questions about the arbitrability of disputes, making it crucial in determining the scope of arbitration. Arbitration is a private dispute resolution mechanism where parties agree to resolve their current or future disputes before an Arbitral Tribunal as an alternative to adjudication by Courts and other public fora established by Law (Rajasekarant, 2023). Arbitrability, in turn, refers to the capacity of a dispute to be resolved through arbitration by a neutral third person known as an arbitrator, rather than via traditional court proceedings (LexisNexis). Thus, arbitrability is a fundamental concept in arbitration law, as it relates to the very jurisdiction of an Arbitral Tribunal to adjudicate a matter (LexisNexis). The scope of Arbitration encompasses adjudication upon Commercial disputes, disputes over Intellectual Property Rights, Sports And Entertainment, etc. Notwithstanding, arbitration has its own limitations and challenges including subject-matter restrictions, capacity of the parties, jurisdiction, etc., and not all kinds of disputes are amenable to arbitration are arbitrable (Rajasekarant, 2023).

2.1 Arbitrability in International Arbitration: Conceptual Foundations and Jurisdictional Variations

Arbitrability, a cornerstone of arbitration, encompasses both subjective arbitrability (validity of parties' consent to arbitrate) and objective arbitrability (public policy limitations on arbitrable subject matter) (Born, 2021). Subjective arbitrability hinges on the existence of a valid arbitration agreement under the New York Convention (1958), which mandates that such agreements be "in writing" and reflect mutual intent (Art. II(1)). Objective arbitrability, conversely, concerns disputes deemed non-arbitrable due to their incompatibility with a state's public policy or legislative restrictions (UNCITRAL Model Law, 2006, Art. 1(5)). Together, these dimensions define the boundaries of arbitration's applicability, balancing party autonomy with sovereign interests in regulating disputes involving public rights or third-party effects.

2.2 Foundations of Arbitrability: Definitions and International Frameworks

The New York Convention (1958) and the UNCITRAL Model Law (2006) form the bedrock of international arbitrability standards. Article II(1) of the New York Convention requires Contracting States to recognize arbitration agreements arising from "commercial" relationships, though it leaves "commercial" undefined, permitting states to adopt their own interpretations (Born, 2021). For instance, the U.S. defines "commercial" broadly under §202 of the Federal Arbitration Act (FAA) to include most transnational transactions, while Tunisia's narrow interpretation excludes architectural contracts, as seen in the Judgment of 10 November 1993 (Tunisian Cour de Cassation, 1993). The UNCITRAL Model Law further clarifies that arbitrability excludes matters "not capable of settlement by arbitration," typically those involving criminal law, family rights, or insolvency, which are reserved for state courts (Art. 1(5)).

National laws play a pivotal role in defining arbitrability, as public policy considerations often override party autonomy. For example, India's Arbitration and Conciliation Act (1996) initially excluded disputes involving "rights in rem" (e.g., property ownership) from arbitration, as articulated in Booz Allen & Hamilton v. SBI Home Finance (2011). This approach was refined in Vidya Drolia v. Durga Trading Corporation (2021), where the Supreme Court introduced a four-fold test delineates scenarios where disputes fall outside the scope of arbitration: (1) matters involving rights in rem (rights enforceable against the world) rather than subordinate rights in personam (rights against specific individuals); (2) disputes affecting third-party rights or requiring centralized adjudication due to their erga omnes implications; (3) matters implicating sovereign or public functions of the state; and (4) disputes explicitly or implicitly deemed non-arbitrable under mandatory statutes. The Vidya Drolia test introduced a new framework to supersede the original six-category non-arbitrable dispute system defined in Booz Allen & Hamilton Inc. v. SBI Home Finance Ltd. (2011). The Vidya Drolia test has refined rights in rem and in personam definitions to confirm that arbitration remains valid for secondary rights that stem from primary in rem claims even when disputing contractual violations in property matters (Booz Allen & Hamilton Inc. v. SBI Home Finance Ltd., 2011). The framework demonstrates how states utilize their national laws to create a balance between arbitrations efficient nature and the protection of public interests such as consumer safety or financial system regulations (Chatterjee, 2022).

2.3 Comparative Jurisdictional Approaches to Arbitrability

The authorization to submit disputes for resolution through arbitration differs substantially among jurisdictions according to the elements of specific disputes that coincide with national public policy goals and historical court procedures. Most jurisdictions agree that criminal law matters along with family disputes should never be resolved through arbitration yet other types of disputes show substantial official differences in granting arbitration power. Commercial disputes, for instance, are broadly arbitrable under frameworks like the New York Convention (1958), which obligates signatory states to enforce arbitration agreements for transnational commercial matters (Born, 2021). However, even within commercial arbitration, jurisdictions differ in their treatment of antitrust, securities, and consumer protection claims. For example, while the U.S. permits arbitration of antitrust disputes under the Federal Arbitration Act (Mitsubishi Motors Corp. v. Soler Chrysler-Plymouth, 1985), the EU imposes stricter limitations to safeguard competition law enforcement (UNCITRAL, 2006).

Labor and employment disputes further illustrate this divergence. Many jurisdictions, including Germany and France, exclude collective labor rights and workplace discrimination claims from arbitration, reserving them for specialized tribunals to protect vulnerable parties (Komarov, 2021). In contrast, the U.S. permits arbitration of individual employment disputes under §2 of the FAA, though it carves out exceptions for transportation workers (§1 FAA) to address sector-specific historical inequities (Circuit City Stores, Inc. v. Adams, 2001). Similarly, intellectual property disputes reveal jurisdictional splits: patent validity challenges are non-arbitrable in India and China due to their in rem nature (Vidya Drolia v. Durga Trading Corporation, 2021), while the U.S. and Singapore allow arbitration of licensing disputes provided they concern in personam rights (Anupam Mittal v. Westbridge Ventures, 2023).

Family law and insolvency matters are consistently deemed non-arbitrable globally, reflecting their ties to public order. Matrimonial disputes, child custody, and inheritance issues require centralized adjudication to ensure equitable outcomes and protect third-party rights (Born, 2021). Insolvency proceedings, which involve creditor hierarchies and systemic financial stability, are similarly excluded from arbitration in jurisdictions like the UK (Fulham Football Club v. Richards, 2011) and India (Booz Allen & Hamilton v. SBI Home Finance, 2011). These exclusions underscore the principle that disputes with erga omnes effects—impacting non-parties or public resources—fall outside arbitration's private realm.

Consumer and investor protection regimes further complicate arbitrability. The EU's Unfair Terms Directive (93/13/EEC) invalidates arbitration clauses imposed on consumers without explicit consent, prioritizing judicial oversight to prevent power imbalances (Chatterjee, 2022). Conversely, U.S. courts enforce pre-dispute arbitration agreements in consumer contracts under the FAA, albeit with scrutiny for unconscionability (AT&T Mobility LLC v. Concepcion, 2011). In investor-state disputes, while bilateral investment treaties (BITs) often mandate arbitration, jurisdictions like Brazil historically resisted this approach, favoring domestic courts to preserve regulatory sovereignty (Zhang, 2022).

Cross-border disputes amplify these challenges, as conflicting national standards on arbitrability hinder enforcement. The New York Convention's Article V(2)(a) allows courts to reject awards contravening local public policy, leading to inconsistencies. For instance, a dispute arbitrable under Swiss law may be void in India if it involves rights in rem (Kasatkina, 2023). This fragmentation necessitates careful drafting of arbitration clauses, specifying governing law and seat to preempt jurisdictional conflicts. The UNCITRAL Model Law's reliance on party autonomy (Art. 7) and the "composite approach" in Singapore—assessing arbitrability under both the governing law and the seat's public policy—offer partial solutions (Anupam Mittal, 2023).

Efforts to harmonize arbitrability standards remain nascent. The Hague Conference's 2019 Judgments Convention promotes cross-border enforcement but excludes arbitration, while UNCITRAL's ongoing reforms aim to address digital disputes without resolving substantive divergences (UNCITRAL, 2022). Regional frameworks like the EU's Recast Brussels Regulation (1215/2012) streamline jurisdictional rules but leave arbitrability to member states. Parties in the absence of international legislation must use creative arbitration methods combining expert decision and mediation protocols (Rose & Shehadeh, 2021) to traverse arbitration rules.

The diverse nature of arbitrability demonstrates fundamental conflicts between contracting parties' freedom of choice against state powers. The expansion of commercial arbitration in worldwide markets does not extend to contentious areas that affect public welfare considerations or involve third-party rights or supervisory oversight. Harmonization requires a controlled balance between procedural freedoms and diverse judicial areas to make arbitration function as an effective modern alternative to traditional litigation but also protect the core principles of legal systems.

2.4 Arbitrability of Smart Contract Disputes: A Prelude

Smart contracts, as self-executing agreements encoded on blockchain platforms, inherently challenge traditional arbitrability frameworks. While they resemble conventional contracts in facilitating commercial transactions, their automated execution and decentralized architecture raise unique questions about consent, jurisdictional anchoring, and compliance with sector-specific regulations (Kaal & Calcaterra, 2020). For instance, a smart contract automating cryptocurrency trades may be arbitrable in Singapore under the Arbitration Act (2001) but void in China due to its crypto ban (Shenzhen Intermediate People's Court, 2023).

The arbitrability of smart contract disputes hinges on whether they fit within existing legal definitions of "commercial" relationships and comply with national public policy. Jurisdictions like the U.K., through its Digital Dispute Resolution Rules (2021), have begun adapting arbitration procedures to blockchain contexts, enabling on-chain enforcement of awards. However, without global consensus on issues like cryptocurrency regulation or decentralized autonomous organizations (DAOs), the arbitrability of such disputes remains fragmented (Rose & Shehadeh, 2021).

3 – CHALLENGES TO ARBITRABILITY OF SMART CONTRACT DISPUTES

Smart contracts have emerged as a transformative technology in digital transactions, introducing automated, self-executing agreements that operate without traditional intermediaries. However, these innovative instruments present unique challenges for arbitration systems designed for conventional contracts. This chapter examines the specific challenges to the arbitrability of smart contract disputes, focusing on the legal hurdles that determine whether such disputes can be legitimately submitted to arbitration and successfully resolved through this mechanism.

3.1 Examining Subjective Arbitrability and the Challenge of Consent in Smart Contract Arbitration

One of the fundamental challenges in determining the arbitrability of smart contract disputes is the issue of consent. Arbitration fundamentally rests on party autonomy, which requires both parties to mutually agree to arbitrate disputes (Lew et al., 2013, p. 187). However, in the context of smart contracts, which are self-executing agreements deployed on blockchain networks, the traditional understanding of contractual consent becomes problematic (Chevalier, 2021). The nature of automated transactions, decentralized execution, and pseudonymous participation creates significant uncertainty about whether parties have truly consented to arbitration in a legally recognizable manner (Chatterjee, 2022). This issue is particularly critical when disputes arise from automated transactions executed without explicit human approval at each stage (Casey & Niblett, 2017).

Traditional arbitration agreements are typically signed explicitly, either in writing or electronically, with clear terms outlining the agreement to arbitrate (Born, 2021). In contrast, smart contracts often operate in a decentralized, automated manner, where users may interact with contract terms without actively reviewing or negotiating them (Savelyev, 2018). If a smart contract includes a pre-coded arbitration clause, the question arises: does executing or interacting with the smart contract imply valid consent to arbitration? Many jurisdictions prohibit arbitration in disputes where consent was not meaningfully obtained (Born, 2021). This aligns with Article V(2)(b) of the New York Convention, which allows refusal of arbitration based on public policy if an agreement lacks proper consent (New York Convention, 1958). Similarly, national arbitration laws, such as the UK Arbitration Act (1996) (s.5), the Indian Arbitration and Conciliation Act (1996) (s.7), and the U.S. Federal Arbitration Act (FAA) (9 U.S.C. § 2), require arbitration agreements to be explicit and voluntary. If a party did not explicitly agree to arbitration, courts in these jurisdictions may rule that no valid arbitration agreement exists, rendering the dispute non-arbitrable (UK Arbitration Act, 1996; The Indian Arbitration and Conciliation Act, 1996; U.S. Federal Arbitration Act, 1925).

Legal scholars have drawn parallels between smart contract arbitration clauses and clickwrap or browsewrap agreements to understand how consent operates in digital contexts (Kaal & Calcaterra, 2020). The courts show a willingness to accept Clickwrap agreements when users execute "I agree" button clicks as valid consent under Specht v. Netscape (2002). Netscape, 2002). Altar ground agreements including browsewrap encounter legal problems because users do not explicitly accept terms (Nguyen v. Barnes & Noble 2014). Barnes & Noble, 2014). The automatic adoption process in smart contracts deployed for decentralized finance (DeFi) and automated token transfers matches the features of browsewrap contracts because users lack an option to manually agree to arbitration terms (Kaal & Calcaterra, 2020). Judicial bodies might doubt whether the absence of active agreement creates sufficient voluntary consent to empower arbitration of resultant disputes from such agreements.

Consumer protection laws create more complexity for the consent requirements that need consideration in smart contract arbitrability disputes. Consumer protection legislation throughout various jurisdictions prohibits forcing consumers into arbitration agreements unless consent is voluntary and they receive proper information about them. Consumer unions within the European Union (European Union, 1993) through 93/13/EEC along with India (Consumer Protection Act, 2019) ban unfair arbitration clause imposition on consumers. A smart contract arbitration clause in consumer agreements might fail to obtain court approval due to evidence showing a lack of consumer agreement thus leading to non-arbitrability of the dispute (Chatterjee, 2022). Under EU consumer protection laws, consumer's informed consent stands as a key requirement so it would be likely that automated arbitration clauses within smart contracts for consumers will face legal challenges (Netscape, 2002). Courts may find that users were not adequately informed of arbitration terms, especially if those terms were buried in smart contract code or linked to an inaccessible external document.

3.2 Challenges to the Objective Arbitrability of Smart Contract Disputes and the Limits Imposed by Public Policy

Public policy restrictions often render smart contract disputes non-arbitrable when the underlying subject matter violates national laws or regulatory frameworks. For instance, China has imposed an outright ban on cryptocurrencies, making contracts based on such assets unenforceable. In contrast, India has not banned cryptocurrencies per se, but the proposed Cryptocurrency and Regulation of Official Digital Currency Bill, 2021 signals a preference for banning private cryptocurrencies while supporting a Central Bank Digital Currency (CBDC). This legislative ambiguity creates uncertainty regarding the legal status of crypto-based smart contracts in India (Mukherjee, 2022). Under Section 23 of the Indian Contract Act (1872), contracts involving unlawful consideration potentially including private cryptocurrencies if later prohibited are deemed void ab initio. Consequently, arbitral tribunals may lack jurisdiction over disputes arising from such agreements, as they could be considered contrary to public policy (Siron & Paesano, 2022). Similarly, China's Shenzhen Intermediate People's Court invalidated an arbitral award involving cryptocurrency transactions, citing the contravention of public policy due to the digital assets involved (Li, 2023).

The legality of the underlying asset or transaction represented by a smart contract directly impacts its arbitrability. As smart contracts increasingly automate transactions involving digital assets, securities, financial instruments, and other regulated assets, they encounter a complex web of national regulations that may restrict arbitrability on public policy grounds. The federal authority enforcing securities ensures that "investment contracts" qualification through the SEC v. W.J. Howey Co. (1946) test. The satisfaction of the Howey Test in smart contracts makes them subject to mandatory court intervention from securities regulators which can bar arbitration of disputes (De Filippi & Wright, 2018). The mandatory financial sector regulatory oversight makes it difficult for arbitration clauses to provide dispute resolution for smart contract controversies.

Besides cryptocurrency regulations, the public policy restrictions also address wider smart contract regulatory requirements. The failure of DeFi platforms to comply with anti-money laundering rules in their sector-specific regulations leads to non-arbitrability because they violate regulatory frameworks (JAMS, 2023; De En Goh, 2022). Decisions stemming from non-compliant smart contracts can lose their arbitrability based on public policy grounds under EU member state legislation according to the Markets in Crypto-Assets (MiCA) regulation of the European Union. The architectural design of blockchain which lacks borders enhances conflicts between parties' abilities to determine contract terms and government-established public policy standards which leads to substantial difficulties when arbitrators need to settle disputes from smart contracts (De En Goh, 2022; European Union, 2023).

The regulatory shifts in cryptocurrency alongside blockchain create an unknown situation about the future arbitrability of smart contract disputes. Future regulations might change the status of arbitrable disputes which are acceptable at present times. Regulatory ambiguity prevents parties from using arbitration to settle their smart contract disputes because new regulations can make their arbitration agreements invalid. The broad assumption that smart contract disputes automatically receive the arbitrability characteristics of traditional contracts faces growing resistance according to Kreutzer (2021). Long-term smart contracts face substantial challenges because regulatory changes during their period could establish new public policy issues that might prevent the arbitration of disputes from obtaining jurisdiction.

The lack of worldwide agreement on blockchain governance rules makes the public policy obstacle to enforcing smart contract arbitration even more difficult to overcome. Some jurisdictions embrace blockchain and smart contracts but numerous territories maintain controlled limitations or total constraints against these technologies (GFMA & GDF, 2024). The divergent regulatory systems lead to substantial difficulties when determining the arbitrability of transnational smart contract disputes because different jurisdictions may have opposing views on what constitutes arbitral jurisdiction. According to the search results "these differing legal interpretations demonstrate the necessity of global consensus for proper smart contract regulation" (De En Goh, 2022). Public policy restrictions pose ongoing barriers to smart contract dispute arbitrability particularly when the disputes cross international borders unless harmonization standards are established.

3.3 Sector-Specific Arbitrability Limitations

The particular nature of various sectors creates obstacles to arbitrability because these industries have specific regulatory requirements that constrain or ban arbitration.

Industry restrictions on smart contracts make disputes excluded from arbitration no matter what parties agree or contract validity exists thus creating legal confusion for blockchain-based payments in regulated markets. Such understanding helps professionals determine the arbitrability of smart contract disputes within different industrial sectors (Law Commission, 2021; De En Goh, 2022).

The gambling and prediction market industry imposes highly restrictive limitations on arbitrability specifically for smart contract disputes. Blockchain-based prediction markets that operate without authorization in the United Kingdom fall void under gambling laws and thus render their disputes non-arbitrable according to the Gambling Act of 2005 and the Law Commission (2021) and Chechetkin v. Payward Ltd. (2022). Payward Ltd., 2022). The automatic payout functionality of these platforms dependent on specified events in their smart contracts is restricted from submission to arbitration when the underlying gambling activities violate regulatory measures. Other jurisdictions worldwide share similar legislation which creates major obstacles for arbitration of disputes arising from gambling-related smart contracts. Decentralized prediction markets encounter substantial issues when they need to function between jurisdictions that have different regulations regarding gambling activities.

Healthcare proves to be a domain that creates substantial barriers to the arbitrability of smart contracts. Smart contracts used for managing medical data exchange and healthcare payments conflict with data privacy rules such as the EU General Data Protection Regulation (GDPR) and the U.S. Health Insurance Portability and Accountability Act (HIPAA) as per Silva et al. (2024), HIPAA (1996) and GDPR (2016). Disputes concerning smart contracts that might violate statutory privacy rights cannot be arbitrated because arbitrators lack the power to decide such violations that violate public policy (Li, 2023). The ability to use blockchain technology for medical record management and pharmaceutical supply chains becomes limited due to the restriction of smart contracts through arbitration.

Singapore approves arbitration in general but smart contracts affecting public infrastructure or essential services face exclusions from arbitration due to national interest requirements (Li, 2023). The public importance of critical infrastructures and public utilities and energy distribution systems that smart contracts automate can make disputes arising from these contracts non-arbitrable according to De En Goh (2022) and Terraform v. 3750 Investors (2023). The prohibition on certain business sectors creates an essential conflict between smart contracts' operational effectiveness and judicial intervention needs in critical areas that generate major hurdles for arbitration dispute resolution in these markets.

Financial services demonstrate substantial restrictions for the arbitrability of smart contracts. The courts of certain jurisdictions together with specialized regulatory tribunals maintain exclusive jurisdiction over some financial disputes. The

Consumer Financial Protection Bureau [CFPB] (2017) as well as Chechetkin v. Payward Ltd. (2022) and Control of Exemption Clauses Ordinance (1990) maintain that laws protecting consumers from financial exploitation restrict arbitration when it comes to retail financial services including smart contracts handling consumer fiscal activities. Payward Ltd., 2022; Control of Exemption Clauses Ordinance, 1990). In India, the Supreme Court in Vidya Drolia v. The Supreme Court of India determined through Durga Trading Corporation (2021) that state functions that cannot be waived by the government are excluded from arbitration. Smart contract disputes in the financial sector that include retail customers or regulated financial sectors experience limitations to their arbitrability because of current restrictions.

The energy industry introduces distinctive arbitrability barriers that affect smart contracts. Utility sector regulations restrict blockchain technology applications with smart contracts for energy trading and grid management and renewable energy authentication according to Beebeejaun and Faccia (2024). Certain jurisdictions limit the arbitrability of smart contract disputes that concern regulated energy markets or utility services because exclusive jurisdiction sits with energy regulatory authorities (Kokaia, 2025; Khan, 2023). The sector-specific regulations create substantial obstacles for blockchain technology expansion in energy markets which reduces the accessibility of arbitration as a conflict resolution mechanism in this sector.

3.4 Regulatory Responses to Smart Contract Arbitrability: Fragmentation and Harmonization Efforts

Smart contracts encounter substantial difficulties during arbitration procedures because the regulatory environment for their arbitrability exists as separate legal frameworks across different jurisdictions. The current regulatory environment leads to contrasting approaches between different authorities who oversee blockchain frameworks and smart contracts as well as arbitration legal structures that directly influence arbitrability decisions. Parties entering into smart contract agreements remain uncertain about their ability to arbitrate disputes when relevant laws do not harmonize on arbitrability terms thus diminishing arbitration as a dispute resolution method for blockchain basis transactions.

Most jurisdictions have not established specific guidelines regarding the arbitrability of smart contracts after they made legal definitions regarding these digital agreements. Smart contracts receive enforcement status in United Kingdom law by the UK Law Commission under current principles of contract law. The UK Law Commission Report from 2021 declared smart contracts fulfill all necessary components of contract formation before recommending minimal legislative changes for enforcement purposes (UK Law Commission Report, 2021). Smart contracts currently face an unclear regulatory environment when it comes to arbitration agreements because the arbitrability of resultant disputes remains uncertain (Law Commission, 2021; Brown, 2023). The unclear boundary between contract recognition and arbitration clarity directly hinders parties who want to settle smart contract disputes through arbitration.

Different states within the United States have implemented varying systems regarding regulations for smart contract arbitration and their associated enforceability. Arizona together with Tennessee has authorized legislation to confirm blockchain-based contracts as valid legal documents. State laws address contract enforcement while they include limited specifications about arbitrability alone (Arizona Revised Statutes, 2024; Tennessee Code Annotated, 2018). Smart contract arbitration continues to raise questions regarding its application of Federal Arbitration Act provisions (Federal Arbitration Act, 1925; Born, 2021) while this law maintains control over arbitration agreements. The diverse legal systems across states lead to substantial mystery about the arbitrability of smart contracts especially when parties from various states or nations engage in cross-border business.

European Union authorities focus on cryptocurrency regulation through the Markets in Crypto-assets Regulation (MiCA) yet they have not established legal procedures for handling smart contract disputes (EU Regulation, 2023). The existing regulatory vacuum produces doubt about how arbitration handles disputes stemming from smart contracts when EU parties are involved or if the contracts operate under EU territory. EU's leading position in world trade and blockchain implementation makes an absence of decisive smart contract dispute arbitration rules create international implications for global blockchain dispute resolution. Cross-border transactions mixing EU and non-EU parties encounter major challenges from uncertainty because they receive different arbitrability decisions based on jurisdictions to which their agreements are subject.

Regulatory efforts to harmonize standards are underway to handle the expanding regulatory sector (Bakhramova 2024). Global institutions such as UNCITRAL acknowledge the necessity to adjust arbitration systems for digital advancement yet they have not established systemic reforms for specific arbitrability of smart contracts. The UNCITRAL Model Law on International Commercial Arbitration (UNCITRAL, 2024) along with its widespread adoption fails to provide direct solutions for blockchain and smart contract arbitrability issues. The absence of specific provisions about smart contract arbitrability in international soft law makes it difficult to reach consistent determinations in arbitrability across different jurisdictions. This issue specifically affects international disputes involving smart contracts under multiple legal frameworks.

The lack of regulatory harmonization has direct implications for the arbitrability of smart contract disputes. As highlighted in the search results, "these developments indicate a growing recognition of smart contracts within legal systems, but significant gaps remain in addressing arbitrability and enforcement within international arbitration frameworks" (Ante, 2020). These gaps create uncertainty for parties seeking to arbitrate smart contract disputes, as the arbitrability of their disputes may vary significantly depending on which jurisdiction's laws apply. This uncertainty undermines the effectiveness of arbitration as a dispute resolution mechanism for smart contracts, potentially driving parties toward less efficient or less predictable alternatives.

4 - RECOMMENDATIONS FOR ADDRESSING ARBITRABILITY CHALLENGES IN SMART CONTRACT DISPUTES: A GLOBAL PERSPECTIVE

The worldwide resolution to the arbitrability problems coming from smart contracts must include both boundary-breaking international cooperation and respect for geographical jurisdiction authorities. Both subjective and objective arbitrability questions related to consent, formalities, and identities, and public policy and sectoral standards need a comprehensive approach for resolution. In order to support blockchain-based arbitration the strategy needs to unify legal standards and implement technological tools while promoting institutions that adjust to decentralized blockchain operations.

4.1 Global Legislative Harmonization of Consent and Formality Standards

A critical priority exists to update the New York Convention's formal validity standards because they need to recognize blockchain-based arbitration agreements. While Article II(1) mandates arbitration agreements to be "in writing," its interpretation must evolve to recognize code as a valid form of written consent as the rigid adherence to traditional notions of "writing" risks rendering blockchain arbitration clauses unenforceable and undermines arbitration's role in digital transactions. Recognizing code as "writing" is critical to preserving party autonomy in decentralized finance (DeFi) and cross-border transactions. Hybrid "Ricardian Contracts," which pair natural language terms with code, demonstrate how legal intent can align with technical execution (Grigg, 2004). However, discrepancies between coded and text-based clauses risk invalidation under strict formalist regimes, as seen in Nguyen v. Barnes & Noble (2014).

The UNCITRAL Working Group III's ongoing reforms to the Model Law on International Commercial Arbitration should explicitly validate smart contract arbitration clauses, drawing inspiration from jurisdictions like Switzerland, India, and Singapore that recognize electronic agreements under broad definitions of "writing" (Born, 2021; UNCITRAL, 2022; Arbitration and Conciliation Act, 1996). For example, Article 12 of Switzerland's Code of Obligations and Section 7 of Singapore's Electronic Transactions Act provide useful frameworks for aligning code-based contracts with traditional legal formalities. Similarly, India's 2015 amendment to Section 7 of the Arbitration and Conciliation Act (1996), which recognizes electronic communications as valid arbitration agreements, can serve as a legislative model (Kasatkina, 2023). However, for such recognition to be effective, it must be accompanied by interpretive guidelines that define "electronic means" to explicitly include blockchain-based interactions ensuring that passive consent via smart contract execution meets voluntariness requirements under both the Federal Arbitration Act and EU Directive 93/13/EEC (Born, 2021; Chatterjee, 2022).

To address consent ambiguities, the Hague Conference on Private International Law could develop a protocol requiring smart contracts to incorporate "active assent" mechanisms, such as cryptographic signatures or multi-factor authentication, ensuring compliance with the EU's Directive on Unfair Terms in Consumer Contracts (93/13/EEC) and analogous frameworks in Asia and North America (Kaal & Calcaterra, 2020). These mechanisms would mitigate browsewrap-style consent issues prevalent in DeFi platforms, where users passively agree to terms through transaction execution (Nguyen v. Barnes & Noble Inc., 2014).

4.2 Harmonizing Public Policy Standards Through Supplementary Protocols

Supplementary protocols should be used to create unified standards for public policy exceptions since their current fragmented enforcement diminishes the arbitrability of cross-border smart contract disputes under the New York Convention. The Convention should have a supplementary protocol that enables the distinction between domestic public policy exceptions from international public policy standards to limit enforcement refusals regarding universally recognized principles including fraud, money laundering, and terrorism financing (Komarov, 2021). A clear separation between domestic rules and fundamental legal principles is essential because national crypto bans that which China currently enforces (Shenzhen Intermediate People's Court, 2023) hold different priorities than international standards leading to enforcement clashes with countries like Singapore and Japan where such transactions remain legal (Li, 2023). The EU's Markets in Crypto-Assets Regulation (MiCA) serves as an exemplar for this protocol to create minimum standards for crypto-asset service providers while permitting arbitration to handle disputes deriving from compliant contracts (EU Regulation, 2023).

Enforcement courts must dismiss public policy objections only when these objections coincide with international ordre public definitions found in instruments such as the UN Convention Against Corruption (2003) or the Financial Action Task Force's (FATF) guidelines (UNCITRAL, 2022) under the proposed protocol. The supplementary protocol requires Indian courts to execute arbitral awards from crypto-related smart contracts under the Indian Contract Act §23 (1872) unless the transaction broke global anti-money laundering policies (Mukherjee, 2022). This approach aligns with the Hague Judgments Convention's (2019) emphasis on distinguishing between parochial policies and fundamental legal principles, ensuring that arbitration remains a viable mechanism for cross-border disputes (Hague Conference, 2019).

To address regulatory flux, the protocol could incorporate a "dynamic incorporation" mechanism, enabling arbitrators to apply the regulatory framework in force at the time of dispute resolution rather than contract formation (Schwarz, 2023). This would stabilize long-term smart contracts, such as decentralized finance (DeFi) agreements, which face uncertainty due to evolving national regulations. For example, a smart contract automating cross-border energy trades under the EU's REMIT regulation would remain arbitrable even if subsequent amendments to energy laws in one jurisdiction rendered it non-compliant locally (Beebeejaun & Faccia, 2024). By prioritizing harmonized standards over fragmented domestic policies, this protocol would reconcile the decentralized nature of blockchain with the need for legal certainty, fostering trust in digital transactions while respecting state sovereignty (De Filippi & Wright, 2018).

4.3 Institutionalizing a Global Arbitrability Clearinghouse for Sector-Specific Disputes

The sector-specific arbitrability challenges posed by smart contracts demand a centralized mechanism to harmonize fragmented regulatory standards and ensure consistent enforcement across jurisdictions (De En Goh, 2022). A Worldwide Arbitration Platform operated by the World Bank International Centre for Settlement of Investment Disputes would address blockchain dispute complexities through systematic classifications of cases based on industry-type legal framework and case ruling standards. Smart contracts operating in finance healthcare and energy sectors require compliance with unique national laws to allow arbitrability between parties. A decentralized finance (DeFi) platform operating across borders falls under the Payment Services Act (2019) as implemented in Singapore not MiCA regulations of the EU making any related arbitration matters ineligible for resolution in the EU

(EU Regulation, 2023; Monetary Authority of Singapore, 2019). A decentralized repository makes it difficult for arbitrators to handle the diverse legal interpretations which results in unpredictable arbitration outcomes that weaken arbitration effectiveness.

The institutional framework structure of ICSID makes it the best choice to administer this clearinghouse operation. ICSID demonstrates decades of experience in resolving international investment disputes through its procedural expertise and neutrality in addressing state sovereignty against investor rights which would prove essential for smart contract disputes with public policy implications (Schreuer, 2001). Using ICSID infrastructure the clearinghouse should build a dynamic database platform to monitor unacceptable situations such as healthcare GDPR violations and unlicensed gambling systems while integrating real-time regulatory checks through API systems. The smart contract enforcement system under the EU's REMIT regulation performs an automated arbitrability review to verify sector compliance before starting arbitration according to Beebeejaun & Faccia (2024). Such a system decreases enforcement uncertainties in lengthy smart contracts since it adapts to changing regulatory landscapes after network launches.

The clearinghouse enables intersystem dialogues by following the OECD's blockchain policy framework to create unified standards for sensitive sectors as per OECD (2023). ICSID could work alongside the ICC along with SIAC to produce standard smart contract clauses that handle pseudonymity and distributed enforcement issues which were present in Kleros v. Anonymous (2023). Anonymous (2023). The Digital Dispute Resolution Rules (2021) of the UK Jurisdictional Taskforce allow modifications on the blockchain while they need widespread adoption to demonstrate systemic effect (UKJT, 2021). The legitimacy and wide reach of ICSID would establish the clearinghouse as a reliable authority that would prevent parties from using regulatory loopholes to manipulate arbitrability outcomes.

4.4 Strengthening the New York Convention's Adaptability

Article II(1) dictates that arbitration agreements must exist in written documentation yet this provision remains incompatible with blockchain technology because its operation depends on code-based mechanisms. Traditional written signatures and explicit consent mechanisms fail to exist in many smart contracts as they use self-executing protocols on decentralized ledgers which generate enforcement gaps because of the Convention's strict formalities (UNCITRAL, 2022). Solidity-based arbitration provisions that run on the Ethereum network might fail to comply with Article II(2)'s "exchange of letters or telegrams" standard because jurisdictions with strict interpretations could find them invalid (Born, 2021). Florida State University requires legislative intervention to bridge the gap between international electronic arbitration laws and blockchain technology advancements since their misalignment produces legal vulnerabilities that compromise arbitration systems handling blockchain transactions.

An annexure to the UNCITRAL Guide on the New York Convention should address code specifically to show it fulfills the requirements of "writing" under its regulations. Jurisdictions like India and Singapore have already modernized their arbitration laws to validate electronic agreements under broad definitions of "writing" (Arbitration and Conciliation Act, 1996, §7; Electronic Transactions Act, Cap. 88), but global inconsistencies persist. The annexure could codify hybrid "Ricardian Contracts" which pair natural language terms with code as compliant with Article II(1), provided they incorporate cryptographic validation (Grigg, 2004). For example, Mattereum's blockchain framework uses cryptographic hashes to align smart contract execution with the U.K. Arbitration Act (1996), demonstrating how technical safeguards can meet legal formalities (Gupta, 2017). This approach would mitigate enforcement risks in cases like Nguyen v. Barnes & Noble (2014), where passive "browsewrap" consent was invalidated, by requiring active cryptographic signatures or multi-factor authentication for coded clauses (Kaal & Calcaterra, 2020).

The annexure should further clarify that cryptographic signatures satisfy the Convention's signature requirement, aligning with the EU's eIDAS Regulation (910/2014) and the U.S. E-SIGN Act (2000), which recognize electronic signatures as legally equivalent to handwritten ones. For instance, Arizona's blockchain-friendly statutes explicitly validate smart contracts under the Uniform Electronic Transactions Act (A.R.S. §44-7061, 2021), ensuring enforceability despite the absence of physical documentation. The proposed annexure would resolve inconsistent standards to protect existing arbitral clauses from nullification when regulating entities modify rules after awards have been issued. This situation aligns with India's planned Cryptocurrency Bill (2021) which threatens to make current arbitration awards void (Mukherjee, 2022).

The annexure requires amendments to establish sequential jurisdictional rules that define arbitration locations in decentralized environments. The requirement of traditional seats presents an obstacle against blockchain's ability to function without borders due to its network stations located across multiple nations. The Hague Judgments Convention (2019) offers a template by prioritizing mutual recognition over territoriality, enabling enforcement of awards rendered through decentralized platforms like Kleros (Agarwal, 2024). For example, the U.K.'s Digital Dispute Resolution Rules (2021) permit tribunals to issue on-chain orders, bypassing national courts for enforcement (Rose & Shehadeh, 2021). By endorsing such mechanisms, the annexure would align the Convention with procedural innovations while preserving its pro-enforcement ethos.

These reforms complement earlier recommendations: legislative harmonization ensures code-based agreements meet formal validity, while the global clearinghouse (Recommendation 3) provides sector-specific guidance on compliance. Concurrently, arbitration institutions like the ICC and SIAC must integrate blockchain-specific procedures, such as appointing arbitrators with dual expertise in law and technology, to operationalize these standards (JAMS, 2024). Without such adaptations, the Convention risks obsolescence, ceding ground to fragmented national regimes that hinder cross-border enforcement.

CONCLUSION

The integration of smart contracts into the global commercial landscape represents a transformative shift in how agreements are formed, executed, and enforced. Yet, this transformation also exposes critical frictions within the existing framework of international arbitration, particularly concerning the arbitrability of disputes arising from decentralized, pseudonymous, and self-executing contracts. The challenges of arbitrability are twofold: subjective arbitrability is hindered by uncertainties around consent, identity, and formality, while objective arbitrability is constrained by inconsistent public policy exceptions and regulatory fragmentation across jurisdictions. The leading legal systems demonstrate major differences regarding the recognition and enforcement of smart contract-related arbitration agreements. Uncoordinated reform efforts will jeopardize the predictability that arbitration is supposed to offer due to inconsistent approaches across different jurisdictions. Technical compatibility alongside world-level uniformity must be established to continue utilizing arbitration as the standard procedure for handling international business conflicts.

A global coordinated effort must establish modernized foundational legal instruments to properly align them with progressive technological developments. The modernization of consent and formality requirements demands a revision of New York Convention definitions regarding valid arbitration agreements. Code-based contracts and blockchain operations must earn status as "in writing" documentation through specific active digital signatures which serve to address ambiguity problems and verify voluntary consent. Multiple legislative improvements organized by Switzerland, India, and Singapore give evidence of effective methods to implement recognition initiatives. Public policy exceptions applied to blockchain-based disputes remain inconsistent which demands the creation of an additional New York Convention protocol. The proposed protocol needs to make a clear separation of national laws from international effects by denying enforcement refusal only for universally accepted legal violations but not for local bans on cryptocurrencies. The infrastructure of a global arbitrability clearinghouse established by ICSID would work towards resolving issues of fragmentation within sectors with strict regulations. The proposed clearinghouse system enables real-time assistance with sector-specific arbitrability limitations by utilizing common databases through interoperable tools to reach regulatory alignment between multiple jurisdictions.

The revisions of UNCITRAL's interpretive guidelines and those produced by related bodies about smart contract technology should replace the arduous process of formal New York Convention amendments. Coded agreements together with consensus validation techniques lead to valid parties' consent provided that such agreements have proper authentication methods. The public policy exception needs to be interpreted purposefully by courts for denying enforcement to apply solely when the transaction violates international ordre public and not local regulatory standards. The arbitrability of smart contracts serves as a bellwether for how effectively international arbitration can adapt to the demands of technological change. By embracing targeted legal reforms, promoting international cooperation, and integrating digital infrastructure into dispute resolution processes, the global arbitration regime can remain both relevant and resilient in the face of an increasingly decentralized commercial world.

REFERENCES

Agarwal, M. (2024, March 18). From social contracts to smart contracts: Navigating decentralization, blockchain, and Kleros arbitration. The Contemporary Law Forum. https://tclf.in/2024/03/18/from-social-contracts-to-smart-contracts-navigating-decentralization-blockchain-and-kleros-arbitration

Ante, L. (2020). Smart contracts on the blockchain – A bibliometric analysis and review. *SSRN*. Advance online publication. DOI: 10.2139/ssrn.3576393

Aristotle. (1932). The rhetoric of Aristotle (Bk I, p. 77), as cited in Malhotra, O. P., & Malhotra, I. (2003). Arbitration and conciliation (2nd ed., p. xxxvii).

Bakhramova, M. (2024). Harmonization of the legal framework for online arbitration. *International Journal of Law and Policy*, *2*(2), 1–15. https://irshadjournals.com/index.php/ijlp/article/download/154/137. DOI: 10.59022/ijlp.154

BasuMallick, C. (2023). What are smart contracts? Types, benefits, and tools. Spiceworks.

Beebeejaun, Z., & Faccia, A. (2024). Blockchain in energy markets: Regulatory challenges. *Journal of World Energy Law and Business*.

Beebeejaun, Z., & Faccia, A. (2024). Electronic alternative dispute resolution, smart contracts, and equity in the energy sector. *Journal of World Energy Law and Business*, *17*(1), 1–25. DOI: 10.1093/jwelb/jwac004

Booz Allen & Hamilton Inc. v. SBI Home Finance Ltd., (2011) 5 SCC 532.

Born, G. (2021). *International commercial arbitration* (3rd ed.). Kluwer Law International.

Brown, S. (2023). Arbitration of cryptoasset and smart contract disputes. Practical Law. https://www.cliffordchance.com/content/dam/cliffordchance/briefings/2023/08/arbitration-of-cryptoasset-and-smart-contract.pdf

Buterin, V. (2014). A next-generation smart contract and decentralized application platform. Ethereum White Paper.

Casey, A. J., & Niblett, A. (2017). Smart Contracts and Consumer Protection: The Missing Piece of the Puzzle. *Stanford Technology Law Review : STLR : An Online High-Technology Law Journal from Stanford Law School*, *20*(2), 126–145.

Chatterjee, S. (2022). Arbitrability and consumer protection. *Journal of International Dispute Resolution*, *13*(3), 45–67.

Chatterjee, S. (2022). Arbitrability of Smart Contracts in India: The Role of Public Policy. *Indian Journal of Arbitration Law*, *11*(2), 203–221.

Chechetkin v. Payward Ltd.[2022] EWHC 2370 (Comm).

Chevalier, M. (2021). From smart contract litigation to blockchain arbitration, a new decentralized approach leading towards the blockchain arbitral order. *Journal of International Dispute Settlement*, *12*(4), 558–584. DOI: 10.1093/jnlids/idab025

Consumer Financial Protection Bureau. (2017). Arbitration agreements rule. 12 C.F.R. § 1040. https://www.consumerfinance.gov/rules-policy/final-rules/arbitration-agreements-rule/

Consumer Protection Act (2019).

Control of Exemption Clauses Ordinance (Cap 71) §15 (1990).

Das, S. (2020). IBM & Mahindra to develop blockchain supply chain finance solutions in India. CCN.

De En Goh, G. R. (2022). Sectoral arbitrability and smart contracts: Regulatory barriers in decentralized ecosystems. *Digital Law Journal*, *3*(4), 71–105. DOI: 10.38044/2686-9136-2022-3-4-71-105

De En Goh, G. R. (2022). Smart contract disputes and public policy in the ASEAN+6 region. *Digital Law Journal*, *3*(4), 32–70. DOI: 10.38044/2686-9136-2022-3-4-32-70

De Filippi, P., & Wright, A. (2018). *Blockchain and the law: The rule of code*. Harvard University Press.

European Union. (1993). Council Directive 93/13/EEC of 5 April 1993 on unfair terms in consumer contracts. Official Journal of the European Communities, L95, 29–34. https://eur-lex.europa.eu/legal-content/EN/TXT/?uri=CELEX%3A31993L0013

European Union. (2023). Regulation (EU) 2023/1114 on Markets in Crypto-Assets (MiCA). Official Journal of the European Union, L 150, 1–59.

Federal Arbitration Act (1925).

Gambling Act. (2005). https://www.legislation.gov.uk/ukpga/2005/19/contents

Garrie, D. B., & Andle, G. A. (2024). *Arbitrating smart contract disputes: A comprehensive approach*. Daily Journal Corporation.

Garrie, D. B., & Andle, G. A. (2024, December 19). Arbitrating smart contract disputes: A comprehensive approach. Daily Journal Corporation. https://www.dailyjournal.com/article/382578-arbitrating-smart-contract-disputes-a-comprehensive-approach

General Data Protection Regulation (GDPR), 2016 O.J. (L 119) 1 (EU).

Global Financial Markets Association (GFMA) & Global Digital Finance (GDF). (2024). The smart contract primer. https://www.gfma.org/wp-content/uploads/2024/10/gfma-gdf-smart-contract-primer-report-2024.pdf

Grigg, I. (2004). The Ricardian contract. *IEEE Security and Privacy*.

Health Insurance Portability and Accountability Act (HIPAA) of 1996, Pub. L. No. 104-191, 110 Stat. 1936.

Howell, B. E., & Potgieter, P. H. (2021). Uncertainty and dispute resolution for blockchain and smart contract institutions. *Journal of Institutional Economics*, *17*(4), 545–559. DOI: 10.1017/S1744137421000138

Howell, J. (2023). Smart contracts vs. traditional contracts: Key differences. 101 Blockchains.

ICC (2023). Arbitration rules and blockchain disputes.

Indian Arbitration and Conciliation Act (1996).

JAMS. (2023). JAMS rules governing disputes arising out of smart contracts. https://www.jamsadr.com/rules-smart-contracts

JAMS. (2023). JAMS Smart Contract Clause and Rules (DRAFT). https://www.jamsadr.com/rules-smart-contracts

Jena, R., & Sahu, R. (2023). *Smart contracts with respect to Indian laws*. DJMR.

Kaal, W. A., & Calcaterra, C. (2020). Blockchain innovation and antitrust regulation. *Harvard Business Law Review Online*, *10*(1), 1–28.

Kasatinka, M. (2022). Dispute resolution mechanism for smart contracts. MUJLT, 16(2). https://cris.maastrichtuniversity.nl/files/152295161/18580-Article_Text-51891-1-10-20220930.pdf

Kasatkina, A. (2023). Blockchain arbitration in India. Indian Review of International Arbitration.

Kasatkina, M. (2022). *Dispute resolution mechanisms for smart contracts*. MUJLT. DOI: 10.5817/MUJLT2022-2-2

Khan, T. (2023). The growing need for arbitration in energy disputes. SCC Online Blog. https://www.scconline.com/blog/post/2023/01/14/the-growing-need-for-arbitration-in-energy-disputes/

Kokaia, L. (2025). Bridging technology and law: Regulating blockchain smart contracts for peer-to-peer renewable energy markets. Georgian Renewable Energy Development Association. https://bm.ge/en/news/bridging-technology-and-law-regulating-blockchain-smart-contracts-for-peer-to-peer-renewable-energy-markets-blog

Komarov, A. S. (2021). Jurisdictional challenges in blockchain-based arbitration: The case of smart contracts. *International Arbitration Review*, *24*(1), 101–127.

Komarov, A. S. (2021). *Jurisdictional challenges in blockchain-based arbitration*. International Arbitration Review.

Komarov, A. S. (2021). Jurisdictional challenges in labor arbitration. *International Arbitration Review*, *24*(1), 101–127.

Kreutzer, L. (2021). Arbitrability and smart contracts: A conceptual and legal analysis. *Journal of International Arbitration*, *38*(2), 145–170.

Kumar, M. G. (2023). *The impact of smart contracts and AI on the traditional contract law in India*. IJLMH.

Law Commission. (2021). Smart legal contracts: Advice to Government. https://lawcom.gov.uk/project/smart-contracts/

Lew, J. D. M., Mistelis, L. A., & Kröll, S. M. (2013). *Comparative International Commercial Arbitration*. Kluwer Law International.

LexisNexis. (n.d.). Arbitrability definition. https://www.lexisnexis.co.uk/legal/glossary/arbitrability

Li, J. (2023, December 1). Guiding Cases 199–201 issued by the PRC Supreme People's Court: Further steps toward a pro-arbitration regime. China Law Vision. https://www.chinalawvision.com/2023/12/uncategorized/guiding-cases-199-201-issued-by-the-prc-supreme-peoples-court-further-steps-toward-a-pro-arbitration-regime/

Malhotra, O. P., & Malhotra, I. (2003). *Arbitration and conciliation* (2nd ed.). LexisNexis Butterworths.

Mistelis, L. A., & Brekoulakis, S. L. (Eds.). (2009). *Arbitrability: International and comparative perspectives*. Kluwer Law International.

Mitsubishi Motors Corp. v. Soler Chrysler-Plymouth, 473 U.S. 614 (1985).

Mukherjee, S. (2022). India's crypto conundrum: Public policy, private currencies and CBDCs. *SSRN*. DOI: 10.2139/ssrn.4206714

Munoz, A., ... (2024, March 22). Commercial arbitration: France. Global Arbitration Review. https://globalarbitrationreview.com/insight/know-how/commercial-arbitration/report/france

Nakamoto, S. (2008). Bitcoin: A peer-to-peer electronic cash system. Bitcoin White Paper.

New York Convention (1958). Convention on the Recognition and Enforcement of Foreign Arbitral Awards.

Nguyen v. Barnes & Noble Inc., 763 F.3d 1171 (9th Cir. 2014).

OECD. (2023). OECD blockchain policy framework. OECD Publishing. https://www.oecd.org/en/topics/digital-finance.html

OECD. (2023). *OECD blockchain policy framework*. OECD Publishing.

Patel v. Mirza, [2016] UKSC 42.

Primavera de Filippi and Aaron Wright. (2018). *Blockchain and the Law: The Rule of Code*. HUP.

Rajasekarant, V. (2023, July 7). Decoding arbitrability and determining the boundaries of arbitration in Indian jurisprudence. SCC Times. https://www.scconline.com/blog/post/2023/07/07/decoding-arbitrability-and-determining-the-boundaries-of-arbitration-in-indian-jurisprudence

EU Regulation 2023/1114. (2023). Markets in Crypto-Assets Regulation.
EU Regulation 2023/1114. (2023). Markets in Crypto-Assets Regulation.

Regulation (EU) 2023/1114, (2023). https://eur-lex.europa.eu/eli/reg/2023/1114/oj/eng

Reuters. (2024). Uber 'clickwrap' contract gets blessing from NY's top court. But there's a twist. Retrieved from https://www.reuters.com/legal/government/column-uber-clickwrap-contract-gets-blessing-nys-top-court-theres

Reuters. (2025). Blockchain agreements: Avoiding ambiguity, manifesting assent. Retrieved from https://www.reuters.com/legal/transactional/blockchain-agreements-avoiding-ambiguity-manifesting-assent-2025-03-11/

Rose, J., & Shehadeh, P.-R. (2021, September 20). Evaluating the UK Jurisdiction Taskforce's "Digital Dispute Resolution Rules, 1.0". Daily Jus. https://dailyjus.com/world/2021/09/evaluating-the-uk-jurisdiction-taskforces-digital-dispute-resolution-rules-1-0

Rose, N., & Shehadeh, A. (2021). Hybrid arbitration models. *Arbitration International, 37*(4), 603–624.

Savelyev, A. (2018). Contract Law 2.0: Smart Contracts as the Beginning of the End of Classic Contract Law. *Information & Communications Technology Law, 26*(2), 116–134. DOI: 10.1080/13600834.2017.1301036

Saxena, V., & Swarna, H. (2024, April 17). The conundrum of enforceability of blockchain arbitration: Learnings from Kleros. Mapping ADR. https://jgu.edu.in/mappingADR/the-conundrum-of-enforceability-of-blockchain-arbitration-learnings-from-kleros/

Schreuer, C. (2001). The ICSID Convention: A Commentary. Cambridge University Press.

Schwarz, M. (2023). Legal enforceability of blockchain arbitration awards: A comparative analysis. *Harvard Journal of Law & Technology, 36*(2), 215–252.

Schwarz, M. (2023). Legal enforceability of blockchain arbitration awards. *Harvard Journal of Law & Technology, 36*(2), 215–252.

Shehata, I. (2018). *Smart contracts & international arbitration*. Kluwer Arbitration Blog. DOI: 10.2139/ssrn.3290026

Shreya Singhal v. Union of India (AIR 2015 SC 1523)

Silva, R.. (2024). Reflections about blockchain in health data sharing: Navigating medicolegal and regulatory challenges. *Journal of Medical Internet Research, 26*(2), e10887941. DOI: 10.1089/jmir.2024.10887941

Singapore International Arbitration Centre (SIAC) Year in Review. (2023). https://siac.org.sg/siac-year-in-review-2023

Siron, D., & Paesano, F. (2022). *Cryptocurrencies in Asia and beyond: Law, regulation and enforcement*. Basel Institute on Governance.

Specht v. Netscape Communications Corp., 306 F.3d 17 (2d Cir. 2002).

Statutes, A. R. § 44-7061 (2024). https://www.azleg.gov/ars/44/07061.html

Supreme Court of Canada. (2019). [2019] 3 S. *CR (East Lansing, Mich.)*, •••, 465.

Supreme Court of India. (2015). M/s. Trimex International FZE Ltd. v. Vedanta Aluminium Ltd., AIR 2015 SC 1523.

Szabo, N. (1996). Smart contracts: Building blocks for digital markets. Extropy Journal, 16.

Tennessee Code Annotated § 47-10-202 (2018). https://www.capitol.tn.gov/Bills/110/Bill/SB1662.pdf

Terraform Pte Ltd v. 3750 Investors [2023] SGHC 289.

UK Jurisdiction Taskforce. (2021). Digital Dispute Resolution Rules. https://mattereum.com/wp-content/uploads/docs/UKJT-Digital-Dispute-Resolution-Rules.pdf

UK Jurisdictional Taskforce. (2021). Digital Dispute Resolution Rules.

UK Law Commission (2021). Legal status of smart contracts and dispute resolution.

UK Law Commission Report (2021). https://lawcom.gov.uk/corporate-document/annual-report-20-21/

UNCITRAL. (2006). *Model Law on International Commercial Arbitration*. United Nations.

UNCITRAL. (2022). Guide to the New York Convention on the Recognition and Enforcement of Foreign Arbitral Awards. United Nations. https://www.uncitral.org/pdf/NYConvention_Guide.pdf

UNCITRAL. (2022). *UNCITRAL model law on international commercial arbitration with 2006 amendments*. United Nations Commission on International Trade Law.

UNCITRAL. (2024). UNCITRAL Model Law on Automated Contracting. https://unis.unvienna.org/unis/pressrels/2024/unisl362.html

UNCITRAL Model Law on International Commercial Arbitration (2006).

Verma, A. D. (2025, March 15). Legal challenges in Web 3.0: Navigating smart contracts, DAOs and blockchain disputes. SCC Online. https://www.scconline.com/blog/post/2025/03/15/legal-challenges-in-web-3-0-navigating-smart-contracts-daos-and-blockchain-disputes/

Vidya Drolia v. Durga Trading Corporation (2021) 2 SCC 1.; Vidya Drolia v. Durga Trading Corporation, (2020) SCC OnLine SC 1018.

Ware, S. J. (2020). Automated Arbitration and the Federal Arbitration Act. *Harvard Journal of Law & Technology*, *34*(1), 151–188.

Werbach, K. (2018). *The blockchain and the new architecture of trust*. MIT Press. DOI: 10.7551/mitpress/11449.001.0001

Winter-Barker, S. (2024, June 27). JAMS publishes artificial intelligence arbitration rules, but are they fit for purpose? Kluwer Arbitration Blog. https://arbitrationblog.kluwerarbitration.com/

Woebbeking, M. K. (2019). *The impact of smart contracts on traditional concepts of contract law*. JIPITEC.

Zachariadis, M., Hileman, G., & Scott, S. V. (2019). Governance and control in distributed ledgers: Understanding the challenges facing blockchain technology. *Information Systems Journal*, *29*(6), 563–580.

Zhang, L. (2022). Arbitrability of IP disputes in China. *Journal of Intellectual Property Law*, *29*(3), 45–67.

Zhang, L. (2022). Investor-state arbitration and sovereignty. *Journal of International Economic Law*, *25*(2), 215–240.

Chapter 12
Data Privacy Case Studies in the European Union

Tamara Phillips Fudge
https://orcid.org/0000-0002-8682-9711
Purdue University Global, USA

ABSTRACT

The General Data Protection Regulation (GDPR) protects the citizens of the European Union against illicit use of their personal data, and since data can traverse continents in mere seconds, implications for this law are worldwide. Today's collection, storage, transport, and other tasks related to data are accomplished by a wide variety of technological means. However, companies are not always following the many mandates of the GDPR. Specific cases involving various technologies offer an opportunity to understand and discuss further the ethical use of personal information as well as the ramifications of disobeying the law.

INTRODUCTION

On May 25, 2018, the European Union issued the General Data Protection Regulation (GDPR), a sweeping set of rules meant to ensure data about every EU individual is secure. In a general sense, this includes data collection, storage, and sharing, but there are more details worthy of exploration. Since data can be transferred electronically anywhere in the world, people and companies in countries outside the EU can be affected by the GDPR, and other governments may be interested in adopting similar guidelines. A brief review of the Regulation's main requirements through its list of principles, plus exploration into encryption and various roles provides a background for individual cases involving a variety of technologies. Each scenario helps to understand application of the technologies, the ethical concerns,

DOI: 10.4018/979-8-3373-3186-7.ch012

and situation results in relation to the GDPR, thereby providing fodder for discussion and critical thinking in the classroom and workplace.

LITERATURE REVIEW: EU AND GDPR

The European Union began in 1957 as the European Economic Community, and is now a partnership of 27 countries, encompassing 447 million people and at least two dozen different languages ("What is the European Union," n.d.). Current members are Austria, Belgium, Bulgaria, Croatia, Cyprus, Czech Republic, Denmark, Estonia, Finland, France, Germany, Greece, Hungary, Ireland, Italy, Latvia, Lithuania, Luxembourg, Malta, Netherlands, Poland, Portugal, Romania, Slovakia, Slovenia, Spain, and Sweden.

The GPDR came about in 2018. Among the main tenets are protecting data from theft, changes, deletion, or other compromises, the need to use encryption, and individual rights such as the right of access, driven by consent (Krasteva, 2024). The right for data to be forgotten, also called the right to erasure, is also required, whether or not the data can still be personally identifiable (Hutt et al., 2023). This is not a new concept; Warren and Brandeis (1890) wrote about the "right to be let alone" as called by a Judge Cooley in an 1879 tort. Intrusions listed in the article include photographs, newspaper articles, and "mechanical devices" plus the understanding that information can be tangible or intangible (Warren & Brandeis, 1890, p. 195). Herath et al. (2023) fittingly assert today's needs have evolved to include "the intersection of human rights, law, cybersecurity, data privacy, and geopolitics" (pp. 6-7).

Notably, the GDPR is all-encompassing, as it applies to all EU individuals' personal data, regardless of the kind of industry or the technology used to process it (Akhlaghpour et al., 2021). Penalties may be levied when rules are broken; organizations can be fined up to €20 million or forfeit up to 4% of annual sales depending on the offense (Krasteva, 2024). The Regulation itself is 88 pages long and was written in 2016 (Regulation 2016/679).

Principles

There are seven principles of the GDPR, which are outlined in Article 5 and provide answers to many of the questions the law may prompt. The wording is as follows:

1. Personal data shall be:
   (a) processed lawfully, fairly and in a transparent manner in relation to the data subject (**'lawfulness, fairness and transparency'**);

(b) collected for specified, explicit and legitimate purposes and not further processed in a manner that is incompatible with those purposes; further processing for archiving purposes in the public interest, scientific or historical research purposes or statistical purposes shall, in accordance with Article 89(1), not be considered to be incompatible with the initial purposes (**'purpose limitation'**);
(c) adequate, relevant and limited to what is necessary in relation to the purposes for which they are processed (**'data minimisation'**);
(d) accurate and, where necessary, kept up to date; every reasonable step must be taken to ensure that personal data that are inaccurate, having regard to the purposes for which they are processed, are erased or rectified without delay (**'accuracy'**);
(e) kept in a form which permits identification of data subjects for no longer than is necessary for the purposes for which the personal data are processed; personal data may be stored for longer periods insofar as the personal data will be processed solely for archiving purposes in the public interest, scientific or historical research purposes or statistical purposes in accordance with Article 89(1) subject to implementation of the appropriate technical and organisational measures required by this Regulation in order to safeguard the rights and freedoms of the data subject (**'storage limitation'**);
(f) processed in a manner that ensures appropriate security of the personal data, including protection against unauthorised or unlawful processing and against accidental loss, destruction or damage, using appropriate technical or organisational measures (**'integrity and confidentiality'**).

2. The controller shall be responsible for, and be able to demonstrate compliance with, paragraph 1 (**'accountability'**).

(Regulation 2016/679, pp. 35-36)

Bailey (2023) explains the lawfulness principle in laymen's terms by stating, "if you can achieve your objective without processing personal data, the basis is no longer lawful" (Lawfulness section). Purpose limitation and data minimization refer to understanding what is being collected and why, and limiting collection to that which is truly necessary. Every entity must ensure accuracy and only store data for the length of time it is used for the originally stated purpose. In terms of integrity and confidentiality, there must be safeguards in place to thwart hacking, accidental loss, and unwanted changes. Lastly, accountability is attained by designating a person or department to be held responsible for ensuring GDPR rules are followed (Bailey, 2023).

COMPLYING WITH THE GDPR

While each principle is important, Integrity and Confidentiality are key technical elements in keeping data safe, and Accountability provides necessary human elements worthy of explanation.

Encryption

In the United States, laws and regulations tend to "navigate a delicate balance between national security and individual rights" (Atadoga et al., 2024, p. 448). Atadoga et al. (2024) explain the GDPR keeps a stronger focus on the rights of the individual. Encryption is recommended, emphasizing confidentiality with end-to-end communication (Atadoga et al., 2024), which limits who is allowed to send and who is allowed to read the data. A technique called pseudonymization in which alternative descriptors are substituted for personally identifiable information is acceptable, but not as secure as encryption (Coos, 2021). Another technique is "data masking," in which data is "shuffled," scrambled, or a substitute is put into place; while this means the data is not readable by humans, it is still technically usable with the right processes applied, and a benefit is that reverse engineering does not work, thereby hampering any hacking efforts (Cobb, 2022). Even though pseudonymizing and masking may be tempting and work in some situations, encryption is still the strongest procedure and less expensive to implement (Coos, 2021).

Encryption is by necessity complicated. It takes plaintext, which is data anyone should be able to read, and changes it into a secret code called ciphertext that must be changed back into plaintext for the recipient to again be able to read it (Aumasson, 2025). Symmetric encryption, where the key to encrypt and decrypt are the same, is often found in messaging apps. Asymmetric encryption, also called public-key, uses one key to encrypt and a different one to decrypt. This might be used in email, website security, and digital signatures, and is considered stronger protection (Poggi, 2021). The technologist assigned to set up encryption must also understand the differences between common algorithms such as Data Encryption Standard (DES), Triple Data Encryption Standard (3DES), Rivest–Shamir–Adleman (RSA), Advanced Encryption Standard (AES), Elliptic Curve Cryptography (ECC), Diffie-Hellman, Blowfish, Twofish, and others (Poggi, 2021), and choose a model that is both practical and secure for the purposes of protecting data while it is being sent from one machine to another ("data in transit") as well as data being stored, which is called "at rest" (Aumasson, 2025).

The GDPR, which specifically mentions encryption only four times, does not specify which standards should be used, only that security measures must be taken

(Coos, 2021). Some organizations can be tapped to assist with administration of their standards as well as certifications and assistance with legal compliance, including:

- European Telecommunication Standards Institute (ETSI) – EU
- European Committee for Electrotechnical Standardization (CENELEC) – EU
- International Telecommunication Union (ITU) – United Nations
- International Organization for Standardization (ISO) – worldwide
- International Electrotechnical Commission (IEC) – worldwide
- Institute of Electrical and Electronics Engineers (IEEE) – worldwide
  (Atadoga, 2024)

Roles

Specific roles are defined within the GDPR to help ensure compliance and enforce the law; these are illustrated in Figure 1 below. The European Data Protection Board (EDPB) oversees conflicts and is comprised of the leaders of each country's authorities (Daigle & Khan, 2020). A Supervisory Authority (SA) is typically a national organization, although some countries such as Germany may divide responsibilities into regions; these are sometimes called Data Protection Authorities (DPAs), and their job is to oversee compliance, issues, and fines in their territory (Arfelt et al., 2019; Daigle & Khan, 2020). A Data Protection Officer (DPO) is to be appointed to ensure compliance; a cybersecurity expert may serve in this capacity (Li et al., 2019). Other roles include the Data Controller, which can be an individual, group of people, or other agency that identifies purpose and how data will be handled, and the Data Processor, again either an individual, group, or agency that will directly process the data per the instructions of the Controller (Akhlaghpour et al., 2021).

Figure 1. Important GDPR Roles

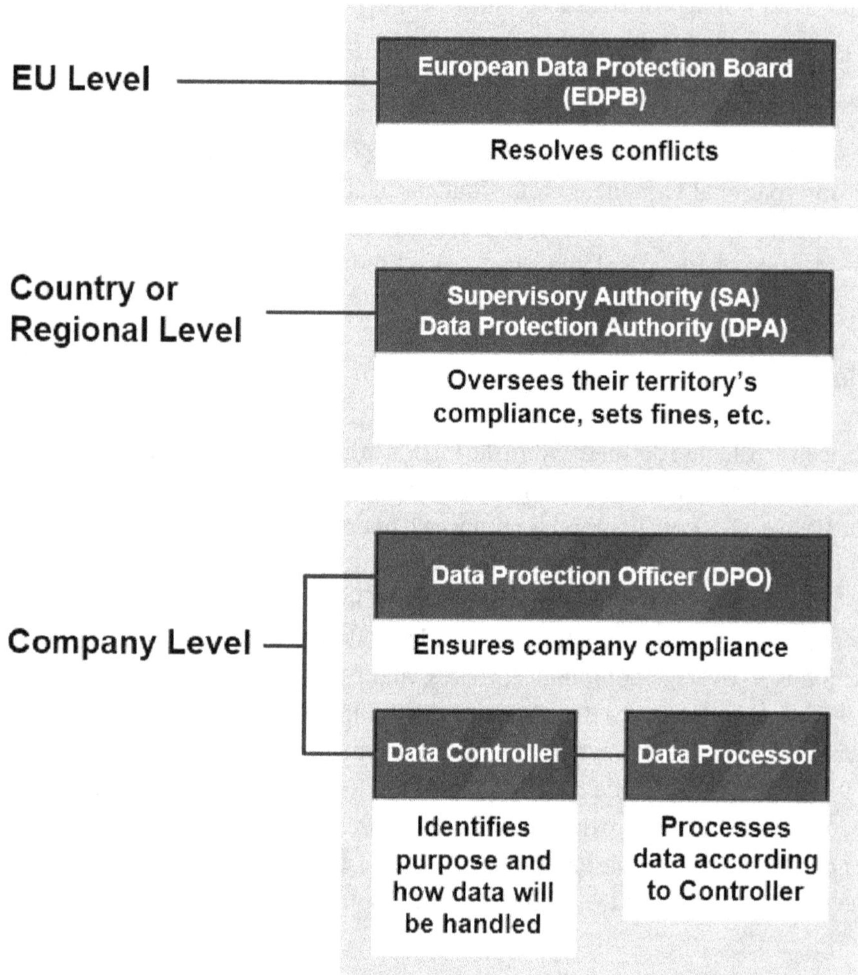

(Fudge, 2025)
based on Akhlaghpour et al., 2021; Arfelt et al., 2019; Daigle & Khan, 2020; and Li et al., 2019

Other Controls

Individual watchdog groups such as "NOYB" (short for "none of your business") also assist in ensuring the GDPR is followed. This Non-Governmental Organization (NGO) is based in Vienna, Austria and focuses on the ePrivacy Directive, limiting their work to commercial ventures rather than governments or other public authorities ("Our general principles," n.d.). They work to instigate or encourage litigation when appropriate, and in other cases, instead bring media attention to issues as a push for ethical outcomes ("About us," n.d.a.).

Another advocacy group is France's La Quadrature du Net (LQND). This organization was first created in 2008 in response to a controversial French law. LQND provides legal and political support regarding technology and data issues, keeps watch over legislative affairs that affect tech users, and works to educate the populace about security, surveillance, and censorship. Among their statements is "we work for a free, decentralised and empowering Internet" ("About us," n.d.b., para. 1).

Education

Training is offered by various vendors for companies to learn about GDPR requirements; this includes in-person training even in the United States, as any data gathered from EU residents or transferred to or from the EU must fulfill compliance ("General Data," 2021).

Each January 28 since 2006 is "Data Protection Day" as designated by the Council of Europe in honor of a treaty signed in 1981 calling for the protection of personal data (Council of Europe, n.d.). Activities in 2025 included special events for high school students, public seminars and lectures, certificates of appreciation, press conferences and other information campaigns via social media, radio, television, and other means (Convention 108, 2025). While this idea originated in Europe, other countries such as Canada, Uruguay, Mauritius, and Ukraine also participated (Convention 108, 2025).

DISCUSSION: CASE STUDIES

The GDPR can require the payment of fines from companies for violating 42 different Articles, although some Articles are invoked more often than others (Wolff & Atallah, 2021). In each of the following scenarios, the technologies have non-controversial applications, but can also be misused. Covered are GPS tracking, CCTV, drones, vehicle dashcams, online test proctoring, AI and language scraping, facial recognition, and DNA data scenarios, with some other incidents listed that may serve well for additional study.

GPS Tracking

Uses of the Technology

Location tracking using the Global Positioning System (GPS) uses a network of satellites, servers dedicated for location data, tracking devices, and wireless networks ("How does GPS," 2024), and location is identified by latitude, longitude, and height (Sathaye et al., 2022). GPS assists companies in keeping track of inventory and can calculate vehicle speed in real time ("How does GPS," 2024). Drones and autonomous cars make use of GPS, consumers are able to see where packages are in real-time by watching web applications that use GPS, and parents can rest well knowing where their children are thanks to its use in mobile devices. An example of an unusual application of this technology is with a utility company in Oklahoma, U.S.A., which created a GPS "panic button" for workers if they find themselves in an emergency and need to tell the company their exact location ("How does GPS," 2024). Recent research by Auerbach et al. (2025) suggest adolescents with suicidal tendencies may be more at risk if they stay at home for long periods, and GPS data from their smartphones might be able to help predict suicidal ideations. In addition, GPS has been suggested by Hammas et al. (2025) as a component to be added to solar energy technologies, with GPS calculating sun position and time to increase the production of energy by about 33%.

Scenario: October 2022, Slovenia

A Slovenian employer installed GPS tracking in eight company vehicles with the intent to protect documents and equipment stored there from theft when their workers were on a work site but not in their trucks ("Safety of property," 2022). These trucks had dual purpose: delivery and passenger transport. The data was processed in an ongoing manner, even when the employees were in their vehicles, and the data was monitored by an outside company ("Safety of property," 2022).

Ethical issues

The GPS remained active when workers were driving said vehicles, this data was captured and retained, and the employer incorrectly claimed the workers in the vehicles were not personally identifiable ("Safety of property," 2022). The ePrivacy Directive, espoused by the Republic of Slovenia, includes protection of traffic and location data, which when "processed and stored by the operator must be deleted or modified in such a way they cannot be linked to a specific or identifiable person once they are no longer needed to transmit messages" (Damjan, 2023). Damjan

(2023) further explains there are three privacy areas, which may be labeled as intimate/family, private, and public lives, and this situation thus encroaches upon the drivers' private lives.

Solution

The Slovenian Supervisory Authority investigated. Their decision acknowledged that keeping property safe is a legitimate use of the technology, but tracking when a worker was in the vehicle with valuable items was unnecessary. The Authority confirmed a violation of GDPR article 6.1 due to the lack of necessity and Article 5.1(c) which requires data minimization. As a result, the company was ordered to stop continuous tracking and record GPS data only on when the vehicles were not occupied by the workers ("Safety of property," 2022). It was suggested the workers be given the capability of turning GPS on when in the vehicle and turning it off when leaving ("Safety of property," 2022). Research did not indicate a fine was levied.

CCTV Monitoring

Uses of the Technology

Close Captioned Television (CCTV) is used in businesses and in smart cities to monitor activity. While this technology has been determined to work well during the daytime, its effectiveness in protecting city streets at night is enhanced with appropriate street lighting as well as other controls within the environment (Chen et al., 2025). Law enforcement may request recordings to help identify those who may be engaged in criminal activity. Company officials can use CCTV to verify work activity, identify or prevent misconduct, or confirm safety procedures are being followed (Sellers, 2018). The technology is not always simple video pictures; it may incorporate facial recognition, read license plates, and through audio sensors can identify sounds such as different kinds of gunshots (Thomas et al., 2022). Koca (2024) adds hand signals can be captured and identified. CCTV cameras have even been used to monitor cattle herds (Modi et al., 2024).

Scenario: March 2023, Spain

A Spanish employer used CCTV to monitor employees at work; this included both video and audio recording (Ayora, 2023). Employees knew there were cameras to capture their workplace visually, but discovered their conversations were being monitored as well only after the employer called to complain they heard news casts in the background instead of the regularly played music (Ayora, 2023).

Ethical issues

While the company had a contract with the CCTV managers that indicated audio would be captured by a microphone, they argued they were not recording, just listening (Ayora, 2023). Concerns may be voiced about interpretation of these recordings, which provide "identity, position, and behavioral patterns of individuals under surveillance" (Koca, 2024, p. 84549). In addition, this affected not just employees, but customers who entered the business (Ayora, 2023).

Solution

Sellers (2018) states the GDPR Article 35 refers to the profiling of employees using CCTV as potentially being excessive. Ayora (2023) adds that Spanish law allows for video cameras but written notification must be visible, and certain areas such as dressing rooms must not be surveilled. With these in consideration, the Agencia Española Protección Datos (AEPD) determined CCTV and monitoring by audio was acceptable, but recording audio lacked consent and necessity. They determined the combined collection of a person's physical image and voice in violation of GDPR article 6 and imposed a €5000 fine (Ayora, 2023). Importantly, it was also stated the mere act of capturing audio was in fact personal data processing, whether or not the audio was recorded. The court document ended aptly invoking GDPR Article 57 allowing the AEPD to make and enforce these decisions and Article 31 which requires cooperation by the company (Ayora, 2023).

Drones

Uses of the Technology

Drones have many uses, including disaster response, wildfire management, search and rescue operations, geospatial mapping, filming or monitoring public events, wildlife tracking, and surveying crime scenes (Hovsha & Brien, 2022; Szira et al., 2023). Drones can incorporate cameras for videography and sensors to determine wind strength and direction, measure heat and humidity; those with microphones can also transmit and record audio. There may be other technologies included as well, such as LiDAR (Light Detection And Ranging) and/or GPS (Hovsha & Brien, 2022). Drone use in the EU is governed by the European Union Aviation Safety Agency (EASA), which clearly shows connections to GDPR's Article 40 and includes a code of conduct to minimize the effect on personal privacy, operate with transparency, and deal with data per the law (European Union Aviation, n.d.), thereby meeting the demands of the principles set forth in Article 6.

The European Union Aviation Safety Agency (2024) published a 468-page rule guide explaining drone regulations set by the EU. The document identifies the need for data protection in accordance with the GDPR, and includes instructions for impact assessment, computer traffic data locks and monitoring, prevention of unauthorized access to any stored data, complaint procedures, and more.

Scenario: 2022, Greece

Greece was already on a humanitarian watch list in during the pandemic when they planned to launch two surveillance systems, Hyperion and Centaur, to monitor activity in political asylum camps on the Aegean Islands using a combination of drones and CCTV (Fotiadis et al., 2022; Stamatoukou, 2024). These were implemented without completing mandatory assessments and identifying data protection officers (Fotiadis et al., 2022).

Ethical Issues

The collection of data through drones and CCTV are intrusive and politically questionable considering those being surveilled are refugees. As Bassi et al. (2019) state, "The GDPR hinges on the assumption that the processing of personal data is a risky activity" (p. 581), and risks involved with drones include physical safety of those on the ground as well as data security issues, identity theft, and potential discrimination. CCTV and facial recognition are additional risks and intrusions on personal lives. Sathaye et al. (2022) add the possibility of GPS drone data being spoofed (faked).

Solution

The Greek Data Protection Authority took notice of the situation in late 2021 and began investigating. Article 38 of the GDPR requires the DPO be selected in a timely fashion, but it was not until a month after the investigation began that one was hired (Fotiadis et al., 2022). It was found Hyperion was in operation for 18 months and Centaur for two months without adequate data protection; in addition, a classified document with payment information was freely available online for five hours before the error was found (Fotiadis et al., 2022). Humanitarian issues were brought up by Homo Digitalis, the Hellenic League for Human Rights, and other rights organizations, and the United Nations High Commissioner for Refugees also wrote a letter condemning the system (Stamatoukou, 2024). The Ministry of Migration and Asylum was then fined €175,000 (Stamatoukou, 2024).

Vehicle Cameras

Uses of the Technology

Cameras are installed on many new vehicles and can easily be added to older vehicles with the purpose of recording surrounding activity. The technology can enhance visual capabilities of the driver such as assisting with parking or viewing what would otherwise be in a "blind spot," but the focus with this scenario is the capability of a "dashcam" to record events such as theft or damage while parked or accidents while driving (Christensen, 2024). Some dashcams simply view what a driver sees looking forward, and some have forward and behind-the-car views. Tesla vehicles have 360-degree angles of viewing thanks to eight company-installed cameras (Christensen, 2024).

Scenario: 2019, Germany and Austria

Volkswagen tested its driver assistance technology in 2019 on public roads in Germany. Law enforcement intercepted the vehicle when it crossed into Austria near Salzburg, and cross-border data as well as collection of traffic data without the knowledge of others on the road were contended ("LfDI," 2022).

Ethical Issues

Dashcam data might be collected, shared with law enforcement, and/or uploaded to the internet without the knowledge and consent of those who were being recorded. This could include license plate numbers (Christensen, 2024) and images of drivers' faces (Ritsema Van Eck & Vellinga, 2022) which could be used for facial recognition. The fact these can be shared violate the GDPR Article 6(3) in which third parties are not to have access (Ritsema Van Eck & Vellinga, 2022). The YouTube "Dashcam Nation" channel, which posts compilations of submitted dashcam recordings they call "Idiots in Cars," is an example of wide sharing. The channel is based in the United States and says their videos are meant to raise awareness on the road regarding safety, but there is no legal disclaimer about data privacy or whether dashcam recordings are accepted by the channel from EU countries (Dashcam Nation, n.d.).

According to a dashcam vendor, laws in the EU governing the use of these cameras vary per country, but are also covered by the GDPR ("Dash cam legality," 2025). In Austria and Germany, dashcams are allowed but must not record continuously or be shared publicly without express written consent; the idea is for it to find use with triggered events (meaning sudden occurrences such as accidents or other damage). According to *Dash cam legality* (2025), recordings in Germany "can be used as evidence in court if the interest in evidence outweighs privacy concerns."

Solution

Because Volkswagen's vehicle crossed into a second country, several DPAs were brought in to evaluate the case. GDPR Article 13 was found to have been violated since there was no identification on the vehicle notifying others of the data collection, plus lack of agreements and prior assessments violated Articles 28 and 35 respectively, and the absence of security measures documentation led to violation of Article 30 ("LfDI," 2022). The company was fined €1.1 million, but it was also noted they complied quickly to remedy errors ("LfDI," 2022).

In another case, Tesla was called out for GDPR issues stemming from dashcam use and the capture of faces and license plates, and learned that lack of protecting data and following the rules of the GDPR can erode public trust ("GDPR compliance," 2023).

Online Test Proctoring

Uses of the Technology

Test-taking has been a component of formal learning for well over 200 years, so with the advent of online learning and the necessities caused by the COVID-19 pandemic, online testing has become commonplace (Woldeab & Brothen, 2024). That being said, cheating on tests has also long been a potential pitfall. Online tests might be left unproctored, which Fendler et al. (2024) claim leads to higher incidents of cheating, and repeated occurrences only teach students "how to cheat more effectively" (p. 36). Institutional reputations can be at stake if their graduates have not learned what the grades imply (Fendler et al., 2024), and more schools than ever are using or considering proctoring software (Woldeab & Brothen, 2024).

Proctored exams usually make use of web cams, keystroke data, facial recognition and physical movement such as eye-tracking, gestures, and posture; they tend to be strictly timed and may include browser "lockdown" (Sakhipov et al., 2025), plus sound analysis and full room scans (Gullo, 2023). These measures help to ensure the student's identity and restricts them from using their textbook, notes, phone, or to surf the internet in a different window looking for answers they are supposed to have learned prior to taking the test. They also gather much data.

Scenario: May 2023, France

A student from the United States filed the first complaint about TestWe software used for proctored online testing at the Distance Learning Institute in Paris (known as IED), claiming the required actions of using the software were unnecessary and overly intrusive (Gullo, 2023).

Ethical Issues

Rensaa (2023) indicates requiring students to obtain web cams and other technology can be a problem, and their interpretation of Article 6 is that schools must offer in-person testing for those who are uncomfortable with online restrictions. This creates a problem, as fully online schools such as IED and other schools which offer online courses may have students all over the world, and requiring major travel to take a test is simply not logical. Proctoring software includes the use of biometrics as well as audio and video of the student's home environment. In the United States, an Ohio court determined the video room scans that show all of the student's surroundings while taking a proctored test to be in violation of the country's Fourth Amendment since it intrudes into their home, which is personal, private space (Gullo, 2023). This kind of proctoring is also considered by some to be "legitimized spyware" (Gullo, 2023, para. 5).

Solution

The plaintiffs in the case were supported by La Quadrature du Net, which asserted the manifold requirements for proctoring by TestWe were "disproportionate to the intended purpose" (Gullo, 2023, para. 9), thereby violating minimization as required by Article 5(1)(c), It is unclear if a GDPR sanction was enforced, but TestWe claims today to be fully in line with GDPR requirements, CNIL standards, and ISO certification ("European reference," n.d.).

AI and Language Scraping

Uses of the Technology

Artificial Intelligence learns from existing data; its Large Language Models (LLMs) "scrape" data from social media and other online sources ("Irish privacy watchdog," 2025) and this is done in order to compile data for the technology to "learn" human language and humor (Desmarais, 2024). This is done by looking for word patterns and ideas to be able to produce output (Amarikwa, 2024).

Scenario: April 2025, Social Media (online)

In mid-2024, The Irish Data Protection Commission and NOYB filed multiple complaints against the social media platform X after it was noted users' data settings had been altered to allow Elon Musk's Grok AI to collect data from over 60 million EU individuals' posts for training (Desmarais, 2024). Users were not notified prior to the changes, and the new settings required them to "opt out" rather than "opt in." Desmarais (2024) cited NOYB's statement that 16 articles of the GDPR were breached, and they filed grievances on behalf of Austria, Belgium, France, Greece, Ireland, Italy, the Netherlands, Spain, and Poland.

Ethical Issues

According to O'Flaherty (2024), Grok AI is known to have spread disinformation during the 2024 U.S. election, and is "prone to hallucinations," (para. 3), which is the term used when AI technology fabricates information. Brooks (2025) reported that Grok 3, the current version of this AI software, has a 94% fail rate for citation accuracy. Privacy issues with the platform go back to its Twitter days, when the U.S. Federal Trade Commission issued fines for how user data privacy was treated (O'Flaherty, 2024). There is apparently a lack of transparency about the data collection and use (Amarikwa, 2024), which violates the GDPR Article 5(1)(a).

According to Amarikwa (2024), there are three kinds of scraping. Screen or HTML scraping pulls data from the code used to build the website. Crawlers do the same but check sites' hyperlinks, too; this is how indexing is done in search engines, for example. Lastly, Application Program Interface (API) scraping is much like HTML scraping but has a different structure. While the processes may be different, the purpose is to pull data from the internet, and consent is not sought (Amarikwa, 2024). The GDPR includes 71 instances of the word "consent" and Article 7 focuses directly on this major aspect of the law; there are also provisions for withdrawal of consent such as in Article 7(3). A related ethical concern is that some companies sell scraped data to AI developers (Amarikwa, 2024). Item 47 of page 9 of the GDPR indicates controllers and/or third parties must consider legitimate purposes for data handling, including "the reasonable expectations of data subjects based on their relationship with the controller" (Regulation 2016/679, p. 9).

In addition, AI technology has an environmental impact; it requires an enormous amount of fresh water to maintain cool temperatures in their companies' data centers, and Gordon (2024) cites a United Nations report describing frequent severe water shortages for at least 2/3 of the world's population.

Solution

On August 8, 2024, X announced Grok AI would no longer use EU data (Desmarais, 2024). However, the Irish DPC was still investigating the issue as of April, 2025 ("Irish privacy watchdog," 2025), indicating the problem is ongoing. Disturbingly, NOYB said "the treatment of personal data is very likely irreversible" in this particular situation (Desmarais, 2024, para. 13).

Facial Recognition

Uses of the Technology

Facial recognition relies on photographic evidence; detection of a human face is the first step, followed by alignment, template generation, and then matching to a known visage in a database (Simmler & Canova, 2025). Figure 2 demonstrates that this is a geometric process.

Figure 2. Facial Recognition: Simple Example

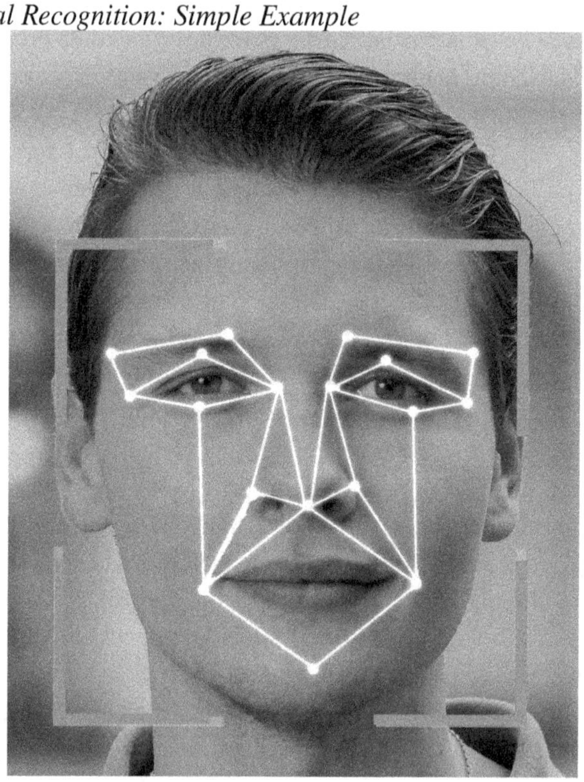

(Tumisu, 2021)

This technology can be used as part of a multi-factor authentication; for example, along with a passcode, users might use a facial scan as a means to unlock their phone. Airports are starting to use this at security checkpoints, and it has been suggested for use in campus safety, personal identification when banking, digital ticketing for sports events, hotel check-ins, and even excluding people from businesses and other locations where they have been known to cause trouble ("14 intriguing," 2023). Gargaro (2024) adds it can be used to identify lost children through age progression imagery developed from photographs. Facial recognition is also used by law enforcement in attempting to identify criminals, often from CCTV image captures. In terms of public safety, facial recognition is a good tool; however, there are concerns about undue surveillance such as tracking people in crowds and the questioned use of this collected data (Gültekin-Várkonyi, 2024).

Scenario: Fall 2024, The Netherlands

Clearview AI was said to have scraped 30 billion photos of real people from the internet without their permission (Poireault, 2024b). While the company is based in the United States, images were taken from people around the world, including in the EU.

Ethical Issues

Simller and Canova (2025) note facial recognition is a form of biometric data and therefore falls under the GDPR. AI imagery is created by extracting and saving tiny pieces of existing images and storing them in a database (Farmer, 2024). The system must then be able to recognize when a human face is presented, and then it will work to match input against templates. As Simmler and Canova (2025) explain, this is done with mathematical methods, and the program then "produces a similarity comparison of a distinct face to that of other faces" (p. 3). Thus, the entire technology relies on images of others, which is both an intellectual property issue and a privacy violation. Reliability may be scrutinized, as the environmental lighting, emotional expressions, and head/chin position may make a difference in the mathematical calculations (Kortli et al., 2020). In addition, there are concerns about the easy transfer of such data from one country to another and the fact that biometrics do not change much over time, presenting a concern should the data be hacked or otherwise compromised (Raposo, 2023).

Solution

Despite the company not having a physical presence in Europe, the GDPR rightly asserted EU citizens' data was included in the company's holdings (Poireault, 2024b). While not part of the European Union, Australia had started a probe into Clearview AI's use of its citizens' photos, but abandoned the investigation just prior to the Dutch charges (Poireault, 2024a). Ultimately, Clearview AI was fined €30.5 million and additionally assessed a €5.1 million penalty for non-compliance with the Dutch Data Protection Authority due to its practice of image theft, claiming a lack of transparency with those whose data appears in the company's database (Poireault, 2024b), which is covered in several GDPR Articles such as the Principles.

DNA Data

Uses of the Technology

DNA profiling has several purposes, including searching for familial relationships and identifying predisposition to genetic diseases (Bergstedt, 2021; Nogel, 2024). It is also used in law enforcement, although in 2009 the EU Council declared "Member States are urged to limit the DNA analysis results to chromosome zones containing no genetic expression" as a means to prevent undue prejudices ("Council Resolution," 2009, III.1). Unidentified human remains have sometimes been identified through DNA matching to known relatives; the passage of time, the condition of the body, and the environment in which the body was found determine procedures and accuracy (Samsuwan et al., 2018). DNA identification in pets has long been known to assist in identifying animal pedigrees (Jeffreys & Morton, 1987).

Scenario A: October 19, 2004, Sweden

An 8-year-old boy on his way to school and an unrelated woman on her way to work were both murdered in a park in Linköping, Sweden, one morning in October 2004. The male assailant was observed leaving the scene, and the knife and a hat left there provided crucial DNA evidence. Local law enforcement requested area men submit to DNA swabs, and around 6000 men volunteered and were tested (Tillmar et al., 2021). In addition to the volunteered data, police DNA databases were checked, but there were still no matches. Law enforcement DNA holdings at the time only identified 15 markers or identifying sequences, further limiting the search for the perpetrator (Wandermurem, 2025). The case remained unsolved for years.

Scenario B: May 1999, the Netherlands

In a similar case five years earlier, a 16-year-old girl from the Netherlands was raped and murdered, and people in her small village believed this was perpetrated by an immigrant. DNA gathered from the scene at the time proved the person responsible was far more likely to be of local heritage. This initial DNA check was done using the Y-chromosome Haplotype Reference Database (YHRD) which connects male lineage (Schiermeier, 2021), and it was suggested this was done at least partially to stop the persecution of refugees in the area and to quiet the media frenzy that followed the murder (Jong & M'charek, 2018).

Ethical issues

These cases were not instances of GDPR violations since they predated the legislation, but instead the cases' resolutions hinged on later rulings allowing legal use of collected genealogical data. Those who send in DNA to commercial companies do so to know more about themselves and their heritage (Bergstedt, 2021); they have not provided specific consent for use by law enforcement.

There is also the concern of ethnic or racial identification in genomic data, plus fears that leaked DNA data may affect health or life insurance options and/or ability to receive medical treatments (Ramanan et al., 2025). Test results must include a sufficient number of markers to ensure accuracy (Nogel, 2024); Y-chromosome Short Tandem Repeat (Y-STR) sequencing (a formal wording for markers) is commonly used today, and since 2017, the Combined DNA Index System (CODIS) in the U.S. used by law enforcement uses 20 markers (Thomas et al., 2024; Katsanis, 2020). Whether this is sufficient could be debated. The U.S. data is relevant in this case, as "the majority of users of personal genome companies are of European descent" (Katsanis, 2020, p. 541); U.S. citizens who use genealogy DNA companies will quite often share ancestry with Europeans. This last fact was one of the issues with the Linköping murders, as familial data gathered in the U.S. traverses into the EU and so is subject to GDPR regulations. It must also be stated that the aforementioned YHRD database underwent scrutiny for its holdings, as there have been too many questions about how DNA was gathered, especially from China (Schiermeier, 2021).

Solutions

The case in Sweden remained unsolved for sixteen years when finally, new legislation allowed police searches for familial DNA on the commercial genealogical sites GEDmatch and Family Tree, which are popular in Sweden (Tillmar et al., 2021). Genealogist Peter Sjölund scoured the available data and was finally able to identify the murderer's ancestral DNA going back 200 years; he was then able to move forward in time to living relatives (Wandermurem, 2025). This path led to two brothers, one of whom was the perpetrator and ultimately admitted to the crime (Tillmar et al., 2021).

Netherlands law at the time of the girl's murder did not allow for forensic familial searches, but eventually it did approve of matching for "externally visible personal characteristics" (Jon & M'charek, 2018, p. 358), and the case was solved in 2012 when the DNA was matched to a local farmer who, once accused, confessed. This predated the GDPR but was covered under the country's then-current data laws.

Of Interest

Netflix's 2025 miniseries *The Breakthrough* provides an account of the Linköping story albeit with some "creative liberties" (Wandermurem, 2025, para. 15).

Other Cases Worthy of Further Study

Hacked Tax Data, Bulgaria, 2019

The National Revenue Agency of Bulgaria was fined €2.6 million in August, 2019 due to leakage of over 6 million citizens' tax data such as PINs, contact information, home addresses, contributions to health insurance, income information, and tax payments (Wolff & Atallah, 2021). Notably, Kottasová (2019) points out that Bulgaria has only about 7 million people; this was a large percentage of the country's population. It is suggested government files might be a preference for some hackers, since passwords can change, but names, ID numbers, birth dates, and similar data collected by governments do not. The 20-year-old hacker – who was ultimately caught – posted the stolen data, and it was freely shared online (Kottasová, 2019).

Non-Compliance, Portugal, 2019

Hospitals hold a great amount of patient data. In 2019, the Centro Hospitalar Barreiro Montijo in Portugal was fined €400,000 for several GDPR violations (de Meneses & Van Quathem, 2018; Monteiro, 2019). An excuse was given that the Comissão Nacional de Protecção de Dados (CNPD) had not been formally assigned as the Authority – this was only a few months after the GDPR was put in place – but this was countered with specific instances of GDPR violations, including:

- Lack of minimization by allowing too many users, in violation of Article 5(1)(c)

- Poor processing procedures, in violation of Article 83(5)(a)
- Poor integrity and confidentiality handling, in violation of Article 5(1)(f)
- Additional procedural errors, in violation of Article 32(1)(b) (Monteiro, 2019)

One of the missteps was the identification of 985 users as doctors by their system, but the hospital only employed 296 doctors, and all "doctors" were able to see all patient files, even those with whom they were not directly associated (de Meneses & Van Quathem, 2018; Monteiro, 2019). Despite the newness of the law, CNPD stated it was still the responsibility of the hospital to keep data safe (de Meneses & Van Quathem, 2018).

Organ Donor Data, The Netherlands, 2020

Organ donor information from 1998 to 2010 in the Netherlands had been stored on hard drives, but the Dutch government admitted in 2020 that during a process of getting rid of paper forms and consolidating data electronically, two such hard drives were lost. These contained the personal data of over 6.9 million people on the country's donor registry and included identification numbers, birth dates, signatures, and other personal information (Cimpanu, 2020). At the time of disclosure there had not been any identity theft occurrences, but it was reported the drives were not encrypted, causing some fears ("6.9 million," 2020). It is not clear if a fine was levied.

Mobile Technology Company Data Leakage, Greece, 2020

For four months in 2020, telecommunications company Cosmote and its companion OTA experienced a data leakage for 10 million subscribers (Fotiadis, 2023). Cosmote was fined €6 million for not protecting data sufficiently and not anonymizing adequately, and OTA was determined to violate GDPR Article 32 with poor security measures and fined €3.25 million; the companies were also told they failed to allocate responsibilities between them properly (European Data Protection Board, 2022). According to Fotiadis (2023), the companies paid the fines but then asked for the decision to be reversed, declaring the fines to be excessive in proportion to the situation. The Data Protection Authority countered the fines could have been substantially higher per law (Fotiadis, 2023).

FURTHER ASSESSMENT

The case studies point to the need to continually assess problems with personally identifiable data. Prince et al. (2024) express concern about individuals' data privacy literacy, which in turn may put their data at risk; better public awareness programs may help, although Zhang et al. (2024) report awareness has somewhat increased over the last few years. The Regulation is complex and takes time, effort, people, and finances for businesses to comply; Zaguir et al. (2024) also suggest practical guides would be of great assistance, and fortunately, there are some online (see the Appendix). Some previously-used business methods have also had to change: Wang et al. (2023) warn companies to exercise caution with ads on their websites and use opt-*in* programs, and while it means making changes from old procedures, this may be ultimately advantageous compared to overly-generalized target marketing. Zhang et al. (2024) add consent mechanisms need to provide better "actionable choices" (p. 8).

Reporting: An Example

When an issue is found, each company is responsible for immediately reporting incidents, and procedures vary per locality. In Ireland, there is a health service data loss incident form giving insight into the kind of information that must go into such a report. Their form states no more than 24 hours must have elapsed since the incident, and information to be provided by the company includes contact information, incident details and timing, whether the compromised data was in electronic or paper format, the causes/nature of the breach, the kind of data disclosed (birth dates, personal identification numbers, criminal records, biometrics, etc.), the number of people whose data is involved and number of records, notification information, and whether or not a backup of the data has been retained. There is a separate section for mobile and storage devices, asking about password protection and other factors. The last two sections require information about what rules were in place prior to the breach and what actions were taken to prevent a repeat incident ("Data breach incident report," 2020).

Wider Reach

Other countries' businesses can be affected by the GDPR. Google was fined €50 million in 2019, accused by France's Commission Nationale de l'Informatique et des Libertés (CNIL) for acquiring and using user data for personalizing ads without consent (Brook, 2019). In July 2021, Amazon was fined €746 million by the Luxembourg National Commission for Data Protection due to targeted marketing in the EU that lacked proper consent ("20 biggest," 2025). Meta endured a larger fine in May 2023, assessed €1.2 billion by the Irish Data Protection Commission due to transfer of European users' personal data to the U.S. without adequate safety measures ("20 biggest," 2025). Microsoft is based in the U.S. but in 2024 was the focus of accusations made by Austrian regulators and NOYB that the 365 Education Office Suite was collecting children's data via cookies and trying to shift responsibility to the schools; the documentation allegedly provided by Microsoft lacks transparency (Dela Cruz, 2024).

According to Akhlaghpour et al. (2021), the GDPR may well have been the inspiration for other governments such as Brazil and the state of California to create comprehensive data regulations. In 2021, China enacted their Personal Information Protection Law (PIPL); like the GDPR and other regulations, this affects anyone doing business with persons in Mainland China, and violations could lead to a range of liabilities which might include criminal investigation (Cui & Qi, 2021).

CONCLUSION

The GDPR provides a strong and detailed framework for the processing of personal data in the EU as well as data that may flow to or from the EU from elsewhere. Case studies show how technology can present problems needing resolution to meet GDPR, and each event has the potential to set precedents affecting individuals worldwide. The incidents illustrate potential for concern and may prove useful in the discussion of tech and data ethics in schools and in the workplace. While technologies constantly change and improve, and potential issues with each can be vastly different – thereby hindering understanding by courts – the fact remains that EU citizens need the law to protect themselves, data authorities and watchdog groups are needed to help enforce the law, and even those who live outside the EU benefit from compliance with the GDPR.

REFERENCES

About us. (n.d.a,). NOYB. https://noyb.eu/en/about-us

About us. (n.d.b.). La Quadrature du Net. https://www.laquadrature.net/about/

Akhlaghpour, S., Hassandoust, F., Fatehi, F., Burton-Jones, A., & Hynd, A. (2021, September). Learning from enforcement cases to manage GDPR risks. *MIS Quarterly Executive*, *20*(1), 199–218. DOI: 10.17705/2msqe.00049

Amarikwa, M. (2024, February 5). Internet openness at risk: Generative AI's impact on data scraping. *Richmond Journal of Law & Technology, 30*(3).

Arfelt, E., Basin, D., & Debois, S. (2019, September). *Monitoring the GDPR.* [Conference paper]. 24th European Symposium on Research in Computer Security (pp. 681-699).

Atadoga, A., Farayola, O. A., Ayinla, B. S., Amoo, O. O., Abrahams, T. O., & Osasona, F. (2024, February 18). A comparative review of data encryption methods in the USA and Europe. *Computer Science & IT Research Journal*, *5*(2), 447–460. DOI: 10.51594/csitrj.v5i2.815

Auerbach, R. P., Bloom, P. A., Pagliaccio, D., Lan, R., Galfalvy, H., Bitran, A., Durham, K., Crowley, R., Joyce, K., Blanchard, A., Chernick, L. S., Dayan, P. S., Greenblatt, J., Khan, L. E., Porta, G., Tse, T. C., Cohn, J. F., Morency, L.-P., Brent, D. A., & Allen, N. B. (2025, January 27). Using smartphone GPS data to detect the risk of adolescent suicidal thoughts and behaviors. *Journal of the American Medical Association*, *8*(1), E2456429. DOI: 10.1001/jamanetworkopen.2024.56429 PMID: 39869336

Aumasson, J.-P. (2025). *Serious cryptography: A practical introduction to modern encryption* (2nd ed.). No Starch Press.

Ayora, M. (2023, December 13). *AEPD (Spain): EXP202205820.* GDPR Hub. https://gdprhub.eu/index.php?title=AEPD_(Spain)_-_EXP202205820#Facts

Bailey, E. (2023, September 22). *GDPR compliance and personal data: The ultimate guide.* Matomo. https://matomo.org/blog/2023/09/gdpr-personal-data

Bassi, E., Bloise, N., Dirutigliano, J., Fici, G. P., Pagallo, U., Primatesta, S., & Quagliotti, F. (2019, November). The design of GDPR-abiding drones through flight operation maps: A win-win approach to data protection, aerospace engineering, and risk management. *Minds and Machines*, *29*(4), 579–601. DOI: 10.1007/s11023-019-09511-9

Bergstedt, E. (2021, May 28). *Solving a double murder arouses international interest.* Linköping University. https://liu.se/en/news-item/kunskap-om-dubbelmords-losning-vacker-internationellt-intresse

Brook, C. (2019, January 21). *Google fined $57M by data protection watchdog over GDPR violations.* Digital Guardian. https://www.digitalguardian.com/blog/google-fined-57m-data-protection-watchdog-over-gdpr-violations

Brooks, B. (2025, March 13). *Musk's Grok 3 '94% Inaccurate': Here's how other AI chatbots fare against truth.* eWeek. https://www.eweek.com/news/ai-chatbot-citation-problem

Chen, R., Fu, C., de Melo, S. N., & Xu, Y. (2025, March). Day and night: Evaluating the impact of CCTV and street lighting on urban crime prevention in Detroit. *Journal of Criminal Justice*, *98*, 102397. DOI: 10.1016/j.jcrimjus.2025.102397

Christensen, T. K. (2024, July). Pre-installed cameras in vehicles: New technology from data protection law perspective. *Computer Law & Security Review*, *53*, 105980. DOI: 10.1016/j.clsr.2024.105980

Cimpanu, C. (2020, March 11). *Dutch government loses hard drives with data of 6.9 million registered donors.* ZD Net. https://www.zdnet.com/article/dutch-government-loses-hard-drives-with-data-of-6-9-million-registered-donors

CISO Mag. (2020, March 12). *6.9 million Dutch donors face identity theft scare.* https://cisomag.com/6-9-million-dutch-donors-face-identity-theft-scare 1

Cobb, M. (2022, September). *Data Masking.* Tech Target. https://www.techtarget.com/searchsecurity/definition/data-masking

Convention 108. (2025, January 24). *Data Protection Day.* Consultative Committee of the Convention for the Protection of Individuals with Regard to Automatic Processing of Personal Data. https://rm.coe.int/final-dpd-2025-compilation/1680b3b2ec

Coos, A. (2021, April 26). *GDPR encryption requirements.* End Point Protector. https://www.endpointprotector.com/blog/gdpr-data-encryption-requirements

Council of Europe. (n.d.). *Data protection day - 28 January.* https://www.coe.int/en/web/data-protection/data-protection-day

Council Resolution. 2009/C 296/01. (2009, November 30). *Official Journal of the European Union.* https://eur-lex.europa.eu/legal-content/EN/TXT/HTML/?uri=CELEX:32009G1205(01)

Cui, S., & Qi, P. (2021, July). The legal construction of personal information protection and privacy under the Chinese Civil Code. *Computer Law & Security Review, 41*, 105560. DOI: 10.1016/j.clsr.2021.105560

Daigle, B., & Khan, M. (2020, June). The EU General Data Protection Regulation: An analysis of enforcement trends by EU Data Protection Authorities. *Journal of International Commerce & Economics,* 1-38. https://www.usitc.gov/publications/332/journals/jice_gdpr_enforcement_0.pdf

Damjan, M. (2023, April 13). The right to privacy in the digital age: A Slovenian perspective. In Wielec, M. (Ed.), *The right to privacy in the digital age: Perspectives on analysis of certain central European countries' legislation and practice* (pp. 273–309). Central European Academic Publishing., DOI: 10.54237/profnet.2023.mwrtpida_8

Dash cam legality in EU (2025 updated). (2025, February 11). DDPAI. https://www.ddpai.com/blog/dash-cam-legality-in-eu

Dashcam Nation. (n.d.). *Idiots in cars.* [YouTube channel]. YouTube. Retrieved April 13, 2025, from https://www.youtube.com/@DashcamNation1

Data breach incident report. (2020, May). Feidhmeannas Seirbhíse Sláinte (Health Service Executive). https://assets.hse.ie/media/documents/data-breach-incident-reporting-form-external.pdf

Data privacy manager. (2025, March 3). *20 biggest GDPR fines so far.* https://dataprivacymanager.net/5-biggest-gdpr-fines-so-far-2020

de Meneses, A. O., & Van Quathem, K. (2018, October 26). *Portuguese hospital received and contests 400,000 € fine for GDPR infringement.* Covington Inside Privacy. https://www.insideprivacy.com/data-privacy/portuguese-hospital-receives-and-contests-400000-e-fine-for-gdpr-infringement

Dela Cruz, J. (2024, June 5). *Microsoft faces children's privacy complaints in Austria over use of 365 Education Suite in schools.* Tech Times. https://www.techtimes.com/articles/305352/20240605/microsoft-faces-children-privacy-complaints-austria-365-education-suite.htm

Desmarais, A. (2024, August 12). Elon Musk hit with nine complaints of breaching EU privacy rules to train AI model. *Euro News.* https://www.euronews.com/next/2024/08/12/elon-musk-hit-with-nine-complaints-of-breaching-eu-privacy-rules-to-train-ai-model

European Data Protection Board. (2022, February 3). *Hellenic DPA: Fines imposed to telecommunications companies due to personal data breach and illegal data processing.* https://www.edpb.europa.eu/news/national-news/2022/hellenic-dpa-fines-imposed-telecommunications-companies-due-personal-data_en

European Union Aviation Safety Agency. (2024, July). *Easy access rules for Unmanned Aircraft Systems (Regulations (EU) 2019/947 and 2019/945).* https://www.easa.europa.eu/en/document-library/easy-access-rules/easy-access-rules-unmanned-aircraft-systems-regulations-eu#group-publications

European Union Aviation Safety Agency. (n.d.) *Code of conduct.* https://www.easa.europa.eu/en/domains/civil-drones/privacy/code-of-conduct

Farmer, L. S. J. (2024, March). Visual literacy in an AI-driven world. *Computers in Libraries, 44*(2), 36–40.

Fendler, R., Beard, D., & Godbey, J. (2024). A robust examination of cheating of unproctored online exams. *Electronic Journal of e-Learning, 22*(5), 26–38. DOI: 10.34190/ejel.22.5.3173

Forbes. (2023, August 18). *4 intriguing new and potential uses for facial recognition technology.* https://www.forbes.com/councils/forbestechcouncil/2023/08/18/14-intriguing-new-and-potential-uses-for-facial-recognition-technology

Fotiadis, A. (2023, April 26). *After a personal data breach affecting 10 million customers, Cosmote & OTE appeal to cancel fine*. Solomon. https://wearesolomon.com/mag/format/feature/after-a-personal-data-breach-affecting-10-millions-customers-cosmote-ote-appeal-to-cancel-fine

Fotiadis, A., Papangeli, I., & Malichudis, S. (2022, September 9). *Asylum surveillance systems launched in Greece without data safeguards.* Balkan Insight. https://balkaninsight.com/2022/09/09/asylum-surveillance-systems-launched-in-greece-without-data-safeguards

Fudge, T. P. (2025, March 30). *GDPR roles by level.* [Image]. Fudgelink: The European Union's General Data Protection Regulation. https://fudgelink.com/GDPR

Gargaro, D. (2024, July 23). *The pros and cons of facial recognition technology.* IT Pro. https://www.itpro.com/security/privacy/356882/the-pros-and-cons-of-facial-recognition-technology

GDPR compliance and data anonymization: Lessons from Tesla's personal data leak in automotive cameras. (2023, December 20). Syntonym. https://www.syntonym.com/posts/gdpr-compliance-and-data-anonymization-lessons

General Data Protection Regulation (GDPR): A compliance guide for the US. (2021, August). IT Governance USA. [Green Paper]. https://www.itgovernanceusa.com/guidance-for-achieving-compliance-with-the-eu-gdpr

Gordon, C. (2024, February 25). AI is accelerating the loss of our scarcest natural resource: Water. *Forbes*. https://www.forbes.com/sites/cindygordon/2024/02/25/ai-is-accelerating-the-loss-of-our-scarcest-natural-resource-water

Gullo, K. (2023, March 31). *After students challenged proctoring software, French court slaps TestWe app with a suspension.* Electronic Frontier Foundation. https://www.eff.org/deeplinks/2023/03/after-students-challenged-proctoring-software-french-court-slaps-testwe-app

Gültekin-Várkonyi, G. (2024, September 30). Navigating data governance risks: Facial recognition in law enforcement under EU legislation. *Internet Policy Review, 13*(3). Advance online publication. DOI: 10.14763/2024.3.1798

Hammas, M., Fituri, H., Shour, A., Khan, U. A., & Ahmed, S. (2025, January). A hybrid dual-axis solar tracking system: Combining light-sensing and time-based GPS for optimal energy efficiency. *Energies, 18*(1), 217. DOI: 10.3390/en18010217

Herath, S., Gelman, H., & Mckee, L. (2023). Privacy harm and non-compliance from a legal perspective. *Journal of Cybersecurity Education. Research and Practice, 2023*(2), 3. DOI: 10.32727/8.2023.18

Hovsha, J., & Brien, D. O. (2022). Drone use cases and their privacy impacts: A taxonomy. *Tilburg Law Review, 27*(1), 60–80. DOI: 10.5334/tilr.281

How does GPS tracking work? (2024, September 3). GPS Insight. https://www.gpsinsight.com/blog/gps-tracking-work

Hutt, S., Das, S., & Baker, R. S. (2023, July). The right to be forgotten and educational data mining: Challenges and paths forward. In Feng, M., Käser, T., & Talukdar, P. (Eds.), *Proceedings of the 16th International Conference on Educational Data Mining* (pp. 251–259). Bengaluru, India. DOI: 10.5281/zenodo.8115655

Irish privacy watchdog investigates Elon Musk's X's use of personal data to train Grok AI chatbot. (2025, April 11). *Associated Press*. https://apnews.com/article/ireland-data-privacy-elon-musk-6458d4cc70f6b77af8034e64f45e752f

Jeffreys, A. J., & Morton, D. B. (1987, February). DNA fingerprints of dogs and cats. *Animal Genetics, 18*(1), 1–15. DOI: 10.1111/j.1365-2052.1987.tb00739.x PMID: 2886082

Jong, L., & M'charek, A. (2018). The high-profile case as 'fire object': Following the Marianne Vaatstra murder case through the media. *Crime, Media, Culture*, *14*(3), 347–363. DOI: 10.1177/1741659017718036 PMID: 30568716

Katsanis, S. H. (2020, August). Pedigrees and perpetrators: Uses of DNA and genealogy in forensic investigations. *Annual Review of Genomics and Human Genetics*, *21*(1), 535–564. DOI: 10.1146/annurev-genom-111819-084213 PMID: 32289230

Koca, M. (2024). Real-time security risk assessment from CCTV using hand gesture recognition. *IEEE Access : Practical Innovations, Open Solutions*, *12*, 84548–84555. DOI: 10.1109/ACCESS.2024.3412930

Kortli, Y., Jridi, M., Al Falou, A., & Atri, M. (2020, January 7). Face recognition systems: A survey. *Sensors (Basel)*, *20*(2), 342. DOI: 10.3390/s20020342 PMID: 31936089

Kottasová, I. (2019, July 21). An entire nation just got hacked. *CNN World*. https://edition.cnn.com/2019/07/21/europe/bulgaria-hack-tax-intl/index.html

Krasteva, V. (2024, December 26). *What is EU GDPR in a nutshell!* Composity. https://composity.com/en/post/eu-general-data-protection-regulation-in-nutshell

LfDI (Lower Saxony) – Volkswagen. (2022, July 26). GDPR Hub. https://gdprhub.eu/index.php?title=LfDI_(Lower_Saxony)_-_Volkswagen

Li, H., Yu, L., & He, W. (2019). The impact of GDPR on global technology development. *Journal of Global Information Technology Management*, *22*(1), 1–6. DOI: 10.1080/1097198X.2019.1569186

Modi, S., Mane, S., Mahadik, S., Kadam, R., Jambhale, R., Mahadik, S., & Mali, Y. (2024). Automated attendance monitoring system for cattle through CCTV. *Revista Electrónica de Veterinaria*, *25*(1), 1025–1034. DOI: 10.69980/redvet.v25i1.724

Monteiro, A. M. (2019, January 3). *First GDPR fine in Portugal issued against hospital for three violations*. IAAP. https://iapp.org/news/a/first-gdpr-fine-in-portugal-issued-against-hospital-for-three-violations

Nogel, M. (2024, June). Some areas where digital forensics can support the addressing of legal challenges linked to forensic genetic genealogy. *Forensic Science International Digital Investigation*, *49*, 301696. DOI: 10.1016/j.fsidi.2024.301696

O'Flaherty, K. (2024, September 9). *What you need to know about Grok AI and your privacy*. Wired. https://www.wired.com/story/grok-ai-privacy-opt-out

Our general principles. (n.d.). NOYB. https://noyb.eu/en/our-general-principles

Poggi, N. (2021, June 15). *Encryption choices: RSA vs. AES explained.* Prey Project. https://preyproject.com/blog/types-of-encryption-symmetric-or-asymmetric-rsa-or-aes

Poireault, K. (2024a, August 21). *Australia calls off Clearview AI investigation despite lack of compliance.* Infosecurity Magazine. https://www.infosecurity-magazine.com/news/australia-calls-off-clearview-ai

Poireault, K. (2024b, September 4). *Clearview AI fined €30.5m by Dutch watchdog over illegal data collection.* Infosecurity Magazine. https://www.infosecurity-magazine.com/news/clearview-ai-fined-30m-netherlands

Prince, C., Omrani, N., & Schiavone, F. (2024). Online privacy literacy and users' information privacy empowerment: The case of GDPR in Europe. *Information Technology & People*, *37*(8), 1–24. DOI: 10.1108/ITP-05-2023-0467

Ramanan, V., Vinod, R., Williams, C., Ramachandran, S., & Venkatasubramanian, S. (2025, February 13). *Genetic data governance in crisis; policy recommendations for safeguarding privacy and preventing discrimination.* ArXiv. DOI: 10.48550/ARXIV.2502.09716

Raposo, V. L. (2023). (Do not) remember my face: Uses of facial recognition technology in light of the General Data Protection Regulation. *Information & Communications Technology Law*, *32*(1), 45–63. DOI: 10.1080/13600834.2022.2054076

Regulation 2016/679 OJ L 119 of the European Parliament and of the Council of 27 April 2016 on the protection of natural persons with regard to the processing of personal data and on the free movement of such data, and repealing Directive 95/46/EC (General Data Protection Regulation). *Official Journal of the European Union, 59,* 1-88. https://eur-lex.europa.eu/legal-content/EN/TXT/PDF/?uri=CELEX:32016R0679

Rensaa, R. J. (2023, May 11). Assessment considerations during lockdown in Norway: An exploratory case study with focus on misconducts in university mathematics. *Cogent Education*, *10*(1), 2210456. DOI: 10.1080/2331186X.2023.2210456

Ritsema Van Eck, G. J., & Vellinga, N. E. (2022, September). The new car safety rules of the GSR in light of the GDPR: An unnecessarily tangled web. *European Journal of Law and Technology*, *13*(1).

Safety of property can be a legitimate interest for GPS tracking, but the measure must be appropriate and necessary. (2022, October 4). European Data Protection Board. https://www.edpb.europa.eu/news/national-news/2022/safety-property-can-be-legitimate-interest-gps-tracking-measure-must-be_en

Sakhipov, A., Omirzak, I., & Fedenko, A. (2025, February 25). Beyond face recognition: A multi-layered approach to academic integrity in online exams. *Electronic Journal of e-Learning*, *23*(1), 81–95. DOI: 10.34190/ejel.23.1.3896

Samsuwan, J., Somboonchokepisal, T., Akaraputtiporn, T., Srimuang, T., Phuengsukdaeng, P., Suwannarat, A., Mutirangura, A., & Kitkumthorn, N. (2018, September 13). A method for extracting DNA from hard tissues for use in forensic identification. *Biomedical Reports*, *9*(5), 433–438. DOI: 10.3892/br.2018.1148 PMID: 30402227

Sathaye, H., Strohmeier, M., Lenders, V., & Ranganathan, A. (2022, August). *An experimental study of GPS spoofing and takeover attacks on UAVs.* [Conference proceedings]. 31st USENIX Security Symposium, Boston, MA. (pp. 3503-3520). https://www.usenix.org/system/files/sec22-sathaye.pdf

Schiermeier, Q. (2021, June 15). Forensic database challenged over ethics of DNA holdings. *Nature*, *594*(7863), 320–322. DOI: 10.1038/d41586-021-01584-w PMID: 34131337

Sellers, F. (2018, February 8). *The GDPR's impact on CCTV and workplace surveillance.* Privacy World. https://www.privacyworld.blog/2018/02/the-gdprs-impact-on-cctv-and-workplace-surveillance

Simmler, M., & Canova, G. (2025, April). Facial recognition technology in law enforcement: Regulating data analysis of another kind. *Computer Law & Security Review*, *56*, 106092. DOI: 10.1016/j.clsr.2024.106092

Stamatoukou, E. (2024, April 3). *Greek Ministry fined over surveillance systems at asylum centres.* Balkan Insight. https://balkaninsight.com/2024/04/03/greek-ministry-fined-over-surveillance-systems-at-asylum-centres

Szira, Z., Varga, E., Csegődi, T. L., & Milics, G. (2023, December 24). The development of drone technology and its regulation in the European Union. *EU Agrarian Law*, *12*(1), 35–41. DOI: 10.2478/eual-2023-0005

TestWe. (n.d.). *The European reference for online exams and certifications.* https://testwe.eu/en

Thomas, A. L., Piza, E. L., Welsh, B. C., & Farrington, D. P. (2022). The internationalization of CCTV surveillance: Effects on crime and implications for emerging technologies. *International Journal of Comparative and Applied Criminal Justice*, *46*(1), 81–102. DOI: 10.1080/01924036.2021.1879885

Thomas, M., Mackes, N., Preuss-Dodhy, A., Wieland, T., & Bundschus, M. (2024). Assessing privacy vulnerabilities in genetic data sets: Scoping review. *JMIR Bioinformatics and Biotechnology*, *5*, e54332. Advance online publication. DOI: 10.2196/54332 PMID: 38935957

Tillmar, A., Fagerholm, S. A., Staaf, J., Sjölund, P., & Ansell, R. (2021, July). Getting the conclusive lead with investigative genetic genealogy – A successful case study of a 16 year old double murder in Sweden. *Forensic Science International. Genetics*, *53*, 102525. DOI: 10.1016/j.fsigen.2021.102525 PMID: 33991867

Tumisu. (2021, January 26). *Man Face*. [Image]. Pixabay. https://pixabay.com/photos/man-face-facial-recognition-5946820. Free for use under the Pixabay Content License; no alterations other than cropping.

Wandermurem, I. (2025, January 2025). *The true story behind Netflix's gripping Swedish crime drama, The Breakthrough.* Time. https://time.com/7205773/the-breakthrough-true-story-netflix

Wang, P., Jiang, L., & Yang, J. (2023, April 11). The early impact of GDPR compliance on display advertising: The case of an ad publisher. *JMR, Journal of Marketing Research*, *61*(1), 70–91. DOI: 10.1177/00222437231171848

Warren, S. D., & Brandeis, L. D. (1890, December 15). The right to privacy. *Harvard Law Review*, *4*(5), 193–220. DOI: 10.2307/1321160

What is the European Union? (n.d.). EU & Me. https://op.europa.eu/webpub/com/eu-and-me/en/WHAT_IS_THE_EUROPEAN_UNION.html

Woldeab, D., & Brothen, T. (2024, August 30). Exploring the impact: How online exam proctoring reduces cheating and enhances course legitimacy. *International Journal of E-learning & Distance Education*, *39*(1), 1–29. DOI: 10.55667/10.55667/ijede.2024.v39.i1.1327

Wolff, J., & Atallah, N. (2021). Early GDPR penalties: Analysis of implementation and fines through May 2020. *Journal of Information Policy*, *11*, 63–103. DOI: 10.5325/jinfopoli.11.2021.0063

Zaguir, N. A., de Magalhães, G. H., & de Mesquita Spinola, M. (2024, June 18). Challenges and enablers for GDPR compliance: Systematic literature review and future research directions. *IEEE Access : Practical Innovations, Open Solutions*, *12*, 81608–81630. DOI: 10.1109/ACCESS.2024.3406724

Zhang, J. H., Koivumäki, T., & Chalmers, D. (2024, November). Privacy vs convenience: Understanding intention-behavior divergence post-GDPR. *Computers in Human Behavior*, *160*, 108382. DOI: 10.1016/j.chb.2024.108382

APPENDIX

Web Links of Interest

Some of these are found in the Reference section, but provided here for quick access:

- GDPR original text in English (88 page PDF):
  https://eur-lex.europa.eu/legal-content/EN/TXT/PDF/?uri=CELEX:32016R0679
- GDPR searchable website:
  https://gdpr-info.eu
- European Commission information on the GDPR:
  https://commission.europa.eu/law/law-topic/data-protection_en
- GDPR Enforcement Tracker to check fines assigned in various countries:
  https://www.enforcementtracker.com
- GDPR Hub for details regarding specific cases:
  https://gdprhub.eu/index.php?title=Welcome_to_GDPRhub
- GDPR.EU site including checklists, sample data processing agreement and other documentation:
  https://gdpr.eu
- GDPR user-friendly guide:
  https://www.gdpreu.org

Chapter 13
Legal and Ethical Challenges on Drone Technology:
Learnings From Indian Skies

Nidhi Kastwar
https://orcid.org/0009-0009-6352-6177
Amity University, Gwalior, India

Aakash Gupta
https://orcid.org/0009-0008-3920-9991
Amity University, Gwalior, India

ABSTRACT

Drone technology is a mixed blessing in the modern tech era. While it offers advantages across various societal sectors, the downsides of unmonitored usage must not be ignored. This paper explores the challenges and opportunities of drone technology and evaluates its use in Indian skies, balancing concerns related to public safety, privacy, criminal justice, and surveillance. The study fills a gap by combining technological and legal perspectives. It critically examines how drones have enhanced existing practices in remote sensing, surveillance, crime scene documentation, search and rescue operations, aerial photography, and agriculture. At the same time, it addresses issues such as threats to individual privacy, unauthorized usage, and the risk of hacking and security breaches. The findings highlight that drones bring significant benefits but also pose societal risks, emphasizing the need for stringent regulations on drone operations in Indian airspace. This research relies on qualitative analysis of secondary data.

DOI: 10.4018/979-8-3373-3186-7.ch013

1. INTRODUCTION

Drone is an informal term for any remotely operated autonomous vehicle, including aerial, ground, or underwater systems. It is an uncrewed aircraft and does not have an onboard human pilot. Drones are increasingly used by state and non-state actors (A. Kumar & Vishwanathan, 2025) and have applications spanning several industries. They are used in military surveillance and strikes (Jackman, 2023), aerial photography and videography (such as buildings and construction sites) (Li & Wu, 2024), delivery services, and other commercial applications (De Oliveira et al., 2024), agriculture (precision farming, crop monitoring, spraying pesticides) (A. P. M. Kumar et al., 2025), and search and rescue operations (Gautam & Johari, 2023). This can be seen in the evolution of drones as a sector. It all began with kites and balloons in the early 20th century. However, today, we have reached the stage where drone taxis are not fiction anymore; they have become a reality. Drones are fast becoming an integral part of society and have applications in various sectors.

Technology often moves in building blocks, with each new phase of technological development becoming only a stepping stone for a new evolutionary form to emerge. The rapid integration of drones into sectors like logistics, agriculture, and surveillance underscores the urgent need for robust legal frameworks to address their dual-use potential. Emerging technologies like drones intersect with critical legal questions around privacy, autonomy, and cross-border governance, necessitating interdisciplinary solutions. Within drone technology, advancements are happening on new age control mechanisms, miniaturization, achieving cost-effectiveness, improved sensors with LIDAR and multi-spectral cameras, enhanced autonomy powered by Artificial Intelligence (AI), capability of multiple drones acting in coordination to monitor large-scale areas (Drone Swarms), amongst others will only shift gears in the widespread adoption of drones even in those sectors where their application seems unlikely at present.

Regulators cannot be oblivious to technological development. Drones have certainly proved to be a double-edged sword. They have been used in smuggling drugs across borders, dropping bombs, unauthorized surveillance, infringing personal privacy, espionage, having flights in restricted airspace, and increasing the risk of air accidents, amongst others. These technological and legal challenges of their unmonitored usage need an appropriate regulatory response. The most important one is integrating the thousands and millions of drones into regulated airspace. Though the Indian Government has taken several regulatory steps to prevent the unmonitored and unauthorized usage of drones, there is scope for improvement incorporating the evolving techno-legal landscape and requirements of the nascent drone industry. By qualitatively analyzing secondary data, this study explores the dual-use nature of drone technology. The study looks at the technical and legal problems caused by drones. It also examines India's current drone laws and ends with suggestions for improvements.

2. LITERATURE REVIEW

2.1 Purpose & Methodology of Review

Considering the recency of the topic, the definitions, enabling technologies, and airspace classifications are constantly changing (Ariante & Del Core, 2025). A literature review is conducted to understand the current drone research from a regulatory and policy perspective. Search queries are conducted on Scopus, Web of Science, Dimenions.AI, and Google Scholar from 2016 to 2025. A content analysis is conducted with two reasons in mind. Firstly, the topic is emerging as Governments are proposing legislation to control the usage of drones. Secondly, content analysis helps incorporate public and practical perspectives based on policy documents, legal rulings, and grey literature, including print and digital media reports, newspapers, and blogs. Figure 1 shows an increasing number of publications on "drone regulations."

Figure 1. Increasing publications on "drone regulations."

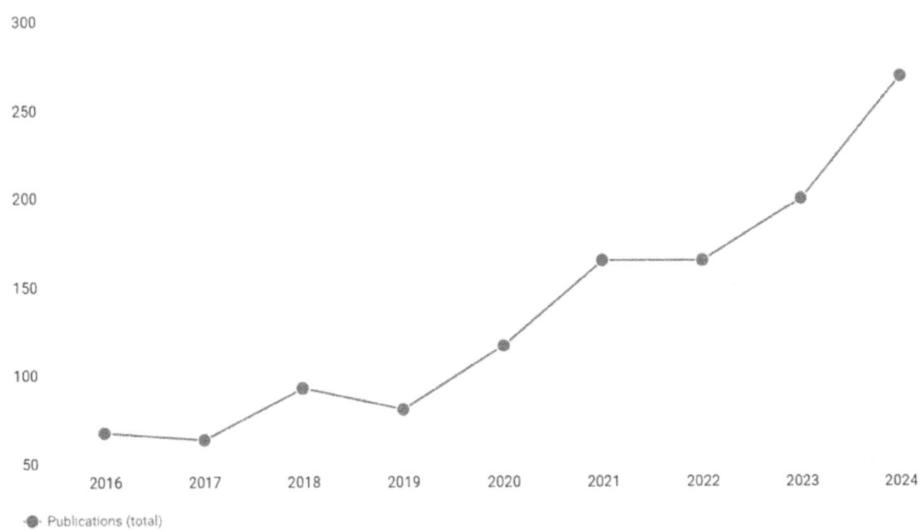

Source: Dimensions.ai; Period: 2016 to 2024

2.2 Research Themes

Key themes that emerged from the literature review are as follows:

1. **Regulatory Development**: This theme includes national policies, international frameworks, and enforcement mechanisms.
2. **Legal and Ethical Considerations**: This theme includes liability, AI integration, and cross-border operations.
3. **Social Perception and Privacy**: These include public acceptance, equity in tech access, and surveillance concerns.

Table 1 presents an extended list of research themes and briefly describes each.

Table 1. Research Themes on Drone and their Regulations and Policies

Research Theme	Scope of the theme
Drone Regulations and Policy Development	• Understanding the current state of drone regulations and policies • Development of a new Drone policy • Enforcement mechanisms and compliance monitoring of drone regulations • Evolving regulatory frameworks and their compliance
Legal and Ethical Implications	• Research into the legal and ethical questions that arise with increased levels of drone autonomy • It questions the liability arising from using technologies like AI within drones.
Cross-Border Drone Operations and International Regulations	• Focus on international regulations and agreements for drones crossing national boundaries. • Challenges in aligning drone regulations at local, national, and international levels. • Harmonization of international drone regulations to promote interoperability and reduce regulatory barriers.
Public Perception and Social Acceptance	• Understanding public/societal attitudes toward drones and their influence on policymaking. • Acceptance of drone technology and regulations. • Community resistance to drone operations (e.g., Amazon Prime Air trials). • Ensuring equitable access to drone technology in rural/urban areas.
Privacy and Data Protection	• Exploring how drone usage impacts individual privacy and the measures needed to safeguard data. • Regulatory responses to surveillance risks posed by drones collecting personal or sensitive data. • Legal implications of drone-collected data (GDPR, CCPA compliance). • Balancing public safety with individual privacy rights.

Data Source: Author compilation from Literature Review

2.3 Research Gap

This literature review identifies a knowledge gap on the topic. The study synthesizes fragmented information on India's evolving drone regulations, technological advancements, and societal impacts into a cohesive analysis. While existing literature covers drone applications and policies separately, this study:

- Integrates techno-legal challenges (e.g., privacy, BVLOS operations, urban air mobility) with India's regulatory response (Drone Rules 2021, UTM Policy).
- Identifies inconsistencies in current policies (e.g., undefined "recreational activities," lack of mandatory safety features) that prior studies may not have systematically critiqued.

3. DRONES: SOARING HIGH, REACHING FAR

3.1 History and Definitions

Drones are closely related to another popular term – 'Unmanned Aerial Vehicles' (UAVs). They are a sort of low-altitude flight. UAVs are aircraft that operate without a human pilot onboard. Strictly speaking, all UAVs are drones, but not all are UAVs. A drone can be operated remotely by a person or programmed to operate autonomously through communication technology, such as the Global Positioning System (GPS), onboard processor (computer), and sensors (Chavekar et al., 2023). So, the European Union (EU) definition of a drone is binary: a drone is either fully autonomous. This dichotomous approach oversimplifies reality and ignores graduated levels of autonomy (Nawaz, 2024). Drones have decent-resolution cameras to capture video and images of remote locations. They vary widely in size, capability, and usage, ranging from hobbyists to utility drones.

The history of drone technology traces back to flying kites and balloons (Franke, 2017; Morton, 2016) and using them as weaponry mode or an eye in the sky in warfare. In World War II, the U.S. Army and Air Forces converted the B-17 and B-24 bombers into remotely piloted aircraft (RPA) and loaded them with explosives (Kreps & Zenko, 2014). Now, drones are used not only in defense and surveillance but also in the civilian sector application. The credit for such wide application goes to technological advancement, making drones more compact, easy, and affordable.

3.2 Market Growth and Economics

Globally, the drone market was $14.1 billion in 2018 and grew at a 20.5% CAGR to $43.1 billion in 2024. Asia, North America, and European markets are the most significant users of drones. As of 2020, the Indian drone market was worth Rs. 2,900 crores. By 2025, the market will grow by a CAGR of 80% to reach Rs. 81,600 crores. The market size is expected to grow at a CAGR of 35% to reach Rs. 2,48,000 crores by 2030. Defence, Commercial, Counter-UAS, Homeland Security (HLS), and Exports are key sectors that use drones. The key industries by value of business services and labor for drones are infrastructure, agriculture, transport, security, media and entertainment, insurance, telecom, and mining.

3.3 Applications by Sectors

Logistics service providers (LSPs) include courier, cargo, and e-commerce companies. Drones deliver parcels and packages over long distances, avoid road traffic, and provide last-mile coverage (Niu et al., 2024). Giants like Amazon have tested drones as a viable option for delivering parcels. In July 2024, Desk to Desk Courier and Cargo (DTDC) and Sky Air Mobility entered into a partnership and launched drone-based delivery services. On their first attempt, DTDC was able to deliver, covering a distance of 7.5 km in mere 3 to 4 minutes. After tasting initial success in Gurugram, leading courier companies such as DTDC strategized clear plans to expand their drone delivery services to other locations following the success (The Hindu Bureau, 2024). The higher operational cost through scale operations can reduce prices and further increase competition in the industry. Also, LPSs are generally sensitive to government policies. There is also a need to amend logistic and shipping laws to accommodate drones as a legal and new mode of transportation for LSPs (Niu et al., 2024).

Drones have become a cheap and effective alternative for gathering data from inaccessible places. So, they can become an integral part of Remote Sensing kits, especially in Geophysics. In this, drones are used for modeling, risk assessment, monitoring, and damage assessment, amongst others (Quamar et al., 2023). Governments across the world use drones for aerial surveillance. Netra, an autonomous and lightweight Unmanned Aerial Vehicle (UAV), is used by the Indian Armed Forces for reconnaissance (PTI, 2010). Drones are used in forensic sciences to conduct search and rescue and surveillance operations, track suspects, gather evidence, and perform routine patrols. Drones have undoubtedly made the work of law enforcement agencies much more efficient and more manageable. The New York Police Department has used drones for crime scene documentation with positive results (Bhuiyan, 2024). Delhi Police also made headlines for utilizing drones for crime scene mapping, evidence collection, and suspect tracking to solve a double murder case (TNN, 2020). Drones are also becoming popular tools for governments to locate and deliver food and essential medical supplies to disaster-affected people.

3.4 Case Studies and Indian Examples

Drones are used in the Panna Tiger Reserve to track animal movement, map their habitats, and locate the growth of invasive alien species (Sudhi, 2017). To accelerate reforestation, the Telangana Government launched India's first seeding campaign, "Hara Bhara," where seed copters were used to plant seeds (Telangana Today, 2021). Drones can revolutionize the stagnating Indian agriculture sector by cutting costs and improving efficiency through precision spraying of herbicides, pesticides, and insecticides, as well as tracking the health of soil and crops and field mapping. These developments show how drones are helping prominent sectors of society. They have proved beneficial not only for the agricultural sector, making it more sustainable where drones are used for monitoring crops (Arza-García & Burgess, 2022) but also for several other sectors like investigation, where drones are used to collect evidence and conduct surveillance (Almusayli et al., 2024). Dones redefined how construction projects are designed, executed, and maintained (Hammad et al., 2021). Similarly, healthcare drones help with timely medicines (Stierlin et al., 2024) without pharmacists, especially when the patient is in a remote location, such as a rural area or island (Miyata et al., 2025). Similarly, the media is using it for aerial photography and for covering events (Garg et al., 2023).

In 2022, Indian Prime Minister Narendra Modi announced that India would become a Drone Hub by 2030 and launched 150 remote pilot certificates at the Drone Festival christened *Bharat Drone Mahotsav* in New Delhi, India. The two-day festival attracted 1600 delegates (Paliwal, 2022). In September 2024, the Government announced affordable Drone Taxis at the Asia Pacific Ministerial Conference. Once they turn into a reality, they have the potential to improve urban travel (Sinha, 2024).

4. SOARING HIGH, FALLING SHORT

4.1 Privacy and Surveillance Concerns

Drones fly at low frequency, have high payload capacity, and can be equipped with high-resolution multi-spectral cameras and super-sensitive sensors. These characteristics make them a robust platform for multiple applications. The drone sector grew rapidly during the COVID-19 pandemic (Martins et al., 2021). However, the drone ecosystem is still in its preliminary stage of development in the civil and commercial environment, considering the risk associated with its use. Countries are still evaluating the implementation of integrated laws on the use of drones (Almazrouei & Ibrahim, 2025). Public concerns about the growing use and demand for drones have not been addressed adequately. Whether or not the operation of the Drone advances society is highly dependent on the intention with which the drone operator is operating the Drone and on the proper adherence to the regulations. Stringent regulations are necessary to ensure the safety and security of the people. Further, education programs should be implemented to improve information dissemination methods to access relevant regulatory information owing to low public awareness of this topic (Gelirli & Tangül, 2025).

Drones are equipped with cameras even when not directed to capture images. They are prone to capturing data for their navigation. Drones fly at such heights and are sometimes so small that they become invisible to the naked eye (ITF, 2021). Thus, they can collect and use information without the awareness of the people in the vicinity. Even if appropriate regulations prevent this, the possibility of hacking leading to the distribution of sensitive information cannot be ignored. Shortly, when the sky is full of drones, their permanent presence could wear away the current understanding of privacy (Kellermann et al., 2020). Infringement of privacy via drones is more concerning for females. Recording personal photos and videos threatens the Right to Privacy and restricts personal liberty. The captured material could be used for extortion and blackmailing. In 2018, a drone was used to illegally surveil the property of Mr. Todd Maxon in Michigan over a zoning dispute without a warrant (Reuters, 2024). The case caught the attention of the media and caused a legal dispute. Several countries began reporting the use of drones for criminal and illegal purposes, calling for legislation about it (Almazrouei & Ibrahim, 2025).

Drones can be misused when they can be used to harass children, residents, and staff by breaching their privacy. For example, the recording of student sessions at Eliada Children's Home in Asheville, North Carolina, was well discussed (Barrows, 2022). Thieves used drones to surveil farmer storage and stole 50 bags of onion (Sanas, 2024). Drones are highly prone to being used by the media to stalk celebrities. It would be almost impossible to stop a drone from doing that as it has high maneuverability and quick responses to recent technological advances. Even if its presence is known, it would be tough to confront the operator immediately as the drones are operated remotely. The Supreme Court of India has included the Right to Privacy under Article 21 of the Indian Constitution in the K.S. Puttaswamy vs Union of India. The case increased the importance of enforcing adequate regulations (The Hindu Net Desk, 2017).

While privacy and surveillance remain critical concerns, the increasing number of drones in shared airspace also introduces a new set of challenges. Many of these challenges are related to safety and air traffic management.

4.2 Airspace and Safety Issues

Accelerated drone use will lead to millions flying in the skies daily. In the USA, Amazon CEO Jeff Bezos is already discussing having a drone to deliver parcels within 30 minutes (Simpson, 2023). The same might happen in other countries in the near to medium future. Increased air traffic due to drones will make the management of airspace complicated. Multiple flight delays and diversions occurred due to multiple drone sightings at Dublin Airport (Gowran, 2023). Due to Drone sightings for 3 to 4 hours at Amritsar Airport, flight services were affected (TOI News Desk, 2024). It will be challenging to differentiate between the public and private space boundaries (Raghunatha et al., 2023). The GIS mapping of airspace is technically cumbersome and is bound to take time for implementation. At the same time, drones are increasingly becoming part of urban air mobility.

Social acceptance of drone trust in institutions that deploy drones differs across stakeholders (Wang et al., 2025). The risk of accidents will increase. In Australia, a Drone crashed on a man, causing a head injury in a photograph competition (Forrest, 2018). The Australian Civil Aviation Safety Authority is an early mover calling for drone regulations (Zenz, 2023). During a life concert in Chennai, India, a Bollywood singer, Benny Dayal, got injured when a drone hit the back of his head (Sharma, 2023). These incidents make the public averse and bring in resistance to drones. So, there is a need to bring in public education and awareness to boost understanding and acceptance (Gelirli & Tangül, 2025). So, there is a need to call for inclusive governance strategies considering all stakeholders. Further, it should be accepted that the challenges are interconnected and require collaborative solutions (Wang et al., 2025).

Beyond airspace management and safety, the potential misuse of drones for criminal activities and security threats further complicates the regulatory landscape.

4.3 Criminal and Safety Risks

Drones are prone to be used for smuggling drugs, tobacco, prohibited goods, weapons, and phones, amongst others, for criminal and terrorist purposes. In Columbia, seven security guards of maximum security Tramacúa prison in Valledupar were caught selling illicit goods, including cell phones, into the jail (Crumley, 2021). In the UK, too, drones were found to be used to smuggle money, cigarettes, drugs, blades, guns, and cell phones to inmates. Further, there is the perceptible threat of usage of suicide drones because of their remote operability, cheapness, and high effectiveness. Further, there are cyber security issues (Dolata & Schwabe, 2023), like hacking, spoofing, malware, and virus threats in information shared by drones (Omolara et al., 2023). Drones can also target sensitive infrastructure of critical national importance, such as power grid systems. A stranger attacked the residence of the Irani prime minister in Baghdad with an explosive-filled drone (Zahra, 2021). In Sweden, drones were used to surveil sensitive government buildings and nuclear power plants. It is frequent to find drones smuggling contraband across sensitive borders like USA-Mexico and India-Pakistan. Five significant recoveries took place in 2022 carrying narcotic substances in Punjab (ANI, 2023), and 181 drones were seized in 2024 concerning smuggling drugs (Bajwa, 2024). Drones also monitor police movement and activity to smuggle drugs safely (Mohammad, 2024). In Jammu and Kashmir's Rajouri district, security forces seized a pistol, two magazines, and some bullets dropped by a Drone near the Line of Control (Majid, 2024). Using drones in forensic sciences may lead to the risk of extensive and haphazard data collection and processing (Somayajula, 2021). Law enforcement agencies must use drones responsibly and strictly adhere to regulations (Rao, 2023).

Drones provide access to goods for last-minute delivery and transporting passengers while decreasing traffic congestion in urban areas. It will also create semi and high-skill jobs in the manufacturing, operation, repair, service, and overhaul sectors. At the same time, logistics operators and last-mile delivery persons might lose jobs to drones (László, 2024). The drone taxi and delivery services may be costlier for the general public to afford, which may lead to less social acceptance, and there is a possibility of social injustice as a new form of privileged class mobility (ITF, 2021).

Considering the criminal and safety risks being posed, it becomes evident that existing laws and policies may not be fully equipped to address emerging challenges. This highlights the need to examine regulatory loopholes.

4.4 Regulatory Loopholes

Drone surveillance intersects well with digital rights and data privacy, primarily when drones are used to collect biometric or location data without consent. Research shows that the public is more worried about privacy than safety or noise with drones (Komasová, 2024). While the Supreme Court of India recognizes the Right to Privacy as a fundamental right under Article 21, there is a lack of enforceable technical or regulatory safeguards in current drone operations to uphold these rights. The Personal Data Protection Act of 2023 has not established binding obligations on drone operators. This regulatory gap becomes particularly significant as drone technology advances further. For example, future drones would have sophisticated data collection methods that outpace the development of corresponding legal protections. As a result, individuals and organizations face uncertainty regarding accountability, redress mechanisms, and the permissible scope of drone-based surveillance without clear, enforceable standards.

Alongside these regulatory gaps, it is equally important to consider the unintended environmental and wildlife impacts resulting from widespread drone adoption.

4.5 Environmental and Wildlife Impact

The negative impact of drones on the environment cannot be neglected. Accelerated drone use will lead to an adverse effect on wildlife, increasing noise pollution and air pollution as the majority of drones are electric-powered. Also, it will not be easy to differentiate between the public and private space boundaries (Raghunatha et al., 2023). Drone accidents can release harmful pollutants into the Air. Noise pollution caused by the operations of drones will impact avian wildlife. Their fly paths might interrupt the daily and seasonal migratory routes of birds. These disruptions highlight the need for comprehensive environmental assessments before large-scale drone deployment. These are particularly required in ecologically sensitive regions. Furthermore, current regulatory frameworks often lack specific provisions addressing the cumulative ecological consequences of widespread drone operations, underscoring the urgency for targeted environmental guidelines and monitoring mechanisms.

These environmental consequences and other emerging issues underscore the necessity for a comprehensive techno-legal framework to govern drone operations effectively.

5. TECHNO-LEGAL LANDSCAPE

Policy and regulations are a well-studied theme in academic research circles on drones. However, considering the technological updates and newer challenges, the study is mainly ongoing and work-in-progress (Ariante & Del Core, 2025). There has been a rapid rise in the usage of Drones by Indian security and law enforcement forces since 2019, owing to a significant rise in diverse threats from drone misuse by non-state actors. Since then, researchers have highlighted challenges in effectively countering drones, especially in border areas (A. Kumar & Vishwanathan, 2025). With the rapid growth of the drone industry in India, the market size is projected to increase to approximately 2,95,000 crores by 2030 (PIB, 2023). Drone technology presently consists of three main elements, i.e., the Drone's central processing unit (CPU), which is known as the flight controller, ground control station (GCS), and wireless links to control information flow. Drone controllers are categorized into visual line-of-sight (VLOS) and beyond visual line-of-sight operations (BVLOS) based on their distance from GCS. Drones are classified into various categories based on their flight range, wing type, endurance weight, and wing load. Some of the popular drone types are multirotor drones, fixed-wing drones, and hybrid-wing drones. Various drones now have crash and collision avoidance systems, which only work with low-power radio-frequency transmitters. Drones also have onboard batteries, communication, and navigation systems (Yaacoub et al., 2020).

In order to successfully regulate drones, the regulations must balance the ethical and legal challenges associated with drone use while allowing such a level of flexibility that it helps in the growth of the drone ecosystem. As drones are an innovation from just a few years ago and are still in development, pre-independence legislation like the Aircraft Act of 1934 and Aircraft Rules of 1937 do not recognize drones separately. Therefore, a mature legal framework was necessary for the drone sector. Researchers have discussed the Indian Drone Policy and Regulatory stand (Rajagopalan & Krishna, 2019).

Artificial Intelligence (AI) is a significant technology that empowers other technologies to offer superior performance and capabilities. AI helps in the navigation system of various autonomous vehicles, autonomous weapons, autonomous ships, drones, UAVs, robots, and other low-altitude flights (Nawaz, 2024; Yaacoub et al., 2020). AI-powered navigation, obstacle avoidance, and swarm coordination/intelligence increasingly power drones to rely on autonomous decision-making systems. This raises urgent legal questions about liability, accountability, and compliance when AI malfunctions lead to harm. Existing Indian regulations, such as the Drone Rules 2021, remain silent on AI-specific safeguards, creating a regulatory void that must be urgently addressed. The lack of AI-specific safeguards in current regulations, such as liability frameworks for algorithmic failures, creates a void of governance (Gaurav et al., 2025). Future drone policies must address these gaps to align with global ethical AI and digital rights debates (Christy et al., 2024). For example, intelligent drones' safety, ethics, and regulation aspects require careful study when used with industrial robotics and AI (Gaurav et al., 2025).

5.1 Cross-Border Drone Operations & International Law

As drones increasingly operate across borders—for surveillance, logistics, and even warfare—the absence of harmonized international drone laws presents a challenge. The lack of mutual recognition of drone certifications and inconsistent privacy laws hinder global governance efforts. The study highlights the need for treaties addressing AI-enabled UAVs, data jurisdiction, and international airspace sovereignty. The absence of harmonized international drone laws mirrors broader challenges in governing digital technologies across borders. This study highlights similar tensions in blockchain and AI governance, advocating for treaties that reconcile sovereignty with interoperability—a model drone regulations could adopt.

5.2 Indian Done Policy & Regulatory Perspective

In 2014, the Directorate General of Civil Aviation (DGCA) banned the civilian use of drones due to safety and security concerns. DGCA also announced that it would be illegal to use drones until proper rules and regulations are formulated (IndiaToday.in, 2014). This was a response to the increased use of drones by e-commerce industries like Amazon and Francesco's Pizzeria, a pizza delivery service based in Mumbai (Gupta, 2014).

The growing demand for drones and advancement in drone technology made it necessary for the DGCA to regulate drones (PIB, 2023). In 2016, DGCA issued draft guidelines regulating the civil use of drones (PTI, 2016). Finally, in August 2018, DGCA issued the Civil Aviation Requirements (CAR 1.0) for remotely piloted aircraft system (RPAS) and their operations to be enabled through the Digital Sky Platform (DSP) (PTI, 2018). However, CAR 1.0 was restrictive for new entrants and was not elaborate enough to deal with the matters related to national security. Leading to this, the Ministry of Civil Aviation issued Unmanned Aircraft System Rules (UAS Rules) in 2021 after receiving recommendations from stakeholders. However, they were more or less the same or even more restrictive than CAR 1.0 (PSL, 2021).

On August 25, 2021, the Indian Ministry of Civil Aviation published liberalized Drone Rules, 2021, replacing the UAS rules, 2021 vide gazette notification. Under the Drone Rules 2021, several licenses, forms, and fees were eliminated, and the registration and certification process was simplified (Mukul, 2021). Later in September, the Indian Government notified the Production-Linked Incentive (PLI)

The scheme for developing the drone ecosystem via which a total amount of INR 120 crore (roughly $16 million) has been sanctioned for drones and drone components spread over 3 Financial Years with an incentive rate of 20% (PIB, 2021). The Directorate General of Civil Aviation (DGCA) is the regulatory authority in India that is responsible for administering drone operations. Under Rule 4 and Rule 5 of Drone Rules 2021, drones are categorized and classified based on their weight and use. The Unmanned aircraft system is categorized into Aeroplane, Rotorcraft, and Hybrid Unmanned Aircraft Systems, and these three are further sub-categorized into Remotely Piloted Aircraft Systems, Model Remotely Piloted Aircraft Systems, and Autonomous and Aircraft Systems. Based on the weight, the Unmanned Aircraft Systems have been classified into five categories mainly (Unit, 2022):

1. Nano Unmanned Aircraft Systems weighing less than or equal to 250 grams

2. Micro Unmanned Aircraft Systems weighing more than 250 grams but less than or equal to 2 kilograms
3. Small Unmanned Aircraft Systems weighing more than 2 kilograms but less than or equal to 25 kilograms
4. Medium Unmanned Aircraft System weighing more than 25 kilograms but less than or equal to 150 kilograms and,
5. Large Unmanned Aircraft Systems weighing more than 150 kilograms.

The Drone Rules 2021 apply only to Unmanned Aircraft Systems with a maximum all-up weight of not more than 500 kg. For the UAS exceeding 500 kg, aircraft rules, 1937 Aircraft Rules, 1937 will be applicable. Additionally, these rules do not apply to the UAS belonging to or used by Naval, Military, Or Air Forces of the Union of India (Desai, 2023). Further, Part III and Part IV of Drone Rules 2021 provide about drones' certification and registration process. The primary requirements for a Drone are Type Certification and a Unique Identification Number (UIN). However, the rules state that no Type Certification is required to operate an Unmanned Aircraft or Model Remotely Piloted Aircraft System. All the applications, registration, and certifications will be made on the Digital Sky Platform, the one-stop platform for all drone services (DigiLaw, 2021). The U.S. has the Defense Innovation Unit's (DIU) Blue Small UAS (sUAS) initiative, which includes the generation of IDs for drones. However, it is clarified that Blue-listed drones are not necessarily technologically superior and that they are not the only option for DoD or U.S. government procurement. So, it highlighted that the list's military suitability does not guarantee optimal use for civilian infrastructure tasks (Salinas & Lewandowski, 2024).

Rules 14 and 15 of The Drone Rules 2021 state that the drones must be registered on the Digital Sky Platform form. The Digital Sky Platform issues a Unique Identification Number (UIN), which shall be linked to the Unique Serial Number provided by the manufacturer. According to Rules, the import of drones will be regulated by the Directorate General of Foreign Trade (DGFT). The Type Certificate shall be issued within 75 days from the application submission date according to Rule 9 (Dhankhar, 2024). The airspace under the Rules was segregated into three zones, i.e., red, yellow, and green, within 30 days of the notification of the rules (Srivastava, 2023). The classification is shown in Figure 2.

Figure 2. Classification of Airspace Map

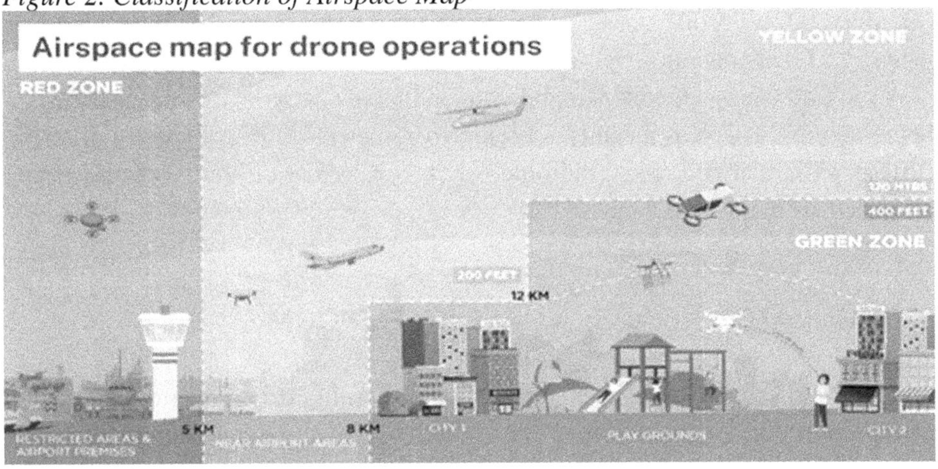

Source: (Srivastava, 2021)

According to the Rules, no approval is required to operate a Drone in a Green Zone, but prior permission is required to operate a UAS in a Red or Yellow Zone. If there is an urgent need, the Central Government may declare a specific area a red zone for ninety-six hours by notifying it through the Digital Sky platform (Rule 24, The Drone Rules, 2021). Rules 26 to 28 of Drone Rules 2021 provide that drone operation should not be done in any manner that can jeopardize the safety and security of a person. No person shall carry arms, ammunition, or dangerous goods in any UAS, respectively (Krishna et al., 2021).

In case of any accident, the Drone operator must mandatorily report it to the directorate General through the Digital Sky platform within forty-eight hours of such an event. The Drone Rules 2021 exempted obtaining the remote pilot license for operating Nano UAS and micro UAS for non-commercial purposes (Banerji, 2021). Rule 12 of the Drone Rules 2021 specifies safety features like No Permission - No Take-off, Geo-Fencing, and real-time tracking Bacon, but such features are not mandatory. Rule 44 provides that in the case of insurance coverage, the provisions of the Motor Vehicles Act, 1988 shall apply mutatis mutandis to Third-party Insurance of UAS. However, a Nano drone may operate without Third-party Insurance. The Rules provide that any contravention of Rule 22, which permits flying Drones in the red zone and yellow zone with prior permission only, and Rule 27, which states that no person shall carry any arms, amongst others, on UAS shell be a cognizable and non-compoundable offense (Majmudar & Partners, 2021).

Following the notification of these rules, the Unmanned Aircraft System Traffic Management (UTM) Policy was published in 2022. In February 2022, Drone (Amendment) Rules 2022 were notified for the amending Drone Rules 2021, whereby the word "Remote Pilot License" was replaced with a "Remote Pilot Certificate" (Indulia, 2022). Further, in 2023, Drone (Amendment) Rules 2023 were notified wherein a Drone operator was allowed to submit a driver's license, voter ID card, or ration card in case of non-availability of an Indian passport (Upadhyay, 2023). In September 2024, DGCA recently notified two frameworks, the Aircraft Engineering Advisory Circular and the Aerodrome Advisory Circular on Vertiports, regarding advanced air mobility (Chopra, 2024).

6. REGULATORY GAPS: A CALL TO REFORM

There are several challenges and issues concerning drone operations and the regulatory framework related to drone use in India. In a two-day National Security Strategies Conference, the Union Home Minister emphasized strengthening the architecture and monitoring Rouge Drones (TNN, 2024). Recently, the Ministry of Defense stressed the importance of following drone regulations and stated that ignorance of rules is a significant concern after an individual is found flying a drone in a No-Drone Zone (C. Kumar, 2024). Several incidents have taken place on the National and International levels, proving that there is a need for stringent regulation regarding regulating Drone use.

Countries are trying to build effective regulatory frameworks that boost the drone ecosystem and reduce the issues and challenges associated with drones (Siddiqui & Muniza, 2025). Liberalized Drone Rules of 2021 lay the strong base for regulating Drone operations and building the UAS ecosystem. However, there is scope for improvement, especially in addressing the challenges of evolving technology. Though the Drone Rules 2021 have demarcated the air space into three zones, i.e., the Red Zone, Yellow Zone, and Green Zone, the Drone Highways are yet to be established. Drone Rules, 2021 states that every person owning a drone shall adopt safety features, which the Central Government shall notify within six months of the publication of the rules. However, such safety features as Geo fencing and NPNT (No Permission - No Take-off) are yet to be made mandatory as the rules have not made it obligatory. There is only a time frame for notifying such safety features, which is 6 months, as mentioned, but there is no time frame for implementing these safety features. The features of prime importance are the safety and security features concerning both human-crewed and uncrewed aerial vehicles.

The rules do not define drones' autonomous operation, making it unclear whether any licenses are required for autonomous drone operations. The Unmanned Aircraft Rules of 2021 require the manufacturer to comply with an authorization procedure before commencing R&D operation. However, the new Drone Rules of 2021 state that any Drone manufacturer can conduct R&D operations without having a Type

Certificate, Unique Identification Number, or any prior permission except that the manufacturer must have a GST Identification Number. No limit has been placed on the Drone's size for R&D purposes, and the rules are also silent about the safety measures to be taken concerning R&D operations (Desai, 2023).

The Drone Rules neither have express restrictions nor give permission for beyond visual line of sight (BVLOS) operations except for a Model Remotely Piloted Aircraft Systems. Therefore, drone regulations regarding Beyond Visual Line of Sight (BVLOS) Operations must be updated, including adequate traffic management landing and specifications (Raghunatha et al., 2023). Further, Model Remotely Piloted Aircraft Systems weighing up to 25 kg are exempted from the Type Certificate requirement and can operate without any restriction in Green Zone. This leads to a possibility that these can be used for unlawful purposes as the term recreational activities is not defined in the rules.

Despite the multiple benefits of drones in forensic science, several issues still need to be addressed. Drone data must be utilized responsibly by the investigators while considering all the ethical considerations relating to data and ensuring that the data is not shared with a third party without compliance with the law. On the other hand, there are several issues on the technical point with Drone use in forensic science, such as the lack of specialized hardware, software, knowledge, and expertise with the investigating agencies and investigators (Almusayli et al., 2024). Another risk that needs to be addressed is the misuse of drone technology by law enforcement agencies in the name of surveillance. The question is whether judicial authorities need search warrants to use a drone for investigation (McNeal et al., 2017).

The Drone Rules of 2021 impose penalties on the offender that are less severe than those outlined in the previous Unmanned Aircraft Rules, 2021. This leads to an apprehension that the Rules might not be an effective deterrent. For, in the case of Venkatesh vs. State, the Madras High Court reviewed a Criminal Revision Case on February 15, 2023. It ruled in favor of Venkatesh, who sought the return of his seized properties, including a remote control, a drone pad, and a digital camera confiscated by police concerning a drone flying over the High Court campus. The petitioner argued that he was not accused and had not used the Drone for illegal activities. The court found that no photograph was taken, and no memory card was recovered. It ordered the return of the properties under conditions of ownership proof and a commitment to refrain from illegal use.

Further, the regulations governing drones provide that any accidents or incidents involving drones must be reported to the Directorate General of Civil Aviation (DGCA) through the Digital Sky Platform. Additionally, such incidents are also communicated to local law enforcement authorities, which may result in the commencement of parallel investigations. The carriage of dangerous goods is prohibited under the Drone Rules, 2021. However, any harmless object carried by a drone or the Drone itself can also endanger or cause injury to any person in case of crash or technology failure. For example, a delivery drone carrying a frozen chicken in Gurugram Sector 50 crashed on the TV antenna of a house, breaking a part of the wall. This Drone crashed near the park where the children often play, which is only at a 10 M distance from the house where delivery has to take place (Dhankhar, 2024).

Furthermore, the definition of an accident under the rules does not include any incident involving property damage (Desai, 2023). The safety investigation procedures provided in the Aircraft (Investigation of Accidents and Incidents) Rules, 2017, can be used as a baseline to formulate the rules concerning accidents via drones in India under the Drone Rules, 2021 (Verma et al., 2022). Drones can be fitted with explosives and can carry deadly chemicals, which is a significant safety and security concern. Flying a Drone over someone's property may lead to trespass and nuisance like discomfort, damage to land, and unauthorized surveillance. The biggest concern with drone operations is privacy violations or surveillance. Drones fly at a low altitude and can potentially collect data that can violate personal privacy and lead to cyber-attacks (Panday, 2017). The Personal Data Protection Act of 2023 is a new legislation with few issues and has yet to prove its efficacy. Drone Rules, 2021, are silent regarding privacy safeguards (S. D. Gupta, 2014).

Concerning drone delivery and drone taxis, proper attention to elements of technology, urban planning, infrastructure, and regulations regulating security and safety issues are much needed. The local authorities are inadequately prepared for the upcoming challenges related to urban air mobility, and the regulations are unclear. The Drone regulations must be an essential catalyst in improving State preparedness and Industry readiness. There are significant concerns about the Government's ability to track who is operating a drone, especially if the Drone is destroyed and cannot be identified (like in the case of suicide drones). This becomes a serious problem when drones carry explosives or dangerous chemicals.

Another issue is a regulatory tussle over who will be responsible for laying down safety standards between manufacturers, operators, and government bodies. The industry would want autonomous and representative industrial federations to recommend safety standards to ensure their liberal character. In contrast, the Government would not want to relax them to minimize accidental harm to life, property, and the environment. Researchers believe that safety aspects are relatively accepted, so it is time to shift focus to other aspects (Komasová, 2024).

7. FUTURE RESEARCH DIRECTIONS

Drone detection is a key challenge and emerging topic. Traditional methods involve audio and vision-based sensing. Technology is progressing to make drone detection more sophisticated, even when drones operate in different environments, drone models, and distances (Jana et al., 2025). Considering that global trends are towards smart cities where drones will be increasingly used, technological progress should focus on integrating geospatial technologies. The inputs from drones can be used in urban planning and administration with smart city integration, such as GIS mapping and airspace management (Manda et al., 2024).

Drones and UAV technologies can benefit from the technological integration of Artificial Intelligence (AI), Machine Learning (ML), and Deep Learning (DL). The convergence of AI and Drone technologies will demand an adaptive legal framework to address algorithmic bias, data protection, and explainability in autonomous decisions. Regulatory sandboxes and real-time audit mechanisms must be developed to ensure legal compliance without stifling innovation. India's ambition to become a Drone Hub by 2030 hinges on its ability to lead in AI-integrated legal governance.

Advanced AI can bring in self-piloting, real-time decision-making, and swarm intelligence. This technology pack can offer object detection, navigation, and obstacle avoidance, improving safety and efficiency. Extensive customization with enterprise-ready tailored solutions with global security standards is expected. Because of progress in hardware technology, drones will have maximized efficiency, superior accuracy, cost optimization, and provide deeper insights. New generation drones have multiple data capture points, follow a lean deployment model, have higher data accuracy (sub 10 cm accuracy, high resolution of 2 to 5 cm per pixel with near real-time updates), and provide advanced data analytics. U.S. (53%) and China (18%) dominate the manufacturing landscape (Salinas & Lewandowski, 2024). However, countries like India have taken up initiatives like Make-in-India that make procuring drone-related hardware easier. Collecting faster and more accurate data through drones will become relatively more straightforward. With relatively lower cost of ownership, managed fleet operations will grow at an unprecedented scale and frequency. Corporations will begin to build sector-specific data intelligence with decision-making and ideation happening on AI-enabled cloud analytics platforms. While all the reasons appear favorable, they bring in newer problems concerning ethics and regulatory issues considering the operation of drones and the capture, storage, and usage of data with them.

8. SUGGESTIONS

Suggestions for Regulatory Reforms: Further reforms in drone regulations are needed. A beginning can be made by modernizing the Aircraft Act 1934 for Beyond Visual Line of Sight (BVLOS) operations of drones, clearly defining "Recreational Activities," and giving explicit legal status to using drones in evidence gathering and crime scene documentation. Additionally, improvements are required in reporting and addressing grievances, implementing a better-unmanned traffic management system, establishing rules for air route scheduling (especially in densely populated areas), and introducing dynamic geofencing. Furthermore, the Aircraft (Investigation of Accidents and Incidents) Rules, 2017, can serve as a guide to include property damages due to drone accidents under the ambit of "Accidents" defined in the Drone Rules 2021—legal recognition of AI-driven drones as autonomous agents should be considered in future drone legislation. Regulatory reforms must mandate transparency in algorithmic decisions and require safety audits for machine learning models deployed in autonomous navigation systems. AI-specific certification mechanisms and liability attribution frameworks will be key to addressing emerging risks.

Suggestions for Institutional and Technological Improvements: The cooperation between Law Enforcement Authorities, Air Traffic Regulators, and DGCA must be institutionalized, with DGCA becoming the primary regulator. Modern practices in airspace allocation, route scheduling, and data protection and sharing standards are imperative. State preparedness for tracing the Drone's actual operator and managing urban airspace will be key to realizing the revolutionary potential of drone technology. There is also an impetus for technology developers to produce new-age "Sense and Avoid Capabilities" in drones to minimize accidents. Thus, a complete overhaul of the regulatory landscape concerning drone technology is essential, focusing on balancing innovation with responsibility.

9. CONCLUSION

Drones have emerged as a transformative technology with vast potential across industries, from agriculture and disaster management to defense and logistics. However, their rapid adoption has highlighted significant regulatory and ethical challenges, including privacy infringement, airspace management, and security risks. While India has taken progressive steps with the Drone Rules 2021, UTM Policy 2022, and other frameworks, gaps remain in addressing evolving technological advancements and operational complexities. Key areas requiring urgent attention include modernizing the Aircraft Act 1934 for BVLOS operations, strengthening privacy safeguards, improving urban air mobility regulations, and enhancing enforcement mechanisms. Additionally, fostering collaboration between regulators, law enforcement, and industry stakeholders is crucial to ensuring safe and responsible drone integration. Balancing innovation with accountability will be essential in harnessing the full potential of drone technology while mitigating its risks. A forward-looking, adaptive regulatory approach is necessary to position India as a global drone hub by 2030, as envisioned by the Government. The future of drones hinges on harmonizing technological progress with robust governance to create a sustainable and secure ecosystem.

REFERENCES

Almazrouei, & Ibrahim, A. (2025). Legislative Confrontation of Drone Crimes in the United Arab Emirates. *AAU Journal of Business and Law, 9*(1), 38. https://doi.org/DOI: 10.51958/AAUJBL2025V9I1P4

Almusayli, A., Zia, T., & Qazi, E.-H. (2024). Drone Forensics: An Innovative Approach to the Forensic Investigation of Drone Accidents Based on Digital Twin Technology. *Technologies*, *12*(1), 11. DOI: 10.3390/technologies12010011

ANI. (2023, December 12). 514 drone sightings since 2022, 121 brought down, says Punjab IGP. *Business Standard*. https://www.business-standard.com/india-news/514-drone-sightings-since-2022-121-brought-down-says-punjab-igp-123121200211_1.html

Ariante, G., & Del Core, G. (2025). Unmanned Aircraft Systems (UASs): Current State, Emerging Technologies, and Future Trends. *Drones (Basel)*, *9*(1), 59. DOI: 10.3390/drones9010059

Arza-García, M., & Burgess, A. J. (2022). Drones in the Sky: Towards a More Sustainable Agriculture. *Agriculture*, *13*(1), 84. DOI: 10.3390/agriculture13010084

Bajwa, H. (2024, October 30). BSF in Punjab intercepts 13 drones in a week, 181 drones seized in 2024 amid rising smuggling concerns. *The New Indian Express*. https://www.newindianexpress.com/nation/2024/Oct/30/bsf-in-punjab-intercepts-13-drones-in-a-week-181-drones-seized-in-2024-amid-rising-smuggling-concerns

Banerji, O. (2021, October 11). The Drone Rules, 2021:An Overview. *iPleaders*. https://blog.ipleaders.in/the-drone-rules-2021-an-overview/

Barrows. (2022, December 17). *It's not a joke or funny' Drone harassing children, staff & therapy horses at Eliada Home*. Abc13news. https://wlos.com/news/local/eliada-home-drone-harassing-harassment-west-asheville-western-north-carolina-children-staff-therapy-horses-nonprofit-organization-privacy-issues

Bhuiyan, J. (2024, November 14). New York City police will send drones to sites of reported robberies and gunshots. *The Guardian*. https://www.theguardian.com/technology/2024/nov/14/nypd-drones-police

Chavekar, A., Mulla, Y., Mane, S., Kumar, S., & Kazi, F. (2023). A Review of Drone Communication Protocols: Current Trends and Future Perspectives. *2023 IEEE International Carnahan Conference on Security Technology (ICCST)*, 1–6. https://doi.org/DOI: 10.1109/ICCST59048.2023.10726850

Chopra, A. (2024, September 27). *Air Taxis by 2026: How aviation will transform India's urban mobility*. Firstpost. https://www.firstpost.com/opinion/air-taxis-by-2026-how-aviation-will-transform-indias-urban-mobility-13819638.html

Christy, V., Manda, V. K., & M. L., G. (2024). Ethical Frameworks for Use in Artificial Intelligence Systems. In J. Gomathi Sankar & A. David (Eds.), *Advances in Computational Intelligence and Robotics* (pp. 122–154). IGI Global. https://doi.org/DOI: 10.4018/979-8-3693-8557-9.ch005

Crumley, B. (2021, December 20). Colombian prison guards use drones to fly contraband – and burgers – into their own jail. *DroneDJ*. https://dronedj.com/2021/12/20/colombian-prison-guards-use-drones-to-fly-contraband-and-burgers-into-their-own-jail/

De Oliveira, F. M. C., Bittencourt, L. F., Bianchi, R. A. C., & Kamienski, C. A. (2024). Drones in the Big City: Autonomous Collision Avoidance for Aerial Delivery Services. *IEEE Transactions on Intelligent Transportation Systems*, *25*(5), 4657–4674. DOI: 10.1109/TITS.2023.3329029

Desai, N. M. (2023, November). *The Global Drone Revolution*. Nishith Desai Associates. https://www.nishithdesai.com/fileadmin/user_upload/pdfs/Research_Papers/The_Global_Drone_Revolution.pdf

Dhankhar, L. (2024, February 17). *Drone delivering frozen chicken crashes at Gurugram*. Hindustan Times. https://www.hindustantimes.com/india-news/drone-delivering-frozen-chicken-crashes-at-gurugram-101708107559623.html

DigiLaw. (2021). *Regulatory Framework for Drones in India*. https://www.digilaw.in/public/research/Regulatory_Framework_for_Drones.pdf

Dolata, M., & Schwabe, G. (2023). Moving beyond privacy and airspace safety: Guidelines for just drones in policing. *Government Information Quarterly*, *40*(4), 101874. DOI: 10.1016/j.giq.2023.101874

Forrest, C. (2018, June 13). 17 drone disasters that show why the FAA hates drones. *TechRepublic*. https://www.techrepublic.com/article/12-drone-disasters-that-show-why-the-faa-hates-drones/

Franke, U. (2017, December 10). Looking Back to the Future: The Beginnings of Drones and Manned Aerial Warfare. *The Strategy Bridge*. https://thestrategybridge.org/the-bridge/2017/12/10/looking-back-to-the-future-the-beginnings-of-drones-and-manned-aerial-warfare

Garg, V., Niranjan, S., Prybutok, V., Pohlen, T., & Gligor, D. (2023). Drones in last-mile delivery: A systematic review on Efficiency, Accessibility, and Sustainability. *Transportation Research Part D, Transport and Environment*, *123*, 103831. DOI: 10.1016/j.trd.2023.103831

Gaurav, A., Gupta, B. B., Arya, V., & Castiglione, A. (2025). Safety, Ethics, and Regulation in Intelligent Drones. In Gupta, B. B., & Colace, F. (Eds.), (pp. 331–346). Advances in Computational Intelligence and Robotics. IGI Global., DOI: 10.4018/979-8-3693-2707-4.ch014

Gautam, T., & Johari, R. (2023). Drone: A Systematic Review of UAV Technologies. In S. Tanwar, S. T. Wierzchon, P. K. Singh, M. Ganzha, & G. Epiphaniou (Eds.), *Proceedings of Fourth International Conference on Computing, Communications, and Cyber-Security* (Vol. 664, pp. 147–158). Springer Nature Singapore. https://doi.org/DOI: 10.1007/978-981-99-1479-1_11

Gelirli, N., & Tangül, H. (2025). A Study on Analyzing the Level of Public Compliance with Drone Laws in Northern Cyprus. *Journal of Aviation*, *9*(1), 53–63. DOI: 10.30518/jav.1543124

Gowran, L. M. (2023, March 6). What's going on with Dublin Airport's drone disruptions? Silicon Republic. *Silicon Republic*. https://www.siliconrepublic.com/machines/dublin-airport-drones-flight-disruptions

Gupta, S. D. (2014, November 8). Drones for all. *Business Standard*. https://www.business-standard.com/article/specials/drones-for-all-114110700900_1.html

Hammad, A., Da Costa, B., Soares, C., & Haddad, A. (2021). The Use of Unmanned Aerial Vehicles for Dynamic Site Layout Planning in Large-Scale Construction Projects. *Buildings (Basel, Switzerland)*, *11*(12), 602. DOI: 10.3390/buildings11120602

IndiaToday.in. (2014, October 13). *Civilian drones banned in India: Report*. India Today. https://www.indiatoday.in/technology/news/story/civilian-drones-banned-in-india-report-222975-2014-10-13

Indulia, B. (2022). *Drone (Amendment) Rules, 2022*. SCC Online Times. https://www.scconline.com/blog/post/2022/02/15/drone-amendment-rules-2022/

ITF. (2021). *Ready for Take-Off? Integrating Drones into the Transport System*. OECD Publishing, Paris. https://www.itf-oecd.org/sites/default/files/docs/take-off-integrating-drones-transport-system.pdf

Jackman, A. (2023). 'Manning' the 'unmanned': Reapproaching the military Drone through learning the/to Drone. *Political Geography*, *104*, 102894. DOI: 10.1016/j.polgeo.2023.102894

Jana, S., Mishra, A. K., & Khan, M. Z. A. (2025). Opportunistic Drone Detection Using CommSense. *IEEE Transactions on Instrumentation and Measurement, 74*, 1–15. DOI: 10.1109/TIM.2025.3545200

Kellermann, R., Biehle, T., & Fischer, L. (2020). Drones for parcel and passenger transportation: A literature review. *Transportation Research Interdisciplinary Perspectives, 4*, 100088. DOI: 10.1016/j.trip.2019.100088

Komasová, S. (2024). Czech society and drones: Experience, norms, and concerns. *Drone Systems and Applications, 12*, 1–14. DOI: 10.1139/dsa-2023-0065

Kreps, S., & Zenko, M. (2014, February 12). The Next Drone Wars. *Foreign Affairs*. https://www.foreignaffairs.com/united-states/next-drone-wars

Krishna, R., Taneja, A., & Rastogi, A. (2021, September 25). *The Drone Rules, 2021: Summary And Key Takeaways—Aviation—Transport—India*. Mondaq. https://www.mondaq.com/india/aviation/1114708/the-drone-rules-2021-summary-and-key-takeaways

Kumar, A., & Vishwanathan, A. (2025). Use of drones in Indo-Pak cross border terrorism: Challenges, regulations and evolving responses. *Asian Politics & Policy, 17*(1), e70003. DOI: 10.1111/aspp.70003

Kumar, A. P. M., Rajesh, P., Kavitha, R., Thiyagarajan, R., & Yallappa, D. (2025). Drones Over Fields. In F. Daya J. L, S. G. Jasmine, & U. Kose, *Digital Farming and Smart Agriculture for Sustainable Future* (1st ed., pp. 206–221). Chapman and Hall/CRC. https://doi.org/DOI: 10.1201/9781003479154-14

Kumar, C. (2024, August 20). MoD urges strict adherence to drone flying rules amid rising popularity. *Times of India*. https://timesofindia.indiatimes.com/india/mod-urges-strict-adherence-to-drone-flying-rules-amid-rising-popularity/articleshow/112652323.cms

László, B. (2024, November 6). *How does drone transport affect the labour market and traditional supply chains?* Flyingcarsmarket.Com. https://flyingcarsmarket.com/how-does-drone-transport-affect-the-labour-market-and-traditional-supply-chains/

Li, R., & Wu, M. (2024). Revealing Urban Color Patterns via Drone Aerial Photography—A Case Study in Urban Hangzhou, China. *Buildings (Basel, Switzerland), 14*(2), 546. DOI: 10.3390/buildings14020546

Majid, Z. M. (2024, July 26). Army seizes arms, ammunition dropped by Drone along LoC. *Deccan Herald*. https://www.deccanherald.com/india/jammu-and-kashmir/army-seizes-arms-ammunition-dropped-by-drone-along-loc-3124211

Majmudar & Partners. (2021). *Drone Rules, 2021: Key Highlights*. https://www.majmudarindia.com/wp-content/uploads/DroneRules-230921-KeyHighlights.pdf

Manda, V. K., Christy, V., & Hlali, A. (2024). Current Trends, Opportunities, and Futures Research Directions in Geospatial Technologies for Smart Cities. In Darwish, D., & Chemingui, H. (Eds.), (pp. 239–270). Advances in Geospatial Technologies. IGI Global., DOI: 10.4018/979-8-3693-8054-3.ch009

Martins, B. O., Lavallée, C., & Silkoset, A. (2021). Drone Use for COVID-19 Related Problems: Techno-solutionism and its Societal Implications. *Global Policy*, *12*(5), 603–612. DOI: 10.1111/1758-5899.13007 PMID: 34899997

McNeal, G. S., Goodwin, W., & Jones, S. (2017). Warrantless Operations of Public Use Drones: Considerations for Government Agencies. *The Fordham Urban Law Journal*, *44*(3), 703–723.

Miyata, J., Tsuchiya, H., Nonaka, F., Aso, Y., Sugahara, M., & Maeda, T. (2025). Demonstration of autonomous fixed-wing drone delivery of prescribed medications in remote islands in Japan. *Journal of General and Family Medicine*, jgf2.768. https://doi.org/DOI: 10.1002/jgf2.768

Mohammad, M. (2024, November 12). *Peddlers Resort To High-End Drone, Encrypted Apps To Deliver Drugs In Kashmir*. ETV Bharat. https://www.etvbharat.com/en/!state/peddlers-resort-to-high-end-drone-encrypted-apps-to-deliver-drugs-in-kashmir-enn24111204985

Morton, T. (2016). *From Kites through Cold War: The Evolution of United States Air Force Manned Airborne ISR* [Doctorate of Philosophy Thesis, School of Advanced Air and Space Studies, Air University]. https://apps.dtic.mil/sti/pdfs/AD1030466.pdf

Mukul, P. (2021, September 2). Explained: How India's new drone rules have been liberalised. *The Indian Express*. https://indianexpress.com/article/explained/india-drone-rules-2021-explained-7471914/

Nawaz, S. A. (2024). Regulating Autonomy in Civilian Drones: Towards a Spectral Approach. *Journal of Intelligent & Robotic Systems*, *110*(2), 46. DOI: 10.1007/s10846-024-02056-9

Niu, B., Zhang, J., & Xie, F. (2024). Drone logistics' resilient development: Impacts of consumer choice, competition, and regulation. *Transportation Research Part A, Policy and Practice*, *185*, 104126. DOI: 10.1016/j.tra.2024.104126

Omolara, A. E., Alawida, M., & Abiodun, O. I. (2023). Drone cybersecurity issues, solutions, trend insights and future perspectives: A survey. *Neural Computing & Applications*, *35*(31), 23063–23101. DOI: 10.1007/s00521-023-08857-7

Paliwal, A. (2022, May 27). *India will be drone hub by 2030: PM Modi at country's biggest drone festival*. India Today. https://www.indiatoday.in/india/story/drone-hub-by-2030-pm-narendra-modi-india-biggest-drone-festival-pragati-maidan-1954855-2022-05-27

Panday, J. (2017, August 28). *India's Supreme Court Upholds Right to Privacy as a Fundamental Right—And It's About Time. Electronic Frontier Foundation*. EFF. https://www.eff.org/deeplinks/2017/08/indias-supreme-court-upholds-right-privacy-fundamental-right-and-its-about-time

PIB. (2021, December 9). *Incentive of Rs. 120 crore has been provided for Indian manufacturers of drone and drone components under PLI Scheme*. https://pib.gov.in/Pressreleaseshare.aspx?PRID=1779782

PIB. (2023, March 20). *Shri Jyotiraditya Scindia highlights various aspects of the growth of the Indian Civil Aviation Industry*. Press Information Bureau, Government of India. https://www.pib.gov.in/PressReleseDetailm.aspx?PRID=1908939

PSL. (2021). *PSL Release—The Unmanned Aircraft System Rules, 2021*. PSL Advocates and Solicitors. https://www.pslchambers.com/wp-content/uploads/2021/07/The-Unmanned-Aircraft-System-Rules-2021.pdf

PTI. (2010, July 3). DRDO develops UAV Netra to aid anti-terrorist operations. *The Hindu*. https://www.thehindu.com/news/national/DRDO-develops-UAV-lsquoNetrarsquo-to-aid-anti-terrorist-operations/article16183692.ece

PTI. (2016, April 27). DGCA releases draft guidelines for unmanned flying devices. *Mint*. https://www.livemint.com/Politics/bAB3DaJLWsn3B5G5AfGS7N/DGCA-releases-draft-guidelines-for-unmanned-flying-devices.html

PTI. (2018, August 27). *Government announces Regulations for Drones*. https://pib.gov.in/newsite/printrelease.aspx?relid=183093

Quamar, M. M., Al-Ramadan, B., Khan, K., Shafiullah, M., & El Ferik, S. (2023). Advancements and Applications of Drone-Integrated Geographic Information System Technology—A Review. *Remote Sensing*, *15*(20), 5039. DOI: 10.3390/rs15205039

Raghunatha, A., Thollander, P., & Barthel, S. (2023). Addressing the emergence of drones – A policy development framework for regional drone transportation systems. *Transportation Research Interdisciplinary Perspectives*, *18*, 100795. DOI: 10.1016/j.trip.2023.100795

Rajagopalan, R. P., & Krishna, R. (2019). India's Drone Policy: Domestic and Global Imperatives. *ICAO Scientific Review: Analytics and Management Research*, *1*, 53–68.

Rao. (2023, September 15). Unmanned eyes in the sky: The rise of forensic drones in crime investigation. *Times of India.* https://timesofindia.indiatimes.com/blogs/forensicsciencetech/224796/

Reuters. (2024, February 12). *Intrusive' drones? U.S. surveillance case tests privacy law.* https://economictimes.indiatimes.com/news/defence/intrusive-drones-us-surveillance-case-tests-privacy-law/articleshow/107629919.cms

Salinas, J. C., & Lewandowski, T. (2024). Blue Unmanned Aircraft Systems Explained: The Current Drone Market, Flight Regulations, and Debunking Common Misconceptions. *Transportation Research Record: Journal of the Transportation Research Board*, (03611981241257509). Advance online publication. DOI: 10.1177/03611981241257509

Sanas, S. (2024, July 15). Onion Heist: Ambegaon Farmer Loses 90000 After Drone Patrol. *The Bridge Chronicle.* https://www.thebridgechronicle.com/news/onion-heist-ambegaon-farmer-loses-90000-after-drone-patrol

Sharma, A. (2023, March 4). Singer Benny Dayal Gets Hit By A Drone During Live Concert In Chennai. *NDTV.* https://www.ndtv.com/offbeat/video-singer-benny-dayal-gets-hit-by-a-drone-during-live-concert-in-chennai-3835053

Siddiqui, H. R., & Muniza, M. (2025). Regulatory Gaps in Drone Surveillance: Addressing Privacy, Security, and Manufacturing Standards. *Annals of Human and Social Sciences*, *6*(1), 415–428.

Simpson, E. (2023, October 19). Amazon pledges parcels in an hour using drone deliveries. *BBC.* https://www.bbc.com/news/business-67132527

Sinha, S. (2024, September 13). 'Air taxis to soon become a reality in India': PM Modi. *Times of India.* https://timesofindia.indiatimes.com/business/india-business/air-taxis-to-soon-become-a-reality-in-india-pm-modi/articleshow/113298314.cms

Somayajula, D. (2021, July 31). *'Eye in the Sky'- India's Drone Operations and Privacy Concerns.* Vidhi Centre for Legal Policy. https://vidhilegalpolicy.in/blog/eye-in-the-sky-indias-drone-operations-and-privacy-concerns/

Srivastava, P. (2021). *Civil Aviation Regulatory Landscape of Indian Drone Ecosystem red.* https://legalaffairs.gov.in/sites/default/files/Civil%20Aviation%20Regulatory%20Landscape%20of%20Indian%20Drone%20Ecosystem%20red.pdf

Srivastava, P. (2023). *Regulatory Landscape of Indian Drone Ecosystem.* Department Of Legal Affairs. https://legalaffairs.gov.in/sites/default/files/Civil%20Aviation%20Regulatory%20Landscape%20of%20Indian%20Drone%20Ecosystem%20red.pdf

Stierlin, N., Risch, M., & Risch, L. (2024). Current Advancements in Drone Technology for Medical Sample Transportation. *Logistics (Basel)*, *8*(4), 104. DOI: 10.3390/logistics8040104

Sudhi, K. S. (2017, March 5). Now, drones to be used for monitoring tigers. *The Hindu*. https://www.thehindu.com/sci-tech/energy-and-environment/now-drones-to-be-used-for-monitoring-tigers/article17408388.ece

Telangana Today. (2021, October 1). *Hara Bhara, India's first aerial seeding campaign launched in Hyderabad*. https://telanganatoday.com/hara-bhara-indias-first-aerial-seeding-campaign-launched-in-hyderabad

The Hindu Bureau. (2024, July 29). DTDC launches drone delivery services in India. *The Hindu*. https://www.thehindu.com/sci-tech/technology/dtdc-launches-drone-delivery-services-in-india/article68459936.ece

The Hindu Net Desk. (2017, August 24). Supreme Court verdict on Right to Privacy. *The Hindu*. https://www.thehindu.com/news/resources/supreme-court-verdict-on-right-to-privacy/article62041731.ece

TNN. (2020, July 17). Delhi Police use Drone to solve double murder. *Times of India*. https://timesofindia.indiatimes.com/city/delhi/delhi-police-use-drone-to-solve-double-murder/articleshow/77009863.cms

TNN. (2024, September 16). *Need to urgently tackle rogue drones, online frauds: Amit Shah*. Times of India. https://timesofindia.indiatimes.com/india/need-to-urgently-tackle-rogue-drones-online-frauds-amit-shah/articleshow/113377061.cms

TOI News Desk. (2024, August 28). Mysterious drone-like object cause 3-hour flight disruption at Amritsar airport. *Times of India*. https://timesofindia.indiatimes.com/india/mysterious-drone-like-object-cause-3-hour-flight-disruption-at-amritsar-airport/articleshow/112864415.cms

Unit, R. (2022, January 28). *The Drone Rules, 2021*. Press Information Bureau, Ministry of Information and Broadcasting, Government of India. https://static.pib.gov.in/writereaddata/specificdocs/documents/2022/jan/doc202212810701.pdf

Upadhyay, D. (2023, October 5). *New Drone rules 2023 for pilots notified; any govt ID, address proof admissible*. Mint. https://www.livemint.com/news/india/new-drone-rules-2023-for-pilots-notified-any-government-id-address-proof-admissible-11696517295150.html

Verma, S., Anukaran, S., & Verma, K. (2022, February 17). *Safety Investigations Of Accidents & Incidents Involving Drones: Addressing The Gaps In Drone Rules In India*. Mondaq. https://www.mondaq.com/india/aviation/1162664/safety-investigations-of-accidents-incidents-involving-drones-addressing-the-gaps-in-drone-rules-in-india

Wang, N., Mutzner, N., & Blanchet, K. (2025). 'We Need Time...': An Expert Survey on Societal Acceptance of Urban Drones. *Science & Public Policy*. Advance online publication. DOI: 10.1093/scipol/scae084

Yaacoub, J.-P., Noura, H., Salman, O., & Chehab, A. (2020). Security analysis of drones systems: Attacks, limitations, and recommendations. *Internet of Things : Engineering Cyber Physical Human Systems*, *11*, 100218. DOI: 10.1016/j.iot.2020.100218 PMID: 38620271

Zahra, Q. A. (2021, November 7). *Failed assassination bid against Iraq's PM ramps up tension*. USA Today. https://www.usatoday.com/story/news/world/2021/11/07/mustafa-al-kadhimi-iraqi-prime-minister-assassination-attempt/6330276001/

Zenz, A. (2023). Safety first: Analysing the problematisation of drones. *Griffith Law Review*, *32*(3), 310–334. DOI: 10.1080/10383441.2024.2303937

KEY TERMS AND DEFINITIONS

Artificial Intelligence (AI): refers to the development of computer systems or machines that can perform tasks that typically require human intelligence. With AI, machines can learn reasoning, problem-solving, perception, and language understanding. AI can be used to enhance drones' autonomy through navigation, obstacle avoidance, and swarm coordination. Current AI systems have several advantages and opportunities but also involve challenges and risks. The challenges include bias, discrimination, privacy invasion, and potential misuse.

Beyond Visual Line-of-Sight (BVLOS): BVLOS refers to drone operation beyond the operator's visual range. BVLOS flights are significant because they enable drones to fly longer distances and cover larger areas. So, there will be an increase in efficiency and versatility. BVLOS operations require advanced technologies such as autopilot systems, GPS and navigation systems, communication systems, and sensor systems. However, BVLOS flights also pose several challenges and risks, such as the potential for collisions with other aircraft, loss of communication links, and the inability to monitor the Drone's surroundings visually.

Drone Swarms: Multiple drones operating in coordination to monitor large-scale areas. They are used in applications of various industries, such as military, agriculture, construction, and entertainment. Drone Swarms are characterized by their autonomy, coordination, scalability, flexibility, and robustness.

Drones: Informally refers to any remotely operated autonomous vehicle (aerial, ground, or underwater). They can be equipped with various sensors and payloads, including cameras, thermal imaging devices, and chemical sensors. They can be used for various applications, such as aerial photography, delivery services, search and rescue operations, agricultural monitoring, environmental monitoring, and border patrol.

Geo-fencing: A safety feature that creates virtual boundaries for drone operations. Geo-fencing can be used for various purposes, such as drone operations, vehicle tracking, personal safety, and property protection. It is implemented using various technologies such as GPS, GIS, Cellular networks, and Satellite imaging.

Unmanned Aerial Vehicles (UAVs): UAVs are aircraft that operate without a human pilot. UAVs come in various sizes and shapes. They range from small quadcopters for recreational purposes to large military-grade drones for reconnaissance, surveillance, and combat missions. Governments and regulatory bodies have established rules and guidelines for the safe and responsible use of UAVs.

Compilation of References

Aaronson, S. A. (2021). Why the WTO Needs to Address Emerging Technologies. *World Trade Review*, *20*(2), 165–182. DOI: 10.1017/S1474745620000532

Aaronson, S. A., & Leblond, P. (2018). Another digital divide: The rise of data realms and its implications for the WTO. *Journal of International Economic Law*, *21*(2), 245–272. DOI: 10.1093/jiel/jgy019

Abed, A. K., & Anupam, A. (2022). Review of security issues in the Internet of Things and artificial intelligence-driven solutions. *Security and Privacy*, *6*(3), e285. DOI: 10.1002/spy2.285

Abidin, M. A. Z., Nawawi, A., & Salin, A. S. A. P. (2019). Customer data security and theft: A Malaysian organization's experience. *Information and Computer Security*, *27*(1), 81–100. DOI: 10.1108/ICS-04-2018-0043

About us. (n.d.a,). NOYB. https://noyb.eu/en/about-us

About us. (n.d.b.). La Quadrature du Net. https://www.laquadrature.net/about/

Acemoglu, D., & Restrepo, P. (2020). Artificial Intelligence, Automation, and Work. In Agrawal, A., Gans, J., & Goldfarb, A. (Eds.), *The Economics of Artificial Intelligence: An Agenda* (pp. 197–236). University of Chicago Press.

Agarwal, M. (2024, March 18). From social contracts to smart contracts: Navigating decentralization, blockchain, and Kleros arbitration. The Contemporary Law Forum. https://tclf.in/2024/03/18/from-social-contracts-to-smart-contracts-navigating-decentralization-blockchain-and-kleros-arbitration

Ahmad, K., Maabreh, M., Ghaly, M., Khan, K., Qadir, J., & Al-Fuqaha, A. (2022). Developing future human-centered smart cities: Critical analysis of smart city security, Data management, and Ethical challenges. *Computer Science Review*, *43*, 100452. DOI: 10.1016/j.cosrev.2021.100452

Ahmad, N. (2009). Restrictions on cryptography in India-A case study of encryption and privacy. *Computer Law & Security Review*, *25*(2), 173–180. DOI: 10.1016/j.clsr.2009.02.001

Ahmed, J., Yildirim, S., Nowostawski, M., Abomhara, M., Ramachandra, R., & Elezaj, O. (2020, March 5). 2020). Towards Blockchain-Based GDPR-Compliant Online Social Networks: Challenges, Opportunities and Way Forward Future of Information and Communication Conference

AI Ethics Lab. (2025). *Promoting and advancing human rights in global AI ecosystems (White paper)*. AI Ethics Lab.

Akhlaghpour, S., Hassandoust, F., Fatehi, F., Burton-Jones, A., & Hynd, A. (2021, September). Learning from enforcement cases to manage GDPR risks. *MIS Quarterly Executive*, *20*(1), 199–218. DOI: 10.17705/2msqe.00049

Al-Abdullah, M., Alsmadi, I., AlAbdullah, R., & Farkas, B. (2020). Designing Privacy-friendly Data Repositories: A Framework for a Blockchain that follows the GDPR [Article]. Digital Policy. *Regulation & Governance*, *22*(5-6), 389–411. DOI: 10.1108/DPRG-04-2020-0050

Albayati, H., Kim, S. K., & Rho, J. J. (2020). Accepting financial transactions using blockchain technology and cryptocurrency: A customer perspective approach. *Technology in Society*, *62*, 101320. DOI: 10.1016/j.techsoc.2020.101320

Alexander, D. (2019). Smart contracts and the law: Reconciling code with contract doctrine. [Check your library database for full access—placeholder journal entry if citing generally.]. *Journal of Business Law*, *20*(3), 45–67.

Alfayan, M., & Hagras, H. (2025). Towards an Explainable Artificial Intelligence approach for smart grid systems. *Discover Artificial Intelligence*, *5*(1), 40. DOI: 10.1007/s44163-025-00261-5

Aljifri, H., & Sanchez Navarro, D. (2003). International legal aspects of cryptography. *Computers & Security*, *22*(3), 196–203. DOI: 10.1016/S0167-4048(03)00305-5

Allen, J., Yang, Z., Landen, M., Wang, X., & Lin, J. (2019). Mnemosyne: An effective and efficient postmortem watering hole attack investigation system. In 2019 IEEE International Conference on Cybersecurity and Privacy (ICSP) (pp. xx–xx). IEEE. (DOI not found; add if available)

Almazrouei, & Ibrahim, A. (2025). Legislative Confrontation of Drone Crimes in the United Arab Emirates. *AAU Journal of Business and Law, 9*(1), 38. https://doi.org/DOI: 10.51958/AAUJBL2025V9I1P4

Almeida, D., Shmarko, K., & Lomas, E. (2022). The ethics of facial recognition technologies, surveillance, and accountability in an age of artificial intelligence: A comparative analysis of US, EU, and UK regulatory frameworks. *AI and Ethics*, *2*(3), 377–387. DOI: 10.1007/s43681-021-00077-w PMID: 34790955

Almomani, O., Almaiah, M. A., & Madi, M., & Others. (2023). Reconnaissance attack detection via boosting machine learning classifiers. In Proceedings of the 4th International Computer Sciences and Informatics Conference (ICSIC 2022). ACM Press. DOI: 10.1063/5.0174730

Almusayli, A., Zia, T., & Qazi, E.-H. (2024). Drone Forensics: An Innovative Approach to the Forensic Investigation of Drone Accidents Based on Digital Twin Technology. *Technologies*, *12*(1), 11. DOI: 10.3390/technologies12010011

Alsaigh, R., Mehmood, R., & Katib, I. (2022). AI explainability and governance in smart energy systems: A review. *Frontiers in Energy Research*, *10*, 107129. DOI: 10.3389/fenrg.2023.107129

Alyas, T., Abbas, Q., Niazi, S., Alqahtany, S. S., Alghamdi, T., Alzahrani, A., Tabassum, N., & Ibrahim, A. M. (2025). Multi blockchain architecture for judicial case management using smart contracts. *Scientific Reports*, *15*(1), 1–17. DOI: 10.1038/s41598-025-92842-8 PMID: 40069277

Amara, N., Zhiqui, H., & Ali, A. (2017). Cloud computing security threats and attacks with their mitigation techniques. *2017 International Conference on Cyber-Enabled Distributed Computing and Knowledge Discovery (CyberC)*, 244-251. DOI: 10.1109/CyberC.2017.37

Amarikwa, M. (2024, February 5). Internet openness at risk: Generative AI's impact on data scraping. *Richmond Journal of Law & Technology, 30*(3).

American Data Privacy and Protection Act (2022).

Anderson, J. P. (1980). *Computer security threat monitoring and surveillance. James P*. Anderson Company.

Anderson, M. R. (2010). Community psychology, political efficacy, and trust. *Political Psychology*, *31*(1), 59–84. DOI: 10.1111/j.1467-9221.2009.00734.x

ANI. (2023, December 12). 514 drone sightings since 2022, 121 brought down, says Punjab IGP. *Business Standard*. https://www.business-standard.com/india-news/514-drone-sightings-since-2022-121-brought-down-says-punjab-igp-123121200211_1.html

Anjum, M. M., Iqbal, S., & Hamelin, B. (2021). ANUBIS: A provenance graph-based framework for advanced persistent threat detection.

Ante, L. (2020). Smart contracts on the blockchain – A bibliometric analysis and review. *SSRN*. Advance online publication. DOI: 10.2139/ssrn.3576393

Anu, P., & Vimala, S. (2017). A survey on sniffing attacks on computer networks. In *Proceedings of the 2017 International Conference on Intelligent Computing and Control*. DOI: 10.1109/I2C2.2017.8321914

An, Y. Z., Zaaba, Z. F., & Samsudin, N. F. (2016). Reviews on security issues and challenges in cloud computing. *IOP Conference Series. Materials Science and Engineering*, *160*(1), 012106. DOI: 10.1088/1757-899X/160/1/012106

Aoki, N.(2020). An experimental study of public trust in AI chatbots in the public sector. Gov. Inf. Q. 37 (4), 101490. http://dx.doi.org/. 101490DOI: 10.1016/j.giq.2020

Apte, S., & Petrovsky, N. (2016). Will blockchain technology revolutionize excipient supply chain management? *Journal of Excipients and Food Chemicals*, *7*(3), 76–78. http://jefc.scholasticahq.com/article/4513-will-blockchain-technology-revolutionize-excipient-supply-chain-management

Araujo, T. (2018). Living up to the chatbot hype: The influence of anthropomorphic design cues and communicative agency framing on conversational agent and company perceptions. *Computers in Human Behavior*, *85*, 183–189. DOI: 10.1016/j.chb.2018.03.051

Arévalo, P., & Jurado, F. (2024). Impact of artificial intelligence on the planning and operation of distributed energy systems in smart grids. *Energies*, *17*(17), 4501. DOI: 10.3390/en17174501

Arfelt, E., Basin, D., & Debois, S. (2019, September). *Monitoring the GDPR*. [Conference paper]. 24th European Symposium on Research in Computer Security (pp. 681-699).

Ariante, G., & Del Core, G. (2025). Unmanned Aircraft Systems (UASs): Current State, Emerging Technologies, and Future Trends. *Drones (Basel)*, *9*(1), 59. DOI: 10.3390/drones9010059

Aristotle. (1932). The rhetoric of Aristotle (Bk I, p. 77), as cited in Malhotra, O. P., & Malhotra, I. (2003). Arbitration and conciliation (2nd ed., p. xxxvii).

Article 29 Data Protection Working Party. (2010, 16 February 2010). *Opinion 1/2010 on the Concepts of "controller" and "processor" (No. 00264/10/EN WP 169).* https://ec.europa.eu/justice/article-29/documentation/opinion-recommendation/files/2010/wp169_en.pdf

Article 29 Data Protection Working Party. (2011, 4 April 2011). *Opinion 12/2011 on Smart Metering.* https://ec.europa.eu/justice/article-29/documentation/opinion-recommendation/files/2011/wp183_en.pdf

Article 29 Data Protection Working Party. (2014, 10 April 2014). *Opinion 05/2014 on Anonymisation Techniques.* https://ec.europa.eu/justice/article-29/documentation/opinion-recommendation/files/2014/wp216_en.pdf

Article 29 Data Protection Working Party. (2017). Guidelines on Data Protection Impact Assessment (DPIA). https://ec.europa.eu/newsroom/article29/item-detail.cfm?item_id=611236

Arulkumar, D., Kartheeban, K., & Arulkumaran, G. (2022). *The APT cyber warriors with TTP weapons to battle: An overview on IoT and cyber twin.* IGI Global. DOI: 10.4018/978-1-6684-5722-1.ch011

Arza-García, M., & Burgess, A. J. (2022). Drones in the Sky: Towards a More Sustainable Agriculture. *Agriculture*, *13*(1), 84. DOI: 10.3390/agriculture13010084

Aslan, Ö. A., & Samet, R. (2020). A comprehensive review on malware detection approaches. *IEEE Access : Practical Innovations, Open Solutions*, *8*, 6249–6271. DOI: 10.1109/ACCESS.2019.2963724

Atadoga, A., Farayola, O. A., Ayinla, B. S., Amoo, O. O., Abrahams, T. O., & Osasona, F. (2024, February 18). A comparative review of data encryption methods in the USA and Europe. *Computer Science & IT Research Journal*, *5*(2), 447–460. DOI: 10.51594/csitrj.v5i2.815

Auerbach, R. P., Bloom, P. A., Pagliaccio, D., Lan, R., Galfalvy, H., Bitran, A., Durham, K., Crowley, R., Joyce, K., Blanchard, A., Chernick, L. S., Dayan, P. S., Greenblatt, J., Khan, L. E., Porta, G., Tse, T. C., Cohn, J. F., Morency, L.-P., Brent, D. A., & Allen, N. B. (2025, January 27). Using smartphone GPS data to detect the risk of adolescent suicidal thoughts and behaviors. *Journal of the American Medical Association*, *8*(1), E2456429. DOI: 10.1001/jamanetworkopen.2024.56429 PMID: 39869336

Aumasson, J.-P. (2025). *Serious cryptography: A practical introduction to modern encryption* (2nd ed.). No Starch Press.

Authenticated e-Discovery. (2025, January 21). *Authenticated e-discovery: Utilizing blockchain for robust security and trust in.* Ankura Angle. https://angle.ankura.com/post/102jsqp/authenticated-e-discovery-utilizing-blockchain-for-robust-security-and-trust-in

Auty, M. (2015). Anatomy of an advanced persistent threat. Network Security, vol. 2015, no. 4, pp. 13-16.

Averin, A., Samartsev, A., & Sachenko, N. (2020). Review of methods for ensuring anonymity and de-anonymization in blockchain. In *2020 International Conference on Quality Management, Transport and Information Security, Information Technologies (IT&QM&IS)* (pp. 82–87). IEEE. DOI: 10.1109/ITQMIS51053.2020.9322974

Ayaburi, E. W. (2022). Understanding online information disclosure: Examination of data breach victimization experience effect. *Information Technology & People, 36*(1), 95–114. DOI: 10.1108/ITP-04-2021-0262

Ayora, M. (2023, December 13). *AEPD (Spain): EXP202205820.* GDPR Hub. https://gdprhub.eu/index.php?title=AEPD_(Spain)_-_EXP202205820#Facts

Bacon, J., Michels, J. D., Millard, C., & Singh, J. (2018). Blockchain Demystified: A technical and Legal Introduction to Distributed and Centralized Ledgers. *Richmond Journal of Law and Technology, 25*(1). https://jolt.richmond.edu/blockchain-demystified-a-technical-and-legal-introduction-to-distributed-and-centralised-ledgers/

Bailey, E. (2023, September 22). *GDPR compliance and personal data: The ultimate guide.* Matomo. https://matomo.org/blog/2023/09/gdpr-personal-data

Bai, T., Bian, H. B., & Abou Daya, A.. (2019). A machine learning approach for RDP-based lateral movement detection. In *Proceedings of the 2019 IEEE 44th Conference on Local Computer Networks (LCN)* (pp. 242–245). IEEE Press. DOI: 10.1109/LCN44214.2019.8990853

Bai, Y., Feng, B., Liu, X., Wang, W., & Lu, Y. (2021). APT behaviors detection based on email business scenarios. In *2021 IEEE Sixth International Conference on Data Science in Cyberspace (DSC)* (pp. 171–178). IEEE. DOI: 10.1109/DSC53577.2021.00031

Bajwa, H. (2024, October 30). BSF in Punjab intercepts 13 drones in a week, 181 drones seized in 2024 amid rising smuggling concerns. *The New Indian Express.* https://www.newindianexpress.com/nation/2024/Oct/30/bsf-in-punjab-intercepts-13-drones-in-a-week-181-drones-seized-in-2024-amid-rising-smuggling-concerns

Bakhramova, M. (2024). Harmonization of the legal framework for online arbitration. *International Journal of Law and Policy*, *2*(2), 1–15. https://irshadjournals.com/index.php/ijlp/article/download/154/137. DOI: 10.59022/ijlp.154

Bakiner, O. (2023). The promises and challenges of addressing artificial intelligence with human rights. *Big Data & Society*, *10*(2), 20539517231205476. DOI: 10.1177/20539517231205476

Balamurugan, M., Narayanan, K., Raghu, N., Arjun Kumar, G. B., & Trupti, V. N. (2025). Role of artificial intelligence in smart grid – A mini review. *Frontiers in Artificial Intelligence*, *8*, 1551661. Advance online publication. DOI: 10.3389/frai.2025.1551661 PMID: 39968172

Banerji, O. (2021, October 11). The Drone Rules, 2021:An Overview. *iPleaders*. https://blog.ipleaders.in/the-drone-rules-2021-an-overview/

Barrows. (2022, December 17). *It's not a joke or funny' Drone harassing children, staff & therapy horses at Eliada Home*. Abc13news. https://wlos.com/news/local/eliada-home-drone-harassing-harassment-west-asheville-western-north-carolina-children-staff-therapy-horses-nonprofit-organization-privacy-issues

Bassi, E., Bloise, N., Dirutigliano, J., Fici, G. P., Pagallo, U., Primatesta, S., & Quagliotti, F. (2019, November). The design of GDPR-abiding drones through flight operation maps: A win-win approach to data protection, aerospace engineering, and risk management. *Minds and Machines*, *29*(4), 579–601. DOI: 10.1007/s11023-019-09511-9

BasuMallick, C. (2023). What are smart contracts? Types, benefits, and tools. Spiceworks.

Beebeejaun, Z., & Faccia, A. (2024). Blockchain in energy markets: Regulatory challenges. *Journal of World Energy Law and Business*.

Beebeejaun, Z., & Faccia, A. (2024). Electronic alternative dispute resolution, smart contracts, and equity in the energy sector. *Journal of World Energy Law and Business*, *17*(1), 1–25. DOI: 10.1093/jwelb/jwac004

Beg, S., Saif, U. R. K., & Anjum, A. (2022). Data usage-based privacy and security issues in mobile app recommendation (MAR): A systematic literature review. *Library Hi Tech*, *40*(3), 725–749. DOI: 10.1108/LHT-04-2021-0147

Belen-Saglam, R., Altuncu, E., Lu, Y., & Li, S. (2023). A Systematic Literature Review of the Tension between the GDPR and Public Blockchain Systems. *4*(2), 100129. https://doi.org/DOI: 10.1016/j.bcra.2023.100129

Bello, G., & Perez, A. J. (2019, 18 April 2019). Adapting Financial Technology Standards to Blockchain Platforms Proceedings of the 2019 ACM Southeast Conference.

Bergquist, J., Laszka, A., Sturm, M., & Dubey, A. (2017, 11 December 2017). On the Design of Communication and Transaction Anonymity in Blockchain-based Transactive Microgrids Proceedings of the 1st Workshop on Scalable and Resilient Infrastructures for Distributed Ledgers, California Consumer Privacy Act.

Bergstedt, E. (2021, May 28). *Solving a double murder arouses international interest.* Linköping University. https://liu.se/en/news-item/kunskap-om-dubbelmords-losning-vacker-internationellt-intresse

Bhattacharya, D. (2022). Digital Yuan (e-CNY): China's official digital currency. *Strategic Analysis*, *46*(1), 93–99. DOI: 10.1080/09700161.2022.2039582

Bhuiyan, J. (2024, November 14). New York City police will send drones to sites of reported robberies and gunshots. *The Guardian*. https://www.theguardian.com/technology/2024/nov/14/nypd-drones-police

Bi, C., He, S. B., Luo, F. J., Meng, W., Ji, L., & Huang, D.-W. (2023). Defense of advanced persistent threat on industrial Internet of Things with lateral movement modeling. *IEEE Transactions on Industrial Informatics*, *19*(9), 9619–9630. DOI: 10.1109/TII.2022.3231406

Binns, R. (2018). Algorithmic accountability and public reason. *Philosophy & Technology*, *31*(4), 543–556. DOI: 10.1007/s13347-017-0263-5 PMID: 30873342

Binns, R., Veale, M., Van Kleek, M., & Shadbolt, N. (2018). 'It's Reducing a Human Being to a Percentage': Perceptions of Justice in Algorithmic Decisions. *Proceedings of the 2018 CHI Conference on Human Factors in Computing Systems*, 1–14. https://doi.org/DOI: 10.1145/3173574.3173951

Bleher, H., & Braun, M. (2023). Reflections on putting AI ethics into practice: How three AI ethics approaches conceptualize theory and practice. *Science and Engineering Ethics*, *29*(3), 21. DOI: 10.1007/s11948-023-00443-3 PMID: 37237246

Booz Allen & Hamilton Inc. v. SBI Home Finance Ltd., (2011) 5 SCC 532.

Born, G. (2021). *International commercial arbitration* (3rd ed.). Kluwer Law International.

Boucher, P. (2022). *How blockchain technology could impact artificial intelligence in industry*. European Parliamentary Research Service. https://www.europarl.europa.eu/thinktank/en/document/EPRS_BRI(2022)729354

Bou-Harb, E., Debbabi, M., & Assi, C. (2014). Cyber scanning: A comprehensive survey. *IEEE Communications Surveys and Tutorials*, *16*(3), 1496–1519. DOI: 10.1109/SURV.2013.102913.00020

Bourguignon, F., Lefèvre, Q., & Schmidt, P. (2023). Building digital sovereignty: Policy frameworks in the EU. *Digital Policy Studies*, *7*(2), 132–149. DOI: 10.2139/ssrn.4412528

Bradford, A. (2020). *The Brussels Effect: How the European Union Rules the World*. Oxford University Press. DOI: 10.1093/oso/9780190088583.001.0001

Brkan, M. (2021). Do algorithms rule the world? Algorithmic decision-making and data protection in the framework of the GDPR and beyond. *International Journal of Law and Information Technology*, *29*(2), 91–121. DOI: 10.1093/ijlit/eay017

Brook, C. (2019, January 21). *Google fined $57M by data protection watchdog over GDPR violations*. Digital Guardian. https://www.digitalguardian.com/blog/google-fined-57m-data-protection-watchdog-over-gdpr-violations

Brooks, B. (2025, March 13). *Musk's Grok 3 '94% Inaccurate': Here's how other AI chatbots fare against truth*. eWeek. https://www.eweek.com/news/ai-chatbot-citation-problem

Brown, S. (2023). Arbitration of cryptoasset and smart contract disputes. Practical Law. https://www.cliffordchance.com/content/dam/cliffordchance/briefings/2023/08/arbitration-of-cryptoasset-and-smart-contract.pdf

Brunton, F., & Nissenbaum, H. (2024). The limits of digital sovereignty. *Surveillance & Society*, *22*(1), 15–30. DOI: 10.24908/ss.v22i1.16012

Bryant, A., & Colledge, B. (2002). Trust in electronic commerce business relationships. *Journal of Electronic Commerce Research*, *3*, 32–39.

Bryson, J. J., & Theodorou, A. (2019). How society can maintain human-centric artificial intelligence. *Nature Machine Intelligence*, *1*(1), 5–6. DOI: 10.1038/s42256-018-0005-2

Bryson, J. J., & Winfield, A. F. (2017). Standardizing ethical design for artificial intelligence and autonomous systems. *Computer*, *50*(5), 116–119. DOI: 10.1109/MC.2017.154

Bulman-Pozen, J., & Seifter, M. (2023). State Constitutional Rights and Democratic Proportionality. *Columbia Law Review*, *123*(7), 1855–1928.

Bunnell, L., Osei-Bryson, K. M., & Yoon, V. Y. (2020). FinPathlight: Framework for an multiagent recommender system designed to increase consumer financial capability. *Decision Support Systems, 134*, 113306. DOI: 10.1016/j.dss.2020.113306

Buolamwini, J., & Gebru, T. (2018). "Gender shades: Intersectional accuracy disparities in commercial gender classification". *Conference on Fairness, Accountability and Transparency*, January 2018, pp. 77-91.

Burgess, R., Klein, M., & Lee, S. (2023). Software dependency and national resilience in smart infrastructure. *Journal of Critical Infrastructure Studies, 11*(4), 256–271. DOI: 10.1016/j.jcis.2023.02.009

Burri, M. (2017). The governance of data and data flows in trade agreements: The pitfalls of legal adaptation. *U.C. Davis Law Review, 51*, 65–132.

Burri, M. (2021). Governing Trade in the Age of Innovation: Towards a New Regulatory Framework for Digital Trade. *Journal of International Economic Law, 24*(2), 1–26. DOI: 10.1093/jiel/jgab002

Burri, M. (2021). Understanding the implications of digital trade for international trade law. *Journal of International Economic Law, 24*(1), 35–62.

Buterin, V. (2014). A next-generation smart contract and decentralized application platform. Ethereum White Paper.

Buterin, V. (2014). A next-generation smart contract and decentralized application platform. *Etherum, January*.

Calhoun, C. S., Bobko, P., Gallimore, J. J., & Lyons, J. B. (2019). Linking precursors of interpersonal trust to human-automation trust: An expanded typology and exploratory experiment. *Journal of Trust Research, 9*(1), 28–46. DOI: 10.1080/21515581.2019.1579730

Calo, R. (2015). Robotics and the Lessons of Cyberlaw. *SSRN, 103*(3), 513–563. DOI: 10.2139/ssrn.2402972

Calo, R. (2018). Artificial intelligence policy: A primer and roadmap. *U.C. Davis Law Review, 51*(2), 399–435.

Calo, R., & Citron, D. K. (2021). The Automated Administrative State: A Crisis of Legitimacy. *Emory Law Journal, 70*(4), 797–846. https://ssrn.com/abstract=3814094

Calo, R., & Kerr, I. (2013). Robotics and the New Cyberlaw. In Lin, P., Abney, K., & Bekey, G. A. (Eds.), *Robot Ethics: The Ethical and Social Implications of Robotics* (pp. 207–223). MIT Press.

Caltagirone, S., Pendergast, A., & Betz, C. (2013). The diamond model of intrusion analysis. *Threat Connect*, *298*(704), 1–61.

Cao, Z., & Zhao, L. (2021, 26 March 2021). A Design of Key Distribution Mechanism in Decentralized Digital Rights Management Based on Blockchain and Zero-Knowledge Proof International Conference on Blockchain Technology

Casey, A. J., & Niblett, A. (2017). Smart Contracts and Consumer Protection: The Missing Piece of the Puzzle. *Stanford Technology Law Review : STLR : An Online High-Technology Law Journal from Stanford Law School*, *20*(2), 126–145.

Cave, S., & Dignum, V. (2019). Algorithms and Values. In Dubber, M., Pasquale, F., & Das, S. (Eds.), *The Oxford Handbook of AI Ethics* (pp. 247–265). Oxford University Press.

Cejka, S., Zeilinger, F., Veseli, A., Holzleitner, M.-T., & Stefan, M. (2020, 2 May 2020). *A Blockchain-based Privacy-friendly Renewable Energy Community* Proceedings of the 9th International Conference on Smart Cities and Green ICT Systems-SMARTGREENS, https://pdfs.semanticscholar.org/1a64/15e5779b204fea30 63c0e2b22f08d7138ba4.pdf

Cejka, S., Zeilinger, F., Stefan, M., Zehetbauer, P., Veseli, A., Burgstaller, K., & Holzleitner, M.-T. (2020). Implementation and Operation of Blockchain-Based Energy Communities Under the New Legal Framework. In Klein, C., Helfert, M., Berns, K., & Gusikhin, O. (Eds.), *Smart Cities, Green Technologies, and Intelligent Transport Systems* (pp. 3–30). Springer.

Cengiz, F. (2023). Blockchain governance and governance via blockchain: Decentralized utopia or centralized dystopia? *Policy Design and Practice*, *6*(4), 446–464. Advance online publication. DOI: 10.1080/25741292.2023.2247203

Centobelli, P., Cerchione, R., Del Vecchio, P., Oropallo, E., & Secundo, G. (2021). Blockchain Technology for Bridging Trust, Traceability and Transparency in Circular Supply Chain. *Information & Management*, *59*(7), 103508. https://doi.org/https:// doi.org/10.1016/j.im.2021.103508. DOI: 10.1016/j.im.2021.103508

Cervi, G. V. (2022). Why and how does the EU rule global digital policy: An empirical analysis of EU regulatory influence in data protection laws. *Digital Society : Ethics, Socio-Legal and Governance of Digital Technology*, *1*(2), 18. DOI: 10.1007/ s44206-022-00005-3

Chander, A. (2019). How Law Made Silicon Valley. *Emory Law Journal*, *68*(2), 357–416. https://scholarlycommons.law.emory.edu/elj/vol68/iss2/3/

Chander, A. (2021). The racist algorithm. *Michigan Law Review, 119*(5), 1023–1044. https://repository.law.umich.edu/mlr/vol119/iss5/5

Chantrel, S. P., Surmann, A., Erge, T., & Thomsen, J. (2021). Participative Renewable Energy Community—How Blockchain-Based Governance Enables a German Interpretation of RED II. *Electricity, 2*(4), 471-486. https://doi.org/https://doi.org/10.3390/electricity2040028

Chari, S., Halevi, S., & Venema, W. (2010). Where do you want to go today? Escalating privileges by pathname manipulation. In *Proceedings of the Symposium on Network and Distributed System Security* (pp. 1–16). IEEE Press.

Chatterjee, S. (2022). Arbitrability and consumer protection. *Journal of International Dispute Resolution, 13*(3), 45–67.

Chatterjee, S. (2022). Arbitrability of Smart Contracts in India: The Role of Public Policy. *Indian Journal of Arbitration Law, 11*(2), 203–221.

Chavekar, A., Mulla, Y., Mane, S., Kumar, S., & Kazi, F. (2023). A Review of Drone Communication Protocols: Current Trends and Future Perspectives. *2023 IEEE International Carnahan Conference on Security Technology (ICCST)*, 1–6. https://doi.org/DOI: 10.1109/ICCST59048.2023.10726850

Chechetkin v. Payward Ltd.[2022] EWHC 2370 (Comm).

Chen, D., & Zhao, H. (2012). Data security and privacy protection issues in cloud computing. *2012 International Conference on Computer Science and Electronics Engineering*, 647-651. DOI: 10.1109/ICCSEE.2012.193

Cheng, H., Lee, J., & Low, K. (2021). Smart contract code audits and the role of expert testimony. *Computer Law & Security Review*, *41*, 105528. DOI: 10.1016/j.clsr.2021.105528

Cheng, Y., & Jiang, H. (2020). How Do AI-driven Chatbots Impact User Experience? Examining Gratifications, Perceived Privacy Risk, Satisfaction, Loyalty, and Continued Use. *Journal of Broadcasting & Electronic Media, 64*(4), 592–614. DOI: 10.1080/08838151.2020.1834296

Chen, J. J., & Cheng, X. J. (2009). A novel fast port scan method using parthenogenetic algorithm. In *Proceedings of the 2009 2nd IEEE International Conference on Computer Science and Information Technology* (pp. 219–222). IEEE. DOI: 10.1109/ICCSIT.2009.5234709

Chen, R., Fu, C., de Melo, S. N., & Xu, Y. (2025, March). Day and night: Evaluating the impact of CCTV and street lighting on urban crime prevention in Detroit. *Journal of Criminal Justice*, *98*, 102397. DOI: 10.1016/j.jcrimjus.2025.102397

Chen, Y. H., Yang, Z., & Ai, C. X. (2023). Data center APT attack detection and defense technology. *Network Security Technology & Application*, *2023*(6), 4–7.

Chen, Y., Pereira, I., & Patel, P. C. (2021). Decentralized Governance of Digital Platforms. *Journal of Management*, *47*(5), 1305–1337. DOI: 10.1177/0149206320916755

Chevalier, M. (2021). From smart contract litigation to blockchain arbitration, a new decentralized approach leading towards the blockchain arbitral order. *Journal of International Dispute Settlement*, *12*(4), 558–584. DOI: 10.1093/jnlids/idab025

Chiarella, M. L. (2023). Digital Markets Act (DMA) and Digital Services Act (DSA): New Rules for the EU Digital Environment. *Athens JL*, *9*(1), 33–58. DOI: 10.30958/ajl.9-1-2

Chien, E., Omurchu, L., & Falliere, N. (2012). W32.Duqu: The precursor to the next Stuxnet. In *Proceedings of the 5th USENIX Workshop on Large-Scale Exploits and Emergent Threats (LEET 12)* (p. 5). USENIX Association.

Children's Online Privacy Protection Act (1998).

Choobineh, M., Arab, A., Khodaei, A., & Paaso, A. (2022). Energy Innovations through Blockchain: Challenges, Opportunities, and the Road Ahead. *The Electricity Journal*, *35*(1), 107059. https://doi.org/https://doi.org/10.1016/j.tej.2021.107059. DOI: 10.1016/j.tej.2021.107059

Chopra, A. (2024, September 27). *Air Taxis by 2026: How aviation will transform India's urban mobility*. Firstpost. https://www.firstpost.com/opinion/air-taxis-by-2026-how-aviation-will-transform-indias-urban-mobility-13819638.html

Chousein, Z., Tetik, H. Y., Sağlam, R. B., Bülbül, A., & Li, S. (2020, 4 November 2020). *Tension between GDPR and Public Blockchains: A Data-Driven Analysis of Online Discussions* [Conference Paper]. International Conference on Security of Information and Networks, https://www.scopus.com/inward/record.uri?eid=2-s2.0-85100648836&doi=10.1145%2f3433174.3433587&partnerID=40&md5=2151aa5536ae1d9f6f5b0029933fede2

Christensen, T. K. (2024, July). Pre-installed cameras in vehicles: New technology from data protection law perspective. *Computer Law & Security Review*, *53*, 105980. DOI: 10.1016/j.clsr.2024.105980

Christidis, K., & Devetsikiotis, M. (2016). Blockchains and smart contracts for the Internet of Things. *IEEE Access : Practical Innovations, Open Solutions, 4*, 2292–2303. DOI: 10.1109/ACCESS.2016.2566339

Christy, V., Manda, V. K., & M. L., G. (2024). Ethical Frameworks for Use in Artificial Intelligence Systems. In J. Gomathi Sankar & A. David (Eds.), *Advances in Computational Intelligence and Robotics* (pp. 122–154). IGI Global. https://doi.org/DOI: 10.4018/979-8-3693-8557-9.ch005

Chukwunweike, J. N., Yussuf, M., Okusi, O., & Oluwatobi, T. (2024). The role of deep learning in ensuring privacy integrity and security: Applications in AI-driven cybersecurity solutions. *World Journal of Advanced Research and Reviews, 23*(2), 2550.

Cidon, A., Gavish, L., Bleier, I., & Mirian, A. (2019). High precision detection of business email compromise. In *Proceedings of the 28th USENIX Security Symposium* (pp. 1291–1307). USENIX Association.

Cihon, P., Maas, M. M., & Kemp, L. (2020). Should AI governance be centralized? Design lessons from history. *Proceedings of the AAAI/ACM Conference on AI, Ethics, and Society*, 228–234. https://doi.org/DOI: 10.1145/3375627.3375857

Cimpanu, C. (2020, March 11). *Dutch government loses hard drives with data of 6.9 million registered donors*. ZD Net. https://www.zdnet.com/article/dutch-government-loses-hard-drives-with-data-of-6-9-million-registered-donors

CISO Mag. (2020, March 12). *6.9 million Dutch donors face identity theft scare*. https://cisomag.com/6-9-million-dutch-donors-face-identity-theft-scare 1

Clark, E., Cho, G., & Hoyle, A. (2003). Online dispute resolution: Present realities, pressing problems and future prospects. *International Review of Law Computers & Technology, 17*(1), 7–25. DOI: 10.1080/1360086032000063084

Clarke, J. (2009). *Blind SQL injection exploitation*. Elsevier. DOI: 10.1016/B978-1-59749-424-3.00005-0

Clarke, R. (1994). Human identification in information systems. *Information Technology & People, 7*(4), 6–37. DOI: 10.1108/09593849410076799

Cobb, M. (2022, September). *Data Masking*. Tech Target. https://www.techtarget.com/searchsecurity/definition/data-masking

Colorado Privacy Act (2021).

Commission Nationale de l'Informatique et des Libertés (CNIL). (2018, September 24). *Blockchain and the GDPR*. CNIL. https://www.cnil.fr/en/blockchain-and-gdpr

Consumer Financial Protection Bureau. (2017). Arbitration agreements rule. 12 C.F.R. § 1040. https://www.consumerfinance.gov/rules-policy/final-rules/arbitration-agreements-rule/

Consumer Protection Act (2019).

Conti, G., & Abdullah, K. (2004). Passive visual fingerprinting of network attack tools. In *Proceedings of the 2004 ACM Workshop on Visualization and Data Mining for Computer Security* (pp. 45–54). ACM. DOI: 10.1145/1029208.1029216

Control of Exemption Clauses Ordinance (Cap 71) §15 (1990).

Convention 108. (2025, January 24). *Data Protection Day.* Consultative Committee of the Convention for the Protection of Individuals with Regard to Automatic Processing of Personal Data. https://rm.coe.int/final-dpd-2025-compilation/1680b3b2ec

Coos, A. (2021, April 26). *GDPR encryption requirements*. End Point Protector. https://www.endpointprotector.com/blog/gdpr-data-encryption-requirements

Council of Europe. (n.d.). *Data protection day - 28 January.* https://www.coe.int/en/web/data-protection/data-protection-day

Council Resolution. 2009/C 296/01. (2009, November 30). *Official Journal of the European Union.* https://eur-lex.europa.eu/legal-content/EN/TXT/HTML/?uri=CELEX:32009G1205(01)

Cowls, J., King, T. C., Hitrova, C., & Floridi, L. (2021). Designing AI for people: Ethics, theory and practice. *Nature Machine Intelligence*, *3*, 896–899. DOI: 10.1038/s42256-021-00412-x

Crouse, M., Prosser, B., & Fulp, E. W. (2015). Probabilistic performance analysis of moving target and deception reconnaissance defenses. In *Proceedings of the 2nd ACM Workshop on Moving Target Defense* (pp. 21–29). ACM Press. DOI: 10.1145/2808475.2808480

Crumley, B. (2021, December 20). Colombian prison guards use drones to fly contraband – and burgers – into their own jail. *DroneDJ*. https://dronedj.com/2021/12/20/colombian-prison-guards-use-drones-to-fly-contraband-and-burgers-into-their-own-jail/

Cui, S., & Qi, P. (2021, July). The legal construction of personal information protection and privacy under the Chinese Civil Code. *Computer Law & Security Review*, *41*, 105560. DOI: 10.1016/j.clsr.2021.105560

Daigle, B., & Khan, M. (2020, June). The EU General Data Protection Regulation: An analysis of enforcement trends by EU Data Protection Authorities. *Journal of International Commerce & Economics,* 1-38. https://www.usitc.gov/publications/332/journals/jice_gdpr_enforcement_0.pdf

Daley, S. (2023). Blockchain and AI: How they integrate and 26 examples. Built In. https://builtin.com/artificial-intelligence/blockchain-ai-examples

Damjan, M. (2023, April 13). The right to privacy in the digital age: A Slovenian perspective. In Wielec, M. (Ed.), *The right to privacy in the digital age: Perspectives on analysis of certain central European countries' legislation and practice* (pp. 273–309). Central European Academic Publishing., DOI: 10.54237/profnet.2023.mwrtpida_8

Daníelsson, J., Macrae, R., & Uthemann, A. (2022). Artificial intelligence and systemic risk. *Journal of Banking & Finance, 140*, 106290. DOI: 10.1016/j.jbankfin.2021.106290

Das, S. (2020). IBM & Mahindra to develop blockchain supply chain finance solutions in India. CCN.

Dash cam legality in EU (2025 updated). (2025, February 11). DDPAI. https://www.ddpai.com/blog/dash-cam-legality-in-eu

Dashcam Nation. (n.d.). *Idiots in cars.* [YouTube channel]. YouTube. Retrieved April 13, 2025, from https://www.youtube.com/@DashcamNation1

Data breach incident report. (2020, May). Feidhmeannas Seirbhíse Sláinte (Health Service Executive). https://assets.hse.ie/media/documents/data-breach-incident-reporting-form-external.pdf

Data privacy manager. (2025, March 3). *20 biggest GDPR fines so far.* https://dataprivacymanager.net/5-biggest-gdpr-fines-so-far-2020

Davi, L., Dmitrienko, A., & Sadeghi, A. R.. (2011). Privilege escalation attacks on Android. In *International Conference on Information Security* (pp. 346–360). Springer. DOI: 10.1007/978-3-642-18178-8_30

De En Goh, G. R. (2022). Sectoral arbitrability and smart contracts: Regulatory barriers in decentralized ecosystems. *Digital Law Journal*, *3*(4), 71–105. DOI: 10.38044/2686-9136-2022-3-4-71-105

De En Goh, G. R. (2022). Smart contract disputes and public policy in the ASEAN+6 region. *Digital Law Journal*, *3*(4), 32–70. DOI: 10.38044/2686-9136-2022-3-4-32-70

De Filippi, P., Mannan, M., & Reijers, W. (2020). Blockchain as a confidence machine: The problem of trust & challenges of governance. *Technology in Society*, *62*, 101284. Advance online publication. DOI: 10.1016/j.techsoc.2020.101284

De Filippi, P., & Wright, A. (2018). *Blockchain and the law: The rule of code*. Harvard University Press.

de Meneses, A. O., & Van Quathem, K. (2018, October 26). *Portuguese hospital received and contests 400,000 € fine for GDPR infringement*. Covington Inside Privacy. https://www.insideprivacy.com/data-privacy/portuguese-hospital-receives-and-contests-400000-e-fine-for-gdpr-infringement

De Oliveira, F. M. C., Bittencourt, L. F., Bianchi, R. A. C., & Kamienski, C. A. (2024). Drones in the Big City: Autonomous Collision Avoidance for Aerial Delivery Services. *IEEE Transactions on Intelligent Transportation Systems*, *25*(5), 4657–4674. DOI: 10.1109/TITS.2023.3329029

de Terwangne, C. (2020). Article 5 Principles Relating to Processing of Personal Data. In Kuner, C., Bygrave, L. A., Docksey, C., & Drechsler, L. (Eds.), *The EU General Data Protection Regulation (GDPR): A Commentary*. Academic., DOI: 10.1093/oso/9780198826491.003.0034

Dela Cruz, J. (2024, June 5). *Microsoft faces children's privacy complaints in Austria over use of 365 Education Suite in schools*. Tech Times. https://www.techtimes.com/articles/305352/20240605/microsoft-faces-children-privacy-complaints-austria-365-education-suite.htm

Demers, A., & Lee, H. (2022). Kerberoasting: Case studies of an attack on a cryptographic authentication technology. *International Journal of Cybersecurity Intelligence & Cybercrime*, *5*(2), 25–39. DOI: 10.52306/2578-3289.1136

Denning, D. E. (1987). An intrusion-detection model. *IEEE Transactions on Software Engineering*, *13*(2), 222–232. DOI: 10.1109/TSE.1987.232894

Desai, N. M. (2023, November). *The Global Drone Revolution*. Nishith Desai Associates. https://www.nishithdesai.com/fileadmin/user_upload/pdfs/Research_Papers/The_Global_Drone_Revolution.pdf

Deshpande, V. (2024). Smart grids integration with AI-powered demand response. *Research Journal of Computer Systems and Engineering*, *5*(1), 45–58.

Desmarais, A. (2024, August 12). Elon Musk hit with nine complaints of breaching EU privacy rules to train AI model. *Euro News*. https://www.euronews.com/next/2024/08/12/elon-musk-hit-with-nine-complaints-of-breaching-eu-privacy-rules-to-train-ai-model

Dhankhar, L. (2024, February 17). *Drone delivering frozen chicken crashes at Gurugram*. Hindustan Times. https://www.hindustantimes.com/india-news/drone-delivering-frozen-chicken-crashes-at-gurugram-101708107559623.html

Dhillon, R., & Sivabalan, P. (2025). Exploring dimensions of governance for different types of blockchain systems. *The British Accounting Review, 101588*, 101588. Advance online publication. DOI: 10.1016/j.bar.2025.101588

Di Minin, E., Fink, C., Hausmann, A., Kremer, J., & Kulkarni, R. (2021). How to address data privacy concerns when using social media data in conservation science. *Conservation Biology, 35*(2), 437–446. DOI: 10.1111/cobi.13708 PMID: 33749044

Diamantopoulou, V., Lambrinoudakis, C., King, J., & Gritzalis, S. (2022). EU GDPR: Toward a Regulatory Initiative for Deploying a Private Digital Era. In Knijnenburg, B. P., Page, X., Wisniewski, P., Lipford, H. R., Proferes, N., & Jennifer, R. (Eds.), *Modern Socio-Technical Perspectives on Privacy* (pp. 427–448). Springer. DOI: 10.1007/978-3-030-82786-1_18

Digicast Technologies. (2023). The impact of blockchain on global trade. https://www.digicast-technologies.com/blockchain-global-trade/

DigiLaw. (2021). *Regulatory Framework for Drones in India*. https://www.digilaw.in/public/research/Regulatory_Framework_for_Drones.pdf

Directive 2019/944 on Common Rules for the Internal Market for Electricity and Amending Directive 2012/27/EU (2019). https://data.europa.eu/eli/dir/2019/944/oj

Dolata, M., & Schwabe, G. (2023). Moving beyond privacy and airspace safety: Guidelines for just drones in policing. *Government Information Quarterly, 40*(4), 101874. DOI: 10.1016/j.giq.2023.101874

Dragu, T., & Lupu, Y. (2021). Digital authoritarianism and the future of human rights. *International Organization, 75*(4), 991–1017. DOI: 10.1017/S0020818320000624

Driver's Privacy Protection Act, (1999).

Dror-Shpoliansky, D. (2022). *Rights in the digital age: Challenges and ways forward (OECD Digital Economy Papers No. 347)*. OECD Publishing.

Duarte, D. (2019). An Introduction to Blockchain Technology from a Legal Perspective and its Tensions with the GDPR. *Cyberlaw Journal of the Cyberlaw Research Centre of the University of Lisbon School of Law*, 1-58. https://papers.ssrn.com/sol3/papers.cfm?abstract_id=3545331

Du, G., & Ruhe, G. (2009). "Does explanation improve the acceptance of decision support for product release planning?", *3rd International Symposium on Empirical Software Engineering and Measurement*, October 2009, pp. 56-68. IEEE. DOI: 10.1109/ESEM.2009.5316049

Duman, S., Kalkan-Cakmakci, K., Egele, M., Demirci, H., & Inan, K. (2016). Email-Profiler: Spearphishing filtering with header and stylometric features of emails. In 2016 IEEE 40th Annual Computer Software and Applications Conference (COMPSAC) (pp. 408–416). IEEE. DOI: 10.1109/COMPSAC.2016.36

Durairaj, D., Gopi, R., Hariharasudan, A., Otola, I., & Bilan, Y. (2020). Reactive Power Optimization and Price Management in Microgrid Enabled with Blockchain. *Energies, 13*(23), 6179. DOI: 10.3390/en13236179

Dutch Data Protection Authority. (2022). *Assessment Framework for AI in Smart Metering Systems*. https://autoriteitpersoonsgegevens.nl

Dutta, R., Das, A., Dey, A., & Bhattacharya, S. (2020, 25 October 2020). Blockchain vs GDPR in collaborative data governance International Conference on Cooperative Design, Visualization and Engineering.

Dzobo, O., Malila, B., & Sithole, L. (2021). Proposed Framework for Blockchain Technology in a Decentralised Energy Network. *Protection Control of Modern Power Systems, 6*(1), 1–11.

Ebbers, F., & Karaboga, M. (2021). Blockchain and Data Protection: An Evaluation of the Challenges and Solutions Mentioned by German Stakeholders. In Ahlemann, F., Schütte, R., & Stieglitz, S. (Eds.), *Innovation Through Information Systems* (Vol. 47, pp. 353–369). Springer., https://doi.org/https://doi.org/10.1007/978-3-030-86797-3_24 DOI: 10.1007/978-3-030-86797-3_24

Ebers, M., Kosta, E., & Schulz, W. (Eds.). (2021). *Law and Artificial Intelligence*. Hart Publishing.

Elia Group. (2023). *Open source architectures for secure energy system operations: Elia tech review*. https://www.eliagroup.eu

Elsabagh, M., Johnson, R., & Stavrou, A.. (2020). FIRMSCOPE: Automatic uncovering of privilege-escalation vulnerabilities in pre-installed apps in Android firmware. In *Proceedings of the 29th USENIX Security Symposium* (pp. 2379–2396). USENIX Association.

ENISA. (2024). *Threat Landscape for Artificial Intelligence in Critical Infrastructure*. European Union Agency for Cybersecurity. https://www.enisa.europa.eu/publications/ai-threat-landscape

ENTSO-E. (2024). Towards autonomous grid operation: Guidelines for AI-based dispatching. https://www.entsoe.eu

Erraissi, A., & Belangour, A. (2018). Data sources and ingestion big data layers: Meta-modeling of key concepts and features. *IACSIT International Journal of Engineering and Technology*, *7*, 3607–3612.

EU Regulation 2023/1114. (2023). Markets in Crypto-Assets Regulation.

Eubanks, V. (2018). *Automating Inequality: How High-Tech Tools Profile, Police, and Punish the Poor*. St. Martin's Press.

European Commission. (2014). Regulation (EU) No 910/2014 of the European Parliament and of the Council of 23 July 2014 on electronic identification and trust services for electronic transactions in the internal market (eIDAS Regulation). *Official Journal of the European Union, L, 257*, 73–114. https://eur-lex.europa.eu/legal-content/EN/TXT/?uri=CELEX%3A32014R0910

European Commission. (2021). *Proposal for a Regulation laying down harmonised rules on artificial intelligence (Artificial Intelligence Act)*. COM(2021) 206 final. https://eur-lex.europa.eu/legal-content/EN/TXT/?uri=CELEX%3A52021PC0206

European Commission. (2021). Proposal for a Regulation laying down harmonised rules on artificial intelligence (Artificial Intelligence Act). https://eur-lex.europa.eu/legal-content/EN/TXT/?uri=CELEX%3A52021PC0206

European Commission. (2021). Proposal for a Regulation of the European Parliament and of the Council Laying Down Harmonised Rules on Artificial Intelligence (Artificial Intelligence Act). https://eur-lex.europa.eu/legal-content/EN/TXT/?uri=CELEX%3A52021PC0206

European Commission. (2022). Energy communities and the internal electricity market. *Official Journal of the European Union*. https://eur-lex.europa.eu/legal-content/EN/TXT/?uri=CELEX%3A52022DC0312

European Commission. (2024). *Digital sovereignty in critical infrastructure: Legal and regulatory framework proposal*. Publications Office of the European Union. https://europa.eu/publications/digital-sovereignty

European Data Protection Board. (2022, February 3). *Hellenic DPA: Fines imposed to telecommunications companies due to personal data breach and illegal data processing*. https://www.edpb.europa.eu/news/national-news/2022/hellenic-dpa-fines-imposed-telecommunications-companies-due-personal-data_en

European Data Protection Supervisor. (2022, 24 August 2022). *EDPS Formal Comments on the Draft Commission Implementing Regulation on Interoperability Requirements and Non-Discriminatory and Transparent Procedures for Access to Metering and Consumption Data*. https://edps.europa.eu/system/files/2022-09/22-08-24_access-metering-and-consumption-data_en.pdf

European Parliament & Council. (2024). *Regulation (EU) 2024/2847 on Cyber Resilience for Digital Products*. Official Journal of the European Union. https://eur-lex.europa.eu/eli/reg/2024/2847/oj

European Parliament. (2018, 27 November 2018). *Report on Blockchain: A Forward-looking Trade Policy*. Retrieved November 6 from https://www.europarl.europa.eu/doceo/document/A-8-2018-0407_EN.html

European Parliamentary Research Service. (2019, July 2019). *Can Distributed Ledgers be Squared with European Data Protection Law?* https://www.europarl.europa.eu/RegData/etudes/STUD/2019/634445/EPRS_STU(2019)634445_EN.pdf

European Parliamentary Research Service. (2022). Artificial Intelligence Act: EU Legislation in Progress. https://www.europarl.europa.eu/thinktank

European Union Agency for Fundamental Rights (FRA). (2020). *Getting the future right – Artificial intelligence and fundamental rights*. https://fra.europa.eu/en/publication/2020/artificial-intelligence-and-fundamental-rights

European Union Aviation Safety Agency. (2024, July). *Easy access rules for Unmanned Aircraft Systems (Regulations (EU) 2019/947 and 2019/945)*. https://www.easa.europa.eu/en/document-library/easy-access-rules/easy-access-rules-unmanned-aircraft-systems-regulations-eu#group-publications

European Union Aviation Safety Agency. (n.d.) *Code of conduct*. https://www.easa.europa.eu/en/domains/civil-drones/privacy/code-of-conduct

European Union. (1993). Council Directive 93/13/EEC of 5 April 1993 on unfair terms in consumer contracts. Official Journal of the European Communities, L95, 29–34. https://eur-lex.europa.eu/legal-content/EN/TXT/?uri=CELEX%3A31993L0013

European Union. (2016). Regulation (EU) 2016/679 of the European Parliament and of the Council of 27 April 2016 on the Protection of Natural Persons with regard to the Processing of Personal Data and on the Free Movement of such Data, and Repealing Directive 95/46/EC (General Data Protection Regulation). *Official Journal of the European Union Law 119/1, 59*.

European Union. (2023). Regulation (EU) 2023/1114 on Markets in Crypto-Assets (MiCA). Official Journal of the European Union, L 150, 1–59.

Farmer, L. S. J. (2024, March). Visual literacy in an AI-driven world. *Computers in Libraries*, *44*(2), 36–40.

Federal Arbitration Act (1925).

Fendler, R., Beard, D., & Godbey, J. (2024). A robust examination of cheating of unproctored online exams. *Electronic Journal of e-Learning*, *22*(5), 26–38. DOI: 10.34190/ejel.22.5.3173

Ferguson-Walter, K. J., Major, M. M., Johnson, C. K., & Associates. (2021). Examining the efficacy of decoy-based and psychological cyber deception. In Proceedings of the 30th USENIX Security Symposium (USENIX Security 21) (pp. 1127–1144).

Financial Crime Academy. (2025). Blockchain and privacy: Navigating the balance between transparency and data protection. https://financialcrimeacademy.org/blockchain-and-privacy/

Finck, M. (2018). Blockchains and Data Protection in the European Union. *European Data Protection Law Review, 4*, 17. https://doi.org/https://doi.org/10.21552/edpl/2018/1/6

Finck, M. (2018). Blockchains: Regulating the Unknown. *German Law Journal, 19*(4), 665-692. https://doi.org/https://doi.org/10.1017/S2071832200022847

Finck, M. (2019). Blockchain and the General Data Protection Regulation: Can distributed ledgers be squared with European data protection law? European Parliamentary Research Service. https://www.europarl.europa.eu/thinktank/en/document/EPRS_STU(2019)634445

FireEye Company. (2015). HAMMERTOSS: Stealthy tactics define a Russian cyber threat group.

Floridi, L. (2020). The fight for digital sovereignty: What it is, and why it matters, especially for the EU. *Philosophy & Technology*, *33*(3), 369–378. DOI: 10.1007/s13347-020-00423-6 PMID: 35194548

Floridi, L., & Cowls, J. (2019). A unified framework of five principles for AI in society. *Harvard Data Science Review*, *1*(1). Advance online publication. DOI: 10.1162/99608f92.8cd550d1

Floridi, L., Cowls, J., Beltrametti, M., Chatila, R., Dignum, V., & Schafer, B. (2022). How to Design AI for a Good Society: Seven Principles. *Minds and Machines*, *30*(1), 1–24. DOI: 10.1007/s11023-020-09503-7

Forbes Technology Council. (2023). The blockchain revolution in cross-border transactions. https://www.forbes.com/councils/forbestechcouncil/2023/09/05/the-blockchain-revolution-in-cross-border-transactions/

Forbes. (2023, August 18). *4 intriguing new and potential uses for facial recognition technology*. https://www.forbes.com/councils/forbestechcouncil/2023/08/18/14-intriguing-new-and-potential-uses-for-facial-recognition-technology

Forrest, C. (2018, June 13). 17 drone disasters that show why the FAA hates drones. *TechRepublic*. https://www.techrepublic.com/article/12-drone-disasters-that-show-why-the-faa-hates-drones/

Fotiadis, A. (2023, April 26). *After a personal data breach affecting 10 million customers, Cosmote & OTE appeal to cancel fine*. Solomon. https://wearesolomon.com/mag/format/feature/after-a-personal-data-breach-affecting-10-millions-customers-cosmote-ote-appeal-to-cancel-fine

Fotiadis, A., Papangeli, I., & Malichudis, S. (2022, September 9). *Asylum surveillance systems launched in Greece without data safeguards.* Balkan Insight. https://balkaninsight.com/2022/09/09/asylum-surveillance-systems-launched-in-greece-without-data-safeguards

Franke, U. (2017, December 10). Looking Back to the Future: The Beginnings of Drones and Manned Aerial Warfare. *The Strategy Bridge*. https://thestrategybridge.org/the-bridge/2017/12/10/looking-back-to-the-future-the-beginnings-of-drones-and-manned-aerial-warfare

Fudge, T. P. (2025, March 30). *GDPR roles by level.* [Image]. Fudgelink: The European Union's General Data Protection Regulation. https://fudgelink.com/GDPR

Fu, Y., Li, H. C., & Wu, X. P.. (2015). Detecting APT attacks: A survey from the perspective of big data analysis. *Journal of Communication, 36*(11), 1–14.

G'sell, F., & Martin-Bariteau, F. (2022). *The impact of blockchains for human rights, democracy, and the rule of law*. Council of Europe Report. DOI: 10.2139/ssrn.4170324

Gaia-X, A. I. S. B. L. (2024). Gaia-X Architectural Framework. Gaia-X AISBL. https://www.gaia-x.eu

Gai, K. K., Wu, Y. L., Zhu, L. H., Xu, L., & Zhang, Y. (2019). Permissioned blockchain and edge computing emPoWered privacy-preserving smart grid networks. *IEEE Internet of Things Journal, 6*(5), 7992–8004. DOI: 10.1109/JIOT.2019.2904303

Galis, M. (2024). Blockchain and data privacy: The future of technology compliance. Forbes Technology Council. https://www.forbes.com/councils/forbestechcouncil/2024/02/15/blockchain-and-data-privacy-the-future-of-technology-compliance/

Gambling Act. (2005). https://www.legislation.gov.uk/ukpga/2005/19/contents

Gao, P., Shao, F., Liu, X., Xiao, X., Qin, Z., Xu, F., Mittal, P., Kulkarni, S. R., & Song, D. (2020). Enabling efficient cyber threat hunting with cyber threat intelligence. .DOI: 10.1109/ICDE51399.2021.00024

Gao, H. (2018). Digital or Trade? The Contrasting Approaches of China and US to Digital Trade Governance. *Journal of International Economic Law*, *21*(2), 297–321. DOI: 10.1093/jiel/jgy015

Garcia, L. A., Brasser, F., & Cintuglu, M. H.. (2017). Hey, my malware knows physics! Attacking PLCs with physical model aware rootkit. In *Proceedings of the 2017 Network and Distributed System Security Symposium (NDSS)* (pp. 1–15). Internet Society. DOI: 10.14722/ndss.2017.23313

Gargaro, D. (2024, July 23). *The pros and cons of facial recognition technology*. IT Pro. https://www.itpro.com/security/privacy/356882/the-pros-and-cons-of-facial-recognition-technology

Garg, V., Niranjan, S., Prybutok, V., Pohlen, T., & Gligor, D. (2023). Drones in last-mile delivery: A systematic review on Efficiency, Accessibility, and Sustainability. *Transportation Research Part D, Transport and Environment*, *123*, 103831. DOI: 10.1016/j.trd.2023.103831

Garrie, D. B., & Andle, G. A. (2024, December 19). Arbitrating smart contract disputes: A comprehensive approach. Daily Journal Corporation. https://www.dailyjournal.com/article/382578-arbitrating-smart-contract-disputes-a-comprehensive-approach

Garrie, D. B., & Andle, G. A. (2024). *Arbitrating smart contract disputes: A comprehensive approach*. Daily Journal Corporation.

Gartner. (2021). Blockchain basics: A guide to identity and trust management. Gartner Research. https://www.gartner.com/en/documents/3991163/blockchain-basics-a-guide-to-identity-and-trust-management

Gasser, U., Budish, R., & Cohen, M. (2024). *Interoperability and control in global tech systems: A European perspective*. Harvard Kennedy School Policy Brief. https://cyber.harvard.edu/interoperability-control

Gasser, U., & Almeida, V. A. F. (2017). A layered model for AI governance. *IEEE Internet Computing*, *21*(6), 58–62. DOI: 10.1109/MIC.2017.4180835

Gaurav, A., Gupta, B. B., Arya, V., & Castiglione, A. (2025). Safety, Ethics, and Regulation in Intelligent Drones. In Gupta, B. B., & Colace, F. (Eds.), (pp. 331–346). Advances in Computational Intelligence and Robotics. IGI Global., DOI: 10.4018/979-8-3693-2707-4.ch014

Gautam, T., & Johari, R. (2023). Drone: A Systematic Review of UAV Technologies. In S. Tanwar, S. T. Wierzchon, P. K. Singh, M. Ganzha, & G. Epiphaniou (Eds.), *Proceedings of Fourth International Conference on Computing, Communications, and Cyber-Security* (Vol. 664, pp. 147–158). Springer Nature Singapore. https://doi.org/DOI: 10.1007/978-981-99-1479-1_11

Gazi, S. (2021). Reimagining a centralised cryptocurrency regulation in the US: Looking through the lens of crypto-derivatives. *Cambridge L. Rev.*, *6*, 97.

GDPR compliance and data anonymization: Lessons from Tesla's personal data leak in automotive cameras. (2023, December 20). Syntonym. https://www.syntonym.com/posts/gdpr-compliance-and-data-anonymization-lessons

GDPRWise. (n.d., n.d.). *GDPR and Online Marketplaces.* Retrieved December 13 from https://gdprwise.eu/news/platforms-required-to-take-more-active-role/

Gefen, D. (1997), Building Users' Trust in Freeware Providers and the Effects of This Trust on Users' Perceptions of Usefulness, Ease of Use and Intended Use, Doctoral dissertation, Georgia State University, Atlanta.

Gelirli, N., & Tangül, H. (2025). A Study on Analyzing the Level of Public Compliance with Drone Laws in Northern Cyprus. *Journal of Aviation*, *9*(1), 53–63. DOI: 10.30518/jav.1543124

General Data Protection Regulation (GDPR), 2016 O.J. (L 119) 1 (EU).

General Data Protection Regulation (GDPR): A compliance guide for the US. (2021, August). IT Governance USA. [Green Paper]. https://www.itgovernanceusa.com/guidance-for-achieving-compliance-with-the-eu-gdpr

General Personal Data Protection Law, (2020).

Ghosh, R. (2021). Digital trade and developing countries: A review of WTO initiatives. *South Centre Policy Brief*, *96*, 1–10.

Gill, S. S., Tuli, S., Xu, M., Singh, I., Singh, K. V., Lindsay, D., Tuli, S., Smirnova, D., Singh, M., Jain, U., Pervaiz, H., Sehgal, B., Kaila, S. S., Misra, S., Aslanpour, M. S., Mehta, H., Stankovski, V., & Garraghan, P. (2019). Transformative Effects of IoT, Blockchain and Artificial Intelligence on Cloud Computing: Evolution, Vision, Trends and Open Challenges. *Internet of Things : Engineering Cyber Physical Human Systems*, *8*, 100118. https://doi.org/https://doi.org/10.1016/j.iot.2019.100118. DOI: 10.1016/j.iot.2019.100118

Giordano, V., Gangale, F., & Fulli, G. (2020). *Smart grid projects outlook 2020: Innovation driving the energy transition*. European Commission JRC Science for Policy Report., DOI: 10.2760/21882

Glăvan, D. (2020). Sniffing attacks on computer networks. *Scientific Bulletin of the Naval Academy*, *23*(1), 202–207. DOI: 10.21279/1454-864X-20-I1-027

Global Financial Markets Association (GFMA) & Global Digital Finance (GDF). (2024). The smart contract primer. https://www.gfma.org/wp-content/uploads/2024/10/gfma-gdf-smart-contract-primer-report-2024.pdf

Godyn, M., Kedziora, M., Ren, Y., Liu, Y., & Song, H. H. (2022). Analysis of Solutions for a Blockchain Compliance with GDPR. *Scientific Reports*, *12*(1), 15021. DOI: 10.1038/s41598-022-19341-y PMID: 36056166

Goldberg, Y. (2015). A primer on neural network models for natural language processing. arXiv. https://arxiv.org/abs/1510.00726

Gont, F., & Chown, T. (2016). Network reconnaissance in IPv6 networks. *RFC*, *7707*, 1–38.

Gordon, C. (2024, February 25). AI is accelerating the loss of our scarcest natural resource: Water. *Forbes*. https://www.forbes.com/sites/cindygordon/2024/02/25/ai-is-accelerating-the-loss-of-our-scarcest-natural-resource-water

Gordon, D. G. (2016). Legal aspects of cloud computing. *Encyclopedia of Cloud Computing*, 462-475. DOI: 10.1002/9781118821930.ch38

Gowran, L. M. (2023, March 6). What's going on with Dublin Airport's drone disruptions? Silicon Republic. *Silicon Republic*. https://www.siliconrepublic.com/machines/dublin-airport-drones-flight-disruptions

Greenleaf, G. (2023). Global data privacy laws 2023: 162 national laws and 20 bills. *SSRN*, *186*, 1–4. DOI: 10.2139/ssrn.4426146

Grier, J. (2023). The blockchain revolution in cross-border transactions. Forbes Technology Council. https://www.forbes.com/councils/forbestechcouncil/2023/09/05/the-blockchain-revolution-in-cross-border-transactions/

Grigg, I. (2004). The Ricardian contract. *IEEE Security and Privacy*.

Guimarães, L. N. (2017). The Dichotomy between Smart Metering and the Protection of Consumer's Personal Data in Brazilian Law. *Brazilian Journal of Public Policy*, *7*(3), 275. DOI: 10.5102/rbpp.v7i3.4898

Gullo, K. (2023, March 31). *After students challenged proctoring software, French court slaps TestWe app with a suspension.* Electronic Frontier Foundation. https://www.eff.org/deeplinks/2023/03/after-students-challenged-proctoring-software-french-court-slaps-testwe-app

Gültekin-Várkonyi, G. (2024, September 30). Navigating data governance risks: Facial recognition in law enforcement under EU legislation. *Internet Policy Review*, *13*(3). Advance online publication. DOI: 10.14763/2024.3.1798

Gupta, S. D. (2014, November 8). Drones for all. *Business Standard*. https://www.business-standard.com/article/specials/drones-for-all-114110700900_1.html

Gurumurthy, A., & Chami, N. (2022). From digital inclusion to data justice: The role of international institutions. *Development Studies Research*, *9*(1), 18–31.

Haber, M. J., & Rolls, D. (2020). *A nuance on lateral movement*. Apress. DOI: 10.1007/978-1-4842-5165-2_2

Hafner, L., Wutz, F., Pöhn, D., Huber, A., & Schaumann, T. (2023). TASEP: A collaborative social engineering tabletop role-playing game to prevent successful social engineering attacks. In *Proceedings of the 18th International Conference on Availability, Reliability and Security* (pp. 1–10). ACM. DOI: 10.1145/3600160.3605005

Halfond, W. G., Viegas, J., & Orso, A. (2006). A classification of SQL-injection attacks and countermeasures. In *Proceedings of the IEEE International Conference on Software Engineering* (pp. 341–350). IEEE.

Hammad, A., Da Costa, B., Soares, C., & Haddad, A. (2021). The Use of Unmanned Aerial Vehicles for Dynamic Site Layout Planning in Large-Scale Construction Projects. *Buildings (Basel, Switzerland)*, *11*(12), 602. DOI: 10.3390/buildings11120602

Hammas, M., Fituri, H., Shour, A., Khan, U. A., & Ahmed, S. (2025, January). A hybrid dual-axis solar tracking system: Combining light-sensing and time-based GPS for optimal energy efficiency. *Energies*, *18*(1), 217. DOI: 10.3390/en18010217

Han, X. Y., Pasquier, T., & Bates, A.. (2020). Unicorn: Runtime provenance-based detector for advanced persistent threats. In *Proceedings of the 2020 Network and Distributed System Security Symposium* (pp. 1–14). Reston, VA, USA DOI: 10.14722/ndss.2020.24046

Haque, A. B., Islam, A. K. M. N., Hyrynsalmi, S., Naqvi, B., & Smolander, K. (2021). GDPR Compliant Blockchains–A Systematic Literature Review. *IEEE Access : Practical Innovations, Open Solutions*, *9*, 50593–50606. DOI: 10.1109/ACCESS.2021.3069877

Harvard, D. C. E. (2025). Building a responsible AI framework: 5 key principles for organizations. https://professional.dce.harvard.edu/blog/building-a-responsible-ai-framework-5-key-principles-for-organizations/

Hayward, R., & Chiang, C. (2015). Parallelizing fully homomorphic encryption for a cloud environment. *Journal of Applied Research and Technology*, *13*(2), 245–252. DOI: 10.1016/j.jart.2015.06.004

Health Insurance Portability and Accountability Act (1996).

Health Insurance Portability and Accountability Act (HIPAA) of 1996, Pub. L. No. 104-191, 110 Stat. 1936.

Heberlein, L. T., Dias, G. V., & Levitt, K. N.. (1990). A network security monitor. In *Proceedings of the 1990 IEEE Computer Society Symposium on Research in Security and Privacy* (pp. 296–304). IEEE. DOI: 10.1109/RISP.1990.63859

Heid, A. K. (2018). "Trust in Homo Artificialis: Evidence from Professional Investors", *American Accounting Association Annual Meeting*, August 2018, Washington USA.

Herath, S., Gelman, H., & Mckee, L. (2023). Privacy harm and non-compliance from a legal perspective. *Journal of Cybersecurity Education. Research and Practice*, *2023*(2), 3. DOI: 10.32727/8.2023.18

Herden, C. J., Alliu, E., Cakici, A., Cormier, T., Deguelle, C., Gambhir, S., Griffiths, C., Gupta, S., Kamani, S. R., Kiratli, Y.-S., Kispataki, M., Lange, G., Moles de Matos, L., Tripero Moreno, L., Betancourt Nunez, H. A., Pilla, V., Raj, B., Roe, J., Skoda, M., & Edinger-Schons, L. M. (2021). Corporate Digital Responsibility. *Sustainability Management Forum Nachhaltigkeits Management Forum*, *29*(1), 13–29. DOI: 10.1007/s00550-020-00509-x

Herian, R. (2018). Regulating Disruption: Blockchain, GDPR, and Questions of Data Sovereignty. *Journal of Internet Law*, *22*(2), 1–16. https://papers.ssrn.com/sol3/papers.cfm?abstract_id=3241228

Herian, R. (2018). Taking Blockchain Seriously. *Law and Critique*, *29*(2), 163–171. https://doi.org/https://doi.org/10.1007/s10978-018-9226-y. DOI: 10.1007/s10978-018-9226-y

Herrnfeld, H.-H., Brodowski, D., & Burchard, C. (2020). *Article-by-Article Commentary: Article 64 Joint controllers* (1st ed.). Bloomsbury Publishing.

Hildebrandt, M. (2016). *Smart Technologies and the End(s) of Law: Novel Entanglements of Law and Technology*. Edward Elgar Publishing., DOI: 10.4337/9781786430232

Hildebrandt, M., & Tielemans, L. (2013). Data Protection by Design and Technology Neutral Law. *Computer Law & Security Review*, *29*(5), 509–521. https://doi.org/https://doi.org/10.1016/j.clsr.2013.07.004. DOI: 10.1016/j.clsr.2013.07.004

Hirth, L., Moser, P., & Nicolosi, M. (2021). Smart grids and AI-based control systems: Lessons from Germany. *Energy Economics*, *95*, 105112. DOI: 10.1016/j.eneco.2021.105112

Hjaltalin, I. T., & Sigurdarson, H. T. (2024). The strategic use of AI in the public sector: A public values analysis of national AI strategies. *Government Information Quarterly*, *41*(1), 101914. DOI: 10.1016/j.giq.2024.101914

Holmes, C., Zhang, Y., & Stodden, V. (2022). Explainable AI in critical infrastructure: Case studies from energy dispatching. *AI & Society*, *37*(2), 251–269. DOI: 10.1007/s00146-021-01211-2

Holzleitner, M.-T., Burgstaller, K., Cejka, S., & Veseli, A. (2020). Electricity Trading via Blockchain in an Energy Community from a Data Protection Point of View. *European Energy & Climate Journal, 9*(2), 33-43. https://ezproxy.um.edu.my/login?url=https://search.ebscohost.com/login.aspx?direct=true&db=edb&AN=145712706&site=eds-live

Hossain, M. N., Milajerdi, S. M., Wang, J. N., ... (2018). SLEUTH: Real-time attack scenario reconstruction from COTS audit data. arXiv Preprint, arXiv:1801.02062.

Hovsha, J., & Brien, D. O. (2022). Drone use cases and their privacy impacts: A taxonomy. *Tilburg Law Review*, *27*(1), 60–80. DOI: 10.5334/tilr.281

How does GPS tracking work? (2024, September 3). GPS Insight. https://www.gpsinsight.com/blog/gps-tracking-work

Howell, J. (2023). Smart contracts vs. traditional contracts: Key differences. 101 Blockchains.

Howell, B. E., & Potgieter, P. H. (2021). Uncertainty and dispute resolution for blockchain and smart contract institutions. *Journal of Institutional Economics, 17*(4), 545–559. DOI: 10.1017/S1744137421000138

Hristea, F., & Caragea, C. (2022). Natural language processing (NLP) and machine learning (ML)—Theory and applications. MDPI. https://www.mdpi.com/books/reprint/6302

Huang, L. (2023). Ethics of artificial intelligence in education: Student privacy and data protection. *Science Insights Education Frontiers, 16*(2), 2577–2587. DOI: 10.15354/sief.23.re202

Huang, T., Liu, J., & Wang, S.. (2021). Survey of the future network technology and trend. *Journal of Communication, 42*(1), 130–150.

Hung, H. T. (2025). Exploring China's cyber sovereignty concept and artificial intelligence governance model: A machine learning approach. *Journal of Computational Social Science, 8*(1), 24. DOI: 10.1007/s42001-024-00346-8

Hunit. (2025). Smart legal contracts. https://smartlegalcontracts.io/

Hussain, S. S., & Sharma, P. (2025). Challenges and Safeguards. *Artificial Intelligence and Accounting: Ethical, Legal, and Social Implications*, 82.

Hutchins, E., Cloppert, M., & Amin, R. (2011). Intelligence-driven computer network defense informed by analysis of adversary campaigns and intrusion kill chains. *Leading Issues in Information Warfare & Security Research, 1*(1), 80–106.

Hutt, S., Das, S., & Baker, R. S. (2023, July). The right to be forgotten and educational data mining: Challenges and paths forward. In Feng, M., Käser, T., & Talukdar, P. (Eds.), *Proceedings of the 16th International Conference on Educational Data Mining* (pp. 251–259). Bengaluru, India. DOI: 10.5281/zenodo.8115655

ICC (2023). Arbitration rules and blockchain disputes.

IEC. (2023). Industrial communication networks - Network and system security – Part 2-1: Establishing an industrial automation and control system security program (IEC 62443-2-1). International Electrotechnical Commission. https://webstore.iec.ch

Ilias, M., Kovács, V., & Delgado, E. (2023). Regulating AI in the energy sector: A scoping review of EU laws. *Energies, 18*(9), 2359. DOI: 10.3390/en18092359

India Information Technology Security Evaluation Center. (2023). Global advanced persistent threat (APT) research report.

Indian Arbitration and Conciliation Act (1996).

IndiaToday.in. (2014, October 13). *Civilian drones banned in India: Report*. India Today. https://www.indiatoday.in/technology/news/story/civilian-drones-banned-in-india-report-222975-2014-10-13

Indulia, B. (2022). *Drone (Amendment) Rules, 2022*. SCC Online Times. https://www.scconline.com/blog/post/2022/02/15/drone-amendment-rules-2022/

Information Commissioner's Office. (2020). Guide to the General Data Protection Regulation (GDPR). ICO. https://ico.org.uk/for-organisations/guide-to-data-protection/guide-to-the-general-data-protection-regulation-gdpr

Interaction Design Foundation. (2025). The Fourth Industrial Revolution. https://www.interaction-design.org/literature/topics/the-fourth-industrial-revolution

Irish privacy watchdog investigates Elon Musk's X's use of personal data to train Grok AI chatbot. (2025, April 11). *Associated Press*. https://apnews.com/article/ireland-data-privacy-elon-musk-6458d4cc70f6b77af8034e64f45e752f

Ismail, F. (2020). Digital Industrialisation and the Developmental State: The Role of the WTO and E-commerce Negotiations. South Centre Research Paper No. 113. https://www.southcentre.int

ISO. (2023). Blockchain and distributed ledger technologies. https://www.iso.org/committee/6266604.html

Itani, W., Kayssi, A., & Chehab, A. (2009). Privacy as a service: Privacy-aware data storage and processing in cloud computing architectures. *2009 Eighth IEEE International Conference on Dependable, Autonomic and Secure Computing*. DOI: 10.1109/DASC.2009.139

ITF. (2021). *Ready for Take-Off? Integrating Drones into the Transport System*. OECD Publishing, Paris. https://www.itf-oecd.org/sites/default/files/docs/take-off-integrating-drones-transport-system.pdf

ITU. (2023). Focus Group on Application of Distributed Ledger Technology. https://www.itu.int/en/ITU-T/focusgroups/dlt/

Jaccard, G., & Tharin, A. (2018, 4 December 2018). *GDPR & Blockchain: The Swiss Take*.

Jackman, A. (2023). 'Manning' the 'unmanned': Reapproaching the military Drone through learning the/to Drone. *Political Geography*, *104*, 102894. DOI: 10.1016/j.polgeo.2023.102894

JAMS. (2023). JAMS rules governing disputes arising out of smart contracts. https://www.jamsadr.com/rules-smart-contracts

JAMS. (2023). JAMS Smart Contract Clause and Rules (DRAFT). https://www.jamsadr.com/rules-smart-contracts

Jamshed, H., Waheed, U., Iqbal, S., Faheem, M., Ashraf, M. W., & Mansoor, Y. (2025). Dynamic smart contracts framework on Ethereum private blockchain for real estate management. *Journal of Engineering (Stevenage, England)*, *2025*(1), e70063. DOI: 10.1049/tje2.70063

Janakiram, M. S. V. (2024). The building blocks of LLMs: Vectors, tokens and embeddings. The New Stack. https://thenewstack.io/the-building-blocks-of-llms-vectors-tokens-and-embeddings/

Jana, S., Mishra, A. K., & Khan, M. Z. A. (2025). Opportunistic Drone Detection Using CommSense. *IEEE Transactions on Instrumentation and Measurement*, *74*, 1–15. DOI: 10.1109/TIM.2025.3545200

Jeffreys, A. J., & Morton, D. B. (1987, February). DNA fingerprints of dogs and cats. *Animal Genetics*, *18*(1), 1–15. DOI: 10.1111/j.1365-2052.1987.tb00739.x PMID: 2886082

Jelovac, D., Ljubojevi'c, C., & Ljubojevi'c, L. (2021). HPC in business: The impact of corporate digital responsibility on ˇbuilding digital trust and responsible corporate digital governance. Digital Policy. *Regulation & Governance*, *24*, 485–497. DOI: 10.1108/DPRG-11-2020-0164

Jena, R., & Sahu, R. (2023). *Smart contracts with respect to Indian laws*. DJMR.

Jensen, M., Schwenk, J., Gruschka, N., & Iacono, L. L. (2009). On technical security issues in cloud computing. *2009 IEEE International Conference on Cloud Computing*, 109-116. DOI: 10.1109/CLOUD.2009.60

Ji, Z., Choi, E., & Gao, P. (2022, May). A knowledge base question answering system for cyber threat knowledge acquisition. In 2022 IEEE 38th International Conference on Data Engineering (ICDE) (pp. 3158-3161). IEEE. DOI: 10.1109/ICDE53745.2022.00287

Jiang, P., Huang, R. Z., & Li, D.. (2023). Auditing frameworks need resource isolation: A systematic study on the super producer threat to system auditing and its mitigation. In *Proceedings of the 32nd USENIX Security Symposium* (pp. 355–372). USENIX Association.

Jobin, A., Ienca, M., & Vayena, E. (2019). The global landscape of AI ethics guidelines. *Nature Machine Intelligence*, *1*(9), 389–399. DOI: 10.1038/s42256-019-0088-2

Jong, L., & M'charek, A. (2018). The high-profile case as 'fire object': Following the Marianne Vaatstra murder case through the media. *Crime, Media, Culture*, *14*(3), 347–363. DOI: 10.1177/1741659017718036 PMID: 30568716

Juliussen, B. A., Kozyri, E., Johansen, D., & Rui, J. P. (2023). The third country problem under the GDPR: Enhancing protection of data transfers with technology. *International Data Privacy Law*, *13*(3), 225–243. DOI: 10.1093/idpl/ipad013

Justo-Hanani, R. (2022). The politics of Artificial Intelligence regulation and governance reform in the European Union. *Policy Sciences*, *55*(1), 137–159. DOI: 10.1007/s11077-022-09452-8

Kaal, W. A., & Calcaterra, C. (2020). Blockchain innovation and antitrust regulation. *Harvard Business Law Review Online*, *10*(1), 1–28.

Kachura, M. (2023). Land ownership goes digital with NFTs in India. Itez. https://itez.com/en/blog/technology/land-ownership-goes-digital-with-nfts

Kadaba, D. M. K., & Aithal, P. S., & KRS, S. (2023). Government initiatives and digital innovation for Atma Nirbhar MSMEs/SMEs: To achieve sustainable and inclusive economic growth. [IJMTS]. *International Journal of Management, Technology, and Social Sciences*, *8*(1), 68–82.

Kalaiselvi, G., Santhosh Kumar, R., Sudharsan, S., & Venkadasubramanian. (2023). Raven: NFT-based land records system using blockchain. IJARSCT. https://www.ijarsct.co.in/Paper9753.pdf

Kaminski, M. E. (2019). The right to explanation, explained. *Berkeley Technology Law Journal*, *34*(1), 189–218. DOI: 10.15779/Z38TD9N83H

Kang, M., Ahmed, S., & Vishwanath, P. (2025). Criminal evidence analysis using blockchain technologies. *International Journal of Creative Research Thoughts*, *13*(3). https://ijcrt.org/papers/IJCRT25A3092.pdf

Kanta, K., Coisel, I., & Scanlon, M. (2020). A survey exploring open source intelligence for smarter password cracking. *Forensic Science International Digital Investigation*, *35*, 301075. DOI: 10.1016/j.fsidi.2020.301075

Kasatinka, M. (2022). Dispute resolution mechanism for smart contracts. MUJLT, 16(2). https://cris.maastrichtuniversity.nl/files/152295161/18580-Article_Text-51891-1-10-20220930.pdf

Kasatkina, A. (2023). Blockchain arbitration in India. Indian Review of International Arbitration.

Kasatkina, M. (2022). *Dispute resolution mechanisms for smart contracts.* MUJLT. DOI: 10.5817/MUJLT2022-2-2

Kaspersky, I. C. S. CERT. (2023). *Industrial cybersecurity incidents in smart grids.* https://ics-cert.kaspersky.com/reports

Kasyapa, M. S. B., & Vanmathi, C. (2024). Blockchain integration in healthcare: A comprehensive investigation of use cases, performance issues, and mitigation strategies. *Frontiers in Digital Health, 6*, 1359858. DOI: 10.3389/fdgth.2024.1359858 PMID: 38736708

Katsanis, S. H. (2020, August). Pedigrees and perpetrators: Uses of DNA and genealogy in forensic investigations. *Annual Review of Genomics and Human Genetics, 21*(1), 535–564. DOI: 10.1146/annurev-genom-111819-084213 PMID: 32289230

Kaufmann, J., & Lawyer, W. R. (2018, 7 August 2018). *Blockchain and the Data Controller.* Retrieved January 8 from https://lrz.legal/images//pdf/Blockchain-meets-Data-Privacy_Blockchain-and-the-Data-Controller.pdf

Kaur, B., & Kour, M. (2025). Impact of Artificial Intelligence on Investment Decision-Making. In AI, Economic Perspectives, and Firm Business Management (pp. 1-12). IGI Global Scientific Publishing. DOI: 10.4018/979-8-3693-7357-6.ch001

Kellermann, R., Biehle, T., & Fischer, L. (2020). Drones for parcel and passenger transportation: A literature review. *Transportation Research Interdisciplinary Perspectives, 4*, 100088. DOI: 10.1016/j.trip.2019.100088

Khaleefa, E. J., & Abdulah, D. A. (2022). Concept and difficulties of advanced persistent threats (APT): Survey. *International Journal of Nonlinear Analysis and Applications, 13*(1), 4037–4052.

Khan, T. (2023). The growing need for arbitration in energy disputes. SCC Online Blog. https://www.scconline.com/blog/post/2023/01/14/the-growing-need-for-arbitration-in-energy-disputes/

Khan, M. A., Saleh, A. M., Waseem, M., & Sajjad, I. A. (2022). Artificial Intelligence Enabled Demand Response: Prospects and Challenges in Smart Grid Environment. *IEEE Access : Practical Innovations, Open Solutions, 10*, 11231–11245. DOI: 10.1109/ACCESS.2022.3231444

Kim, D. (2021). The convergence of digital, physical and biological systems. Korea Economic Institute. https://keia.org/wp-content/uploads/2021/10/KEI_SMA_Dongwoo-Kim_FINAL.pdf

Kim, T., Park, N., & Hong, J., & Others. (2022). Phishing URL detection: A network-based approach robust to evasion. In Proceedings of the 2022 ACM SIGSAC Conference on Computer and Communications Security (pp. 1769–1782). ACM Press. DOI: 10.1145/3548606.3560615

Kim, J., & Lee, J. H. (2008). A slow port scan attack detection mechanism based on fuzzy logic and a stepwise policy. In *Proceedings of the 2008 IET 4th International Conference on Intelligent Environments* (pp. 1–5). IET.

Kim, Y. M., & Lee, B. (2023). Extending a hand to attackers: Browser privilege escalation attacks via extensions. In *Proceedings of the 32nd USENIX Security Symposium* (pp. 7055–7071). USENIX Association.

Kirchschlaeger, P. G. (2024). Blockchain ethics. *Philosophies, 9*(1), Article 2.

Koca, M. (2024). Real-time security risk assessment from CCTV using hand gesture recognition. *IEEE Access : Practical Innovations, Open Solutions, 12*, 84548–84555. DOI: 10.1109/ACCESS.2024.3412930

Kokaia, L. (2025). Bridging technology and law: Regulating blockchain smart contracts for peer-to-peer renewable energy markets. Georgian Renewable Energy Development Association. https://bm.ge/en/news/bridging-technology-and-law-regulating-blockchain-smart-contracts-for-peer-to-peer-renewable-energy-markets-blog

Kokolakis, S. (2017). Privacy attitudes and privacy behavior: A review of current research on the privacy paradox phenomenon. *Computers & Security, 64*, 122–134. DOI: 10.1016/j.cose.2015.07.002

Komarov, A. S. (2021). *Jurisdictional challenges in blockchain-based arbitration*. International Arbitration Review.

Komarov, A. S. (2021). Jurisdictional challenges in blockchain-based arbitration: The case of smart contracts. *International Arbitration Review, 24*(1), 101–127.

Komarov, A. S. (2021). Jurisdictional challenges in labor arbitration. *International Arbitration Review, 24*(1), 101–127.

Komasová, S. (2024). Czech society and drones: Experience, norms, and concerns. *Drone Systems and Applications, 12*, 1–14. DOI: 10.1139/dsa-2023-0065

Kortli, Y., Jridi, M., Al Falou, A., & Atri, M. (2020, January 7). Face recognition systems: A survey. *Sensors (Basel), 20*(2), 342. DOI: 10.3390/s20020342 PMID: 31936089

Kottasová, I. (2019, July 21). An entire nation just got hacked. *CNN World.* https://edition.cnn.com/2019/07/21/europe/bulgaria-hack-tax-intl/index.html

Kour, M. (2025). Navigating the Fintech Wave and Its Background and Challenges. In Algorithmic Training, Future Markets, and Big Data for Finance Digitalization (pp. 121-132). IGI Global Scientific Publishing. DOI: 10.4018/979-8-3693-6386-7.ch005

Kovacs, L., Nguyen, H., & Petrov, R. (2022). Machine learning in power system operations: Challenges and opportunities. *Electric Power Systems Research, 206,* 107739. DOI: 10.1016/j.epsr.2021.107739

Kranenburg-Hanspians, K. v., Kaulartz, M., & Runte, C. (2019, January 2019). *The Tension between GDPR and the Rise of Blockchain Technologies.* https://cms.law/en/media/international/files/publications/publications/the-tension-between-gdpr-and-the-rise-of-blockchain-technologies

Krasteva, V. (2024, December 26). *What is EU GDPR in a nutshell!* Composity. https://composity.com/en/post/eu-general-data-protection-regulation-in-nutshell

Kreps, S., & Zenko, M. (2014, February 12). The Next Drone Wars. *Foreign Affairs.* https://www.foreignaffairs.com/united-states/next-drone-wars

Kreutzer, L. (2021). Arbitrability and smart contracts: A conceptual and legal analysis. *Journal of International Arbitration, 38*(2), 145–170.

Krishna, R., Taneja, A., & Rastogi, A. (2021, September 25). *The Drone Rules, 2021: Summary And Key Takeaways—Aviation—Transport—India.* Mondaq. https://www.mondaq.com/india/aviation/1114708/the-drone-rules-2021-summary-and-key-takeaways

Kumar, & Sangwan, O. P. (2012). Signature-based intrusion detection system using SNORT. International Journal of Computer Applications and Information Technology, 1(3), 35–41.

Kumar, A. P. M., Rajesh, P., Kavitha, R., Thiyagarajan, R., & Yallappa, D. (2025). Drones Over Fields. In F. Daya J. L, S. G. Jasmine, & U. Kose, *Digital Farming and Smart Agriculture for Sustainable Future* (1st ed., pp. 206–221). Chapman and Hall/CRC. https://doi.org/DOI: 10.1201/9781003479154-14

Kumar, C. (2024, August 20). MoD urges strict adherence to drone flying rules amid rising popularity. *Times of India.* https://timesofindia.indiatimes.com/india/mod-urges-strict-adherence-to-drone-flying-rules-amid-rising-popularity/articleshow/112652323.cms

Kumar, A., & Sharma, D. K. (2025). A Blockchain based Solution for Efficient and Secure Healthcare Management. *International Journal of Critical Infrastructures, 21*(2), 10060627. Advance online publication. DOI: 10.1504/IJCIS.2025.10060627

Kumar, A., & Vishwanathan, A. (2025). Use of drones in Indo-Pak cross border terrorism: Challenges, regulations and evolving responses. *Asian Politics & Policy, 17*(1), e70003. DOI: 10.1111/aspp.70003

Kumar, M. G. (2023). *The impact of smart contracts and AI on the traditional contract law in India*. IJLMH.

Kumar, N., Kumar, K., Aeron, A., & Verre, F. (2025). Blockchain technology in supply chain management: Innovations, applications, and challenges. *Telematics and Informatics Reports, 18*, 100204. DOI: 10.1016/j.teler.2025.100204

Kumar, P., & Gautam, S. (2025). Blockchain Technology in the Investment Domain: A Bibliometric Analysis. *International Journal of Electronic Finance, 1*(1), 10061055. Advance online publication. DOI: 10.1504/IJEF.2025.10061055

Kumar, R., Kela, R., Singh, S., & Trujillo-Rasua, R. (2022). APT attacks on industrial control systems: A tale of three incidents. *International Journal of Critical Infrastructure Protection, 37*, 100521. DOI: 10.1016/j.ijcip.2022.100521

Kuznetsov, V., Pashkov, D., Bezvershenko, L., et al. (2023). *Operation triangulation: iOS devices targeted with previously unknown malware*.

La Torre, M., Botes, V. L., Dumay, J., & Odendaal, E. (2019). Protecting a new Achilles heel: The role of auditors within the practice of data protection. *Managerial Auditing Journal, 36*(2), 218–239. DOI: 10.1108/MAJ-03-2018-1836

Laatikainen, G., Li, M., & Abrahamsson, P. (2023). A system-based view of blockchain governance. *Information and Software Technology, 157*, 107149. DOI: 10.1016/j.infsof.2023.107149

Lacity, M. C., & Willcocks, L. P. (2016). A new approach to automating services. *MIT Sloan Management Review, 58*, 41–49.

Laksamana, Patria, Suharyanto Suharyanto, and Yohanes Ferry Cahaya. (2022). Determining factors of continuance intention in mobile payment: Fintech industry perspective. Asia Pacific Journal of Marketing and Logistics, ahead-of-print.

Lambrellis, D. (2022). Algorithms, Source Code, and the JSI: Balancing Innovation and Regulatory Autonomy. *Legal Issues of Economic Integration, 49*(1), 59–84.

László, B. (2024, November 6). *How does drone transport affect the labour market and traditional supply chains?* Flyingcarsmarket.Com. https://flyingcarsmarket.com/how-does-drone-transport-affect-the-labour-market-and-traditional-supply-chains/

Laux, J., Wachter, S., & Mittelstadt, B. (2024). Three pathways for standardisation and ethical disclosure by default under the European Union Artificial Intelligence Act. *Computer Law & Security Review*, *53*, 105957. DOI: 10.1016/j.clsr.2024.105957

Law Commission. (2021). Smart legal contracts: Advice to Government. https://lawcom.gov.uk/project/smart-contracts/

Le Coq, C., & Jaunziems, D. (2025). AI in the energy transition: Insights from Energy Talk 2025. *Free Policy Briefs*. https://freepolicybriefs.org/2025/06/02/ai-energy-transition

Lehmann, M. (2018). Who owns blockchain? *Harvard Journal of Law & Technology*, *31*(2), 567–588.

Lemieux, V. L. (2016). Trusting records: Is blockchain technology the answer? *Records Management Journal*, *26*(2), 110–139. DOI: 10.1108/RMJ-12-2015-0042

Lemke, T. (2023). Digital dependencies and the future of sovereignty: An infrastructure perspective. *European Review of Digital Politics*, *9*(1), 45–63. DOI: 10.1007/s41469-023-00612-1

Lessig, L. (2009). *Code and Other Laws of Cyberspace*. Basic Books.

Levitin, A. J. (2017). Pandora's Digital Box: The Promise and Perils of Digital Wallets. *University of Pennsylvania Law Review*, *166*(2), 305–376. https://www.jstor.org/stable/45154936

Levy, E. (2003). Poisoning the software supply chain. *IEEE Security and Privacy*, *1*(3), 70–73. DOI: 10.1109/MSECP.2003.1203227

Lew, J. D. M., Mistelis, L. A., & Kröll, S. M. (2013). *Comparative International Commercial Arbitration*. Kluwer Law International.

LexisNexis. (n.d.). Arbitrability definition. https://www.lexisnexis.co.uk/legal/glossary/arbitrability

LfDI (Lower Saxony) – Volkswagen. (2022, July 26). GDPR Hub. https://gdprhub.eu/index.php?title=LfDI_(Lower_Saxony)_-_Volkswagen

Li, J. (2023, December 1). Guiding Cases 199–201 issued by the PRC Supreme People's Court: Further steps toward a pro-arbitration regime. China Law Vision. https://www.chinalawvision.com/2023/12/uncategorized/guiding-cases-199-201-issued-by-the-prc-supreme-peoples-court-further-steps-toward-a-pro-arbitration-regime/

Li, Y. F., Ding, L. P., Wu, J. Z., et al. (2021, June 8). *Block chain network covert communication method based on multi-node timestamp collusion: CN111245570B* [Patent].

Li, Z. (2020, 10 June 2020). *Standardisation of Blockchain and Distributed Ledger Technologies—A Legal Voice from the Data Protection Law Perspective* EURAS Annual Standardisation Conference–Standards for Digital Transformation: Blockchain and Innovation https://papers.ssrn.com/sol3/papers.cfm?abstract_id=3892298

Li, H. (2018). Deep learning for natural language processing: Advantages and challenges. *National Science Review*, *5*(1), 24–26. https://academic.oup.com/nsr/article/5/1/24/4107792. DOI: 10.1093/nsr/nwx110 PMID: 34691827

Li, H., Yu, L., & He, W. (2019). The impact of GDPR on global technology development. *Journal of Global Information Technology Management*, *22*(1), 1–6. DOI: 10.1080/1097198X.2019.1569186

Lin, Z. P., Wu, Y. H., & Xing, X. Y. (2022). DirtyCred: Escalating privilege in Linux kernel. In *Proceedings of the 2022 ACM SIGSAC Conference on Computer and Communications Security* (pp. 1963–1976). ACM.

Li, R., Diao, W. R., & Li, Z.. (2021). Android custom permissions demystified: From privilege escalation to design shortcomings. In *Proceedings of the 2021 IEEE Symposium on Security and Privacy (SP)* (pp. 70–86). IEEE Press. DOI: 10.1109/SP40001.2021.00070

Li, R., & Wu, M. (2024). Revealing Urban Color Patterns via Drone Aerial Photography—A Case Study in Urban Hangzhou, China. *Buildings (Basel, Switzerland)*, *14*(2), 546. DOI: 10.3390/buildings14020546

Liu, B. J., Johansson, B. S., & Paulsson, V. (2025). AI-enabled predictive analytics in smart grids: The case of Sweden. *Linköping Electronic Conference Proceedings*, *42*(3), 49–65. https://doi.org/DOI: 10.5560/liu.diva-portal.1956031

Liu, B., Xu, E., Wang, J., Wei, Z., Xu, L., Zhao, B., & Su, J. (2011). Thwarting audio steganography attacks in cloud storage systems. *2011 International Conference on Cloud and Service Computing*, 259-265. DOI: 10.1109/CSC.2011.6138530

Liu, X., Riaz, S., & Farooq, M. (2022). AI in Swedish local smart grids: A case study. *Sustainable Energy Technologies and Assessments*, *51*, 101092. DOI: 10.1016/j.seta.2022.101092

Liu, Y., Lu, Q., Yu, G., Paik, H. Y., & Zhu, L. (2022). Defining blockchain governance principles: A comprehensive framework. *Information Systems*, *109*, 102090. DOI: 10.1016/j.is.2022.102090

Liu, Y., Lu, Q., Zhu, L., Paik, H. Y., & Staples, M. (2023). A systematic literature review on blockchain governance. *Journal of Systems and Software*, *197*, 111576. Advance online publication. DOI: 10.1016/j.jss.2022.111576

Li, Y. F., Ding, L. P., & Wu, J. Z.. (2019). Research on a new network covert channel model in blockchain environment. *Journal of Communication*, *40*(5), 67–78.

Liyanaarachchi, G., Deshpande, S., & Weaven, S. (2021). Online banking and privacy: Redesigning sales strategy through social exchange. *International Journal of Bank Marketing*, *39*(6), 955–983. DOI: 10.1108/IJBM-05-2020-0278

Li, Z. (2021). Confronting Algorithm Bias Risks: Will Blockchain Provide New Opportunities or Challenges for Data Protection Law? *Dublin Law & Politics Review* *2*(43). https://doi.org/https://ssrn.com/abstract=3946608

Lobschat, L., Mueller, B., Eggers, F., Brandimarte, L., Diefenbach, S., Kroschke, M., & Wirtz, J. (2021). Corporate digital responsibility. *Journal of Business Research*, *122*, 875–888. DOI: 10.1016/j.jbusres.2019.10.006

Lokanan, M. E. (2014). How senior managers perpetuate accounting fraud? Lessons for fraud examiners from an instructional case. *Journal of Financial Crime*, *21*, 411–423. DOI: 10.1108/JFC-03-2013-0016

Lu, S. (2022). Data privacy, human rights, and algorithmic opacity. *California Law Review*, *110*(Dec), 1423–1472.

Luthander, R., Widén, J., & Munkhammar, J. (2020). Self-consumption and self-sufficiency of solar photovoltaic systems with battery storage: A study of Swedish households. *Renewable Energy*, *106*, 193–201. DOI: 10.1016/j.renene.2016.12.044

Madan, V., & Kour, M. (2024), "Fintech and Mobile Payments in Transition: A Study of Adoption Challenges", *2024 IEEE International Conference on Interdisciplinary Approaches in Technology and Management for Social Innovation (IATMSI)*, (Vol. 2, pp. 1-6). IEEE. DOI: DOI: 10.1109/IATMSI60426.2024.10502648

Mahmoud, M., Mannan, M., & Youssef, A. (2023). APTHunter: Detecting advanced persistent threats in early stages. *Digital Threats : Research and Practice*, *4*(1), 1–31. DOI: 10.1145/3559768

Majid, Z. M. (2024, July 26). Army seizes arms, ammunition dropped by Drone along LoC. *Deccan Herald.* https://www.deccanherald.com/india/jammu-and-kashmir/army-seizes-arms-ammunition-dropped-by-drone-along-loc-3124211

Majmudar & Partners. (2021). *Drone Rules, 2021: Key Highlights.* https://www.majmudarindia.com/wp-content/uploads/DroneRules-230921-KeyHighlights.pdf

Malaquias, R. F., & Hwang, Y. (2019). Mobile banking use: A comparative study with Brazilian and US participants. *International Journal of Information Management*, *44*, 132–140. DOI: 10.1016/j.ijinfomgt.2018.10.004

Malhotra, O. P., & Malhotra, I. (2003). *Arbitration and conciliation* (2nd ed.). LexisNexis Butterworths.

Manda, V. K., Christy, V., & Hlali, A. (2024). Current Trends, Opportunities, and Futures Research Directions in Geospatial Technologies for Smart Cities. In Darwish, D., & Chemingui, H. (Eds.), (pp. 239–270). Advances in Geospatial Technologies. IGI Global., DOI: 10.4018/979-8-3693-8054-3.ch009

Mandiant Intelligence Center. (2013). APT1: Exposing one of India's cyber espionage units.

Mantelero, A. (2013). The EU Proposal for a General Data Protection Regulation and the Roots of the 'Right to be Forgotten'. *Computer Law & Security Review*, *29*(3), 229–235. https://doi.org/https://doi.org/10.1016/j.clsr.2013.03.010. DOI: 10.1016/j.clsr.2013.03.010

Mars, A., & Gouider, M. S. (2017). Big data analysis to feature opinions extraction of customers. *Procedia Computer Science*, *112*, 906–916. DOI: 10.1016/j.procs.2017.08.114

Martinez, J., Ruiz, A., Puelles, J., Arechalde, I., & Miadzvetskaya, Y. (2019). Smart Grid Challenges Through the Lens of the European General Data Protection Regulation. In Siarheyeva, A., Barry, C., Lang, M., Linger, H., & Schneider, C. (Eds.), *Advances in Information Systems Development* (Vol. 39, pp. 113–130). Springer., https://doi.org/https://doi.org/10.1007/978-3-030-49644-9_7 DOI: 10.1007/978-3-030-49644-9_7

Martin, K. D., Kim, J. J., Palmatier, R. W., Steinhoff, L., Stewart, D. W., Walker, B. A., Wang, Y., & Weaven, S. K. (2020). Data Privacy in Retail. *Journal of Retailing*, *96*(4), 474–489. DOI: 10.1016/j.jretai.2020.08.003

Martins Gonçalves, R., Mira da Silva, M., & Rupino da Cunha, P. (2023). Implementing GDPR-Compliant Surveys Using Blockchain. *Future Internet, 15*(4), 143. DOI: 10.3390/fi15040143

Martins, B. O., Lavallée, C., & Silkoset, A. (2021). Drone Use for COVID-19 Related Problems: Techno-solutionism and its Societal Implications. *Global Policy, 12*(5), 603–612. DOI: 10.1111/1758-5899.13007 PMID: 34899997

Mazurczyk, W., & Caviglione, L. (2021). Cyber reconnaissance techniques. *Communications of the ACM, 64*(3), 86–95. DOI: 10.1145/3418293

McKendrick, E. (2021). *Contract law: Text, cases, and materials* (9th ed.). Oxford University Press.

McKnight, H., & Chervany, N. L. (2002). What trust means in E-commerce customer relationships: An interdisciplinary conceptual Typology. *International Journal of Electronic Commerce, 6*(2), 35–59. DOI: 10.1080/10864415.2001.11044235

McLean, S., & Deane-Johns, S. (2016). Demystifying Blockchain and Distributed Ledger Technology–Hype or Hero? *Computer Law Review International, 17*(4), 97-102. https://doi.org/https://doi.org/10.9785/cri-2016-0402

McNeal, G. S., Goodwin, W., & Jones, S. (2017). Warrantless Operations of Public Use Drones: Considerations for Government Agencies. *The Fordham Urban Law Journal, 44*(3), 703–723.

MDPI. (2023). Use of blockchain-based smart contracts in logistics and supply chains. https://www.mdpi.com/2079-9292/12/6/1340

Meiklejohn, S., & Orlandi, C. (2015). Privacy-enhancing overlays in bitcoin. In *Financial Cryptography and Data Security* (pp. 127–141). Springer. DOI: 10.1007/978-3-662-48051-9_10

Mengelkamp, E., Gärttner, J., & Weinhardt, C. (2018). Decentralizing energy systems through local energy markets: A blockchain-based market approach. *Computer Science -. Research for Development, 33*, 207–214. DOI: 10.1007/s00450-017-0360-9

Menon, S., & Jain, K. (2024). Blockchain Technology for Transparency in Agri-Food Supply Chain: Use Cases, Limitations, and Future Directions. *IEEE Transactions on Engineering Management, 71*, 106–120. Advance online publication. DOI: 10.1109/TEM.2021.3110903

Merlo, V., Pio, G., Giusto, F., & Bilancia, M. (2022). On the Exploitation of the Blockchain Technology in the Healthcare Sector: A Systematic Review. *Expert Systems with Applications, 213*, 118897. DOI: 10.1016/j.eswa.2022.118897

Meyer, D. (2018, 27 February 2018). *Blockchain Technology is on a Collision Course with EU Privacy Law*. https://iapp.org/news/a/blockchain-technology-is-on-a-collision-course-with-eu-privacy-law/

Mik, E. (2017). Smart contracts: Terminology, technical limitations and real-world complexity. *Law, Innovation and Technology*, *9*(2), 269–300. DOI: 10.1080/17579961.2017.1378468

Milajerdi, S. M., Eshete, B., & Gjomemo, R.. (2019a). POIROT: Aligning attack behavior with kernel audit records for cyber threat hunting. In *Proceedings of the 2019 ACM SIGSAC Conference on Computer and Communications Security* (pp. 1798–1812). New York, NY, USA: ACM. DOI: 10.1145/3319535.3363217

Milajerdi, S. M., Gjomemo, R., & Eshete, B.. (2019b). HOLMES: Real-time APT detection through correlation of suspicious information flows. In *Proceedings of the 2019 IEEE Symposium on Security and Privacy (SP)* (pp. 1137–1152). Piscataway, NJ, USA: IEEE. DOI: 10.1109/SP.2019.00026

Milčiuvienė, S., Kiršienė, J., Doheijo, E., Urbonas, R., & Milčius, D. (2019). The Role of Renewable Energy Prosumers in Implementing Energy Justice Theory. *Sustainability (Basel)*, *11*(19), 5286. DOI: 10.3390/su11195286

Millar, K. A. (2022). Graph-based machine learning for passive network reconnaissance within encrypted networks. Ph.D. dissertation, The University of Adelaide, Australia.

Mirchandani, A. (2018). The GDPR-Blockchain Paradox: Exempting Permissioned Blockchains from the GDPR. *Fordham Intellectual Property. Media and Entertainment Law Journal*, *29*, 1201.

Mistelis, L. A., & Brekoulakis, S. L. (Eds.). (2009). *Arbitrability: International and comparative perspectives*. Kluwer Law International.

Mistral, A. I. (2024). Tokenization guide. https://docs.mistral.ai/guides/tokenization/

Mitsubishi Motors Corp. v. Soler Chrysler-Plymouth, 473 U.S. 614 (1985).

Mittelstadt, B. D., Allo, P., Taddeo, M., Wachter, S., & Floridi, L. (2016). The ethics of algorithms: Mapping the debate. *Big Data & Society*, *3*(2), 1–21. DOI: 10.1177/2053951716679679

Miyata, J., Tsuchiya, H., Nonaka, F., Aso, Y., Sugahara, M., & Maeda, T. (2025). Demonstration of autonomous fixed-wing drone delivery of prescribed medications in remote islands in Japan. *Journal of General and Family Medicine*, jgf2.768. https://doi.org/DOI: 10.1002/jgf2.768

Modi, S., Mane, S., Mahadik, S., Kadam, R., Jambhale, R., Mahadik, S., & Mali, Y. (2024). Automated attendance monitoring system for cattle through CCTV. *Revista Electrónica de Veterinaria, 25*(1), 1025–1034. DOI: 10.69980/redvet.v25i1.724

Moghe, U., Lakkadwala, P., & Mishra, D. K. (2012). Cloud computing: Survey of different utilization techniques. *2012 CSI Sixth International Conference on Software Engineering (CONSEG)*, 1-4. DOI: 10.1109/CONSEG.2012.6349524

Mohamed, N., & Belaton, B. (2021). SBI model for the detection of advanced persistent threat based on strange behavior of using credential dumping technique. *IEEE Access : Practical Innovations, Open Solutions, 9*, 42919–42932. DOI: 10.1109/ACCESS.2021.3066289

Mohamed, R., Eltamaly, A. M., & Abdelaziz, A. Y. (2021). AI-based adaptive energy management for prosumer networks. *International Journal of Electrical Power & Energy Systems, 129*, 106810. DOI: 10.1016/j.ijepes.2020.106810

Mohammad, M. (2024, November 12). *Peddlers Resort To High-End Drone, Encrypted Apps To Deliver Drugs In Kashmir*. ETV Bharat. https://www.etvbharat.com/en/!state/peddlers-resort-to-high-end-drone-encrypted-apps-to-deliver-drugs-in-kashmir-enn24111204985

Monteiro, A. M. (2019, January 3). *First GDPR fine in Portugal issued against hospital for three violations*. IAAP. https://iapp.org/news/a/first-gdpr-fine-in-portugal-issued-against-hospital-for-three-violations

Monteiro, J. A., & Teh, R. (2017). Provisions on Electronic Commerce in Regional Trade Agreements. WTO Working Paper ERSD-2017-11. https://www.wto.org

Morton, T. (2016). *From Kites through Cold War: The Evolution of United States Air Force Manned Airborne ISR* [Doctorate of Philosophy Thesis, School of Advanced Air and Space Studies, Air University]. https://apps.dtic.mil/sti/pdfs/AD1030466.pdf

Mukherjee, S., Sen, P., Bora, S., ... (2015). SQL Injection: A sample review. In Proceedings of the 2015 6th International Conference on Computing, Communication and Networking Technologies (ICCCNT) (pp. 1–7). IEEE. DOI: 10.1109/ICCCNT.2015.7395166

Mukherjee, S. (2022). India's crypto conundrum: Public policy, private currencies and CBDCs. *SSRN*. DOI: 10.2139/ssrn.4206714

Mukul, P. (2021, September 2). Explained: How India's new drone rules have been liberalised. *The Indian Express*. https://indianexpress.com/article/explained/india-drone-rules-2021-explained-7471914/

Munoz, A., ... (2024, March 22). Commercial arbitration: France. Global Arbitration Review. https://globalarbitrationreview.com/insight/know-how/commercial-arbitration/report/france

Musiani, F. (2025). Infrastructuring digital sovereignty: An agenda for digital self-determination. *Frontiers in Communication*, *10*, 1562072. DOI: 10.3389/fcomm.2025.1562072

Nachbar, T. B. (2021). Algorithmic fairness, algorithmic discrimination. *Florida State University Law Review. Florida State University. College of Law*, *48*(2), 509–558.

Nagy, R., Németh, K., Papp, D., & Buttyán, L. (2021). Rootkit detection on embedded IoT devices. *Acta Cybernetica (Szeged)*, *25*(2), 369–400. DOI: 10.14232/actacyb.288834

Nakamoto, S. (2008). Bitcoin: A Peer-to-Peer Electronic Cash System | Satoshi Nakamoto Institute. *Bitcoin.Org*.

Nakamoto, S. (2008). Bitcoin: A peer-to-peer electronic cash system. Bitcoin White Paper.

Nakamoto, S. (2008). Bitcoin: A peer-to-peer electronic cash system. https://bitcoin.org/en/bitcoin-paper

Narayanan, A., Bonneau, J., Felten, E., Miller, A., & Goldfeder, S. (2016). Bitcoin and Cryptocurrency Technologies: A Comprehensive Introduction. In *Bitcoin and Cryptocurrency Technologies: A Comprehensive Introduction*. Princeton University Press.

Narayanan, A., Bonneau, J., Felten, E., Miller, A., & Goldfeder, S. (2016). *Bitcoin and cryptocurrency technologies: A comprehensive introduction*. Princeton University Press.

Nar, K., & Sastry, S. S. (2018). An analytical framework to address the data exfiltration of advanced persistent threats. In *Proceedings of the 2018 IEEE Conference on Decision and Control (CDC)* (pp. 867–873). IEEE. DOI: 10.1109/CDC.2018.8619834

National Conference of State Legislatures. (2021). Blockchain legislation. NCSL. https://www.ncsl.org/research/financial-services-and-commerce/blockchain-state-legislation-and-regulations.aspx

Nawaz, S. A. (2024). Regulating Autonomy in Civilian Drones: Towards a Spectral Approach. *Journal of Intelligent & Robotic Systems*, *110*(2), 46. DOI: 10.1007/s10846-024-02056-9

Nemitz, P. (2018). Constitutional democracy and technology in the age of artificial intelligence. *Philosophical Transactions. Series A, Mathematical, Physical, and Engineering Sciences, 376*(2133), 20180089. DOI: 10.1098/rsta.2018.0089 PMID: 30323003

Neuburger, J. (2018). *Blockchain, personal data and the GDPR right to be forgotten*. Lexology.

New York Convention (1958). Convention on the Recognition and Enforcement of Foreign Arbitral Awards.

Nguyen v. Barnes & Noble Inc., 763 F.3d 1171 (9th Cir. 2014).

NIST. (2023). *Managing AI risks in critical energy systems: Technical guidance*. National Institute of Standards and Technology., DOI: 10.6028/NIST.SP.1276

Niu, B., Zhang, J., & Xie, F. (2024). Drone logistics' resilient development: Impacts of consumer choice, competition, and regulation. *Transportation Research Part A, Policy and Practice, 185*, 104126. DOI: 10.1016/j.tra.2024.104126

Nogel, M. (2024, June). Some areas where digital forensics can support the addressing of legal challenges linked to forensic genetic genealogy. *Forensic Science International Digital Investigation, 49*, 301696. DOI: 10.1016/j.fsidi.2024.301696

Nykyri, M., Kärkkäinen, T. J., Levikari, S., Honkapuro, S., Annala, S., & Silventoinen, P. (2022). Blockchain-Based Balance Settlement Ledger for Energy Communities in Open Electricity Markets. *Energy, 253*, 124180. https://doi.org/https://doi.org/10.1016/j.energy.2022.124180. DOI: 10.1016/j.energy.2022.124180

O'Flaherty, K. (2024, September 9). *What you need to know about Grok AI and your privacy*. Wired. https://www.wired.com/story/grok-ai-privacy-opt-out

OECD. (2023). *Artificial Intelligence in Society: Industrial Applications and Legal Trends*. OECD Publishing. https://www.oecd.org/going-digital/ai/

OECD. (2023). *OECD blockchain policy framework*. OECD Publishing.

OECD. (2023). OECD blockchain policy framework. OECD Publishing. https://www.oecd.org/en/topics/digital-finance.html

OECD. (2023). *OECD Framework for the Classification of AI Systems*. OECD Publishing. https://www.oecd.org/going-digital/ai/classification

Office of the UN High Commissioner for Human Rights. (2022). *The right to privacy in the digital age (A/HRC/51/17)*. United Nations.

Ofgem. (2024, April 3). Ofgem fears 'AI collusion' in energy market. *The Times*. https://www.thetimes.co.uk/article/03ofgem-q6dspmr3r

Olislaegers, S. (2011, September 5). 2011). *Early Lessons Learned in the ENDORSE Project: Legal Challenges and Possibilities in Developing Data Protection Compliance Software* IFIP PrimeLife International Summer School on Privacy and Identity Management for Life, Omar, I. A., Jayaraman, R., Salah, K., Yaqoob, I., & Ellahham, S. (2021). Applications of Blockchain Technology in Clinical Trials: Review and Open Challenges. *Arabian Journal for Science and Engineering, 46*, 3001–3015. https://doi.org/https://doi.org/10.1007/s13369-020-04989-3

Omolara, A. E., Alawida, M., & Abiodun, O. I. (2023). Drone cybersecurity issues, solutions, trend insights and future perspectives: A survey. *Neural Computing & Applications, 35*(31), 23063–23101. DOI: 10.1007/s00521-023-08857-7

Organisation for Economic Co-operation and Development. (2022, June 10). *Recommendation of the Council on Blockchain and Other Distributed Ledger Technologies (OECD/LEGAL/0470)*. OECD. https://legalinstruments.oecd.org/en/instruments/OECD-LEGAL-0470

Osnos, E. (2018)." Can Mark Zuckerberg fix Facebook before it breaks democracy?", The New Yorker,10,September,2018.Retrievedfrom https://www.newyorker.com/magazine/2018/09/17/can mark-zuckerberg-fix-facebook-before-it-breaks democracy.

Our general principles. (n.d.). NOYB. https://noyb.eu/en/our-general-principles

Outlook India. (2025). Blockchain in Indian judiciary: Use cases and challenges. https://www.outlookindia.com/xhub/blockchain-insights/blockchain-in-indian-judiciary-use-cases-and-challenges

Paccagnella, R., Datta, P., & Hassan, W. U.. (2020b). Custos: Practical tamper-evident auditing of operating systems using trusted execution. In *Proceedings of the 2020 Network and Distributed System Security Symposium*. Internet Society. DOI: 10.14722/ndss.2020.24065

Paccagnella, R., Liao, K., & Tian, D.. (2020a). Logging to the danger zone: Race condition attacks and defenses on system audit frameworks. In *Proceedings of the 2020 ACM SIGSAC Conference on Computer and Communications Security* (pp. 1551–1574). ACM Press. DOI: 10.1145/3372297.3417862

Pagallo, U. (2013). *The Laws of Robots: Crimes, Contracts, and Torts*. Springer., DOI: 10.1007/978-94-007-6564-1

Paliwal, A. (2022, May 27). *India will be drone hub by 2030: PM Modi at country's biggest drone festival*. India Today. https://www.indiatoday.in/india/story/drone-hub-by-2030-pm-narendra-modi-india-biggest-drone-festival-pragati-maidan-1954855-2022-05-27

Palmiotto, F., & Menéndez González, N. (2023). Facial recognition technology, democracy and human rights. *Computer Law & Security Review*, *50*, 105857. DOI: 10.1016/j.clsr.2023.105857

Panagariya, A. (2022). Digital revolution, financial infrastructure and entrepreneurship: The case of India. *Asia and the Global Economy*, *2*(2), 100027. DOI: 10.1016/j.aglobe.2022.100027

Panday, J. (2017, August 28). *India's Supreme Court Upholds Right to Privacy as a Fundamental Right—And It's About Time. Electronic Frontier Foundation*. EFF. https://www.eff.org/deeplinks/2017/08/indias-supreme-court-upholds-right-privacy-fundamental-right-and-its-about-time

Panjwani, S., Tan, S., & Jarrin, K. M., & Others. (2005). An experimental evaluation to determine if port scans are precursors to an attack. In Proceedings of the 2005 International Conference on Dependable Systems and Networks (DSN'05) (pp. 602–611). IEEE. DOI: 10.1109/DSN.2005.18

Pan, X., González, R., & Weber, F. (2025). The paradigm shift in the energy sector through green innovation. *Energy Research & Social Science*, *102*, 103076. DOI: 10.1016/j.erss.2024.103076

Park, J. Y., Ryu, J. P., & Shin, H. J. (2016). Robo advisors for portfolio management. *Advanced Science and Technology Letters*, *141*, 104–108. DOI: 10.14257/astl.2016.141.21

Park, S. (2024). Bridging the global divide in AI regulation: A contextual, coherent, and commensurable framework. *SSRN*, *33*(1), 125–175. DOI: 10.2139/ssrn.4950781

Patel v. Mirza, [2016] UKSC 42.

Patel, A., Taghavi, M., Bakhtiyari, K., & Celestino Júnior, J. (2013). An intrusion detection and prevention system in cloud computing: A systematic review. *Journal of Network and Computer Applications*, *36*(1), 25–41. DOI: 10.1016/j.jnca.2012.08.007

Patel, K. (2018). Artificial Intelligence in Finance. *IJSART*, *4*(4), 2787–2788.

Pavlou, P. (2003). Consumer acceptance of electronic commerce: Integrating trust and risk with the technology acceptance model. *International Journal of Electronic Commerce*, *7*(3), 101–134. DOI: 10.1080/10864415.2003.11044275

Pearson, S., & Benameur, A. (2010). Privacy, security and trust issues arising from cloud computing. *2010 IEEE Second International Conference on Cloud Computing Technology and Science*, 693-702. DOI: 10.1109/CloudCom.2010.66

Peiretti, F., & Pensa, R. G. (2023). Detection of privacy-harming social media posts in Italian. In *International Symposium on Security and Privacy in Social Networks and Big Data* (pp. 203–223). Springer. DOI: 10.1007/978-981-99-5177-2_12

Peng, L., Feng, W., Yan, Z., Li, Y., Zhou, X., & Shimizu, S. (2020). Privacy Preservation in Permissionless Blockchain: A Survey. *Digital Communications and Networks*, *7*(3), 295–307. https://doi.org/https://doi.org/10.1016/j.dcan.2020.05.008. DOI: 10.1016/j.dcan.2020.05.008

Pentland, A. (2021). Building the new economy: A data commons. *Communications of the ACM*, *64*(9), 37–39.

Personal Data Protection Act (2012).

Personal Data Protection Act, (2019).

Peters, J., Akoto, N., & Mbogo, A. (2022). Geopolitical asymmetries in digital infrastructure. *International Journal of Critical Infrastructure Protection*, *38*, 100519. DOI: 10.1016/j.ijcip.2022.100519

PIB. (2021, December 9). *Incentive of Rs. 120 crore has been provided for Indian manufacturers of drone and drone components under PLI Scheme*. https://pib.gov.in/Pressreleaseshare.aspx?PRID=1779782

PIB. (2023, March 20). *Shri Jyotiraditya Scindia highlights various aspects of the growth of the Indian Civil Aviation Industry*. Press Information Bureau, Government of India. https://www.pib.gov.in/PressReleseDetailm.aspx?PRID=1908939

Poggi, N. (2021, June 15). *Encryption choices: RSA vs. AES explained*. Prey Project. https://preyproject.com/blog/types-of-encryption-symmetric-or-asymmetric-rsa-or-aes

Pohrmen, F. H., Das, R. K., & Saha, G. (2019). Blockchain-Based Security Aspects in Heterogeneous Internet-of-Things Networks: A Survey. *Transactions on Emerging Telecommunications Technologies*, *30*(10), e3741. https://doi.org/https://doi.org/10.1002/ett.3741. DOI: 10.1002/ett.3741

Poireault, K. (2024a, August 21). *Australia calls off Clearview AI investigation despite lack of compliance*. Infosecurity Magazine. https://www.infosecurity-magazine.com/news/australia-calls-off-clearview-ai

Poireault, K. (2024b, September 4). *Clearview AI fined €30.5m by Dutch watchdog over illegal data collection.* Infosecurity Magazine. https://www.infosecurity-magazine.com/news/clearview-ai-fined-30m-netherlands

Polcumpally, A. T., Pandey, K. K., Kumar, A., & Samadhiya, A. (2024). Blockchain governance and trust: A multi-sector thematic systematic review and exploration of future research directions. *Heliyon, 10*(12), 32975. DOI: 10.1016/j.heliyon.2024.e32975 PMID: 38984295

Potter, A., Highams, H., Kazmi, T., Young, A., Kerpauskaite, K., Stylianou, T., Ashcroft, V., & Kateifides, A. (2020, 26 March 2020). *Comparing Privacy Laws: GDPR v. Australian Privacy Act.* https://www.dataguidance.com/sites/default/files/gdpr_v_australia.pdf

Power Ledger. (2019, 2019). *Power Ledger Whitepaper.* Retrieved March, 4 2023 from https://www.powerledger.io/company/power-ledger-whitepaper

Premalatha, J., & Sathya, K. (2020). Integration of Blockchain into IoT. In Kumar, S. A. P., Velliangiri, S., & Karthikeyan, P. (Eds.), *Internet of Things* (1st ed., pp. 121–134). CRC Press., DOI: 10.1201/9781003032441-8

Primavera de Filippi and Aaron Wright. (2018). *Blockchain and the Law: The Rule of Code.* HUP.

Prince, C., Omrani, N., & Schiavone, F. (2024). Online privacy literacy and users' information privacy empowerment: The case of GDPR in Europe. *Information Technology & People, 37*(8), 1–24. DOI: 10.1108/ITP-05-2023-0467

Privacy Act (1988).

Przegalinska, A., Ciechanowski, L., Stroz, A., Gloor, P., & Mazurek, G. (2019). In bot we trust: A new methodology of chatbot performance measures. [CrossRef]. *Business Horizons, 2019*(62), 785–797. DOI: 10.1016/j.bushor.2019.08.005

PSL. (2021). *PSL Release—The Unmanned Aircraft System Rules, 2021.* PSL Advocates and Solicitors. https://www.pslchambers.com/wp-content/uploads/2021/07/The-Unmanned-Aircraft-System-Rules-2021.pdf

PTI. (2010, July 3). DRDO develops UAV Netra to aid anti-terrorist operations. *The Hindu.* https://www.thehindu.com/news/national/DRDO-develops-UAV-lsquoNetrarsquo-to-aid-anti-terrorist-operations/article16183692.ece

PTI. (2016, April 27). DGCA releases draft guidelines for unmanned flying devices. *Mint.* https://www.livemint.com/Politics/bAB3DaJLWsn3B5G5AfGS7N/DGCA-releases-draft-guidelines-for-unmanned-flying-devices.html

PTI. (2018, August 27). *Government announces Regulations for Drones.* https://pib.gov.in/newsite/printrelease.aspx?relid=183093

Putz, B., Menges, F., & Pernul, G. (2019). A Secure and Auditable Logging Infrastructure Based on a Permissioned Blockchain. *Computers & Security*, *87*, 101602. https://doi.org/https://doi.org/10.1016/j.cose.2019.101602. DOI: 10.1016/j.cose.2019.101602

Qi An Xin Technology Group Inc. (2023). *Global advanced persistent threats (APT) mid-2023 report.*

Quamar, M. M., Al-Ramadan, B., Khan, K., Shafiullah, M., & El Ferik, S. (2023). Advancements and Applications of Drone-Integrated Geographic Information System Technology—A Review. *Remote Sensing*, *15*(20), 5039. DOI: 10.3390/rs15205039

Radu, R. (2021). Steering the governance of artificial intelligence: National strategies in perspective. *Policy and Society*, *40*(2), 178–193. DOI: 10.1080/14494035.2021.1929728

Raghunatha, A., Thollander, P., & Barthel, S. (2023). Addressing the emergence of drones – A policy development framework for regional drone transportation systems. *Transportation Research Interdisciplinary Perspectives*, *18*, 100795. DOI: 10.1016/j.trip.2023.100795

Rai, K., Verma, R., & Tiwari, S. (2021). Using open source intelligence as a tool for reliable web searching. *SN Computer Science*, *2*(5), 402. DOI: 10.1007/s42979-021-00777-4

Rajagopalan, R. P., & Krishna, R. (2019). India's Drone Policy: Domestic and Global Imperatives. *ICAO Scientific Review: Analytics and Management Research*, *1*, 53–68.

Rajasekarant, V. (2023, July 7). Decoding arbitrability and determining the boundaries of arbitration in Indian jurisprudence. SCC Times. https://www.scconline.com/blog/post/2023/07/07/decoding-arbitrability-and-determining-the-boundaries-of-arbitration-in-indian-jurisprudence

Rajeshwar, J., ... (2025). Blockchain for legal evidence management: Enhancing transparency and security in judicial systems. International Journal of Engineering Studies. https://theaspd.com/index.php/ijes/article/download/419/361/1426

Rajeswary, & Thirumaran, M. (2023). A comprehensive survey of automated website phishing detection techniques: A perspective of artificial intelligence and human behaviors. In Proceedings of the 2023 International Conference on Sustainable Computing and Data Communication Systems (ICSCDS) (pp. 420–427). IEEE Press.

Ramanan, V., Vinod, R., Williams, C., Ramachandran, S., & Venkatasubramanian, S. (2025, February 13). *Genetic data governance in crisis; policy recommendations for safeguarding privacy and preventing discrimination*. ArXiv. DOI: 10.48550/ARXIV.2502.09716

Ramos, L. F. M., & Silva, J. M. C. (2019, 3 April 2019). *Privacy and Data Protection Concerns regarding the Use of Blockchains in Smart Cities* [Conference Paper]. International Conference on Theory and Practice of Electronic Governance, ICEGOV 2019, https://www.scopus.com/inward/record.uri?eid=2-s2.0-85066637109&doi=10.1145%2f3326365.3326410&partnerID=40&md5=d7539ba4cf6c8e1f65143f1f9e752526

Rao. (2023, September 15). Unmanned eyes in the sky: The rise of forensic drones in crime investigation. *Times of India*. https://timesofindia.indiatimes.com/blogs/forensicsciencetech/224796/

Raposo, V. L. (2023). (Do not) remember my face: Uses of facial recognition technology in light of the General Data Protection Regulation. *Information & Communications Technology Law*, *32*(1), 45–63. DOI: 10.1080/13600834.2022.2054076

RBI. (2022). Report on trend & progress of banking in India 2021-22.Retrieved from: https://rbi.org.in/Scripts/AnnualPublications.aspx?head=Trend%20and%20Progress%20of%20Banking%20in%20India

Rebecchi, K., Todd, L., & Hagège, H. (2024). Teaching responsible creativity: A path to ethical innovation. *Discover Education*, *3*(1), 103. DOI: 10.1007/s44217-024-00164-0

Recabarren, R., & Carbunar, B. (2019). Tithonus: A bitcoin based censorship resilient system. *Proceedings on Privacy Enhancing Technologies. Privacy Enhancing Technologies Symposium*, *2019*(1), 68–86. DOI: 10.2478/popets-2019-0005

Rechkoska-Shikoska, U., & Shikoski, B. (2025). Cloud computing, security and legal issues. *A Research Agenda for Cybersecurity Law and Policy*, 205-215.

Red Hat. (2016). *Kernel local privilege escalation 'dirty COW*. Red Hat Customer Portal.

Rees, D. (2020). Smart contracts and the evidential challenges of intent. *Law, Innovation and Technology*, *12*(2), 145–163. DOI: 10.1080/17579961.2020.1815401

Regulation (EU) 2023/1114, (2023). https://eur-lex.europa.eu/eli/reg/2023/1114/oj/eng

Regulation 2016/679 OJ L 119 of the European Parliament and of the Council of 27 April 2016 on the protection of natural persons with regard to the processing of personal data and on the free movement of such data, and repealing Directive 95/46/EC (General Data Protection Regulation). *Official Journal of the European Union, 59,* 1-88. https://eur-lex.europa.eu/legal-content/EN/TXT/PDF/?uri=CELEX:32016R0679

Reijers, W., Wuisman, I., Mannan, M., De Filippi, P., Wray, C., Rae-Looi, V., Cubillos Vélez, A., & Orgad, L. (2021). Now the Code Runs Itself: On-Chain and Off-Chain Governance of Blockchain Technologies. *Topoi*, *40*(4), 821–831. Advance online publication. DOI: 10.1007/s11245-018-9626-5

Renda, A. (2022). Artificial intelligence in the EU: Policy, regulation, and ethics. *European Journal of Risk Regulation*, *13*(1), 7–27. DOI: 10.1017/err.2021.44

Rensaa, R. J. (2023, May 11). Assessment considerations during lockdown in Norway: An exploratory case study with focus on misconducts in university mathematics. *Cogent Education*, *10*(1), 2210456. DOI: 10.1080/2331186X.2023.2210456

Rese, A., Ganster, L., & Baier, D. (2020). Chatbots in retailers' customer communication: How to measure their acceptance? *Journal of Retailing and Consumer Services*, *56*, 102176. DOI: 10.1016/j.jretconser.2020.102176

Reuters. (2024). Uber 'clickwrap' contract gets blessing from NY's top court. But there's a twist. Retrieved from https://www.reuters.com/legal/government/column-uber-clickwrap-contract-gets-blessing-nys-top-court-theres

Reuters. (2024, February 12). *Intrusive' drones? U.S. surveillance case tests privacy law*. https://economictimes.indiatimes.com/news/defence/intrusive-drones-us-surveillance-case-tests-privacy-law/articleshow/107629919.cms

Reuters. (2025). Blockchain agreements: Avoiding ambiguity, manifesting assent. Retrieved from https://www.reuters.com/legal/transactional/blockchain-agreements-avoiding-ambiguity-manifesting-assent-2025-03-11/

Reyes, C. L. (2016). Moving beyond bitcoin to an endogenous theory of decentralized ledger technology regulation. *Villanova Law Review*, *61*(2), 191–234.

Riaz, S., Alwahaibi, A., & Farooq, M. (2021). Autonomous frequency control using reinforcement learning. *Renewable Energy*, *173*, 1274–1282. DOI: 10.1016/j.renene.2021.04.052

Riss, A. (2023). Blockchain and NFT revolution in land registries and real estate. DEV Community. https://dev.to/ahmmrizv9/blockchain-and-nft-revolution-in-land-registries-and-real-estate-341k

Ritsema Van Eck, G. J., & Vellinga, N. E. (2022, September). The new car safety rules of the GSR in light of the GDPR: An unnecessarily tangled web. *European Journal of Law and Technology*, *13*(1).

Riva, G. M. (2020). What Happens in Blockchain Stays in Blockchain. A Legal Solution to Conflicts Between Digital Ledgers and Privacy Rights. *Frontiers in Blockchain*, *3*, 36. DOI: 10.3389/fbloc.2020.00036

Roberts, H., Cowls, J., Hine, E., Morley, J., Wang, V., Taddeo, M., & Floridi, L. (2023). Governing artificial intelligence in China and the European Union: Comparing aims and promoting ethical outcomes. *The Information Society*, *39*(2), 79–97. DOI: 10.1080/01972243.2022.2124565

Robinson, N., Valeri, L., Cave, J., Starkey, T., Graux, H., Creese, S., & Hopkins, P. P. (2010). The cloud: Understanding the security, privacy and trust challenges. SSRN *Electronic Journal*. DOI: 10.2139/ssrn.2141970

Rolling Out. (2025). 2025 global privacy, AI, and data security regulations. BigID. https://bigid.com/blog/2025-global-privacy-ai-and

Rose, J., & Shehadeh, P.-R. (2021, September 20). Evaluating the UK Jurisdiction Taskforce's "Digital Dispute Resolution Rules, 1.0". Daily Jus. https://dailyjus.com/world/2021/09/evaluating-the-uk-jurisdiction-taskforces-digital-dispute-resolution-rules-1-0

Rose, N., & Shehadeh, A. (2021). Hybrid arbitration models. *Arbitration International*, *37*(4), 603–624.

Rossi, A. (2019). *Legal Design for the General Data Protection Regulation. A Methodology for the Visualization and Communication of Legal Concepts*. University of Bologna.

Roy, S., Sharmin, N., Acosta, J. C., Kiekintveld, C., & Laszka, A. (2023). Survey and taxonomy of adversarial reconnaissance techniques. *ACM Computing Surveys*, *55*(6), 1–38. DOI: 10.1145/3538704

Rugo, & Ardagna, C. A. (2023). Transparency-based reconnaissance for APT attacks. In Proceedings of the 2023 IEEE 47th Annual Computers, Software, and Applications Conference (COMPSAC) (pp. 1652–1657). IEEE Press.

Ruhnau, O., & Qvist, S. A. (2022). Storage requirements in a 100% renewable European power system: Extreme events and integration of sector coupling. *Energy*, *238*, 121963. DOI: 10.1016/j.energy.2021.121963

Ryan, M. D. (2011). Cloud computing privacy concerns on our doorstep. *Communications of the ACM*, *54*(1), 36–38. DOI: 10.1145/1866739.1866751

Saari, A., Sinclair, S., Leshinsky, R., & Junnila, S. (2025). Best practices for blockchain-driven digital transformation in cross-industry settings. *Digital Business*, *5*(2), 100127. DOI: 10.1016/j.digbus.2025.100127

Saberi, S., Kouhizadeh, M., Sarkis, J., & Shen, L. (2019). Blockchain technology and its relationships to sustainable supply chain management. *International Journal of Production Research*, *57*(7), 2117–2135. DOI: 10.1080/00207543.2018.1533261

Sadeghian, A. (2024). Detecting the most vulnerable nodes in the AND-OR graph using MITRE ATT&CK.

Saeidi, S. P., Sofian, S., Saeidi, P., Saeidi, S. P., & Saaeidi, S. A. (2015). How does corporate social responsibility contribute to firm financial performance? The mediating role of competitive advantage, reputation, and customer satisfaction. *Journal of Business Research*, *68*(2), 341–350. DOI: 10.1016/j.jbusres.2014.06.024

Safety of property can be a legitimate interest for GPS tracking, but the measure must be appropriate and necessary. (2022, October 4). European Data Protection Board. https://www.edpb.europa.eu/news/national-news/2022/safety-property-can-be-legitimate-interest-gps-tracking-measure-must-be_en

Sakhipov, A., Omirzak, I., & Fedenko, A. (2025, February 25). Beyond face recognition: A multi-layered approach to academic integrity in online exams. *Electronic Journal of e-Learning*, *23*(1), 81–95. DOI: 10.34190/ejel.23.1.3896

Salahdine, F., & Kaabouch, N. (2019). Social engineering attacks: A survey. *Future Internet*, *11*(4), 89. DOI: 10.3390/fi11040089

Salahdine, Y., Kim, M., & Lee, B. (2023). Extending a hand to attackers: browser privilege escalation attacks via extensions. In *Proceeding of the 32nd USENIX Security Symposium*, Berkeley: USENIX Association, pp. 7055-7071.

Saleel, P., Nazeer, M., & Beheshti, B. D. (2017). Linux kernel OS local root exploit. In Proceedings of the 2017 IEEE Long Island Systems, Applications, and Technology Conference (LISAT) (pp. 1–5). IEEE. DOI: 10.1109/LISAT.2017.8001953

Salinas, J. C., & Lewandowski, T. (2024). Blue Unmanned Aircraft Systems Explained: The Current Drone Market, Flight Regulations, and Debunking Common Misconceptions. *Transportation Research Record: Journal of the Transportation Research Board*, (03611981241257509). Advance online publication. DOI: 10.1177/03611981241257509

Saltz, J. S., & Dewar, N. (2019). Data science ethical considerations: A systematic literature review and proposed project framework. *Ethics and Information Technology*, *21*(3), 197–208. DOI: 10.1007/s10676-019-09502-5

Samsuwan, J., Somboonchokepisal, T., Akaraputtiporn, T., Srimuang, T., Phuengsukdaeng, P., Suwannarat, A., Mutirangura, A., & Kitkumthorn, N. (2018, September 13). A method for extracting DNA from hard tissues for use in forensic identification. *Biomedical Reports*, *9*(5), 433–438. DOI: 10.3892/br.2018.1148 PMID: 30402227

Sanas, S. (2024, July 15). Onion Heist: Ambegaon Farmer Loses 90000 After Drone Patrol. *The Bridge Chronicle*. https://www.thebridgechronicle.com/news/onion-heist-ambegaon-farmer-loses-90000-after-drone-patrol

Sanchez, T. W., Brenman, M., & Ye, X. (2024). The ethical concerns of artificial intelligence in urban planning. *Journal of the American Planning Association*, •••, 1–14.

Sanka, A. I., Irfan, M., Huang, I., & Cheung, R. C. C. (2021). A survey of breakthrough in blockchain technology: Adoptions, applications, challenges and future research. In *Computer Communications* (Vol. 169). DOI: 10.1016/j.comcom.2020.12.028

Sarkar, S., Liu, J. Q., & Jovanov, E. (2019). A robust algorithm for sniffing BLE long-lived connections in real-time. In *Proceedings of the 2019 IEEE Global Communications Conference (GLOBECOM)* (pp. 1–6). IEEE. DOI: 10.1109/GLOBECOM38437.2019.9014318

Saroj, S., Battacharjee, S., & Sharma, R. (2023). Quantum algorithms for intelligent demand response in smart grids. *Applied Sciences (Basel, Switzerland)*, *13*(2), 657. DOI: 10.3390/app13020657

Sathaye, H., Strohmeier, M., Lenders, V., & Ranganathan, A. (2022, August). *An experimental study of GPS spoofing and takeover attacks on UAVs.* [Conference proceedings]. 31st USENIX Security Symposium, Boston, MA. (pp. 3503-3520). https://www.usenix.org/system/files/sec22-sathaye.pdf

Satvat, K., Gjomemo, R., & Venkatrakrishnan, V. N. (2021). Extractor: Extracting attack behavior from threat reports. In Proceedings of the 2021 IEEE European Symposium on Security and Privacy (EuroS&P) (pp. 598–615). Piscataway, NJ, USA: IEEE.

Savelyev, A. (2018). Contract Law 2.0: Smart Contracts as the Beginning of the End of Classic Contract Law. *Information & Communications Technology Law*, *26*(2), 116–134. DOI: 10.1080/13600834.2017.1301036

Saxena, V., & Swarna, H. (2024, April 17). The conundrum of enforceability of blockchain arbitration: Learnings from Kleros. Mapping ADR. https://jgu.edu.in/mappingADR/the-conundrum-of-enforceability-of-blockchain-arbitration-learnings-from-kleros/

Saxena, A., & Shukla, R. K. (2021). Artificial intelligence and blockchain fusion: A technology forecast towards 2030. *Technological Forecasting and Social Change*, *166*, 120601. DOI: 10.1016/j.techfore.2021.120601

Schellinger, B., Völter, F., Urbach, N., & Sedlmeir, J. (2021, 4 January 2022). *Yes, I Do: Marrying Blockchain Applications with GDPR* Hawaii International Conference on System Sciences 2022

Scheurman, T. (2021). Comparing Social Media Content Regulation in the US and the EU: How the US Can Move Forward with Section 230 to Bolster Social Media Users' Freedom of Expression. *San Diego Int'l LJ*, *23*, 413.

Schiermeier, Q. (2021, June 15). Forensic database challenged over ethics of DNA holdings. *Nature*, *594*(7863), 320–322. DOI: 10.1038/d41586-021-01584-w PMID: 34131337

Schiff, D. (2022). Education for AI, not AI for education: The role of education and ethics in national AI policy strategies. *International Journal of Artificial Intelligence in Education*, *32*(3), 527–563. DOI: 10.1007/s40593-021-00270-2

Schreuer, C. (2001). The ICSID Convention: A Commentary. Cambridge University Press.

Schwab, K. (2016). The Fourth Industrial Revolution. World Economic Forum. https://www.weforum.org/about/the-fourth-industrial-revolution-by-klaus-schwab

Schwarz, M. (2023). Legal enforceability of blockchain arbitration awards. *Harvard Journal of Law & Technology*, *36*(2), 215–252.

Schwarz, M. (2023). Legal enforceability of blockchain arbitration awards: A comparative analysis. *Harvard Journal of Law & Technology*, *36*(2), 215–252.

Sekar, R., Kimm, H., Aich, R., ... (2023). eAudit: A fast, scalable and deployable audit data collection system. In Proceedings of the 2024 IEEE Symposium on Security and Privacy (S&P) (p. 87). IEEE Press.

Sellers, F. (2018, February 8). *The GDPR's impact on CCTV and workplace surveillance.* Privacy World. https://www.privacyworld.blog/2018/02/the-gdprs-impact-on-cctv-and-workplace-surveillance

Sen, N. (2018). Understanding the role of the WTO in international data flows: Taking the liberalisation or the regulatory autonomy path? *Journal of International Economic Law, 21*(2), 323–348. DOI: 10.1093/jiel/jgy021

Sethi, A., & Makwana, F. (2024). Smart contracts for supply chain management using blockchain. *International Journal of Innovative Research in Technology, 11*(1), 326–331.

Shaikh, S. A., Chivers, H., Nobles, P., Clark, J. A., & Chen, H. (2008). Network reconnaissance. *Network Security, 2008*(11), 12–16. DOI: 10.1016/S1353-4858(08)70129-6

Shany, Y. (2023). Digital rights and the outer limits of international human rights law. *German Law Journal, 24*(S3).

Shao, W., Jia, C., Xu, Y., Qiu, K., Gao, Y., & He, Y. (2020). Attrichain: Decentralized Traceable Anonymous Identities in Privacy-Preserving Permissioned Blockchain. *Computers & Security, 99*, 102069. https://doi.org/https://doi.org/10.1016/j.cose.2020.102069. DOI: 10.1016/j.cose.2020.102069

Sharma, A. (2023, March 4). Singer Benny Dayal Gets Hit By A Drone During Live Concert In Chennai. *NDTV*. https://www.ndtv.com/offbeat/video-singer-benny-dayal-gets-hit-by-a-drone-during-live-concert-in-chennai-3835053

Sharma, A. (2024, January 12). *Understanding smart contracts in blockchain: A complete overview.* Medium. https://medium.com/@sharma1991ais/understanding-smart-contracts-in-blockchain-a-complete-overview-1d879381cfc

Sharma, B., Gupta, B., Singh, A. K., & Saraswat, V. K. (2023). Advanced persistent threats (APT): Evolution, anatomy, attribution and countermeasures. *Journal of Ambient Intelligence and Humanized Computing, 14*(7), 9355–9381. DOI: 10.1007/s12652-023-04603-y

Shehata, I. (2018). *Smart contracts & international arbitration*. Kluwer Arbitration Blog. DOI: 10.2139/ssrn.3290026

Shreya Singhal v. Union of India (AIR 2015 SC 1523)

Siddiqui, H. R., & Muniza, M. (2025). Regulatory Gaps in Drone Surveillance: Addressing Privacy, Security, and Manufacturing Standards. *Annals of Human and Social Sciences, 6*(1), 415–428.

Silva, L. V., Barbosa, P., Marinho, R., & Brito, A. (2018). Security and privacy aware data aggregation on cloud computing. *Journal of Internet Services and Applications, 9*(1), 6. DOI: 10.1186/s13174-018-0078-3

Silva, R.. (2024). Reflections about blockchain in health data sharing: Navigating medicolegal and regulatory challenges. *Journal of Medical Internet Research*, *26*(2), e10887941. DOI: 10.1089/jmir.2024.10887941

Simmler, M., & Canova, G. (2025, April). Facial recognition technology in law enforcement: Regulating data analysis of another kind. *Computer Law & Security Review*, *56*, 106092. DOI: 10.1016/j.clsr.2024.106092

Simpson, E. (2023, October 19). Amazon pledges parcels in an hour using drone deliveries. *BBC*. https://www.bbc.com/news/business-67132527

Sim, W. L., Chua, H. N., & Tahir, M. (2019, 19 November 2019). *Blockchain for Identity Management: The Implications to Personal Data Protection IEEE Conference on Application, Information and Network Security (AINS)*, Pulau Pinang, Malaysia. DOI: 10.1109/AINS47559.2019.8968708

Singapore International Arbitration Centre (SIAC) Year in Review. (2023). https://siac.org.sg/siac-year-in-review-2023

Singh, A. P. (2025). Blockchain technology: Core mechanisms, evolution, and future implementation challenges. arXiv. https://arxiv.org/html/2505.08772v1

Sinha, S. (2024, September 13). 'Air taxis to soon become a reality in India': PM Modi. *Times of India*. https://timesofindia.indiatimes.com/business/india-business/air-taxis-to-soon-become-a-reality-in-india-pm-modi/articleshow/113298314.cms

Siron, D., & Paesano, F. (2022). *Cryptocurrencies in Asia and beyond: Law, regulation and enforcement*. Basel Institute on Governance.

Siu, R. C. (2023). Social, political, and economic dimensions of the instituted process of central bank digital currency: The case of the digital Yuan. *Journal of Economic Issues*, *57*(2), 458–465. DOI: 10.1080/00213624.2023.2201610

Sivasubramaniam, S., Dlabolová, D. H., Kralikova, V., & Khan, Z. R. (2021). Assisting you to advance with ethics in research: An introduction to ethical governance and application procedures. *International Journal for Educational Integrity*, *17*(1), 1–18. DOI: 10.1007/s40979-021-00078-6

Smith, J., Zhao, L., & Patel, N. (2024). Governing the green transition: The role of AI investments in renewable energy adoption. *Sustainability*, *17*(12), 5538. DOI: 10.3390/su17125538

Somayajula, D. (2021, July 31). *'Eye in the Sky'- India's Drone Operations and Privacy Concerns*. Vidhi Centre for Legal Policy. https://vidhilegalpolicy.in/blog/eye-in-the-sky-indias-drone-operations-and-privacy-concerns/

Song, Z., Yan, E., Song, J., Jiang, R., Yu, Y., & Chen, T. (2025). A Blockchain-Based Digital Identity System with Privacy, Controllability, and Auditability. *Arabian Journal for Science and Engineering*, *50*(10), 7027–7051. DOI: 10.1007/s13369-024-09178-0

Son, Y. B., Im, J. H., Kwon, H. Y., Jeon, S. Y., & Lee, M. K. (2020). Privacy-Preserving Peer-to-Peer Energy Trading in Blockchain-Enabled Smart Grids using Functional Encryption. *Energies*, *13*(6), 1321. https://doi.org/https://doi.org/10.3390/en13061321. DOI: 10.3390/en13061321

Specht v. Netscape Communications Corp., 306 F.3d 17 (2d Cir. 2002).

Sri, S. G. A., & Bhaskari, L. (2018). A Study on Blockchain Technology. *IACSIT International Journal of Engineering and Technology*, *7*, 418. DOI: 10.14419/ijet.v7i2.7.10757

Srivastava, P. (2021). *Civil Aviation Regulatory Landscape of Indian Drone Ecosystem red.* https://legalaffairs.gov.in/sites/default/files/Civil%20Aviation%20Regulatory%20Landscape%20of%20Indian%20Drone%20Ecosystem%20red.pdf

Srivastava, P. (2023). *Regulatory Landscape of Indian Drone Ecosystem*. Department Of Legal Affairs. https://legalaffairs.gov.in/sites/default/files/Civil%20Aviation%20Regulatory%20Landscape%20of%20Indian%20Drone%20Ecosystem%20red.pdf

Stamatoukou, E. (2024, April 3). *Greek Ministry fined over surveillance systems at asylum centres*. Balkan Insight. https://balkaninsight.com/2024/04/03/greek-ministry-fined-over-surveillance-systems-at-asylum-centres

Statutes, A. R. § 44-7061 (2024). https://www.azleg.gov/ars/44/07061.html

Stewart, H., & Jürjens, J. (2018a). Data security and consumer trust in FinTech innovation in Germany. *Information and Computer Security*, *26*(1), 109–128. DOI: 10.1108/ICS-06-2017-0039

Stewart, H., & Jürjens, J. (2018b). Fintech and trust: A qualitative study of customers' attitudes towards fintech and their data protection concerns. *Journal of Financial Services Marketing*, *23*, 225–237.

Stierlin, N., Risch, M., & Risch, L. (2024). Current Advancements in Drone Technology for Medical Sample Transportation. *Logistics (Basel)*, *8*(4), 104. DOI: 10.3390/logistics8040104

Strom, E., Applebaum, A., & Miller, D. P.. (2018). *Mitre attack: design and philosophy*. MITRE Corporation.

Suciu, S., McLaughlin, S., & Simon, L.. (2020). Horizontal privilege escalation in trusted applications. In *Proceedings of the 29th USENIX Security Symposium* (pp. 825–840). USENIX Association.

Sudhi, K. S. (2017, March 5). Now, drones to be used for monitoring tigers. *The Hindu*. https://www.thehindu.com/sci-tech/energy-and-environment/now-drones-to-be-used-for-monitoring-tigers/article17408388.ece

Suganya, S., & Damodharan, P. (2013). Enhancing security for storage services in cloud computing. *2013 International Conference on Current Trends in Engineering and Technology (ICCTET)*, 396-398. DOI: 10.1109/ICCTET.2013.6675995

Sule, M. J., Zennaro, M., & Thomas, G. (2021). Cybersecurity through the lens of digital identity and data protection: Issues and trends. *Technology in Society*, *67*, 101734. DOI: 10.1016/j.techsoc.2021.101734

Supreme Court of Canada. (2019). [2019] 3 S. *CR (East Lansing, Mich.)*, •••, 465.

Supreme Court of India. (2015). M/s. Trimex International FZE Ltd. v. Vedanta Aluminium Ltd., AIR 2015 SC 1523.

Swammy, Sarah, Richard Thompson, Marvin Loh, Sarah Swammy, Richard Thompson, and Marvin Loh. (2018). A Vision for the Future: The Bermuda FinTech Story. Crypto Uncovered 173.

Swan, M. (2015). *Blockchain: Blueprint for a new economy*. O'Reilly Media.

Szabo, N. (1996). Smart contracts: Building blocks for digital markets. Extropy Journal, 16.

Szabo, N. (1997). The idea of smart contracts. Nick Szabo's Papers and Concise Tutorials. https://www.fon.hum.uva.nl/rob/Courses/InformationInSpeech/CDROM/Literature/LOTwinterschool2006/szabo.best.vwh.net/smart_contracts_idea.html

Szira, Z., Varga, E., Csegődi, T. L., & Milics, G. (2023, December 24). The development of drone technology and its regulation in the European Union. *EU Agrarian Law*, *12*(1), 35–41. DOI: 10.2478/eual-2023-0005

Taddeo, M., & Floridi, L. (2018). How AI can be a force for good. *Science*, *361*(6404), 751–752. DOI: 10.1126/science.aat5991 PMID: 30139858

Takabi, H., Joshi, J. B., & Ahn, G. (2010). Security and privacy challenges in cloud computing environments. *IEEE Security and Privacy*, *8*(6), 24–31. DOI: 10.1109/MSP.2010.186

Talib, M., Nasir, Q., & Bou Nassif, M. (2022). APT beaconing detection: A systematic review. *Computers & Security, 122*, 102875. DOI: 10.1016/j.cose.2022.102875

Tan, E., Mahula, S., & Crompvoets, J. (2022). Blockchain governance in the public sector: A conceptual framework for public management. *Government Information Quarterly, 39*(1), 101625. DOI: 10.1016/j.giq.2021.101625

Tapscott, D., & Tapscott, A. (2016). *Blockchain revolution: How the technology behind Bitcoin is changing money, business, and the world*. Penguin Books.

Tashev, T. (2025). Anatomy of an LLM: Tokens, weights and parameters. Webopedia. https://www.webopedia.com/technology/llm-tokens-weights-parameters/

Tatam, M., Shanmugam, B., Azam, S., & Kannoorpatti, K. (2021). A review of threat modeling approaches for APT-style attacks. *Heliyon*, *7*(1), e05969. DOI: 10.1016/j.heliyon.2021.e05969 PMID: 33506133

Tatar, U., Gokce, Y., & Nussbaum, B. (2020). Law Versus Technology: Blockchain, GDPR, and Tough Tradeoffs. *Computer Law & Security Review, 38*, 105454. https://doi.org/https://doi.org/10.1016/j.clsr.2020.105454. DOI: 10.1016/j.clsr.2020.105454

Telangana Today. (2021, October 1). *Hara Bhara, India's first aerial seeding campaign launched in Hyderabad*. https://telanganatoday.com/hara-bhara-indias-first-aerial-seeding-campaign-launched-in-hyderabad

Tennessee Code Annotated § 47-10-202 (2018). https://www.capitol.tn.gov/Bills/110/Bill/SB1662.pdf

Terraform Pte Ltd v. 3750 Investors [2023] SGHC 289.

TestWe. (n.d.). *The European reference for online exams and certifications*. https://testwe.eu/en

Thaler, R. H., & Sunstein, C. R. (2009). *Nudge: Improving Decisions about Health, Wealth, and Happiness*. Penguin Books.

The Hindu Bureau. (2024, July 29). DTDC launches drone delivery services in India. *The Hindu*. https://www.thehindu.com/sci-tech/technology/dtdc-launches-drone-delivery-services-in-india/article68459936.ece

The Hindu Net Desk. (2017, August 24). Supreme Court verdict on Right to Privacy. *The Hindu*. https://www.thehindu.com/news/resources/supreme-court-verdict-on-right-to-privacy/article62041731.ece

Thomas, A. L., Piza, E. L., Welsh, B. C., & Farrington, D. P. (2022). The internationalization of CCTV surveillance: Effects on crime and implications for emerging technologies. *International Journal of Comparative and Applied Criminal Justice*, *46*(1), 81–102. DOI: 10.1080/01924036.2021.1879885

Thomas, M., Mackes, N., Preuss-Dodhy, A., Wieland, T., & Bundschus, M. (2024). Assessing privacy vulnerabilities in genetic data sets: Scoping review. *JMIR Bioinformatics and Biotechnology*, *5*, e54332. Advance online publication. DOI: 10.2196/54332 PMID: 38935957

Thompson, A., & Voon, T. (2016). Data localisation requirements and the WTO. *World Trade Review*, *15*(4), 701–722.

Thompson, S. (2020). Blockchain signatures and eIDAS: A qualified mismatch? [Database access required—placeholder journal entry.]. *Journal of European Law*, *26*(4), 233–247.

Tian, D. H., Ma, R., Jia, X. Q., & Hu, C. (2019b). A kernel rootkit detection approach based on virtualization and machine learning. *IEEE Access : Practical Innovations, Open Solutions*, *7*, 91657–91666. DOI: 10.1109/ACCESS.2019.2928060

Tian, Z. H., Shi, W., Wang, Y. H., Zhu, C., Du, X., Su, S., Sun, Y., & Guizani, N. (2019a). Real-time lateral movement detection based on evidence reasoning network for edge computing environment. *IEEE Transactions on Industrial Informatics*, *15*(7), 4285–4294. DOI: 10.1109/TII.2019.2907754

Tillmar, A., Fagerholm, S. A., Staaf, J., Sjölund, P., & Ansell, R. (2021, July). Getting the conclusive lead with investigative genetic genealogy – A successful case study of a 16 year old double murder in Sweden. *Forensic Science International. Genetics*, *53*, 102525. DOI: 10.1016/j.fsigen.2021.102525 PMID: 33991867

TNN. (2020, July 17). Delhi Police use Drone to solve double murder. *Times of India*. https://timesofindia.indiatimes.com/city/delhi/delhi-police-use-drone-to-solve-double-murder/articleshow/77009863.cms

TNN. (2024, September 16). *Need to urgently tackle rogue drones, online frauds: Amit Shah*. Times of India. https://timesofindia.indiatimes.com/india/need-to-urgently-tackle-rogue-drones-online-frauds-amit-shah/articleshow/113377061.cms

TOI News Desk. (2024, August 28). Mysterious drone-like object cause 3-hour flight disruption at Amritsar airport. *Times of India*. https://timesofindia.indiatimes.com/india/mysterious-drone-like-object-cause-3-hour-flight-disruption-at-amritsar-airport/articleshow/112864415.cms

Trade Council. (2024). The role of blockchain in international trade. https://tradecouncil.org/wp-content/uploads/2024/10/Theroleofblockchainininternat ionaltrade.pdf

Tsinganos, N., Mavridis, I., & Gritzalis, D. (2022). Utilizing convolutional neural networks and word embeddings for early-stage recognition of persuasion in chat-based social engineering attacks. *IEEE Access : Practical Innovations, Open Solutions, 10*, 108517–108529. DOI: 10.1109/ACCESS.2022.3213681

Tucker, P., & Mahnken, T. (2024). The geopolitics of code: Strategic software in critical infrastructure. *Survival: Global Politics and Strategy*, *66*(1), 77–95. DOI: 10.1080/00396338.2024.1697780

Tumisu. (2021, January 26). *Man Face.* [Image]. Pixabay. https://pixabay.com/photos/man-face-facial-recognition-5946820. Free for use under the Pixabay Content License; no alterations other than cropping.

Turing. (2023). Blockchain in supply chain: Benefits, use cases & applications. https://www.turing.com/resources/blockchain-for-supply-chains

Tyagi, A. K., Nair, M. M., Niladhuri, S., & Abraham, A. (2020). Security, Privacy Research issues in Various Computing Platforms: A Survey and the Road Ahead. *Journal of Information Assurance Security and Communication Networks*, *15*(1), 1–16. www.mirlabs.net/jias/index.htm

UK Jurisdiction Taskforce. (2021). Digital Dispute Resolution Rules. https://mattereum.com/wp-content/uploads/docs/UKJT-Digital-Dispute-Resolution-Rules .pdf

UK Jurisdictional Taskforce. (2021). Digital Dispute Resolution Rules.

UK Law Commission (2021). Legal status of smart contracts and dispute resolution.

UK Law Commission Report (2021). https://lawcom.gov.uk/corporate-document/annual-report-20-21/

UNCITRAL Model Law on International Commercial Arbitration (2006).

UNCITRAL. (2006). *Model Law on International Commercial Arbitration*. United Nations.

UNCITRAL. (2017). *Model Law on Electronic Transferable Records*. United Nations Commission on International Trade Law.

UNCITRAL. (2022). Guide to the New York Convention on the Recognition and Enforcement of Foreign Arbitral Awards. United Nations. https://www.uncitral.org/pdf/NYConvention_Guide.pdf

UNCITRAL. (2022). *UNCITRAL model law on international commercial arbitration with 2006 amendments*. United Nations Commission on International Trade Law.

UNCITRAL. (2024). UNCITRAL Model Law on Automated Contracting. https://unis.unvienna.org/unis/pressrels/2024/unisl362.html

UNCTAD. (2021). *Digital Economy Report 2021: Cross-border data flows and development*. United Nations.

UNCTAD. (2023). Global report on blockchain and its implications on trade facilitation. https://unctad.org/system/files/official-document/tcsdtlinf2023d1_en.pdf

UNESCO. (2021). *Recommendation on the Ethics of Artificial Intelligence*. United Nations Educational, Scientific and Cultural Organization.

UNHRC. (2021). *Report of the Office of the United Nations High Commissioner for Human Rights on the right to privacy in the digital age*. United Nations Human Rights Council.

Unit, R. (2022, January 28). *The Drone Rules, 2021*. Press Information Bureau, Ministry of Information and Broadcasting, Government of India. https://static.pib.gov.in/writereaddata/specificdocs/documents/2022/jan/doc202212810701.pdf

Upadhyay, D. (2023, October 5). *New Drone rules 2023 for pilots notified; any govt ID, address proof admissible*. Mint. https://www.livemint.com/news/india/new-drone-rules-2023-for-pilots-notified-any-government-id-address-proof-admissible-11696517295150.html

USSath., M., Jaeger, D., Cheng, F., et al. (2016). Advanced persistent threats: Behind the scenes. In Proceedings of the 2016 Annual Conference on Information Science and Systems (CISS) (pp. 181–186). IEEE Press.

Utz, M., Johanning, S., Roth, T., Bruckner, T., & Strüker, J. (2023). From Ambivalence to Trust: Using Blockchain in Customer Loyalty Programs. *International Journal of Information Management*, *68*, 102496. https://doi.org/https://doi.org/10.1016/j.ijinfomgt.2022.102496. DOI: 10.1016/j.ijinfomgt.2022.102496

Van Dijk, J. A. G. M. (2020). *The digital divide*. Polity Press.

Van Vuuren, T., Roberts-Lombard, M., & Van Tonder, E. (2012). Customer satisfaction, trust and commitment as predictors of customer loyalty within an optometric practice environment. *Southern African Business Review*, *16*, 81–96.

Vander Goot, M. J., Hafkamp, L., & Dankfort, Z. (2021). Customer Service Chatbots: A Qualitative Interview Study into the Communication Journey of Customers. *Lecture Notes in Computer Science, 12604*, 190–204. DOI: 10.1007/978-3-030-68288-0_13

Vanhove, S. (2020, 16 September 2020). *Peer-to-Peer Electricity Trading: Challenges for the Distribution System Operator (DSO) under EU Law International Conference on the European Energy Market (EEM)*, Stockholm, Sweden.

Vanin, F. N. S., Policarpo, L. M., Righi, R. R., Heck, S., da Silva, V. F., Goldim, J., & da Costa, C. A. (2023). A Blockchain-Based End-to-End Data Protection Model for Personal Health Records Sharing: A Fully Homomorphic Encryption Approach. *Sensors (Basel), 23*(1), 14. https://doi.org/https://doi.org/10.3390/s23010014. DOI: 10.3390/s23010014 PMID: 36616613

Vannucci, V., & Pantano, E. (2020). Do I Lose my Privacy for a Better Service? Investigating the Interplay between Big Data Analytics and Privacy Loss from Young Consumers' Perspective. In *Retail Futures* (pp. 193–205). Emerald Publishing Limited. DOI: 10.1108/978-1-83867-663-620201021

Vatanparast, R., & Moon, M. J. (2023). The digital standards race: Who governs blockchain standards? *Global Policy, 14*(2), 260–274.

Veale, M., & Edwards, L. (2018). Clarity, surprises, and further questions in the Article 29 Working Party draft guidance on automated decision-making and profiling. *Computer Law & Security Review, 34*(2), 398–404. DOI: 10.1016/j.clsr.2017.12.002

Verma, A. D. (2025, March 15). Legal challenges in Web 3.0: Navigating smart contracts, DAOs and blockchain disputes. SCC Online. https://www.scconline.com/blog/post/2025/03/15/legal-challenges-in-web-3-0-navigating-smart-contracts-daos-and-blockchain-disputes/

Verma, S., Anukaran, S., & Verma, K. (2022, February 17). *Safety Investigations Of Accidents & Incidents Involving Drones: Addressing The Gaps In Drone Rules In India*. Mondaq. https://www.mondaq.com/india/aviation/1162664/safety-investigations-of-accidents-incidents-involving-drones-addressing-the-gaps-in-drone-rules-in-india

Vidya Drolia v. Durga Trading Corporation (2021) 2 SCC 1.; Vidya Drolia v. Durga Trading Corporation, (2020) SCC OnLine SC 1018.

Virginia Consumer Data Protection Act, (2021).

Vo, D., & Delahunty, M. (2020). The GDPR and blockchain: Incompatible or mutually reinforcing? *European Data Protection Law Review, 6*(3), 324–335. DOI: 10.21552/edpl/2020/3/9

Voigt, P., & Von dem Bussche, A. (2017). *The EU General Data Protection Regulation (GDPR): A Practical Guide*. Springer International Publishing. DOI: 10.1007/978-3-319-57959-7

Voss, W. G. (2021). Data Protection Issues for Smart Contracts. In Corrales, M., Fenwick, M., & Wrbka, S. (Eds.), *Smart Contracts: Technological, Business and Legal Perspectives* (pp. 79–100). Hart Publishing., DOI: 10.5040/9781509937059.ch-004

Wachter, S., & Mittelstadt, B. (2019). A Right to Reasonable Inferences: Re-Thinking Data Protection Law in the Age of Big Data and AI. *Columbia Business Law Review, 2019*(2), 494–620. https://ssrn.com/abstract=3248829

Wachter, S., Mittelstadt, B., & Floridi, L. (2017). Transparent, explainable, and accountable AI for robotics. *Science and Engineering Ethics, 23*(3), 611–628. DOI: 10.1007/s11948-016-9768-6 PMID: 33157874

Wallach, H. (2018). Computational social science≠ computer science+ social data. *Communications of the ACM, 61*(3), 42–44. DOI: 10.1145/3132698

Walters, R., Trakman, L., & Zeller, B. (2019). *Data Protection Law: A Comparative Analysis of Asia-Pacific and European Approaches* (1 ed.). Springer. https://doi.org/ DOI: 10.1007/978-981-13-8110-2

Walters, N. (2019). Privacy Law Issues in Blockchains: An Analysis of PIPEDA, the GDPR, and Proposals for Compliance. *Canadian Journal of Law and Technology, 17*(276). https://doi.org/https://papers.ssrn.com/sol3/papers.cfm?abstract_id=3481701

Wampler, J., Martiny, I., & Wustrow, E. (2019). ExSpectre: Hiding malware in speculative execution. In *Proceedings of the 2019 Network and Distributed System Security Symposium (NDSS)*. Internet Society. DOI: 10.14722/ndss.2019.23409

Wandermurem, I. (2025, January 2025). *The true story behind Netflix's gripping Swedish crime drama, The Breakthrough.* Time. https://time.com/7205773/the-breakthrough-true-story-netflix

Wang, C., Ren, K., Lou, W., & Li, J. (2010). Toward publicly auditable secure cloud data storage services. *IEEE Network, 24*(4), 19–24. DOI: 10.1109/MNET.2010.5510914

Wang, C., Wang, Q., Ren, K., & Lou, W. (2010). Privacy-preserving public auditing for data storage security in cloud computing. *Proceedings - IEEE INFOCOM*, 1–9. DOI: 10.1109/INFCOM.2010.5462173

Wang, D., Zhao, J., & Wang, Y. (2020). A Survey on Privacy Protection of Blockchain: The Technology and Application. *IEEE Access : Practical Innovations, Open Solutions*, *8*, 108766–108781. https://doi.org/https://doi.org/10.1109/ACCESS.2020.2994294. DOI: 10.1109/ACCESS.2020.2994294

Wang, N., Mutzner, N., & Blanchet, K. (2025). 'We Need Time…': An Expert Survey on Societal Acceptance of Urban Drones. *Science & Public Policy*. Advance online publication. DOI: 10.1093/scipol/scae084

Wang, N., Zhou, X., Lu, X., Guan, Z., Wu, L., Du, X., & Guizani, M. (2019). When Energy Trading Meets Blockchain in Electrical Power System: The State of the Art. *Applied Sciences (Basel, Switzerland)*, *9*(8), 1561. DOI: 10.3390/app9081561

Wang, P., Jiang, L., & Yang, J. (2023, April 11). The early impact of GDPR compliance on display advertising: The case of an ad publisher. *JMR, Journal of Marketing Research*, *61*(1), 70–91. DOI: 10.1177/00222437231171848

Wang, Q., Wang, C., Ren, K., Lou, W., & Li, J. (2011). Enabling public Auditability and data dynamics for storage security in cloud computing. *IEEE Transactions on Parallel and Distributed Systems*, *22*(5), 847–859. DOI: 10.1109/TPDS.2010.183

Wang, R., Xu, C., Dong, R., Luo, Z., Zheng, R., & Zhang, X. (2023). A Secured Big-Data Sharing Platform for Materials Genome Engineering: State-of-the-Art, Challenges and Architecture. *Future Generation Computer Systems*, *142*, 59–74. DOI: 10.1016/j.future.2022.12.026

Wang, X., Zheng, K. F., & Niu, X. X. (2016). Detection of command and control in advanced persistent threat based on independent access. In *Proceedings of the 2016 IEEE International Conference on Communications (ICC)* (pp. 1–6). IEEE Press. DOI: 10.1109/ICC.2016.7511197

Ware, S. J. (2020). Automated Arbitration and the Federal Arbitration Act. *Harvard Journal of Law & Technology*, *34*(1), 151–188.

Warren, S. D., & Brandeis, L. D. (1890, December 15). The right to privacy. *Harvard Law Review*, *4*(5), 193–220. DOI: 10.2307/1321160

Weber, R. H. (2019). The law and ethics of decentralised autonomous organisations. *European Journal of Risk Regulation*, *10*(2), 241–258.

Werbach, K. (2018). *The blockchain and the new architecture of trust*. MIT Press. DOI: 10.7551/mitpress/11449.001.0001

Werbach, K. (2022). Digital Asset Regulation: Peering into the Past, Peering into the Future. *Wm. & Mary L. Rev.*, *64*, 1251.

What is the European Union? (n.d.). EU & Me. https://op.europa.eu/webpub/com/eu-and-me/en/WHAT_IS_THE_EUROPEAN_UNION.html

Winfield, A. F. T., Michael, K., Pitt, J., & Evers, V. (2019). Machine ethics: The design and governance of ethical AI and autonomous systems. *Proceedings of the IEEE, 107*(3), 509–517. DOI: 10.1109/JPROC.2019.2900622

Winston, M. (2022). Wrapping code: Smart contracts and contractual safeguards. [Available via HeinOnline/academic databases.]. *Harvard Journal of Law & Technology, 35*(1), 115–140.

Winter-Barker, S. (2024, June 27). JAMS publishes artificial intelligence arbitration rules, but are they fit for purpose? Kluwer Arbitration Blog. https://arbitrationblog.kluwerarbitration.com/

Woebbeking, M. K. (2019). *The impact of smart contracts on traditional concepts of contract law*. JIPITEC.

Woldeab, D., & Brothen, T. (2024, August 30). Exploring the impact: How online exam proctoring reduces cheating and enhances course legitimacy. *International Journal of E-learning & Distance Education, 39*(1), 1–29. DOI: 10.55667/10.55667/ijede.2024.v39.i1.1327

Wolff, J., & Atallah, N. (2021). Early GDPR penalties: Analysis of implementation and fines through May 2020. *Journal of Information Policy, 11*, 63–103. DOI: 10.5325/jinfopoli.11.2021.0063

World Bank. (2020). *Blockchain: Opportunities for Private Enterprises in Emerging Markets*. International Finance Corporation.

World Economic Forum. (2020, April 6). Supply chains are in chaos. Here's how to make them more resilient. *World Economic Forum*. https://www.weforum.org/stories/2020/04/supply-chains-resilient-covid-19/

World Economic Forum. (2025). *Global Risks Report 2025*. World Economic Forum. https://www.weforum.org/publications/global-risks-report-2025/

World Scientific. (2025). Industry 4.0: Converging technologies in the global economy. https://worldscientific.com/doi/pdf/10.1142/9789811203930_0001

World Trade Organization. (1994). General Agreement on Trade in Services. Marrakesh Agreement Establishing the World Trade Organization, Annex 1B.

World Trade Organization. (2021). Joint Statement Initiative on E-Commerce: Negotiating Texts. https://www.wto.org/english/tratop_e/ecom_e/ecom_e.htm

Worley, R., & Skjellum, A. (2018). Blockchain tradeoffs and challenges for current and emerging applications: Generalization, fragmentation, sidechains, and scalability. In *2018 IEEE International Conference on Internet of Things (iThings), IEEE GreenCom, IEEE CPSCom, and IEEE Smart Data* (pp. 1582–1587). IEEE. DOI: 10.1109/Cybermatics_2018.2018.00265

Wright, A., & De Filippi, P. (2015). Decentralized blockchain technology and the rise of lex cryptographia. Social Science Research Network (*SSRN*). https://doi.org/ DOI: 10.2139/ssrn.2580664

Wu, H., Yao, Q., Liu, Z., Huang, B., Zhuang, Y., Tang, H., & Liu, E. (2024). Blockchain for finance: A survey. In *IET Blockchain* (Vol. 4, Issue 2). DOI: 10.1049/ blc2.12067

Wu, M. (2020). Digital Trade-Related Provisions in Regional Trade Agreements: Existing Models and Lessons for the Multilateral Trade System. RTA Exchange Working Paper. International Centre for Trade and Sustainable Development. https:// rtaexchange.org

Yaacoub, J.-P., Noura, H., Salman, O., & Chehab, A. (2020). Security analysis of drones systems: Attacks, limitations, and recommendations. *Internet of Things : Engineering Cyber Physical Human Systems*, *11*, 100218. DOI: 10.1016/j. iot.2020.100218 PMID: 38620271

Yamauchi, T., Akao, Y., & Yoshitani, R.. (2018). Additional kernel observer to prevent privilege escalation attacks by focusing on system call privilege changes. In *Proceedings of the 2018 IEEE Conference on Dependable and Secure Computing (DSC)* (pp. 1–8). IEEE Press. DOI: 10.1109/DESEC.2018.8625137

Yang, J., Ma, C., Hsiao, S., & Liu, J. (2024). Blockchain governance: A bibliometric study and content analysis. *Technology Analysis and Strategic Management*, 1–15. Advance online publication. DOI: 10.1080/09537325.2024.2337347

Yang, J., Zhao, Y., Han, C., Liu, Y., & Yang, M. (2022). Big data, big challenges: Risk management of financial market in the digital economy. *Journal of Enterprise Information Management*, *35*(4/5), 1288–1304. DOI: 10.1108/JEIM-01-2021-0057

Yan, Y., Huang, C., Wang, Q., & Hu, B. (2020). Data mining of customer choice behavior in internet of things within relationship network. *International Journal of Information Management*, *50*, 566–574. DOI: 10.1016/j.ijinfomgt.2018.11.013

Yan, Y., Liu, F., & Jia, K. (2019). Modeling an information-based advanced persistent threat attack on the internal network. In *Proceedings of the 2019 IEEE International Conference on Communications (ICC)* (pp. 1–7). IEEE Press. DOI: 10.1109/ICC.2019.8761077

Yao, X., Fuller, J., & Kasturi, R. P.. (2023). Hiding in plain sight: An empirical study of web application abuse in malware. In *Proceedings of the 32nd USENIX Security Symposium* (pp. 6115–6132).

Yeom, S., Choi, S., Chi, J., & Park, S. (2021). Blockchain-Based Employment Contract System Architecture Allowing Encrypted Keyword Searches. *Electronics (Basel), 10*(9), 1086. DOI: 10.3390/electronics10091086

Yeung, K. (2018). Algorithmic regulation: A critical interrogation. *Regulation & Governance, 12*(4), 505–523. DOI: 10.1111/rego.12158

Yeung, K., Howes, A., & Pogrebna, G. (2020). AI governance by human rights–centered design, deliberation and oversight: An end to ethics washing. *Law, Innovation and Technology, 12*(2), 311–333.

Yu, S., Wang, C., Ren, K., & Lou, W. (2010). Achieving secure, scalable, and fine-grained data access control in cloud computing. *2010 Proceedings IEEE INFOCOM*.

Yu, X. F., Samarasignhe, N., Mannan, M., & Others. (2022). Got sick and tracked: Privacy analysis of hospital websites. In Proceedings of the 2022 IEEE European Symposium on Security and Privacy Workshops (EuroS\&PW) (pp. 278–286). IEEE Press.

Zachariadis, M., Hileman, G., & Scott, S. V. (2019). Governance and control in distributed ledgers: Understanding the challenges facing blockchain technology. *Information Systems Journal, 29*(6), 563–580.

Zaguir, N. A., de Magalhães, G. H., & de Mesquita Spinola, M. (2024, June 18). Challenges and enablers for GDPR compliance: Systematic literature review and future research directions. *IEEE Access : Practical Innovations, Open Solutions, 12*, 81608–81630. DOI: 10.1109/ACCESS.2024.3406724

Zahra, Q. A. (2021, November 7). *Failed assassination bid against Iraq's PM ramps up tension*. USA Today. https://www.usatoday.com/story/news/world/2021/11/07/mustafa-al-kadhimi-iraqi-prime-minister-assassination-attempt/6330276001/

Zaidan, E., & Ibrahim, I. A. (2024). AI governance in a complex and rapidly changing regulatory landscape: A global perspective. *Humanities & Social Sciences Communications, 11*(1), 1121. DOI: 10.1057/s41599-024-03560-x

Zarifis, A., & Cheng, X. (2022). A model of trust in fintech and trust in Insurtech: How Artificial Intelligence and the context influence it. *Journal of Behavioral and Experimental Finance*, *36*, 100739. DOI: 10.1016/j.jbef.2022.100739

Zarifis, A., Kawalek, P., & Azadegan, A. (2021). Evaluating if trust and personal information privacy concerns are barriers to using health insurance that explicitly utilizes AI. *Journal of Internet Commerce*, *20*(1), 66–83. DOI: 10.1080/15332861.2020.1832817

Zarsky, T. Z. (2016). The Trouble with Algorithmic Decisions: An Analytic Road Map to Examine Efficiency and Fairness in Automated and Opaque Decision Making. *Science, Technology & Human Values*, *41*(1), 118–132. DOI: 10.1177/0162243915605575

Zenz, A. (2023). Safety first: Analysing the problematisation of drones. *Griffith Law Review*, *32*(3), 310–334. DOI: 10.1080/10383441.2024.2303937

Zhang, J. H., Koivumäki, T., & Chalmers, D. (2024, November). Privacy vs convenience: Understanding intention-behavior divergence post-GDPR. *Computers in Human Behavior*, *160*, 108382. DOI: 10.1016/j.chb.2024.108382

Zhang, J., & Zhang, Z. M. (2023). Ethics and governance of trustworthy medical artificial intelligence. *BMC Medical Informatics and Decision Making*, *23*(1), 7. DOI: 10.1186/s12911-023-02103-9 PMID: 36639799

Zhang, L. (2022). Arbitrability of IP disputes in China. *Journal of Intellectual Property Law*, *29*(3), 45–67.

Zhang, L. (2022). Investor-state arbitration and sovereignty. *Journal of International Economic Law*, *25*(2), 215–240.

Zhang, Q., Yuan, Z., & Li, J. (2023). Neural decision-making in electric power dispatch: Enhancing resilience and responsiveness. *Energy Reports*, *9*, 1587–1599. DOI: 10.1016/j.egyr.2022.12.005

Zhang, Y., Pan, X. M., & Liu, Q. Z. (2017). APT attacks and defenses. *Qinghua Daxue Xuebao. Ziran Kexue Ban*, *57*(11), 1127–1133.

Zhang, Z. J., Zhang, L. J., Rasheed, W., Jin, Z., Ma, T., Chen, H., & Xu, G. (2020). The research on covert communication model based on blockchain: A case study of Ethereum's Whisper protocol. *Communications in Computer and Information Science*, *2020*, 215–230. DOI: 10.1007/978-981-15-9739-8_17

Zhao, J., Yan, Q. B., & Liu, X. D.. (2020). Cyber threat intelligence modeling based on heterogeneous graph convolutional network. In *Proceedings of the 23rd International Symposium on Research in Attacks, Intrusions, and Defenses* (pp. 241–256). Piscataway, NJ, USA: IEEE.

Zheng, Z., Xie, S., Dai, H.-N., Chen, W., Chen, X., Weng, J., & Imran, M. (2020). An Overview on Smart Contracts: Challenges, Advances and Platforms. *Future Generation Computer Systems*, *105*, 475–491. DOI: 10.1016/j.future.2019.12.019

Zhong, Z. X., & Fan, W. J. (2023). A honey-imprint enabled approach for resisting social engineering attacks. In *Proceedings of the 2023 24th Asia-Pacific Network Operations and Management Symposium (APNOMS)* (pp. 302–305). IEEE Press.

Zhou, Y., Wang, X., & Liu, J. (2020). Real-time decision automation for power dispatch using deep reinforcement learning. *IEEE Transactions on Smart Grid*, *11*(4), 3282–3293. DOI: 10.1109/TSG.2019.2962102

Zhou, Y., Zhang, Y., & Liu, C. (2021). Distributed edge intelligence for smart grid systems. *IEEE Internet of Things Journal*, *8*(7), 5338–5350. DOI: 10.1109/JIOT.2020.3023428

Zhuk, A. (2025). Beyond the blockchain hype: Addressing legal and regulatory challenges. *SN Social Sciences*, *5*(11), 11. DOI: 10.1007/s43545-024-01044-y

Zuboff, S. (2019). *The Age of Surveillance Capitalism: The Fight for a Human Future at the New Frontier of Power*. PublicAffairs.

Zyskind, G., Nathan, O., & Pentland, A. (2015). *Decentralizing privacy: Using blockchain to protect personal data. In 2015 IEEE Security and Privacy Workshops*. IEEE., DOI: 10.1109/SPW.2015.27

About the Contributors

Ionica Oncioiu's research focuses on the intersection of law and digitalization, particularly in areas such as security risk management, ethical decision-making, and legal frameworks within the digital economy. Her expertise encompasses the evolving legal challenges businesses face in the digital age, with a focus on ensuring compliance with both national and international laws in domains like network security, data protection, and cybersecurity. Her publications in IGI reflect her expertise and evolving interest in the digital economy, with several books published between 2013 and 2020, covering subjects such as: Business Innovation, Development, and Advancement in the Digital Economy (2013) Driving Innovation and Business Success in the Digital Economy (2016) Ethics and Decision-Making for Sustainable Business Practices (2017) Network Security and Its Impact on Business Strategy (2018) Throughput Accounting in a Hyperconnected World (2019) Improving Business Performance Through Innovation in the Digital Economy (2020)

***

Munir Ahmad is a seasoned professional in the realm of Spatial Data Infrastructure (SDI), Geo-Information Productions, Information Systems, and Information Governance, boasting over 25 years of dedicated experience in the field. With a PhD in Computer Science, Dr. Ahmad's expertise spans Spatial Data Production, Management, Processing, Analysis, Visualization, and Quality Control. Throughout his career, Dr. Ahmad has been deeply involved in the development and deployment of SDI systems specially in the context of Pakistan, leveraging his proficiency in Spatial Database Design, Web, Mobile & Desktop GIS, and Geo Web Services Architecture. His contributions to Volunteered Geographic Information (VGI) and Open Source Geoportal & Metadata Portal have significantly enriched the geospatial community. As a trainer and researcher, Dr. Ahmad has authored over 50 publications, advancing the industry's knowledge base and fostering innovation in Geo-Tech, Data Governance, and Information Infrastructure, and Emerging Technologies. His commitment to Research and Development (R&D) is evident in his role as a dedicated educator and mentor in the field.

Mohammad Al-Khaldy is an Assistant professor of Business Intelligence and Data Analytics at University of Petra, Jordan. He completed his PhD in Atrificial Intelligence and Data Science for the University of Hull -United Kingdom - 20017. Alkhaldy's research interests include data analytics, machine learning, predictive analytics, NLP, and decision support systems. His research has been published extensively in academic journals and conferences. Alkhaldy taught a variety of courses in Artificial intelligence and business intelligence, including Data Mining, Business Analytics, Computer Programming, Intelligent business systems, Data Visualization, and machine learning. Alkhaldy is a member of Jordan Computers Society, and Arab Robotics & AI Association. He also a reviewer for several other academic conferences and journals.

Amjad Aldweesh is a computer associate professor interested in the Blockchain and Smart contracts technology as well as cyber security. Amjad has a Bachelor degree in computer science. He has a MSc degree in advanced computer science and security from the University of Manchester with distinction. Amjad is the second in the UK and the first in the middle east to have a PhD in the Blockchain and Smart contracts technology from Newcastle University.

Ashiv Choudhary is currently an Assistant Professor and Research Fellow, Centre for Alternative Dispute Resolution (CADR) at Jindal Global Law School, O.P. Jindal Global University. He is also Faculty Advisor for ADR HOC - Knowledge Steez. He holds LL.M. in Comparative and International Dispute Resolution from Queen Mary University of London with Distinction in Dissertation titled 'Arbitrability of Patent Issues – An analysis from Indian and Global Perspective'. He has published several articles in peer reviewed Indian as well as International law journals. His primary areas of interest are Alternate Dispute Resolution, Arbitration, Indian Penal code, Law of Torts, Civil Procedure Code, etc.

Tamara Phillips Fudge is a full-time professor in the graduate technology programs at Purdue University Global. She has won fellowships and awards for innovation and teaching, and has taught a wide variety of topics, including web development, human-computer interaction, systems analysis and design, and those featuring documentation, diagramming, problem-solving, and presentation. Her career started with music degrees from Indiana University and Florida State University. She sang opera, oratorio, and in recital; her compositions have been heard on Public Radio, at various universities, and a state choral convention. She taught vocal and choral music, piano, pedagogy, foreign language diction, opera production, music theory, composition, and related courses in the traditional college classroom for 20-odd years. For 7 years, she was a weekend correspondent for the Quad-City Times (Davenport, IA). Following a brief stint as an agent/registered representative selling life and health insurance and variable products, she returned to school with a keen interest in technology and has since distinguished herself in online teaching, coordination of large projects, and curriculum development.

Lalit Goyal Associate Professor, Graduate School of Business Tula's Institute, NAAC Grade A+ Accredited Institute. Dhoolkot Road, Dhoolkot Dehradun, Uttarakhand Email id- lalitgoyalmbafinance@gmail.com

Aakash Gupta is currently an Associate Professor of Law at Amity University Gwalior, India. He has obtained the degree of LL.M. from M.L.B. Government College of excellence Jiwaji University, Gwalior. He has obtained his PhD degree in Law from Jiwaji University and cleared UGC NET exmination in 2012. Prior to Amity University, he was working as an Assistant Professor of Law Prestige Institute of Management & Research Gwalior from 2018 to 2023 and in Madhav Law College Gwalior from 2014 to 2018. He has also worked as Guest Lecturer in SOS in Law, Jiwaji University till 2014. He has more than 13 years of experience in Academic and Litigation. His area of Interest in Constitutional Law and Criminal Law. He has 12 International / National Publications to his credit. He has attended various seminar, webinars and workshops and delivered special lectures in EML on numerous occasion. He has published 1 book and presented chapters in 5 books. He has also developed a unique pedagogy to teach law subjects in a poetic form.

Manya Gupta, Assistant Professor position in the School of Law, at Graphic era hill university Dehradun With my specialized expertise in Constitutional Law, Centre-State Relations, Labour Law, Investment and Competition Law, and the Law of Torts, I am confident I would make a valuable addition to your esteemed University. As a qualified legal educator, I hold the UGC NET qualification and have completed my Ph. D., L.L.M. & B.COM.LLB(Hons), focusing on the significance of DNA and fingerprint evidence in the Indian judicial system.

Pooja Jaiswal received the B.Sc. degree in Science from J.K. Institute of Applied Physics & Technology, University of Allahabad (U.P.) in 2007. She received the B.Tech & M.Tech degree in Electronics and communication from J.K. Institute of Applied Physics & Technology, University of Allahabad (U.P.) in 2010 & 2012. Her research interest includes Quantum computing and Image Processing with Deep learning and their applications. Presently she is pursuing PhD from J.K. Institute of Applied Physics & Technology, University of Allahabad, India.

Radhey Shyam Jha, Associate Professor & Head, Law College Dehradun, Uttaranchal University Dehradun, Email id - radhey.shyamjha@gmail.com

Karisma previously served as an Assistant Professor at the Tunku Abdul Rahman University of Management and Technology. She is currently an independent researcher. Her research pursuits revolve around the intersection of law and technology, emphasising interdisciplinary and comparative perspectives. Specifically, she explores the applicability of blockchain technology in the energy sector, delving into the associated legal and regulatory dimensions. Her commitment to excellence manifests in several high-quality research papers she has published and presentations she has delivered at international conferences. Her profound understanding of foundational aspects, astute insights, and expertise in decentralised systems make her an exceptional candidate for the presented research opportunity.

Nidhi Kastwar is a Law Researcher. She is currently pursuing her Ph.D. from Amity Law School, Amity University Gwalior, Madhya Pradesh. Prior to this, she worked as an Assistant Professor in Amity Law School, Amity University Gwalior from January 2022 to March 2024. In addition to this, she has qualified for UGC NET in 2020. She has participated in various Faculty Development Programmes, and National and International conferences and has published articles in reputed journals. She completed her LL.M in Constitutional Law and is a gold medal holder from Amity Law School Amity University Gwalior, M.P in 2019 and her B.A.LL.B (H) from Jiwaji University, Gwalior, M.P. in 2018 and she is a merit holder.

Vinay Kumar Kasula has a Master's in Technology from Osmania University, followed by a second Master's from Northwest Missouri State University. His academic journey has been driven by a deep-rooted interest in research and advanced technologies. This passion led him to pursue and complete a Ph.D. at the University of the Cumberlands, where he graduated in 2024, focusing on areas including Blockchain, Artificial Intelligence, Deep Learning, Machine Learning, Data Analytics, and Cybersecurity. With over a decade of industry experience, currently as a Senior Systems Analyst, he has applied and expanded his expertise in these domains, continually exploring and integrating innovative solutions to meet evolving technological challenges. This blend of education, research, and practical experience fueled his commitment to advancements in these cutting-edge fields.

Bhargavi Konda works as a senior systems analyst in the human resources information systems department for a healthcare company. She mainly works with data analysis and generates reports for various departments in the organization. She has been one of the major contributors in maintaining employee records, supporting all HR departments, and especially working with payroll operations from her team. She earned her master's degree from Osmania University (2001-2004). She received the gold medal and Star Student of the Year awards for her outstanding performance. She was placed in an IT consulting company right after her master's, and she worked as an Oracle technical consultant from 2004 to 2012. In that period, she was awarded the Outstanding Trainer award for her commitment and dedication. She has experience implementing applications in the banking and manufacturing sectors. She was passionate about higher studies, so she started to pursue a Ph.D. in IT in 2019. She earned a Ph.D. degree in Information Technology in the year 2024 from the University of the Cumberlands. She is excited to work on many journals and publications in the future and wants to continue her research. She can be contacted at email: Bhargavikonda@ieee.org.

Manjit Kour is working as Professor at University Business School at Chandigarh University. She holds a PhD in Business Management from IK Gujral Punjab Technical University, India. She has a good research record with several research papers published in reputed journals. She is an editorial board member and reviewer of many reputed journals including Scopus and ABDC-indexed journals. Her areas of interest include sustainability, green practices, Fintech, online marketing trends and business ethics.

Harsh Mahaseth is an Associate Professor and Senior Research Fellow (Centre for ADR) at Jindal Global Law School, O.P. Jindal Global University, India. He has worked as a visiting faculty at NALSAR University of Law and Mahindra University. He has recently been listed as one of the Top-Cited International Law Scholars in India, a list created by the Indian Blog of International Law that contains names of legal stalwarts of India. Harsh is the co-founder of Collegelt, a platform to help people connect with students and alumni while applying to universities abroad. He previously held the position of Assistant Dean at O.P. Jindal Global University, and the position of Assistant Director at the Nehginpao Kipgen Center for Southeast Asian Studies.

Mădălina Mihăilescu is a PhD university lecturer and dean of the Faculty of Exact Sciences and Engineering at Hyperion University in Bucharest. Her academic activity focuses on areas such as automation, applied computer science and new digital technologies. She coordinates bachelor's and master's programs, actively contributing to the modernization of the curriculum and the promotion of interdisciplinary research. She has participated in numerous scientific conferences and published papers in specialized journals. Through her involvement, she supports the connection between the university environment, industry and technological innovation, strengthening the prestige of the institution at national and international levels.

Venktesh Mishra has completed his B.Tech degree in Electronics & Instrumentation Engineering from U.P. Technical University Lucknow, India in 2006 and M. Tech degree in Electrical Engineering from MNNIT Prayagraj, India in 2013. He has completed his Ph.D. from University of Allahabad; Allahabad, India in the area of application of Power Electronics converter in renewable energy sources. He has published several papers in international journals and conferences. His area of interest includes Power electronics and Wind Energy Conversion Systems and Quantum computing. Venktesh Mishra, working as Associate Professor since last 16 years in field of Department of Electronics and Communication Engineering, United College of Engineering and Research Naini, Prayagraj, U.P., India, 211010.

Deepak Mudgil is an aspiring student pursuing M Tech Cyber Security from the Department of Computer Science & Engineering at DIAT, Pune.

Tushar received a B.Tech degree in electronics and communication from U.P.T.U., Lucknow (U.P.), in 2007. I received the M.B.A. degree in R.T.M. from Jiwaji University, Gwalior (M.P.), in 2009. I am a "gold medalist" in M.E. in Communication Control and Networking from M.P.C.T. Gwalior, M.P. My research interests include antenna and microwave communication, QCA design, and deep learning and their applications. Presently I am pursuing a Ph.D. and acting as an assistant professor at the United College of Engineering & Research, Prayagraj, India.

Nandita Pradhan is the head of the ECE and CRT department. She did B.E. in Electronics and Telecommunication Engineering in 1985, M.E. in Communication Systems from the Govt. Engineering College, Jabalpur in 1991 and Ph.D. in Electronics and Communication Engineering from AKTU, Lucknow. She began her professional journey as a Lecturer in the Department of ECE at Government Engineering College, Jabalpur in 1985 and served in that position until 1997. Currently she worked as a Head of the Department of ECE in United Group of Institutions, Prayagraj, India.

Payal Sharma, is an Assistant Professor at Acropolis Faculty of Management and Research, Indore, India. She has a PhD in Management from Devi Ahilya Vishwavidyalaya, Indore. Her research areas includes Psychological Capital, Organizational Climate, Fintech, Student Employability and Entrepreneurship. She has has experience in providing hands-on training in different research tools and methodology. She has conducted various Faculty Development and Management

Development Programs in different areas including SPSS, Bibliography, Research, Perception, Joharry Window, and Personality Assessment.

Prabhat Chandra Shrivastava is an Assistant Professor in the Department of Electronics and Communication at the University of Allahabad, Prayagraj. He completed his Ph.D. and M.Tech from MNNIT Allahabad and his B.E. from RGPV Bhopal. He has more than 10 years of experience in teaching and research. His main areas of work include Architecture of Digital Filter Design, Digital Signal Processing, Artificial Intelligence (AI), Machine Learning (ML), and Smart Agriculture. He has worked on useful projects like predicting plant health using AI, analyzing ECG signals for heart problems, and recognizing Indian classical music with deep learning. Dr. Shrivastava has published many research papers in international journals and conferences. He has also qualified the GATE exam five times and received fellowships during his M.Tech and Ph.D. studies. He is passionate about using technology to solve real-life problems in agriculture.

Ayushi Singh is a Lecturer at OP Jindal Global University. She holds an LL.M. in International Law from the University of Cambridge and a PG Diploma in International Trade and Business Laws from ISIL. She has previously worked in different capacities with OECD, UNESCAP and WTO.

Sweta Singh holds a B.Tech. in Electronics and Communication Engineering (U.P.T.U Lucknow), M.Tech. in VLSI Design (Banasthali Vidyapeeth, Rajasthan), and a D.Phil. in Electronics and Communication Engineering (University of Allahabad, Prayagraj). She has over 12 years of teaching and research experience, having served at reputed institutions including MNNIT Prayagraj, BBS CET Prayagraj, K.N.I.T. Sultanpur, Government Girls' Polytechnic, Faizabad and Dr. R.M.L. Avadh University Faizabad. Her research interests include microstrip patch antennas, MIMO systems, reconfigurable antennas, VLSI architecture, and 5G/ satellite communication. Dr. Singh has published several papers in reputed journals and international conferences (IEEE, Springer, PIERC), and contributed to multiple book chapters in the field of wireless communication. She actively participates in FDPs, workshops, and training programs, and is dedicated to academic excellence, innovation, and student mentorship. Currently she is working as an Assistant Professor in the Department of Computer Science Engineering & Technology at United University, Rawatpur, Prayagraj

Nidhi Tyagi, Associate Professor, Department of Humanities & Social Sciences, Graphic Era Deemed to be University Dehradun, Uttarakhand, tyagi1234nidhi@gmail.com

Akhila Reddy Yadulla holds an MS in Computer Science from Northwestern Polytechnic University in 2016, an MS in Information Technology Management from Campbellsville University in 2019, and a Ph.D. in Information Technology from the University of the Cumberlands in 2024. She is an accomplished Senior Software Engineer with over eight years of experience in Java full-stack development and expertise in the Software Development Life Cycle. Dr. Yadulla is proficient in Java, Spring Boot, Hibernate, RESTful APIs, Angular, React, Microservices, SQL/NoSQL databases, DevOps, and Agile methodologies. Her research focuses on Cybersecurity, Artificial Intelligence, Data Science, Big Data, Blockchain Technologies, Amazon Web Services, and Machine Learning. She combines deep technical knowledge, advanced problem-solving skills, and AI-driven innovative solutions in cutting-edge technologies. Notably, she led a team in developing a secure and scalable microservices architecture for significant telecommunication and banking platforms, resulting in a major increase in system performance. She can be contacted at email: Akhilareddyyadulla@ieee.org.

Mounica Yenugula is a skilled IT professional with a strong academic background and an experienced Cloud Engineer. She holds a Ph.D. in Information Technology from the University of Cumberlands, where her research focused on critical security and trust issues in cloud environments. Her academic journey began with a Bachelor of Technology in Electronics and Communication Engineering from Koneru Lakshmaih University and continued with a Master of Science in Electrical Engineering from California State University, Los Angeles. As a certified Cloud Engineer, Mounica has successfully implemented cloud solutions within the financial sector, driving digital transformation. Her active involvement in the Women in IT community and her role as a judge for the Globee Awards demonstrate her commitment to industry advancement and innovation. She can be contacted at email: ymounica.phd@ieee.org.

Index

N

O

P

S

T

U

V

www.ingramcontent.com/pod-product-compliance
Lightning Source LLC
LaVergne TN
LVHW080348011026
849161LV00009B/2234